IN DA

IN DANGER
UNDAUNTED

The Anti-Interventionist Movement
of 1940–1941
as Revealed in the Papers of
the America First Committee

EDITED BY

Justus D. Doenecke

HOOVER INSTITUTION PRESS

Stanford University, Stanford, California

Hoover Press Publication 384

First printing, 1990

Manufactured in the United States of America
Printed on acid-free paper

96 95 94 93 92 91 90   9 8 7 6 5 4 3 2 1

Library of Congress Cataloging-in-Publication Data

In danger undaunted : the anti-interventionist movement of 1940–1941
as revealed in the papers of the America First Committee / edited by
Justus D. Doenecke.
       p.   cm. — (Hoover archival documentaries)
  (Hoover Press publication ; 384)
  Includes bibliographical references.
  ISBN 0-8179-8841-6 (alk. paper).
  ISBN 0-8179-8842-4 (pbk. : alk. paper)
  1. America First Committee.   2. World War, 1939–1945—United
States.   3. United States—Neutrality.   I. Doenecke, Justus D.
II. America First Committee.   III. Series.
D753.147   1989   89-35269
940.53'73—dc20   CIP

CONTENTS

Acknowledgments / ix

Preface / xi

INTRODUCTION

The Origins and Activities of the America First Committee / 1

DOCUMENTS

Selected Documents of the America First Committee / 79

Name Index / 471

Topic Index / 483

ACKNOWLEDGMENTS

The author is greatly indebted to the staff of the Hoover Institution on War, Revolution and Peace at Stanford, California, for sponsoring this project. In particular, I wish to thank Dr. Robert Hessen, general editor of the Hoover Archival Documentaries, for his countless hours of labor and continual words of encouragement. Other staff members who went out of their way to expedite this research include Mr. Charles Palm, associate director for library and archives; Dr. Adorjan I. de Galffy, former assistant archivist; Mr. Ronald Bulatoff, archival specialist; and Dr. Elena Danielson, associate archivist. Ms. Ann Wood, senior editor of the Hoover Institution Press, was exceptionally cooperative in expediting the publication of this book, and Ms. Janet Schilling did a most careful job of copyediting.

Mrs. Ruth Sarles Benedict, former director of America First's research bureau, graciously responded to my lengthy inquiries. Mrs. Rosemary Allen Little, librarian of public administration, politics, and law of Princeton University Library, made sure that I received the special Princeton file of America First papers donated by Sterling Morton. Dr. Robert S. Wood, former director of the Herbert Hoover Presidential Library, was especially generous in sharing his unmatched knowledge of the former president. I am also indebted to the staffs of Houghton Library of Harvard University; the Bancroft Library of the University of California; Sterling Memorial Library of Yale University; the Swarthmore College Peace Collection; the archives division of the New York Public Library; the Wisconsin State Historical Society; the University of Oregon; the Library of Congress; the Chicago Historical Society; and Providence College.

Other scholars also helped to expedite this project. Acting with a generosity unmatched in academe, Dr. James T. Patterson of Brown University and Dr. Eugene Lewis of New College of the University of South Florida provided a critical reading of the entire introduction. Special mention must go to Dr. J. Garry Clifford of the University of Connecticut for a critique based upon a matchless knowledge of Roosevelt's foreign policy. In an act of kindness rare among scholars, Garry also shared sources and leads at an early stage of this research. I benefited from the analysis of Dr. Raymond G. O'Connor, professor emeritus of the University of Miami, who possesses a thorough knowledge of naval operations in the years 1940–41.

Over the years, the Institute of Humane Studies (IHS), now located at

George Mason University in Fairfax, Virginia, and the Liberty Fund of Indianapolis, Indiana, have generously given me the equivalent of several years of support to investigate twentieth-century American policymakers and their critics. In particular I owe a debt to Mr. Leonard P. Liggio, former IHS president, and to Mr. Kenneth S. Templeton, Jr., past executive secretary of the Liberty Fund. The John Anson Kittredge Education Fund, whose chairman is Dr. Ernest R. May, also supported this research. Dr. Robert Benedetti, provost of New College of the University of South Florida, strongly encouraged all scholarly endeavor.

PREFACE

From September 1939, when Hitler invaded Poland and thereby triggered World War II, to December 1941, when Japan attacked Pearl Harbor, Americans vigorously debated their nation's role in the conflict. At stake was the possible entrance of the United States into the greatest war in world history, a move bound to affect the nation for decades to come.

Yet both interventionists and anti-interventionists had one thing in common: they were composed of extremely diverse coalitions. Neither group shared economic doctrines, social bases, or political affiliation. Within the interventionist camp were Wall Street financiers, New York City labor leaders, southern Democrats noted for their domestic conservatism, and presidents of Ivy League universities. Among the anti-interventionists were midwestern Republican congressmen, followers of the radio demagogue Father Charles E. Coughlin, the labor coterie surrounding John L. Lewis, and leaders of the Chicago business community. Former participants in the old progressive movement were on both sides. Members of the German-American Bund were strong isolationists, as were Trotskyists and, until June 22, 1941, Stalinists.

Opponents of intervention found their voice in the America First Committee (AFC), established in September 1940 to oppose the interventionism of President Franklin D. Roosevelt and his administration.

Since 1942, the AFC papers have been deposited in the archives of the Hoover Institution on War, Revolution and Peace. The 338 manuscript boxes contain national, state, and local records. In carton upon carton—sometimes unexpectedly—one finds material illuminating many aspects of U.S. policy, for the collection constitutes an invaluable record of one of the most vigorous action groups ever to appear in the United States. For those concerned with opinion making and economic elites, the AFC papers contain lists of major contributors, national committee members, prominent endorsers (including leaders in the black community), and those who offered confidential financial support. For those curious about student activism, the collection explores the world of the university, where two future presidents of the United States were among AFC ranks. For those who study mass opinion making, there are critiques of radio commentators, press opinion, and Hollywood films. For those interested in pressure groups, the collection is replete with AFC internal memorandums, an organizational prospectus, and candid appraisals of its own strengths and weaknesses. Historians of U.S. politics will appreciate the analysis of legislation offered by America First's Washington office. Lend-Lease, convoys, draft renewal, arming merchant ships, a possible war referendum—fresh material is offered on all these topics, and on tensions with Japan as well.

Although we have several excellent histories of America First and of anti-interventionism in general, we have not yet let Roosevelt's foes speak for themselves.[1] Until now, no documentary collection or anthology devoted to their perspective has appeared. Although the historical monograph can offer balance and perspective, only the sources themselves can convey the logic, complexity, and passion of the anti-interventionist position.

This volume is drawn entirely from the Hoover Institution's America First Collection. It reveals why many Americans, including some of great power and influence, sought to keep their country out of the war, doing so despite the likelihood that Hitler would overrun Europe if the United States did not enter on England's side. Given the enormity of what was already known about Hitler's internal regime and its imperialistic ambitions, it must seem a mystery to those living many years later why so many Americans opposed fighting the German führer. This book of documents helps solve that mystery.

NOTES

1. Manfred Jonas, *Isolationism in America, 1935–1941* (Ithaca, N.Y.: Cornell University Press, 1966); Wayne S. Cole, *Roosevelt and the Isolationists* (Lincoln: University of Nebraska Press, 1983); Wayne S. Cole, *America First: The Battle against Intervention, 1940–1941* (Madison: University of Wisconsin Press, 1953); Michele Flynn Stenehjem, *An American First: John T. Flynn and the America First Committee* (New Rochelle, N.Y.: Arlington House, 1976).

INTRODUCTION

*The Origins and Activities of the
America First Committee*

The world of the late twentieth century is rooted in the 1940s; the outcome of World War II altered the face of the globe and left the United States dominant. Yet in 1940 and 1941, when the outcome was much in doubt, the Roosevelt administration committed the nation to a policy of all aid short of war.

Most historians praise U.S. policy of the 1940s, and World War II has gone down in history as "the good war." In that scenario, Franklin D. Roosevelt was wise and courageous in supporting the Allied powers. If at times he lacked candor, he did educate his fellow citizens to the dangers posed by Axis domination of the Eurasian continent and to the need to support the victims of German and Japanese aggression. Indeed, the war was in truth what Roosevelt had originally called it—"the war for survival."

Although few Americans lack some awareness of the nature and impact of World War II, many have forgotten—or never really learned—the steps by which their country was drawn ever closer to conflict. On September 1, 1939, Hitler invaded Poland, and within two days Britain and France declared war on Germany. World War II had begun. Roosevelt quickly announced that the United States would "remain a neutral nation." Within three weeks, however, he urged Congress to remove an arms embargo that had been one of the linchpins of U.S. neutrality legislation. In acceding to Roosevelt's request and thereby authorizing "cash and carry" exports of munitions to belligerents, Congress acted in full awareness that such a move would aid the Allies, who still controlled the Atlantic sea lanes. The legislation also gave the president authority to delineate combat zones, areas that U.S. ships and citizens were forbidden to enter. On November 4, 1939, Roosevelt defined the zone as comprising the entire Baltic Sea and the whole Atlantic area from southern Norway to the British Isles, the Low Countries, and southern France.

In the late spring of 1940, the German blitzkrieg swung through the Low Countries, and Roosevelt called for all-out assistance to Britain and France. By June 22, however, France had surrendered, and Britain began fighting for her life in an unprecedented air battle. During the summer, with Roosevelt's firm backing, Congress passed the first peacetime selective service act in U.S. history. The law affected sixteen and a half million men between the ages of twenty-one and thirty-six. Those conscripted would be trained for one year, then enter the reserves. On September 3, by executive agreement, Roosevelt transferred some fifty overage destroyers to Great Britain in return for eight bases in the Western Hemisphere.

Then, after defeating Wendell L. Willkie in the November presidential race, he called on the nation to become "the great arsenal of democracy." Congress responded in March 1941 by passing the Lend-Lease Act, a comprehensive measure that gave the president broad discretionary powers to aid the Allies, including the authority to sell, transfer, exchange, and lease arms and other war materials overseas whenever he deemed such activity vital to U.S. defense.

Between April and July 1941, Roosevelt made other interventionist moves, including the creation of military bases on Greenland, the proclamation of an unlimited national emergency, and the landing of U.S. troops on Iceland. On June 22, 1941, when Germany invaded the Soviet Union, Roosevelt promptly ensured that the Russians would receive U.S. lend-lease assistance. On July 26, he responded to Japan's occupation of Indochina by freezing all Japan's assets in the United States. This move severed Japan's major source of oil, and tensions mounted toward the breaking point.

At the end of the summer, joining with Prime Minister Winston Churchill of Great Britain, the president signed the Atlantic Charter, a declaration of war aims that included "the final destruction of Nazi tyranny" and "the establishment of a wider and permanent system of general security." Congress extended army service for draftees by eighteen months, though this "draft renewal" bill squeezed through the House of Representatives by only one vote. On September 4, when a German submarine stationed off the coast of Iceland fired on the U.S. destroyer *Greer,* Roosevelt responded by instructing U.S. naval warships to shoot German and Italian war vessels on sight.

By autumn, the United States was fighting an undeclared war in the Atlantic. After attacks on other U.S. ships—in particular the *Kearny* and the *Reuben James*—resulted in loss of life, Congress repealed the major remaining restrictions in the 1939 Neutrality Act, allowing U.S. merchant vessels to be armed and to pass through the war zone to British ports.

Perhaps Roosevelt did not foresee committing ground forces overseas but planned merely to supply weapons and participate in air and sea engagements. It is just as plausible that he believed that he could not achieve maximum industrial and manpower mobilization without total war, that Britain and the Soviet Union alone could not defeat the Axis, and that an equal voice at the peace table could be earned only by participating fully in the conflict. One thing, however, is not in dispute: by 1941 the president was willing to risk war to ensure Allied survival.

Roosevelt gave his reasons repeatedly. In his "fireside chat" of December 29, 1940, he claimed that "the Nazi masters of Germany" had made it clear that they sought "to enslave the whole of Europe, and then to use the resources of Europe to dominate the rest of the world." If Britain were defeated, "the Axis powers will control the continents of Europe, Asia, Africa, Australasia, and the high seas—and they will be in a position to bring enormous military and naval resources [to bear] against this hemisphere." The Americas, he went on, "would be living at the point of a gun." He continued this theme in his third inaugural address, delivered on January 20, 1941: "We would rather die on our feet than live on our knees."[1]

In the president's eyes, the Axis threat was not purely military. Speaking to the Pan-American Union on May 27, 1941, Roosevelt claimed that Germany posed a major economic challenge. By exploiting "slave labor in the rest of the world," Hitler would be able to undersell U.S. goods everywhere. In order to survive, Roosevelt said, the United States would have to radically restructure its economy. Wages and hours would be regulated, collective bargaining abolished, and prohibitive tariffs enacted. "The whole fabric of working life as we know it—business, manufacturing, mining, agriculture—all would be mangled and crippled under such a system."[2]

Roosevelt did not neglect matters of ideology. In December 1940 he noted that Hitler himself had denied any possibility of ultimate peace between Germany's political philosophy and that of the West. In September 1941 Roosevelt called Germany "an enemy of all law, all liberty, all morality, all religion." In October he referred to a secret German plan to "abolish all existing religions" and replace them with "an international Nazi church."[3]

If the danger was as great as Roosevelt portrayed it, anti-interventionism could only jeopardize the United States. How indeed could anyone suggest that the United States refrain from rescuing the embattled British? In December 1940 Roosevelt challenged those who sought a negotiated peace: "Such a dictated peace would be no peace at all. It would be only another armistice, leading to the most gigantic armament race and the most devastating trade wars of all history." Roosevelt might concede, as he did on May 27, 1941, that those "who shut their eyes to the ugly realities of international banditry" were "sincere" and "patriotic." But then he said that such people were playing into Axis hands; at worst, they were downright subversive. Whatever their motive, Americans must immunize themselves against the "tender whispering of appeasers that Hitler is not interested in the Western Hemisphere" or "the soporific lullabies that a wide ocean can protect us from him."[4]

Roosevelt and those who shared his perspective thought of their foes as isolationists. Strictly speaking, an isolationist opposes binding commitments or obligations. Guarding American freedom of action, isolationists sought— as one scholar notes—"to leave America free to determine when, where, how, and whether the United States should involve itself abroad."[5] In the eyes of the Roosevelt administration, however, isolationism connoted an ostrich-like apathy, mixed with the hope that Hitler's appetite for conquest would be sated once he controlled Europe. Little wonder most so-called isolationists spurned the term, with its connotation of naïveté, preferring less pejorative labels such as anti-interventionist, non-interventionist, and nationalist.

Roosevelt's barbed retorts did not prevent a large body of Americans from opposing each step toward intervention. Many factors came into play. Particularly haunting was the memory of the Great War. An entire generation had been raised on the revisionist histories of Sidney Bradshaw Fay, Harry Elmer Barnes, and Walter Millis. Moreover, the novels of Ernest Hemingway and the plays of Lawrence Stallings portrayed a conflict that was neither purposeful nor glorious. It was, as one character noted in John Dos Passos's *1919* (1932), "a goddam madhouse."[6] And if the horrors of trench warfare and gassed troops were not enough, there was the unjust Versailles Treaty, that "orgy in ink" as Sen. Henrik Shipstead (Farmer-Labor–Minn.) called it, perceived as an unjust diktat that gave birth to communism, fascism, and Nazism.[7]

The anti-interventionists believed that the inevitable aftermath of any new conflict would be worldwide depression, with accompanying social disintegration. Conservatives saw the capitalist system in peril, believing that full-scale mobilization must lead to inflation, price and wage controls, and compulsory unionization; thus socialism would be the war's one lasting result. Prominent aviator Charles A. Lindbergh was even more apprehensive: "God knows what will happen before we finish it [World War II]—race riots, revolution, destruction."[8]

Liberals were equally apprehensive. To them, the sensationalist exposés of the Senate Committee Investigating the Munitions Industry were most alarming. It was popularly called the Nye Committee after Sen. Gerald P. Nye (R-N.D.) and was in session from 1934 to 1936. The committee excoriated the "merchants of death," the profiteers who supposedly manipulated the Wilson administration into World War I. Similarly, a new war would engulf the nation in "armament economics," a sure harbinger of fascism. Workers would receive low wages, farmers low prices. Then strikes would be outlawed. On M-Day, or Mobilization Day, a centralized defense force would assume dictatorial powers and in the process conscript at least a million men. After the immediate and artificial war boom ended, the grim aftermath of 1929 would again be at hand. Civil liberties would be abrogated, national censorship imposed, and the clampdown would be so severe that the antics of the Creel Committee (the official U.S. propaganda agency during World War I) and the repressive espionage and sedition laws of 1917 and 1918 would seem mild by comparison.[9]

The dissenters had other arguments. They denied that Axis domination of the European continent endangered U.S. security. In fact, they argued, the United States could remain the one major power unscathed by global war. If the nation could stay aloof from the struggle, perhaps supplying the

British and Chinese but without risking combat, it could preserve the strength needed to play the pivotal role in postwar reconstruction.

Moreover, the anti-interventionists argued, the United States could survive quite well. Whatever dreams Hitler had at that stage, including possible global conquest, were irrelevant. Even if he sought military occupation of the entire world, the United States could remain secure. It could create an impregnable defense, while reorganizing the economy of the Western Hemisphere to keep its citizens employed, its raw materials flowing. As for the ideological problem of living in a world "half slave, half free," the United States had survived amid tyrannies before and would undoubtedly do so again.

When war broke out in 1939, anti-interventionist sentiment was diffuse and unorganized. Only in the summer of 1940, after France had fallen and after the interventionists had established well-organized and well-financed pressure groups, did opponents of Roosevelt's foreign policy undertake a major organizational effort, one that centered on the America First Committee. The committee, formally organized that September, coordinated all efforts to oppose Roosevelt's proposals for providing lend-lease assistance, arming merchant ships, and escorting war supplies to Allied ports. The AFC also criticized other administration moves such as the occupation of Iceland, the drafting of the Atlantic Charter, and the placing of economic pressures on Japan.

By the time the Japanese bombed Pearl Harbor on December 7, 1941, the AFC had 450 units and at least a quarter of a million members. It had held massive rallies, distributed tons of literature, sponsored national radio speakers, and supplied research data to members of Congress. In the process, it forced Roosevelt to be far more circumspect in his legislative proposals and to make some interventionist moves surreptitiously, such as authorizing naval escorts in the Atlantic.

It is hardly surprising that interventionists attacked America First: its leaders and members were portrayed by their foes and in much of the press as unpatriotic, appeasement-minded, indeed downright subversive. It is probably not sheer coincidence that when one looks at later *Who's Who* entries of those who occupied crucial AFC posts—chairman, national director, director of organization, publicity director—their America First activities go unmentioned.

Origins

The events of the spring of 1940 were crucial to the origin of the America First Committee. One shock followed another. First Denmark fell, then Norway, then Belgium and the Netherlands, finally France—and Americans suddenly realized that Nazi Germany dominated most of Western Europe. In addition, the fate of England, the bulwark of Allied resistance, was much in doubt. Rumors circulated that Britain would soon be invaded and that the United States would be at war by Christmas.

In response to those traumatic events, public sentiment shifted rapidly. In September 1939 polls indicated that Americans above all sought to avoid war. But by November 1940 a majority of Americans told pollsters they preferred all-out war to Britain's defeat.[10]

If the interventionists welcomed the destroyer bases deal and the military draft, they still saw Britain in peril. Hence, they wanted major weapons sent to the besieged isles, including pursuit planes, tanks, high-speed torpedo craft (mosquito boats), and four-engine bombers (Flying Fortresses). They also sought loans so Britain could pay for these items.

This pressure, spearheaded by Kansas editor William Allen White's Committee to Defend America by Aiding the Allies (CDAAA), greatly alarmed anti-interventionists. To send such valuable weapons overseas, they believed, was totally irresponsible because a still weak United States sorely needed such weapons for its own defense. Still more appalling, acting as a surrogate belligerent would eventually lead the nation into a futile and ruinous war. Moreover, if the United States transported such goods and extended loans, it would be violating its own neutrality legislation. As yet, though, aside from a few pacifist groups, no major national organization was devoted solely to fighting intervention.

The events of 1940 were distressing to R. Douglas Stuart, Jr., a student at the Yale University Law School. Son of the first vice president of Quaker Oats, Stuart had graduated from Princeton University in 1937. His studies in government and international relations had convinced him, he said later, that "the U.S. had gained nothing and lost a great deal through participation in World War I." Soon after graduation, Stuart spent several months in Europe, where his belief was reinforced. By the spring of 1940 he was meeting informally with students who feared direct U.S. involvement and with such kindred spirits among the Yale law faculty as Edwin M. Borchard and Fred Rodell.[11]

Late in the spring of 1940, Stuart and four other law students—among them future president Gerald R. Ford and future Supreme Court justice Potter Stewart—launched a petition aimed at organizing college students into a nationwide anti-interventionist organization. Their efforts centered on enforcing the key provisions of the Neutrality Act of 1939: banning loans to belligerents and blocking the shipment of war goods abroad. Insisting on cash-and-carry, the students said, "We demand that Congress refrain from war, even if England is on the verge of defeat." In a history of the America First Committee completed in October 1942, Ruth Sarles tells how the Yale group began its activities. Sarles, who directed the AFC research bureau in Washington, D. C., begins her narrative with their petition. [Document 1]

The law students soon enlarged their focus, seeking supporters not only among college graduates but in all areas of national leadership. Stuart's New Haven home served as the national headquarters, and his wife, Barbara, was his first full-time assistant. Kingman Brewster, Jr., the articulate anti-interventionist chairman of the *Yale Daily News*, was particularly apprehensive about the country's direction; he took on the challenge of recruiting such prominent intellectuals as historian Charles A. Beard. [Document 2]

In part because Stuart grew up in Chicago, serious organizing started there. Early in July he met with Gen. Thomas S. Hammond, president of the Whiting Corporation, and with investor Sterling Morton. Morton's outspoken opposition to Roosevelt's foreign policy is evident in his address to the National Small Business Men's Association. His speech touched on many themes dear to anti-interventionists, including the need for a small, mobile army; the difficulties Germany would have in invading the United States; and the desirability of U.S. trade with Japan. [Document 3]

Hammond and Morton proposed that Gen. Robert E. Wood lead the group. Wood, the sixty-one-year-old board chairman of Sears, Roebuck, was widely respected as one of America's leading and most progressive business-men. He had helped to revolutionize the techniques of merchandising, fostered welfare capitalism, and backed much of the early New Deal. True, he had broken with the Roosevelt administration over pump-priming, the Wagner National Labor Relations Act, and what he saw as the president's apparent willingness to risk war. But, less isolationist than many White House critics, he supported cash-and-carry, conscription, and the president's call of May 1940 for 50,000 planes within the next calendar year.[12] Although it took a great deal of convincing to secure Wood's leadership, on July 15, 1940, he agreed to serve as acting chairman.[13]

Stuart and his friends spent the summer recruiting supporters.[14] Thanks to his father's generosity, Stuart secured a rent-free office in the Board of Trade building. Initially three desks, a filing cabinet, and a telephone composed his total facilities. The group originally called itself the Emergency Committee to Defend America First, but late in August it renamed itself the America First Committee.

Even before the national organization was formally established, the first defection took place: Gerald R. Ford, former All-American center in football at the University of Michigan, resigned from the original student executive committee. Ford had been an enthusiastic recruiter for America First. Yet, because he was an assistant football coach at Yale, he feared that the athletic association might frown on his activities and that his job could be in jeopardy.[15]

In other ways, though, the founders were in luck. By late July, William H. Regnery, a Chicago textile manufacturer and president of the Western Shade Cloth Company, promised substantial contributions if the organization was launched. Wood invited twenty-nine prominent Americans to serve as sponsors, and many responded.[16]

Publicizing the AFC

In order to promote the AFC, on September 4 the new organization made its first public announcement. Officially naming Stuart as national director, it proclaimed four principles:

1. The United States must build an impregnable defense for America.

2. No foreign powers, nor group of powers, can successfully attack a *prepared* America.

3. American democracy can be preserved only by keeping out of the European war.

4. "Aid short of war" weakens national defense at home and threatens to involve America in war abroad.

The committee also outlined its proposed activities:

1. To bring together all Americans, regardless of possible differences on other matters, who see eye-to-eye on these principles. (This does not include Nazis, Fascists, Communists, or members of other groups that place the interest of any other nation above those of our own country.)

2. To urge Americans to keep their heads amid rising hysteria in times of crisis.

3. To provide sane national leadership for the majority of the American people who want to keep out of the European war.

4. To register this opinion with the President and the majority of Congress.[17]

The AFC's aims and policies were articulated in more detail by Clay Judson, executive committee member and prominent Chicago attorney. In a letter to Wood written within three weeks after the AFC was formed, Judson stressed the primacy of national defense and the ruinous consequences of full-scale belligerency. If the United States kept supplying Britain with weapons used "to kill Germans," he said, Germany would be justified in attacking U.S. commerce. Recalling with disillusionment the entry of the United States into World War I, Judson wrote, "The parallel between the present time and 1916–1917 is complete." [Document 4]

On September 5 General Hugh Johnson officially launched the committee with a nationwide radio broadcast. Johnson, a flamboyant personality, was a Scripps-Howard columnist and had directed the National Recovery Administration. He stressed themes that America First would repeat continually: First, the U.S. military was far too undermanned and underequipped to send ships, tanks, or Flying Fortresses to Britain. The army had fewer than three hundred first-line combat planes and only fifty-nine heavy bombers. It also lacked enough modern equipment to outfit 100,000 men. Second, Britain—far from ever being the first line of U.S. defense—had, in the admittedly distant past, acted most aggressively in the Western Hemisphere, once in Mexico and once in Venezuela. It also took territory in Honduras and the Falkland Islands in defiance of the Monroe Doctrine. In addition, at Munich, the British showed their unreliability by tossing Czechoslovakia "to the wolves." Third, although the interventionists claimed that Hitler would menace the Atlantic if Britain fell, the United States could shift its fleet from the Pacific, where it had no serious material interests at stake. In fact, as far as U.S. activities in the Pacific went, one could only deduce, "We are out there to help preserve the British Empire in Asia."[18]

In Johnson, the AFC was using a former New Dealer and Democrat to assault interventionism, and it remained strictly neutral throughout the 1940 presidential campaign. It shunned Wendell Willkie, the Republican nominee, partly because his views could scarcely be distinguished from Roosevelt's. Both candidates favored a vigorous defense program and aid to Britain "short of war" but voiced strong opposition to entering the conflict. More important, the heavily Republican AFC leadership undoubtedly realized that many Democrats opposed intervention and that some who voted for Roosevelt could be enrolled in the AFC ranks.[19] When columnist John T. Flynn proposed a pre-election broadcast, sponsored by the AFC and attacking the president, the directors objected. As Clay Judson noted, the AFC was not organized to promote or oppose candidates; rather it was established to foster non-interventionist principles.[20]

On September 21, 1940, America First held its first directors' meeting, one devoted primarily to promotional activities. General Wood served as chairman. Other directors attending included Regnery, Stuart, and Clay Judson. Bruce Barton—advertising executive and Republican congressman from New York City's "silk-stocking district"—was authorized to organize a series of radio programs that would include speeches by such luminaries as Wood, Johnson, Sen. Robert M. La Follette (Progressive-Wis.), Sen. David I. Walsh (D-Mass.), Sen. Arthur Capper (R.-Kan.), and the radio commentator Boake Carter.[21]

The AFC's immediate concern was to counter the militant wing of the CDAAA, which sought the release of secret bomb sights and of twenty-five Flying Fortresses to Britain.[22] Noting a Gallup poll indicating that 52 percent of the people favored underwriting a British victory by "all aid short of war," Stuart wrote Johnson on September 24, 1940, "Until today this trend has not been effectively stopped. The dangers in 'aid short of war' have not been analysed." Hence, on October 3, 1940, the AFC started placing advertisements in the press warning against sending weapons overseas: "We need guns. We need men. We need ships enough for a two-ocean navy independent of any other power. Let nobody take them away from us. Let nobody give them away." Self-made "emergencies" might mean war with Japan and instantly thereafter with Germany. The message was clear: "*Peace* at home or *war* abroad? Think America! you can decide if you act now!"[23]

But how to act? The advertisements created a demand for leadership that the AFC, not yet a membership organization, was ill equipped to supply. Many contributors asked how they could join the organization, something that caught the committee totally unprepared.(A year later the organization that had begun with a one-room office and a lone stenographer ended up with ten rooms and sixty-eight employees.)[24]

As Christmas 1940 grew closer, fear of war had not lessened. Although the Greeks were driving the Italians out of Albania and the British were taking the initiative in Libya, Germany had made significant gains in the east. Hungary, Romania, and the rump state of Slovakia announced their adherence to the Tripartite Pact, joining the alliance of Germany, Italy, and Japan.

Britain was relying on a blockade of the European continent and a massive bombing of Germany. Once Britain received the assistance needed to match the strength of the Axis, Churchill told Roosevelt, it would land troops on the continent and, it hoped, deliver the telling blow. With the possibility that Britain could hold out, perhaps even win the war, interventionists demanded all-out aid. Immediately after the 1940 elections, Roosevelt started speaking—both privately and publicly—of allotting to Britain half of all the munitions and the latest bombers being produced in the United States.[25]

In the eyes of the anti-interventionists, however, Britain was in worse shape than ever, and talk of massive aid only made the AFC leadership more apprehensive. "People are waking up to the fact that we have drifted terribly close to the brink of war," Stuart wrote. "Britain is about at the end of her rope. Her shipping losses are higher than in 1917. The interventionists are desperate and are launching a whirlwind attack on the Neutrality Act." [Document 5]

The retired diplomat William R. Castle, a member of the AFC's national committee and a confidant of former president Herbert Hoover's, shared Stuart's suspicions. He was convinced that Roosevelt sought U.S. involvement. He hoped that through its press contacts the AFC would scotch the rumor that U.S. warships would escort British merchantmen to England. Roosevelt, he feared, would try to get around the neutrality law by using British ships and ordering the navy to protect them, something—Castle claimed—the president had a right to do as commander in chief.[26]

Stuart too saw trouble ahead. He noted that Britain's heavy shipping losses might cause the United States to enter the forbidden combat zone, that is, the seas surrounding Britain that had been banned to U.S. shipping since November 1939, when the Neutrality Act was passed.[27] "The next sixty days will tell the tale," he wrote Wood. [Document 6]

The committee also prepared to oppose credits to Great Britain. The 1939 Neutrality Act had forbidden all credits to belligerents. In addition, the Johnson Act of 1934 prohibited private loans to governments in default of their obligations to the U.S. government and its citizens, a category that certainly included Great Britain. William Benton, vice president of the University of Chicago and a retired advertising executive, went so far as to say that he would approve loans only if the treasures of the British Museum were put up as collateral. [Document 7]

Although Benton's proposal did not get much hearing, the AFC strongly debated the credits issue. Meeting on December 17, it decided not to oppose loans to belligerents. Although such a position appears a bit incongruous for an anti-interventionist body, Stuart noted that his uncle, Edward L. Ryerson, Jr., an AFC national committeeman who had been vocal in opposing any ban on credits, was board chairman of Inland Steel, a firm doing "a tidy little steel business" with the British.[28]

By early December, *Time* reported that the AFC had 60,000 members, eleven local chapters, and "an organization drive that was going like a house afire." Just before Christmas, Stuart could report to a major donor that the organization had able personnel and clear lines of command.[29]

Amid its anxieties over Roosevelt policy and its efforts to become a mass organization, the AFC experienced trouble with a rival organization. On December 17, 1940, at New York's Hotel Lexington, Iowa editor Verne Marshall announced the formation of the No Foreign War Committee (NFWC). Originally the NFWC was intended to serve simply as a coordinating body for various pacifist, civic, business, and veterans groups. O. K. Armstrong, a leader in the American Legion, agreed to head the group, but Marshall created an entirely new and militant organization. Thus, instead of the No Foreign War *Campaign* headed by the moderate and conciliatory Armstrong, the No Foreign War *Committee* emerged, led by the strident and volatile Marshall.[30]

Stuart believed that Marshall's backers were undermining the AFC by organizing a rival group. [Document 8] At first, the AFC attempted to cooperate with the NFWC, but a unity meeting between Wood and Marshall left the general convinced that Marshall was in a state of nervous exhaustion. As Ruth Sarles writes of the meeting, "It terminated with the two factions severing negotiations completely." By January 24, 1941, the AFC felt compelled to inform its chapters that it had no connection with Marshall's NFWC.[31]

Organization

For the AFC to succeed, respected leaders were essential, both to lend their prestige and to contribute their wealth and talents. Recruitment for the national committee, however, was not easy, even among those sympathetic to the anti-interventionist cause.

Some individuals, particularly those from the world of publishing, claimed to be in general agreement but wanted to keep their independence. Others—such as the New York district attorney Thomas E. Dewey, a leading presidential contender in 1940—pleaded too many responsibilities.[32] Still others sought to avoid controversy. Robert Maynard Hutchins, president of the University of Chicago, replied, "I am in as much trouble as the University can stand already."[33] Several figures disagreed with what they saw as the AFC's emphasis. The historian Will Durant responded, "We should not enter the war and should stick to international law; but I can't reconcile myself to the replacement of the British empire—vicious in its origins, but liberal in its development—by a despotism so openly hostile to the liberties that have made Western civilization." Former U.S. vice president Charles G. Dawes, board chairman of Chicago City Bank and Trust Company, withdrew from the embryonic national committee in August 1940. Though initially suspicious of Roosevelt's interventionist measures, he soon found himself advocating all-out aid to Britain short of war.[34]

The AFC's political conservatism also alienated some potential allies. Many of its most publicized contributors had attacked the New Deal, and the AFC often advanced arguments that appealed to big business. As the liberal economist Stuart Chase observed, "General Wood's outfit is undoubtedly splendid but I just don't want to appear on the same letterhead with some of his buddies."[35]

Then there was the matter of isolationism. Charles Clayton Morrison, editor of the *Christian Century*, wished "to see the United States assume a pacific responsibility in world affairs," something he feared "may not be congenial to the leadership of America First." [Document 9] Others found the AFC too nationalistic. The international lawyer John Foster Dulles wrote that he was

> very much opposed to our getting into war; on the other hand I am not an isolationist. I believe strongly that our present troubles are primarily due to the inevitable break-down of a world order based on super-nationalism.[36]

Dulles was not alone. Felix Morley, former Pulitzer prize–winning editor of the *Washington Post* and president of Haverford College, sympathized with most AFC aims and even spoke at an AFC luncheon. But he declined membership on the national committee on the grounds that he had been a staunch supporter of the League of Nations; in addition, he opposed the various neutrality acts for failing to distinguish between aggressor and victim.[37]

In February 1941, when Congress passed the Lend-Lease Act, there were more rejections. Hugh R. Wilson, a former ambassador to Germany, argued that head-on opposition to intervention was doomed to failure and moreover would give a false impression of national disunity.[38]

Occasionally a possible recruit said he could do more good elsewhere. Ray Lyman Wilbur, president of Stanford University and Herbert Hoover's secretary of the interior, told Wood he had joined the CDAAA to "keep it from running to extremes."[39] As late as September 1941, Professor Edwin M. Borchard, who had influenced the original Yale group, claimed his influence with Congress would be greater if he remained aloof. [Document 10]

Some prominent Americans, such as Democratic wheelhorse James A. Farley, apparently never responded. Other suggestions the AFC itself vetoed. For example, in December 1940 one AFC staff member wrote Stuart: "On second thought Frank Lloyd Wright may not be a good man to have on the committee. He is a great architect but he has quite a reputation for immorality."[40]

It would, however, be a mistake to dwell on those who decided not to join the committee. The list of national committee members is impressive. Some resigned for various reasons, but others remained steadfast.[41] Upon joining, Ryerson expressed alarm at the prowar hysteria he perceived in the summer of 1940.[42] General Hugh Johnson pointed graphically to the horrors of war: "Why do I shrink from a new crop of faceless, armless, legless men?" [Document 11]

New York advertising executive Chester Bowles also remained, despite his liberal domestic views, saying: "Obviously we cannot build a wall around ourselves in an attempt to exist regardless of what goes on in other parts of the world." [Document 12] He was so strongly opposed to entering the war that he supported Senators Robert A. Taft (R-Ohio) and Burton K. Wheeler (D-Mont.) as presidential candidates.[43] In July 1941 Bowles critically appraised possible war objectives. [Document 13]

But some national committee members defected. Two leading pacifists resigned almost immediately after the group was formed. The prominent liberal editor Oswald Garrison Villard denied that the AFC's focus on defense was either necessary or desirable: "I believe it carries within it the seeds of death for our democracy." Similarly, Albert W. Palmer, president of the Chicago Theological Seminary, submitted an entire brief for Christian pacifism, one that went so far as to claim that all wars in U.S. history had been "bad and unnecessary."[44]

AFC leaders attributed some resignations to interventionist pressure. When Eddie Rickenbacker withdrew in February 1941, Wood suspected that the World War I ace feared losing valuable mail delivery contracts for Eastern Air Lines, the firm he headed. Actress Lillian Gish told Wood she had been blacklisted by both Hollywood and the legitimate theater, but said she had been promised a $65,000 film contract if she severed her ties with the AFC without revealing why she resigned.[45]

Occasionally the AFC dropped national committee members it found embarrassing. Avery Brundage, prominent Chicago builder and president of the American Olympic Association, had aroused suspicions that he was pro-Nazi. Henry Ford seemed tainted by his sponsorship of an anti-Semitic weekly, the *Dearborn Independent*, during the 1920s. Although the famous auto manufacturer publicly repudiated his earlier views, the committee found it too risky to retain his name on its masthead.[46]

Some prominent Americans, though untapped for the national committee, were rumored to be sympathetic to the AFC position. They included St. Louis manufacturer Stuart Symington, later secretary of the air force and a Democratic senator from Missouri, and Bernard M. Baruch, the famed financier who headed the War Industries Board in 1918. With others, such as Maj. Albert G. Wedemeyer, support for the AFC was never in doubt.[47]

Occasionally the AFC benefited greatly from what, in effect, was a silent partner. Herbert Hoover did not formally join America First, for he was spearheading the National Committee on Food for the Small Democracies, an effort to feed some 27 million Europeans, mostly women and children. Five nations under German occupation—Norway, Holland, Belgium, Poland, and France—should, Hoover argued, have the right to import food. A neutral international organization would protect food supplies from the Germans. Because such a proposal involved lifting Britain's blockade, most interventionists attacked Hoover's efforts. He nonetheless attracted support from some of them, including Gen. John J. Pershing and Sen. John H. Bankhead (D-Ala.). They undoubtedly recalled that in World War I a similar Hoover effort had not interfered with waging the war.[48]

Hoover did not want to tie his relief efforts to those of the AFC, so he used his close friend William Castle as an informal liaison. In addition, in July 1941 Hoover attempted in vain to have Chief Justice Charles Evans Hughes speak on the radio against intervention. During 1941 Hoover tapped millionaire Jeremiah Milbank to contribute to the AFC, and the AFC in turn reprinted Hoover's speeches and endorsed his relief efforts.[49] Although the AFC never gave any reason for the endorsement, its motives were obvious: the food plan would relieve suffering, reduce tensions between the Axis and the Allies, and bring Hoover, a prominent anti-interventionist, into international policy making.

The AFC's national chairman and board of directors were no mere figureheads but made the crucial decisions. Chairman Wood appeared at committee headquarters in Chicago almost daily; he personally approved every significant decision. Yet he always sought to surrender his post, and at the outset he hoped Eddie Rickenbacker, Verne Marshall, or financier Joseph P. Kennedy would accept the leadership. The seven-member board of directors, or executive committee, usually made major policy; the national committee seldom met.[50]

The twenty-four-year-old Stuart and the Chicago staff executed the policies formulated by the directors and the national committee. At first

Stuart was national director, but in April 1941 the directors changed his post to a less exalted one: executive secretary and assistant to the chairman. He was in charge of local chapters, speakers, and advertisements and of supervising the Washington research staff and lobby. Some senior AFC leaders sharply criticized him, in particular AFC vice chairman and former Democratic party organizer Janet Ayer Fairbank, but he possessed what historian Wayne S. Cole calls "selfless idealism." More pertinent, Stuart was a good executive, with the ability to grow in the job.[51] His staff was by and large a young one and in some cases politically liberal as well.[52]

Several individuals exercised a supervisory function in local areas. In a sense, they were deputies of the national headquarters.[53] John T. Flynn, chairman of the New York chapter and national committeeman, was undoubtedly the most important of these. A noted journalist and writer on economics, Flynn had long attacked Wall Street speculation and proposed to curb war profits. By 1939 he suspected that Roosevelt sought to bolster the nation's sagging economy by undertaking ventures abroad. Flynn served as national chairman of the Keep America Out of War Congress, a coordinating body composed primarily of pacifists and socialists. In November 1940 the New Republic dropped his weekly column because of its anti-interventionism, but he retained a forum in the Scripps-Howard papers.[54] A staunch liberal, he was particularly alert to the danger that fascists might infiltrate the AFC. [Document 14]

Certain divisions of the AFC were particularly important. The speakers bureau arranged some 126 public addresses in thirty-two states. The bureau for research and congressional liaison contributed a series of position papers entitled "Did You Know?" which gave the anti-interventionist perspective on disputed issues. The bureau was directed by Ruth Sarles, a young woman who held a master's degree in international relations from American University and who had edited Peace Action, the monthly bulletin of the National Council for the Prevention of War.[55]

Local chapters were in many ways the nucleus of the committee, though they could often be its curse as well. They were invaluable in arranging rallies, distributing literature, and launching mail campaigns. But national headquarters could not always exercise the needed supervision, much less assure itself of competent chapter leaders. Even the Washington, D.C., chapter had trouble recruiting an able executive.[56]

Politically, the AFC had a conservative cast. Although it was officially neutral, Republicans everywhere predominated. Many rally speakers directly attacked Roosevelt and the New Deal.[57] Moreover, Stuart, Wood, and Fairbank supported Scribner's Commentator, a monthly publication rightist enough to include articles praising France's Marshal Pétain and Portugal's Doctor Salazar. The AFC even lent them a mailing list.[58]

Although strongly critical of Roosevelt, the AFC never sought to impeach him. In a letter to all chapter chairmen, Stuart said such talk "tends to make the Committee seem partisan, political, and personally hostile to Mr. Roosevelt." Much AFC support, he went on, was drawn from Roosevelt backers, and the polls showed that his popularity had reached its zenith. Besides, impeachment was a legal matter, involving formal charges.[59]

AFC conservatism was in part determined by the nature of the contributors. Initially Wood and Regnery underwrote the organization. Donors of a hundred dollars or more provided two-thirds of the national committee's income. Eight businessmen alone supplied over $100,000: they included Regnery; Harold L. Stuart, a Chicago investment banker and national committeeman; and H. Smith Richardson of the Vick Chemical Company of New York.[60] Particularly revealing is the roster of large contributors, and here several things should be noted. First, major parts of the Chicago business orbit gave extremely heavily.[61] Second, manufacturing was disproportionally represented in contributions as compared with finance, communications, and transportation. Third, an usually large number of family-owned firms were donors. Fourth, agriculture-based enterprises, such as meat packing, were heavily represented. Fifth, many contributors were from industries far more dependent on civilian consumers than on military orders. To all such interests, war would accelerate higher taxes and promote industrial unionism. Lying ahead were the risks of postwar reconversion and the sudden draining of federal credit and contracts. Not only would socialism be "the road ahead"—a phrase John Flynn later made popular—but depression was inevitable. Conversely, if the nation did not enter the war, the survival of capitalism in the United States could well be ensured. In addition, an economic link between agriculture and industry would ensure U.S. self-sufficiency.[62]

To focus on big business alone, however, would give a misleading picture. Most individual contributions, particularly to local chapters, were quite small, and donating was a real sacrifice for some supporters.

Several donors sent notes with their gifts. Young John F. Kennedy mailed a hundred dollars, adding, "what you are all doing is vital." Stuart asked Kennedy, about to travel to Latin America, to work full time for the committee. "Everyone seems to be against us but the *people*," Stuart wrote to the future president.[63]

Certain groups were deliberately recruited. Richard A. Moore, later the AFC director of publicity, organized College Men for Defense First (CMDF), a group that included actor José Ferrer and New Frontiersman R. Sargent Shriver. In practice the CMDF acted as an AFC conduit, and it formally merged with the committee the day before the Pearl Harbor attack.[64] Veterans also were targeted, although in 1941 the AFC could not dissuade the American Legion from backing Roosevelt's foreign policy, including aid to the Soviet Union. The AFC was able to prevent the 1940 convention of the American Farm Bureau Federation from adopting a pro-war resolution, but it found direct recruiting of farmers difficult. Labor participation, if anything, was even sparser, and few leaders of the Congress of Industrial Organizations, the American Federation of Labor, or the railroad brotherhoods were listed as AFC sponsors. Stuart did tap Kathryn Lewis, daughter of CIO president John L. Lewis, for the national committee; she obviously represented that most prominent U.S. labor leader. There were some sporadic efforts to recruit blacks, and late in the summer of 1941, Washington attorney Perry Howard, Republican patronage broker, organized a Negro division.[65]

Despite its conservative cast, America First contributed to several pacifist and socialist groups.[66] Socialist party leader Norman Thomas did not join, but he spoke at two massive AFC rallies, received AFC funds for Sunday broadcasts, and undertook two college tours sponsored by the committee. In May 1941, defending himself to a fellow socialist, Thomas claimed it a grave mistake "to retire to some monastery to preserve our purity." If socialists were to avoid war, they must reach the masses, and here is where the AFC was so crucial. Suggestions to organize anti-interventionist New Dealers as a distinct body, however, were never acted on.[67]

The Committee's General Position

Once money was raised and leaders recruited, the AFC wasted no time in publicizing its views. In a series of instructions for speakers drafted during the lend-lease debate, America First offered its own interpretation of the nature and causes of what was to become World War II. It is not the least of ironies that an organization backed by believers in capitalism advanced in part a modified Leninist argument: namely, that the conflict was fundamentally a struggle between competing empires. Expressing a viewpoint popular in the 1930s, the AFC speakers bureau still thought in terms of "imperialist war" and "have-not" powers. Of course, unlike the communists, the AFC saw the Soviet Union as simply another imperialist regime.

The war, said the speakers bureau, was simply "another chapter in the series of conflicts between European states that have been going on in war and peace for hundreds of years." A new German empire was attempting to compete with well-established ones, and when Britain learned that Germany would be expanding at Britain's expense, not that of the Soviet Union, it declared war on the Third Reich. [Document 15] The bureau denied that Nazism embodied a worldwide revolution. In fact, if the United States preserved its democracy, it would insulate itself from National Socialism. [Document 16] Even if Britain were victorious, it would be unable to restore the governments destroyed by Germany. Moreover, any restored states would be too small to defend themselves, and the unstable political order created by the Versailles peace would simply continue. [Document 17] One thing remained clear: neither the survival of democracy nor the preservation of the global balance of power was at stake.

The speakers bureau drafted questions designed to embarrass CDAAA speakers. For example, the AFC denied that war could destroy the ideologies of Nazism, fascism, or communism. "How can philosophies be stamped out?" it asked. In an effort to show that the mere existence of a hostile ideology contained no threat, the bureau noted that the United States had enjoyed "quite amicable" trade relations with the German and Italian dictatorships until war broke out in 1939. [Document 18]

The AFC accused the Roosevelt administration of participating in the war without the consent of Congress or the people. [Document 19] In so doing, it said, the United States was neglecting its two primary concerns: preserving a democratic form of government and building an adequate national defense. [Document 20] Certainly there was no indication that U.S. belligerence would preserve democracy. [Document 21] And it was equally certain that the American people had made no commitment to fight outside the Western Hemisphere. [Document 22]

The AFC staff also promoted specific books, including Charles A. Beard's *A Foreign Policy for America* (1940), Norman Thomas's *We Have a Future* (1940), and Maj. Gen. Johnson Hagood's *We Can Defend America* (1937). [Document 23] It also kept tabs on friendly elements within the press and held Hanson W. Baldwin, military columnist for the *New York Times,* in particularly high esteem. Occasionally it praised specific articles, even if they appeared in such interventionist magazines as *Life* and *Collier's.*[68]

If the AFC had a solution to the international crisis, it lay in a negotiated peace.[69] Negotiation was the one real alternative to the continuous fighting— and to what it saw as the perilous interventionism of Franklin D. Roosevelt. Even the popular slogan "V for Victory" was suspect, and Lindbergh and Stuart suggested an alternative, "A is for America." Although the AFC as an organization did not officially endorse the position, it promoted pleas for negotiation made by others.[70]

Furthermore, its individual leaders were far from silent on the whole matter of war and peace aims. In January 1941 General Wood claimed a victorious Germany would seek economic control of Europe but would leave most states politically independent.[71] Two weeks later, Clay Judson claimed that a compromise peace would give the world a chance to recover from the wreckage of war. [Document 24] In February, Castle noted that John Cudahy, a former ambassador to Belgium, had told him a negotiated peace was Britain's only hope. [Document 25][72]

Sarles kept careful tabs on any peace talk. In late May 1941 she suspected that John Winant, U.S. ambassador to Great Britain, had come home with Hitler's latest peace proposal. [Document 26] In July she noted that any peace could be made only on Hitler's terms. Hence, for America First publicly to urge peace in the abstract, or to make specific peace proposals, would be self-defeating. It was better, she wrote Stuart, to have local chapters study peace aims. [Document 27] Another month later, she was even more pessimistic. The president, she said, had decided on a limited war, not involving mass numbers of army troops but drawing upon American marines and sailors.[73] [Document 28]

The German invasion of the Soviet Union led to more peace talk. In October 1941, Sarles suspected that a victorious Hitler might propose a peace, while resigning as chancellor because his work was done. Bowles thought that Britain, seeing ahead the possibility of the Soviet Union's defeat, might make peace in return for German restoration of the Western democracies. Stuart, also looking at the Russian front, asked Robert Hutchins to launch a mediation movement. [Document 29] In November, Flynn predicted that if the Soviet Union fell, Roosevelt would abandon Britain. America First, he continued, should support prominent clergy in an independent peace effort. [Document 30] Wood, however, was uncertain whether the time was ripe, and the matter of negotiation was not raised again.[74]

The Roosevelt administration had continually stressed that Germany posed a devastating military threat. Many historians have concurred, claiming that Hitler's goals far surpassed rectification of the Versailles treaty. His "Greater Germany" was merely a way station to larger aims—hegemony in Europe, including the Soviet Union; the projection of German power overseas; a broader global struggle with the United States.[75] But even though Hitler had continually expressed hostility toward the United States, the AFC denied that Hitler could conquer it. To America First there was a great difference between intention and capability, and it focused on what it saw as great weaknesses in the German war machine.

On this point, materials prepared for speakers raised important questions: Was the United States next on Germany's list of conquests? [Document 31] Would it not be better to fight now, with allies, than later without them? [Document 32] Could the prestige acquired by a victorious Nazism bring fascism to the United States? [Document 33] What damage could a German "fifth column" do? [Document 34]

Another series of questions centered on German designs overseas: Could Germany invade the continental United States from any European base? [Document 35] From the Caribbean or Central America? [Document 36] From any base south of the Caribbean? [Document 37] What would happen if Germany defeated Britain and then sought Canadian and Caribbean outposts? [Document 38] Or sought French and Dutch colonies as bases for an assault on the United States? [Document 39]

A third group of questions centered on naval defense. Excluding the British navy, was not the combined tonnage of the Axis powers greater than that of the United States? [Document 40] If Germany captured the British fleet and used the shipbuilding facilities of the nations it had conquered, could it isolate the United States from the rest of the world? [Document 41] Was the British fleet the first line of a U.S. defense? [Document 42]

America First had to confront other arguments as well. Interventionists warned constantly that an Axis victory would result in a crippling loss of U.S. markets and raw materials. Therefore the AFC had to devise rebuttals on such questions as How dependent is the U.S. economy on foreign trade? [Document 43] Could Germany capture world commerce and thereby strangle American industry? [Document 44] Must the United States fight in order to secure needed tin and rubber? [Document 45] Could Germany cause the world to abandon the gold standard, thereby making U.S. currency valueless? [Document 46]

The speakers bureau stressed that the United States already held the lion's share of Latin American trade and was doing as much business as Germany, Italy, England, France, and Japan together. It noted that needed raw materials were located in the Western Hemisphere, an area the U.S. Navy could protect. [Documents 47–49]

In addition, the position papers of the AFC's research bureau argued that even if Hitler were victorious over Europe, North Africa, and the Near East, he could not destroy U.S. trade; that Germany might well find victory over the Soviet Union counterproductive; and that within the Western Hemisphere lay all raw materials needed for U.S. industry. [Documents 50–52] While denying the administration's claim that the United States faced an oil shortage, the AFC sought economic integration of the entire hemisphere. [Documents 53 and 54][76] The research bureau was especially critical of Roosevelt's economic policies. Accusing the administration of poorly allocating raw materials and misinterpreting the Lend-Lease Act, it found the United States on the verge of another depression. [Documents 55 and 56]

General Wood maintained that the United States could always dominate the trade of the upper half of Latin America. The products of the continent's temperate zone, however—Brazil's cotton, Chile's copper and nitrates, and Argentina's meat, cotton, and wool—were bound to compete with U.S. goods. "We cannot sell unless we buy," the general said, "and that is a far greater obstacle than all nazidom."[77]

The anti-interventionist economic argument at its most sophisticated level can be found in excerpts from an eighty-four-page manuscript, "The Economic Consequences of American Intervention," written by Lawrence Dennis. Dennis was a journalist and economist who advocated what he called "a desirable fascism," by which he meant nationalization of banks and major monopolies, redistribution of wealth and income through progressive taxation, subsidization of small enterprises and farming, one-party rule, and reorganization of the Congress on vocational lines. Two weeks before Pearl

Harbor, Wood sought to raise funds for the publication of Dennis's manu-script, possibly under the signature of someone better known and less controversial.[78]

Hitler, said Dennis, could not deprive the United States of its Latin American markets. Neither, for that matter, would Japan be able to withhold rubber from the United States even if it conquered Southeast Asia. More-over, by skillful use of the economic weapon of barter, the United States would be able to build a powerful economic presence in the Western Hemisphere. If Germany dominated all the Near East and Africa and Europe to the Urals, the United States could not only ward off German economic penetration, it could actually emerge, claimed Dennis, a much stronger power. [Document 57]

If Dennis's manuscript had been published under AFC auspices, it would have constituted the most extensive public challenge yet to the interventionist economic arguments popularized by columnist Walter Lipp-mann and diplomat Douglas Miller. Lippmann had claimed that Germany would undersell the United States, Miller that the United States would become a Nazi economic colony. Publication of the manuscript would also have shown the AFC was willing to sponsor, at least surreptitiously, the views of a man who espoused a corporate state and who would soon be branded in the popular press as "America's No. 1 fascist author."[79]

From Lend-Lease to Draft Extension

Most AFC attention did not focus on such broad theories. Instead it centered on Roosevelt's specific legislative proposals. On December 7, 1940, Church-ill wrote the president, claiming that Britain could no longer pay cash for U.S. arms. Within ten days, Roosevelt said publicly that the United States must keep aid flowing; moreover, he would soon show how this could be done. In his fireside chat of December 29, the president foresaw disastrous consequences if Britain fell, and on January 6, he outlined his program to provide lend-lease assistance.[80]

The lend-lease bill was sweeping in scope. It authorized the president to provide military articles and information to any country "whose defense the President deems vital to the defense of the United States." Terms for transfer were left completely to the president's discretion. The terms "defense article" and "defense information" permitted virtually anything to fall under one of the two categories if the president desired.[81]

For the committed America Firster, the bill meant nothing but trouble. On the day after it was submitted, Wood promised AFC opposition "with all the vigor it can exert." The president was not simply asking for a blank check; he sought "a blank check book with the power to write away our manpower, our laws and our liberties." A committee advertisement said the bill permitted the president to do just about anything: send U.S. warships and merchant vessels into war zones, give unlimited funds to other nations, turn over the entire United States Navy as well as every gun and bullet in the army, cancel any law on the statute books, make military alliances with any nation, and take the United States into war whenever, wherever, and against whomever he wished. To Stuart, the United States would be stripping her own defense, making her security increasingly dependent on a British victory.[82]

Writing to Harvard president James B. Conant, Clay Judson challenged the major interventionist premise: that it was more important to defeat Hitler than to stay out of war. [Document 24] Full-scale entry, Judson said, would only destroy America's freedom. He challenged Conant's suggestion that the United States might limit its assistance to air and sea power. Defeating Germany would require an invasion of the European continent, and any such invasion would involve "losses of such magnitude that civilization itself will shudder."

During the lend-lease debate, AFC leaders—Wood, Castle, and prominent Iowa Republican Hanford MacNider—testified before the appropriate congressional committees. The AFC provided speakers for hundreds of meetings and mailed a weekly newsletter to 1,250 of those speakers. It circulated many petitions, with the Chicago chapter alone gathering over 700,000 signatures. At least 2,600 transcribed speeches were sent to radio stations. New chapters were organized virtually daily; by late February 1941, 648 embryonic chapters were on the AFC books. The research division prepared major position papers [Document 58], which were often reprinted by several newspapers, including the Hearst chain, and entered into the *Congressional Record*.[83]

Wood's own alternative to lend-lease centered on selling spare U.S. ships to Britain and on providing long-term credits for food and war supplies. Three criteria, however, would have to be met: namely, that it was impossible for Britain to pay; that the transfer violated no U.S. neutrality laws; and that the goods be carried in Britain's own vessels.[84]

Not everyone who opposed entry into the war backed the AFC's position on lend-lease. Thomas Dewey opposed mass protest, declaring that discussion should be left to Congress. He wrote Wood, "The dangers of the bill are so apparent that I cannot believe the American people will willingly give such broad powers to one man under the present circumstances." A. Whitney Griswold, a political scientist who had originally encouraged the Yale group, considered it crucial to keep the United Kingdom and British navy out of German hands. [Document 59] Princeton historian Raymond J. Sontag claimed outright defeat of the bill would fatally weaken America's international prestige. [Document 60][85] Editor and critic John Chamberlain endorsed aid to Britain, but insisted on outright transfer of British bases to the United States and a genuine negotiated peace. [Document 61]

For at least one correspondent, the AFC was too ambivalent. The author Lincoln Colcord found the committee trying to "carry water on both shoulders": it endorsed aid to Britain in principle when strict neutrality was called for. [Document 62] Stuart, in a most revealing reply, said Colcord was correct in thinking that an absolutely neutral stand was more rational, but that Colcord should be aware of the intense public sentiment and the fact that "logical consideration[s] do not prevent those who advocate strict neutrality from being widely and hopelessly discredited."[86]

The AFC possessed few illusions about defeating the bill. Late in January 1941 the Washington bureau predicted passage in some form by May 15. It noted the trade-offs within the Senate and saw proposed amendments as innocuous. Even more troublesome, Britain faced only an even chance of surviving the coming summer. [Document 63]

Yet in public, the AFC claimed actual defeat of the measure was possible, *"provided the strong opposition sentiment in Congress is brought out by repeated encouragement from home"* (emphasis in original). It found useless a much-touted time limit on foreign use of U.S.-made defense materials, for possession was nine-tenths of the law. It asserted that administration witnesses were unable to say how the United States could even be invaded. Most important, it maintained that the bill would immediately result in a war in which the United States would have to supply from 5 to 10 million troops. [Document 64]

The House passed the bill on February 8 by a vote of 260 to 165. Most of the amendments adopted were merely expressions of intent; they did not curb any power granted by the new law. The most important concession—a $1.3 billion limit on appropriations—stripped the opponents of their chief argument, that the measure involved abdication of congressional responsibility and granted the president a blank check. It was not an effective ceiling, however, as the president could decide how to price defense articles.[87]

Once the debate shifted to the Senate, America First increased its pressure. On February 12 an AFC newsletter noted concurrent proposals to curb personal liberty and the ineffectiveness of the House amendments. [Document 65] A day later, the Washington office issued the first of a series of confidential reports indicating that Britain faced certain defeat and implying that lend-lease would be futile. One predicted a German campaign in the Balkans and a direct attack on the British Isles. [Document 66] Others forecast the imminent fall of Greece, the closing of the Suez Canal, and further German penetration of the entire Mediterranean area, including Spain. [Documents 67–70]

Even before the Senate debate on lend-lease opened, however, the

Washington bureau knew the bill would pass. On March 8 the Senate passed it 60 to 31, and within ten days Roosevelt signed it. A Gallup poll showed that over half the respondents favored lend-lease.[88]

Wood said publicly that the AFC must see that lend-lease was enforced in such manner as to avoid European and Asian conflicts. In particular, America First vigorously opposed the use of U.S. merchant vessels and naval convoys. The AFC took credit for a provision in the bill that allegedly prevented the delivery of war goods to Britain. When the word "transferring" was stricken from the authorization, the president—the AFC claimed—was prevented from sending goods into war zones in U.S. merchant ships convoyed by U.S. war vessels.[89]

Privately General Wood was discouraged enough to consider resigning the chairmanship. Yet, despite initial discouragement, the committee continued. On March 28, at a director's meeting, Judson and Ryerson saw naval escorts as inevitable and maintained that the AFC could accomplish little. Wood and Fairbank, however, said the AFC must continue as long as funds were available. Moreover, some congressmen, in analyzing the administration victory, saw the anti-interventionist cause as far from lost. [Document 71][90]

Ironically, given that Roosevelt's proposal was so heavily debated, for the rest of 1941 lend-lease was neither outstandingly novel nor notably altruistic. For two years, Roosevelt had envisaged the European democracies as America's front line and had presented the United States as "the great arsenal of democracy." Yet the supplies were no gift, for repayment was postponed, not waived. Later administration discussions revealed that "consideration" would not necessarily be in money or even in kind; instead it involved a commitment to the U.S. conception of the postwar world economy. The United States would press Britain into abolishing her commercial system of Imperial Preference and thereby eliminate discriminatory tariffs against U.S. goods.

In 1941 Britain received no great benefit. Only later was the British Commonwealth given some $31 billion in supplies and the Soviet Union some $11 billion. Throughout 1941 lend-lease provided only 1 percent of Britain's munitions total. (Another 7 percent came from the United States under older contracts, which the British paid for in cash.)[91]

The bill did mark a significant turning point, however. By assuming responsibility for Britain's long-term purchases, Roosevelt relieved the British government of a costly and cumbersome burden and demonstrated his faith in Britain's survival. With that irrevocable commitment, a genuine Anglo-American alliance was forged.

Another point should be noted. The AFC never called for a British defeat. Wayne Cole writes that nearly all committee leaders sympathized with the British and hoped they would not lose. Moreover, they officially discouraged anti-British statements per se. Yet, as Cole also notes, many

America Firsters could justly be called Anglophobes. The AFC was unsparing in spreading anti-British stories, including them in bulletin after bulletin, and leaving the decided impression that the British were a singularly ungrateful people. It did not need the warning it received from birth control advocate Margaret Sanger: "You are fighting not the invasion of redcoats but the invasion of British charm, flattery, diplomacy at the Nth degree."[92]

The AFC was particularly cool toward Union Now, formally named Federal Union. Union Now was a plan advanced by Clarence K. Streit, former League of Nations correspondent for the *New York Times*, by which the United States would first federate with Britain, then with the democracies of Western Europe. The AFC responded with the slogan "British Union Now? Soviet Union Next?" and then a full-scale position paper prepared by the research bureau. [Document 72][93]

More important than such attacks were AFC estimates of Britain's chances. During the lend-lease debates, speakers were given material claiming Britain faced little danger of an all-out blitzkrieg. [Document 73] Most of the time, however, the AFC stressed Britain's peril. In December 1940 Stuart saw Britain in sorry condition [Document 6], and in May 1941 Ruth Sarles reported on Britain's weakness. [Document 74] At one point, she thought Churchill might resign. [Document 75] In November, Wood claimed that Britain was either unwilling or unable to invade Germany.[94]

Given its deep-rooted suspicions of Britain and pessimism about an Allied victory, the AFC strongly opposed escorts. During the lend-lease debate, Roosevelt had said that escorting ships through a danger zone invariably involved "shooting," and "shooting comes awfully close to war." Yet once lend-lease was passed, the CDAAA announced the slogan "Deliver the Goods to Britain Now," a policy the AFC saw as making war inevitable. In March, America First responded to such demands by adding two sentences to its statement of principles: "In 1917 we sent our American ships into the war zone and this led us to war. In 1941 we must keep our naval convoys and merchant vessels on this side of the Atlantic."[95]

Roosevelt did little to alleviate their anxieties. On April 11, 1941, he announced that the United States was occupying Greenland. In addition, he began extending Atlantic neutrality "patrols" as far as necessary to protect the hemisphere. Secretly he assured Churchill that the United States Navy would radio to British craft the location of enemy ships west of twenty-five degrees longitude.[96] Stuart warned Wood that Roosevelt's "patrols" might serve as a smoke screen for "convoys." Other AFC leaders shared Stuart's general anxiety. Early in April, Sterling Morton suggested that America First concede that the United States was already a belligerent. [Document 76] Wood replied, denying that the nation had underwritten a complete victory for Britain. [Document 77] By the middle of April, Sarles suspected that the United States would get into war within the month. She also noted rumors of sending U.S. troops to Cape Verde, especially if the Germans moved toward Dakar.[97]

Particularly alarming was the use of U.S. ships to transport lend-lease goods. Congressional anti-interventionists caucused over convoy issues, while the AFC launched an anti-convoy mail campaign. Rep. Hamilton Fish (R-N.Y.) offered the slogan "No Convoys—No War," which the committee immediately made its own. The AFC also supported a resolution of Sen. Charles W. Tobey (R-N.H.) that would have prohibited U.S. escorts for British ships.[98]

Some optimism remained in the AFC ranks, which saw at least one setback as apparently for the best. When, on April 30, Tobey's bill died in committee, Sarles considered its failure encouraging, for it gave the AFC something to focus on. "As long as we still have a convoy resolution to fight for I think we are in a better strategic position," she said. [Document 78] She noted that it was a group of anti-interventionist senators who opposed bringing Tobey's convoy motion to a vote. [Document 79][99]

Yet, despite administration efforts to downplay the escort issue, Sarles saw it as a real one, especially since U.S. merchant vessels would be going into the dangerous Red Sea zone. [Document 79] There were other reasons for indignation as well. When the administration began to seize Axis ships, a move authorized by Congress, the AFC's *Washington News Letter* saw the United States violating international law.[100]

On May 27, 1941, Pan American Day, Roosevelt delivered a radio address in which he accused the Nazis of seeking world domination. Germany, he asserted, might soon be within striking distance of the Western Hemisphere. To resist the Nazis, the Allies must control the seas. The United States must not only step up shipbuilding, but must also expand its patrols far into the North Atlantic. In addition, he proclaimed an unlimited national emergency, although he neither committed the United States to convoys nor sought repeal of the Neutrality Act.[101]

The AFC responded quickly. The *Washington News Letter* offered a lengthy analysis of Roosevelt's speech, noting that all specific assumption of emergency powers must be preceded by individual proclamations. [Document 80][102] Sarles was apprehensive, for she saw Roosevelt ignoring both Congress and his previous antiwar pledges. [Document 26] On June 4, in another *Washington News Letter*, editor Kendrick Lee claimed the budding defense boom hid impending unemployment and saw the German conquest of Crete as proving the folly of convoys. [Document 81]

For the United States, however, naval warfare began in earnest on June 10. On that day, Americans learned that a German submarine, *U-69*, had sunk the *Robin Moor*, a merchant vessel flying the U.S. flag, some twenty days earlier. The incident took place in the South Atlantic, seven hundred miles from both the bulge of Brazil and the west coast of Africa. No lives were lost.

America First kept close tabs on the incident, fearing that the administration would exploit the sinking to accelerate entry into the war. Congress's seeming lack of anxiety was most reassuring to the AFC. Sarles noted from

Capitol Hill, "There has not been great excitement." Although interventionists stressed that the ship transported no munitions, the research bureau
showed that the *Robin Moor* was carrying contraband. [Document 82] AFC
national headquarters drew its own lesson: If U.S. ships insisted on carrying
cargo that both belligerents labeled contraband, they must accept the risk.[103]
Moreover, as the research bureau noted, any arming of merchant vessels
would lead to war. [Document 83]

The ship issue temporarily subsided. In a broadcast made on June 20,
Roosevelt invoked the doctrine of freedom of the seas. The United States,
he said, would not yield to "piracy."[104] Unlike Woodrow Wilson in the case
of the *Sussex,* he did not do what the AFC most feared—use the *Robin
Moor* incident to take more radical measures. Yet the AFC research bureau
vigorously protested, accusing the president of violating international law
by his efforts to help one belligerent defeat another. [Document 84]

By late July the committee believed it was making progress. It boasted
that it had defeated escorts; caused Roosevelt to postpone and rewrite his
"national emergency" speech, originally scheduled for early May; and
eliminated the clause in a conscription renewal bill permitting troops to be
stationed outside the hemisphere.[105] Particularly heartening were the AFC
rallies where Senator Wheeler, Senator Nye—and most important—Col.
Charles Lindbergh addressed capacity crowds.

Lindbergh had joined the national committee on April 17, 1941, an event
that made national news. In the previous few months his ties to America
First had grown increasingly close. When, in March, *Collier's* had published
Lindbergh's anti-interventionist "A Letter to Americans," the AFC strongly
promoted the piece, even going so far as to gather endorsements. During
the spring, Wood—who desperately wanted to return to full-time work at
Sears, Roebuck—kept asking Lindbergh to become committee chairman.
The Lone Eagle refused, claiming he was so controversial that he would
split the AFC. Besides, he said, he needed the time to write.[106]

As one of his biographers notes, Lindbergh's membership gave the
committee a much-needed boost. His solo trans-Atlantic flight in 1927 had
made him the foremost hero of a jaded generation, and for many even his
bitter feud with the press had not tarnished his halo. Lindbergh was
undoubtedly the only anti-interventionist whose mass appeal had any chance
of rivaling the president's. As the AFC's most popular speaker, he could
recruit new members and rally enthusiasm. Indeed, his appeal occasionally
reached beyond his fellow conservatives, and the liberal Chester Bowles
was not beyond envisioning him president of the United States. [Document
85]

Yet in some ways, Lindbergh's allegiance was a mixed blessing. His anti-
interventionism was so intense that he exposed himself to attack in a way
that many America Firsters did not. In testifying before the House Foreign
Affairs Committee against lend-lease, he had gone so far as to say that he

wanted neither side to win. Furthermore, though he privately opposed Germany's treatment of the Jews, he had never condemned the persecutions publicly. (Lindbergh feared that such condemnation would increase interventionist sentiment.) He also refused to return a Nazi decoration bestowed on him in 1936, and three years later, in 1939, he called for building "our White ramparts."[107]

Even General Wood was concerned when, late in May 1941, Lindbergh publicly called for "new leadership," as Roosevelt had recently been re-elected for another term.[108] Further criticism came on August 29, 1941, when Lindbergh suggested at Oklahoma City that "before this war is over, England herself may turn against us, as she has turned against France and Finland." (He undoubtedly was referring to Britain's attack on the French fleet at Mers-el-Kebir, the interception of three Finnish ships, and a blockade of the northern Finnish port of Petsamo.) Even before his Des Moines speech (see below), Lindbergh's presence on AFC platforms had increased the attacks on the organization, and the press spent far more time attacking the AFC than covering its efforts to prevent full-scale U.S. entry into the war. As Cole writes, "One can only guess whether the patterns would have been substantially different if Lindbergh had never joined the Committee."[109]

Even as noted a figure as Lindbergh had difficulty proving he spoke for the majority of Americans. The polls consistently showed the public favoring the president's specific interventionist moves. Because the surveys always indicated that Americans would risk war to aid Britain, the AFC sought to argue with the results and how they were obtained. Bowles was particularly concerned. On April 25 he noted the Gallup polls expressing "the same old fundamental confusion," namely, that Americans wanted to stay out of the war while supporting something as warlike as convoys. [Document 86] He wrote Roy Larsen, the publisher of *Life*, claiming that poll respondents appeared "totally unaware of the seriousness of the British situation." Furthermore, they failed to realize that "Any war between Hitler and ourselves would be long and exhausting." [Document 87] Conservative public relations executive James P. Selvage accused the Gallup organization of doctoring questionnaires to make the nation appear more interventionist than it really was. [Document 88] Commented John T. Flynn, "The trouble with the Gallup poll is that the man who asks the question gets into long discussions with the person questioned and can easily shape the answers to suit himself."[110] The AFC commissioned Ross Stagner, a Dartmouth psychologist, to analyze national polls, provided Robert Hutchins with funds to take an independent university survey, and privately financed questionnaires by several anti-interventionist congressmen.[111]

The AFC had a different idea about how to measure the true tenor of public opinion: a national advisory referendum on the issue of war or peace. As endorsed by the national committee in June 1941, such a referendum would bind neither president nor Congress, but would definitely establish that Americans wanted no all-out conflict. Ruth Sarles, who had worked for the Ludlow war referendum in 1938, planned strategy. But the AFC chapters did not respond enthusiastically. At the last national committee meeting before Pearl Harbor, Stuart reported that neither anti-interventionists in Congress nor the AFC chapters were confident about securing the referendum's adoption.[112]

When on June 22, 1941, Germany invaded the Soviet Union, the New York chapter offered extensive discussion. It stressed Hitler's long-standing desire for Soviet resources; Britain and France, by interfering with Hitler's ambition between the time of Britain's guarantee to Poland and the Molotov-Ribbentrop pact, had only succeeded in destroying the nations of Western Europe. [Document 89] Chapter chairman Flynn commented that Hitler never sought England or France anyhow, for unlike the Soviet Union they could not supply him with agricultural and oil resources. Writing of England, Flynn said, "That little island cannot grow enough food for herself. If Hitler got England she would just be a big WPA [Works Progress Administration] project on his hands!"[113]

To America Firsters, aid to the Soviet Union was out of the question, and Lindbergh went so far as to tell an AFC rally, "I would a hundred times rather see my country ally herself with England, or even with Germany, with all her faults, than the cruelty, the godlessness, and the barbarism that exists in Soviet Russia."[114]

When the administration sought all possible aid to the Soviets, the AFC tried to exploit these longheld fears. Late in June it issued a position paper in which it claimed that shipping war goods to the Soviet Union via Vladivostok risked American lives. [Document 90] Early in July it released a report accusing the administration of falsely claiming that Alaska was threatened and of exploiting this fear on behalf of aid to the Soviets. [Document 91] On October 8 the AFC research bureau produced a six-page memo challenging Roosevelt's statement to the press that the Soviet constitution protected the free exercise of religion.[115]

Such warnings were in vain. Although most Americans detested both communism and the Soviet Union, they saw Germany—with its domination of Europe—as by far the greater danger. Once Hitler attacked, Roosevelt promised to assist the Soviet Union. As a start, he refused to apply the neutrality statute that would have forbidden such aid. At the end of July he sent his leading adviser, Harry Hopkins, to Moscow on a fact-finding mission. Hopkins reported that if aided promptly, the Soviets could stop the German advance.[116]

On September 18 supplementary lend-lease legislation—including assistance to the Soviet Union—was introduced in the House. Almost immediately Sarles reported to Stuart that its passage was ensured, but she closely followed the course of the bill. [Document 92] General Wood deemed it unwise to fight the comprehensive aid proposal, but he suggested an amendment prohibiting any of the appropriation from going to the Soviets. When the House voted overwhelmingly in favor of the new bill, America First declared it had been apparent from the outset that a steamroller was at work.[117]

The AFC kept a watchful eye on the Soviet campaign. On August 1 the research bureau issued a lengthy memorandum offering the intriguing argument that Germany's conquest of the Soviet Union could weaken, not strengthen, the Reich. [Document 51] Several major AFC leaders were confident that this victory would soon take place, at which point Britain would be forced to make peace. For example, in the middle of October former U.S. Rep. Samuel B. Pettengill (R-Ind.), a close adviser to the committee, thought Britain might "throw Russia to the dogs to save her empire," only offering token bombing against Germany. Then, once Germany had defeated the Soviets, it would be so exhausted that it would be forced to make peace. [Document 93][118]

During the debate over the Soviet Union, America First stressed the dangers of domestic communism. To Bowles, the American Communist Party presented a far more lasting danger than Nazism. [Document 85] The committee occasionally sought to pin the communist label on interventionist leaders. Conversely, the communists bitterly fought America First. Before Germany invaded the Soviet Union, they accused the AFC of being as imperialistic as its interventionist counterparts. When in June the communists suddenly desired U.S. intervention, they did all they could to paint the AFC as a pro-Nazi organization.[119]

Early in July, Sarles found the AFC increasing in strength, something she explained in part by the Russo-German war. Yet she noted rumors concerning U.S. military involvement in Iceland, the extension of the Atlantic patrol, and the fortification of the coast of Brazil. Stuart feared that U.S. ships were actively engaging the German navy; he denied, however, that the United States was already in the war. The administration, he told Wood, could not undertake something so unconstitutional.[120]

There was still cause for alarm. On July 11 the research bureau issued a memorandum warning that the United States might seize Dakar and the Cape Verde Islands. [Document 94] It also noted the construction of U.S. bases in northern Ireland and could not resist pointing out that one construction contract went to a subsidiary of J. P. Morgan.[121]

The most important event of summer, however, concerned Iceland. On July 7, 1941, Roosevelt announced that four thousand U.S. troops had landed in Reykjavik. Were the Germans to occupy that strategic island, said the president, they would pose an intolerable threat to all "the independent nations of the New World." Hostile naval and air bases there would menace Greenland, shipping in the North Atlantic, and the steady flow of munitions to Britain, the last item "a broad policy clearly approved by Congress."[122]

In the eyes of the AFC, Roosevelt's Iceland move had brought the nation perilously close to war. On July 9 the research bureau accused the administration of placing U.S. troops within shooting range of Hitler's forces and doing so within the German war zone. [Document 95][123] The AFC also found Roosevelt's apparent flouting of the Constitution highly objectionable. Iceland had been a sovereign state in personal union with Denmark, but Germany's occupation of Denmark in 1940 had given the Icelandic parliament an opportunity to control its own foreign affairs. Iceland's prime minister, Hermann Jonasson, had cabled Roosevelt on July 1, 1941, that Iceland was ready to entrust its protection to the United States provided U.S. forces withdrew on the conclusion of war. Yet Stuart claimed Roosevelt had specifically violated the Constitution, for that document stipulated that all treaties must be approved by the Senate before taking effect. According to Flynn, "If the President, without the consent of Congress, can occupy Iceland, he can occupy Syria or Ethiopia."[124]

Although the occupation of Iceland undoubtedly brought the United States closer to conflict, AFC concerns did not carry much weight. By presenting the Iceland move as essentially a defensive one, Roosevelt received strong congressional backing, and a national poll indicated 61 percent of the public in favor, with only 20 percent opposed.[125]

In just a little over a month after the United States occupied Iceland, Roosevelt met secretly with Churchill. Conferring from August 9 to 12 at Placentia Bay, Newfoundland, the two leaders drafted a common statement of global aims informally labeled the Atlantic Charter, discussed possible responses to Japan's moves, and formulated procedures for U.S. patrols halfway across the Atlantic—if the president so ordered.

At first, the AFC protest against the charter was somewhat muted. Wood offered cautious praise. Not only was there no specific promise of convoys, but the eight-point manifesto might "find a receptive hearing even in Germany." On August 14 Fred Burdick, the AFC's congressional liaison, reported from Washington that Congress did not see warlike commitments resulting.[126]

Yet, within the AFC, there was deep pessimism as well.[127] Sarles suspected that the eight points were declared to undercut any peace Hitler might be considering. In addition, the summit meeting could be followed by joint British-U.S. activity in the Far East. [Document 96] Sarles said that Britain could only fund its war effort through exports, and to balance its payments, Britain would have to retain its tariffs—article IV of the charter notwithstanding—against the United States. [Document 92] The culmination of the AFC's response to the charter came in a series of position papers prepared by the research bureau. From the outset, the bureau believed the charter was really a set of war aims, not an opening for peace negotiations. The papers compared the provisions in the charter to President Woodrow

Wilson's Fourteen Points, denied that they were legally binding, and offered a point-by-point critique. [Documents 97–99][128]

At the very moment Roosevelt and Churchill were meeting, America First was confronted with another administration move, and this time the committee was far less militant than in the case of lend-lease. The Selective Service Act, passed in September 1940, had limited the draftees to twelve months' service and had prohibited stationing them outside the Western Hemisphere. In April 1941 George C. Marshall, the army chief of staff, told a House committee that selectees were going home at the end of their year of service. In his biennial report of July 3, however, Marshall noted with alarm that as many as 75 to 90 percent of the regular officers were reservists, men whose term was coming to an end. As far as enlisted men were concerned, Marshall found the outlook equally grim: the number of selectees usually ran from 25 to 50 percent of the total forces. Hit particularly hard would be such crucial support forces as engineers, heavy artillery, and anti-aircraft. The historian Forrest C. Pogue reports Marshall's perspective: "The Chief of Staff faced the prospect of seeing National Guard members, reserve officers, and trained selectees melt away within a few months." A few days after Marshall made his report, the War Department requested that limits on time in service and geographic location be lifted.[129]

On July 14 Roosevelt's congressional advisers flatly told him the House would never tamper with the restrictive draft law. Roosevelt did manage to secure endorsement for lifting the one-year limit, but only at the price of retaining the ban on serving outside the hemisphere. Nor did the public strongly back the president, as shown by an opinion poll indicating that only 51 percent favored eliminating the one-year limit.[130]

In a special message sent to Congress on July 21, Roosevelt wrote, "Within two months, disintegration, which would follow failure to take Congressional action, will commence in the armies of the United States." He noted that the 1940 law allowed Congress to extend the one-year training period if danger persisted. Claiming that the peril was "infinitely greater" than it had been a year before, he asked Congress to "acknowledge" a national emergency. Of course, Roosevelt realized that if Congress declared such an emergency, it could automatically bring into force the provisions of the 1940 act empowering the president to hold the soldiers "for the duration." Marshall still sought a law extending the time period—indefinitely in fact—and as the Senate Military Affairs Committee supported him, Congress braced itself for another fight.[131]

Suspecting that the administration ultimately sought authority to send troops overseas, Wood protested. Calling it a bald request for a new American Expeditionary Force, Wood feared Roosevelt would claim that the president is empowered to fight anywhere in the world.[132] In a letter to his fellow anti-interventionist and chairman of the Senate Military Affairs Committee, Robert R. Reynolds (D-N.C.), Wood suggested alternative legislation, centering on incentives for reenlistment. [Document 100]

In a series of position papers, the research bureau argued that the draft renewal was not needed for U.S. defense, accused the administration of breaking faith, and denied that the current army faced disaster. [Documents 101 to 103] National headquarters released a short bulletin advancing the argument that, the president's claims notwithstanding, the nation was in far less danger than it had been a year earlier. [Document 104]

Yet once Roosevelt dropped his proposal to send troops outside the hemisphere, the AFC took no official stand on the controversy. General Wood, a reserve officer, believed that if he opposed a proposal made by the army chief of staff he would be accused of disloyalty.[133] Pettengill similarly advised against taking a position, doing so on political grounds. [Document 105] The Chicago headquarters followed Pettengill's advice. Calling on chapters to "follow the middle road," Page Hufty, director of organization, issued Bulletin #444. The AFC, said the bulletin, always stood for the strongest possible defense while opposing any legislation that permitted sending U.S. troops to the battlefield.[134]

Such formal neutrality did not mean that the AFC was truly disinterested. It tacitly opposed the bill, and in some cases more than tacitly.[135] The research bureau denied that a national emergency existed. [Document 106] It warned that any congressional proclamation of such an emergency would endanger servicemen and threaten a variety of civilian freedoms. [Documents 107 and 108] Just as important, the research bureau assisted the bill's opponents. Burdick predicted the bill would fail.[136] Ruth Sarles, however, felt undercut by Hufty's Bulletin #477, which barred formal chapter action against draft renewal, for she believed the AFC should exert more overt opposition. [Document 28]

The bill's sponsors encountered difficulties. On August 7, by a comfortable margin, the Senate modified the administration proposals. It offered only an eighteen-month extension (General Marshall had opposed any time limit), provided for a pay raise after one year's service, and sought to expedite the release of men over age twenty-eight. On August 12, the House narrowly passed the same bill, 203–202. The sudden news that Vichy France was on the verge of capitulating to Germany, claimed Sarles, provided the necessary support. Marshall's biographer, Forrest Pogue, credits the AFC with leading an effective opposition.[137]

The close vote has often been misunderstood. Even if the bill had been defeated, there would have been one compromise: draftees would still have had to serve from six to twelve months longer. Furthermore, when the bill passed, many AFC leaders were by no means despondent. Stuart wrote, "It turned out perfectly." Burdick referred to *a big moral victory*, "the best thing that could have happened." [Documents 109 and 110; emphasis in original] Pettengill preferred passage by one vote to defeat by one vote.

[Document 111] The 203 representatives who supported the bill, he said, were now forced to show their constituents that they opposed entering the war. In fact, he found the AFC at the peak of its potential usefulness. Hufty noted that forty more congressmen opposed the extension of service than had opposed lend-lease. "You are winning this fight," he wrote AFC backers.[138]

Controversies Concerning the AFC

Legislative proposals such as lend-lease and draft renewal generated intense bitterness, as did Roosevelt's decision to occupy Iceland and to aid the Soviet Union. By the summer of 1941 the debate had become intemperate, and the AFC found the media hostile. America First was particularly concerned about Hollywood's role in promoting U.S. entry into war. Many films advanced an interventionist perspective; few—if any—were anti-interventionist.[139] The AFC called for theater boycotts.[140] Equally important, it assisted a Senate investigation of the motion picture industry.

Flynn was particularly active. He drafted the original Senate resolution submitted by Senators Nye and Bennett Champ Clark (D-Mo.), gathered the initial two thousand dollars for research, supervised the viewing of some seventy-five films, and wrote Nye's radio speech of August 1 demanding an inquiry. In a letter to Stuart, Flynn revealed his grand design. [Document 112][141]

The AFC found segments of the press highly suspect. Stuart was particularly critical of Henry R. Luce's *Time* and *Life*, claiming that their apparent objectivity made them all the more deadly. The committee even saw the more dispassionate *New York Times* as exercising a double standard, offering heavy-handed descriptions of AFC meetings but not of communist-sponsored ones.[142]

America First carefully monitored radio broadcasting. One survey of broadcasts in the New York area, made in December 1940, showed a large preponderance of interventionist programs. [Document 113] Only by proving gross inequity could the AFC expect to have its views presented, and even then, in Sarles's words, "it had to scratch and claw at the networks, to cajole and humor, to plead and threaten."[143] The AFC met with some success, however: it coordinated speaking engagements for anti-interventionists, whether they were addressing AFC meetings or others, and supplied anti-interventionists to debate at formal forums.

Originally, in the fall of 1940, when the AFC was organized, all sides tried to avoid polemics. By the summer of 1941, however, abuse had become the norm, so much so that Cole believes the AFC's effectiveness was seriously undermined. Interior Secretary Harold L. Ickes found the AFC composed of "anti-democrats, appeasers, labor baiters, and anti-Semites." In July 1941, when several AFC postcards critical of Roosevelt reached recruits stationed in training camps, Secretary of War Henry L. Stimson told a press conference: "This comes very near the line of subversive activities against the United States—if not treason."[144]

The press made similar accusations. *Time* called the AFC a "garden" in which "the weeds had gotten out of hand," a group full of "Jew-haters, Roosevelt-haters, England-haters, Coughlinites, politicians, demagogues."[145] Early in March 1941 an interventionist group called Friends of Democracy, Inc., published a pamphlet labeling the AFC "a Nazi transmission belt." One of the most vitriolic attacks came from the Right Reverend Henry W. Hobson, Episcopal bishop of Southern Ohio and chairman of the militantly interventionist Fight For Freedom Committee. In a cable sent in October 1941, Hobson called America First "the first fascist party in this nation's history." [Document 114] Such hostility took a particularly ugly turn when efforts were made, often with success, to prevent AFC meetings from being held. For example, in May 1941 the Miami county commissioners voiced objection, as did the Oklahoma City council in August.[146]

These activities helped create a climate of opinion in which dissent became suspect. As Castle confided to his diary after trying to launch the Philadelphia chapter, "there are lots of people who are willing to work if they can do it without being seen, but are afraid their friends would criticize them if they came out in the open."[147] Bowles expressed particular dismay at the silence of labor and farm groups. [Document 115]

The Roosevelt administration was itself involved in harassment. The president secretly had the Federal Bureau of Investigation examine AFC activities several times and also had a private investigator and grand jury at work. Roosevelt's investigations, the FBI's included, could not prove subversion, causing historian Richard W. Steele to suggest that the president's "judgment was strongly conditioned by the hopes of using the loyalty issue to smear his critics."[148]

All this is not to say the AFC was free of fascist infiltration. In December 1940 the German chargé d'affaires Hans Thomsen boasted, "We have good relations with both isolationist committees [AFC, NFWC] and support them in various ways." Perhaps the greatest blot on the AFC record was its frequent use of Laura Ingalls as a speaker late in 1941. Ingalls, an aviatrix, accepted funds from the German government to promote anti-intervention. It is highly questionable, though, whether the Nazis or their supporters had gained much influence within the AFC.[149]

The AFC also sought to sever any ties with the extreme right in general. Yet purging the rank-and-file members could be difficult, and monitoring mass meetings was almost impossible. Morton wrote Wood, "I don't consider such undesirable attendance as a reason for discontinuing meetings, any more than rod-riding by criminals is reason to discontinue railway freight service. But we should, perhaps, emulate the railroads by policing these meetings as carefully as possible."[150]

Pro-Nazism was not the only charge the AFC had to face. Another was anti-Semitism. The overwhelming majority of Jewish Americans undoubtedly favored some degree of intervention, a fact that made committee leadership particularly eager to recruit Jews. Two Jews had been members of the national committee: philanthropist Lessing Rosenwald and former congresswoman Florence Prather Kahn (R-Calif.). Rosenwald resigned almost immediately, however, and Kahn did so within several months. Jews helped staff the New York chapter, holding such offices as office manager, publicity director, and research director. Sidney Hertzberg, the AFC's first publicity director, was Jewish, as was James Lipsig, a major drafter of AFC position papers. The AFC denounced anti-Semitism and tried to avoid anti-Semitic speakers.[151]

Anti-Semitism was not absent, however, and the press publicized any manifestations. Anti-Semites were quite vocal at some rallies, including those held in New York's Madison Square Garden, attached anti-Jewish remarks to their contributions (though some were returned), and led several local chapters. Some AFC leaders supported Father Coughlin, and Coughlin reciprocated by endorsing the AFC. A private letter by Castle, expressing "no particular affection" for Jews and New Dealers, was reprinted in the New York tabloid *PM*, resulting in negative publicity for the committee.[152]

Yet controversy remained relatively mild until Lindbergh claimed that the "Jewish people" were among America's leading prowar groups. On September 11, 1941, Lindbergh spoke over nationwide radio while addressing an AFC rally at Des Moines. He had long privately expressed anger over Jewish interventionism, but in Des Moines he made his views public.[153] Because of the furor his speech aroused, and because of its impact on the AFC, the relevant portion is reproduced in full here.

It is not difficult to understand why Jewish people desire the overthrow of Nazi Germany. The persecution they suffered in Germany would be sufficient to make bitter enemies of any race. No person with a sense of the dignity of mankind can condone the persecution of the Jewish race in Germany. But no person of honesty and vision can look on their pro-war policy here today without seeing the dangers involved in such a policy, both for us and for them.

Instead of agitating for war, the Jewish groups in this country should be opposing it in every possible way, for they will be among the first to feel its consequences. Tolerance is a virtue that depends upon peace and strength. History shows that it cannot survive war and devastation. A few far-sighted Jewish people realize this, and stand opposed to intervention. But the majority still do not. Their greatest danger to this country lies in their large ownership and influence in our motion pictures, our press, our radio, and our Government.

I am not attacking either the Jewish or the British people. Both races, I admire, but I am saying that the leaders of both the British and the Jewish races, for reasons which are as understandable from their viewpoint as they are inadvisable from ours, for reasons which are not American, wish to involve us in the war. We cannot blame them for looking out for what they believe to be their own interests, but we must also look out for ours. We cannot allow the natural passions and prejudices of other peoples to lead our country to destruction.[154]

Not suprisingly, interventionists strongly attacked the speech. But it met with strong opposition from anti-interventionist ranks as well and caused several resignations from the national committee. To Bowles, Lindbergh's remarks "sounded definitely anti-Semitic," though Bowles denied the colonel harbored such feelings "in even the slightest degree." [Document 116] In writing a friend, Herbert Hoover said, "Lindbergh's anti-Jewish speech is, of course, all wrong. And I fear it will hurt all of us who are opposed to war." Pacifist leader Frederick J. Libby called for immediate clarification, citing the claim of Sen. Guy M. Gillette (D-Iowa) that "for the first time we are on the defensive." [Document 117][155]

Flynn was particularly upset. As soon as he heard of the speech, he phoned Stuart and Wood from New York. It was incredible, he said, that Lindbergh, acting alone, literally committed the America First movement to open attack on the Jews. [Document 118] In a letter to Lindbergh, Flynn claimed that New York's Jewish population was practically unanimous for war and that, as a whole, the Jewish people wanted war. Furthermore, they had tried to brand all war opponents anti-Semitic or pro-Nazi, a responsibility that "should be brought home to them. But this is a far different matter from going out on the public platform and denouncing 'the Jews' as the warmongers. No man can do that without incurring the guilt of religious and racial intolerance and that character is poison in a community like ours."[156]

Some anti-interventionists claimed Lindbergh oversimplified matters to the point of distortion. Norman Thomas, for example, wrote Stuart, "Not all Jews are for war and Jews have a right to agitate for war if we have a right to agitate against it. The point in both cases is the way the job is done and here I think a great many besides Jews have been at fault. What about [columnist] Dorothy Thompson and [publisher] Henry Luce? What about economic forces making for war?" Within two weeks, Thomas told Stuart he could no longer speak under AFC auspices.[157]

Other anti-interventionists said administration backers should look at beams in their own eyes before pointing out motes in others. For instance,

Gregory Mason, professor of journalism at New York University and chairman of the Stamford-Greenwich-Norwalk AFC, claimed that at any charity event for Great Britain, "you'll find a very high percentage of names of wealthy snobs who would shun a Jew as they would a leper."[158]

Some anti-interventionists shared Lindbergh's beliefs, yet thought the speech unwise. Anne Morrow Lindbergh claimed her husband was naming the prowar forces "truthfully, moderately, and with no bitterness or rancor." But she recognized that the public would interpret the address as Jew-baiting, that anti-Semites would rally to his ranks, and that the path to war would not be impeded.[159] Several figures on the national committee, however, were quick to support Lindbergh. Gen. Thomas Hammond, the Chicago manufacturer and chairman of the Chicago chapter, said Lindbergh had handled the "Jewish problem" with courage. [Document 119] Physiologist Anton J. Carlson of the University of Chicago found the overwhelming majority of Jews "even more violently pro-war than our national Administration." Novelist Kathleen Norris claimed Lindbergh's remarks were harmless. Putting the Jews in the same company as the president, the administration, and the pro-British partisans need not cause Jews "either shame or anger."[160]

Just a week after he had spoken, Lindbergh met with the national committee. On September 18, it debated for eight hours. In her account of the meeting, Ruth Sarles notes general support for Lindbergh's position and the reasoning behind this support. [Document 120] The AFC statement, released on September 24, denied Lindbergh and his fellow AFC members were anti-Semitic. It blamed the interventionists for raising the issue of race, and it invited Jews to enter its ranks.[161]

Stuart was disturbed about the AFC response, though he did not indicate what he would have preferred. He called the statement the best that people with diverse views could draft. Rep. Karl E. Mundt (R-S.D.), a significant AFC liaison in the House, reassured Stuart that America First had not lost status in Congress. Norman Thomas, however, argued that even silence was preferable to the statement produced. [Document 121] Sen. Hiram Johnson (R-Calif.) concurred, writing with reference to Washington, "Everything is hell here." On October 3, at an AFC rally in Fort Wayne, Indiana, Lindbergh claimed that his remarks had been distorted, his motives and meanings "falsely ascribed." He did not "speak out of hate for any individuals or any people."[162]

The Lindbergh speech, and the AFC response to it, damaged America First. More than ever, particularly in light of Roosevelt's efforts to repeal the Neutrality Act, the AFC needed to mobilize all of its resources. Yet, at an inopportune time Lindbergh had given his opponents a golden opportunity to discredit the entire anti-interventionist movement. Lindbergh saw himself speaking out against "the danger to this country" with courage and integrity. But he juxtaposed "the Jewish race" against "our interests," and he offered a view of Jewish power that bordered on the conspiratorial. In no way could the AFC have gained from the Des Moines speech. And the loss was inestimable.[163]

The Final Months

Just a week before Lindbergh spoke, the Navy Department announced that the destroyer *Greer*, enroute to Iceland with mail, was attacked some 175 miles south of Reykjavik. The attack had failed, the news bulletins of September 4 reported. The German torpedoes had missed their mark.

On September 11, the very day of Lindbergh's Des Moines address, Roosevelt spoke over nationwide radio. He claimed that a German submarine "first fired upon this American destroyer without warning, and with deliberate design to sink her." (The president failed to mention that the *Greer* had been tracking a German submarine for over three hours while a British plane was dropping four depth charges.) To meet this "act of piracy," U.S. naval vessels and aircraft were ordered to shoot Axis submarines and raiders "on sight." "Our patrolling vessels and planes," Roosevelt said, "will protect all merchant ships—not only American ships but ships of any flag—engaged in our defensive waters," an area he defined as "a vast expanse of the Atlantic Ocean."[164]

Roosevelt also mentioned previous sinkings. The U.S. freighter *Steel Seafarer*, flying the U.S. flag, had been bombed on September 8 while en route to an Egyptian port. A day later the State Department announced the loss of the *Sessa*, reported to have been sunk near Greenland several weeks earlier while carrying supplies to Iceland. Twenty-four crew members were lost; the rest were rescued. The ship was not legally entitled to U.S. protection, however, as it was sailing under Panamanian registry, a common subterfuge used to evade Neutrality Act restrictions.

Speaking for the AFC, Wood accused Roosevelt of initiating "an undeclared war in plain violation of the Constitution." He asked, "American shipowners hide behind a foreign flag to make some money. Are American men to die for their 'dividends'? "[165]

Other anti-interventionists were just as quick to respond. Judson commented, "Obviously Germany cannot sit by and see her enemies supplied without trying to prevent it." Indeed, Judson added in an indirect reference to the Hoover food plan, it was Britain who was acting like the "pirate" by prohibiting food from reaching the starving babies of occupied Europe. Borchard of Yale, an advocate of strict neutrality, claimed Roosevelt had no right to send U.S. ships to belligerent ports. [Document 10] The New York chapter bulletin observed, "Any naval officer who insists that the Germans shot first will have to confess that he disobeyed the president's order." It added, "You are in plain view of a conspiracy, an intrigue so to manage events that we cannot escape the war."[166] The research bureau issued a position paper accusing the president of initiating an undeclared war without popular consent. [Document 122]

By September 17, Wood was considering adjourning the AFC. Believing that Roosevelt's "shoot-on-sight" speech had put the nation at war, he—as a former army officer—saw himself under the authority of his commander in chief, the president. Hence, Wood reasoned, the AFC should cease further activities until the 1942 congressional elections. He wrote Hanford Mac-Nider, the AFC vice chairman, saying, "I would be in favor of stopping right now were it not for the fact that if we did so now, the matter would be linked up with the Lindbergh speech at Des Moines and taken as a repudiation of Lindbergh." Lindbergh himself, however, hoped that the AFC would continue. Much was still unforeseen, he said, and he preferred to go down fighting.[167] For the moment, Wood did not give up hope.

Others, though, also had second thoughts about continuing. MacNider wanted Congress to vote directly on war, saying, "I think we can make a stirring appeal to get this ghastly business over with one way or another, so the people can get back to the rebuilding of this nation before it's too late." [Document 123] The Minnesota meatpacker Jay C. Hormel, in a letter of resignation from the national and executive committees, claimed the U.S. economy was geared to war, the nation engaging in limited naval warfare. "End this thing," he wrote, referring to the conflict. [Document 124]

While the AFC was debating adjournment, the sinking of U.S.-owned merchant vessels continued. On September 16, the State Department announced that the *Montana*, a U.S. freighter under Panamanian registry, was sunk between Greenland and Iceland. No one was injured. Three days later, the *Pink Star*, another U.S.-owned vessel flying the Panamanian flag, was torpedoed in the same general locale. Some of the crew were lost. The AFC responded to the *Pink Star* incident by issuing another position paper, this one presenting the entire practice of Panamanian registry as an evasion of both the Neutrality and the Lend-Lease Acts. [Document 125] Such protests halted neither U.S. shipments nor the sinking of U.S.-owned merchant ships, and in October four more were lost.[168]

All this time, the United States engaged in military convoying. According to a report Churchill secretly made to his cabinet, on September 1, U.S. warships would be ordered to escort ships to and from Iceland, at which point the British would take over. Slightly more than two weeks later, the U.S. Navy did begin escorting its first British convoys. U.S. "defensive waters" now extended as far as ten degrees west longitude, some four hundred miles off the Scottish coast. There, for roughly three-quarters of the Atlantic, U.S. vessels were to escort friendly convoys and destroy any Axis ships encountered on the way.[169]

Such orders were bound to lead to incidents, and on October 17 the

Navy Department announced the torpedoing near Iceland of the *Kearny*, a crack destroyer scarcely a year in service. The ship was responding to an appeal from a Canadian convoy that had been attacked by a wolf pack raid some four hundred miles away. Although it was damaged, not sunk, eleven lives were lost, and Americans saw their first casualty list of World War II.

On October 27 Roosevelt responded to the sinking with a blistering Navy Day speech. Through the *Kearny*, he said, the United States itself had been attacked. Wood replied that the *Kearny* was engaged in convoy duty, protecting deliveries to a belligerent. Here indeed, commented the general, was final proof of the administration's warlike intention.[170]

The greatest crisis was still ahead. On October 31, six hundred miles west of Iceland, a German U-boat sank the U.S. destroyer *Reuben James*, part of a five-destroyer group escorting forty-four ships. This time 45 men were saved, 115 lost. The AFC had only one response: to request an investigation by the Senate Naval Affairs Committee. The proposal was made by over two hundred chapter leaders the day after the attack, along with calls to withdraw U.S. troops from Iceland and to order U.S. naval vessels out of the war zone.[171]

With U.S. ships now being sunk, the administration worked harder than ever to repeal the Neutrality Act of 1939. The act forbade U.S. vessels from entering combat zones designated by the president. Roosevelt, of course, realized that Britain would receive far more aid if U.S. ships could sail directly to its borders. He also mentioned that although U.S. destroyers were escorting the merchant ships, these freighters—particularly those flying the U.S. flag—should assist in their own defense by mounting a gun or two.

Fully aware that draft renewal had passed by narrowest of margins, Roosevelt did not seek immediate repeal of the whole act; instead he focused on the sections affecting the Atlantic war. The crucial provisions were Section 2, which banned U.S. vessels from entering belligerent zones; Section 3, which authorized the president to proclaim combat zones around belligerent countries; and Section 6, which prohibited the arming of U.S. merchant vessels. Of these, the least controversial was the last one, particularly as escorts were already under way. Therefore the administration decided to test opinion in the House, where opposition seemed stronger, by asking it to approve only the repeal of Section 6. If the House did so, the Senate would be asked to repeal all three sections, after which the House would vote again, this time on the more comprehensive Senate bill. On September 14, several weeks before Roosevelt asked for repeal of Section 6, Sarles surmised administration strategy. [Document 126]

Speaking on October 9, Roosevelt urged Congress to permit the arming of U.S. merchant ships, which should then be permitted to enter combat zones and deliver lend-lease goods directly to the ports of friendly belligerents. "Although the arming of merchant ships does not guarantee their safety, it most certainly adds to their safety," the president said. The ships could choose whether to shoot the enemy on sight or keep their distance until help arrived. Fearing that Congress might not approve the immediate lifting of combat zone restrictions, Roosevelt did not push the proposal; he hoped, however, that it would receive "earnest and early attention."[172]

The AFC responded immediately, beginning an effort that would result in thousands of pamphlets, dozens of meetings, and the flooding of Congress with letters and telegrams. Wood accused Roosevelt of "asking Congress to issue an engraved drowning license to American seamen." He maintained that freedom of the seas did not involve supplying one side only. Furthermore, Britain was in little need of U.S. shipping. Hitler, so Wood believed, would not deliberately sink U.S. ships going to Iceland, but he would certainly strike at those going all the way to the British Isles. On October 13, the AFC research bureau issued a lengthy position paper: it stressed that not a single American life had been lost on any ship flying the U.S. (not Panamanian) flag, recalled that in World War I arming merchant ships provoked submarine attack, and noted that British naval officers stationed in Iceland had denied that such arming offered much protection.[173]

The AFC kept careful tabs on the debate. Sarles outlined the opposition's political strategy. [Document 127] Among some "insiders," however, there was only moderate optimism. Senator Wheeler, for example, did not think the armed ship bill could be defeated.[174] Pettengill gave the administration a wide margin. [Document 93]

The prediction was a bit off, for the House approved the bill 259 to 138. Only two days of committee hearings were held, so the opposition had little chance to present its case. News of the *Kearny,* made public on October 17, the day the House voted, undoubtedly increased the majority. Two days after the bill passed, a Gallup poll indicated 72 percent of the American people favored arming merchant ships but only 46 percent supported their entrance into combat zones.[175]

The administration followed through on its strategy. Officially, the Senate was only concerned with repealing Section 6. But in reporting out the bill, the Foreign Relations Committee added provisions permitting U.S. vessels to carry cargoes and passengers to belligerent destinations and to areas the president had previously defined as combat zones.

In opposing the measure, the AFC worked closely with the minority on the Foreign Relations Committee to line up witnesses.[176] Its research bureau released a fifty-five page memorandum, which included data attempting to prove U.S. ships were not needed to deliver goods to Britain. [Document 128]

The predictions varied. Burdick saw a chance for the bill's defeat, particularly given the imminent defection of Southern senators. [Document 129] Wood predicted that if the combat zone amendment passed, anti-interventionists in Congress would introduce a war resolution.[177] It would not be an advisory referendum, but an outright and binding congressional vote on war against Germany. Pettengill found some anti-interventionists strongly in favor of the proposal and gave several reasons why he considered the tactic wise. [Document 130] Such a move, he believed, was the only thing that would bring prowar congressmen up short. Otherwise, they would give away the whole case by inches, still insisting before their constituents that they never voted for war. [Document 93]

On October 20 the national committee appointed Fairbank, Judson, and AFC staff member Richard Moore to draft a supporting statement. Two days later, over Wood's signature, it released an open letter to Roosevelt. It began, "The America First Committee, in the interests of peace, honor and constitutional government, respectfully asks that you cause to be submitted to Congress a resolution for the declaration of a state of war between the United States and the German Reich." According to Robert E. Sherwood, a dramatist and historian, Roosevelt thought that if the issue ever came to a direct vote, it would meet with "certain and disastrous defeat."[178]

On November 7, after eleven days of bitter debate, the Senate voted 50 to 37 to amend the Neutrality Act drastically, permitting merchantmen to be armed and U.S. ships to enter the war zone. Although the margin was reasonably comfortable, it was smaller than on most administration proposals since war had begun.

Wood's response was surprisingly upbeat. He noted that some administration supporters had suddenly taken the anti-interventionist position.[179] If there was a corresponding reaction in the House, whose vote on abolishing combat zones approached, the president might still lose. Sarles later claimed if the Senate had acted just two days earlier, the margin would have been so narrow that the House would not have concurred easily.[180] John T. Flynn commented, "There is a chance of our winning," as he devised alternative strategies for victory and defeat. [Document 30]

Such optimism was unfounded. Six days after the Senate tally, the House voted 212 to 194 to abolish combat zones, thereby permitting U.S. ships to carry goods directly to belligerent ports. Four days later Roosevelt signed the bill.

The AFC staff believed the administration victory was rooted in unprecedented pressure and—in all seriousness—in congressional inebriation. Yet it had genuine reason to be encouraged.[181] The congressmen who opposed revision, Wood noted, represented about 50 percent of the American voters. The AFC organization department boasted "We Are at Our Greatest Strength." In a private letter, Flynn called the close vote "a staggerer for the President." Roosevelt, he continued, was "in a terrible spot," as he stood more than ever between "the war-minded madmen" who were growing increasingly angry with him and "an opposition to war which . . . can destroy him." [Document 131] In Burdick's words, *time is on our side*."[182]

After his victory, Roosevelt remained cautious. Since the crucial parts of the Neutrality Act had been repealed, the president was empowered to send armed convoys directly across the Atlantic. Yet only on November 25 did the administration decide to do so. At that time, it decided to send unarmed vessels to Lisbon and armed vessels to Archangel; ships flying the U.S. flag would start sailing to Britain, but presumably as part of a British escort. Only the decision about Lisbon was made public. Hence, the initiative remained in the hands of Hitler, who sought more than ever to avoid incidents.[183]

The AFC remained fearful of a new American Expeditionary Force (AEF). On December 4 the *Chicago Tribune* and *Washington Times-Herald* published the War Department's sweeping (and until that point, secret) contingency plans—the drafting of 10 million men, a joint U.S.-British invasion by July 1, 1943, and a 5-million-man AEF in 215 divisions. The source of the leak was never revealed.[184] Burdick reported that the exposé would probably save millions of American lives. "It caught the war crowd flat-footed," he wrote. [Document 132] Sarles called the exposé "a shot in the arm." [Document 133]

Defeat on the neutrality issue reinforced one decision the AFC had already made: to enter politics directly. When 227 AFC members, representing 119 chapters, met in Washington on November 1, they unanimously endorsed for reelection those in Congress who had upheld "provisions of the present Neutrality Act which prohibit the entry of American flag ships into combat zones or belligerent ports." Conversely, they sought to defeat neutrality foes. On November 28, the national committee concurred, calling for "a non-partisan political program" and authorizing Wood to appoint a bipartisan advisory committee.[185] Five days before the Pearl Harbor attack, Stuart outlined his organization and suggested leading personnel. [Document 134] Chester Bowles was enthusiastic but stressed that activities should be limited to the war issue. [Document 12]

The move, however, did not meet with unanimous consent. Political activity, commented Castle, might result in the ouster of some otherwise able people from Congress. [Document 135] MacNider, a dark-horse presidential candidate the previous year, resigned from the AFC over the matter. He called himself "a rabid Republican" who could never be nonpartisan. [Document 136][186]

Despite these objections and some defections, however, such talk raised AFC morale. To Flynn, the decision would "steam up our whole organization," though he did point out some hazards. [Document 137][187] Stuart wrote on December 1:

Opposition to the New Deal's war policy is mounting. On every side we see small business; the Church; even Labor beginning to awake and comprehend the disaster that war means to them. We can be the catalytic agent which brings together all these elements and transforms them into a cohesive political force.[188]

According to a Gallup poll taken in the fall of 1941, 16 percent of the voters would have supported candidates of a keep-out-of-war party headed by Lindbergh, Nye, and Wheeler. Cole suspects that this percentage was significant enough to swing some close elections. Wood thought that if the AFC could unseat only a few Roosevelt backers, non-interventionists could control the majority of the House.[189]

All such dreams came to naught, not because of tensions with Germany, but because of the U.S. confrontation with Japan. Although the AFC paid far less attention to Asia than to Europe, few, if any, committee leaders welcomed conflict with Japan. Even reports of a Japanese offensive against Southeast Asia, manifested in February 1941, did not make the AFC more belligerent. Japan, declared the speakers bureau, was "not going to pull Germany's chestnut from the fire." If war between the United States and Japan did break out, Japan would be able to conquer British Malaya, the Dutch East Indies, and the Philippines; it could, however, do little damage east of Hawaii. [Document 138] The research bureau denied that Japan sought conflict. [Document 139]

Throughout the spring of 1941, the AFC kept tabs on the Far East. In May, Sarles noted various peace rumors. [Document 26] Yet, while calling for continued peace with Japan, the *Washington News Letter* asked how the administration could "froth at the mouth against the Axis, and at the same time continue to appease Japan, a member of the Axis, by shipping her war material."[190]

In July tensions between the United States and Japan suddenly increased. Vichy France permitted Japan to occupy eight air and two naval bases in South Indochina. Aware that Japan was thereby given military control over all Indochina, the Roosevelt administration retaliated on July 26 by freezing Japanese assets, a move that soon ended all exports to Japan.

The AFC saw no threat in Japan's Indochina action. Its research bureau challenged Under Secretary of State Sumner Welles, who claimed Japan's move threatened the Philippines and endangered the U.S. supply of rubber and tin. [Document 106] The New York chapter bulletin found the Japanese simply imitating the United States, "which holds the Philippines after driving out the Spaniards and subjugating the population."[191]

When, on August 6, Secretary of State Cordell Hull warned Japan not to invade Thailand, some America First Committee leaders expressed apprehension. Five days later, the AFC directors were alarmed enough to pass a special resolution opposing war with Japan. Soon Sarles reported the United States might well fight if Japan moved toward the Dutch East Indies or Singapore. [Document 96][192]

Yet, late in the summer of 1941, some America First personnel were still optimistic. On August 28 Burdick reported a growing belief on Capitol Hill that the crisis with Japan would be settled amicably, though he personally saw more popular support for a war with Japan than for one with Germany. [Document 140] By the end of August, Flynn envisioned the two nations brought "to their senses." As late as October 3, Sarles perceived the situation as serious but not hopeless. [Document 92] In mid-November, Flynn wrote Wood, "The Japanese situation is working to keep the Administration from a war commitment in either ocean." [Document 30][193]

By December 1, 1941, negotiations had broken down, although diplomatic relations were not formally severed. Burdick noted the apprehension of congressional anti-interventionists. [Documents 141 and 142] On the day before the Japanese struck at Pearl Harbor, the New York chapter bulletin blamed the United States for the crisis. The administration, it said on December 6, had made impossible demands on Japan to remove its troops from Siamese borders and to end the China war. Sarles confessed on the same day that she could get no lead on the Far Eastern situation; undaunted, she suggested that the AFC stress the difficulties of fighting an Asian war.[194]

When the Japanese attacked Hawaii, some AFC leaders were not surprised. Lindbergh wrote in his diary, "We have been prodding them into war for weeks. They have simply beaten us to the gun." Wood commented about Roosevelt, "Well, he got us through the back door."[195] Castle was more startled. Both Japan and the United States, he believed, lacked statesmanship. [Document 143] Reporting to Wood from Washington, Sarles found "the men on the Hill" had experienced "a profound sense of shock"; the damage at the Hawaiian base, she noted, was far greater than the public had been told. [Document 144] On December 20 she noted many in Washington were still skeptical about Secretary of the Navy Frank Knox's official account of the attack. [Document 145]

Final Strategy

The AFC saw no alternative but to close ranks with the rest of the nation. On the evening of December 7, national headquarters issued a brief statement: "The America First Committee urges all those who have subscribed to its principles to give their support to the war effort of this country until the conflict with Japan is brought to a successful conclusion. In this war the America First Committee pledges its aid to the President as commander in chief of the armed forces of the United States." As Lindbergh noted, "I can see nothing to do under these circumstances except to fight."[196]

The AFC was confronted with the most important decision of its short history: whether to disband. On December 8, national headquarters canvassed all chapter chairmen. It posited four alternatives, including complete termination. [Document 146] Within twenty-four hours, cables came pouring into the central office, all but a half dozen urging that the AFC continue in wartime.[197] Some leading congressional figures concurred, among them La Follette, Jr., and Hiram Johnson. [Document 147]

Other important anti-interventionists, however, wanted to end all committee activity. Any alternative action, said General Hammond, would be misunderstood. In her survey of Congress, Sarles noted that Senator Taft believed the AFC's major job, keeping the United States out of war, was over. [Document 147] Castle suggested a compromise: close down the individual chapters, but preserve records and membership lists in case action was needed again. [Document 148] Morton favored dissolution or complete suspension, with the option of later mobilizing opinion against what he saw as excessive internationalism.[198]

On December 11 a special meeting of the national committee voted to dissolve the AFC. In no way regretting its past activities, it said, "Our principles were right. Had they been followed, war could have been avoided." [Document 149] At first glance, this action appears somewhat surprising. Wood had wanted the AFC to adjourn, not disband. Lindbergh too sought mere adjournment, telling Wood such a course "would be burning no bridges." But minutes before the national committee met, it received news that Germany and Italy had declared war on the United States, an event that tipped the scales for complete dissolution. There were only two dissenting votes, one cast by industrialist Robert R. Young.[199]

The dissolution gave AFC leaders few qualms. Wood told Lindbergh if the committee merely adjourned, the chapters would "gradually fall apart or get into the hands of extremists or radicals," people who might "give the government an excuse to attack us on the grounds of subversive activities."[200]

At the same time, the battle was deemed a noble one. Bowles felt "as confident as I have ever been in my life" that the future would prove "the rightness" of the AFC's policies. Representative Mundt praised the AFC for strengthening the nation's defenses. "Historians poring through the archives," he said, would find ample data with which to vindicate the AFC position. William H. Regnery still had hopes for a new organization, one that would take an active part in the coming elections. Senator Wheeler wrote Wood, "I feel that we did everything we could to keep this country out of war. We lost and the warmongers have won. They wanted war, and they have it, and now they have it, they do not know what to do with it."[201]

And so the fate of the AFC was sealed. The battle of America First was over.

Conclusion

On one level, the AFC was a failure. Congress passed every bill the committee opposed, and public opinion polls seldom comforted the foes of intervention. More important, the United States entered a war the AFC saw as destructive to the nation's security and ruinous to the republic's form of government. Anti-interventionism as a political posture was discredited ever after.

Seldom if ever in the history of the United States have political "outsiders"—that is, people excluded from the decision-making process—defined a political agenda. In 1940 and 1941 the president set the agenda, determined the issues, and chose the timing. AFC broadcasts, petitions, telegrams, and rallies were all reactive. As an emergency action group, the AFC lacked the time and resources to offer a comprehensive alternative to Roosevelt's program, even if the president himself was as much improviser as architect. Aside from a visceral anti–New Dealism voiced by many AFC speakers, the AFC never supplemented foreign policy with any domestic program. Perhaps even more important, except for what one can find latent in AFC position papers, it offered no real vision of America's place in a postwar world. The AFC had no declaration, position paper, or manifesto that offered a comprehensive scenario, an all-encompassing alternative view. Truly, the AFC was caught in what was once called "the conservative dilemma": with no general program of its own (and by the nature of the organization such a program would be difficult to design), it could only respond to initiatives, not set its own.

Yet America First cannot be dismissed so quickly. Despite its limitations, both internal and external, it did surprisingly well. It helped generate a public sentiment that forced Roosevelt to be more circumspect in such demands on Congress as draft renewal and more secretive about such warlike moves as escorting British vessels. The AFC took credit for a number of things: a lend-lease amendment preventing actual delivery of war goods to Britain; Roosevelt's failure to announce convoys in his "national emergency" address of late May 1941; elimination of an administration-sponsored clause in the original draft renewal bill explicitly permitting American troops to be stationed outside the hemisphere. It is hard to trace specific influence, but obviously the committee helped generate enough public sentiment to make the president more cautious. In addition, as Cole notes, anti-interventionist strength in Congress increased throughout 1941, in large part because of AFC efforts.[202]

In a sense, committee strategy was quite successful. The AFC ignored or sought to undermine polls that consistently showed Americans more desirous of defeating Germany than of keeping out of war. Instead, it stressed that the public, by and large, opposed entering the war as a full-fledged belligerent. By defining the issue as war or peace, the committee could make strategic retreats after each defeat. If the Pearl Harbor attack had not taken place, and if Hitler had exercised restraint in the Atlantic, the America First Committee might have won its major battle.[203]

Given the public's moderately interventionist sentiments, the hostility to the AFC exhibited by many opinion makers, and the fact that Roosevelt's party controlled Congress, the AFC probably could not have been much more effective. Even though Lindbergh's Des Moines speech made the committee vulnerable in a way it had not been before, it is doubtful whether in November 1941 it really determined the success of neutrality revision.

At its best, America First supplied rationale and data needed for intelligent decision making. Some of its arguments, particularly as expounded in its position papers, could—if thoroughly debated—have done much to elevate the political dialogue. But the debate far too often became one big exercise in mud slinging, for which the AFC must bear part of the blame. The fiery anti-British tone in some bulletins as well as in AFC speeches by Wheeler and Nye, Lindbergh's Des Moines address, the rhetoric used at some rallies, the welcoming of Coughlinites—all sullied the committee's reputation. Of course, the greater responsibility goes to those with greater power, and the interventionists—and the Roosevelt administration in particular—bear a heavy burden for censorship efforts, secret political intimidation, and irresponsible accusations.

In retrospect, there is much about the committee that is surprising. Although long associated in the public mind with the great debate over intervention, America First was not launched until the debate was well under way. Indeed, more time had passed between Hitler's invasion of Poland and the committee's official founding on September 4, 1940, than between its establishment and the bombing of Pearl Harbor. Moreover, the AFC originally did not recruit rank-and-file members, being primarily a publicity organization. One might even argue that mass membership was thrust upon a woefully unprepared AFC leadership.

Also surprising, given its general reputation, was the political moderation of the staff. Neither Wood and Stuart nor the great bulk of the Chicago and Washington personnel were vehemently anti–New Deal or Roosevelt-haters. The most visible opponent of the New Deal was Flynn, and his critique came from the left, not the right.

One could even claim that initially America First did not embody the more militant brands of isolationism represented by Lindbergh or Col. Robert R. McCormick, publisher of the *Chicago Tribune*. Wood had endorsed William Allen White's original Non-Partisan Committee for Peace through the Revision of the Neutrality Law, a group advocating cash-and-carry just after World War II broke out in 1939. At that time, William Castle favored repeal of the arms embargo.[204] Clay Judson had served as president of the Chicago Council on Foreign Relations.

At the outset the committee was not particularly anti-British. During the battle over lend-lease, General Wood claimed to favor all-out aid short of war, doing so, he said, as a matter of "cold-blooded realism." When one has a potential antagonist such as Germany, he said, it is well to wear him down. Similarly, both Janet Fairbank and Edward Ryerson, Jr., stressed aid to

Britain within legal bounds.[205] It was only in the heat of battle, as the Roosevelt administration became more openly interventionist, that the AFC took on a more anti-British and overtly neutralist tone.

Overall, the committee contributed to the nation's political vitality. By rallying dissenting opinion, it forced debate on major administration measures and did so amid attacks that were often as sweeping as they were unfair. The health of any democracy depends on the degree of tolerance it grants its dissenters. Although the administration argued that the AFC threatened national unity, suppression of the committee would have almost guaranteed the destruction of any consensus. As this collection of documents shows, the AFC was an intensely patriotic group that could offer cogent arguments against intervention. If Americans had failed to speak out against what they saw as threats to the nation's security, they would have been abdicating their responsibilities as citizens. America First remained undaunted, advancing arguments concerning U.S. survival in an Axis-dominated world, and it did so amid intimidation from the highest levels at home. In later times, when the United States entered undeclared wars with little or no previous debate, such activism would be sorely missed.

NOTES

1. *New York Times*, December 30, 1940, p. 7; January 21, 1941, p. 1.

2. Ibid., May 28, 1941, p. 6.

3. Ibid., December 30, 1940, p. 7; September 12, 1941, pp. 1, 4; October 28, 1941, p. 4.

4. Ibid., December 30, 1940, p. 7; May 28, 1941, p. 6; September 12, 1941, pp. 1, 4.

5. Wayne S. Cole, "Isolationism," in Otis L. Graham, Jr. and Meghan Robinson Wander, eds., *Franklin D. Roosevelt, His Life and Times: An Encyclopedic View* (Boston: G. K. Hall, 1985), p. 211.

6. Dos Passos cited in Mark Sullivan, *Our Times*, vol. 6: *The Twenties* (New York: Scribner's, 1935), p. 375.

7. Henrik Shipstead cited in *Congressional Record*, October 16, 1939, p. 451.

8. Entry of April 25, 1941, *The Wartime Journals of Charles A. Lindbergh* (New York: Harcourt Brace Jovanovich, 1970), p. 478.

9. Among the works presenting this scenario are Rose M. Stein, *M-Day: The First Day of War* (New York: Harcourt Brace, 1936); Mauritz A. Hallgren, *The Tragic Fallacy: A Study of America's War Policies* (New York: Alfred A. Knopf, 1937), pp. 413–33; Stephen and Joan Raushenbush, *The Final Choice: America between Europe and Asia* (New York: Reynal and Hitchcock, 1937), chap. 11; C. Hartley Grattan, *The Deadly Parallel* (New York: Stackpole Sons, 1939); and Norman Thomas and Bertram

D. Wolfe, *Keep America Out of War: A Program* (New York: Frederick A. Stokes, 1939).

10. For a Gallup poll that reveals the shift in public sentiment, see *New York Times*, September 22, 1940, p. 34.

11. Wayne S. Cole, *America First: The Battle against Intervention, 1940–1941* (Madison: University of Wisconsin Press, 1953), pp. 10–11; Michele Flynn Stenehjem, *An American First: John T. Flynn and the America First Committee* (New Rochelle, N.Y.: Arlington House, 1976), pp. 13–14.

12. For Wood's background, see Justus D. Doenecke, "General Robert E. Wood: The Evolution of a Conservative," *Journal of the Illinois State Historical Society* 71 (August 1978): 162–75; and Doenecke, "The Isolationism of General Robert E. Wood," in John J. Schacht, ed., *Three Faces of Midwestern Isolationism* (Iowa City: Center for the Study of the Recent History of the United States, 1981), pp. 11–22.

13. For initial planning, see R. D. Stuart, Jr., to R. E. Wood, August 2 and 14, 1940, Box 63, the Papers of the America First Committee (hereafter cited as AFC Papers), Hoover Institution on War, Revolution and Peace, Stanford, Calif.; R. D. Stuart, Jr., to K. Brewster, August 19, 1940, Box 65, AFC Papers.

14. Ruth Sarles, "A Story of America First," unpublished manuscript, 1942, on deposit at the Hoover Institution, pp. 45–49.

15. See two undated letters from Gerald R. Ford to R. D. Stuart, Jr., and one undated letter from Ford to Barbara and R. D. Stuart, Jr., Box 66, AFC Papers.

16. For early backers, see Cole, *America First*, pp. 13–14; Sarles, "Story," pp. 50–58. Those promising to act as silent supporters included Merle Thorpe, editor of *Nation's Business;* Frank B. Jewett, vice-president of American Telegraph and Telephone Company and president of Bell Telephone Laboratories; Captain Joseph M. Patterson, publisher of the *New York Daily News;* and Roy W. Howard, board chairman of the Scripps-Howard newspaper chain (Barbara S. Stuart to "Mr. Brown," July 16, 1940, Box 66, AFC Papers).

17. Cole, *America First,* pp. 15–16.

18. Hugh Johnson, "Defend America First," address delivered over NBC network, September 5, 1940, in *Vital Speeches*, October 1, 1940, pp. 763–65.

19. In an interview given to *PM*, a tabloid published in New York City, Stuart went so far as to say he might vote for Roosevelt (*PM*, October 3, 1940). He continued that he had backed Senator Robert A. Taft (R-Ohio), a staunch anti-interventionist, for the Republican nomination, but had found Wendell Willkie too closely tied to the banking house of J. P. Morgan. Just before the election, Stuart wrote, "While it hurts for an ex-New Dealer to admit it I am voting for Wendell Willkie. Hope all my conservative roomies feel better." R. D. Stuart, Jr., to W. Don Stuart, November 1, 1940, Box 292, AFC Papers.

20. Minutes of the directors meeting, November 1, 1940, Box 337, AFC Papers.

21. Minutes of the directors meeting, September 21, 1940, October 7, 1940; minutes, national committee, October 25, 1940, Box 337, AFC Papers.

22. Walter Johnson, *The Battle against Isolation* (Chicago: University of Chicago Press, 1944), pp. 119–20. White repudiated the request, fearing that it connoted too much pressure on the administration after the destroyer bases deal. Within several months, however, such demands were adopted by the CDAAA. Ibid., pp. 121–22.

23. R. D. Stuart, Jr., to H. Johnson, September 24, 1940, Box 60, AFC Papers. For the Gallup poll cited by Stuart, see *New York Times,* September 22, 1940, p. 34. For the AFC ad, see *New York Times,* October 3, 1941, p. 21.

24. "One Year of America First—An Amazing Story of Democracy in Action" (pamphlet printed in Chicago by the America First Committee, 1941).

25. William L. Langer and S. Everett Gleason, *The Undeclared War, 1940–1941* (New York: Harper, 1953), p. 231; Robert Dallek, *Franklin D. Roosevelt and American Foreign Policy, 1932–1945* (New York: Oxford University Press, 1979), p. 252; *New York Times,* November 9, 1940, p. 1.

26. W. R. Castle to R. D. Stuart, Jr., November 19, 1940, Box 63, AFC Papers.

27. Stuart was quite justified in his estimate. On December 8, 1940, Churchill wrote Roosevelt, reporting that from June 2 to November 24, 1940, Allied and neutral shipping losses amounted to 569 vessels or 2,401,192 gross tons. Langer and Gleason, *Undeclared War,* p. 232.

28. Minutes of the directors meeting, December 17, 1941, Box 337, AFC Papers. Within a day, Clay Judson wrote Stuart, declaring that perhaps the Neutrality Act of 1939 forbade loans by individuals. Moreover, any loans from the U.S. government would certainly require an amendment to the Johnson Act of 1934. C. Judson to R. D. Stuart, Jr., December 18, 1941, Box 63, AFC Papers. For Stuart on Ryerson, see R. D. Stuart, Jr., to H. MacNider, December 18, 1940, Box 286, AFC Papers.

29. *Time,* December 23, 1940, p. 13; and R. D. Stuart, Jr., to Lunsford Richardson, December 23, 1940, Box 290, AFC Papers.

30. For the background of Marshall and his organization, see Justus D. Doenecke, "Verne Marshall's Leadership of the No Foreign War Committee," *Annals of Iowa* 41 (Winter 1973): 1153–72. General Hanford MacNider, Iowa cement manufacturer and formerly national commander of the American Legion, had originally been offered the NFCW chairmanship, but had turned it down. Entry of December 12, 1940, Lindbergh, *Wartime Journals,* pp. 426–28.

31. On cooperation efforts, see memorandum of Harry Schnibbe to John T. Flynn, enclosed with letter dated April 14, 1942, Box 21, the papers of John T. Flynn, University of Oregon (hereafter cited as Flynn Papers); on the Wood-Marshall meeting, see Sarles, "Story," p. 103; on the AFC warning, see R. L. Bliss, Bulletin #23, January 24, 1941, Box 278, AFC Papers.

32. For Dewey's erstwhile anti-interventionism, see Barry K. Beyer, *Thomas E. Dewey, 1937–1947: A Study in Political Leadership* (New York: Garland, 1979), pp. 264–67; Richard Norton Smith, *Thomas E. Dewey and His Times* (New York: Simon and Schuster, 1982), pp. 303, 333. For his response to America First, see T. E. Dewey to R. E. Wood, February 25, 1941, Box 59, AFC Papers.

33. R. M. Hutchins to R. E. Wood, July 25, 1940, Box 21, AFC Papers. In May

1941, Hutchins gave an anti-interventionist speech in which he said, "I have not joined the America First committee. I do not like its name. I should like to join a committee for humanity first." Hutchins, "Should We Do Whatever Is Necessary to Insure a British Victory?" *Town Meeting* 6 (May 26, 1941): 16–17. Hutchins gave much informal advice and openly aided the AFC in a public opinion survey. See Joseph L. Jaffe, Jr., "Isolationism and Neutrality in Academe, 1938–1941" (Ph.D. diss., Case Western Reserve University, 1979), pp. 21–81. Conversely, the AFC promoted Hutchins's speeches (e.g., R. L. Bliss, Bulletin #146, March 22, 1941, Box 278, AFC Papers).

34. W. Durant to R. E. Wood, December 31, 1940, Box 289, AFC Papers; C. G. Dawes to R. E. Wood, August 20, 1940, Box 289, AFC Papers.

35. S. Chase to Philip La Follette, August 29, 1940, the papers of Philip La Follette, Wisconsin State Historical Society, Madison, Wisconsin (hereafter cited as La Follette Papers). When asked again, he said of the organizations, "I think I'll let them age a little, like wine." S. Chase to R. D. Stuart, Jr., November 12, 1940, Box 35, AFC Papers. Chase did give the AFC permission to reprint one of his articles, which was published under the title "Four Assumptions about the War" (S. Chase to R. E. Wood, January 1, 1941, Box 59, AFC Papers).

36. Morrison helped sponsor the Chicago chapter. He also introduced the isolationist Senator Burton K. Wheeler (D-Mont.) at an AFC rally. *Congressional Record,* speech of April 27, 1941, pp. A2248–50. For Dulles, see J. F. Dulles to W. R. Castle, Jr., November 22, 1940, Box 63, AFC Papers. Dulles's wife contributed $950 to the New York chapter. Stenehjem, *American First,* p. 182. Dulles's law firm, Sullivan and Cromwell, gave free legal advice when the AFC was dissolved. Memorandum, May 28, 1942, Box 21, Flynn Papers.

37. F. Morley to R. E. Wood, January 4, 1941, the papers of Felix Morley, Herbert Hoover Presidential Library, West Branch, Iowa; entry of May 24, 1941, the diary of Felix Morley (hereafter cited as Morley diary), Hoover Presidential Library.

38. H. R. Wilson to R. E. Wood, February 14, 1941, Box 56, AFC Papers.

39. R. L. Wilbur to R. E. Wood, December 31, 1940, Box 68, AFC Papers. See also R. L. Wilbur to R. E. Wood, September 25, 1941, Box 68, AFC Papers.

40. S. Hertzberg to R. D. Stuart, Jr., December 3, 1940, Box 66, AFC Papers. Hertzberg was undoubtedly referring to Wright's unconventional sexual behavior.

41. National committee members not otherwise identified in this volume include J. Sanford Otis, vice-president of Central Republic Bank of Chicago; Samuel Hopkins Adams, author; Otto Case, treasurer of the state of Washington; Mrs. Bennett Champ Clark, wife of the Democratic senator from Missouri; Irving S. Cobb, author; Wilbur E. Hammaker, Methodist bishop of the Rocky Mountain states; William L. Hutcheson, first vice-president of the American Federation of Labor; Frank O. Lowden, former governor of Illinois; Ray McKaig, master of the Idaho National Grange; Clarence Manion, dean of the University of Notre Dame College of Law; Mrs. John P. Marquand, wife of a prominent novelist; Gregory Mason, anthropologist and journalist; Isaac Pennypacker, Philadelphia attorney; George N. Peek, agricultural economist; Carl G. Snavely, Cornell University football coach; Louis J. Taber, master of the National Grange; Mrs. Burton K. Wheeler, wife

of the Democratic senator from Montana; George H. Whipple, Nobel prize–winning physician at the University of Chicago; Edwin S. Webster, Jr., senior partner of Kidder, Peabody; and Maj. Alford J. Williams, flyer and Scripps-Howard columnist. National committee members who resigned and whose resignations are not otherwise mentioned in this volume include Charles Francis Adams, Boston banker and former secretary of the Navy (December 3, 1940); Thomas N. McCarter, president of the New Jersey Public Service Company (September 29, 1941); and M. W. Thatcher, general manager of the Farmers' Union Grain Terminal Association of St. Paul, Minnesota. Sarles, "Story," pp. 121–25.

42. Ryerson in ibid., p. 52.

43. C. Bowles to R. A. Taft, May 28, 1940, Box 75, the papers of Robert A. Taft, Library of Congress; C. Bowles to Philip La Follette, July 8, 1940, La Follette Papers.

44. O. G. Villard to R. D. Stuart, Jr., October 5, 1940, Box 292, AFC Papers; A. W. Palmer to R. D. Stuart, Jr., November 8, 1940, Box 65, AFC Papers. Stuart had written Palmer, wanting him to reconsider his decision to withdraw. When the AFC was formed, Stuart claimed, it was convinced that it should make clear it was not a pacifist organization. The committee sought, Stuart told Palmer, to avoid being smeared as appeasers. Within a week or so, however, the AFC abandoned the policy, for it realized that it had alienated many people who shared its general opposition to war (R. D. Stuart, Jr., to A. W. Palmer, November 1, 1940, Box 65, AFC Papers).

45. For Wood and Stuart on Rickenbacker, see R. D. Stuart, Jr., to P. Hufty, February 2, 1941, Box 64, AFC Papers. For Rickenbacker's pessimism, see *New York Times*, December 11, 1940, p. 1, and December 24, 1941, p. 4. For Gish, see confidential memo, R. A. Moore, August 28, 1941, Box 287, AFC Papers.

46. For Brundage, see R. D. Stuart, Jr., to K. Brewster, October 7, 1940, Box 292, AFC Papers. For Ford, see minutes of the directors meeting, December 3, 1940, Box 337, AFC Papers.

47. Symington mentioned in E. Jeffrey to R. L. Bliss, February 17, 1941, Box 2, AFC Papers; Baruch in Hugh Johnson to R. E. Wood (cable), February 23, 1941, Box 57, AFC Papers; Albert C. Wedemeyer, *Wedemeyer Reports!* (New York: Henry Holt, 1958), pp. 25–26, 34–35.

48. For accounts of the Hoover plan, see Hoover press statement, *New York Times*, August 12, 1940, p. 1; Hoover, reply to British statement, ibid., October 7, 1940, p. 1.

49. On Hughes, see R. E. Wood to H. Hoover, June 2, 1941, Box 55; H. Hoover to R. E. Wood, July 19, 1941, Box 60, AFC Papers. On Milbank, see R. E. Wood to H. Hoover, July 8, 1941. Box 55; H. Hoover to R. E. Wood, July 11, 1941, Box 55; H. Hoover to Mrs. Jeremiah Milbank, July 11, 1941, Box 82, Papers of Herbert Hoover (hereafter cited as Hoover Papers), Hoover Presidential Library. On food plan, see minutes, national committee, October 20, 1941, Box 337, AFC Papers. Moreover, within two weeks after Pearl Harbor, Stuart thanked Hoover for the frequent advice the AFC had received from him. "If the country had heeded your words," Stuart said, "it would not be facing these tragic days ahead." R. D. Stuart,

Jr., to H. Hoover, December 17, 1941, Box 132, AFC Papers. Hoover, in responding, said he had "been filled at all times with profound admiration for the magnificent battle you have made." H. Hoover to R. D. Stuart, Jr., December 18, 1941, Box 132, AFC Papers.

50. For Rickenbacker, see R. D. Stuart, Jr., to H. MacNider, August 30, 1940, Box 63, AFC Papers. For Marshall, see Cole, *America First*, p. 17. For Kennedy, see R. D. Stuart, Jr., to H. Smith Richardson, December 30, 1940, Box 65, AFC Papers. The fact that all directors were also on the national committee served to minimize friction between the two groups. For general bureaucratic structure, see Cole, *America First*, pp. 17–24.

51. Cole, *America First*, pp. 23–26. For change in Stuart's title, see minutes of the directors meeting, April 10, 1941, Box 337, AFC Papers. The directors were responding to criticism made by Janet Ayer Fairbank, vice chairman and director of AFC operations in Illinois and Iowa, who accused Stuart of amateurism and incompetence. Cole, *America First*, pp. 20, 24. For complaints in turn concerning Fairbank's treatment of Stuart and the staff, see Tutor Gardiner to R. E. Wood, August 15, 1941; Page Hufty to R. E. Wood, August 15, 1941, and October 28, 1941, all Box 284, AFC Papers.

52. Earl Jeffrey, director of state organization, was a Chicago advertising executive who had worked on Hoover's campaign in 1928 and on Alfred M. Landon's in 1936. Robert L. Bliss, director of organization until May 1941, had held publicity posts with the J. Walter Thompson advertising firm and *PM*, a New York tabloid. Harry C. Schnibbe, assistant director of organization with the task of establishing chapters, was a recent alumnus of Fordham University, where he had written a strong anti-interventionist column for the undergraduate newspaper. Richard A. Moore was director of organization in June and July of 1941, at which point he was made national director in charge of publicity. A graduate of Yale Law School, he had been an attorney in New York. Page Hufty, who replaced Moore as director of organization in July, was a financier based in Washington and Palm Beach. Kendrick Lee, editor of various AFC weekly newsletters, and Ruth Sarles, AFC Washington representative and director of the research bureau, had worked for pacifist organizations. Fred Burdick, in charge of congressional liaison, had served as chief of news and editorial analysis for the Works Progress Administration, a major New Deal agency, and had served on the staff of several Texas newspapers. Sidney Hertzberg, director of publicity and advertising until March 1941, was a prominent socialist journalist who had served on the staff of the *New York Times*, *Time*, and *Current History*. Joseph R. Boldt, Jr., eastern field representative, had worked for the *New York Times*'s editorial library and held a master's degree in history from Rutgers. James Lipsig, research assistant in Washington and a socialist, was an attorney who had served both the American Civil Liberties Union and the American Labor Party, a New York State party backed by liberal trade unions. Given such a staff, it was not really curious for the liberal monthly *Common Sense* to say that the AFC was "largely dominated by realistic liberals." See "Review of the Month," *Common Sense*, February 1941, p. 50.

53. Local supervisors of the AFC included John Wheeler (son of the Montana senator) of Los Angeles, John T. Flynn of New York, Janet Ayer Fairbank of Chicago,

banker Walter Gosgriff of Salt Lake City, Lansing Hoyt of Milwaukee, and former senator David Aiken Reed (R-Pa.) of Pittsburgh (Sarles, "Story," p. 331).

54. For material on Flynn's career, see Stenehjem, *American First;* Richard Clark Frey, Jr., "John T. Flynn and the United States in Crisis, 1928–1950," (Ph.D. diss., University of Oregon, 1969); Ronald Radosh, *Prophets on the Right: Profiles of Conservative Critics of American Globalism* (New York: Simon and Schuster, 1975), pp. 197–273.

55. Sarles offers an impressive list of people, in Congress and out, who spoke under AFC auspices. Sarles, "Story," pp. 86–88. The AFC paid much attention to the advice of Congressman Karl Mundt (R-S.D.), who offered candid estimates of the strengths and weaknesses of those congressmen who might speak for the committee. See K. Mundt to R. D. Stuart, Jr., April 17 and April 21, 1941, Box 278, AFC Papers.

The bulletins of the bureau for research and congressional liaison were sent regularly to approximately thirty-five senators, 250 congressmen, and 700 editors, writers, and columnists. Sarles later claimed she did not know how widely they were used, but she found hardly a day when there was not some evidence of AFC research in House or Senate proceedings. Sometimes a whole line of argument was traceable to a "Did You Know?" bulletin. The Library of Congress was a frequent client, requesting reference on points made in these bulletins. Sarles, "Story," p. 96. Sarles attended hearings and was the AFC laison with the Senate. Socialist lawyer James Lipsig worked as statistician and researcher. He had sole responsibility for producing "Did You Know?" Cushman Reynolds, editor of the weekly newsletter *Uncensored* and coauthor of *Strategy of the Americas* (1941), aided Lipsig, particularly on military matters. Kendrick Lee sometimes substituted for Reynolds. Fred Burdick covered radio broadcasting for House members, but often reported on their general sentiments. See R. D. Stuart, Jr., to S. B. Pettengill, July 30, 1941, Box 62, AFC Papers. Among the early staff members were Frank Hanighen, later cofounder of *Human Events,* and Murray Kempton, later a prominent journalist.

56. Hoover's secretary of war, Patrick J. Hurley, was originally considered as chapter leader, but he feared that his position as reserve officer might prohibit such activity. See the diary of William R. Castle (hereafter cited as Castle diary), Houghton Library, Harvard University, December 26, 1940; R. D. Stuart, Jr., to W. R. Castle, January 4, 1941, Box 63, AFC Papers. Similarly, General Stanley D. Embick wanted to head the chapter, but was still in active service. See Castle diary, January 11, 1941. Another candidate was Frank C. Waldrop, political editor of the *Washington Times-Herald.* However, the newspaper's publisher, Eleanor M. ("Cissy") Patterson, did not want to tie her newspaper to any single organization. See Castle diary, December 20, 1940. The wife of Senator Bennett Clark ended up heading the chapter.

57. Cole, *America First,* p. 172. One must, however, beware of oversimplifying. Stuart himself was no economic conservative, generally supporting the New Deal and hoping after graduation to work for the National Labor Relations Board, a decided prounion body. At one time the press considered General Wood close enough to the Roosevelt administration to suggest he might lead the National Industrial Recovery Administration. Before America First was organized, Castle

thought of Wood as "one of the President's most able henchmen as he is the most intelligent." Stuart in Stenehjem, *America First*, pp. 13–14; Doenecke, "General Robert E. Wood," pp. 164–68; Castle Diary, September 29, 1939.

58. R. D. Stuart, Jr., to C. S. Payson, April 30, 1941, Box 62, AFC Papers; Stanton B. Leeds, "The Real Petain," *Scribner's Commentator* 10 (July 1941): 13–18; Paul R. Sanders, "Europe's Mildest Dictator," *Scribner's Commentator* 11 (November 1941): 31–36; and George T. Eggleston, *Roosevelt, Churchill, and the World War II Opposition: A Revisionist Autobiography* (Old Greenwich, Conn.: Devin-Adair, 1979), pp. 120–24, 133.

59. Letter dated July 23, 1941, Box 29, AFC Papers. When a chapter passed a proimpeachment resolution, it was reprimanded by national headquarters. P. Hufty to chairmen, October 25, 1941, file of AFC materials, Princeton University Library (hereafter cited as Princeton file). The AFC also called for the immediate destruction of a scurrilous pamphlet sent anonymously to a chapter entitled "The Condition of Our Leader." R. L. Bliss, Bulletin #215, April 21, 1941, AFC Papers.

60. For major donors, see Cole, *America First*, pp. 31–33, 74.

61. "Contributions from National Committee Members and Contributors of Larger Amounts: Received thru November 29, 1941," Box 338, AFC Papers. AFC staffer Hertzberg saw a division on foreign policy between eastern financiers and midwestern industrialists. S. Hertzberg to Lester Markel, February 25, 1941, Box 285, AFC Papers.

62. For a general discussion of this reasoning, see Justus D. Doenecke, "Power, Markets, and Ideology: The Isolationist Response to Roosevelt Policy, 1940–1941," in Leonard Liggio and James J. Martin, eds., *Watershed of Empire: Essays on New Deal Foreign Policy* (Colorado Springs, Colo.: Ralph Myles, 1976), pp. 132–61.

63. J. F. Kennedy to R. D. Stuart, Jr., n.d., Box 79, AFC Papers. R. D. Stuart, Jr., to J. F. Kennedy, April 29, 1941, Box 79, AFC Papers. In a letter to Wood, Stuart wrote that Joseph P. Kennedy "is planning to contribute through his son Jack." Letter dated March 29, 1941, Box 18, AFC Papers.

64. Included on the letterhead of College Men for Defense First, as having given permission to use their names as of March 10, 1941, were several individuals who later became prominent. *Beloit:* W. Willard Wirtz (1933 graduate), Kennedy and Johnson's secretary of labor; *University of Chicago:* Cyrus Leroy Baldridge (1911), artist; *Haverford:* Fred Rodell (1926), legal scholar; *Northwestern:* Harold H. Velde (1931), later a congressman from Peoria prominent in anti-subversive investigations; *Princeton:* José Ferrer (1933), actor; Devin A. Garrity (1927), publisher; Jonathan B. Bingham (1936), later New York congressman; *Yale:* Richard M. Bissell, Jr. (1932), assistant professor of economics at Yale, later deputy director of plans, Central Intelligence Agency; Kingman Brewster (1941), later president of Yale; Peter H. Dominick (1937), later senator from Colorado; Richard A. Moore (1936), later special counsel to President Nixon; Edward L. Ryerson (1908), board chairman, Inland Steel; R. Sargent Shriver, Jr. (1938), student, Yale law school, class of 1941, later director of the Peace Corps and the Office of Economic Opportunity. All names in letterhead, R. E. Moore to R. D. Stuart, Jr., April 18, 1941, Box 64, AFC Papers.

65. For American Legion action, see *New York Times*, September 18, 1941, p. 1. For recruiting of farmers, see Sarles, "Story," p. 107; Cole, *America First*, pp. 77–78.

The AFC was unsuccessful with William Green, president of the American Federation of Labor. See W. Green to R. E. Wood, December 23, 1940, Box 285, AFC Papers. Late in March 1941, Hertzberg reported that the AFC had antagonized the CIO by having Henry Ford on the national committee, the AFL by having Kathryn Lewis. Moreover, while most of the leading AFC industrialists had notorious antiunion attitudes, a number had been involved in tough labor disputes. Even the antiwar labor leadership had to play along with the administration, so as to prevent too many restrictions on unions, while the rank and file saw the war's continuation meaning jobs and higher wages. S. Hertzberg to R. D. Stuart, Jr., and R. L. Bliss, March 25, 1941, Box 285, AFC Papers.

For the closeness of Kathryn Lewis to her father, see Melvyn Dubovsky and Warren R. Van Tine, *John L. Lewis: A Biography* (New York: Quadrangle, 1977), pp. 294–95. But when Stuart suggested Philip Murray, vice president of Lewis's Congress of Industrial Organizations, Miss Lewis said it was inadvisable, undoubtedly reflecting her father's sentiments. See Kathryn Lewis to R. D. Stuart, Jr., October 30, 1940, Box 282, AFC Papers. Lewis himself expressed admiration for Wood's antiinterventionist efforts, indicating at one point that he might be willing to speak on behalf of the committee. John L. Lewis to R. E. Wood, May 6, 1941, Box 4, AFC Papers.

For efforts to recruit blacks, see letterhead of black division, Box 34, AFC Papers.

66. For AFC contributions to the National Council for the Prevention of War, the Keep America Out of War Congress, and the KAOWC youth affiliate called the Youth Committee Against War, see R. D. Stuart, Jr., to Alice L. Dodge, January 2, 1941, Box 285, AFC Papers. For the Women's International League for Peace and Freedom, see Dorothy Detzer to R. E. Wood, February 14, 1941, Box 59, AFC Papers. For the Ministers No War Committee, see Cole, *America First*, p. 227. For a description of the leading socialist-pacifist coalition, see Justus D. Doenecke, "Noninterventionism of the Left: The Keep America Out of the War Congress, 1938–1941," *Journal of Contemporary History* 12 (April 1977): 221–36.

67. Stenehjem, *American First*, p. 53. Material on subsidizing Thomas's tours is found in R. D. Stuart, Jr., to E. S. Webster, Jr., April 22, 1941, the Papers of the Socialist Party (hereafter cited as Socialist Party Papers), Duke University Library; Mary Hillyer to R. D. Stuart, Jr., April 25, 1941, Box 61, AFC Papers; R. D. Stuart, Jr., to N. Thomas, May 22, 1941, the papers of Norman Thomas (hereafter cited as Thomas Papers), New York Public Library; Howard Rae Penniman, "The Socialist Party in Action: The 1940 National Campaign" (Ph.D. diss., University of Minnesota, 1942), 177; Fay Bennett to R. D. Stuart, Jr., plus memo, June 6, 1941, Box 291, AFC Papers; N. Thomas to R. D. Stuart, Jr., August 8, 1941, Thomas Papers. For Thomas on purity, see N. Thomas to Joe Friedman, May 26, 1941, Thomas Papers. (One of Thomas's sons worked on Long Island for the AFC. N. Thomas to Grace Milgram, July 28, 1941, Thomas Papers.) For New Deal group, see S. Hertzberg to C. Bowles, January 13, 1941, Box 35, AFC Papers. Among the names suggested were reformer Josephine Roche; former agricultural official Gardner Jackson; econo-

mist Eliot Janeway; journalist Richard Neuberger; Lloyd K. Garrison, dean of the University of Wisconsin law school; Mary Farquarson, state senator in Oregon; and Eli Oliver of the American Labor Party.

68. Other AFC endorsements included Herbert Hoover's *Shall We Send Our Youth to War?* (1939) and Fleming MacLiesh and Cushman Reynolds's *Strategy of the Americas* (1941). (Reynolds worked for the AFC research bureau.) Hugh S. Johnson's *Hell-Bent for War* (1941) was similarly boosted, and one AFC bulletin told every American to read it. The committee subsidized one book of its own, an anthology entitled *We Testify* (1941), edited by Nancy Schoonmaker and Doris Fielding Reid. Both were staff members of the New York chapter. Hoover endorsed in R. L. Bliss, Bulletin #77, February 20, 1941, Box 278, AFC Papers; MacLiesh and Reynolds in Bliss, Bulletin #223, March 26, 1941, Box 279, AFC Papers; Johnson in Bliss, Bulletin #204, April 17, 1941, Box 279, AFC Papers; Schoonmaker and Reid in J. T. Flynn to Harrison Smith, June 26, 1942, Box 21, Flynn Papers.

One AFC bulletin quoted Lord Arthur Ponsonby's *Falsehood in War-Time* (1928), in which a pacifist member of parliament said antiwar statements of rulers "must be placed on a par with the declarations of men who pour paraffin about a house knowing they are continually striking matches and yet asserting they do not want a conflagration" (P. Hufty, Bulletin #628, October 14, 1941, Box 279, AFC Papers). Similarly cited was British writer Hilaire Belloc's *Cruise of the Nona* (1925), which claimed that England had deceived the Americans by stressing the danger of invasion by the Central Powers (P. Hufty, Bulletin #655, October 25, 1941, Box 279, AFC Papers). In October 1941 the AFC issued a bulletin containing excerpts from C. Hartley Grattan's *The Deadly Parallel* (1939), defining what it meant to be a "continental American" (P. Hufty, Bulletin #606, October 6, 1941, AFC Papers). Wood personally endorsed Jerome Frank's *Save America First* (1938), saying that Frank's treatment of continental Europe would be particularly valuable to the AFC (R. E. Wood to R. D. Stuart, Jr., January 3, 1941, Box 57, AFC Papers).

The AFC continually promoted Baldwin's articles from *Harper's* and *Reader's Digest*. See, for example, R. L. Bliss, Bulletin #223, April 28, 1941; R. A. Moore, Bulletin #371, June 28, 1941, Box 279, AFC Papers. Moreover, General Wood said Baldwin alone among military commentators had shown calm perspective and thorough knowledge (R. E. Wood to H. Baldwin, May 8, 1941, the papers of Robert E. Wood (hereafter cited as Wood Papers), Hoover Presidential Library. When Baldwin wrote an article in *Life* on August 4, 1941, entitled "Blueprint for Victory," Page Hufty claimed it was one of the most effective pieces yet written for the AFC (P. Hufty to J. Lipsig, August 8, 1941, Box 3, AFC Papers).

Among the recommended journal articles were Congressman Ross A. Collins, "Do We Want a Mass Army?" (*Reader's Digest*, June 1941, in R. A. Moore, Bulletin #319, June 14, 1941, Box 279, AFC Papers) and Al Williams, "I Rebuke Seversky" (*Scribner's Commentator*, July 1941, in P. Hufty, Bulletin #487, August 12, 1941, Box 279, AFC Papers). Although it branded the Luce publications *Time* and *Life* interventionist propaganda (R. A. Moore, Bulletin #402, July 10, 1941, Box 279, AFC Papers), it endorsed a *Life* article dated August 18, 1941, entitled "This is What Soldiers Complain About," in which draftees found themselves performing pointless tasks (P. Hufty, Bulletin #506, August 20, 1941, Box 279, AFC Papers). And though it gave *Collier's* a similar label, it endorsed Charles A. Lindbergh's "Letter to

Americans," published in that magazine on March 29, 1941 (R. L. Bliss, Bulletin #145, March 22, 1941, Box 278, AFC Papers), and General Johnson Hagood's "Generals Never Learn" in the issue of August 23, 1941 (Bulletin #559, September 18, 1941, Box 279, AFC Papers).

69. For the prevalence of this sentiment in the anti-interventionist movement at large, see Justus D. Doenecke, "Germany in Isolationist Ideology, 1939–1941: The Issue of a Negotiated Peace," in Hans L. Trefousse, ed., *Germany and America: Essays on Problems of International Relations and Immigration* (New York: Brooklyn College Press, 1980), pp. 215–26.

70. For "A is for America," see C. A. Lindbergh to R. D. Stuart, Jr., July 22, 1941, Box 60, AFC Papers; Stuart broadcast cited in R. A. Moore, Bulletin #741, August 6, 1941, Box 279, AFC Papers.

For the AFC lack of endorsement of negotiated peace, see R. E. Wood to J. Art Haughwout, June 7, 1941, Box 68, AFC Papers; R. E. Wood to H. MacNider, June 14, 1941, Box 286, AFC Papers. Among the peace appeals used in AFC publicity were Rep. John W. Vorys's (R.-Ohio) plea for a peace offensive; editor David Lawrence's call for a peace commission; Wheeler's claim that Rudolf Hess, deputy führer, had flown to England specifically to offer peace proposals; journalist Freda Utley's plea in the October 1941 *Reader's Digest* entitled "Must the World Destroy Itself?"; and the Citizens Peace Petition Committee, headed by pacifist minister John Haynes Holmes. See Vorys in R. A. Moore, Bulletin #383, July 2, 1941; Lawrence in Bulletin #403, July 10, 1941; Wheeler in Moore, Bulletin #404, July 10, 1940; Utley in P. Hufty, Bulletin #629, October 14, 1941, all Box 279, AFC Papers.

71. R. E. Wood to R. J. Finnegan, January 22, 1941, Box 292, AFC Papers. See also R. E. Wood to Roy Howard, December 14, 1940, Wood Papers; R. E. Wood to B. E. Maidenberg, July 11, 1941, Box 286, AFC Papers.

72. See also C. Judson to R. M. Hutchins, May 19, 1941, Box 283, AFC Papers; W. R. Castle to R. D. Stuart, Jr., March 11, 1941, Box 63, AFC Papers; Flynn, *New York Times*, May 31, 1941, p. 9; C. A. Lindbergh to R. E. Wood, June 6, 1941, Wood Papers.

73. Sarles was not the only AFC leader who opposed suggesting a negotiated peace. To Hanford MacNider, Iowa manufacturer and AFC vice chairman, suggesting a negotiated peace was "just as much intervention and misguided meddling as what the President is doing." H. MacNider to R. E. Wood, July 11, 1941, Box 286, AFC Papers. Wood replied the AFC had not made negotiated peace a prime committee objective, though various AFC speakers had often mentioned it. R. E. Wood to H. MacNider, July 14, 1941, Box 286, AFC Papers. In November 1941, Lindbergh feared that the United States might end up guaranteeing a peace that could not possibly last. Entry of November 14, 1941, Lindbergh, *Wartime Journals*, p. 557.

74. R. Sarles to R. D. Stuart, Jr., October 18, 1941, Box 41; C. Bowles to R. D. Stuart, October 16, 1941, Box 59, AFC Papers. Hutchins consented to lend his name to a mediation movement, but refused to assume leadership. James Covill Schneider, "The Anxieties of Neutrality: Chicago Public Opinion and American Foreign Policy" (Ph.D. diss.; University of Wisconsin at Madison, 1979), p. 285. For Wood, see R. E. Wood to J. T. Flynn, November 19, 1941, Box 290, AFC Papers.

75. Alton Frye, *Nazi Germany and the American Hemisphere, 1933–1941* (New Haven: Yale University Press, 1967); James V. Compton, *The Swastika and the Eagle: Hitler, the United States, and the Origins of World War II* (Boston: Houghton Mifflin, 1967); Andreas Hillgruber, *Germany and the Two World Wars* (Cambridge, Mass.: Harvard University Press, 1981).

76. For material on oil, see "Oil-Out for Britain," *Did You Know?* #18, August 11, 1941, Box 280, AFC Papers. That bulletin, as well as Documents 62 and 63, were prepared by Cushman Reynolds. Much of this research was done in response to a comment by Senator D. Worth Clark that greatly embarrassed at least one AFC staffer, Ruth Sarles of the research bureau. See R. Sarles to R. D. Stuart, Jr., August 8, 1941, Box 67, AFC Papers. The Idaho Democrat, a strong isolationist, told reporters in Washington that the United States "should take over control" of all Latin America and Canada by establishing puppet governments. *New York Times*, July 30, 1941, p. 8

77. R. E. Wood, "Our Foreign Policy," address to Chicago Council on Foreign Relations, October 4, 1940, in *Congressional Record*, October 14, 1940, p. A6302.

78. For Dennis's thought, see Justus D. Doenecke, "Lawrence Dennis: Revisionist of the Cold War," *Wisconsin Magazine of History* 55 (Summer 1972): 275–86, and Doenecke, "The Isolationist as Collectivist: Lawrence Dennis and the Coming of World War II," *Journal of Libertarian Studies* 3 (Summer 1979): 191–208. For the background of Dennis's manuscript and its links to America First, see J. M. Richardson to R. D. Stuart, Jr., July 18, 1941, Box 286; R. L. Bliss to Doris Fielding Reid, August 19, 1941, Box 280; R. E. Wood to G. Eggleston, September 30, 1941 and November 25, 1941, Box 292; undated memo, "Mr. Holland," to R. A. Moore, Box 292; Jane Conway to R. E. Wood, November 28, 1941, Box 292, AFC Papers; O. John Rogge, *The Official German Report* (New York: Thomas Yoseloff, 1961), pp. 298, 353.
Although critics of the AFC greatly exaggerated Dennis's ties to the organization, such AFC figures as Wood, Sarles, and Senator Wheeler all read Dennis's weekly bulletins or his more ponderous works. R. Sarles to S. Hertzberg, March 20, 1941, Box 67, AFC Papers; R. E. Wood to R. E. Wood, Jr., May 2, 1941, Wood Papers; B. K. Wheeler to R. E. Wood, July 15, 1941, Box 55, AFC Papers. Dennis contributed only ten dollars to the national headquarters, but he was once Wood's guest and was close to some New York chapter leaders. L. Dennis to R. E. Wood, October 4, 1941, Wood Papers; Cole, *America First*, p. 122.

79. Walter Lippmann, "The Economic Consequences of a German Victory," *Life*, July 22, 1940, pp. 64–69; Douglas Miller, *You Can't Do Business with Hitler* (Boston: Little Brown, 1941); Dennis as fascist, *Life*, January 17, 1944, p. 15.

80. W. Churchill to F. D. Roosevelt, December 7, 1940, in Francis L. Loewenheim, Harold D. Langley, and Manfred Jonas, eds., *Roosevelt and Churchill: Their Secret Wartime Correspondence* (New York: E. P. Dutton, 1975), pp. 122–26; Roosevelt press conference, *New York Times*, December 18, 1941, pp. 1, 10; speech, ibid., December 30, 1940, p. 6; message to Congress, ibid., January 7, 1941, p. 4.

81. *New York Times*, January 11, 1941, pp. 1, 3.

82. Wood, *New York Times*, January 12, 1941, p. 7; undated AFC advertise-

ment, Princeton file; R. D. Stuart, Jr., to D. McDonald, January 10, 1941, Box 62, AFC Papers.

83. Cole, *America First*, pp. 42–49; Schneider, "Anxieties," p. 160. By March, the AFC had printed and distributed 1.5 million folders and pamphlets, 500,000 auto stickers, 750,000 buttons, and 15,000 large posters. It had answered 100,000 separate requests for information and mailed over 750,000 items. *Chicago Tribune*, March 10, 1941. For the AFC's line-by-line analysis of the lend-lease bill, see entry of D. Worth Clark, "A Factual Analysis of H.R. 1776," entered February 27, 1941, *Congressional Record*, A901–902.

84. R. E. Wood to R. J. Finnegan, January 22, 1941, Box 292, AFC Papers.

85. T. E. Dewey to R. E. Wood, January 13, 1941, Box 59, AFC Papers. In responding to Griswold, Stuart expressed sadness over the state of his thinking (R. D. Stuart, Jr., to A. W. Griswold, January 29, 1941, Box 60, AFC papers). Stuart, a former student of Sontag's, replied to his professor that war was by no means inevitable. "To be quite frank," he continued, "defeatism is our most dangerous enemy. If the 85% of the people who are opposed to war would just stop letting themselves be pushed around by the other 15%, our problem would be solved." R. D. Stuart, Jr., to R. J. Sontag, February 20, 1941, Box 67, AFC Papers.

86. R. D. Stuart, Jr., to L. Colcord, February 8, 1941, Box 59, AFC Papers.

87. Warren F. Kimball, *The Most Unsordid Act: Lend-Lease, 1939–1941* (Baltimore, Md.: Johns Hopkins Press, 1969), pp. 195–216.

88. For pessimism, see Document 68. Suddenly in late February the Washington bureau briefly became optimistic. See confidential memos, February 28 and March 3, 1941, Box 65; R. L. Bliss, Bulletin #88, March 4, 1941, Box 278, AFC Papers. For Gallup poll, see *New York Times*, March 7, 1941, p. 10.

89. *New York Times*, March 9, 1941, p. 33. For Wood statement, see ibid. For AFC's taking credit, see "One Year of America First" (pamphlet).

90. For resignation issue, see Sarles, "Story," p. 508. For continuation, see minutes of the directors meeting, March 28, 1941, Box 337, AFC Papers.

91. For material on the previous two paragraphs, see David Reynolds, *The Creation of the Anglo-American Alliance, 1937–41: A Study in Competitive Co-operation* (Chapel Hill: University of North Carolina Press, 1981), pp. 166–67; Thomas A. Bailey and Paul B. Ryan, *Hitler vs. Roosevelt: The Undeclared Naval War* (New York: Free Press, 1979), p. 113.

92. Cole, *America First*, pp. 33–37. For an example of anti-British views, see P. Hufty, Bulletin #615, October 9, 1941, Box 279, AFC Papers. For Sanger, see her letter to AFC, June 6, 1941, Box 51, AFC Papers.

93. Streit's plan is found in his books *Union Now: The Proposal for Interdemocracy Federal Union* (New York: Harper and Bros., 1940) and *Union Now with Britain* (New York: Harper and Bros., 1941); AFC slogan in R. A. Moore, Bulletin #388, July 3, 1941, Box 279, AFC Papers.

94. See also Document 127; and R. E. Wood to S. Kent Costikyan, November 18, 1941, Box 56, AFC papers.

95. Roosevelt press conference, *New York Times*, January 22, 1941, p. 1; CDAAA in R. L. Bliss, Bulletin #133, March 18, 1941, Box 278; revised principles, Bulletin #142A, March 21, 1941, Box 278, AFC Papers.

96. Roosevelt press conference, *New York Times*, April 11, 1941, pp. 1, 4; F. D. Roosevelt to W. Churchill, April 11, 1941, in Loewenheim, et al., eds., *Roosevelt and Churchill*, pp. 137–38.

97. R. D. Stuart, Jr., to R. E. Wood, April 26, 1941, Box 69, AFC papers. For sentiments similar to Wood's, see W. R. Castle to S. Morton, August 8, 1941, the papers of Sterling Morton (hereafter cited as Morton Papers), Chicago Historical Society. For Sarles, see also her letters to Kendrick Lee, April 13, 1941, Box 34, AFC Papers, and April 20, 1941, Box 34, AFC Papers.

98. On the congressional caucus, see K. Mundt to R. E. Wood, April 1, 1941, Box 286; on the mail campaign, R. L. Bliss, Bulletin #177, April 2, 1941, Box 278; on the Fish slogan, R. L. Bliss, Bulletin #207, April 19, 1941, Box 279, AFC Papers; on the Tobey resolution, R. L. Bliss, Bulletin #232, May 2, 1941, Box 279; *Washington News Letter* #9, April 15, 1941, p. 2, Box 281, AFC Papers.

99. For examples of optimism, see K. Mundt to R. D. Stuart, Jr., April 21, 1941, Box 62; R. Sarles to K. Lee, May 4, 1941, Box 34; W. R. Castle to R. D. Stuart, Jr., April 22, 1941, Box 63, AFC Papers. Sarles noted that some anti-interventionist senators did not look upon Tobey as a first-rate strategist. He was a man who "unfortunately breaks out in a rash of moral indignation at the drop of a hat." See R. Sarles to R. D. Stuart, Jr., May 18, 1941, Box 34, AFC Papers. Lindbergh thought the measure should have been withdrawn, as it certainly would have been defeated (*Wartime Journals*, May 16, 1941, p. 90).

100. *Washington News Letter* #13, May 15, 1941, p. 3, Box 284, AFC Papers.

101. Text of Roosevelt speech, *New York Times*, May 28, 1941, p. 2.

102. To be on the safe side, the AFC offered statements from prominent legal authorities who found no basis for such a declaration. Bulletin #296, June 5, 1941, Box 279, AFC Papers. See also R. A. Moore, Bulletin #311, June 11, 1941, Box 279, AFC Papers, which quoted various congressional figures who either downplayed emergency powers or called for continued antiwar activity.

103. For lack of anxiety, see Burdick reports of interviews with congressmen, June 11, 13, 18, 1941, Box 65, AFC Papers; R. Sarles to K. Lee, June 14, 1941, Box 34, AFC papers. For the opinion of the national headquarters on contraband, see R. A. Moore, Bulletin #339, June 20, 1941, Box 279, AFC Papers.

104. Text of Roosevelt speech, *New York Times*, June 21, 1941, p. 6.

105. P. Hufty, Bulletin #427, July 19, 1941, Box 279, AFC Papers.

106. During the summer of 1940, Lindbergh encouraged the formation of the AFC. He attempted to enlist Henry Ford in committee ranks. When people sent him contributions after an anti-interventionist speech, he returned the checks, enclosed an America First circular, and added his own endorsement. Then, when he gave $100 to the AFC, he allowed this move to be made public. See entries of September 13–16, 1940, Lindbergh, *Wartime Journals*, pp. 387–89; Wayne S. Cole,

Charles A. Lindbergh and the Battle against American Intervention in World War II (New York: Harcourt Brace Jovanovich, 1974), p. 119.

In "A Letter to Americans" (*Collier's*, March 29, 1941, pp. 14–15, 76), Lindbergh claimed that France and Britain had refused to take part in a European "re-adjustment" while there was still time; that the United States lacked essential tanks and cannon; that the United States had fewer fighting planes than Germany produced in a single week; and that the British continually avoided discussion of war aims, peace terms, or means of achieving victory. The United States, he said, had no means of invading Europe, much less imposing her ideology on the peoples of Germany, the Soviet Union, Italy, or Japan. For AFC endorsement, see R. L. Bliss, Bulletin #201, April 16, 1941, Box 279, AFC Papers.

For examples of Wood's invitation to become chairman, see his letters to Lindbergh, March 29 and April 11, 1941, Wood Papers. For examples of Lindbergh's replies to Wood, see letters of April 8, 1941, and June 4, 1941, Wood Papers.

107. For Lindbergh on victory, see testimony, House Foreign Affairs Committee, *Hearings*, January 23, 1941, p. 378. For Lindbergh on persecution of Jews, see entry of November 13, 1938, *Wartime Journals*, pp. 115–16. For reason for not condemning Germany publicly, see Senate Foreign Relations Committee, *Hearings*, February 6, 1941, p. 522.

Norman Thomas, who genuinely admired Lindbergh, noted the aviator's influence would be far greater if he would emphasize his personal opposition to fascism, make clear that continued independence of Britain and her self-governing dominions was essential, and clarify his statement—made in a speech given August 4, 1940— that suggested U.S. cooperation with a victorious Germany. Thomas wrote Lindbergh, "I do not think you meant to imply that American business is temporarily to share with the German state the profits of exploitation, yet some of your friends so interpret your remarks." N. Thomas to C. A. Lindbergh, August 9, 1940, Thomas Papers.

For Lindbergh on "White ramparts," see his "Aviation, Geography, and Race," *Reader's Digest*, November 1939, pp. 64–67. For criticism from a friendly source, see Norman Thomas to Comrade Waldron, November 29, 1940, Thomas Papers; Thomas, "The Case of Lindbergh," *Socialist Call*, May 17, 1941, p. 6. For extensive treatment of the German decoration, see Colonel Truman Smith's report, "Air Intelligence Activities: Office of Military Attaché, American Embassy, Berlin, Germany, August 1935–April 1939," in Robert Hessen, ed., *Berlin Alert: The Memoirs and Reports of Truman Smith* (Stanford, Calif.: Hoover Institution Press, 1984), pp. 131–34.

108. R. E. Wood to C. A. Lindbergh, June 2, 1941, Wood Papers. The aviator's wife, Anne Morrow Lindbergh, in reading the speech before he delivered it, feared his words would be taken as a call for insurrection. See her entry of May 28, 1941, *War Within and Without: Diaries and Letters, 1939–1944* (New York: Harcourt Brace Jovanovich, 1980), p. 192. Lindbergh responded that he claimed only to advocate opposition by constitutional methods. R. A. Moore, Bulletin #305, June 10, 1941, Box 279, AFC Papers; C. A. Lindbergh to R. E. Wood, June 6, 1941, Wood Papers. The original speech is covered in *New York Times*, May 30, 1941, pp. 1, 8.

109. Oklahoma City speech, *New York Times*, August 30, 1941, p. 5; Cole, *Lindbergh*, p. 123.

110. For Flynn, see Stenehjem, *American First*, p. 76.

111. For Stagner's role, see R. D. Stuart, Jr. to R. Stagner, April 29, 1941; R. Stagner to R. E. Wood, May 1, 1941; R. D. Stuart, Jr. to R. Stagner, May 7, 1941, Box 67, AFC Papers. For Stagner's analysis of the Gallup poll, see "An Analysis of American Institute of Public Opinion Polls Relating to Intervention in the European War," *Congressional Record*, May 9, 1941, pp. 3840–42.

The Hutchins poll indicated strong opposition to full-scale U.S. entry in the war and to the stationing of U.S. forces on bases in Africa, the Azores, or the Cape Verde Islands. But approximately two-thirds of those polled opposed any American offer to mediate the European war. A clear majority favored war if the Western Hemisphere was attacked. Cooperating university presidents included Raymond Kent, University of Louisville; Henry Noble MacCracken, Vassar College; Alan Valentine, University of Rochester; Albert W. Palmer, Chicago Theological Seminary; and Ray Lyman Wilbur, Stanford University; and the Reverend Harry Emerson Fosdick. Samuel E. Gill, who headed a New York public relations firm, conducted the survey. The best coverage of the Hutchins poll is found in Jaffe, "Isolationism," pp. 53–64. The poll was virtually ignored except for a hostile account in *Time*, July 28, 1941, p. 12.

The congressmen who sent out questionnaires were Paul Shafer (R-Mich.), Knute Hill (D-Wash.), Harry Sauthoff (Farmer-Labor–Wis.), and Hamilton Fish—all vehement foes of intervention who, not surprisingly, found their constituents strongly opposed to war. Fish was given particular attention, as he represented Roosevelt's own district. The AFC backed off from any referendum in hostile territory, however, as when Sen. Robert Rice Reynolds (D-N.C.) warned that any referendum in his own state would be prowar. Cole, *America First*, pp. 59–60.

The AFC both gave money and contributed staff to a poll conducted by the strongly anti-interventionist *New York Daily News*. It sponsored a poll of various campuses by the *Yale Daily News*. It financed a survey challenging the claim of *Life* magazine that Neosho, Missouri—a "typical midwestern town"—was interventionist. See "Neosho," *Life*, May 26, 1941, pp. 96–102, 105–8. It funded a poll of 35,000 Roman Catholic clergy by the Catholic Laymen's Committee for Peace, a group headed by the chairman of the Brooklyn AFC chapter. See Cole, ibid., p. 60; Stenehjem, *American First*, p. 87.

112. For the national committee endorsement, see minutes, national committee, June 23, 1941, Box 337; press release, June 28, 1941, Box 36, AFC Papers. For earlier participation by Ruth Sarles, see R. Sarles to K. Lee, April 12, 1941, Box 34, AFC Papers. For the enthusiasm of the Washington staff, see P. Hufty to R. D. Stuart, Jr., June 24, 1941, Box 3, AFC Papers. For words of caution, see J. T. Flynn to N. Thomas, March 17, 1941, Thomas Papers; W. R. Castle to R. D. Stuart, Jr., March 29, 1941, Box 63, AFC Papers. For Sarles's activity, see R. Sarles to R. D. Stewart [*sic*], June 26, 1941, Box 34; undated memo, R. Sarles to R. D. Stuart, Jr., Box 67, AFC Papers; for AFC Chapters, see Cole, *America First*, p. 59; minutes, national committee, November 28, 1941, Box 337, AFC Papers.

113. Flynn in Stenehjem, *American First*, p. 89.

114. Lindbergh, address of July 2, 1941, San Francisco, in *Congressional Record*, July 7, 1941, p. A3283.

115. Prepared from data gathered by the National Catholic Welfare Conference,

the AFC memo cited instances of persecution and included statements by Pope Pius XI, Episcopal Bishop William Manning of New York, and the American Jewish Congress. "Freedom [?] of Religion in Communist Russia," October 8, 1941, Box 279, AFC Papers. For Roosevelt's original comments, see *New York Times*, October 1, 1941, p. 9.

116. For the best discussion of this issue, see Ralph B. Levering, *American Opinion and the Russian Alliance, 1939–1945* (Chapel Hill: University of North Carolina Press, 1976), pp. 41–59. See also Bailey and Ryan, *Hitler vs. Roosevelt*, p. 215.

117. R. Sarles to R. D. Stuart, Jr., September 19, 1941, Box 67, AFC Papers; R. E. Wood to R. D. Stuart, Jr., October 6, 1941, Box 68. On House vote, see P. Hufty, Bulletin #630, October 14, 1941, Box 279, AFC Papers.

118. Early in September, the bulletin of the New York chapter noted that no military expert believed Russia could hold out. A month later, the same journal said the collapse of the Soviet Union was inevitable, at most two months away (issues of September 6, 1941, p. 3; October 4, 1941, p.3).

Committee leadership was as confident in private. Stuart predicted a German victory, though he feared it would tempt the administration to make "some sort of desperate move" to keep Britain in the war. If a declared war could be avoided until January, he continued, the Soviet Union probably would have been conquered or made peace, and England would have negotiated a settlement with Germany. R. D. Stuart, Jr., to C. Bowles, October 11, 1941, Box 59, AFC Papers; R. D. Stuart, Jr., to J. C. Hormel, September 19, 1941, Box 60, AFC Papers. Lindbergh wrote General Wood on October 27, "The collapse of the Russian armies may easily bring the demand in England for negotiation." C. A. Lindbergh to R. E. Wood, October 27, 1941, Wood Papers.

Pettengill had been a Democratic congressman representing South Bend, Indiana. He also wrote a syndicated newspaper column, "The Gentleman from Indiana," and the book *Smoke-Screen* (1940), which attacked the New Deal. He soon became one of the most respected of the AFC's advisers.

119. For use of communist label, see the remarks made about Albert Parry, director of Chicago's Fight for Freedom Committee (P. Hufty, Bulletin #561, September 19, 1941, Box 279, AFC Papers). For communist and extreme left opinion, see editorial, *New Masses*, January 7, 1941, p. 4; Joseph Starobin, "Double-Talk in Foreign Policy," ibid., January 28, 1941, p. 6; Morris Watson, *Brooklyn College Vanguard*, May 16, 1941; editorial, "FDR creates an Emergency," *New Masses*, June 10, 1941, p. 3; and a series of articles written in the fall of 1941 by Harlan Crippen in *US Week* and by John L. Spivak in *New Masses*.

120. R. Sarles to R. D. Stuart, Jr., July 3, 1941, Box 55, AFC Papers; R. D. Stuart, Jr., to R. E. Wood, July 7, 1941, Box 59, AFC Papers.

121. R. A. Moore, Bulletin #415, July 15, 1941, Box 279, AFC Papers.

122. Text of the Roosevelt message, *New York Times*, July 8, 1941, p. 3.

123. Lindbergh had hitherto been optimistic about the United States remaining at peace; he now saw the occupation as the most serious step the United States had yet taken. Referring to Iceland as a European island, not an American one, he said

its occupation involved "a great hazard." Stuart claimed U.S. troops sent there would have been much safer if the United States had first informed Germany. Acting out of sheer ignorance, Germany might have attacked U.S. vessels accidently discovered in her declared war zone. Entry of July 8, 1941, Lindbergh, *Wartime Journals*, p. 515; R. D. Stuart, Jr., to Armand May, July 19, 1941, Box 61, AFC Papers.

124. For Iceland's status, see Langer and Gleason, *The Undeclared War*, p. 575; for Stuart, see letter to Armand May, July 19, 1941, Box 61, AFC Papers; Flynn in Wayne S. Cole, *Roosevelt and the Isolationists, 1932–45* (Lincoln: University of Nebraska Press, 1983), p. 432.

125. *New York Times*, July 18, 1941, p. 5.

126. *New York Times*, August 15, 1941, p. 5, press release, August 14, 1941, Box 278, AFC Papers. In his statement, Wood did question the phrase in the Atlantic Charter "after the final destruction of the Nazi tyranny." The general asked, "Does this mean, as some will doubtless claim, that the President has committed the United States to entrance· in the European war to destroy the existing German government, or does it imply only a wish on the part of Churchill?"
Wood would have found little comfort in Churchill's boast, made to his cabinet upon his return, that Roosevelt had promised to "wage war," but "not declare it." Once the president arrived home, however, he did not issue relevant orders (Reynolds, *Creation*, p. 216; Bailey and Ryan, *Hitler vs. Roosevelt*, pp. 165–66). For Burdick's report, see memo, August 14, 1941, Box 65, AFC Papers. See also C. Judson to P. F. La Follette, August 15, 1941, Box 283, AFC Papers.

127. See P. F. La Follette to C. Judson, August 18, 1941, Box 283, AFC Papers; S. B. Pettengill to R. E. Wood, August 22, 1941, Box 286, AFC Papers; New York chapter bulletin, August 23, 1941, p. 1. The New York chapter suspected secret military commitments while Pettengill spoke vaguely about Roosevelt's "fantastic scheme of Anglo-American world imperialism."

128. Al Hamilton to N. Thomas, August 15, 1941, Thomas Papers.

129. Forrest C. Pogue, *George C. Marshall: Ordeal and Hope, 1939–1942* (New York: Viking, 1966), p. 147.

130. Dallek, *Franklin D. Roosevelt*, p. 277; poll, *New York Times*, August 6, 1941, p. 9.

131. Text of Roosevelt message, *New York Times*, July 22, 1941, p. 6; Pogue, *Marshall*, p. 149.

132. *New York Times*, July 5, 1941, p. 24; C. Pugh, Bulletin #389, July 3, 1941, Box 279, AFC Papers.

133. Wood in Cole, *Roosevelt*, p. 437.

134. P. Hufty, Bulletin #444, July 28, 1941, Box 279, AFC Papers. Hufty soon reiterated his position, doing so the day the Senate voted on the bill. He said AFC chapters could not formally oppose the pending legislation on behalf of America First. However, individual AFC members might express their views in letters to Congress, public statements, or in any other manner. Bulletin #477, August 7, 1941, Box 279, AFC Papers.

135. Few AFC units were as feisty as the New York chapter. Its bulletin warned against any emergency declared by Congress, for under such a proclamation, the president would seek authority to send drafted soldiers to any continent. *"You must stop this scheme immediately,"* it cried. New York chapter bulletin, July 26, 1941, pp. 1, 2. Quotation from page 1.

Chapter director Flynn strongly criticized Hufty's Bulletin #444. Writing Hufty directly, Flynn said, "Here are the Senators and Representatives who are collaborating with us making a desperate battle in Congress to stop this damnable and fraudulent scheme to push us one more step to war, and our national headquarters telling members to step from behind the Senators in so crucial a fight." The proposal had nothing to do with national defense, he continued, but was founded on the utterly fraudulent position that the army was going to melt away. See J. T. Flynn to P. Hufty (copy), June 30, 1941, Box 56, AFC Papers.

136. Cole, *America First*, pp. 101–102, Burdick reports of July 25, 29, 30, 31, August 1, 4, 8, 11, all in 1941, Box 65, AFC Papers.

137. Sarles, "Story," p. 228. On August 12, Marshal Pétain, France's chief of state, had pledged his regime to collaborate in Hitler's new order. For Pogue, see *Marshall*, p. 152.

138. R. D. Stuart, Jr., in Cole, *America First*, p. 102. S. Pettengill to R. E. Wood, August 14 and 15, 1941, Box 292, AFC Papers; P. Hufty, Bulletin #503, August 20, 1941, Box 279, AFC Papers.

139. One AFC bulletin warned against propaganda found in such films as *The Mortal Storm*, which showed Nazis terrorizing a Jewish scientist; Alfred Hitchcock's *Foreign Correspondent*, in which a reporter stumbles upon a Nazi plot led by a seemingly "innocent" head of a peace society; *The Great Dictator*, which had Charlie Chaplin turning Hitler into a buffoon; *That Hamilton Woman*, which used the famous romance of Lord Nelson to draw clear parallels between the dangers of Napoleon's France and Hitler's Germany; *The Ramparts We Watched*, a full-length March of Time production that recreated U.S. entry into World War I from an interventionist position. One Nazi film, *Victory in the West*, was listed. Other films listed include *Mystery Sea Raider*, *After Mein Kampf*, *The World in Flames*, and *They Dare Not Love*. P. Hufty, Bulletin #453, July 30, 1941, Box 279, AFC Papers.

Local units added to this list. For example, the AFC chapter bulletin of St. Louis, in the issue of August 1941, added such films as *Night Train*, *Convoy* (which showed a sea battle between a German raider and a British cruiser convoying a fleet of merchantmen across the Atlantic), *Escape* (in which a young American got his mother out of a Nazi concentration camp), *I Married a Nazi* (an American girl in Germany finds out what dictatorship means), *Manhunt* (dealing with a would-be assassin of Hitler), *Flight Command*, and *Sergeant York* (dealing with the famed hero of World War I). (Box 278, AFC).

140. P. Hufty, Bulletins #452 and 453, July 30, 1941, Bulletin, #501, August 19, 1941, Box 279, AFC Papers; *New York Times*, September 20, 1941, p. 6.

141. Wayne S. Cole, *Senator Gerald P. Nye and American Foreign Relations* (Minneapolis: University of Minnesota Press, 1962), pp. 185–87; Frey, "Flynn," p. 223; R. E. Wood to John J. Wheeler, August 11, 1941, Box 286, AFC Papers. When Wood told an executive of Columbia Pictures that the investigation was in no way

sponsored by the AFC, he was being a bit inaccurate. R. E. Wood to Stanton Griffis (copy), October 31, 1941, Box 285, AFC Papers.

142. *Time* and *Life* had denied, claimed Stuart, that Germany could survive an active campaign, asserted that the German people were starving and hated their leaders, predicted that the British blockade would defeat Germany within two years, asserted that Hitler's campaign had no chance of success, and insisted that the German soldier fought only because he was forced to. R. D. Stuart, Jr., to K. Lee, R. Sarles, R. E. Wood, May 2, 1941, Box 57, AFC papers. The AFC noted a *New York Times* story that stressed the Coughlinites, German accents, and opposition to Britain found at a Madison Square Garden rally. But it found the newspaper silent about visible communist presence at an interventionist meeting held less than two months later. P. Hufty, Bulletin #432, July 22, 1941, Box 279, AFC papers.

143. Sarles, "Story," p. 112.

144. Cole, *America First*, pp. 104–105; Ickes, *New York Times*, April 14, 1941, p. 19; Stimson, *New York Times*, July 25, 1941, p. 1. Such staunch Democrats as Senate Majority Leader Alben W. Barkley of Kentucky rushed to the defense of Senator Wheeler, under whose congressional frank the AFC messages had been mailed, and Stimson soon apologized. In its reply, the AFC noted that contrary to Stimson's implication, the postcards did not attack draft renewal. In fact, they were mailed before General Marshall proposed to extend the service of army personnel. The cards were sent to over a million people whose names came from a magazine mailing list. Page Hufty, AFC director of organization, accused Stimson of attempting to divert public attention from Wheeler's accusation that between 12,000 and 20,000 American troops had landed in Suez. Bulletin #441, July 25, 1941, Box 279, AFC papers. At the same time, Hufty told chapters to remove the names of all military personnel from the file. He commented, "As you know America First has always been strongly in favor of adequate national defense and believes that a high morale among the personnel of the armed forces is vital." Bulletin #442, July 25, 1941, Box 279, AFC Papers.

145. *Time*, October 6, 1941, p. 20.

146. While claiming that the great majority of AFC leaders and members were "patriotic Americans," the Friends of Democracy, Inc., juxtaposed quotations of Hitler with those of Wheeler and Nye. It asserted that Nazi sympathizers in New York, Chicago, and Detroit recruited members and raised money for the committee. It also cited endorsement of the AFC by German and Italian propaganda agencies. "The America First Committee—Nazi Transmission Belt" (pamphlet; New York: Friends of Democracy, Inc., 1941).

Reactions varied among the AFC leadership. Chester Bowles called for a direct response, and John T. Flynn issued an answer on behalf of the New York chapter. However, Clay Judson and Sterling Morton said the AFC should ignore the attack, and neither the directors nor the national committee made any response. C. Bowles to R. D. Stuart, Jr., March 13, 1941, Box 292, AFC Papers; Flynn, *New York Times*, March 15, 1941, p. 6; C. Judson to R. E. Wood, March 20, 1941, Box 282, AFC Papers; S. Morton to R. D. Stuart, Jr., March 24, 1941, Box 282, AFC Papers.

For coverage of the unsuccessful attempt of the Miami city commissioners to keep the AFC from holding a rally at which Philip La Follette, former Progressive governor of Wisconsin, would speak, see *New York Times*, May 4, 1941, p. 9; May 6, 1941, p. 8; May 11, 1941, p. 34. Most of the time, however, the censors got their way, as seen by instances at Atlanta, Oklahoma City, California's Alameda County (Berkeley and Oakland), and the Carnegie Institute of Technology (Pittsburgh). For Atlanta, see ibid., July 10, 1941, p. 1; Oklahoma City, ibid., August 27, 1941, p. 7; Alameda County, *Daily Californian* (University of California at Berkeley), September 17, 1941, p. 1; Carnegie Tech, *New York Times*, May 11, 1941, p. 34. The manager of the Philadelphia Academy of Music, in prohibiting the AFC, wrote the local committee chairman, "Since the Academy of Music is not in Germany or any of its allied countries and since Mr. Hitler has not taken over, the Academy of Music is not available." Sarles, "Story," p. 318.

147. For endorsers of the AFC who did not want their views publicized, see General Charles P. Summerall, president of the Citadel and former army chief of staff, to R. E. Wood, October 20, 1940, Box 291; journalist Dorothy Dunbar Bromley to S. Hertzberg, January 19, 1941, Box 12, AFC Papers; Walter Davenport, associate editor of *Collier's*, to J. T. Flynn, March 10, 1941, Box 21, Flynn Papers. For Castle, see Castle Diary, February 28, 1941.

148. See, for example, F. D. Roosevelt to Stephen T. Early, undated penciled memo, Official File #4330, the papers of Franklin D. Roosevelt (hereafter cited as Roosevelt Papers), Franklin D. Roosevelt Presidential Library, Hyde Park, N.Y.; J. Edgar Hoover to S. Early, with attached report, March 1, 1941, Official File #4330, Roosevelt Papers. For secondary accounts based on much examination of FBI material, see Richard W. Steele, "Franklin D. Roosevelt and His Foreign Policy Critics," *Political Science Quarterly* 94 (Spring 1979): 15–32, Cole, *Roosevelt*, pp. 485–87. In October 1941 Hoover wrote Wood, declaring, "At no time has the FBI directly or indirectly at any place in the United States tapped the wires, interfered with the mail, or checked the membership lists of the America First Committee." J. E. Hoover to R. E. Wood, October 17, 1941, Box 60, AFC Papers. One historian has found that federal agents did monitor AFC operations. See Steele, "Franklin D. Roosevelt," p. 23.

149. Thomsen in *Documents on German Foreign Policy, 1918–1941*, Series D, Volume 11 (Washington, D.C.: U.S. Department of State, 1949), p. 949. For Ingalls, see Cole, *America First*, pp. 121, 124. Usually, the AFC tried to remain alert. It told members of the German-American Bund they were unwelcome, ousted several San Francisco leaders at the request of a Jewish organization, and, after a lengthy battle, forced the pro-German publishing house of Flanders Hall to drop the unauthorized label—"An America First publication"—from its books. See J. T. Flynn to *Free American and Deutscher Weckruf und Beobachter*, copy in R. L. Bliss, Bulletin #257, May 15, 1941, Box 55, AFC Papers; Cole, *America First*, p. 119. For the Flanders Hall controversy, see the series of letters between AFC officials and publisher Sigfrid Hauck, Box 280, AFC Papers. For Flynn's anxieties, see Document 20.

The AFC sought investigation by the FBI and by Congressman Martin Dies (D-Tex.), chairman of the House Un-American Activities Committee. Dies initiated an investigation, which was under way when the AFC dissolved. R. E. Wood to Martin Dies, January 27, 1941, November 13, 1941, in Sarles, "Story," pp. 326–28. For investigation, see Sarles, p. 329. Although the FBI did not accept the AFC offer, at one point FBI agents did check AFC membership against enrollments in the German-American National Alliance, a Nazi group. R. L. Bliss to Chicago FBI, March 13, 1941, Box 285, AFC Papers; R. D. Stuart, Jr., to J. A. Fairbank, June 9, 1941, Box 60, AFC.

150. For example, the AFC withdrew recognition of its Oklahoma representative, Don Lohbeck, who was chief aide to the populist demagogue Gerald L. K. Smith. See R. D. Stuart, Jr., to AFC staff, July 16, 1941, Box 18, AFC Papers. Janet Ayer Fairbank defied General Wood's order to organize a joint meeting with the Citizens Keep America Out of War Committee of Chicago or We, the Mothers, Mobilize for America, as she considered both groups too extreme. J. A. Fairbank to R. E. Wood, November 19, 1941, Box 284, AFC papers. For Morton, see letter to R. E. Wood, May 29, 1941, Box 56, AFC papers.

151. For an example of accusations of anti-Semitism, see Michael Straight, "The Anti-Semitic Conspiracy," *New Republic*, September 22, 1941, pp. 362–63, which sought to link the AFC to virulently anti-Semitic groups. For Jewish opinion, see Alfred O. Hero, Jr., *American Religious Groups View Foreign Policy: Trends in Rank-and-File Opinion, 1937–1969* (Durham, N.C.: Duke University Press, 1973), pp. 22–25, 283–85. For efforts to recruit Jews, see, for example, R. D. Stuart, Jr., to J. A. Fairbank regarding Hugo Sonnenschein, December 23, 1940, Box 20; R. E. Wood to Julius Minor, January 2, 1941, Box 286; R. D. Stuart, Jr., to Ira Hirschmann, November 15, 1940, Box 292, AFC papers. Three Jews were on the New York chapter's executive committee, including the wives of editor Paul Palmer and journalist John Gunther. Sarles, "Story," p. 332.

Hertzberg said, "I happen to be one of the Jews—and I know many others who dare not say so—who believe our entry into the war will ultimately mean greater torture for the Jews than even the victory of Hitler in Europe." S. Hertzberg to Lester Markel, February 25, 1941, Box 292, AFC papers. For denunciations of anti-Semitism, see R. Sarles to P. Hufty, October 6, 1941, Box 291, AFC papers; Cole, *America First*, pp. 133–34.

152. For rallies, see Cole, *America First*, pp. 133–40. For Coughlin movement, see R. D. Stuart, Jr., to Ida C. Mullins (copy), January 6, 1941, Box 285; R. E. Wood to R. A. O'Connor, July 9, 1941, Box 56; R. E. Wood to A. M. Latham, August 14, 1941, Box 286, AFC Papers; Wood cited in *Social Justice*, July 28, 1941, p. 16. For Coughlin's endorsements, see, for example, *Social Justice*, October 7, 1940, p. 17; June 16, 1941, p. 20. For some Coughlin reservations, see ibid., June 9, 1941, p. 20; July 7, 1941, p. 20. For Castle's comments see *PM*, March 20, 1941. In a letter written to Stuart the following day, Castle denied he was anti-Semitic. His phrasing was "perhaps a little unfortunately worded," but he did not expect private letters to be published in a newspaper. Letter dated March 21, 1941, Box 63, AFC Papers. See also Castle Diary, December 14, 1940, where the former diplomat said he could not help agreeing with many of Verne Marshall's "ideas" on the Jews.

153. See, for example, entry of June 30, 1939, Lindbergh, *Wartime Journals*, p. 218; August 23, 1939, p. 245; October 10, 1940, pp. 404–5.

154. For complete text, see Sarles, "Story," pp. 372–76.

155. For resignation from national committee, see Edward L. Ryerson, Jr., to R. D. Stuart, Jr., September 29, 1941, Box 337; Kathryn Lewis, September 29, 1941,

Box 292, AFC Papers. Some prominent Jewish sponsors of the New York chapter also resigned, including Hearst columnist Charles Fleischer (Stenehjem, *American First*, p. 136). Columbia University law professor Philip C. Jessup and publisher Frank E. Gannett suddenly became reluctant to join the AFC (P. C. Jessup to R. E. Wood, September 22, 1941, Box 23, AFC Papers; P. C. Jessup to J. T. Flynn, October 24, 1941, Box 21, Flynn Papers; Gannett in Cole, *Lindbergh*, p. 177). Some condemnations from Roosevelt critics were quite blunt. See, for example, Hugh Johnson to John P. Lewis, September 16, 1941, copy of cable, Box 291, AFC Papers; broadcaster Quincy Howe, entry of September 15, 1941, in Lindbergh, *War Within*, September 15, 1941, p. 225; Hearst press, *San Francisco Examiner*, September 14, 1941, p. 1; Bernard Baruch, letter to *San Francisco Examiner*, October 5, 1941, p. 1; New York attorney Jonathan B. Bingham to AFC, September 14, 1941, Box 289, AFC Papers. Among the other anti-interventionists who opposed the speech were Scripps-Howard columnist Al Williams, *PM*, September 18, 1941, p. 11; prominent Oklahoma Republican Herbert K. Hyde, ibid., p. 11; H. Smith Richardson to Flynn, September 23, 1941, Box 21, Flynn Papers; the diary of journalist William Henry Chamberlin, entry of October 10–17, 1941, Providence College Library.

For the Hoover statement, see H. Hoover to Joseph Scott, September 14, 1941, Box 118, Hoover Papers. In speaking to Lindbergh directly, Hoover was much more moderate. Lindbergh, *Wartime Journals*, entry of October 6, 1941, p. 546–47. See also Selden Rodman, editor of *Common Sense*, to Alfred Bingham, September 16, 1941, the papers of Alfred Bingham, Yale University Library.

156. Letter dated September 15, 1941, Box 21, Flynn Papers. Flynn tried to organize a special Jewish division to counter charges of anti-Semitism, but the branch was never formed (Stenehjem, *American First*, p. 58).

157. N. Thomas to R. D. Stuart, Jr., September 10 [12], 1941, N. Thomas to R. D. Stuart, Jr., September 23, 1941, Box 66, AFC Papers. See also *American Guardian*, September 19, 1941, p. 3; Socialist Party press release, September 23, 1941, Socialist Party Papers; *Chicago Tribune*, September 13, 1941; p. 10; September 20, 1941, p. 10; Boake Carter, *San Francisco Examiner*, September 19, 1941, p. 11; J. A. Fairbank to N. Thomas, September 24, 1941, Thomas Papers.

158. For the Mason comment, see D. G. Mason to Thomas Caldecot Clubb (copy), September 19, 1941, Box 34, AFC papers.

159. Entry of September 11, 1941, *War Within*, pp. 220–221. For comments questioning the wisdom of the Des Moines speech, see also W. R. Castle to R. D. Stuart, Jr., September 17, 1941, Box 63; Oswald Garrison Villard to George Gordon Battle (copy), September 23, 1941, Box 283; Wilbur E. Hammaker, Methodist bishop of Denver, to R. D. Stuart, Jr., September 22, 1941, Box 291; S. Morton to R. D. Stuart, Jr., Box 291, AFC Papers; Dorothy Detzer, executive secretary, Women's International League for Peace and Freedom, to Emily Greene Balch, September 22, 1941, the papers of the Women's International League for Peace and Freedom, Swarthmore College Peace collection; *Commonweal*, September 26, 1941, p. 532; *Christian Century*, September 24, 1941, p. 1168.

160. A. J. Carlson to John P. Lewis (copy), September 16, 1941, Box 285; K. Norris (cable) to R. D. Stuart, Jr., September 24, 1941, Box 291, AFC Papers. See

also Cole, *Nye*, p. 190; attorney and reformer Amos Pinchot to S. Stanwood Menken, October 4, 1941, Box 281, AFC Papers.

161. At first, the AFC itself was cautious. In a bulletin for all chapters, the national headquarters claimed the Lindbergh speech had often been misquoted, so it should be read carefully by all chapters and by as many members as possible. P. Hufty, Bulletin #553, September 15, 1941, Box 279, AFC Papers. At another point, Hufty claimed that of the immense volume of mail received by AFC on the matter, only 11 percent differed with Lindbergh. P. Hufty, Bulletin #574, September 22, 1941, Box 279, AFC Papers. For the official AFC statement, *New York Times*, September 25, 1941, p. 4.

162. R. D. Stuart, Jr., to N. Thomas, September 24, 1941, Box 66; K. Mundt to R. D. Stuart, Jr., September 26, 1941, Box 61, AFC Papers; Hiram Johnson to Hiram Johnson, Jr., September 27, 1941, the papers of Hiram Johnson, Bancroft Library, University of California, Berkeley; Lindbergh, *New York Times*, October 4, 1941, p. 1.

163. For thoughtful discussions of this matter, see Cole, *America First*, pp. 153–54, and Cole, *Lindbergh*, p. 185.

164. Text of Roosevelt speech, *New York Times*, September 12, 1941, pp. 1, 4.

165. Sarles, "Story," pp. 280–81. Wood also released a statement by fifty-eight prominent Americans denouncing the speech. Among the signers were such respected academics as Philip C. Jessup, Ray Lyman Wilbur, Edward S. Corwin, and Charles A. Beard. Cole, *America First*, p. 161.

166. C. Judson to P. Hufty, September 12, 1941, Box 283, AFC Papers; New York chapter bulletin, September 20, 1941, p. 2.

167. For meeting of September 17, see entries of September 17 and 18, 1941, Lindbergh, *Wartime Journals*, pp. 540–41; R. E. Wood to H. MacNider, September 22, 1941, the papers of Hanford MacNider (hereafter cited as MacNider Papers), Hoover Presidential Library.

In a letter to Wood dated September 23, Lindbergh offered additional reasons for keeping the AFC alive. The Gallup poll had shown opposition to war rising to 83 percent; the Soviets had suffered heavy reverses; there was at least an even chance of a negotiated peace before the next spring; dissolution demoralized AFC supporters while encouraging the opposition. Text of letter in Sarles, "Story," pp. 283–84. When Lindbergh again met with AFC leaders on October 4, he thought the rank-and-file members would see the AFC showing weakness at the very moment when it should be fighting the hardest. Wrote Lindbergh, "We cannot let these people down at the very moment they have a right to expect us to stand firm." Wood agreed, but thought that the AFC action in regard to adjournment should probably be decided by the action Congress took on the neutrality bill. See entry of October 4, 1941, Lindbergh, *Wartime Journals*, pp. 544–46.

168. On October 3, the sinking of the *I. C. White*, a tanker owned by Standard Oil of New Jersey, was announced. Sailing from Curacao to Cape Town, it was hit some six hundred miles east of Pernambuco, Brazil. It flew the Panamanian flag and was carrying fuel oil. On October 21 and 22, Washington announced several sinkings. The *Bold Venture* was sunk five hundred miles off Iceland. It too held Panamanian

registry, and was bound for England with a cargo of cotton, steel, and copper. The *Lehigh* was torpedoed some seventy-five miles away from Freetown, Sierra Leone. A freighter of the United States Line and flying the American flag, it was headed from Spain to the Gold Coast. Its cargo was ballast, not contraband. The Standard Oil tanker *W. C. Teagle* was sunk in the North Atlantic. It was reportedly flying the British flag and was part of a convoy.

169. Bailey and Ryan, *Hitler vs. Roosevelt*, p. 165; Reynolds, *Creation*, p. 216.

170. Text of Roosevelt speech, *New York Times*, October 28, 1941, p. 4; Wood statement, October 27, 1941, Box 278, AFC Papers. MacNider wrote Wood and, in referring to Roosevelt, said, "I am completely convinced he is crazy or we are." Letter dated October 28, 1941, Box 286, AFC Papers.

171. AFC press release, November 2, 1941, Princeton file.

172. Text of Roosevelt message, *New York Times*, October 10, 1941, p. 4.

173. Wood, ibid.; full text in AFC research bureau, "Did You Know?" #28, October 25, 1941, pp. 32–33, Box 280, AFC Papers; R. E. Wood to B. K. Wheeler, October 9, 1941, Box 55, AFC Papers; AFC research bureau, "Did You Know?" #27, October 13, 1941, Box 280, AFC Papers.

174. Senator Wheeler believed, though, that America First could prevent the repeal of the neutrality act, and in particular the sending of U.S. ships into a combat zone. B. K. Wheeler to R. E. Wood, October 14, 1941, Box 55, AFC Papers.

175. Congressman Mundt blamed the majority members of the House Foreign Affairs Committee for barring open hearings. He found considerably more opposition in the House than he expected. If the country had more time to register its opinions in Washington, or if Congress had access to all the information brought out secretly in cross-examination, opponents of the bill might have won. K. Mundt to John Cudahy (copy), October 18, 1941, Box 61, AFC Papers. For Gallup poll, see *New York Times*, October 19, 1941, p. 5.

176. Sarles, "Story," p. 254.

177. R. E. Wood to H. MacNider, October 29, 1941, Box 286, AFC Papers.

178. National committee, minutes, October 20, 1941, Box 337, AFC Papers; *New York Times*, October 23, 1941, p. 4; press release, October 22, 1941, Princeton file; Robert E. Sherwood, *Roosevelt and Hopkins: An Intimate History* (New York: Harper, 1948), p. 382.

179. Among the supporters of the administration who became anti-interventionist were Harold H. Burton (R-Ohio), Millard E. Tydings (D-Md.), "Cotton Ed" Smith (D-N.C.), Theodore G. Bilbo (D-Miss.), Harry F. Byrd (D-Va.), Henry Cabot Lodge (R-Mass.), Charles S. McNary (R-Ore.), Francis T. Maloney (D-Conn.), and Ralph Owen Brewster (R-Me.).

180. For Wood statement, see press release of November 8, 1941, Box 278, AFC Papers. For AFC perception, see Sarles, "Story," p. 266. Castle was less confident. He wrote Stuart, "The strange thing is that all this push to get into war now should go on at the time Mr. Churchill says the crisis is passed. I don't understand this country." Letter dated November 10, 1941, Box 63, AFC Papers.

181. R. Sarles to R. D. Stuart, Jr., November 19, 1941, Box 34, AFC Papers; Burdick report, November 26, 1941, Box 284, AFC Papers.

182. Wood statement, November 14, 1941, Box 278, AFC Papers; organization department, Bulletin #687, November 14, 1941, Box 279, AFC Papers; Burdick report, November 27, 1941, Box 284, AFC Papers.

183. Roosevelt's moves, Reynolds, *Creation*, pp. 219–20; Hitler's caution, Compton, *The Swastika and the Eagle*, pp. 161–73; Saul Friedländer, *Prelude to Downfall: Hitler and the United States, 1939–1941* (New York: Knopf, 1967), pp. 256–61, 290–95. Bailey and Ryan stress that Roosevelt was already achieving his main goal, to protect the flow of lend-lease supplies, without intolerable losses. He could tangle with no more submarines than he was doing, even if war had been formally declared. At the time of Pearl Harbor, U.S. armed forces were totally unprepared for major operations. Hence some military experts, both U.S. and British, claimed the United States could best aid the embattled Allies by keeping its nominal neutrality. See p. 227. Reynolds finds it likely that, had it not been for Pearl Harbor, limited and undeclared hostility would have continued for many months. See p. 220.

184. In the middle of November, Burdick noted that the War Department ordered some 5.7 million wool service coats, 7 million barracks bags, and 4.2 million field jackets. He asked if preparations were being made for "a huge A.E.F. to be sent to Africa, Europe, Russia and Asia?" Burdick report, November 19, 1941, Box 284, AFC Papers. Herbert Hoover continually pressed Stuart to track down such rumors and bring them to public attention. R. D. Stuart, Jr., to R. Sarles (copy), November 11, 1941, the papers of the Keep America Out of War Congress (hereafter cited as KAOWC Papers), Swarthmore College Peace Collection. Sarles noted rumors of American planes in Africa and American military "observers" in the Middle East. R. Sarles to R. D. Stuart, Jr., November 21, 1941, Box 67, AFC Papers. For both the story of the War Department's plans and the Washington reaction, see the *Chicago Tribune*, December 4, 1941, pp. 1, 10, and the *New York Times*, December 5, 1941, p. 3.

185. AFC press release, November 2, 1941, Princeton file. Cole (*America First*, pp. 181–82) finds it significant that the resolution made the vote on neutrality repeal the determining criteria for AFC support. Coming when the debate was still under way, the AFC obviously hoped to bolster the opposition. For national committee, see minutes, November 28, 1941, Box 337, AFC. On November 25 Stuart noted the AFC was attempting to establish a political advisory committee. He hoped Hoover, Landon, Taft, Wheeler, the two Clarks, John Cudahy (former minister to Belgium), Norman Thomas, and Phil La Follette would serve. R. D. Stuart, Jr., to R. Sarles (copy), November 25, 1941, KAOWC Papers.

186. MacNider did not resign alone. Ellen French Vanderbilt Fitz Simons noted that political activity would necessarily involve efforts on behalf of some Democrats, efforts that would be incompatible with her position as vice chairman of the Republican National Committee. E. F. V. Fitz Simons to R. D. Stuart, Jr., November 28, 1941, Box 290, AFC Papers.

187. Wood replied that he concurred. R. E. Wood to J. T. Flynn, November 19, 1941, Box 290, AFC Papers.

188. R. D. Stuart, Jr., to J. Cudahy, December 1, 1941, Box 292, AFC Papers.

189. Poll, *New York Times*, September 21, 1941; Cole and Wood in Cole, *America First*, pp. 187–88.

190. For expressions that tensions with Japan appear to have relaxed, see *Washington News Letter* #8, March 21, 1941, p. 2, Box 281; ibid. #11, April 29, 1941, p. 3, Box 284, AFC Papers; R. Sarles to K. Lee, June 7, 1941, R. Sarles to R. D. Stuart, Jr., July 3, 1941, Box 67, AFC Papers. For quotation, see *Washington News Letter* #13, May 15, 1941, Box 284, AFC Papers.

191. The chapter's executive committee saw Southeast Asia lying in Japan's sphere of influence, not America's: "If we claim the right to intervene to prevent Japan's acquisition of bases in Indo-China, Japan has an equal right to prevent our acquisition of bases in Brazil." New York AFC executive committee, New York chapter bulletin, August 2, 1941, pp. 1, 2.

192. Sarles feared the United States would consider occupation of Siam a threat to Manila. R. Sarles to R. D. Stuart, Jr., August 9, 1941, Box 67, AFC Papers. Hull's warning, said the New York chapter bulletin, would only weaken Britain's hold on the millions of political and industrial slaves it held in India. Issue of August 16, 1941, p. 3. See also C. Bowles to R. D. Stuart, Jr., August 8, 1941, Box 59, AFC Papers. For AFC directors, see Cole, *America First*, p. 192.

193. Stenehjem, *American First*, p. 113. See also New York chapter bulletin, September 6, 1941, p. 3. In late November, Burdick concurred. "The Japanese situation does not look too bad," he wrote. "We all have noticed that when a couple of boys are thinking of fighting that if they talk it over they never do. It is much the same with nations." Burdick, general report, November 24, 1941, Box 284, AFC Papers.

194. Burdick, general report, December 4, 1941, Box 284, AFC Papers; and New York chapter bulletin, December 6, 1941, pp. 1, 3.

195. Lindbergh and Wood, entry of December 8, 1941, in Lindbergh, *Wartime Journals*, pp. 560–61.

196. AFC statement in Cole, *America First*, p. 193; entry of December 8, 1941, Lindbergh, *Wartime Journals*, p. 561.

197. Sarles, "Story," p. 752.

198. T. Hammond to R. D. Stuart, Jr., December 10, 1941, Box 284, AFC Papers; S. Morton to A. R. Wurtele, December 11, 1941, Morton Papers.

199. Wood in Stenehjem, *American First*, p. 118; C. A. Lindbergh to R. E. Wood, December 26, 1941, Wood Papers. Lindbergh later said once he had learned Germany and Italy had declared war, he favored dissolution. See entry of March 2, 1942, *Wartime Journals*, p. 598. Young said in 1953, "I felt then and still feel that if the Committee could only have kept going some of these people who will become national heroes could have been made to pay for their sins by their liberty or perhaps even their lives." See Arthur Goodard, ed., *Harry Elmer Barnes: Learned Crusader* (Colorado Springs, Colo.: Ralph Myles, 1968), pp. 292–93.

200. R. E. Wood to C. A. Lindbergh, December 12, 1941, Wood Papers.

201. Bowles in Stenehjem, *American First,* p. 118; K. Mundt to H. MacNider, December 23, 1941, MacNider Papers; W. H. Regnery to F. J. Libby, December 12, 1941, the papers of the National Council for the Prevention of War, Swarthmore College Peace Collection; B. K. Wheeler to R. E. Wood, December 22, 1941, Box 55, AFC Papers.

202. P. Hufty, Bulletin #427, July 24, 1941, Box 279; Cole, *America First,* p. 197.

203. For AFC argument, see, for example, R. L. Bliss, Bulletin #183, April 8, 1941, Box 278. For strategic retreats, see Cole, *America First,* pp. 66–67.

204. "Telegram by William Allen White and List of Members of the Committee," in *Congressional Record,* October 14, 1939, pp. A619–20; Castle Diary, November 3, 1939.

205. R. E. Wood to Robert McE. Schauffer, January 23, 1941, Box 55, AFC Papers; Schneider, "Anxieties," p. 152.

DOCUMENTS

Selected Documents of the American First Committee

EDITOR'S NOTE

The printed version of the various documents conforms as closely as possible to the original version, with several exceptions. Obvious spelling, punctuation, and typographical errors have been corrected. Although in most cases the documents are complete, at times passages are omitted that are purely personal, or that do not pertain to the topic under examination. For example, issues of the AFC *Washington News Letter* are not produced in their entirety. Also excerpted are "A Story of America First," a 760-page manuscript completed in October 1942 by Ruth Sarles, director of the AFC research bureau; "The Economic Consequences of American Intervention," a 76-page manuscript written by economist and political theorist Lawrence Dennis and never published by the AFC; an analysis of radio commentators, which was part of a general report on radio in the New York area during early December 1940; and a 57-page report attempting to justify the prohibition of American shipping to belligerent ports.

List of Selected Documents

1. Ruth Sarles, "A Story of America First," pp. 43–44.
2. Kingman Brewster to R. Douglas Stuart, Jr., undated [c. July 1940], Box 65.
3. Sterling Morton, Address to National Small Business Men's Association, August 12, 1940, Box 285.
4. Clay Judson to Robert E. Wood, September 24, 1940, Box 63.
5. R. Douglas Stuart, Jr., to Jay C. Hormel, December 4, 1940, Box 290.
6. R. Douglas Stuart, Jr., to Robert E. Wood, December 5, 1940, Box 63.
7. William Benton to Robert M. La Follette, Jr., December 17, 1940, Box 292.
8. R. Douglas Stuart, Jr., to Robert E. Wood, December 8, 1940, Box 285.
9. Charles Clayton Morrison to Robert E. Wood, May 8, 1941, Box 286.
10. Edwin Borchard to Robert E. Wood, September 24, 1941, Box 68.
11. Hugh S. Johnson to R. Douglas Stuart, Jr., January 8, 1941, Box 35.
12. Chester Bowles to R. Douglas Stuart, Jr., November 28, 1941, Box 55.
13. Chester Bowles to R. Douglas Stuart, Jr., July 30, 1941, Box 59.
14. John T. Flynn to Robert E. Wood, June 5, 1941, Box 284.
15. Speakers Bureau, "How did the present war start?" undated [1941], Box 205.
16. Speakers Bureau, "Is the present war, as many people claim, a 'world revolution'?" undated [1941], Box 205.
17. Speakers Bureau, "For what aims is the war being fought?" undated [1941], Box 205.
18. Speakers Bureau, "Questions posed to speakers of the William Allen White Committee," undated [1941], Box 278.

19. Speakers Bureau, "Is America now taking part in the war?" undated [1941], Box 205.

20. Speakers Bureau, "What, strictly on the basis of our own national interests, should our part be?" undated [1941], Box 205.

21. Speakers Bureau, "If our national interest doesn't require us to go to war, shouldn't we go anyway to keep democracy alive in the world?" undated [1941], Box 205.

22. Speakers Bureau, "Isn't it part of our responsibility as a world power to take a hand settling problems that menace world peace and security?" undated [1941], Box 205.

23. Page Hufty, "America First Book List," Bulletin #476, August 7, 1941, Box 279.

24. Clay Judson to James B. Conant, February 3, 1941, Box 283.

25. William R. Castle to R. Douglas Stuart, Jr., February 14, 1941, Box 63.

26. Ruth Sarles to R. Douglas Stuart, Jr., May 31, 1941, Box 51.

27. Ruth Sarles to R. Douglas Stuart, Jr., July 3, 1941, Box 55.

28. Ruth Sarles to R. Douglas Stuart, Jr., August 9, 1941, Box 67.

29. R. Douglas Stuart, Jr., to Robert M. Hutchins, October 29, 1941, Box 60.

30. John T. Flynn to Robert E. Wood, November 11, 1941, Box 55.

31. Speakers Bureau, "Suppose we don't help England and Germany beats her," undated [1941], Box 56.

32. Speakers Bureau, "Even if war with Germany is not a certainty, wouldn't it be best to fight now to avoid even the possibility of a war without allies?" undated [1941], Box 205.

33. Speakers Bureau, "Will the prestige acquired for Nazism by German military victories bring fascism here without even an attack by Hitler?" undated [1941], Box 205.

34. Speakers Bureau, "Could Germany defeat us without fighting by the use of her 'Fifth Column' in this country?" undated [1941], Box 205.

35. Speakers Bureau, "If Germany does decide to fight us could she invade the continental United States from any European base?" undated [1941], Box 205.

36. Speakers Bureau, "Could Germany get bases on the islands of the Caribbean Sea, or in Central America, from which to fight us?" undated [1941], Box 205.

37. Speakers Bureau, "Suppose Germany were able to acquire land, naval and air bases somewhere south of the Caribbean, could she carry on a large-scale war against us?" undated [1941], Box 205.

38. Speakers Bureau, "If England was defeated, could Germany take Canada and British colonies in the Caribbean and attack us?" undated [1941], Box 205.

39. Speakers Bureau, "What about French and Dutch colonies?" undated [1941], Box 205.

40. Speakers Bureau, "Excluding the British Navy, is not the combined tonnage of Axis powers greater than that of the United States?" undated [1941], Box 205.

41. Speakers Bureau, "If Germany captured the British fleet and used to the fullest the ship-building facilities in the conquered countries, could she isolate us from the rest of the world?" undated [1941], Box 205.

42. Speakers Bureau, "Is it true the British fleet is America's first line of defense, the one force that separates us from totalitarianism?" undated [1941], Box 205.

43. Speakers Bureau, "To what extent does our economic life depend on foreign trade?" undated [1941], Box 205.

44. Speakers Bureau, "It is said that if Germany wins, she will capture our world trade and defeat us by strangling our industry. Is this true?" undated [1941], Box 205.

45. Speakers Bureau, "Need we fight in Asia or Africa for rubber and tin, both of which are indispensable materials?" undated [1941], Box 205.

46. Speakers Bureau, "Can Germany cause the gold standard to be abandoned throughout the world—that is, abolish the use of gold as currency—and thereby make our money useless?" undated [1941], Box 205.

47. Speakers Bureau, "What is the general situation in regard to Latin American trade?" undated [1941], Box 278.

48. Speakers Bureau, "What strategic war materials do we lack in the United States?" undated [1941], Box 278.

49. Speakers Bureau, "The Strategic Materials" (chart), undated [1941], Box 278.

50. Research Bureau, "Buy or Die," *Did You Know* no. 6, July 5, 1941, Box 280.

51. Research Bureau, "Swastika Over Sickle," *Did You Know* no. 15, August 1, 1941, Box 280.

52. Research Bureau, "The All-American Front," *Did You Know* no. 17, August 8, 1941, Box 280.

53. Research Bureau, "The Economics of Hemisphere Defense," *Did You Know* no. 23A, September 19, 1941, Box 280.

54. Research Bureau, "All-Out Aid for the Western Hemisphere," *Did You Know* no. 23B, September 22, 1941, Box 280.

55. Research Bureau, "Priority Orphans," *Did You Know* no. 25, September 30, 1941, Box 280.

56. Research Bureau, "Lease-Lend for War," *Did You Know* no. 26, October 4, 1941, Box 280.

57. Lawrence Dennis, "The Economic Consequences of American Intervention," unpublished manuscript, undated [1941], excerpts from pp. 55–76, Box 292.

58. "The Economic Consequences of the Lease-Lend Program," undated [1941], pp. 7–21, Box 279.

59. A. Whitney Griswold to R. Douglas Stuart, Jr., January 16, 1941, Box 60.

60. Raymond J. Sontag to Robert E. Wood, February 6, 1941, Box 85.

61. John Chamberlain to Mark Prentiss, December 30, 1940, Box 35.

62. Lincoln Colcord to Robert E. Wood, January 6, 1941, Box 59.

63. Washington Office, General Memo, January 29, 1941, Box 64.

64. *Washington News Letter* #1, January 31, 1941, Box 284.

65. *Washington News Letter* #3, February 12, 1941, Box 284.

66. Washington Office, General Memo, February 13, 1941, Box 65.

67. Washington Office, General Memo, February 18, 1941, Box 284.

68. Washington Office, General Memo, February 20, 1941, Box 65.

69. Washington Office, General Memo, February 23, 1941, Box 65.

70. Washington Office, General Memo, March 4, 1941, Box 65.

71. Fred Burdick, "Highlights of Interviews with Representatives," undated [1941], Box 65.

72. Research Bureau, "Union Now?" *Did You Know* no. 16, August 6, 1941, Box 280.

73. Speakers Bureau, Memo on English Defenses, undated [1941], Box 278.

74. Ruth Sarles to R. Douglas Stuart, Jr., May 24, 1941, Box 67.

75. Ruth Sarles to Richard A. Moore, June 4, 1941, Box 34.

76. Sterling Morton to Robert E. Wood, April 3, 1941, Box 286.

77. Robert E. Wood to Sterling Morton, April 7, 1941, Box 286.

78. Ruth Sarles to Kendrick Lee, May 4, 1941, Box 34.

79. Ruth Sarles to Kendrick Lee, May 18, 1941, Box 34.

80. *Washington News Letter* #15, May 30, 1941, Box 284.

81. *Washington News Letter* #16, June 4, 1941, Box 284.

82. Research Bureau, "Memorandum on Contraband Material in the Cargo of the Robin Moor," *Did You Know* no. 1, June 18, 1941, Box 280.

83. Research Bureau, "Memorandum on Arming United States Merchant Vessels," *Did You Know* no. 2, June 21, 1941, Box 280.

84. Research Bureau, "Freedom of the Seas," *Did You Know* no. 3, June 26, 1941, Box 280.

85. Chester Bowles to R. Douglas Stuart, Jr., July 15, 1941, Box 59.

86. Chester Bowles to R. Douglas Stuart, Jr., April 25, 1941, Box 292.

87. Chester Bowles to Roy Larsen, April 30, 1941, Box 292.

88. James P. Selvage to George Gallup, with covering letter to R. Douglas Stuart, Jr., April 29, 1941, Box 67.

89. Statement of New York Chapter, June 23, 1941, Box 126.

90. Research Bureau, "Lease-Lend Aid to Russia," *Did You Know* no. 4, June 27, 1941, Box 280.

91. Research Bureau, "Wings over Nome?" *Did You Know* no. 5, July 1, 1941, Box 280.

92. Ruth Sarles to R. Douglas Stuart, Jr., October 3, 1941, Box 285.

93. Samuel B. Pettengill to Robert E. Wood, October 16, 1941, Box 286.

94. Research Bureau, "Our African Outpost," *Did You Know* no. 8, July 11, 1941, Box 280.

95. Research Bureau, "Our Iceland Outpost," *Did You Know* no. 7, July 9, 1941, Box 280.

96. Ruth Sarles to R. Douglas Stuart, Jr., August 15, 1941, Box 67.

97. Research Bureau, "Eight Points for War or Peace: 1) What Do They Mean?" *Did You Know* no. 19, August 23, 1941, Box 280.

98. Research Bureau, "Eight Points for War or Peace: 2) What Legal Effect Do They Have?" *Did You Know* no. 20, August 23, 1941, Box 280.

99. Research Bureau, "Eight Points for War or Peace: 3) Can They Work?" *Did You Know* no. 21A and B, September 2, 1941, Box 280.

100. Robert E. Wood to Robert R. Reynolds, July 17, 1941, Box 288.

101. Research Bureau, "Another A.E.F.?" *Did You Know* no. 9, July 15, 1941, Box 280.

102. Research Bureau, "Soldiers Until . . .?" *Did You Know* no. 10, July 17, 1941, Box 280.

103. Research Bureau, "Long-Term Conscription," *Did You Know* no. 11, July 17, 1941, Box 280.

104. Page Hufty, " 'Danger' Greater—or A.E.F.?" Bulletin #433, July 23, 1941, Box 279.

105. Samuel B. Pettengill to R. Douglas Stuart, Jr., July 22, 1941, Box 62.

106. Research Bureau, "Nobody Knows the Trouble We're In," *Did You Know* no. 12, July 24, 1941, Box 280.

107. Research Bureau, "The Shape of Things to Come?" *Did You Know* no. 13, July 30, 1941, Box 280.

108. Research Bureau, "Say, Is This the U.S.A.," *Did You Know* no. 14, July 31, 1941, Box 147.

109. Fred Burdick, General Letter, August 12, 1941, Box 65.

110. Fred Burdick, General Letter, August 13, 1941, Box 65.

111. Samuel B. Pettengill to R. Douglas Stuart, Jr., August 13, 1941, Box 64.

112. John T. Flynn to R. Douglas Stuart, Jr., August 4, 1941, Box 64.

113. Samuel E. Romer to Sidney Hertzberg, Memo on Network Commentators, December 6, 1940, pp. 4–5.

114. Henry W. Hobson to Robert E. Wood, October 21, 1941, Box 288.

115. Chester Bowles to Sidney Hertzberg, January 16, 1941, Box 35.

116. Chester Bowles to R. Douglas Stuart, Jr., September 19, 1941, Box 291.

117. Frederick J. Libby to R. Douglas Stuart, Jr., September 22, 1941, Box 292.

118. Teletype Messages between John T. Flynn, Robert E. Wood, and R. Douglas Stuart, Jr., September 12, 1941, Box 284.

119. Thomas S. Hammond to Robert E. Wood, September 16, 1941, Box 291.

120. Ruth Sarles, "A Story of America First," pp. 356–59.

121. Norman Thomas to R. Douglas Stuart, Jr., September 29, 1941, Box 292.

122. Research Bureau, "One-Man War," *Did You Know* no. 22, September 13, 1941, Box 280.

123. Hanford MacNider to Robert E. Wood, September 20, 1941, Box 292.

124. Jay C. Hormel to Robert E. Wood, December 4, 1941, Box 286.

125. Research Bureau, "Jekyll-and-Hyde Ships," *Did You Know* no. 24, September 23, 1941, Box 280.

126. Ruth Sarles to Page Hufty, September 14, 1941, Box 284.

127. Ruth Sarles to R. Douglas Stuart, Jr., October 16, 1941.

128. Research Bureau, "Are American Bottoms Needed to Deliver Materiel to Britain?" *Did You Know* no. 28, October 25, 1941, Box 280.

129. Fred Burdick, General Report, October 30, 1941, Box 292.

130. Samuel B. Pettengill to R. Douglas Stuart, Jr., October 8, 1941, Box 292.

131. John T. Flynn to Robert E. Wood, November 16, 1941, Box 55.

132. Fred Burdick, General Report, December 4, 1941, Box 284.

133. Ruth Sarles to R. Douglas Stuart, Jr., December 6, 1941, Box 284.

134. R. Douglas Stuart, Jr., Memo to Robert E. Wood, December 2, 1941, Box 55.

135. William R. Castle to R. Douglas Stuart, Jr., November 22, 1941, Box 55.

136. Hanford MacNider to Robert E. Wood, December 4, 1941, Box 292.

137. John T. Flynn to Robert E. Wood, December 3, 1941, Box 284.

138. Speakers Bureau, "If Germany could not defeat us alone, might not she and her ally Japan beat us with a war on two fronts?" undated [1941], Box 205.

139. Washington Office, General Report, February 21, 1941, Box 284.

140. Fred Burdick, General Report, August 28, 1941, Box 65.

141. Fred Burdick, General Report, December 2, 1941, Box 284.

142. Fred Burdick, General Report, December 3, 1941, Box 284.

143. William R. Castle to R. Douglas Stuart, Jr., December 8, 1941, Box 290.

144. Ruth Sarles to Robert E. Wood, December 10, 1941, Box 292.

145. Ruth Sarles to R. Douglas Stuart, Jr., December 20, 1941, Box 67.

146. R. Douglas Stuart, Jr., to All Chapter Chairmen, December 8, 1941, in Ruth Sarles, "A Story of America First," pp. 757–759.

147. Ruth Sarles to R. Douglas Stuart, Jr., December 10, 1941, Box 291.

148. William R. Castle to R. Douglas Stuart, Jr., December 10, 1941, Box 284.

149. National Committee, Minutes, December 11, 1941, Box 337.

"A Story of America First"
Ruth Sarles

From Stuart's Whitney Avenue home, plans were formulated for a nation-wide organization of college graduates who would lead the opposition to war in their respective cities.

The simplest method of organization was employed. The group elected an executive Committee made up of Yale Law School men, representative of different sections of the country. They were Eugene Locke, of Dallas, Texas, a graduate of the University of Texas in 1937; Gerald Ford, Grand Rapids, Michigan, a graduate of the University of Michigan in 1935 [Gerald R. Ford, Republican congressman from Michigan, 1948–1973; president of the United States 1974–1977]; Potter Stewart of Cincinnati, Ohio, Yale 1937 [associate justice, United States Supreme Court, 1958–1981]; and Bob Stuart [R. Douglas Stuart, Jr., student at Yale University Law School; national director (1940–41), then executive secretary (1941), America First Committee; later president, board chairman, Quaker Oats Company; U.S. ambassador to Norway]. Stuart was chosen Secretary.

A statement of policy for the embryo group was drawn up. It demanded first that the United States expend all energy on building an impenetrable hemisphere defense. It warned that democracy here would be endangered by involvement in a European war and opposed further aid to England beyond the limitations of the "cash and carry act" (the Neutrality Law) in the belief that it would lead to war.

Following is the exact text of the first set of four principles as agreed upon by the Yale students:

> We believe that the United States must now concentrate all its energies on building a strong defense for this hemisphere.
>
> We believe that today our American democracy can only be preserved by keeping out of war abroad.
>
> We oppose any increase in supplies to England beyond the limitations of cash and carry in the belief that it would imperil American strength and lead to active American intervention in Europe.
>
> We demand that Congress refrain from war, even if England is on the verge of defeat.

A petition blank was mimeographed, topped by the statement of principles and describing, beneath the space for names and addresses, the purpose of the blank. "The national group of graduate students who initiated this petition," it asserted, "are unsubsidized, non-pacifist, and without political affiliation. Its efforts are confined to the one issue outlined above."

The petition was circulated among friends, acquaintances, suggested sympathizers and every obtainable list of college names. Two were sent to each person. They were asked to obtain as many signatures as possible of people in accord with the stated principles. Bundles of petitions and letters were shipped to contacts at Princeton and Harvard. The signed petitions were to be returned to Stuart.

A letter accompanying the petition listed the Executive Committee and explained their purpose. The letter disclosed that men in eight States, including several former college editors and all-American football players, had already agreed to devote their summer to the work of organizing the opposition to war.

In a few weeks the signed petitions were rolling in, and to the new names listed additional petitions were sent. The framework for an organized opposition to war was being hastily thrown up around young college graduates in important centers of the Nation.

DOCUMENT 2

Kingman Brewster to R. Douglas Stuart, Jr. undated [c. July 1940]

So far my fussing around has not accomplished very much. Ogilby is adamant [Remsen Brinkerhoff Ogilby, president of Trinity College, Hartford, Conn.]. If possible I'll get hold of him for advice, but I am positive that he cannot be wheedled into the organization. Beard is apparently taking the same aloof line [Charles A. Beard, noted historian, never joined the AFC, though he did endorse it]. I'm going down to see him Wednesday. The delay was necessary because he has no phone and is not likely to be in New Milford. It took some correspondence from myself and Whit [A. Whitney Griswold, assistant professor of government and political science, later president, Yale University] and some waiting but he will see me and appears very willing to give us personal advice and support. I will sound him out particularly on pamphleteering. Whit has many reservations as to his name value to us anyway. He's so doctrinaire on the subject that his strength is well located by everyone anyway. A letter from Arthur Ballantine, Jr. [son of Arthur Ballantine, under secretary of the U.S. Treasury,

1932–1935] is full of distress about what to do with enlisted enthusiasts. Great problem. Can't do much without money—hence I suggested that the thing to do was raise money.

As I gather it indirectly the Eastern tide of participationist feeling is rising. As I wrote Arthur there are two great dangers. First the campaign to give part of our fleet to Britain. (For publicity purposes I would express it this way. "Part of our fleet" sounds like a much larger national crime than "50 destroyers." After all that's what it amounts to, for destroyers would be the most necessary defensive weapon with which to repel the Nazi invasion that Messrs. White and Sherwood are so sure is imminent) [William Allen White, editor of the *Emporia Gazette* and national chairman of the Committee to Defend America by Aiding the Allies; Robert E. Sherwood, playwright and outspoken interventionist]. The second danger is the great cloud of fatalism that would settle over the land if conscription would become a fact. It would in some ways be pretty hard to go about work with much zest if you were on call for a man whose views are antithetical to yours. Further, don't let anyone sell you on the idea that Willkie is the great peace hope [Wendell L. Willkie, president of the Commonwealth and Southern Company and Republican candidate for president, 1940]. It is too discouragingly obvious from the press reports that he's playing pretty cozy with the W.A.W. outfit [William Allen White's Committee to Defend America by Aiding the Allies]. For my part the organization would lose all value were it to be in any way partisan. I hope my last blast along this line didn't seem too cocky or impertinent, but I feel very strongly on this point even though I am in a private dither about who to vote for.

I have only two constructive suggestions: Dr. Marsh, President of Boston University, may be a likely committee member. He made an excellent speech decrying war hysteria and interventionist muddle-headedness at the commencement of the Boston University summer session. His name is Daniel L. Marsh. Another man whose services might be enlisted is Hanson Baldwin. He is military affairs expert for the N.Y. Times so could not give you his name and keep his job. However his recent piece in the August Harpers is the best statement of the military position of this country that I have ever seen. He would be of inestimable value, if not for research at least to put you in touch with military people in active service who feel free to have an opinion.

I find I am terribly in arrears academically. I'm getting panicky about my Senior thesis which is supposed to be first drafted by the time college opens. I even gave up the Nantucket Regatta, so you can see all is not horseplay. I do hope you can get Hoover signed up [Herbert Hoover, president of the United States, 1929–1933]. Somehow he sums up all that was best in the old politics. But of course he too must be compensated with someone on the other side of the fence. But there I go in unconstructive out of taste advice, so I'll shut up until I have something to offer. Will be glad to hear from you how things are going.

DOCUMENT 3

Address to National Small Business Men's Association
Sterling Morton
August 12, 1940

The National Small Business Men's Association is doing a public service in asking an expression of opinion on the probability, need, or reasons for the United States becoming involved in the war. Taxation to pay for preparations for war will surely fall heavily on the small business man, as well as on the wage-earner, as rich individuals and corporations are already taxed to the point of diminishing returns.

I believe in strong national defense. Every young man should put in at least six months of compulsory service, in the army or navy by those fitted for military duty, and in labor battalions of C.C.C. [Civilian Conservation Corps] camps by the others. But as the leading military experts (until subjected to administration pressure) have maintained that a mobile, well-equipped army of half a million men, equally divided between regulars and national guardsmen, properly backed by trained reserves, is adequate for the defense of this continent, emergency recruiting of a larger army must be suspect as an endeavor to create—and use—an expeditionary force.

One must also suspect this sudden hysterical clamor for defense. Is the condition much different from that of September 1939, or September 1938, for that matter? Military men knew of German preparations. Lindbergh [Charles Lindbergh, the aviator] and others had told of the might of the German air force, of the power of the German army. Anyone who had traveled in France realized the decline in French morale and the lack of popular support for a war against Germany. France's socialistic or communistic kind of government (a close relative of the New Deal) had broken down the strong individualism and patriotism of that country. It had sent essential war equipment and planes to help the Communists in Spain, but, unlike the Germans, had apparently learned nothing from the Spanish campaigns. The country was seriously divided—cursed with self-seeking politicians.

The British defenses, on land and in the air, were notoriously weak. Yet their rulers meddled in all European affairs, blowing hot and cold, friends of Germany one day, enemies the next, aiding France now, Germany then, trying to keep any one power from becoming too strong. In June, Russia was hailed as a member of the "Democratic Front"; in September, the headlines screamed "Moscow's Treason!" The League of Nations had become a farce.

What a mess for us to meddle in! The eventual outcome of meddling is involvement. Should not need for defense measures, if so urgent now, have been recognized before? Why are the demands for money increased each week? Is it possible that now the public approves spending for national defense (whereas it objected to pump-priming), the spenders use defense as just another way to spend money, to create a false prosperity, to influence the voters in the November election?

The thinking man naturally wonders who is going to attack us. The answer given is, (1) Germany; (2) Japan. High authority gives us time-tables for German bombers, yet the same authority takes no steps to assure us intercepting air bases at such places as Trinidad, or Bermuda. South America is put forth as a danger spot. The Germans, if they get to Rio, are twice as far from New York as they now are at Brest! The President's distinguished fifth cousin's book on the River of Doubt shows that the Amazon and Orinoco jungles are about the most impenetrable in the world. We are told that the ideology of dictatorships will permeate South America. Informed persons know that, with possibly one or two exceptions, South America is now completely dictator-ruled. We are told that we would lose our South American trade. Well, in this country we have the Sherman and Clayton laws to insure competition. If our goods and services are not good enough to hold their place in the world, should we force them down the throats of our South American neighbors? And if our form of government is not attractive to other nations, should we force it on them at the point of a bayonet or by economic blockade?

The failure of the British in Norway shows the difficulties of an attempted invasion of North America. The greatest sea power in the world, operating about 250 miles from home bases, could not maintain a small expeditionary force in Norway against the opposition of shore-based aircraft, small sea-borne craft, and a determined, well-trained land force. Multiply that distance by ten, add the opposition of our Navy, and one does not greatly fear that the Germans can land an army in North America, or maintain it after it had been landed.

A reasonable, realistic policy toward Japan would eliminate many dangers in the Pacific. The present Secretary of War [Henry L. Stimson], when Secretary of State, completely reversed the traditional policy of this country, that is, friendship for Japan, reportedly at the instigation of Britain. We opened up Japan; we stopped the Russo-Japanese War at a time when the Japanese effort had passed its peak and the Russian power was augmenting.

Japan is our second-best overseas customer. It is claimed that those parts of China which have been taken over and given peace, order, and a stable government by Japan have greatly increased their trade with the United States. The heavy Chinese emigration to Manchuria must have some reason.

Is it wise or sensible constantly to insult and challenge our second-best customer? Japan would surely be only too anxious to make a reasonable treaty with the United States, giving formal recognition to the Monroe Doctrine and other principles dear to our hearts, in return for recognition of the de facto Japanese position in the Orient. Why not salve Japanese pride by allowing quota immigration on equality with other nations? As long as we have a one-ocean navy, why pick fights in two oceans?

We are told that the Japanese want to take over the Dutch East Indies, and if they do our supplies of rubber and tin would be shut off. Is this a good argument? History and experience show that the Japanese are extremely anxious to develop and exploit the resources of their possessions, to sell their produce abroad in exchange for goods they need.

We should follow the advice of [George] Washington: We should maintain friendly relations with all nations, grant special favors to none. We should remember that the Monroe Doctrine was just as emphatic against American interference in Europe as against European interference in the Americas. We should not meddle in the internal affairs of other nations. If they wish to be ruled by a Hitler, a Stalin, a Petain [Henri Philippe Pétain, who held the title "chief of state" in the Vichy government], or a Haile Selassie [emperor of Ethiopia deposed by Italian forces in 1936], that is their business, not ours. We have no mission to impose our ideas of government on others.

Let us assure a reasonable national defense; let us solve our own domestic problems while other nations solve theirs in their own way; let us adopt a "live and let live" policy. Above all, let us cultivate peace and friendship with all the world.

DOCUMENT 4

Clay Judson to Robert E. Wood
September 24, 1940

I am delighted that you are to give a talk before the Chicago Council on Foreign Relations. [On October 4, 1940, Wood gave a major address to the Council on Foreign Relations of Chicago. Entitled "Our Foreign Policy," it outlined various AFC positions. It was reprinted in full in the *Congressional Record*, October 14, 1941, pp. A6301–303.] You will do a splendid job, and we may all be surprised at the volume of approval which your address will elicit. So far the Council has been deluged with rather sensational talks on the other side of the picture, all of them calculated to get us into this war.

The main objectives of the America First Committee are so sound that we should all be glad of the opportunity to express them publicly. From my standpoint there are four fundamental principles in which the America First Committee believes.

(1) It believes in the defense of America, and by this it means primarily the United States and so much of the balance of this hemisphere as may from time to time be necessary for the safety of this country. The Committee does not believe that there is any danger of a successful invasion of this country. Invasion would be impossible now because any nation which might conceivably be interested in any such wild adventure is otherwise occupied. If we adequately prepare, no nation in the future will dare consider it, or if it does try will not have the slightest chance of success.

(2) The Committee believes that this country's first line of defense is its own navy, its own airplanes, and the oceans which separate it from Europe and Asia.

(3) This government should not give away its ships and planes, both because this weakens our first line of defense and because it is a big step toward participation in this war. If our government continues to furnish large numbers of warships, planes, tanks and weapons to Great Britain with which to kill Germans, it is inevitable that Germany will look upon America as an enemy and will feel justified in undertaking acts of sabotage in this country and in attacking our commerce. The parallel between the present time and 1916–1917 is complete. We believe that this country should immediately check the movement toward war which has been gaining in volume during the past few months.

(4) We are against this country entering the war because we believe that not only our welfare, but perhaps the welfare of civilization itself, depends upon the maintenance of peace and the processes of democracy in the United States. The first thing which would happen should we enter this war would be the loss of all democratic forms of government. This war would not be as easy for us as the last one. If we enter it we would have to fight it through to a military victory. This would mean that America would bear the main burden of crushing the German war machine at the cost of almost everything we have in the way of wealth, and at a terrible cost to us in the lives of the best young men of the nation. If the greatest of the

world's democracies enters into this destructive war the ground will indeed be made fertile for all Communist and Fascist ideas.

In my opinion the question is between war and peace, and all the other arguments are of importance only as they relate to that major issue. That it is imperative for us to reconsider the present trends is every day becoming more and more apparent. On Monday of this week a leading editorial in the Chicago Daily News quoted Mr. Roosevelt's statement that "We will not send our Army, Navy or air forces to fight in foreign lands outside of the Americas, except in case of attack"; and Mr. Willkie's similar statement that "If you elect me President, no American boys will ever be sent to the shambles of the European trenches." The Daily News had this to say about those remarks:

> And if war comes, and however it comes, our sole aim, from that moment on, will be to win. And if victory depends on taking the offensive in foreign lands, we will take that offensive. So why pretend that we will never again send troops abroad, when we do not know, and no one can possibly know, whether we will or not.
>
> In other words, Mr. Roosevelt and Mr. Willkie, in making such statements as they made on Sept. 12 and Sept. 14, respectively, were talking bunk. In a situation as serious as that now confronting the United States we think the people are deserving, from both candidates, of something a little better.

We agree that it is bunk to consider that this country may be half in and half out of this war. The policy which is now being pursued will lead us into the thick of the conflict just as surely as it did in 1917 immediately after Mr. Wilson had been elected on the platform "He kept us out of war." The one possible way of avoiding a war in times like these is by the exercise of calm self-restraint. That and the building up of an impregnable defense would make an attack on us unthinkable or if it does come will deprive it of any possibility of success.

I hope you will forgive me for having written so fully on this question. I did it partly because I wanted to get my own ideas on paper, and partly because you might be able to cull one or two thoughts from it for use in your talk. The soundness of your views and your courage in expressing them and in taking a stand at this time mark you as one of the leading citizens of America today. I cannot begin to express to you my great admiration and gratitude for what you are doing.

DOCUMENT 5

R. Douglas Stuart, Jr., to Jay C. Hormel
December 4, 1940

As I told you I've spent the last few hectic days in the East contacting the many people who have suddenly shown a marked interest in the work of the Committee.

You will be very pleased to learn that this Friday in New York John T. Flynn [economist and journalist] is having a luncheon meeting of a number of very prominent men to form the New York America First Committee.

I have probably already told you that about a week and a half ago an excellent organization was set up in Kansas City. Mr. MacNider [Hanford "Jack" MacNider, Iowa manufacturer, past national commander of the American Legion, past minister to Canada] went over for the initial meeting. Last Friday, Nov. 29, a branch was launched in Washington under Mrs. Bennett Champ Clark [wife of the Democratic senator from Missouri; chairman, Washington Chapter, AFC] and Mr. Wm. Castle [William R. Castle, former U.S. ambassador to Japan and under secretary of state]. Today, December 4, Senator Robert Taft [R-Ohio] and Mrs. Taft formed a Cincinnati chapter of the Committee, and are all set to go to town.

You have no idea how much support is suddenly appearing on the horizon. People are waking up to the fact that we have drifted terribly close to the brink of war. Britain is about at the end of her rope. Her shipping losses are higher than in 1917. The interventionists are desperate and are launching a whirlwind attack on the Neutrality Act. This will culminate in Jan.

In the meantime we've really got to do a job. Our program must rapidly expand. The next sixty days will tell the tale. We've got to do the best publicity job that's ever been done during these critical weeks, and the trouble is, we just don't have the dough.

Here are some of the things we must do.

1. *Publicity*.

    Every newspaper in the United States should receive at least one news release from this Committee every week. They'll use the material we send them. You cannot convince me that the two releases sent air mail every day to every paper in the country by the White Committee has not been responsible for much of the stuff that has permeated our papers and affected the thinking of the people during the last few months.

Mr. Williams is a good man on merchandising a product but he has not had any sense for the "political" issues that are involved in this job; i.e. he just hasn't got a feel for this type of stuff. As a result, I have secured a man named Sidney Hertzberg [socialist journalist; former staff writer for *Time, Current History,* and the *New York Times*] who has been with Time, Inc. et al, who will do an excellent job. He feels so strongly about our point of view that about a year ago he resigned from *Time* to operate on a shoe string a Writers' Anti-War Bureau which has played a tremendously important part in piercing the veil of propaganda, for the benefit of other writers. Their idea has been to influence the influencers of opinion. Obviously, he is in touch with news outlets. I am terribly pleased he has agreed to come.

2. *Advertising*.

Now that we need advertising the most, we have no funds for this work. Every large community in the country ought to be faced with this question through the medium of a newspaper broadside—"What are the people of Minneapolis doing to keep this country out of war?" This ad would wake them up to the facts and urge them to get to work by establishing a Minneapolis organization.

We've got to keep ourselves constantly out in front as a rallying point to give confidence to those people who would otherwise be scared to lift their heads.

3. *Education*.

Most people fail to realize that the most important decisions made by Congress are made in committees. Thus, the two most important committees with which we must be concerned are the Foreign Relations Committee in the Senate, and the Foreign Affairs Committee in the House. My theory here is that we ought to shoot where our shot will do the most good. Thus, if we select those districts from which the members of these Committees come, we will, by taking twenty-three of the forty-eight states in the United States, do practically as good a job as we could have done by covering the entire forty-eight—of course at less than one-half the cost.

As you know, General Wood's speech was entered in the Congressional Record and we have had reprints made. These have been franked by Senator Wheeler [Burton K. Wheeler, D-Mont.]. Thus, we have the cheapest possible mailing piece, the cost of printing and distribution being only $340.00 per hundred thousand.

You, of course, know that it is possible to distribute this mail without knowing the names of the individual persons merely by sending the required number to each rural route or postoffice throughout the entire country. The Postmaster will distribute these to each postoffice box holder or rural free delivery box holder in his district.

For example, we could cover every farmer in the United States by spending $15,000.00. During the winter months the farmers do a lot of reading and are apt to read most of their mail carefully. I don't think we could do anything much more important than to spend $15,000.00 to cover the entire country with General Wood's speech, or some equally effective expression of our point of view.

As a further example of what I mean, Senator George [Walter F. George, D-Ga.] has just been made Chairman of the Foreign Relations Committee of the Senate. He, next to F.D.R. and Hull [Cordell Hull, secretary of state], is probably the most important influence on our foreign policy in this country. As a result, we have covered his State of Georgia with franked copies of General Wood's speech. I honestly think this is a very smart plan.

4. *Research Bureau.*

There are two needs in this regard.

a. A Research Bureau of possibly one or two individuals established in Washington would be a tremendous help to Senators and Congressmen who are fighting our battle in Washington. Each time the President lets go some trial balloon to condition American thinking, e.g. statements that imply that Hitler would have little difficulty steaming up the Hudson River almost any day now—such statements could be knocked into a cocked hat merely by intelligent analysis of the possibilities. And if Senator Shipstead [Henrik Shipstead, Farmer-Labor–Minn.] could, the next day, get up and show this was perfectly ridiculous and have the facts at his disposal, we'd make the interventionists' job a pretty tough one. But the darned trouble is, Senators are so harassed by petty tasks, constituents, etc., that they just don't have time enough to prepare this kind of material.

b. None of us here in our office in Chicago have nearly enough time to even read the paper carefully, much less the Congressional Record. If our news releases are going to make sense, they've got to be based on facts, figures, and items of current importance. If Frank Mayer were in Chicago it would be marvelous for us, the amount of stuff on which we need help—Frank Mayer in Minneapolis is a lot of help, but we need more help right here in Chicago.

I am enclosing a statement of our financial position. It doesn't look so good. We want to repay Mr. Regnery [William H. Regnery, Chicago businessman; president, Western Shade Cloth Company] as much as we possibly can. His contribution should be no more than $10,000.00 at the most.

While we have $16,000.00 in the till, we have almost $15,000.00 in commitments. The balance of $3000.00 is just barely enough to meet personnel, office, and miscellaneous printing expenses during the ensuing month. Obviously, we are terribly handicapped by lack of funds.

I am also enclosing a copy of the response from your chain letter idea. I really am very pleased with it, but the sum is not overwhelming.

Mr. Henry Ford has not come through with a damned cent. He won't even answer the General's letter. I can't figure the situation out.

In closing, let me once again impress upon you the importance of your help now. If the babies down in Washington get control of everything through a war emergency any gold that you've got buried won't be worth a great deal. $5000.00 now may well turn the scale, but of course, we will be deeply grateful for anything that you can send us.

DOCUMENT 6

R. Douglas Stuart, Jr., to Robert E. Wood
December 5, 1940

First let me say that I think it's perfectly swell that you are making the two addresses that you are in the East. It is high time that we, as members of this Committee, got out and expressed our point of view to the public.

I am just putting down on paper a few ideas which I have had on my mind. They may or may not be of some assistance in the preparation of your talk.

There is a lot of talk today about the extension of credit to Great Britain. The analysis of the actual facts indicate that Britain has, today, about two billion in cash in this country.

On the other hand, reading between the lines of the European dispatches, we see that Britain's shipping plight is more severe than it ever has been in her history. Censors have allowed the statement to pass that the shipping losses exceed the rate of shipping losses in April of 1917. Shipment of fruit to Britain has been curtailed entirely; meat rationing has been severely increased; several ports are closed. This all leads me to but one conclusion. This talk about credit is smoke-screen. The real issue and real problem is shipping.

Therefore, although the interventionists do not admit it today, they are going to make a desperate attempt to amend the neutrality act so as to allow American vessels to enter the combat zone. This is the real issue facing the country today. Tremendous attacks will be made on Congress, when it reconvenes in January to make this change. The interventionists' groups will stop at nothing. They are now desperate. For this reason I feel that our major emphasis should be placed on opposition to the modification of the neutrality act.

Also in line with the sinking which I discussed with you yesterday, I believe it would be very wise to take a position as favoring humanitarian aid both to Great Britain and to the five little democracies. People are sympathetic with the conditions over there, and believe we are being too selfish. If we could encourage such medical Red Cross aid, I think we would be in a much stronger position.

While you are in New York I do hope you will be able to see some of the following persons:

First, I have written you about Mrs. Dodge [Mrs. Hartley Dodge, formerly Geraldine Rockefeller]. Jim Farley [James A. Farley, former postmaster general and national chairman of the Democratic party] would be a tremendous addition to our Committee. We need support from the Catholics. Hugh Wilson, a much respected career diplomat [ambassador to Germany, 1938–1939], has just resigned as a result of his divergence of views on the present international situation.

You are, of course, meeting with Mr. Payson [Charles Shipman Payson, New York financier, copublisher of *Scribner's Commentator*] and Mr. Milbank [Jeremiah Milbank, New York banker, copublisher of *Scribner's Commentator*]. I believe both of these men will readily understand our position once they have talked with you. The difficulty has been heretofore this scrupulous commentator group, Stewart and Eggleston [Douglas M. Stewart, New York Stock analyst and copublisher of *Scribner's Commentator*; George Eggleston, editor of *Scribner's Commentator*] have always served as intermediaries. I have been suspicious of them, and they have been suspicious of both you and myself.

Mr. Milbank has promised several people that he is going to spend a tremendous amount of money in this work. I think it is terribly important that we convince him that we can do the job.

As you know, Mr. Hoover is terribly interested in the work we are doing. He has promised me that he will, after the completion of his committee to promote relief to the little democracies, give us all of the time that he possibly can. It would be grand if you could drop in and have a little chat with him.

It seems to me that you are absolutely right in that the next sixty days will tell the tale. I hope you will impress upon all of the members of the Committee that every bit of help they can give us is terribly important. No longer must this Committee be a group of older men—in agreement with our general objective—that only give this work a small percentage of their time and interest. I believe the White committee is an object lesson to us all. Men on that committee have given tremendous amounts of their energy to their particular cause. We must do the same if we are going to beat them.

DOCUMENT 7

William Benton to Robert M. La Follette, Jr. December 17, 1940

Of my many inner resistances to loaning money to the British, one of my principal centers around such words as "credit" and "loans."

If we are going to begin to pass out money to the British, let us call the money a "gift," and force the public to know what's being done with its money—or let us make sure that it really is a "loan."

I have an idea which I think I mentioned to you once before, and which I am again emboldened to suggest because I'm not at all sure it's as crazy as it sounds at first glance. This idea at least dramatizes the issue.

The British Museum is worth billions. I assume that today it's mostly stored away in vaults. (When it isn't, when there's no war on, my hunch is that you'll mostly find Americans wandering through the marble halls anyway.) Our people want art treasures, value museums, crave culture, would much rather have the treasures of the British Museum to show for their money than nothing at all.

Let the British Government ship the British Museum to this country and agree to keep it here for ten years. Parts of it could be put on tour, as the Italian painting exhibit was put on tour a couple of years ago. This wouldn't be bad propaganda from the British standpoint, and I think it would be pretty smart propaganda for the politicians who really delivered something for the taxpayers' money. The balance could be put on exhibit in Washington or at the leading museums of the country.

If the British pay the money back within ten years, they get their museum back. If they don't, the museum is ours.

This is the way business is done between private individuals. It's high time that we at least thought of business in such terms between taxpayers of different countries.

At any rate, the British refusal to send over their museum, as an evidence of good faith, dramatizes that what they are really asking for is "gifts," and not loans at all.

Does this idea sound crazy and visionary, or can it be successfully tossed into the political arena? My hunch is that Colonel McCormick [Robert R. McCormick, publisher, *Chicago Tribune*], Joe Patterson [Captain Joseph M. Patterson, publisher, *New York Daily News*] and many another would go to town for it.

DOCUMENT 8

R. Douglas Stuart, Jr., to Robert E. Wood
December 8, 1940

Just a note as a reminder of some of the things that I hope you can do while in New York.

1. *John T. Flynn*. Mr. Flynn had a very successful luncheon meeting last Friday. They are proceeding rapidly to set up a formal New York America First Committee. Mr. Flynn is expecting a call from you. I hope you can get together with him. He does have some money leads.

2. *Jeremiah Milbank*, 44 Wall Street. Mr. Milbank is the man who is reputed to have promised to give a million dollars toward keeping this country out of the European war. He is the man who is behind this man Douglas Stewart, of Scribner's Commentator. He is also close to Payson. I am afraid that Stewart and O. K. Armstrong, about whom Mr. MacNider told you, have given us a good smearing in Mr. Milbank's eyes.

(a) They accuse us of being New Deal sympathizers. Specifically, they feel that we are a magnet planted by the New Deal to attract all anti-war sentiment and then diffuse it. I must confess that is quite a theory. They point to my statement in P. M. and to your past association with Mr. Roosevelt to prove their point.

(b) They feel, perhaps, that having a Jew on the Committee is a mistake [a reference to Lessing J. Rosenwald, board chairman of Sears, Roebuck; philanthropist]. This attitude makes me concerned about their anti-Semitism.

(c) They have heard that Mr. Bliss [Robert L. Bliss, AFC director of organization until May 1941; previously held publicity posts with J. Walter Thompson and *PM*], who has come out here as our Director of Organization, was in the past associated with P. M. This is absolutely true, but it does not follow from that that he is planted here by P. M. to sabotage our efforts. Mr. Lunsford Richardson [executive, Vick Chemical Corporation], who is paying his expenses, checked carefully on his background before he came out here. He had been a bright, able young publicity man who was intrigued by Ralph Ingersoll's [publisher of *PM*] scheme of a completely new and different newspaper. I think I would have been too. A week before we even contacted Mr. Bliss he had parted company with P. M. Bill Benton [retired advertising executive; vice president of the University of Chicago] of Chicago University, and Chester Bowles [founder and board chairman, Benton and Bowles advertising firm; later U.S. price administrator, governor of Connecticut, and ambassador to India] praise him to the skies. Any person who has worked the way he has out here convinces me that he is no saboteur.

(d) Mr. Stewart and Mr. Eggleston have spread the story that we are slow in answering our mail. I will agree that this has been the case, but we are certainly doing our best and I think we are now in a position to handle it efficiently. It has taken a certain amount of time to build up an organization through which mail can flow in all channels. Mr. Stewart, to be quite frank, has been sent 50,000 copies of your speech to be distributed on his mailing list, as he suggested, and has never even replied to my letter advising him that these were being sent.

3. *Charles Payson.* I think the same story that applies to Mr. Milbank applies to Payson. He married Joan Whitney and is probably the money behind Scribner's Commentator. He is closely associated with Milbank.

4. *Mrs. M. Hartley Dodge*, 350 Fifth Avenue and Madison, New Jersey. As you know, Mrs. Dodge was Geraldine Rockefeller. My friend Mrs. Carl Hanna, from Cleveland, says she is terribly aroused and annoyed by her friends' interventionist ideas. She wants to do everything she can to help the America First Committee. According to Mrs. Hanna, she has given over a quarter of a million dollars to certain political work in the past. I think we should get a substantial contribution from her.

5. *Hugh R. Wilson*. As you know, he has just resigned from the State Department because of disagreement with their foreign policy. Any man who has given his life to the State Department must feel very strongly and have been moved by very deep convictions to take such a drastic step. I am sure he is with us. He would be a valuable man to have on our side. I hope you can see him in either New York or Washington.

6. *Hugh Johnson* [director of conscription during World War I; director, National Recovery Administration, 1933–34; columnist, Scripps-Howard press]. As I told you at luncheon at the Chicago Club yesterday, we need several able exponents of our point of view to make addresses on important occasions. We could use a man like this at least three times a week. While Hugh Johnson may have gotten himself in trouble in the East, he is still the best man we could get in the Midwest and Far West. If we were able to pay Johnson something beyond his expenses I feel that he would be sufficiently interested to take on the job. We need him badly.

7. *President Roosevelt*. I agree with Hertzberg that it would be well for you to talk with F. D. R. I am sure it would have quite an effect on his thinking. It would lay the groundwork for future trips to Washington in times of crisis to present a strong protest against the trend. The almost weekly trips made by the White Committee have had a whale of an effect.

As Mr. MacNider informed you, this *Scribner's Commentator*–Lindbergh group have a plan for a "no foreign war" campaign, although they profess that they are only undertaking a series of meetings throughout the country, not seeking to do any organizational work. Mr. Hoover, Mr. Castle, and Mr. MacNider are convinced that they are planning a competing organization. This is very definitely a mistake. Their argument is that the America First Committee cannot secure the cooperation of certain pacifist and church groups. As the enclosed letter from Frederick J. Libby, head [executive secretary] of the National Council for Prevention of War (the most potent old-line peace organization), indicates, this is no longer true. Through these other groups, and perhaps Mr. MacNider, we could work out a plan of cooperation just as effectively as the Scribner's Commentator–O. K. Armstrong group could. As you know, Mr. MacNider has checked up on this fellow Armstrong and discovered that his Legion background isn't really so hot. He would, of course, have to be the guiding spirit of this "no foreign war" campaign. I think the thing to do is to try to work out a plan of cooperation with the America First Committee.

I will speak to both Phil Follette [Philip Fox La Follette, former governor of Wisconsin, 1931–1933 and 1935–1939] and Hanford MacNider about the plan we discussed at luncheon, but I trust that you are writing them also.

DOCUMENT 9

Charles Clayton Morrison to Robert E. Wood
May 8, 1941

This is in reply to yours of May 2. I have been delayed in acknowledging your letter because of absence from the city.

I wish I were more certain about the implications of membership on the National Committee of America First. I am heart-whole in my agreement with the committee on the matter of keeping America out of the war, and will go to any length to further the great work which the committee is doing on this score. I detect, however, in certain expressions by leading members of the committee and its adherents a commitment to a policy of isolationism with which I do not agree. I am not a pacifist nor an isolationist but a non-interventionist.

If, despite the brave fight you and your committee are making to keep the country out of war (in which fight I devoutly wish to do my bit), the country is led to war by the Administration, I am not so sure of our complete agreement in the policy that would thereafter be pursued. I wish to see the United States assume a pacific responsibility in world affairs which I fear may not be congenial to the leadership of America First. I have taken the slogan, America First, to mean not necessarily an isolation-ist policy except insofar as this war is concerned. As I said in my speech at the Wheeler meeting here, I adopt as my own the slogan of your committee, which I take to be in its fullest expression, *Defend* America first.

I have made it a long-time practice to stay off of committees and boards of all kinds. This I have done because I am primarily interested in main-taining complete independence for The Christian Century. I suggest that it may be better for me to give my hearty support to the work you are now doing and to any further work that the committee may undertake which meets my approval, without making any further commitments. You may be assured that in the present emergency anything I can do I will be only too glad to do. I found the task of speaking at the Wheeler meeting a thor-oughly congenial one.

I much appreciate the implication of friendliness in your letter, and I pay my tribute to you and your colleagues for the courage and energy with which you have organized American sentiment against a national action which I regard as profoundly wrong.

DOCUMENT 10

Edwin Borchard to Robert E. Wood
September 24, 1941

The importance of the work done by the America First Committee and the malicious smears of which it has been made a target would ordinarily lead me immediately to accept your invitation of September 22nd.

Nevertheless, there are considerations which I think are important, considerations which kept me from joining the Committee on the occasion of the original invitation of Douglas Stuart, a former student of mine. In spite of the fact that this administration knows that I am not sympathetic to what they are doing, they call upon me from time to time for advice. In addition, I represent interests before the Department which might be injured by my openly joining the Committee. Again, I am called upon by Senators and others from time to time and occasionally take public positions. This influence is I think better and more convincing if I refrain openly from joining a committee whose object is, so to speak, partisan—in the best possible way, I admit—and which sponsors speakers and policies which oblige it to be partisan.

Perhaps I am wrong, but I think my influence with Senators and members of Congress is greater than it would be, however small it is, if I retain a certain detached position, without concealing the fact, however, which I have made clear, that I oppose the entrance of the United States into this war. I have gone so far as to sponsor meetings of the America First Committee around this section of the country, which shows where my loyalty lies. But under the circumstances I still think it better not to join the Committee as a member.

I have not seen any discussion of the legal questions involved in Mr. Roosevelt's discovery that the freedom of the seas is being impaired. Our noble President is actually undertaking to maintain the proposition that the United States Government has the right to send American ships, armed and unarmed, and even foreign ships under American protection, to carry munitions to one belligerent, and that the other belligerent has no right to stop these shipments. Whether there is any qualification to this claim I do not know, but the assertion that there is such a thing as American defense waters, presumably involving thousands of square miles of open ocean, is without legal support. The only legal ground on which he could stand against Germany's claim is the fact that there is no legal right of Germany to rope off parts of the high seas and call them a war zone, if by that term there is implied an intention to exclude peaceful shipping. But the shipping the President talks about is not peaceful shipping but war supplies, which not only are contraband but, when sent by the United States Government, utterly illegal if, as I presume he claims, we are not in the war. Only an open legal belligerent can do what the President is undertaking to do, and in that sense he did get Congress to pass the lease-lend act which only a belligerent can adopt. Perhaps he will be able more plausibly to assert that when Congress passed that act they implicitly declared war and thus conformed with the constitutional provision. This would be slippery as usual, but it might be deemed plausible by enough of our people exposed to confusion. The President's attack on Germany's war zone, however, would be considerably weakened by his own illegal claim of a defense zone so wide that no limitations appear to have been placed upon it. His claim amounts to an ultimatum that no German ship or airplane can attack an American or foreign ship carrying munitions to Great Britain or to any territory occupied by Great Britain. Such a claim has no legal foundation.

DOCUMENT 11

Hugh S. Johnson to R. Douglas Stuart, Jr. January 8, 1941

Why anybody should ask me my reasons for not wanting to get into war is beyond me. Why do I want to avoid pestilence, poverty, starvation and the most hideous forms of human suffering? Why do I not seek the reduction of homes to blackened rafters, the ends of glistening white human bones sticking through the quivering shreds of bloody flesh, the destitution and languishing of children, the shattering and dissolution of loving families, the abuse of the aged, the blasting of whole landscapes, the ruin of farms and cities, the bankruptcy of nations, the destruction of democracy, the overturning of altars and the coming of anti-Christ? Why do I shrink from a new crop of faceless, armless, legless men—dragging out blasted lives with no more pride in their own strength, manhood, beauty and virility than a toad in a cesspool.

If war is necessary to preserve more of our own people against these things than the number of soldiers who will suffer them, then, as a soldier, I am willing and eager. But to walk into war for the stubbornness, pride or ambition of any man or group of men when it is wholly unnecessary—no. And if I were one of those men I would seek to curb my enthusiasm at least long enough to consider my eventual dreadful responsibility at the bar of my country's opinion if she and I lived, and the more awful judgment of a just God who loves his human children if I died—which I and they most surely shall.

DOCUMENT 12

Chester Bowles to R. Douglas Stuart, Jr. November 28, 1941

I wish I could be in Chicago today for your meeting at which, I gather, you will discuss the possibility of throwing the America First organization into politics.

It would, it seems to me, be a mistake to attempt to establish the Committee as a political party in itself. The men and women who have gone to make up America First agree most emphatically that we must keep out of the war. But I don't believe that there would be many other subjects on which you could get broad agreement.

Some America First members are reactionary, some are conservatives, some are middle-of-the-roaders, and some are strong liberals. I am afraid you would have a rather hopeless time in getting them to agree on such subjects as deficit, spending, labor relations, monopolies, social security, etc.

For this reason I am sure you would confine America First's interest in politics purely to a question of the war. On that basis I don't see why it isn't a sensible and perfectly legitimate thing to do.

The Anti-Saloon League, many years ago, developed an organization through which it could throw its weight, in any given State or Congressional district, behind one candidate or the other. Sometimes it picked a Democrat and sometimes a Republican, and usually all issues were secondary to the one burning issue of to drink or not to drink.

The CIO [Congress of Industrial Organizations] and, to a less extent, the AFL [American Federation of Labor] use the same technique today.

Both of these labor organizations study the candidates in all the different Congressional and State elections and either give or withhold their endorsement, depending on a candidate's attitude toward labor in general and pending labor legislation in particular.

America First could easily follow this precedent on the issue of war and it would be an excellent way of keeping the various Local and State chapters together during the next year. It would give them something to think about and to work towards. And in the election of 1942, the work of these various chapters might be extremely effective.

Any pressure group can, of course, apply more pressure in a political election than its members may justify. A candidate for Congress, for instance, might readily credit a local America First group with the full power to deliver to his opponent the complete anti-war vote of that district. Actually, no matter how well a group is organized, the votes it can deliver are limited. But the candidates can never be quite certain.

Norman Thomas [leader of the American Socialist Party] and his wife are spending the week-end with us and I will talk to them about this whole problem.

I understand from Bill that General Wood would like to have Mr. Thomas serve on a political steering committee with Bob Taft, Wheeler and others.

One of the most important things for America First during the coming months is, I am sure, to keep its skirts completely clean so far as anti-Semitism and Fascism, either domestic or foreign, are concerned. I know how conscious you are of this danger and what a wonderful effort you have made to fight it every time it has become a problem.

The request of the Chicago chapter to the F.B.I. for complete examination of its donors and members was excellent, and I should think that you would ask all the different chapters to do the same thing.

Most of the chapters would probably follow your suggestion and thus secure a clean bill of health from a recognized Government agency. Some probably either would not or could not arrange a check of this kind, but at least the national organization could say that it had done everything in its power to guard itself against any questionable people who might try to ride along on our coat tails.

P.S. I wrote an article for the December issue of Common Sense that may interest you—"What's Wrong with the Isolationists by a Non-Interventionist."

The thing I criticized, of course, was Isolationism which, I believe, is largely the result of Interventionism in the time of war.

Obviously we cannot build a wall around ourselves in an attempt to exist regardless of what goes on in other parts of the world.

Our present position illustrates that neutrality laws and even a strong determination to stay out of war will not necessarily keep us out once the drums start beating and the British begin to call for help. Thus our only hope, over a period of time, of staying out of war is to do all we can to see that major wars do not occur. That calls for world cooperation in time of peace, a more sensible attitude toward tariffs, etc., etc.

Actually one of my own strongest arguments against our entering the war is that it will surely lead to bitterness and disillusionment and peace time Isolationism.

I hope that doesn't sound too complicated. Perhaps you better get the article and read it yourself. I hope you will agree with at least some of it!

DOCUMENT 13

Chester Bowles to R. Douglas Stuart, Jr.
July 30, 1941

I should think that the "A for America" suggestion might be a good one. But somehow it hasn't the positive quality which the "British V" campaign has developed.

I am glad to hear that you are going on the radio. When and what time? I do want to hear you if I possibly can.

If you have time, do devote some attention to the objective that the British, and perhaps soon ourselves, will be fighting for.

Will we be asked to fight for the preservation of the British Empire? If that is so, the victory may already be won as, according to all the current rumors, Hitler is perfectly willing to make peace on that basis.

Are we fighting to protect our physical security against an attack by Hitler and the Japanese? If so, any bloodshed at the present moment seems rather unnecessary with Hitler involved five thousand miles away and every thoughtful military and naval authority in agreement that no army can actually invade us if we do even a 50 per cent good job of preparation.

Are we going to fight to eliminate sin and establish virtue throughout the world? Then the first thing we must do is place high on the list of our war-time objectives the freedom of India, the Malay States, Palestine, Africa, and the Philippines.

Are we fighting for foreign trade? Then as a business investment the war makes little sense since our total foreign trade has never amounted to more than six or seven billion dollars a year, and any first-class war will eat up thirty billion dollars in a year without even stopping for breath.

If we are going to attempt to run the world with England, what kind of a world do we want? Are only democratic nations to be allowed to join our club? Are we going to dominate the world by force and establish our lines of justice in Africa, India and the Far East?

What responsibilities will our Army and Navy be given five, ten, twenty years after the war?

What is the scheme? What is the plot? What is the idea? Where are we headed? Who has made these decisions? When were they debated?

I believe, Bob, that one of the weaknesses in the America First movement has been our own lack of a positive program. We have, to a certain extent at least, been negative.

Perhaps that is because the membership of the America First Committee is distinctly varied and it will be difficult for us to get any agreement among the different elements, ranging all the way from left wing radicals to right wing reactionaries, on just what kind of a world we should strive for.

DOCUMENT 14

John T. Flynn to Robert E. Wood
June 5, 1941

I understand you are to be here on Tuesday and I am dropping you this line before that time. I hope I may have an opportunity for a private word with you, but this letter will tell you what is on my mind. And let me say at the outset that this is for your eyes alone.

For some reason I have a kind of intuition that we are approaching the end of this episode. We are going to be either in or out pretty soon I feel. What is bothering me is what may happen if the war should end soon and we should find ourselves with something of a victory on our hands.

I have been sensing the presence—somewhat vague perhaps but none the less serious—of various forces which have an eye on the America First Committee. If the war should end soon without our getting in, there is no doubt that the Committee is going to occupy a position of immense prestige. There is also no doubt that the war crisis will be succeeded very soon by a peace crisis and there is no doubt that there are men and groups who would like to lay hold of the prestige of the America First Committee to advance their several ambitions and objectives. Some of these are no more serious or mysterious than the politicians. God forbid that we should be so weak as to let some of these birds take possession of this Committee. I am not nearly so disturbed about them as I am about some other forces which are somewhat more mysterious and a little more difficult to put one's finger on. It is not to be denied that there is a powerful anti-semitic under-current moving around the country. It is here in New York among some men who are both wealthy and powerful. God knows the Jews have given plenty of people good cause to be indignant at them. They have made my road so difficult that at times it has been hard to hold my patience and my tongue. I am sure they have not made it pleasant for you either. But in spite of that, I am sure that neither you nor I want to see this fine movement degenerate into a piece of equipment in the hands of intoler-ance when the intolerance breaks out and the under-current becomes a wave. Strictly between ourselves, I think I see some signs of such persons snooping about and perhaps intruding themselves into positions where they may be able to grab this movement, at least its machinery, when its war job is done.

Probably you yourself have caught a whiff of this. I live in continued fear of the rise of some kind of fascist movement in America when this damna-ble war hysteria runs out. It will be a nice, respectable movement domi-nated by fascist ideas but never calling itself fascist. It will be a kind of America First movement but in a very different sense from that in which we have used the name. The question is how we can protect this movement from falling into the hands of any such group or any other kind of group. If the United States declares war on Germany the problem, it seems to me, would be easy—to dissolve the America First Committee right away. But if the war ends with a clear-cut victory for our staying out of it, then the question will arise whether we ought not to dissolve immediately just the same. I see one objection to that. There would be nothing to prevent some other set of people from organizing a new America First and getting by adoption the prestige of this organization. I think some lawyers could circumvent that for us.

The issue of our organization has been a clear-cut one—to keep out of the war. But the issues which will arise after the war crisis and in the peace crisis will be very different, very complicated and members of our Committee and our individual members who could agree so whole-heartedly on keeping out of the war will find themselves split into three or four or more widely divergent political philosophies. It will not be possible to unite this movement behind any one of them and I think we ought not to allow any one of them to run off with it.

I have not discussed this with anyone here because the time has not seemed ripe to do it and I am not wholly sure which ears would be most hospitable to it. But I do feel I should unbosom myself to you. I hope we may have a chance to talk about it at the earliest opportunity.

There is so much peace talk in the air that it is difficult to dismiss it completely. The desperate plight of Britain and the apparent impossibility of the President getting a declaration of war for a long time to come seems to add plausibility to these rumors. I earnestly pray they are true.

DOCUMENT 15

"How did the present war start?"
Speakers Bureau
undated [1941]

A. The present war is another chapter in the series of conflicts between European states that have been going on in war and peace for hundreds of years. For the last two centuries Europe has been divided into nation-states of varying sizes and economic power. Large states have tried to absorb small states, and Great Britain, separate from the continent and head of a great empire, has naturally tried to maintain the status quo in order that no state or combination of states should grow powerful enough to challenge her supremacy.

Napoleon, Bismarck, Kaiser Wilhelm II, and Hitler have all made attempts to bring most of continental Europe under one hand. All succeeded for a time, but the first three were unable finally to compete against

England, or, in the case of Bismarck and the Kaiser, France and England. Hitler is making the same effort, twenty years after the last German defeat.

The present war differs from the last in many particulars. It is, for example, a war between democracy and Nazism because those are the political forms of the major contenders, whereas in the war of 1914–18 the governments of both Germany and England were political democracies operating under limited monarchies. It differs from the last war also in that Russia and Italy are today on the side of Germany whereas twenty years ago they were allies of Britain.

In another sense, however, the present war is a continuation of the last. Germany was defeated by the Allied Powers and the United States after she had attempted to expand her empire and in so doing has threatened the older empires of Britain and France.

The post-war republic of Germany, in addition to being a government just coming into power, had the burden of meeting the obligations imposed by the Allies and trying to compete with established imperialist powers when she had no colonies of her own. This proved impossible and the republic finally gave way to the cruel fascism of Adolf Hitler and the Nazis. Once in power, the Nazis revived the idea of a German empire and began the "Drang noch Osten" (drive to the East). Thus England and France were threatened once more. When it became clear to British statesmen, after the signing of the Soviet-Nazi pact, that Germany's expansion would be at the expense of her interests and not of Russian territory, England declared war on the Third Reich.

Whatever the ideological conflict in this war, and it is one in which nearly all Americans side with the democratic powers, it is primarily a struggle to settle a problem that has arisen from the confusion and unreality of the European state system. That problem has been fought over several times, and no solution has been forthcoming. Americans, deciding on their relation to the war, must remember that what is involved is the organization of a continent from which most of us fled at times when it was facing much the same trouble as today. Thus, a participant in the war should know how to solve those problems and be willing to be responsible for effecting a just solution.

DOCUMENT 16

"Is the present war, as many people claim, a 'world revolution'?"
Speakers Bureau
undated [1941]

A. The present war is, in a sense, a revolution. It is by no means a world revolution, for it is still far from engaging even half the world. But it is true that Germany is interested in the spread of her form of government as well as in extending her state power. This is largely in order that she may extend her power, but it still has revolutionary aspects.

The Nazi government and economy were designed to promote war. In place of the system of individual enterprise in America and England and the purely state enterprise in Russia, Germany has a system in which individuals own property but the state retains and uses the power to commandeer both property and money for its own uses, chiefly for war. She is spreading this system to the conquered countries and will continue to do so if she conquers any more countries. But a great deal of nonsense is being talked about Nazism as world revolution. If America maintains her democracy, she will have freedom of choice and Nazism will have little chance unless most of the people want it, which is most unlikely.

DOCUMENT 17

"For what aims is the war being fought?"
Speakers Bureau
undated [1941]

A. On Germany's part the war is being fought to gain an Empire, on England's part to preserve an Empire.

England has given no clear statement of war aims. Her spokesmen have said that they wish to topple Nazi power, but they have not said what they intend to put in its place. It is also assumed that England wishes to restore the governments which have been destroyed by Germany. Whether she will be able to do this, even if she wins, is doubtful; whether it is completely desirable to do so is even more doubtful, since many people believe that the small nation-states would be forever incapable of defending themselves. In any case, such a restoration would bring Europe back to the status quo of before the war, and that is the condition out of which the present war grew.

Many people believe that England will set up a kind of Federal Union scheme to organize Europe along the lines of the United States. The British government has announced no such intention. Since one way in which Britain can survive is by keeping a division in Europe which gives her the balance of power, it is reasonable to believe that England wants exactly the opposite of Federal Union. But it is true that many powerful people in England regard this as the proper solution, and it may be that a strong effort will be made to force its adoption.

The question then to be asked is whether such a scheme can work. There is no evidence that the European nations have ever been able to live together in unity as the peoples of our continent have. This is not necessarily the fault of the people of the various nationalities and is more likely the result of the conflicts between the different economic and social orders.

A similar scheme, the League of Nations, was introduced after the last war. It was a dismal failure, and instead of union the last war produced Hitler, Mussolini, and Stalin. Americans, disappointed in that effort, are determined to stay out of that effort. Today the question is whether the aims of this war are any more likely to solve European problems than those of the last war. Since the aims are so similar, there is every reason to believe that the results will be similar.

DOCUMENT 18

*"Questions posed to speakers of the William Allen White
Committee"*
Speakers Bureau
undated [1941]

In the event that America gives full aid to Britain—financial, military and human—what guarantee will the British Empire give to America?

And when England is victorious because of our aid, will she include the

U.S. at her council tables? Can we expect this in the light of the British Empire's past performance and her international policies?

Do we not have the right to demand of the British Empire what she is going to do with our aid, whether it be financial or whether it be military? In other words, at the conclusion of the war, taking for granted that the British Empire will be victorious, what will the U.S. get out of war?

If the U.S. enters the war and gives all her aid, what will the U.S. be fighting for—Democracy? The preservation of Democracy? Didn't we fight for Democracy in 1917 and didn't we have to swallow a pretty bitter pill at the conclusion of that engagement?

Do the members of the William Allen White Committee believe that with the destruction of Hitler, Nazism as an ideology will also be destroyed? Or Fascism? Or Communism? This same question holds true of Mussolini or Stalin.

Is it not true that, with the destruction of Hitler, whether he be destroyed morally, whether he be assassinated, whether he should happen to be killed in the course of the war, whether he dies of acute indigestion, Nazism—because of the education of the children of Germany, because the youth of Germany is so imbued with the philosophy of Nazism—will continue? Is it not true that the U.S. will still find herself living in the same world with the Nazi form of Government and with a Nazi dictator whether it is Hitler, or Goering or Goebbels or some other German who will rise to the same zenith as Hitler?

The William Allen White Committee speaks glibly of stamping out Nazism. How is this to be done? How can philosophies be stamped out? Would we have any more success in stamping out Nazism than we would have if we attempted to stamp out Mohammedanism? If it is to be attempted, shouldn't this work be started right here in America First?

Isn't Nazism merely a term of a profound belief? Because the U.S. does not believe along the lines of Nazi belief, or Fascist belief or Communist belief does not mean that these beliefs will discontinue to exist.

The death of Hitler would not kill the Nazi belief. Wouldn't a crushed and beaten Germany continue along Nazi lines in its thinking and in its living? And wouldn't the Nazi belief become even stronger in the hearts and minds of the German people because of defeat?

Do the members of the William Allen White Committee believe that the nations of Europe desire democracy for themselves? Has the youth of Europe any use for democratic principles? Would they be content or happy to live under a democratic form of Government? Isn't it true that the youth of Europe in the larger areas such as Russia, Germany, Italy, Czechoslovakia, Austria, Spain and even France tried the democratic way of life and found that for their particular problems it did not work and discarded it?

Isn't it much wiser for the U.S. to reserve her finances, her military equipment and her men for herself? Wouldn't this be sounder economy?

And if we give full aid to Britain, if we send all of our military output and our men to Britain's side, what guarantee do we have that the British Empire and the U.S. closely allied in total war would be successful?

Is it not possible, even with the strength of this alliance, that the war would go on for many years and Germany combined with Italy and Japan could still prove too great an adversary to completely conquer?

Does the problem not boil down to "what is the greater risk?"

The question often arises "Can a free and democratic U.S. live side by side with a dictator nation?" This question is posed on the premise that Hitler will defeat England and in the event of such a defeat, could we live in a dictator world?

The U.S. managed to live side by side with Italy during the past 12 years and to trade with her. The trade relations have been quite amicable although during this time Italy has been a dictator nation. This was also true of Germany up to the time of the outbreak of the present war with England and from the moment that Hitler took power in Germany.

Merely because our thinking does not coincide with the thinking or philosophies of the majority of the peoples of Europe does not mean that we cannot live in the same world with those peoples. We have managed to trade with China and Japan ever since the beginnings of America and yet the American people are not Buddhists nor believers of Confucius, nor is the government of the U.S. based on Buddhistic or Confucian philosophies.

The William Allen White Committee advocates the sending of ships and planes to England—as many as America can produce. Machines are useless without *men* to run them. Can these machines be sent without *men*?

DOCUMENT 19

"Is America now taking part in the war?"
Speakers Bureau
undated [1941]

A. America is at present taking a very large part in the war. Although we are not formal allies of England and still maintain relations with Germany, we have, because of the actions of the President, very definitely been put on the side of England. We have a defense agreement with Canada, which is part of the British Empire. We are selling arms to England and not to Germany. We have turned over part of the United States Navy to Great Britain. A large proportion of materials supposedly made for our own defense are being turned over to the British. We are cooperating with them in all sorts of trade ventures, thereby acting against Germany.

All this has been done under the orders of the Chief Executive. In November 1939 we repealed the arms embargo provision of the Neutrality Act. This was done by Congress, presumably at the request of the people, who agreed to the proposition after a campaign in the press which emphasized that repeal would make the act even more "neutral." Since then, many un-neutral acts and acts that could be considered warlike under international law have been committed by President Roosevelt without the consent of, without even having consulted, Congress or the people.

Most of the American people, 83 percent according to one of our public opinion polls, want America to stay out of the European war under all circumstances. A majority also wants to help England. The task, then, is to see that our help to England stays short of war and acts of war.

DOCUMENT 20

"What, strictly on the basis of our own national interests, should our part be?"
Speakers Bureau
undated [1941]

A. It is difficult, of course, to define our national interests, but it is always safe to assume that our chief national interest is the maintenance of our democracy and the well-being of our own American people. It is true that we have a stake in the maintenance of democracy throughout the world. It is also true that many Americans have commercial interests abroad which they are naturally interested in protecting. It is far from certain, however, that this war or our involvement in it will protect any of those interests.

Our part should be first of all to protect our own democracy. Since experience has taught us that democracy vanishes in wartime, it would seem that the surest way to keep our form of government is to avoid involvement. We should also seek an adequate national defense to make sure that we can maintain our territorial integrity in the event we are attacked by a foreign power.

If, after announcing their intention to stay out of the war, as they have repeatedly done, the American people wish to aid Great Britain, they should do so. But they should make certain to keep aid and direct participation separate.

DOCUMENT 21

*"If our national interest doesn't require us to go to war,
shouldn't we go anyway to keep democracy alive in the world?"*
Speakers Bureau
undated [1941]

A. There is no guarantee that this war will keep democracy alive in the world, and, indeed, there is reason to believe that the war, if it lasts long enough, and spreads far enough, will kill democracy.

It is true that democracy will have a better chance if England can maintain her freedom. The British Isles are a repository of democratic sentiment, and it would surely be tragic for the cause of representative government if Britain went under.

However, we in the United States in wartime sacrifice many essentials of democracy; in a long and unpopular war, the sacrifice might well become permanent. And even though England still has most of her traditional freedoms, there is no assurance that these can be maintained if the going gets much harder.

War and Nazism both destroy democracy. Our best guarantee is to stay out of war, and make sure then fascism does not attack us from inside or out.

DOCUMENT 22

"Isn't it part of our responsibility as a world power to take a hand in settling problems that menace world peace and security? With modern communications developed as they are, can we still be isolationist?"
Speakers Bureau
undated [1941]

A. We have no responsibilities that our people do not wish to undertake. We have no international commitments, agreed to by the people or their representatives, outside this hemisphere.

Even if we did, it would not be a signal for going to war everytime there was one. Americans naturally wish security and peace for the rest of the world, but it is not entirely within their powers to bring these things about. We are a powerful nation, but not powerful enough to make the whole world follow our lead.

America must size up what it is within her strength to do, choose her own path, and proceed along it. The people want to help Britain so long as they can do so and still stay out of war. That much they have undertaken, no more, and they have no further responsibilities, unless they wish them.

DOCUMENT 23

"America First Book List"
Page Hufty
Bulletin #476, August 7, 1941

The following is a selected reading list of a few of the publications which present in detail the case of the non-interventionists.

United We Stand—Baldwin, Hanson. Distinguished military expert of the *New York Times* writes a clear and penetrating analysis of the military problem of defense and presents a specific program for hemispheric defense.

We Can Defend America—Hagood, Major General [Johnson]. Expert officer of the U.S. Army outlines a sound and invulnerable national defense program.

America and a New World Order—Howard, Graeme K. [vice president in charge of overseas operations, General Motors Corporation]. A study of the consequences of a Hitler victory and an economic program to make the U.S. supreme in the face of dictatorship abroad.

A Foreign Policy for America—Beard, Charles A. The distinguished historian submits a foreign policy designed to meet challenging world conditions and at the same time to realize the democratic "aims" of America.

We Have a Future—Thomas, Norman. The distinguished social thinker and Socialist candidate for President presents a thoughtful and realistic interpretation of America's destiny in a world of change.

Road to War—Millis, Walter [editorial writer, *New York Herald-Tribune*]. The noted economist and social thinker contributes a brilliant general analysis of the war.

Giddy Minds and Foreign Quarrels—Beard, Charles A. The most significant of contemporary American historians has published this classic analysis of the economic and social causes of the last war and America's foreign policy.

And So to War—Herring, Hubert. The editor of *Uncensored* discusses neutrality and foreign trade.

Words That Won the War—Mock [James R.] and Larson [Cedric]. A piercing expose of the propaganda techniques used to indoctrinate the American people in the past war.

How to Sell War in Three Easy Lessons—*Science News Letter*. Jan. 31, 1939. A startling account of the propaganda tactics of the notorious Creel Committee, bureau of information in the country during the last war.

How We Advertised America—Creel, George [chairman, Committee on Public Information, 1917–1919]. The director of the propaganda ministry of the United States during the last war boasts of his ingenuity in this amazing "confession."

That War Prosperity—Stewart, Maxwell [associate editor, *Nation*; editor, Public Affairs pamphlets]. A noted economist shatters the illusion that war brings prosperity to the people and describes the devastating results of the last war on the economic structure of America.

Merchants of Death—Englebrecht, H., and Hanighen, F. An expose of the inhuman manipulation of the munitions industries in precipitating the last war.

The Fruits of Victory—Angell, Norman [British internationalist and economist]. Penetrating study of the consequences of the last war and the insanity of the dictated peace.

Woodrow Wilson and World Settlement—Baker, R. S. [Ray Stannard Baker, journalist and author]. A disheartening but challenging study of a great President's struggle against ruthless and selfish diplomats and exhausted and bitter peoples in his vain attempt to establish a just peace following the last war.

American Farm Program—Gee, W. An analysis of our agricultural problems and policies which would be detrimentally affected by war.

A more exhaustive bibliography can be obtained on request.

DOCUMENT 24

Clay Judson to James B. Conant
February 3, 1941

I appreciate your courtesy in having written me so fully and frankly of your views as you did on December 27th. I regret that the pressure of other affairs has delayed my replying to you. Although a good deal of water has gone over the dam since that date and the specific question now before the country is the "Lease-Lend Bill," it seems to me that the fundamental issues are still the same.

Though I have no hope of influencing you in any way, I am going to trespass on your time once again in order that the real differences between us may be perfectly clear. My reason for doing this, since I cannot hope to affect your views, is personal only, based on my admiration for you as a fine American and my affection for an old friend. Whatever our disagreement, it should not be based on any misunderstanding.

Incidentally, we should not lose sight of the fact that we are in absolute agreement on the fundamentals. We both cherish the fundamentals of democracy. We both detest dictatorship, whether it be of the Communist or the Nazi variety. We both, I am sure, would agree that the welfare of Americans is and should be the primary, if not the sole objective, of America's foreign policy. It is only when we arrive at the course of action to be pursued that disagreement arises. Even so we both believe in an impregnable defense, a strong army, air force, and navy for this country. I believe, however, that though we may help England all we can within the limits of the present neutrality laws and without weakening our own defense, we should not aid her to the point of depriving ourselves of necessary weapons or to the point of certain involvement in the war, as for example by having our own navy convoy ships through the blockade or by opening our harbors to her as naval bases. I believe further that the maintenance of peace for our country in this war is more important than a British victory. You believe, on the contrary, in any aid necessary to insure British victory, including actual participation in the war.

With this background I would like to refer to certain parts of your letter.

First: You inadvertently misquote, or misinterpret, my position when you state: "I agree entirely when you say that the answer to the question, 'Is this our war?' must be based not on our emotional reactions." This statement is followed by your assertion that in the picture which I have drawn of war I have been as emotional as you have.

My argument was not that our decision should not be based on any emotion. All decisions are, at least in part, based on some emotion. What I said was that it should not be based on emotions aroused by the bombings of London or the hatred of dictatorship; that is to say, on our sympathy with, or antipathy for, some foreign country. Our policy should be determined by its effect on America and Americans, and it would be utterly wrong, as well as impossible, to completely ignore our emotions on this score. In short, our national policy should be based on our concern, and it may even be an emotional concern, for the American people. What war would mean for them is a legitimate and a necessary part of this concern, although I never hear it mentioned by the interventionists! On the other hand, emotional concern for the people of Great Britain, though it should and does arouse our sympathies and practical humanitarian responses, should play no part in the determination of our national policy.

Second: You maintain that I attempt to look into the future just as much as you do when I say that a war to crush Germany, and its aftermath, would destroy democracy and individual freedom. In a sense you are perfectly right, of course, for we must always reach a conclusion as to the effect of proposed action, before we can intelligently decide upon the merits of that action. It is all a question of the reasonableness of our conclusions. I think it is reasonable to believe that an all-out total war will be destructive of democracy and individual freedom. You apparently think this doubtful, but you do not hesitate to paint fantastic and fearful pictures of what Germany would do to us after this war if she is not beaten. I think that is emotional speculation, pure and simple. I am certain that Germany could only succeed in ruining herself if she were mad enough to attempt to invade this hemisphere, particularly with the problem of occupied European countries on her hands. Further, it seems clear to me that our losses would be less and our chances of success greater in a hypothetical future war which Germany is assumed to be planning to wage against us in this hemisphere, many thousands of miles from her own bases, than they would be today if we are foolish enough to be dragged into this war which we would have to fight on the other side of the ocean.

Third: You say my statement that this is the most destructive war which the world has yet known cannot be substantiated. It is too soon for statistical proof of that statement now, but when this war has passed into history, I believe its truth will be plain. This is a *total* war. A far larger percentage than ever before of all productive resources is centered on war and destruction. And before Germany could be beaten, as you insist she must be, the destruction of property would be equalled by the destruction of human life. Even today, though the loss of life due to direct military operations is not great as compared with that of the last war, the tremendous damage done to the physical and mental welfare of millions of human beings by the several blockades should not be overlooked. Even if I exaggerate the effect of this war, it is still certainly bad enough by any standard to be ruinous for those ideals which we in America should seek to uphold.

Fourth: With rather plain implications, you ask me personally how much I know about Germany and the present regime, stating that you have made a particular study of that country. I have no doubt that your studies have been more exhaustive than mine. I have only been in Germany twice, once for several months in 1918–19 as a member of our Army of Occupation; once again for a brief visit in 1930. But for 25 years my hobby has been the broad strategy involved in the foreign policies of this country, and I have tried to keep posted on the current situation in Germany and elsewhere. In 1924, in a brief review of the life of General W. V. Judson, I wrote that during the years 1914 to 1917 he had "developed many of his ideas with respect to our national policies, ideas which he had been formulating throughout a lifetime of thought on questions of international strategy." Since he happened to be my father, I spent a good many years discussing with him the very type of question which is now involved, a question which cannot be answered by our hatred of Hitler or our admiration for Churchill.

You also ask me whether I have read Erika Mann's contribution to "Zero Hour." I have just read it, but before that I had read her other book about Nazi Germany, and I have heard both Miss Mann and her father speak. I have always felt that Nora Waln's book "Reaching for the Stars" gave a more complete picture of the Hitler regime than any other work of its general character.

But my knowledge or lack of knowledge of events in Germany has nothing to do with the real issue. The question is whether we should go to war, and the wickedness of Adolph Hitler, however important that may be for propaganda purposes (have you forgotten the picture painted of the Kaiser in 1917?) is not, or should not be, the answer. The true answer is found in the primary interests and objectives of this country, namely, its safety and the preservation of democracy and the American way of life.

You ask whether the answer does not *all* turn on our estimate of what the totalitarian powers would do if they are not defeated in this war. (Are you including Russia, and do you want to defeat her too?) My answer is No, it does not *all* turn on that estimate. That estimate must be made, but we must also estimate what the result will be if we go into a war to crush Germany. On that side it seems to me that those who argue for full participation of this country have a definite blind spot. You do say that it seems quite possible that by use of naval and air power alone England and the United States might overthrow Hitler. I do not believe that you can seriously support any such contention. Responsible authority in England has been quoted to the effect that a re-invasion of the Continent is necessary if victory is to be achieved. Germany, with an over-powering air force, and an army of perhaps 5,000,000 men, has not been able to beat England. Nor has she been able to subdue any other nation without an invasion. England lacks the man power for any such effort. Her navy would be useful in bringing about a victory, but mainly by creating a bridge across which invading troops (including American troops) will enter, after a supreme air force has made this possible. But it is inconceivable that this can be accomplished without losses of such magnitude that civilization itself will shudder from the impact.

We are faced with two alternatives; (1) join in this terrible war so that Germany may be crushed, or (2) stay out of this war, with the probable result that there will be a stalemate and a negotiated peace. To my way of thinking we make a terrible mistake, particularly with respect to the United States of America and its interests, not to explore the possibility of such a peace, but to jump at the conclusion that it is impossible. A dictated peace could come about in two ways, first, after a crushing defeat of England, or second, after a crushing defeat of Germany. Today a compromise between these two undefeated powers would give the world a chance, but in place of encouraging such a policy of peace, its opponents call those who urge it, those Americans who are doing their level best to keep this country out of the holocaust, "appeasers," which on the tongue of a member of the war group has come to be a term of vile reproach.

To avoid war now all that the men of this generation can do is to keep out of war now. To avoid war by making war seems to me absurdly bad logic and a hopeless doctrine. It has been preached for 2500 years, first, perhaps by the ancient Greeks.

I believe that our greatest service to the American people is to preserve peace and democracy here. I believe that we must and can make this country a citadel of democracy which cannot be overthrown. I believe that if we avoid war in Europe now, we may not have to fight any war within the foreseeable future, and that in any event we should avoid war now and trust that our children may be as wise as we are when they are running this country. I believe that if we join this European war we will not crush dictatorship, though we may win a military victory, for Fascism and Communism are the results of war and not of peace.

Let us have faith in this nation, in its power, its courage, its ideals. Let us not be panic-stricken by the fantastic future which is painted of Adolph Hitler leading his 80,000,000 tired Germans to a victory over 200,000,0000 people of Europe and Africa and the Near East, and then again leading those 80,000,000 still more tired Germans across 3,000 miles of sea to the conquest of 200,000,000 people in the Western Hemisphere.

I deeply regret that you do not see eye to eye with me on these points since you are in a position of large responsibility and influence for the welfare of the youth of America, and it is the youth of this country which will pay the greatest penalty for war.

With continued respect and affection, but sorrow that your convictions are such that war (now or tomorrow) seems to you the only rational step for our country, I remain . . .

DOCUMENT 25

William R. Castle to R. Douglas Stuart, Jr.
February 14, 1941

I hope you have had a thoroughly successful time on your trip in the East. I had to go to New York yesterday, as I told you, to talk with Cudahy [John Cudahy, former ambassador to Poland and Belgium] and Lindbergh about Cudahy's expedition to Germany to get news for Life. He says that he has the promise of the Germans that he will be given a free hand and he has the absolute promise of Life to print precisely what he sends in. I don't trust the German promise, and I am terribly afraid that Life may kill what he writes by printing their own comments at the end. However, it is worth trying.

What Cudahy believes, and this is confidential, is that if he gives the real facts it will tend to show people in this country that a negotiated peace is the only sensible and reasonable thing at the moment. And that the chances for England to survive this spring, if conditions are as he fears, are almost nil. Lindbergh frightened me on the subject because his sources of information are pretty good, and he insists that the Germans have not even begun their air attack on England, that they have been trying to see what they could do and to map out the ground. He says that he does not believe Britain has over 5,000 fighting planes at the most and that Germany has at least 25,000. Also, of course, the German training schools for pilots are endless in number and that they seem to have plenty of people. Losses in the war so far are very few if one thinks of it as a world war.*

I talked very strongly with Cudahy about his own attitude because he is completely with us and yet feels that because Roosevelt appointed him to office and because he is a personal friend, he cannot come out and say so. After I jumped on him with both feet, he did say that he felt he would have a perfect right to insist this country ought not to get into the war. I said that also that was all we wanted, that we did not in the least want him to come out in any attack on his friend, Roosevelt. But, you can bet both Lindbergh and I didn't pull any of our punches when we were talking about the President's war policy. Of course, Cudahy thought he could silence us by making fun of Willkie, but that didn't do much good because we agreed.

It was great seeing you when you were here.

* Can't you make a point here—that we mustn't think of it to become thought of as a world war—that that's part of our game to keep it on basis of British-German squabble in the mind of America.

DOCUMENT 26

Ruth Sarles to R. Douglas Stuart, Jr.
May 31, 1941

Here are a few reactions to the President's speech [on May 27, 1941, Roosevelt addressed the nation and proclaimed an unlimited national emergency] that will interest you, and a few additional items:

The general reaction on the Hill among the men I talked with, and from reports of conversations others have had, is that while the speech was perhaps not so bad as they had feared, nevertheless everything is there that *may* indicate strong action in the near future. In other words, while the speech gave very definite reason for believing that the President indicated his recognition that the country is not ready for war, he laid the basis to go ahead whenever *he* thinks it necessary without consulting Congress.

His complete ignoring of Congress in the speech was a matter of some comment here.

I believe that as time goes on, the speech will become more significant.

Undoubtedly, he hoped to push his anti-war pledges further into the background through this speech. Which means AF has got to keep them definitely in the foreground. I hope you will consider some trick way of keeping them constantly before AF members—perhaps have eight or ten of them attractively printed on large cards, to be stuck up on walls, in windows, etc.

One Washington writer calls our present state "belligerency short of war." He comments that if the public doesn't support what the President said in his speech, the commitments won't stick.

I have heard nothing on the Hill about a definite attempt to get action on the Neutrality law. As to convoys, while it may be that we are past that stage, as the Administration has spread abroad, there are a number who don't agree. There is talk of rewriting Tobey's resolution and introducing it in slightly different form [Sen. Charles W. Tobey (R-N.H.) introduced a Senate resolution opposing convoys]; what that form will be, I do not know. Rep. Curtis [Carl Curtis (R-Neb.)] is still keeping his discharge petition going, but does not expect to put on a drive as yet, pending some action in the Senate. (Rumor is that Taft wants to rewrite the Tobey resolution.) David Lawrence [president and editor, *United States News*; newspaper columnist] thinks convoys the logical next step. Senator Reynolds [Robert Rice Reynolds (D-N.C.), chairman, military affairs committee] looks for convoys.

I felt that the President's reference to the Nazi-Communist bedfellows of those "sincere" people who are urging staying out had particular significance for AF. I think it was the day following the speech that Alsop and Kintner [Joseph Alsop and Robert Kintner, Washington columnists] devoted a whole column to AF and its questionable supporters. Alsop and Kintner so frequently act as sounding boards. Possibly their column was the tip-off that that is the tack the Administration will take increasingly to smear us. If you have any way of doing it gently, it might be a good idea to warn local groups to be especially careful of their supporters.

I am sending to Ken Lee [Kendrick Lee, editor of AFC newsletters] copies of the Attorney General's letter of October 1939 which lists the emergency powers of the President. I had this mimeographed for distribution on the Hill, since it was out of print.

There are persistent rumors of peace; they are redoubled with Winant's [John G. Winant, ambassador to Great Britain; former governor of New Hampshire] return. It is said that the President has had Hitler's latest peace proposals for some time, that Winant has come home to discuss them with him. These are the main outlines: Britain keeps her fleet, her independence, and her self-governing dominions. She gives back to Germany her old colonies. Britain keeps something in North Africa, presumably her interest in Egypt. The rest of Africa is jointly administered by Britain, Germany and France. (I don't know where Italy is to come in.) Britain is through in the Mediterranean. Gibraltar is demobilized. Norway is independent. Alsace-Lorraine returns to Germany "forever." Holland and Belgium become a single kingdom. Czechoslovakia and Yugoslavia are done for, and so is Poland. Russia keeps what she now has and gets Persia in addition. In the Far East, the war in China will cease. Japan is to have certain economic rights in China and the Dutch East Indies. If all this can be accomplished, then Hitler will spring some disarmament proposal.

Don't ask me to vouch for this—I can't. But these in general are the terms that have been rumored around here for some time, and Winant's return revives them again. As I remember, they are quite similar to terms published in a Japanese newspaper about two months ago.

One other rumor about Winant deserves mention. It is said he came home at his own request, being very unhappy as to what he finds in England—little disposition toward greater social justice after the war is over, and that was his grand passion as head of the ILO [International Labor Office].

Another peace rumor has to do with the Far East, and that is that we have asked Japan to let us know what she wants. There are several straws in the wind indicating that we may be seriously attempting to resolve this war in the Far East. I have not been able to find any substantial backing for the rumor that we have brought most of our Pacific fleet through the Canal.

DOCUMENT 27

Ruth Sarles to R. Douglas Stuart, Jr.
July 3, 1941

Herewith, at long last, another message on the state of the nation!

There is no doubt but that we are in a much stronger position for the time being, as a result of the Russian-German war. As is always the case when one side takes the lead, a number of things seem to be coming our way. The Knox statement has caused a number of people to hold back. [On June 30, 1941, Knox claimed that the German-Russian war gave the United States an unparalleled opportunity to "clear the Atlantic of the German menace." *New York Times,* July 1, 1941, pp. 1, 14.] Coming along about the same time as Senator Wheeler's resolution for investigation of any actual shooting, it has helped us greatly. Senator Walsh's determination to hold hearings on the Wheeler resolution is significant, since he rarely goes off the deep end.

The report of the House Military Affairs Committee published last Sunday gives point to the widespread dissatisfaction with the defense effort. Note the excellent articles by Hanson Baldwin that have been appearing in the New York Times since last Saturday on the exact status of the army and navy.

These polls that are being conducted in various congressional districts have had a grand effect, I think. You undoubtedly saw in the Wednesday papers a report of the President's press conference, where he revealed that the Fish poll [Congressman Hamilton Fish (R-N.Y.), with AFC financing, sponsored a poll in his congressional district, which was also the district of President Roosevelt. Voters there opposed intervention nine to one.] had got under his skin.

Senator George's statement on the floor of the Senate last Saturday was a tonic. [On June 28, 1941, Senator George had accused the administration of using "totalitarian methods" in advancing its foreign policy. He requested assurance that the American people, through Congress, had the ultimate decision.] As I wrote earlier in the week, I hope America First will make important use of some of his statements, particularly in connection with the advisory referendum campaign; he said some fine things about the right and duty of the people to express their opinions.

It should be noted that the occasion for Senator George's outburst was H. R. 4700, a bill providing for "priorities in transportation by merchant vessels in the interests of national defense." This measure gives tremendous powers to the Maritime Commission, requiring that merchant vessels secure warrants from the Commission (see Congressional Record, June 28th, page 5777). I hear the rumor that Senator George is closely tied up with various shipping and railroad interests, which would explain in part his outburst.

Congressman Woodrum's statement on the floor of the House the same day was also noteworthy. [On June 28, 1941, Congressman Clifton A. Woodrum (D-Va.) warned the administration against adopting an interventionist program.]

I think these statements from two Democrats have done more than anything else to stiffen the backbone of the opposition in Congress.

I am morally certain that the stiffening opposition in Congress and elsewhere had a great deal to do with the failure of the War Department to ask for a formal declaration of a national emergency to enable it to send troops anywhere, as also rumored late last week (I think the Saturday papers had this story).

Mr. Burdick [Fred Burdick, congressional liaison, AFC] has probably reported to you on the Tuesday night meeting of the non-interventionist bloc. About forty attended. Nothing startling happened, but the timing of the meeting was excellent, coming just as stay out sentiment was grouping up on every side. I understand that the group resisted several suggestions that they go all out for impeachment of Secretary Knox, feeling that they ought not deviate from the line of keeping the country out of war. Several men will probably continue along this line, but it will not be an organized job. The men will probably hammer on keeping the war-making power in the hands of Congress. They will also continue to try to keep the administration on the defensive. Senators Vandenberg and Hiram Johnson attended the meeting, I believe, for the first time. Another meeting will probably be held in about two weeks. There was only one Democrat, Congressman Knute Hill [D-Wash.], a fact which I shall not ignore in talking with the men.

I am enclosing Congressman Knutson's [Harold Knutson (R-Minn.)] resolution calling on Congress to declare a state of war between Germany and Russia, a power given Congress under the Neutrality Act.

I enclose also Senator Wheeler's resolution referred to above.

Also, Mr. Tinkham's [Congressman George Holden Tinkham (R-Mass.)], which won't get anywhere.

I sent you the other day a copy of the new advisory referendum resolution introduced in the House.

Apparently for the time being the threat inherent in the property seizure bill as first introduced is removed. Not two days after the President had asked for its passage in its original form, Assistant Secretary of War Patterson [Robert P. Patterson, under secretary of war, 1940–45; secretary of war, 1945–47] appeared before the Senate Military Affairs Committee and proposed a substitute measure that was quite mild. Senator Reynolds tells me that this bill is nothing more, really, than the Maritime Act of 1936, plus certain features of the Lease-Lend Bill, plus certain features of a bill passed last October, granting certain powers to lay up reserves of important materials.

Probably in a short time there will be a bill asking for more funds to carry out the Lease-Lend Act.

As far as I can find out now, after next Wednesday or Thursday the House will do little until about the 20th, when the tax bill is expected; it may take them four days to pass it and after that they may take a recess. I am not yet clear on the Senate picture.

I suppose you have read as many interpretations of the German-Russian war as I have. One that made sense to me was written by Roscoe Drummond, excellent correspondent for the Christian Science Monitor. He says that it was not for materials or territories that Germany made her drive on Russia now; that in the past Russia had been immobilized by diplomacy, and now must be immobilized by the defeat of her armies before the decisive stage of the war. Drummond remarked that Hitlerism cannot stand competing totalitarianism any more than it can stand competing democracy.

There are lots of rumors floating around, of course. Although I cannot guarantee it, I believe that we have extended our Atlantic patrol consistently further east, and also west—reinforced by the Pacific fleet. There is a story that part of the regular army has been sent to Iceland. Also that National Guard units are being trained as special anti-aircraft batteries for use on board merchant ships.

Along with rumors about the forthcoming treaty with Brazil is the story that we are already fortifying and occupying strategic positions along the coast of Brazil.

There is more and more talk of inflation, some say by the end of the year it will be very noticeable. Important price rises are now being admitted as almost inevitable; some go so far as to say they will go up 50%.

John Maynard Keynes [British economist], the British advocate of forced savings, is still here, working quietly. Some people look for the adoption here of his forced savings plan in some form by next winter, as a substitute for more taxes.

Rumors of a deal with Japan persist, but I have nothing new on this. I may have written you a couple of weeks ago a fairly dependable story that Hull was seeing the Japanese Ambassador quietly at his hotel with frequency.

One more item on Congress which I neglected to include above: One Senator who has pretty good judgment says that an armed ship bill would not stand a chance in the Senate—there are too many *Southern* Senators against it.

I hope you have noted the interesting situation over committee chairmanships that has developed since Senator Harrison's [Pat Harrison (D-Miss.)] demise. The enclosed Tom Stokes story tells the tale.

I have not yet written you anything specific on mediation, as you requested because I have been looking for some formula that could be used publicly and would make sense. I have not found any suggestions that seem realistic to me, that get around the objection to urging a peace now because it would so obviously be made under Hitler's terms. I have felt that for an important organization like America First to urge it now would put obstacles in the way of its accomplishments; obviously when a government is committed to a policy that may end up in the war, we could not expect it to be receptive to proposals that would seem to weaken the force and effect of that policy.*

If Hitler defeats Russia as is likely, it may be he would feel that he was then free to organize the whole of Europe as he pleases, and might make a proposal for ending the war that England would not feel she had to turn down. I am interested in Senator Taft's saying that he would not be surprised if there were a reasonable peace proposal by fall (don't quote him).

To me, this means that if persons of influence could now be talking quietly with the President, and talking on realistic terms of a possible peace, they might get somewhere. I cannot see how America First could now push it publicly. However, I still believe that America First could be recommending to local chapters the study of what is required to build an enduring peace when the war is over. There have been a number of concrete plans proposed, most of which I have read. You might want to make up a packet of literature on the subject and urge that before fall, one or two meetings be devoted to discussion of the subject.

At the same time, if men of the calibre of Dr. Hutchins [Robert

---

* unless offered so quietly & influentially that the govt. can—if it will—eventually offer them to the country as its own.

Maynard Hutchins, president, University of Chicago] and others you may know feel moved to try to get to the President, I hope they will do so.

One comment on Knox's speech: I have checked this morning with several of my newspaper friends and others, and as yet I do not discover a clear lead as to whether Knox's speech was intended as a trial balloon for some new foreign policy move, or whether it was just Secretary Knox sounding off. Arthur Krock [Washington correspondent, *New York Times*] calls it a "scouting expedition into the public mind" (New York Times—July 2nd).

DOCUMENT 28

Ruth Sarles to R. Douglas Stuart, Jr. August 9, 1941

This fight on the extension of the time of service for selectees has certainly given the Administration the jitters. As of late yesterday, when I left the House, some who were for it were saying that if it got through by 5 votes they would be lucky. I suppose that the outcome depends on how much heat the Administration is able to turn on the wavering Democrats over the weekend. My fear is that they can swing enough men to pass it, although it is quite likely restricting amendments will be written in.

There is an interesting difference between the way "our" men are going at it in the House and in the Senate. If our men in the Senate had voted for the Burton [Sen. Harold H. Burton (R-Ohio)] (one-year) amendment, it would have gone through. But they preferred to maintain their purity; the result was that we got eighteen months. The Mundt [Rep. Karl Mundt (R-S.D.), informal adviser to the AFC] group in the House is saying vote for all restricting amendments.

For your information, as of yesterday the Kansas delegation was solid against it; Pennsylvania solid; Ohio all but two; Indiana all but one; Illinois probably all but Sabath [Rep. Adolph J. Sabath (D-Ill.)]; etc.

I suppose you have been watching with interest as I have the way the Republicans in the House have taken a new lease on life. I am interested in the way they are playing for labor support; I understand that the CIO is likely to be lined up solid. While I think the Republican declaration the other day (you have seen it, haven't you—if not let me know) was a fine thing, I am not too impressed—prefer to reserve judgment and see if they translate their vigorous words into action.

Incidentally, I was interested in the chapter bulletin #477 [which was dated August 7 and which denied that the National Committee had taken any position on the draft]. Somebody did a great job of pitching a curved ball! I'd appreciate it if you would wire me when a thing like this is contemplated. While I understood AF's reason for not coming out flatly in opposition to extension, it was a vitally important step in the development of the whole war program, and I think we should have been playing it up this way. I have been walking a tightrope here in Washington and only hope and pray my foot doesn't slip!

I rather look for a new drive on the advisory referendum after this selective service thing is out of the way, chiefly in anticipation of a probable Administration move within a few weeks to lift the Western Hemisphere ban.

It is interesting that a number of Washington observers with whom I have checked who don't ordinarily go off half-cocked think there's considerable in the tales of a Churchill-Roosevelt meeting somewhere on the blue. I suppose that if by Monday the outcome of the Selective service extension is in doubt, we can look for a hysteria-creating radiogram of some sort that will swing men into line to put it through.

I think I have told you that I have not been convinced that the President is for getting into the war. Well, I am about to change my mind. Story is, from a usually reliable source, that the President has definitely made up his mind to a limited war. As few casualties as possible, of course, and use only the Marines and the Navy overseas. (This does not make sense to me; the number of Marines is fairly limited—I have 50,000 in my mind—and we have used up many of them so far, what with our numerous outposts in the Atlantic and the Pacific.) Undoubtedly a police force in most South American countries, for which we would use the Army.

Story continues, that purpose of Hopkins [Harry Hopkins, Roosevelt's most trusted adviser and confidant; administrator, Lend-Lease] trip was to talk Britain out of some other contracts, particularly airplanes and aviation supplies, and then turn them over to China, Russia and Dutch East Indies in the belief that with an adequate air force in the Far East Japan could be "sterilized." It is said that our government would consider occupation of Siam a threat to Manila.

Same story—all possibility of a negotiated peace is dead; FDR is against it and would back Churchill; together, they are powerful enough to put it through.

To sum up, we are getting in fast. An attempt will be made to make every move possible. There will be no declaration of war if it can possibly be avoided.

Now, for a few points of my own. Seems to me Germany is likely to take over Portugal, which would give her easy access to the now heavily guarded Azores. (I understand Portugal has been sending large numbers of troops there.) That would then call for a corresponding move on our part to head off the German threat to Latin America. Perhaps we will then try something at Sierra Leone. I think there is a good possibility the lifting of the Hemisphere ban will never be brought before Congress by the Administration.

Wish Winston and FDR would decide their places in history would be more secure if they came back with a dramatic peace move—perhaps that's our best hope.

DOCUMENT 29

R. Douglas Stuart, Jr., to Robert M. Hutchins October 29, 1941

Thanks very much for your note. I hated like the dickens to haunt you about testifying while you were on vacation. But the country must be saved and we can't get very far without turning to persons like yourself.

Bill Benton advises me he has sent you a copy of the interesting report of his Southport neighbor's recent conversation with Truman Smith [Lieutenant Colonel Truman Smith, military attaché for air with the U.S. Embassy in Berlin, 1935–39].

From this it would seem Russia is all through. With the collapse of Russia, it strikes me that several things become obvious:

1) Germany cannot be defeated with an AEF [American Expeditionary Force].

2) Even if an AEF is sent, England will lose more by continuation of the war than she will by making peace now (viz., Freda Utley's [British journalist. For her article, see "Must the World Destroy Itself?" *Reader's Digest*, October 1941, pp. 17–24.] article in the October Reader's Digest).

3) England will be more receptive to the idea of a mediated peace than ever before.

4) A clear-cut geographical basis for peace has been established.

At this psychological moment it is barely possible we could show Roosevelt that he could be a world savior by supporting England in a mediated peace. If he would do this, it would completely justify his foreign policy and give him his place in history.

Although our previous survey [the AFC had Hutchins prepare a poll of American opinion] did not show great support for the idea of mediated peace, the idea has never been supported with an effective publicity program.

If you believe that the foregoing makes sense, you are the best qualified person in the country to advance a mediated peace at this time.

I submit that the best and most dramatic way to present [the] idea would be a full-page advertisement signed by you and run on a nation-wide scale. I believe I can secure the necessary funds.

I feel like a heel intruding on your pleasant vacation in the West but this seems so darned important.

P.S. You might be interested in the enclosed questions we prepared for John Cudahy for use in a debate with Senator Pepper on the subject of a negotiated peace. Cudahy has become a regular trooper!

P.P.S. I have been intending for some time to thank you for giving the General such a fight talk—it helped like blazes. His morale is immensely improved.

[Questions referred to in the P.S.]

1. Do you believe in buying time with other nations' blood?

2. Knowing that England, as her own general staff admits, cannot win the war without a huge AEF—and knowing the American people are opposed to such an AEF—have we any right to discourage England from making peace?

3. If you believe that the war can be won by blockading the continent of Europe, do you think that a just and lasting peace can be obtained or that the cause of democracy can be advanced by the slow starvation of the women and children of France, Belgium, Holland, Denmark, Norway—and finally the people of Germany itself?

4. Knowing that a prostrate Europe turned to totalitarianism after the last

war, what makes you think that new Hitlers, Mussolinis and Stalins will not rise up from the ruins of the 10-year war which you are advocating?

5. Do you think any of the following countries could be in a more desperate situation than they are today if we had encouraged them to make peace instead of having encouraged them to fight? (Jugoslavia, etc.)

6. In what respect do you disagree with the teaching of Christ, "Blessed are the peacemakers"?

DOCUMENT 30

John T. Flynn to Robert E. Wood
November 11, 1941

I am writing you about our probable course after Thursday. What will happen on Thursday I cannot say. As you know, Ham Fish is in charge of the fight in the House with Karl Mundt and John Voorhis [Rep. John M. Vorys (R-Ohio)]. Fish is erratic, but when his eye is clearly on the objective and he is in agreement with his colleagues, as happens in this case, he is a good fighter. Mundt and Voorhis have their feet on the ground. Fish and Mundt tell me that the fight is going to be very close. There is a chance of our winning, despite the rosy claims of the opposition. But I think we must admit it is only a chance. In any case, I am writing you about what we should do should we win in the House and what our course should be should we lose.

If we win, it seems to me the victory will be a very, very solid one. The effect upon the British may well be decisive and if the Russian resistance continues to crumble, the whole stage may well be set for a peace in Europe. It seems to me we might proceed very wisely if, after the vote, the America First Committee remained quiet for a while. I mean that we might hold off the meetings for the time being, though we should try for studio radio time at which those of our speakers who specialize in reason rather than emotion should be utilized to talk very simple common sense to the people. But immediately we should take measures to strike the peace note in the most effective way. My own notion is that we should get hold of Fosdick [Harry Emerson Fosdick, pastor, Riverside Church, New York; national radio preacher], Archbishop Beckman [Francis J. L. Beckman, Roman Catholic Archbishop, Dubuque, Iowa], Dr. Stamm [Frederick K.

Stamm, pastor, Clinton Avenue Community Church, Brooklyn, N.Y.] and as many other leading representatives of all denominations as we can to form a great inter-church movement for peace. I feel sure Fosdick and Beckman would be interested in this. They should immediately by mail attempt to get the signed allegiance of a huge number of ministers of all denominations to this movement. Sending out these letters, handling the details of organization would cost some money. Our committees could lend some personnel to handle the job and make some contributions to it. The amount involved would not be great. I think ten or fifteen thousand names could be signed up and it is possible that two or three or five hundred sponsors, including the more important clergymen, could be gotten. It should be independent and not be in any way connected with America First, save that we would inspire it and aid it in every way possible. Such a committee, representing so vast a church group, could, I think, go to the radio people and demand time in which all the leading clergymen of the country could talk. A Peace Sunday could be set apart. I think the pulpits of the nation could be made to ring with the cry and the prayer for peace.

On the other hand, what should be our course if we should lose the fight on Thursday? What troubles me is your letter indicating your belief that this would be the end. Certainly repeal of Sections 2, 3 and 6 will put it in the hands of the President to get war going, but it may very well be that he will not want to use it immediately and it may very well be that he will not be able to use it immediately. There is a feeling in some quarters that it will be a month or two before anything very important is done under this new proposed grant of power and there is also a still more well-defined feeling that the President feels the chief purpose of this legislation is to buck up the morale of the British—it seems to be doing something for them at a moment when the question of peace threatens to bob up in London at any moment. It is true that we will be at the mercy of an incident, but it is also true that the other side may be at the mercy of an incident. There is no telling what may happen before an actual state of war is created. We have no right to throw away that last chance of saving the country. The Japanese situation is working to keep the Administration from a war commitment in either ocean. Therefore we cannot throw away the hope of peace yet.

On this point I offer two considerations. One is this. England can make peace with Germany much more easily as long as she is in a position to make that peace alone, rather than if we are actually at war with Germany. In the latter case England could scarcely make peace without our agreement. She would be in the bad position of deserting her ally by a separate peace. It is of the most vital importance that England should be in a position to make this peace, whereas if we, on the passage of neutrality repeal, come out and say the nation is at war, that war is a fact, it puts the war groups in a perfect position to declare that we are actually in a war. And I have a strong feeling that once this fact is so, Roosevelt will want the British in the war as long as he possibly can keep them there. Therefore we must do nothing which will encourage the assumption that the nation is at war with Germany, until all hope has passed.

The second point is this. Roosevelt is thoroughly unscrupulous. He will break his promises to England as quickly as he breaks them to the American people. If Russia should fall in the next month or five weeks definitively, and Roosevelt should decide that joining in an all-out war is too dangerous a job for him, he will ditch the British with as little conscience as he ditched all his party platforms. There are always chances that the whole European situation may change in our favor. Suppose we should announce that this fight is over, that the nation is at war with Germany. Then suppose that Roosevelt should deny that this is so and then suppose that in a couple of months some shift in the scene should make it advantageous for him to let the British step out and that peace should come—what a trumpeting there would be from the White House. He would tell the American people that he had promised to keep them out of war and that he had made good his promise, that if he had listened to the America First Committee he would have done none of the things which he had done to make us a factor for Germany to reckon on and that in the end, if he had listened to America First the nation would actually be at war and beyond the pale of peace and that he had kept the country out of war even after the isolationists had said we were in the war.

It seems to me every dictate of strategy calls upon us to assert that the nation is not at war with Germany, that while the repeal of the neutrality act puts into the hands of the President the power to put us into war, nevertheless we will not be at war until he actually uses that power, that Congress has abdicated completely to the dictator, but there are still the American people to reckon with and that the America First Committee will resist any involvement to the end.

The vote in the Senate is the greatest we have had by long odds, showing that the movement against war and against the President has been growing, that our power has been growing and the power of the other side diminishing [the Senate had recently voted to arm merchant ships and to permit U.S. craft into combat zones]. In the face of that situation we dare not say to our followers that at the peak of our strength we are going to quit. Every day I see scores and some days hundreds of these plain, simple people who look to us to save them. I get discouraged, as all of us do at times, but when I see these people and hear their simple faith in us I know that we have to fight to the end, no matter what the cost may be. The story has gotten around that you are to step out as soon as the Neutrality Act is repealed. I do pray that you will not do that, and that whatever you have decided to do, you will not act immediately and that in no case shall the America First Committee or its leaders be responsible for announcing the moment when the nation is at war. I know the situation is difficult for you. It is difficult for all of us, but I earnestly plead with you not to act at once. Let us wait at least a little while and see what turn events take.

DOCUMENT 31

"Suppose we don't help England and Germany beats her. Are we next on Germany's list?"
Speakers Bureau
undated [1941]

A. Probably Hitler thinks that he would someday like to defeat the United States, and certainly he has included us among the "pluto-democracies." But what Hitler wants and what he is able to do are very different things.

The chances are, however, that Hitler, being a smart though unscrupulous man, knows that the United States is a pretty big order and has no wish to tangle with us, at least for the present. But even if he should, in his mania, try to attack us, we know from the experience of England what a job he would have on his hands. It is ridiculous to compare us with countries like Denmark, Austria, Czechoslovakia, and other small countries of Europe. Those were directly over the German border. We are three thousand miles from Europe over a great sea. He has had difficulty negotiating twenty miles of English Channel; three thousands miles are 150 times as far.

DOCUMENT 32

"Even if war with Germany is not a certainty, wouldn't it be best to fight now to avoid even the possibility of a war without allies?"
Speakers Bureau
undated [1941]

A. Definitely, "No."

The Ally in question can of course be nobody else than Britain—plus the Empire's Dominions. Of the Dominions: Eire refuses to enter the war; for all military purposes so does South Africa; Canada is our ally anyway in the Western Hemisphere by last September's agreement [on August 18, 1940, after conferring with Prime Minister Mackenzie King, Roosevelt announced that a permanent Canadian-American Defense Board would be established]; Australia and New Zealand are fighting in northeastern Africa, and apparently in India—neither area is of any military or much economic concern to us, and most right thinking Americans believe that Britain's manner of policing India should undergo considerable alteration. Australia and New Zealand themselves must be thought of in hard boiled terms of Far Eastern policy.   .

This leaves Britain herself. Regardless of sentimental attachments, quite justifiable ones, for Britain, some very basic thinking must be done before we become her full military ally. (There is no point in quibbling about it, we are now Britain's full economic ally, whether or not it seems entirely rational that we should be.)

In discussing the British fleet in question, we will show that the British fleet is not our first line of defense. Thus becoming Britain's military ally rests largely on that natural sympathy. Is this a sufficient basis—in the military long run?

Here is one angle from which to think about it—probably the most important angle. How good an ally would Britain be? An ally sometimes can be as much of a liability as an asset—as Germany discovered in Austria's case and the allies discovered in the cases of Italy and Tsarist Russia in 1918, and as Nazi Germany may now be discovering in the case of Italy. Our intervention in Europe would definitely not insure a British victory. With Britain's industry impaired—perhaps by 40 per cent, some say—with her shipping being destroyed, and with American defense production unlikely to reach anything close to a peak before 1942 (and having in the meantime to supply both Britain and the United States), and with us able to furnish no more than a handful of troops for many months, for whatever purpose Britain might want our troops, and with Japan apparently waiting for our fleet to leave Hawaii so that she can pounce on the Indies (unless we alter our Far Eastern policy, abandon the Philippines and all interest in Singapore, the Indies and Australia, which also means an alteration in British policy), there is not much chance of our doing any more for Britain in the next few months, when she really needs it, than we are doing now. On the other hand, if Britain survives the next few months she might eventually win the war.

Thus, if we entered the war now, sent a few men, a lot of ships and planes, and then England fell anyway—whether by invasion, or through destruction of industries and shipping, or if she were forced to negotiate a peace to avoid falling, we might very well suffer what military men call "defeat in detail," i.e. a defeat far away from our main defense positions that seriously impairs our capacity to defend our main position, when we certainly would have retained our full strength had we not so exposed ourselves. Certainly the British suffered such a defeat in Norway; in a strictly technical sense they can be said to have suffered such a defeat in Flanders. Attempting to save the British Isles, flanked as they are by enemy bases, ringed as they are by submarines, and open as they are to air attack, stands a chance of being the greatest "defeat in detail" in history. And even if we saved them, the effort stands a good chance of stopping right there and ultimately still being "defeat in detail." Britain, at best, is an exposed salient in mighty precarious military position as far as the United States is concerned.

DOCUMENT 33

"Will the prestige acquired for Nazism by German military victories bring fascism here without even an attack by Hitler?"
Speakers Bureau
undated [1941]

A. Certainly a German military victory will increase the prestige of Fascism, here and everywhere. But it will not be nearly enough to make this country go fascist if a vigilant watch is kept over our democracy. To answer such a question in the affirmative is to belie weakness in our own system. Weaknesses there are, but none that cannot be overcome by our democratic methods.

DOCUMENT 34

*"Could Germany defeat us without fighting by the use of her
'Fifth Column' in this country?"*
Speakers Bureau
undated [1941]

A. No. The "Fifth Column" danger has been grossly over-rated. There are
agents of the Nazis here, just as there are agents of other foreign governments. There are Americans who sympathize with these foreign governments. There always have been such "Fifth Columnists," but they have
been never powerful or numerous enough to upset the government.

The way to handle the "Fifth Column" danger is to keep a close watchout
for its members and to keep the avenues of democracy clear. As long as
democracy is in the saddle, there will be machinery for exposing foreign
agents and sympathizers and apprehending them when they break our laws.

Actually, the Fifth Column was not the cause of any European country's
downfall. Countries fall because of their own inner weakness. The Fifth
Column may have helped, but it could never have gotten anywhere if the
inner weaknesses had not already been present.

DOCUMENT 35

*"If Germany does decide to fight us could she invade the
continental United States from any European base?"*
Speakers Bureau
undated [1941]

A. Competent military experts don't believe it is possible. Even if the U.S.
Navy, already the most powerful in the world, soon to be more powerful in
its own waters than all European navies combined, were defeated, the
invaders would still have to face American planes, mine fields, harbor and
coast defenses, and finally the U.S. Army, and in addition the armed forces

of our hemispheric allies—at least Canada and presumably Mexico. Meanwhile even a defeated navy would not be entirely swept from the seas; there would remain a few cruisers, destroyers, submarines, motor torpedo boats, with which to harry enemy lines. Supply itself is the most difficult problem of all for it takes a minimum of 7½ tons of shipping to transport a single soldier across the sea and a minimum of 13 tons of shipping a month to keep him in fighting provisions. And, too, we would have the use of an entire air force—both naval and army. The invader unless he established advanced bases—most of which we now have from Newfoundland to Guiana—could not attack except with such planes as could come by aircraft carrier. For, including our own flying fortresses and long-range patrol bombers, there is not more than a handful of military planes today which can cross an ocean, let alone cross it with a bomb load, drop the bombs, and fly back to a home base. Such raids would be sporadic, suicidal and unprofitable to the invader. Even this handful would lack protection from pursuit planes which are short-ranged.

The proposition of invading the United States from Europe is so fantastic that even the most rabid interventionists have stopped seriously raising it.

DOCUMENT 36

"Could Germany get bases on the islands of the Caribbean Sea, or in Central America, from which to fight us?"
Speakers Bureau
undated [1941]

A. The only way Germany could acquire such bases is by defeating the United States fleet and air forces, and such detachments of the Marine Corps and Army as would be supporting them. For we already are ringing the Caribbean with bases on Guantanamo Bay in Cuba, in Puerto Rico, the Virgin Islands, Jamaica (Br.), Antigua (Br.), Santa Lucia (Br.), Trinidad (Br.). Down below the Caribbean in British Guiana, and up above in the British owned Bahamas and in Britain's Bermuda.

Experts have long considered the Caribbean Sea to be an American lake—even before rights to naval and air bases in British colonies were acquired. And behind the Caribbean lie the vast defenses of the Panama

Canal. So great are the chances against an invader's penetrating the Caribbean—except for sporadic, futile raids—that only the most alarmist prophets conceive of its being done—provided that the bases, the fleet and the air forces are ready.

DOCUMENT 37

"Suppose Germany were able to acquire land, naval and air bases somewhere south of the Caribbean, could she carry on a large-scale war against us?"
Speakers Bureau
undated [1941]

A. It is conceivable that Hitler could muster a fleet too big for us to fight very far from our own bases unless the so-called 2-Ocean Navy had been completed. Such a fleet would have to include the British fleet nearly intact. This does not mean that such a fleet could penetrate the Caribbean where, in addition to our own fleet operating with the tremendous advantage of being close to its own bases, it would meet the full power of our air force. The Caribbean would remain an American lake. But such a naval superiority might permit Hitler to land in Brazil, below the "Bulge" (down where we have the least economic interest and consequently the least influence, and where Hemisphere defense will always be weighed in realistic accord with the immediate situation and not in accord with any vague Hemisphere ideal). Presumably Hitler's fleet would have operated from an advance base in West Africa's own "bulge," from Dakar in French Senegal, or Bathurst in British Gambia. These ports are only 1700 miles from Natal on the "Bulge" of Brazil.

What now? Could Hitler successfully attack North America? Not very well by sea. By sea he would only be able to move against our concentration of strength in the Caribbean, against a ring of bases with naval power backed by air power. Our naval strength would be growing all the while. Meanwhile he would have to protect a 1700-mile overseas supply line back to Dakar or Bathurst, a line which could be harried by our submarine and surface raiders; and he would have to protect another long maritime supply line either from West Africa to Europe, or direct from Brazil to Europe. For it would be many years before Brazil or West Africa could be sufficiently industrialized to support the land, naval and air forces Hitler would be needing. To protect these lines he would have to disperse numerous units of his fleet and so weaken its concentrated fighting power.

Not very well by air either. He would find himself operating from airfields in the jungles and mountains of northern South America, airfields difficult to build, more difficult to supply. He might send out sporadic raids against Caribbean bases and the Panama Canal. But only through criminal negligence on our part could anything happen to the Canal.

Even more difficult would be land attack. First he would have to assemble a large army, by vulnerable overseas transport; then supply that army by vulnerable overseas transport; then he would have to move the army north: by sea via overseas transport to perform the difficult operation of landing on hostile well-defended shores; or by land through mountains and jungles some of which are untracked. Such an expedition sounds fantastic to sensible ears.

Meanwhile, nobody can calculate the trouble he would have with the native South American populations, whether they would join him or fight him guerilla fashion—in their own land. Still less can anybody calculate what might be going on behind him in Europe where whatever unification had been accomplished would inevitably be on a very wobbly basis. And the Soviet Union would certainly have to be "appeased" before any large-scale drive (it could hardly be anything less) could be launched against the Americas.

DOCUMENT 38

"If England was defeated, could Germany take Canada and British colonies in the Caribbean and attack us?"
Speakers Bureau
undated [1941]

A. She could not—at least not until she had won a terrific battle for which our forces would be prepared. The same factors that would prevent Germany from attacking continental United States or anywhere in the Caribbean area would go into operation. We have a defense agreement with Canada, bases of our own in British-owned Newfoundland, Bermuda and the Bahamas, bases of our own in the British West Indies. Even if this were not true, our Navy and air force would be strong enough to be pitted against any attack on Canada or the islands.

DOCUMENT 39

"What about French and Dutch colonies?"
Speakers Bureau
undated [1941]

A. Although we have no bases of our own in them, French and Dutch colonies are already virtually surrounded by U.S. bases built or building. Such military and naval bases as they are (and they aren't much) in French and Dutch colonies could not be reached from Europe without first defeating us on the sea and in the air.

DOCUMENT 40

"Excluding the British Navy, is not the combined tonnage of
Axis powers greater than that of the United States?"
Speakers Bureau
undated [1941]

A. According to a report of Secretary of the Navy Knox, the approximate total combatant tonnage of Germany, Italy and Japan amounts to 1,835,000; of the United States, 1,250,000. Concerning the quality and service of the fleets of the Axis powers, Knox testified before the Senate Foreign Relations Committee, as reported in the Chicago Sunday Tribune, February 2. When asked if the German fleet had been built for operation in home waters or for long range operations, Knox answered, "I should imagine it was designed to operate in European waters." Knox said further that it would take a "long time" to change a short range fleet into one which could operate at long range, thousands of miles from its home ports. Both German and Italian navies were home water fleets, he conceded. Concerning our own fleet, Knox states that there was no single fleet which outranks ours, and that there is none with greater fighting range.

Hanson Baldwin has the following to say on this question: (Reader's Digest, Sept., 1940) "Our fleet, in being and authorized, will be by far the world's greatest. The combined tonnage of all four potential enemy navies (this includes Russia's) is now somewhat superior to ours, but in so small a ratio as to offer no danger. Russia is negligible as a sea power. Italy's fleet is composed of high-speed, short-range ships for Mediterranean service. Some of Germany's ships have small cruising range, for duty in the North Sea. Japan's navy has been built primarily for service in the Far East. Of the five then, ours is really the only blue water navy. The totalitarian powers could muster tenuous superiority only if their own waters were stripped of all naval protection, and even then, our own fleet, a tactical, unified whole, fighting in close proximity to its own bases, aided by shore-based aircraft and submarines, would have an insuperable advantage over a conglomeration of ill-adjusted ships operating thousands of miles from bases. Even our small Atlantic squadron, contrary to general belief, would *not* be a pushover for any power; nevertheless, it ought to be strengthened."

DOCUMENT 41

"If Germany captured the British fleet and used to the fullest the ship-building facilities in the conquered countries, could she isolate us from the rest of the world?"
Speakers Bureau
undated [1941]

A. In Questions No. 14 and 17 we have shown that a European naval coalition that included the British fleet might force us into a position of quartersphere, as opposed to Hemisphere defense, but that it would not mean that a successful attack could be launched against North America and the Caribbean. Moreover, this could only be done with very perfect background conditions in Europe.

But this assumes that the attack would come 1) before the "2-Ocean Navy" was completed, 2) and before that building program could be augmented. Much propaganda, without any accompanying explanation, has been written about the 6 to 1 (more or less) shipbuilding advantage our potential enemies would have over us, should Hitler win. There is a great deal of fallacious reasoning in this argument, even if the 6 to 1 ratio is accepted without question.

1) Only a few nations in the world are at present equipped to build battleships and heavy cruisers which are [the] backbone of modern naval strength: Britain, certainly; Germany, certainly; what was France, certainly; Italy, if she can get the armor plate; Japan, if she can get the steel; the United States, most certainly. This cuts into the 6 to 1.

2) 6 to 1 applies at best to the strictly present situation. But we are already adding to our shipbuilding capacity. And nobody knows how much we can add to it in sheer plant capacity, or in speed.

3) Furthermore, 90 per cent or more of a ship, especially "more" in the case of a warship, is steel. And steel is what the industry of the United States is built upon. The plain fact is that the United States has approximately one half the world's steel-making capacity, is now planning to expand it. From 1916 to 1921, the United States showed herself capable of keeping up with the world in naval building, capable enough to scare the British into the 5-5-3 ratio. Unless the attack came immediately, there is no reason to believe that the U.S. is going to be badly outbuilt. And the naval race would be suicidal for the whole world unless stopped by agreement.

DOCUMENT 42

"Is it true the British fleet is America's first line of defense, the one force that separates us from totalitarianism?"
Speakers Bureau
undated [1941]

A. There is no disputing the contention that the possession of the British fleet by a friendly power makes the Atlantic defense of the United States a simple matter. However, the United States fleet is at least as powerful as the

British fleet by itself, and would quite possibly defeat it in pitched battle if the battle were fought not too far from American waters. If the British fleet should be combined with other European navies in an assault against the Americas, its effect might be to make complete Hemisphere defense impractical (see Question No. 14). But it would not reduce the effectiveness of what is called Quartersphere defense—that is, defense of North America and the Caribbean. But even so, an attack against South America (below the "bulge" of Brazil) could only be undertaken by Hitler under very special circumstances—including unity behind him in Europe. And at best it would be a far bigger gamble than Hitler has yet dared. The fact is that Hitler has done very little gambling, as any military expert will tell you, despite the bravado of his speeches.

The only responsible conclusion to draw is that if the British fleet is in unfriendly hands we must look to our Atlantic defenses, think twice about grandiose schemes of Hemisphere defense. In this sense, a friendly British fleet is a luxury, not an indispensability. To say that the British fleet is the one force that separates us from totalitarianism is false; the one force that separates us from totalitarianism is our own determination not to embrace it.

DOCUMENT 43

"To what extent does our economic life depend on foreign trade?
Speakers Bureau
undated [1941]

A. In 1937, the last "good" normal pre-war for American business, the national income was $69.8 billion dollars. Only 5 percent of this total was accounted for by exports. This is the normal ratio—sometimes the proportion is a little more, sometimes a little less—except that, when the trade channels of the world are disrupted by war, the percentage may rise. Britain and France normally used to derive 20 to 25 percent of their income from foreign trade. Since only 5 percent of our income is derived from foreign trade, we are very close to a position of saying "take it or leave it" so far as foreign trade is concerned. Yearly 35 percent of our exports go to Canada and Latin America, channels which presumably can be kept open, and the remainder could, in a pinch, be absorbed by the home market—by raising the purchasing power of under privileged portions of our domestic population. A few important export products, notably cotton and wheat, could not be absorbed that way; but foreign markets for cotton and wheat have been shrinking for years and eventually some other domestic solution must be found for them.

In recent years our exports have been distributed about as follows: to Canada 16 percent, to Latin America 16 percent, to Europe 40 percent, to Asia and the Pacific 20 percent, to all other countries 8 percent. But the important thing to remember is that 40 percent of our exports is only 2 percent of our total national income—except when the peculiar economics of war alters the situation. But war is an economic quicksand.

Exports can be, as they have in the past, increased by subsidization of foreign purchasing power, but that in the end is unprofitable. But under no circumstances are they worth the price of modern war to the people of the United States.

This total view of the export problem is not changed when our own foreign investments are considered. Big as those investments are they do not bulk large in the national economy. And many of them—like the World War debts and those Peruvian bonds—have in the past proved unprofitable.

Present foreign investment is about $10 billion, or one third less than the popular estimate of the cost of the defense program. This is the active "collectable" investment as estimated shortly before the war began. It does not include World War debts, nor some $10 billion of private debts that must be written off as uncollectable—a fact significant in any consideration of foreign trade.

An interesting detail of our foreign investments is the case of China, where we frequently have taken a threatening position in order to maintain the so-called Open Door. Yet our total investment in China is only $132 million plus another $40 million of missionary property. The total is less than the cost of two battleships. Stuart Chase [popular economist and writer] has estimated that only a few days of war in the Pacific would cost more than a generation of profit on our China investment. For Americans the Open Door is a sentimental concept, and no sentimentality is worth much of a price—certainly not the price of war.

DOCUMENT 44

"It is said that if Germany wins, she will capture our world trade and defeat us by strangling our industry. Is this true?"
Speakers Bureau
undated [1941]

A. Although as a nation it cannot be said of us that we must "export or die" as conceivably can be said of both England and Germany, there is another fact about our foreign trade. We import as well as export. Most of our imports are mineral raw materials and the products of tropical agriculture. Although our foreign trade is relatively unimportant in our own economy, our trade figures bulk large in world commerce. And we are the world's greatest market for other people's raw materials. A few raw materials we buy abroad because we cannot produce them at home. A few we could produce at home we buy abroad because foreign production is cheaper. A great many we buy in Latin America, mostly in northern and western parts least accessible to Hitler, and there are others we could buy in Latin America which we now import from Asia and Africa (notably tin and possibly rubber). There is no raw material so indispensable that we need fight outside this hemisphere for it. Two facts emerge from this: one is that as long as we are able to control most of South America Hitler cannot strangle the really essential part of our foreign trade; the other is that since we are the greatest raw material market in the world, he would only be cutting off his nose to spite his face if he successfully withheld raw materials from us.

DOCUMENT 45

"Need we fight in Asia or Africa for rubber and tin, both of which are indispensable materials?"
Speakers Bureau
undated [1941]

A. No.
Several successful synthetic rubbers are now being marketed. Industrialists, engineers, Fortune Magazine and the National Defense Advisory

Commission have all testified that they could be put into mass production in a short time. Meanwhile there is enough rubber on hand to tide us over for many months and that amount is growing. Moreover, within 10 years, Brazilian production could be restored to its former pre-eminence.

There is enough tin in Bolivia to take care of our needs. Plans are already afoot to smelt Bolivian tin here instead of in England where it has been smelted heretofore. Meanwhile, there are large stocks on hand and more is being accumulated. Half the tin we consume (and we consume half the world's production) is used to coat the thin sheets of iron of which "tin" cans are made. The cans could, if necessary, be coated with silver or aluminum.

DOCUMENT 46

"Can Germany cause the gold standard to be abandoned throughout the world—that is, abolish the use of gold as currency—and thereby make our money useless?"
Speakers Bureau
undated [1941]

A. Many people believe that if Germany wins she would not trade, or allow the countries under her domination to trade, with countries using gold as the medium of exchange values. This conclusion is based on the assumption that Germany would take such action in order to be able to compete at no disadvantage with the United States, which now has nearly three-quarters of the world's mined gold in her possession.

Germany might wish to take such action, but it is difficult to believe that she would be able to do so. Gold is the traditional measure of value for commodities and services, and to achieve a stable world currency something of the same sort would have to be used if gold were abolished. In any event, it is nonsense to believe, as many people seem to, that Germany would put us back on the barter system our remote ancestors knew, when goods were exchanged for other goods with no currency in use at all. Germany would, of course, try to rig the money used in world trade to her own advantage, as she has tried to do in South America and as England is now doing there; but it is hard to see how in the long run she could seriously affect our money system. Certainly foreign trade is becoming more or less nationalized in every country in the world, including the United States. This movement has been most marked in Germany. But Hitler is not the sole reason for the world-wide trend.

It is entirely possible that a German victory would force changes in the old system of currency based on gold. If it is unlikely that the total abolition of gold would come about, it is not improbable that changes in its value would result. But gold is not real wealth. America's real wealth lies in her mines, factories, power plants, farm lands, and manpower. These would remain. They would give us our real bargaining power. Our gold policy over the past few years has mostly been a way of subsidizing certain gold-producing nations, including the U.S.S.R. and Japan along with the British Empire. It has increased our wealth hardly at all, and changes in its value, or even the unlikely event of its total abolition, should not wreck our economy.

DOCUMENT 47

"What is the general situation in regard to Latin American trade?"
Speakers Bureau
undated [1941]

A. The U.S. has the lion's share already; it does about as much business with Latin America as Germany, England, France, Italy and Japan *put together*. We have competed and are competing very successfully with Japanese slave labor (daily wage is about 25¢) and German barter and British imperialism, for we do about as much business with Latin America as England, Germany, France, Italy and Japan *put together*. Why shouldn't we continue to do so? As a matter of fact, plans for doing so have already been considered by the Administration: A. A. Berle of the State Department [assistant secretary of state] sponsored a cartelization and barter scheme in May, 1940 for all the Americas (see Fortune Magazine, September, 1940).

These conclusions were arrived at from Fortune Magazine and from the data given in a report issued by the Latin American section of the Department of Commerce, September, 1940. The total exports of twenty Latin American countries (Cuba, Haiti, the Dominican Republic and all others south of the Rio Grande) were $1.84 billions in 1938 and $1.87 billions in 1939; total imports were $1.47 and $1.34 respectively. The percentages taken and given were:

From (or to)	% of Total Exports		% of Total Imports	
	1938	1938	1938	1939
The U.S.	30.5%	34.9%	30.3%	40.3%
The British Isles (excluding Eire)	16.8	16.4	11.5	10.5
Germany	10.4	6.3	16.2	12.9
Japan, France and Italy	6.0	6.9	8.8	7.5

Most of the balance is accounted for by trade among the Latin American countries themselves.

Latin America's export trade with Europe and Japan, therefore, totaled in 1938 $625,000. Which would you choose: to take this over *at a dead loss* (improbable) or fight a war costing $40 billion a year for several years?

DOCUMENT 48

"What strategic war materials do we lack in the United States?"
Speakers Bureau
undated [1941]

A. In only three is the situation really bad. The following data are summarized from a pamphlet prepared by the Commodities Division of the Army and Navy Munitions Board, issued in March 1940.

Strategic materials are defined as "those essential to national defense, for the supply of which in war dependence must be placed in whole, or in substantial part, on sources outside the continental limits of the United States; and for which strict conservation and distribution control measures will be necessary."

Critical materials are defined as "those essential to national defense, the procurement problems of which in war would be less difficult than those of strategic materials either because they have a lesser degree of essentiality or are obtainable in more adequate quantities from domestic sources; and for which some degree of conservation and distribution control will be necessary." These will not be here considered; they are aluminum, asbestos, cork, graphite, hides, iodine, kapok, opium, optical glass, phenol, platinum, tanning materials, toluol, vanadium, and wool.

H. G. S. summarizes and interprets the data thus:

1. Our own mines or fair-to-satisfactory substitutes are available for 7 of the 14 materials: coconut shell char, mercury, mica, quinine, rubber, silk, and tungsten. This leaves 7.

2. Latin American or Canadian sources are adequate for 3 more: antimony, nickel, quartz crystal.

3. Inferior substitutes are available for one: manilla fibre.

4. This leaves 3 in which the situation is bad: tin, manganese and chromium. Although the tin situation is less bad than that of the other two, we should lay in extensive stock piles of all three. This we are doing. We should also encourage as much as possible the development of Bolivian tin mines.

DOCUMENT 49

The Strategic Materials

Speakers Bureau
undated [1941]

Material	Main Uses	Possible Substitutes	Main Present Source	Possible War-time Sources
1. Antimony	Batteries	None	87% from Latin America	Latin America
2. Chromium	Special steels	None	Russia, Africa	Cuba produces a totally unsatisfactory 7% of our imports.

Material	Main Uses	Possible Substitutes	Main Present Source	Possible War-time Sources
3. Coconut shell char	Gas masks	Synthetic chemicals	South Seas	Substitutes entirely satisfactory at present.
4. Manganese	Special steels	None	Russia, Africa	Cuba produces 25% of our imports; but only stock files could fill our needs.
5. Manilla fibre	Rope	Mostly unsatis factory	Philippines	Central Ameri can sources are increasing; inferior substitutes might have to be used.
6. Mercury	Explosives, etc.	None	⅔ from Spain, ⅓ from our mines	Our own mines will be adequate
7. Mica	Electrical equipment	Synthetic chemicals	India	Substitutes will be adequate.
8. Nickel	Special steels	None	Canada	Canada
9. Quartz crystal	Radios	None	Brazil	Brazil
10. Quinine	In malaria	Synthetic chemicals	East Indies	None except for fair synthetics.
11. Rubber	Countless, indispensable	Synthetic chemicals	East Indies	Could reclaim ¼ of needs; synthetics are being produced rapidly and will be fairly adequate.
12. Silk	Parachutes	Synthetic chemicals	Japan, China	Synthetics are almost entirely satisfactory.
13. Tin	"Cans," solder, etc., etc.	None in most cases	Asia, Bolivia	Some substitutes are satisfactory; Bolivia is fair; need stock-piles.
14. Tungsten	Special steels	Molybdenum	Asia, U.S., Bolivia	Molybdenum and domestic mines.

DOCUMENT 50

Buy or Die

"Did you know that Hitler, even if victorious over Europe and the Mediterranean countries, cannot dominate our trade?"
No. 6, July 5, 1941

The Claim

They (the dictatorships) would fasten an economic strangle-hold upon our several nations. . . . Wages and hours would be fixed by Hitler. . . . The American farmer would get for his products exactly what Hitler wanted to give. He would face obvious disaster and complete regimentation (President Roosevelt, in his "unlimited emergency" speech of May 27, 1941, reported in Christian Science Monitor, May 28).

The Answer

However, the import requirements of Nazi Europe are so large and so varied that she is scarcely in a position to buy or refrain from buying at will. Her exports are wanted, but are not indispensable. Barring the use of force, her position in world markets will be as weak or as strong as her capacity to pay for the goods she needs. Clearly this is an issue whose outcome cannot be dictated entirely by Nazi Europe ("Nazi Europe and World Trade," published by the Brookings Institution, June, 1941, page 184).

The United States can undersell totalitarian countries in world trade, according to Bernard M. Baruch, formerly chairman of Woodrow Wilson's War Industries Board, now a national defense consultant to the Roosevelt Administration . . . Mr. Baruch pointed out that Germany, not the United States, would be 'on the spot' economically if Germany were to win control of the European continent (in interview reported in The Wall Street Journal, June 6, 1941).

The "Economic Menace"

Interventionists originally sought to frighten the American people into willingness to support American entry into the current war by lurid tales of military invasion of the Western Hemisphere by the triumphant Nazi war machine. When that theory was exploded by the military facts, the interventionists dug up the "Economic Menace." The American people were told that a Nazi-dominated Europe threatened our very way of life; that our trade would collapse before the ingenuity of the Nazis; that we would be subdued without the necessity of military attack. The "economic" theory could be advanced persuasively because there was little evidence available of either its accuracy or its falsity. Presumably, the absence of evidence accounts for the fact that the President was persuaded to adopt the theory in his "unlimited emergency" speech of May 27. Now the evidence is available; the "economic" theory is shown to have little basis in economic fact.

Nazi Europe

We can test the "economic" theory. Assume that the Nazis have military control of the entire continent of Europe (for the moment we can except the Soviet Union and the Soviet-dominated states). Make the further (and unlikely) assumption that they are able to unify the numerous nationalities of Europe, suppress or alleviate the age-old hatreds, obtain willing and eager cooperation from the sullen millions of their victims, and co-ordinate the productive capacities of the continent into one integrated, centrally controlled, economic and political unit. That unit would comprise twenty-one countries (Albania, Austria, Belgium, Luxembourg, Bulgaria, Czechoslovakia, Denmark, France, Germany, Greece, Hungary, Italy, Netherlands, Norway, Poland, Portugal, Rumania, Spain, Sweden, Switzerland, and Yugoslavia). Assume further that the Nazis are able to bring into that unit the eleven non-European countries which border the Mediterranean Sea (Algeria, Morocco, Tunisia, Libya, Tangier Zone, Egypt, Turkey, Syria, Lebanon, Palestine and Cyprus). Such assumptions are more than generous to the advocates of the "economic" theory of conquest: they give the Nazis control over countries in Europe, North Africa and the Near East which are yet unconquered.

How Strong Is Nazi Europe

The popular impression fostered by interventionists is based on the assumption that the Nazi regime has been greatly strengthened economically by its conquests, especially in its power to influence trade relations with the nations of the Western Hemisphere. That impression is shown to be far from accurate in a current study published by the Brookings Institution, a conservative and eminently authoritative research institution ("Nazi Europe and World Trade," by Cleona Lewis, published in June, 1941). In this memorandum are discussed the resources and needs of a Nazi-controlled Europe as Dr. Lewis has analysed them. Other aspects of the problem will be treated in subsequent memoranda.

Hitler's Problems

Dr. Lewis's study is based upon two "control" years, 1929 and 1937. The first year was chosen because the Dawes Plan and American loans had made it a prosperous one. The second was chosen because it was one of great business activity and normal trade relations for Germany—it was before the economies of European countries had been seriously distorted by "the purchase and storage of goods for war purposes" (page 3). Since no accurate data are available, no consideration is given to the cost, time and difficulties, obviously tremendous, of repairing the damage to productive capacities caused by the devastation and dislocations of war. In view of the staggering nature of the reconstruction problems, the study is reasonable in assuming that the 1929 and 1937 figures mark the maximum potential resources of Nazi Europe for several years to come. So vast would be the reconstruction job that Hitler would face that the strength attributed to Nazi Europe in the study probably exceeds its actual strength. The study does not consider the possibility that the total volume of European production might increase under more efficient cultivation or resources and more efficient industrial operation. That possibility lies entirely in the realm of speculation, and is subject to a multitude of factors. Even the famed German ingenuity cannot do very much to expand food and industrial raw material production in Europe. The study makes it clear that Europe's "climate, soil, and topography, and the poverty of its subsoil, all place limitations on its domestic output" (page 175).

Nazi Trade Weaknesses

Except for these speculative qualifications which can be too easily over-emphasized, the study shows clearly that Nazi Europe—if it ever comes—will be in no position to dictate the nature and terms of world trade or of the trade of the Western Hemisphere countries. Paradoxical as it may sound, "Germany's supply problem has not been solved by her seizure of neighboring territories. On the contrary, it has been made more difficult. Raw-material imports, in particular, are considerably larger for the whole area than they were for Germany alone—whether they are measured in absolute or relative terms" (page 178). Despite the fact that Nazi Europe furnishes the "living space" the Nazis claimed was vital to Germany's existence, Germany's trade position is now weaker than before the war.

The Nazi Reich—Buyer

This is because Germany, before entry upon her career of aggression, was ultimately dependent upon outside sources for food and raw materials. Far from attaining independence of foreign sources for food and raw materials by her conquests, Germany has become more dependent than ever before upon foreign sources. The old Reich, both in 1929 and 1937, managed to maintain a slightly larger volume of exports than of imports, to sell more than she bought. Consequently she was in a position to drive a good bargain (page 178). Her foreign trade was fairly stable from 1925 through 1937, with foods and raw materials accounting for about 90%, usually, of her imports, and manufactured goods making up from 65% to 80% of her exports. This ratio held good, in the main, even despite the much-exaggerated Nazi trade drive and Nazi attempts to force surplus manufactured goods down the throats of Latin American and other foreign trade countries (pages 8–9).

Nazi Europe—Larger Buyer

Of the 20 European countries assumed to be under Nazi sway, only three really complement and help the Nazi economy by being exporters of foods and raw materials, and importers of manufactures (Bulgaria, Rumania, Yugoslavia). Ten others are helpful to the Nazis in part. Six of these (Denmark, Hungary, Netherlands, Poland, Portugal, and Spain) dovetail with the German economy in that they export more food than they buy, and import more manufactured goods than they sell; but they are dependent, like the old Germany, for most of their raw materials on outside sources. The four others in this second group (Albania, Greece, Norway, and Sweden) also help the old Reich in that they can supply raw materials and buy manufactures; but these countries are a detriment in that they must buy foods from outside sources. The last six [seven] states (Austria, Belgium, Luxembourg, Czechoslovakia, France, Italy, Switzerland) are like Germany in that they must sell their manufactured goods to the outside world, and must buy foods and raw materials. These are the large industrial countries whose subjugation is popularly supposed to constitute a great triumph for the Nazis. Actually, they furnish little opportunity for additional economic "living space." Once they are linked with Germany as a unit in Nazi Europe, they must buy from outside sources twice as much foodstuffs as the old Reich and almost three times as many raw materials, and they must sell almost twice as many manufactures. They have made Germany's presumed goal, independence of outside sources, much more difficult of attainment (pages 11–13).

The Mediterranean Countries

These figures are not changed materially even if the Nazis control the eleven non-European countries bordering the Mediterranean Sea. On the basis of 1937 data, the latter provide only about 19% of the food and 8% of the raw materials needed by Nazi Europe, and take only 16% of the manufactured goods which Nazi Europe must sell. In short, "larger Germany would have to import more food and raw materials, and find larger markets for manufactures, than were required for the old Reich" (pages 15–16).

What the effect of the conquest of Soviet Russia and Great Britain would be will be considered in detail in another memorandum. Nevertheless, it should be stated here that the subjugation of Russia would not ease the economic problems of a Nazi Europe as much as has been popularly supposed. In 1929 and 1937 Russia's exports of foods and raw materials amounted to no more than four percent of Nazi Europe's needs (including Mediterranean countries). Nor is Russia much of a market for Nazi Europe's manufactured goods (page 16).

Buy Or Die

Nazi Europe therefore must import or die. Without food imports, Europe's population must go on short rations, because of shortages of cereals, fats, vegetable oils, meats, and dairy products. Without raw material imports, the textile industries would be crippled (for lack of sufficient supplies of cotton, wool, silk, jute, flax and hemp); the leatherworking industries would be gravely impaired; large-scale synthetic rubber production would be necessary, which would in turn create new raw material needs. Without industrial mineral imports, "manufacturing, mining, transportation, communication and even agriculture would be severely handicapped." Machines and machine tools could no longer be made because of the lack of alloy metals and bearing metals. The automotive and electrical industries would suffer from lack of asbestos, mica, non-synthetic oils, copper and other minerals. There would be enough coal unless (a very likely probability) the resort to synthetic production of rubber, hosiery, and gasoline caused a coal shortage (pages 175–177).

Nazi Europe will have to import. Without imports, even the manufacture of the goods which she must sell in order to buy more food and more raw materials will be crippled. Nazi Europe will be in no position to buy or not to buy, as she pleases, and therefore drive a hard bargain or dictate her own terms. *The bargaining advantage will rest with the Western Hemisphere countries and the other countries of the world which have for sale the products Nazi Europe needs.*

DOCUMENT 51

Swastika over Sickle

"Did you know *that even if Nazi Germany conquers Communist Russia, the enlarged German economy may be weakened rather than strengthened?*"
No. 15, August 1, 1941

The Claim

With these (Russia's) great natural resources at his command, Hitler would be vastly nearer than he is today to the domination of the earth. Any anxiety over his supplies of raw materials that may plague him today would cease to worry him (H. N. Brailsford, British journalist just arrived in America from London. Baltimore Sun, June 23, 1941).

The Answer

German exploitation of Russian resources must be considered as a very long-range project of the Nazis . . . . many of the raw materials that will be used to prepare the (invasion) campaign cannot be replaced from Russian supplies even in the event of victory (J. G. Simonds. New York Herald-Tribune, July 17, 1941).

The United States can undersell totalitarian countries in world trade, according to Bernard M. Baruch, chairman of President Wilson's War Industries Board (from an interview as reported in the Wall Street Journal, June 6, 1941).

Scare Story

Did You Know #6 analyzes the economic position of Germany, assuming that Hitler had conquered all of Europe plus the countries of Asia and Africa which border the Mediterranean Sea. The conclusion was that Nazi Europe would be forced to import even more food and raw materials, and discover even larger export markets for her manufactures than were required by the old Germany. Therefore, an enlarged Germany—despite her new "living space"—would be in no position to dictate the terms on which she would trade. Since June 22, interventionists have been making a great to-do over the effect of a possible Russian collapse. They have been seeing a Germany, already fat from the conquest of Western Europe, emerging from the Russian war still more powerful, and ready to run the world's international trade on any terms that Adolf Hitler might care to devise—with nobody in position to talk back. Actually, when the facts are examined, this nightmarish concept is seen to have little foundation. The conquest of Russia would contribute little to Germany's bargaining power. For the present, at least, it would contribute little to Germany's available wealth. That is if trade and production figures mean what they say. Germany's economy still would be unbalanced as ever (See Did You Know #6) and the German dream of self-sufficiency as remote as ever from realization.

Big Picture

The effect on world commerce of the unification of Nazi Europe into one economy which included the whole of the continent west of the Soviet Union and all the countries of Africa and Asia bordering on the Mediterranean has been studied by Cleona Lewis of the Brookings Institution in her recent book "Nazi Europe and World Trade." Basing her study on the two carefully selected years 1937 and 1929, Dr. Lewis makes clear that such a Europe would be a net importer of food and many essential raw materials such as oil, copper and lead without which a modern industrial state cannot exist. Because Europe still would have to buy these materials Dr. Lewis concludes that Hitler would be no more able to dictate the terms of world trade than he was before the war. Europe simply does not produce enough food, and nobody can dig minerals from the earth which are not there. If the undeveloped expanses of the Soviet Union were to become a part of Nazi Europe—or Nazi Eurasia—Dr. Lewis finds that Germany's position would hardly be improved at all. Remember that a Nazi Europe includes the African and Near Eastern countries which border the Mediterranean, then add Russia. From Dr. Lewis's tables (pp. 15–16) the following facts can be deduced: Russia's *total* exports to *all* countries of foodstuffs amounted to only 14 per cent of a Nazi Europe's *net* imports of foodstuffs in 1937, to only 11 per cent in 1929; Russia's *total* exports to *all* countries of raw materials amounted to only 8 per cent of a Nazi Europe's *net* imports in 1937, to only 9 per cent in 1929. ("Net" figures are used for a Nazi Europe to allow for trade between countries included here in the total Nazi economy—such as wheat shipped from Algiers to Europe, or copper shipped from Cyprus.) Obviously, then, a Nazi economy that included Russia and the Baltic countries once dominated by Russia would still have to buy food and raw materials in the world market—or die.

Oil Drama

Overall statistics of net imports and total exports are meaningful to economists, but they sometimes are both meaningless and dull to those unfamiliar with them. However, the statistics of eggs and gasoline, bread and steel and other specific products tell a story clear to everybody who knows that nations and their armies must be fed and equipped to live and act by farms and mines and factories. The most dramatic raw material of modern war is oil, the most dramatic statistics are oil statistics. In the public eye at least, oil is even more dramatic if not more important than steel, aluminum, copper and wheat. Without the oil to drive them, Hitler's Luftwaffe and his Panzer divisions would be impotent. Because the Soviet Union is the world's second producer of oil, interventionist alarmists see in the possible conquest of the Russians the acquisition by Hitler of a tremendous new oil supply to fuel his engines of war and perhaps dominate the world's oil trade. To hold this view is to overlook the facts of oil in Russia. Great as it is, Russian production does not compare with that of the U.S. The Russian oil may not do Hitler very much good. What *Fortune* has to say about Russia's oil production and consumption is pertinent:

> . . . the Soviet industrial machine is extraordinarily dependent on oil, and its needs are constantly rising. According to one estimate, oil meets 15 per cent of the U.S.S.R.'s total fuel requirements, most vital of which are concerned with the national food supply. In the first place, more than 60 per cent of all Soviet motor fuel produced last year, according to the Soviet press, was consumed by the half-million tractors on the Soviet farms. The tractors are no luxury; since the slaughter of 15 million horses by peasants rebelling against collectivization, mechanized farming has been a necessity. Moreover, at the point of food consumption kerosene is the standard cooking fuel. ("Soviet Industry," *Fortune,* July 1941, p. 84.)

None to Spare

If a conquered Russia were deprived of most of the oil she produces, her economic life would be reduced to a hopeless state of non-productivity, which would be small help to the Nazis in war or peace. In addition, Russia, despite her huge total oil output, actually is acutely short of regular gasoline and aviation gasoline, two oil products in which the Nazis are presumed to be interested (L. E. Frechtling—New York Times, June 29, 1941). Moreover, during recent years, oil exports have dropped from 6,000,000 tons in 1932 to 1,5000,000 tons in 1938 and "even that amount was released only because certain imports were needed badly enough to warrant the sacrifice" (*Fortune*, ibid). Russia agreed to ship 900,000 tons of oil into Germany in 1940 in return for a quantity of machinery. Both sides fell down on deliveries. Russia shipped only 700,000 tons of oil. Because Russia had added some 550,000 tons of Polish oil to her production, the Germans are supposed to have upped their demand to 1,000,000 tons for 1941. Russia's inability to deliver on the new agreement may or may not have helped bring the Nazi invasion. At any rate, the new agreement was a hardship, for by the end of

1940 the Soviet government had been obliged to introduce even stricter rationing of oil consumption than ever before. As *Fortune* (ibid) concludes: "It is evident that Soviet Russia has no oil to spare."

The Cupboard Is Bare

Because it is so easy to regard the vast expanses of Russia, especially the "black earth" region of the Ukraine, as one huge granary, it is commonly supposed that annexation of the Russian economy would not only break the British blockade in war but render a Nazi Europe so self-sufficient in food that the food-exporting nations of the Western Hemisphere would have to approach Hitler on bended knee, imploring him to buy their wheat and corn on any terms he deigned to name. To hold this view is—as in the case of oil—to ignore the facts. According to a statement made public July 9, 1941, by Paul S. Willis, President of the Associated Grocery Manufacturers of America, Russia has not been an important exporter of food since the World War, and her own deficiencies have been considerable. Only by deliberately starving the Russians could Hitler receive much food from Russia. A successful "scorched earth" policy on the part of Russia would make it still more difficult—at least for the discernible future. At best, Hitler would be faced with a serious dilemma. To get much oil out of Russia he must curtail the use of tractors on the Soviet farms. To get much food out of Russia he must keep the tractors running full blast and starve the Russians, thus lowering their productivity (J. G. Simonds, New York Herald Tribune, July 17, 1941). Moreover, food is already short in Russian cities (New York Times, July 17, 1941). The plain fact is that, in the past, the area included here in a Nazi Europe has imported about 60 per cent of its grain, about 15 per cent of its vegetable oils, about 50 per cent of its tobacco, and nearly all of its coffee from the Western Hemisphere; the same area has, in the past, consumed less than one-half of one per cent of Russia's grain production (Cleona Lewis, "Nazi Europe and World Trade," pp. 23, 57). It is obvious that even a victorious Hitler must buy food, and buy food in the Western Hemisphere. The Western Hemisphere can make it a seller's market, and therefore can dictate terms to Hitler.

Ores of War

A Nazi Europe would be able to show little gain in the discernible future in the matter of raw materials, should it annex the total Soviet economy. Unless Soviet industry is to be abandoned, Russia has little surplus coal and iron for export. However, a Nazi Europe is approximately self-sufficient in these basic minerals. Russia is an importer of aluminum, the key metal in the airplane industry, and thus adds nothing to the Nazi airplane industry, which would have to continue to draw on deposits in France, Hungary,

Germany and the Balkans. Russia also is an importer of copper without which there can be no electrical industry. So is a Nazi Europe, which ordinarily draws on the Western Hemisphere for 80 per cent of its supply (Cleona Lewis, ibid, p. 86; J. G. Simonds, ibid). About 50 per cent of the lead Nazi Europe requires for the storage batteries of automobiles, trucks, tanks, tractors and submarines, for type metal, and for many chemical industries must be imported; normally, about two-thirds of the imports come from the Western Hemisphere (Cleona Lewis, ibid, pp. 90, 129). Russia has no important lead deposits under exploitation (J. G. Simonds, ibid). Two important alloys essential to certain high grade steels present a somewhat different picture. Chromium, for stainless steel, though mined in the Balkans, is a serious Nazi deficiency. By stripping Soviet industry, Nazi Europe could utilize Russia's mine production (Cleona Lewis, ibid., p. 108). Russia is the world's No. 1 producer of manganese, indispensable in the purifying of steel. In 1937, the manganese imports of Nazi Europe amounted to 50 per cent of Russia's production (Cleona Lewis, ibid, p. 107). Nevertheless, it is believed that Russia could fill all Nazi Europe's needs (J. G. Simonds, ibid). Nazi Europe has next to no nickel, the essential alloy in armor plate. Neither the Finnish mines—now in Nazi Europe—nor the Russian can begin to make up the deficiency (Cleona Lewis, ibid, p. 108; J. G. Simonds, ibid). Other important mineral deficiencies of Nazi Europe which Russia is unprepared to make up include tin, tungsten, antimony, vanadium, and molybdenum, all essential to a productive economy, both in war and in peace.

Cotton No King

Nor would a Nazi Europe gain much in the way of non-mineral industrial raw materials by conquering Russia and adding the Russian economy to her own. The three most important materials in this class probably are cotton, wool and rubber. A Nazi Europe which included Egypt would have cotton, but it would not have enough by two-thirds (Cleona Lewis, ibid, p. 61). The United States, of course, is the principal source of supply. Russia could supply only a small amount of low grade cotton (J. G. Simonds, ibid). A Nazi Europe must depend on outside sources for most of its wool supply (Cleona Lewis, ibid). Russia has no wool available for Nazi Europe (J. G. Simonds, ibid). Nobody knows precisely, but Nazi Europe is possibly self-sufficient in *synthetic* rubber—at least for military needs. But if this is true, it is at the expense of her coal supply from which the ersatz material is made. Nazi Europe has no natural rubber. Neither has Russia—save for an inferior grade made from a plant called kok-saghyz (*Fortune*, ibid, p.90). Russia also manufactures inferior grades of ersatz rubber in unknown amounts (*Fortune*, ibid, p. 91).

DOCUMENT 52

The All-American Front

*"Did you know that the Western Hemisphere by itself possesses
all the materials necessary for American industry in war or
peace?"*
No. 17, August 8, 1941

The Claim

If Hitler wins, we can expect . . . a growing shortage of certain critical
materials, which up to now have been secured from the Old World. These
shortages . . . might mean dangerous deficiencies in certain areas of our defense
program and in the supply of many goods commonly used in the United States.
(Douglas Miller, "You Can't Do Business with Hitler," pages 206–207.)

The Answer

In so far as strategic raw materials vital to the waging of war are concerned, our
hemispheric self-sufficiency is, therefore, more than adequate to practically any
demand. (Hanson W. Baldwin, in "United We Stand," page 87.)

In these days of uncertainty and fear, Americans are prone to believe the
repeated contentions of the alarmists. A claim frequently voiced is that the
United States is so dependent upon sources outside the Western Hemisphere for its supplies of vital materials that we would be crippled should
the Axis powers seize far-off lands whose names are strange to Americans.
Examination of the facts refutes this claim. We need not go to war for rubber
or tin; American boys need not fight and die in Dong Dang or Bangkok. The
Western Hemisphere is self-sufficient in terms of raw material resources.

We Are Strong

These resources are the iron, copper, aluminum, coal, tin, rubber, nickel,
manganese, oil, and cotton (to mention a few) without which modern
industry, modern living standards—and modern war—would be impossible.
Actually, the U.S. is blessed as is no other nation in the sufficiency of its raw
materials and in its capacity to convert them into necessary, useful goods
(Fleming MacLiesh & Cushman Reynolds, "Strategy of the Americas," p.
12). The U.S. normally produces two fifths of the world's steel (and could

produce far more), three fifths of its oil, one third of its coal, one third of its copper, four fifths of its sulphur, one quarter of its lead, three tenths of its zinc, and sizable portions of most of the rest of the basic raw materials (Hanson W. Baldwin, "United We Stand," p. 311). Some students even think that by careful regimentation, and by the development of substitutes, the U.S. could be entirely, though uncomfortably, self-sufficient. But that is an extreme view (MacLiesh & Reynolds, ibid).

All Here

There are some basic materials which are not produced at all in the U.S., or of which insufficient quantities are produced. In the past, some of these materials have been imported from Asia, Africa and Europe, as well as from Canada and Latin America. With a few minor exceptions, all of them—with proper development—can be procured within the Western Hemisphere (MacLiesh and Reynolds, ibid, p. 13; Baldwin, ibid, pp. 85–87; Hubert Herring, "Good Neighbors," pp. 343–344).

Vital Materials

The Army and Navy Munitions Board lists as "strategic" fourteen materials "for which strict conservation and control measures" are necessary because their sources are entirely or substantially outside the continental limits of the U.S. They are: antimony, chromium, coconut shell char, manganese, manila fiber, mercury, mica, nickel, quartz crystal, quinine, rubber, silk, tin, tungsten (MacLiesh & Reynolds, ibid, pp. 14–37). The Board also lists fifteen materials as "critical" which are produced in somewhat more substantial quantities at home than the "strategic" materials or are somewhat less important in themselves. They are: aluminum, asbestos, cork, graphite, hides, iodine, kapok, opium, phenol, optical glass, platinum, tanning materials, toluol, vanadium, wool (MacLiesh & Reynolds, ibid, pp. 37–42). Some control has been imposed over our supplies of these materials, and steps have been taken to build up reserve supplies (stockpiles). Further, study of the available sources of these materials, one by one, shows the self-sufficiency of the Western Hemisphere. (The following information is from MacLiesh & Reynolds, ibid., pp. 14–42. See also Baldwin, ibid, pp. 308–314; Herring, ibid, pp. 343–344.)

Strategic

Antimony, an important steel alloy: increased production in Mexico, Bolivia and in the U.S. can negate our present reliance on China. *Chromium,* another steel alloy, also required in chemical industries: increased production in Cuba, in Brazil, where reserves are hardly touched, in Canada, and on the U.S. Pacific Coast, could negate reliance on Turkey, U.S.S.R., Southern Rhodesia, and the Philippines. *Coconut Shell Char*, used for gas mask filters and other chemical appliances: coconuts from the coasts of tropical America would serve as well as coconuts from the Far Eastern tropics for these and other purposes—and there are substitutes. *Manganese (ferrograde)*, indispensable in the purification of steel: Cuba and Brazil (if her reserves were developed) could supplant the U.S.S.R., Africa's Gold Coast and India; and increased domestic production, already under way, will be a further help. *Manila Fiber*, for marine cordage: it can be grown all over Central America as easily as in the Philippines, and there are substitutes and a stockpile. *Mercury*, essential in the detonators of artillery shells, in many precision instruments, and in the chemical industries: expanded domestic production, plus increased production in Mexico—and Bolivia— make up for the loss of Spanish and Italian sources. *Mica*, essential to radio, automotive and aviation industries for insulation: strategic mica can be produced in the U.S., Canada, Argentina and Brazil—though more expensively than in India and Madagascar—and there are laboratory substitutes. *Nickel*, essential to armor plate: 85 to 90 per cent of the world's supply comes from Canada. *Quartz Crystal*, one type of which is essential to certain radio equipment: the strategic type comes from Brazil. *Quinine*, for malaria: it can be grown in Peru and Brazil as easily as in the Netherlands Indies; there is a large stockpile; and there are two laboratory substitutes.

Strategic, Too

Rubber, most dramatic of U.S. raw material deficiencies, is of thousand-fold indispensability: domestic consumption has already been ordered cut about 25 per cent by OPM (New York Times, June 20, 1941), but large stocks on hand, plus a growing synthetic industry, will prevent any real emergency, whatever happens in the Netherlands Indies and British Malaya. Moreover, as a long range solution to the rubber problem, there is the slowly expanding production of Brazil, Central America and Haiti. *Silk*, for ladies stockings and lingerie, for the powder bags for larger artillery shells, and for parachutes, comes from Japan: further production for civilian consumption has been stopped by OPM (New York Times, July 27, 1941), but there are stocks on hand, and nylon, rayon and other substitutes are available. Eventually, raw silk may be produced in Brazil (Herring, ibid). *Tin*, only a little less dramatic than rubber, for tin cans, solders and bearings: the government stockpile, now slightly more than a year's requirements (Baltimore Sun, July 30, 1941), the new smelter in construction at Texas City to smelt 18,000 tons of Bolivian tin a year, the use of glass and other substitutes (New York Times, July 10, 1941)—these can offset the much publicized reliance on the Netherlands Indies and British Malaya. *Tungsten*, another steel alloy: a stockpile, increased domestic production, and the new three-year contract to buy Bolivia's entire output (New York Times, May 22, 1941) relieve worry about what would happen if the Burma Road were blocked by the Japanese and the Chinese supply cut off; moreover, molybdenum, on which the U.S. has a world monopoly, can be used instead.

Critical

Aluminum means airplanes—and pots and pans: the present shortage is due to a lack of manufacturing capacity and to bad planning; there is enough readily extractable ore in the U.S., and in the Guianas in South America, to make the planes, the pots, the pans. *Asbestos,* for insulation against heat: it comes from Canada. *Cork* probably cannot be produced in this Hemisphere, but substitutes can be, and there is a stockpile. *Graphite,* for foundry facings, crucibles, electrodes, "lead" pencils: it could be procured in Mexico and Canada instead of Ceylon, Madagascar and Korea. *Hides:* necessary imports are procurable from Argentina, Uruguay, Paraguay, Brazil, Canada and elsewhere in this Hemisphere where cattle are raised. *Iodine:* Chile is the principal source. *Kapok,* from a tree in the East Indies and Malaya, is used to stuff life preservers and furniture: it could be grown all over tropical America—and there are substitutes. *Opium:* there is a stockpile. *Optical Glass,* for range-finders, cameras and microscopes: U.S. industry can produce it. *Phenol,* for plastics, is made from coal tar. *Platinum,* for the electrical industry: Colombia, Canada and Alaska could produce more than we need. *Tanning Materials,* to make leather: they come from various parts of South America, notably Argentina. *Toluol,* for TNT, is made from soft coal or petroleum. *Vanadium,* another steel alloy: the U.S. produces half what it uses, the rest comes from Peru. *Wool,* for uniforms—and civilian clothes: in a pinch, expanded domestic production, and increased imports from Argentina and Uruguay, could offset reliance on Australia and New Zealand; and there is a stockpile.

Progress Report

To list the Western Hemisphere sources of the "strategic" and "critical" materials is not to say that hemisphere self-sufficiency is an accomplished fact. In Washington, there has been a serious lack of raw material planning for the defense program (not to mention peacetime production). The tangled aluminum situation is only the most conspicuous example (Uncensored, July 19, 1941). Not until this summer has OPM adopted measures to preclude dangerous shortages of tin and rubber by restricting consumption (Uncensored, July 19, 1941; New York Times, June 20, 1941). Hemisphere sources are only being scratched. For instance, the difficulty of bucking the British-controlled international tin cartel in Bolivia (MacLiesh & Reynolds, ibid, pp. 28–29) has prevented the building of a smelter in this country capable of turning out more than 20 per cent of U.S. needs—despite the fact that Bolivia could produce several times that amount. However, the Defense Supplies Corporation and the Metals Reserve Company (subsidiaries of the RFC) have bought since last November 250,000 tons of Latin American copper (mostly from Chile), 300,000 tons of Chilean nitrates, and 18,000 tons of Brazilian manganese (of which production could be expanded enormously). Huge purchases of wool and hides have already been made from Argentina and Uruguay. The Metals Reserve Company has contracted to buy Bolivia's entire output of tungsten for three years, and tungsten flows in from Peru, Mexico and Argentina. Extra zinc and lead have been bought in Latin America. The U.S. recently concluded an agreement with Brazil under which the U.S. will for two years purchase Brazil's entire export surplus of rubber, titanium, nickel, iron, zirconium, bauxite (aluminum ore), industrial diamonds, mica crystals, beryllium, chromite and manganese. The U.S. expects to buy Mexico's entire production of mercury and to import pig lead from Mexico, Peru and Canada (Pan American News, July 3, 1941; Uncensored, July 19, 1941). But the flow of imports is being impeded because ships have been diverted to the British (Washington Times Herald, July 7, 1941; see also House Hearings on H. J. Res. 77, 77th Congress, p. 9). Despite the slow progress in importing the vast current raw material production of Latin America and in assisting in the development of those resources toward full production, it is evident that the United States has little to fear with regard to its requirements in basic raw material wealth—even in the remote event that Hitler not only gains a military decision, but also succeeds in organizing the European economy (see Did You Know #6, #15).

(With these facts in mind, the claim that a Nazi Europe would rule world trade can be examined further. It has already been pointed out that a Nazi Europe must buy tremendous quantities of foodstuffs and raw materials in a seller's market [Did You Know, #6], and that even the conquest of Russia would not materially supply those needs [Did You Know, #15]. This study reveals that the Western Hemisphere need not rely upon any area under Nazi control for needed materials. In subsequent studies, attention will be given to other phases of the problem of world trade should the Nazis control Europe and Russia: the economic, the military, and the political factors involved in opposing a Western Hemisphere economy to the strength of Nazi Europe.)

DOCUMENT 53

The Economics of Hemisphere Defense

"Did you know *that the manner in which the Administration is carrying out the Lease-Lend bill is crippling our policy of hemisphere defense?*"
No. 23A, September 19, 1941

All-American Front

Did You Know #17 showed that the Western Hemisphere has the raw material resources to keep its factory wheels turning, and its living standards rising *even if* Adolph Hitler controls the raw materials of *all* the other continents of the world.

Arms Not Enough

The present memoranda (23A and 23B) describe in broad terms the necessary economic basis which must precede and undergird any adequate program of hemisphere defense. Vice-President Henry A. Wallace has declared that "The American Republics can minimize the possibility of ultimate military attack if they unify their economic power." (*Economic Union for the Americas,* University of Chicago Round Table, June 30, 1940.) The theory of military defense for the Western Hemisphere has already been endorsed by 86% of the people. (Gallup Poll, *Washington Post,* May 14, 1941.) But it is axiomatic that nations tend to throw their military weight on the side of those countries with which their economic interests are identified. Therefore, a hemisphere economic plan *must* evolve by which the United States satisfies, to a far greater degree than heretofore, the trade needs of Latin America. Otherwise, the nations to the south will be forced into the hands of European and Asiatic dictators. Now, with European trade cut off by the war, the opportunity has come to weld together, once and for all, the economies of North and South America. Such a program will not be achieved without sacrifice on our part, but the long-term dividends will far outweigh the immediate cost. In considering such a plan, this memorandum (23A) discusses 1) problems arising out of Latin America's trade with the United States, and with Europe [and] 2) present obstacles in the way of increased inter-American trade. Did You Know 23B will discuss 1) proposed plans for an integrated Western Hemisphere economy, and 2) steps already taken for inter-American cooperation.

World Market

Latin America as a whole operates on a semi-colonial economy (*Fortune,* December, 1937). That is, its raw materials are produced—largely by foreign capital—shipped to industrial Europe or the United States, processed into manufactured articles, and finally sold back into the world market. Obviously then, Latin American nations are in general dependent, for their foreign exchange, upon the world prices of raw materials. (*The Foreign Trade of Latin America,* U.S. Tariff Commission, Part 1, p. 44, 45.) When the world price for Latin American raw material exports is low, our neighbors to the South have less money with which to buy the exports of the United States and other exporting nations, and also lack exchange to apply on their foreign debts.

Latin America Must Sell

It is essential that total exports from Latin America exceed total imports into that area if 1) she is to be able to pay for her imports, 2) pay interest on her already large debts to foreign governments and foreign banks, 3) pay for shipping services which are now almost entirely in the hands of non-Latin American nations. Other than exports, there are three main ways by which Latin America has been assisted in meeting her outside obligations; 1) money spent by travelers in Latin America, 2) disbursements in Latin America by foreign-owned concerns, 3) shipment of gold and silver to the United States. (ibid. p. 98.)

Trade with Europe and U.S.

In the past Latin America *as a whole* has had a greater trade with continental Europe *as a whole* than with the United States. (ibid. p. 39.) There are two obvious reasons for such a situation. In the first place, Latin America is one of the great food baskets for Europe, whereas the United States is relatively self-sufficient in foodstuffs. (*Foreign Commerce Weekly,* Feb. 15, 1941.) In the second place, the prices of raw materials which Latin America sells have tended to fall faster than the prices of our manufactured goods. (*Fortune,* September, 1940.) The inevitable result was that Latin America became more and more short of foreign exchange. Nevertheless, in all but two of the ten years from 1929 to 1939, the value of the goods the United States bought from Latin America has been greater than the value of the goods Latin America bought from us. (*Foreign Trade of Latin America,* p. 98.) Moreover, the United States has been the largest *single* buyer of Latin American materials and the largest *single* seller to Latin America. (ibid. p. 40.) In 1938, for instance, the United States took 30% of Latin American exports; United Kingdom took 17%; and Germany, despite her much publicized trade drive, took only 11%. (ibid. p. 39.) In the same year the United States supplied Latin America with 34% of her imports; United Kingdom supplied 12%; and Germany only 16%. (ibid. p. 40.)

Short Sighted U.S.

There are two less obvious causes tending to hurt United States trade with Latin America. The first reason is our slipshod buying methods. For instance, before the present European War it was almost impossible to buy American dollars in Uruguay. Our trade was stymied. This situation came about because one year we would buy up the entire output of wool. The next year, if wool was a fourth of a cent cheaper in Australia, we would buy practically none from Uruguay. Consequently, Uruguay preferred to make five-year barter deals with Germany and Italy because of the guarantee of definite long-term production. This was the only way to avoid periodic anarchy in one of Uruguay's major industries. Mexico and Argentina have made similar protests about our hit-or-miss trade policies. (Carleton Beals, *Pan America* p. 305.) The second factor holding back United States trade with Latin America results partially from the abovementioned trade policies. In the past, the Axis nations either concluded barter agreements, whereby the amount of products traded had equal value, thereby leaving no financial residue; or if a specific barter trade resulted in an Axis nation owing some monetary balance to a Latin American country, the monetary balance was paid in "aski" money; i.e. money which could be used only in the purchase of other goods from the same Axis nation. Thus despite the increase in South American trade with Axis nations during the depression, no more dollar exchange was available with which to purchase goods from the United States. Likewise, payments for imports from Latin America by the British Empire are made in "blocked" sterling; i.e. money which is only good for the purchase of products made in countries belonging to the sterling bloc, consisting mainly of the territories making up the British Empire. (*Foreign Commerce Weekly*, February 15, 1941.) To the extent that Latin American countries sell their goods to countries using blocked currencies (in effect, bilateral trade agreements) the opportunity for other nations to increase their sales in the markets of Latin America will be materially reduced. (*Foreign Trade of Latin America*, p. 103.)

Priorities in the Way

Moreover, of late we have placed obstacles in our own path. These grow out of the confusion within the present Administration in Washington as to where the aid-to-Britain program ends and where our own hemisphere defense program begins. The nature of the impediments can be described in one word: priorities. Price Administrator Leon Henderson and former

OPM Priorities Director Edward R. Stettinius, Jr., have objected to shipping steel, machinery, chemicals, etc., to Latin America, contending that
these products were sorely needed right here at home. (*Newsweek*, July 21,
1941.) Among other duties, Coordinator of Inter-American Affairs Nelson
Rockefeller's Committee within the Office for Emergency Management is
directed to "Formulate, recommend, and execute programs in the commercial and economic fields which, by the effective use of governmental and
private facilities, will further the commercial well-being of the Western
Hemisphere." (Executive Order, July 30, 1941.) Nevertheless he has flatly
stated: "The *front* line (of the defense program) is the aid-to-England
program. The *second* line of defense is the hemisphere program." (Hearings
before the Subcommittee of the Committee on Appropriations, House of
Representatives, 77th Congress, on the Second Deficiency Appropriation
Bill for 1941, p. 688.)

Ships Needed

Such an attitude does not augur well for the solution of the most pressing of
all the immediate problems, namely the bottleneck in ships because of our
lease-lend program, which provides for the release to Britain of 2,000,000
tons of U.S. shipping. (How the tanker part of this ship transfer scheme has
created an oil "shortage" in the United States was described in Did You
Know #18.) In addition the Navy requisitioned 15 new freighters from the
Moore-McCormack lines Pan American run. This was the greatest number
of ships demanded from any foreign-run line. It is not at all surprising that
the resulting ship shortage facing Brazil and Uruguay has created the
prospect of coal rationing in those countries despite the fact that there is
plenty of bituminous coal waiting at Virginia ports. Moreover, shipments at
Buenos Aires and Montevideo are 3 months in arrears, and although
Brazilian manganese is needed in our own defense program—the manganese
is piling up on Brazilian docks. Unless some new and stern authority is put
behind the Latin American drive, inter-American economic relations seem
due for still further disruption. For the United States giant ship-building
effort will further tighten up priorities on the steel and machinery desired
by the Latins. Furthermore the present ship shortage will grow even more
acute in coming weeks if the United States takes over the New York-to-
Iceland run for the British. (*Newsweek*, July 21, 1941.)

Home Trade Needed

Due largely to the nature of their products, the inadequate intracontinental
transportation facilities, and to the early established overseas connections,
the trade between Latin American nations themselves has heretofore been
relatively small. In the aggregate, the 20 nations of Latin America had

furnished the markets for less than 10% of each other's exports. (*Foreign Commerce Weekly*, February 15, 1941.) Another factor operating here is that only a small aristocratic fringe of the population ever sees cash income as high as $1000 a year, while over 50% of Latin American families probably live on less than $100 cash income a year (Duncan Aikman, *Survey Graphic*, March, 1941).

7 Trading Nations

The import and export trade of Latin America is largely concentrated in 7 of the 20 nations. These countries are: Argentina, Brazil, Venezuela, Mexico, Cuba, Chile, and Colombia. In fact, these countries accounted for 85% of total Latin American exports in both 1938 and 1939. The ten countries south of Panama customarily account for over 75% of all Latin American imports. The United States customarily takes about one-third of all Latin American exports and supplies approximately the same percentage of Latin American imports. (*Foreign Trade of Latin America*, pp. 31, 32, 36, 37, 39, 40.)

Trade Bonds with U.S.

A hasty statement to the effect that a unified Europe would automatically control Latin America's foreign trade simply ignores trade statistics. For instance, when regional trade figures are examined the importance of trade with the United States, in relation to total trade (import and export combined), is seen to average approximately 50% in the Caribbean area. (*Foreign Trade of Latin America*, p. 46.) Significantly, these are the countries closest to the United States and they guard the vital defense areas of the Caribbean, the Gulf of Mexico, and the Panama Canal. On a trade basis, it is clear that a Hitler Europe would have a hard time persuading these countries that their economic welfare did not rest on co-operation with the United States. Moreover, in vital Brazil, trade with the United States constitutes nearly 30% of the total: in west coast South American countries—Bolivia, Chile, Ecuador, and Peru—nearly 25%: and in east coast countries—Argentina, Paraguay, and Uruguay—over 10%. (*Foreign Trade of Latin America*, pp. 46, 47.) This then is the overall trade picture of Latin America.

Argentine Problems

But Latin America is not a unit. Latin America is twenty countries, each with problems of its own. Space limits us to only a brief glance at the two largest countries—Argentina and Brazil. The difference between their economic problems demonstrates that Latin America is not a unit. A dramatic picture of a hemisphere economic stumbling block is given by Duncan Aikman. (*Survey Graphic*, March 1941.) He tells of a 4,000,000 ton corn

surplus in Argentina which cannot be moved because Europe is blockaded—
and which threatens 27,000 railroad workers with unemployment. He tells
of a·400,000,000 bushel Argentine wheat surplus cut off from its normal
European market. At the same time the United States itself has unsalable
export surpluses of wheat (150,000,000 bushels) and corn. In Argentina,
those who desire a working hemisphere economy discover the knottiest
problem. For in 1938, Argentina sold 52% of her exports to European
powers, and only 9% to the United States. (Hubert Herring, *Good Neighbors*, p. 344.) Since the United States cannot furnish an outlet for those food
surpluses, Argentina's overproduction constitutes a permanent problem to
be handled by those who would devise an economic plan for the hemisphere.
Whether this food surplus *must* be sold only in Europe is another question
which is considered below.

Bonds with Brazil

Brazil is on the other side of the trade statistics fence. In relation to total
trade (import and export combined), trade with the United States makes up
virtually 30%. (*Foreign Trade of Latin America*, p. 47.) In the past, coffee
has been the major Brazilian export to the United States. (ibid. p. 54.) But
Brazil is the principal present, and potential, source of strategic raw materials in Latin America. (Carleton Beals, *Survey Graphic*, March 1941.) As a
supplier of these vital raw materials, Brazil furnishes a large share of the key
to military defense of the hemisphere. (MacLiesh & Reynolds, *Strategy of
the Americas*, pp. 43, 44.)

DOCUMENT 54

All-Out Aid for the Western Hemisphere

"Did you know *how far we have progressed in creating a
Western Hemisphere economy?*"
No. 23B, September 22, 1941

What to Do

Some proposed programs for the economic defense of the Western Hemisphere assume, in varying degrees, that a world revolution in trade methods

is now gradually taking place. Huge continental trading groups, buying and selling the products of many nations through one agency, are envisaged by some as the only method of assuring equality of treatment to small nations which, by themselves, are in a relatively disadvantageous bargaining position. Such is the view of Dr. Carlos Davila, former provisional President of Chile and former Chilean Ambassador to the United States. He declares that continental monopoly of foreign trade is the only method of saving hemisphere markets for the United States. (*How Should We Meet Totalitarian Aggression in the Americas?* Town Meeting of the Air, November 25, 1940.)

World Trade Problems

Even before the present European War the so-called "free" flow of multilateral trade had been interrupted by 1) bilateral trade agreements 2) outright barter agreements with Axis nations 3) absence of the gold standard (and of any one accepted world monetary standard) with the result that gold could not be used to settle international trade balances 4) uneasy state of world affairs resulting in an upset of international credits. (Adolf A. Berle, Jr., *New Directions in The New World*, p. 39.)

Buy the Surpluses?

Duncan Aikman suggests two plans, of which the first would be a highly expensive, but relatively simple, *emergency* program utilizing the cartel system. This system calls on the United States to buy up stocks of everything which the Germans could possibly demand in Latin America, at prices, in cash or barter, better than the Germans could pay. (Usually proponents of this system state that the cash which the United States would pay Latin America would be good only for the purchase of United States, or at least Western Hemisphere, products.) Aikman contends that we could sell the stocks to Europe at our own terms, or give them away to distressed populations in the Western Hemisphere, or sink them in the ocean. (*Survey Graphic*, March, 1941.) Establishment of a hemispheric surplus commodities corporation is reported to be under consideration by agricultural officials. (*Washington Star*, August 17, 1941.) But Carleton Beals who, according to *Time* magazine is, "now the best informed living writer on Latin America," opposes both the cartel plan and such modifications of it as have been suggested. "The problems are too complex, the nature of the countries and their governments too divergent. . . . A general goal and plan are possible, but the details should be fluid and dependent upon circumstances." (*Pan America*, p. 428.)

New Tactics Needed

However, Beals agrees that we can no longer permit the illusion of a pacific world of free intercourse (as postulated by the Hull reciprocal trade treaties) to block the establishment of our true security (ibid. p. 495). Neither can we continue to make irresponsible loans to other countries with which they buy our own goods (and those of our potential enemies) (ibid. p. 495).

Build up Latin America?

Beals suggests the following economic program for the hemisphere (ibid. pp. 506, 507, 508, 513, 514):

1) An economic plan based on mutual benefit.

2) Promotion of production of strategic materials as near to the United States as possible. These raw product industries must be controlled by (and eventually owned by) the country in which they are located, or by native capital. Investments by our government or by our private capital should be for a limited period, with guarantees of eventual transferral. In 1939, Davila outlined such a long range solution to the Inter-American Financial and Economic Advisory Committee. His plan called for the setting up of corporations with mixed United States and Latin American capital, whose main function would be to develop in Latin American countries new fields of mineral, agricultural, and industrial production which would not compete with the production of the United States. (*How Should We Meet Totalitarian Aggression in the Americas?* p. 9.)

3) Loans to be made only for specific industries (not unearmarked sums to governments). These industries should usually be complementary to, not competitive with, our own. (Aikman believes that a sound hemisphere defense industry development program would, by increasing the purchasing power of Latin Americans, also help to relieve the food surplus problems.) (*Survey Graphic*, March, 1941.)

4) Utilization of new trade methods, such as guaranteed trade quotas and prices, organized purchasing power, tariff reductions and rebates, preferential tariffs, long-term agreements and contracts, even buying subsidies.

5) The setting aside of a percentage of tariff receipts from Latin American products to provide funds for preliminary scientific research, mechanical supervision, sanitation, the further development of rubber plantations etc.

A Mutual Benefit Plan

Such a program would raise the living standards of the Latin American people so that they would gradually emancipate themselves from dictatorships; a larger market would be created for American goods; a greater interchange of commodities would take place between the Latin American countries, thus lessening the degree of their pre-war economic dependence on Europe and the Orient. Thus, we would have secured for ourselves the strategic materials which we are now forced to buy at exorbitant prices from the British and Dutch Empires. At the same time we would strengthen our economic bonds with our southern neighbors and minimize any totalitarian economic threat. However, the Argentine beef and wheat surpluses, and the Brazilian cotton surpluses, should, Beals feels, be allowed to reach their natural outlets in Europe and in the Orient. Under the plan discussed above, these purchases would not be sufficient to wean Latin American nations away from the democratic bloc.

Free Trade?

Adolf A. Berle, Jr., Assistant Secretary of State, urges business men to concentrate less on maintaining a favorable balance of trade, and realize anew that other nations can buy from us only if we buy from them. (As pointed out earlier (Did You Know 23A), this postulate is increasingly true in the present era of bilateral and totalitarian trade agreements.) Berle, maintaining firmly his faith that the day of free commerce will return, states the obvious when he says that we must back this faith by evolving a mechanism for temporary exchange credits. In the case of countries where there is no prospect of an immediate balance of trade, Berle would have the United States extend long-term credits until those nations become financially stronger. Indeed, he would prefer that the powers of the Export-Import Bank be expanded so that the individual American exporter is financed by the Bank, allowing the ultimate risk of payment to fall on the national resources. (Adolf A. Berle, Jr., *New Directions in the New World*, pp. 39–43.)

What's Been Done—Loans

That popular person known as the man-on-the-street, and high government officials in both North and South America, *talk* constantly of hemisphere defense. What has actually been *done* on the economic front? (Except where otherwise noted, the following information is taken from *Foreign Commerce Weekly*, September 6, 1941.) Inasmuch as money is the oil which makes the economic gears mesh, it is important to examine the work of the Export-Import Bank. Since the beginning of the European War this government agency has loaned over $255,000,000 in the Western Hemisphere, all but $25,000,000 of which has gone to Latin America. The Bank has authorized loans to all the southern countries except Bolivia, El Salvador, Guatemala, Honduras, and Mexico. Latin American countries receiving loans in excess of $20,000,000 are, in order of size of loan: Brazil, Argentina, Cuba, Chile, and Colombia. Loans have been made for the improvement of highways, railroads; for the purchase of United States agricultural and industrial machinery; and for the creation of public utilities. A loan has been made for the large-scale production of commercial rubber in Haiti. The latter program means a rise in the living standards of our southern friends and consequently a greater ability to buy ever increasing amounts of the exports of the United States. Moreover, it is an industry which will produce products which we formerly had to buy from sources outside the hemisphere. Finally, increased prosperity in Latin America assures the repayment of the loans extended by our government. Both the Export-Import Bank and the Treasury have made loans for the purpose of stabilizing the shaky currencies of some Latin American nations. The fly in the gravy of the Export-Import loans is that the Latin American nations have so far been able to spend only $92,000,000. The correct name for the fly is "priorities." Because United States industry is glutted with lease-lend orders for Britain, China, and Russia, as well as for our own defense efforts, Latin American orders have more or less fallen by the wayside. Some attempt is now being made by the Department of Commerce to place Latin American orders with some of the small business houses in the United States. It remains to be seen how far the lease-lend program will be allowed to stab-in-the-back our attempt at building a hemisphere economy. (*Newsweek*, September 22, 1941.) It has been charged that too many of the Export-Import loans have been made primarily with an eye to increasing the exportation of United States heavy goods to Latin America, and too few loans made for the development of products complementing the United States economy. (*Foreign Policy Reports*, June 15, 1941.)

What's Been Done—Trade

The shipping shortage has been helped somewhat by an agreement utilizing for inter-American trade, some 80 Axis-controlled ships, hitherto immobilized in Latin American harbors. A quota system has been adopted by the coffee producing nations in order to maintain a stable price structure. Similar arrangements are in the offing among the cacao and wheat producing countries. Exports to the United States have been greatly increased mainly because of the raw material buying program which is part of our rearmament effort. In the first 6 months of 1941 United States imports from Latin America had a greater value than the imports for the full year of 1938. Although in 1940, United States imports from Latin America were up $170,000,000 over 1938, the increase was almost wholly accounted for by imports of gold. (*Washington Star*, September 16, 1941.) Such imports contribute little to a sound economic program for the hemisphere. On the plus side of the raw material ledger is the fact that Brazil has already banned the export of defense materials to all countries *except* the United States. (*Washington Post*, June 19, 1941.) Somewhat similar arrangements have either been concluded or are in the discussion stage with several other Latin American nations. (*New York Times,* September 19, 1941.) Inter-American trade has been completely withdrawn from the hands of pro-Axis traders by President Roosevelt's proclamation of a blacklist.

What's Been Done—Raw Materials

The Department of Agriculture has undertaken exploratory surveys in Latin America looking toward the greater development of tropical agriculture. This is particularly significant because products grown in this area would be almost wholly complementary to the agricultural products of the United States. Moreover, there is tremendous room for expansion in this field because more than two-thirds of Latin America lies within the tropical zone. (M. W. Williams, *The People and Politics of Latin America,* p. 2.) The Inter-American Development Commission, with national councils in each of the South American countries, is making continuous studies aimed at developing Latin American industrialization in those fields for which the United States is now forced to look to other continents. Thus we see that while halting steps have been taken in the right direction, to date the surface has hardly been scratched.

DOCUMENT 55

Priority Orphans

"Did you know *that priorities have created a depression in the midst of the defense boom?*"
No. 25, September 30, 1941

We need not swap the gain of better living for the gain of better defense. I propose to retain the one and gain the other. (President Roosevelt at Chickamauga, 1940 and quoted in the *Saturday Evening Post,* September 27, 1941.)

It is a picture of factories made idle by lack of raw materials to turn out civilian goods, of men made idle by lack of materials to work with, of single-industry towns blighted by a spurious prosperity based on production of goods that we can't wear, or eat, or live in. Every person will be touched, and many will be touched harshly, by the defense program. (Leon Henderson, Price Control Administrator, *New York Times,* July 15, 1941.)

We Told You So

In February, 1941, while Congress was debating the Lease-Lend Bill, the research staff of the America First Committee issued a 21 page study entitled *The Economic Consequences Of The Lease-Lend Program*. Therein we demonstrated that if a huge arms program for the British was *superimposed* upon the already existing program for the defense of America, certain serious economic consequences would follow. We pointed out that our present industrial capacity was not sufficient for such an undertaking, and that we would, therefore, have to do one of two things, either expand our plant capacity or ration our existing plant capacity. We added that if rationing was resorted to, we would also have to institute the priority system. The study also pointed out that priorities represent one of the costs of extraordinary expansion of production of a highly specialized class of goods—unless plant capacity is expanded at the same time. We said that when priorities came there would be more or less serious dislocations for industry with a resulting downward trend of employment among industrial workers. To avoid these consequences, we suggested that it would be possible, at best, to *share* with Britain some of the arms which we were already producing for our own defense.

World War Told You So

The study also recalled that during the World War the industrial production of the United States had risen sharply from the depression levels of 1914 to hit its peak in 1916 because of vast war orders from abroad, but receded during the remaining years of the conflict despite huge war expenditures by our own government. *Prices* rose, but because the limits of our industrial capacity had about been reached in 1916, no greater amounts of *goods* were produced. Finally, the obvious point was made that if, in the present similar situation, the lease-lend program was forced through *before* our industrial capacity was expanded, prices would rise but not production; i.e., the cost of the program would be multiplied without any comparable advance in arms production. This, we said, meant inflation. And as stated above, industry and industrial workers would suffer grave hardships.

You Didn't Listen

But the lease-lend program was pushed through. And now, apparently, we are not only to produce arms for our own defense, but also for Britain, and also for China, and also for our "sister republic" Russia, and for all the "Free" governments-in-exile, and also for ????. Moreover, we did not first take the time to expand our industrial capacity. For one thing industry was reluctant to invest in plant capacity which would be of little use once the

war was over. In the second place, those two Republican jokers in the New
Deal, Messrs. Stimson and Knox, were bleating daily about the crisis that
would come to the United States in the next 30 or 60 or 90 days. The
impression was deliberately created by Administration spokesmen that there
was no time to do things efficiently. Such an attitude made it inevitable that
America should enter a depression in the midst of a war "boom."

Priority Dangers

The present memorandum does not discuss the results of over-concentration
of defense contracts in the hands of a few large companies. It covers only
the unemployment resulting from the priority system, and the effect of
priorities on small businessmen. Priorities are the *alternative to* expansion
of capacity; their purpose is to ration materials when demand exceeds
supply. Priorities mean that those industries whose products are *most*
essential in supplying the armed forces, and in meeting the *basic* needs of
the civilian population, have first call on available power, fuel, raw materials,
and labor. Those industries next in line on the scale of wartime necessity
are then supplied, and so on. Obviously then, any administrator vested with
the power of priority control may, by curtailing raw materials, power, fuel,
and transportation, be able to put a business or an entire industry out of
business overnight (*Defense and Economic Dislocation*, published by the
Research Institute of America, Inc., September 12, 1941). Remembering
then that as of March 1941 unemployment in the United States was estimated by the National Industrial Conference Board at 7,600,000 persons,
while other estimates were even higher (ibid.); and that the slowness with
which we expanded our industrial capacity to meet the increased demands
resulting from the superimposition of the lease-lend program on our own
defense program necessitated the priority system, let us look at some
examples of "priority orphans."

Exit Small Business

The first outspoken recognition on the part of the Administration that serious
dislocations were impending as a result of the lease-lend program came in a
statement by Peter Nehemkis, Jr., special assistant to the Chief of the
Defense Contract Service. In an address to the field officers of the Service
he said: "Already not less than 10 entire industries . . . must either close
down or enter a new line of production. Indeed, before the end of this
summer, we may expect to find one third of American industry faced with
the grim reality of 'guns versus butter,' and as the tempo of the war economy
gains increased momentum, you may expect to find, for a time, not less but
more unemployment; not less but more idle machines. It is one of the
ironies of our defense effort that its total effect may well be to obliterate the

smaller enterprises from the American scene. . . ." (ibid.) It was as simple as that! The elimination of thousands of small businessmen and the resulting unemployment of many more thousand American workmen is indeed an irony.

Defense Unemployment

Yet as far back as November 1940, the militant noninterventionist labor leader John L. Lewis had warned in his annual report as president of the CIO that "Unless substantial economic offsets are provided to prevent this nation from becoming wholly dependent upon the war expenditures, we will come sooner or later to the dilemma which requires either war or depression. . . . We need not sacrifice butter for guns." (*New York Times*, November 18, 1940.) But, as a result of the policies adopted by the Administration, August 8, 1941, found Leon Henderson, then head of the Office of Price Administration and Civilian Supply, testifying before the House Banking and Currency Committee that in the next few months unemployment would increase by 2,000,000. He estimated that this figure constituted a 25% increase in the total number of unemployed. (*Defense and Economic Dislocation.*)

Closed Factories

As early as June 1941, stories began to appear heralding the 50% cut in automobile production for 1942 (*Washington Times-Herald* June 28, 1941). There soon followed stories of an impending 50% cut in refrigerator production and a 30% cut in home washing machine output. In some quarters it was estimated that a 50% reduction in refrigerator output would mean a layoff of about 15,000 employes. (*Wall Street Journal*, August 15, 1941). Shortages of copper, aluminum, zinc, etc., continued to grow. Office of Production Management officials stated that the swiftly mounting impact of priorities in diverting strategic materials away from nondefense factories "will assume perfectly appalling proportions before many weeks," resulting, according to some estimates, in the shutdown of from 5,000 to 6,000 factories. (*Washington Post*, August 8, 1941.)

Ghost Towns

The biggest aluminum firm in Manitowoc, Wisconsin, has already laid off half its factory force of 2600 and many of its office workers. Presently almost all of Manitowoc's aluminum employes may be workless. Similar reports come in from aluminum towns in Ohio, Pennsylvania, and West Virginia. (*Forbes*, September 15, 1941, quoted in *Reader's Digest*, October 1941.)

Zippers Leave Towns

Meadville, Pennsylvania, is the zipper capital of the country. Talon, Inc., turns out 1,200,000 zippers a day. In a week it could make all the zippers our soldiers and sailors could possibly use. (ibid.) Depending directly on the zipper industry for a livelihood are 6000 people, more than half of the town's factory employes. These people man three huge plants in Meadville and another one in nearby Erie. Talon, Inc., pays out 68% of the town's factory payrolls. Already, because of material shortages, 800 workers have been laid off. The remaining 5000 employes can be employed on materials now in stock, only until November 1. Moreover, a priority shutdown of Talon and of half a dozen other slide fastener factories in the same situation in other American cities indicates a further staggering dislocation among 20,000 zipper using customers in 100 or more industries affecting a quarter of a million workers. (*Washington Post*, September 23, 24, 1941.)

Priority Orphans

A refrigerator firm in Evansville, Indiana states that it will have to discharge 1150 men. Similar reports come from refrigerator plants in Dayton, Ohio; Grand Rapids, Michigan; and Los Angeles, California. Washing machine factories in Newton, Iowa; and in Sandusky, Ohio are about to discharge numerous employes. The same stories are heard from stove manufacturers in Belleville, Illinois; jewelry manufacturers in Attleboro, Massachusetts. (*Forbes*, ibid.) In and near Jamestown, N.Y., are some 37 furniture plants employing more than 3000 men, or over one-fourth of the factory workers in the area. Factory owners say that layoffs began three months ago and that more serious layoffs are in prospect. (*Washington Post*, September 25, 1941.) Small manufacturers of medicinal supplies in the New York City area have reported that they are faced with shutdowns because of the diversion of basic chemicals to industrial armament uses. (*New York Times*, June 3, 1941.)

You Can't Do Business. . . .

Completing a state survey, the defense industries board of the Wisconsin Council of Defense reports that of 385 Wisconsin industrial concerns reporting, 247 stated that unless there was quick improvement in getting supplies, a total of 15,340 workmen would be without jobs. (*Wall Street Journal*, August 30, 1941.) Employing 1,500,000 workers in direct construction and another 4,500,000 in related fields, America's third largest industry, building construction, may soon be completely paralyzed, according to Harry C. Bates, president of the Bricklayers Union and chairman of the American Federation of Labor's Committee on Housing. (*Anti-War News Service*, September 24, 1941.) A survey of 6,000 manufacturers revealed that nine out of ten of the nation's small non-defense manufacturers believe they will soon be forced to drastically reduce operations. (Press Release, Chamber of Commerce, September 7, 1941.) Walter D. Fuller, president of the National Association of Manufacturers, has predicted that 90,000 of the nation's manufacturers may "be hit—some fatally—by the stringency of defense material rationing." (Press Release, National Association of Manufacturers, September 21, 1941.) The same trade association has estimated that 3,000,000 workers will be partly or wholly unemployed in the next six months. (*Washington News*, September 25, 1941.)

Blackout

The Office of Production Management is reliably understood to have prepared secretly a list of more than forty industries, embracing thousands of business concerns, which face drastic retrenchment or complete shutdown as a result of raw material starvation, according to Leo M. Cherne, executive secretary of the Research Institute of America, Inc. (*New York Times*, September 2, 1941).

Unemployment as Usual

Of course, the most dramatic picture of priority unemployment is among the automobile workers in Michigan. Governor [Murray D.] Van Wagoner has told a Congressional investigating committee headed by Representative [John H.] Tolan [Democrat] of California that "the nation will see economic chaos within three months" unless priorities on materials and labor are lightened in favor of industrial production for civilian use. In Michigan alone, he said, 100,000 workers will be thrown out of non-defense jobs by January. (*New York Times*, September 24, 1941.) R. J. Thomas, president of the United Automobile Workers, C.I.O., who, with his union, supports aid to Britain but opposes an A.E.F., told the same Congressional committee that last winter's 'business as usual' policy which was followed by the motor industry would mean 'unemployment as usual' for the workers in the coming months. (*New York Times*, September 25, 1941.)

More Guns, Less Butter

And so it goes. There are the unemployed from the restricted import industries; the 175,000 of the silk industry, the 156,000 of the cork industry; the 42,000 rubber workers who will have lost their jobs by the end of this year. There are the Office of Production Management unemployed, thrown out of the nondefense industries because OPM's failure to expand the production of raw materials has placed all strategic raw materials on the priority list. (*New Republic*, August 25, 1941.) To top this tragic and unnecessary picture, we find Donald Nelson [executive vice president and chairman of the executive committee, Sears Roebuck; varied wartime posts, including chairman of the War Production Board, 1942–1944], newly appointed executive director of the Supply Priorities and Allocation Board, telling us that from now on Americans face a lower standard of living. (*New York Herald-Tribune*, September 16, 1941.)

Fascist Soil

One observer, the well-known author Marquis W. Childs, points out that the tragedy is that the severity of the blow might have been greatly tempered if there had been over-all planning coupled with over-all authority. But responsibility within the Government was divided, and political considerations were allowed to enter in. (*Washington Star*, August 17, 1941.) We had the British experience as a warning. In England 20,000 small businesses closed down within two months after England entered the war and another 20,000 were forced to close early in 1940. (*New York Times*, July 20 and August 24, 1941.) A similar danger here was foreseeable, for Peter Nehemkis, quoted earlier in this memorandum, pointed out some time ago that "If through national defense we permit a blackout of small business to take place, we shall richly have cultivated the soil for a fascist economic dictatorship."

In Aid of Small Business

To protect the interests of small businessmen and their employes, there has been organized in the House of Representatives a Small Business Committee under the chairmanship of Representative [Charles A.] Halleck [Republican] of Indiana. The Senate has a similar committee headed by Senator [James E.] Murray [Democrat] of Montana. Halleck's committee seems to have been the more active of the two groups. The Tolan committee, as pointed out earlier, is concerned with the problems of migratory labor. Yet little can be expected in the way of alleviating the effects of our new depression unless there is a radical change in the approach taken by the Administration. Indeed, as *United States News* points out in its issue of October 3, 1941, "Except from a political point of view, Government isn't greatly concerned about the prosperity of individual business. It does not care greatly if corporation debts can't be paid or even if many of them are bankrupt."

DOCUMENT 56

Lease-Lend for War

"Did you know *that the President's misinterpretation of the Lease-Lend law has brought us to the verge of all-out war and another depression?*"
No. 26, October 4, 1941

More Money Wanted

There is now pending before Congress a request by the President for a second lease-lend appropriation, this time for the sum of $5,985,000,000. In the six months since the Lease-Lend law (H.R. 1776) was adopted, and the first appropriation of $7,000,000,000 granted, the avowed purpose of the Lease-Lend law has been so perverted by the Administration that we have been brought to the verge of an all-out shooting war. For that reason alone, the pending appropriation should be refused. But, in addition, this second request should be denied because it is nothing more than part of a program to eliminate Congressional control over vast sums of money for years to come, and because Lease-Lend aid to date has had a detrimental effect upon our own defense program and upon our domestic economy.

Promise Versus Performance

The most ardent supporter of aid-short-of-war to Britain and her Allies must pause and take heed when he finds that the Lease-Lend law which he supported, and which was sold to the Congress and the people as a measure which was designed, and would be used, to keep us out of war, has instead been so misinterpreted and so misused as to bring us to the very verge of war. The most ardent supporter of aid-short-of-war must pause and take heed when a review of the past six months discloses that the Lend-Lease law, as applied by the President, is not the Lend-Lease law which was adopted by Congress in March, 1941, especially when it may be argued by interventionists that approval means approval of the President's actions.

Aid Short of War

The adoption of the Lend-Lease law was urged by the President and his Cabinet members in order that we might become the "arsenal of democracy." This policy was urged as most likely to keep the United States out of war (President Roosevelt—fireside chat, Dec. 29, 1940; Secretary Stimson—Hearing before Senate Foreign Relations Committee on S.275, p. 125, Hearing before House Foreign Relations Committee on H.R. 1776, p. 118; Secretary Knox—Hearing before Senate Foreign Relations Committee on S.275, pp. 209, 242). In their statements, and in the statements of Administration leaders during the Congressional debate, there was no intimation that the bill was also to make the United States the "transportation system" of democracy by imposing upon us the duty of delivering lease-lend aid, or that we were to be the "policeman" of democracy, charged with the duty of patrolling war zones on the seas to ensure delivery. Opponents of the bill charged that its terms were so vague and the powers granted by it to the President so sweeping that we might find ourselves charged with the threefold burden of being at once "arsenal," "transportation system," and "policeman," with participation in the war as the inevitable outcome. But the Congressional sponsors of the bill ridiculed these charges.

President's Neutrality Pledge

The Lease-Lend bill was discussed against the background of the Neutrality Act of 1939. That Act, adopted as a sign of national strength, not fear or weakness, expressly forbade American ships and American citizens to travel to countries proclaimed by the President to be at war, and further forbade such travel into combat zones which he should declare (Sec. 2, 3—*Congressional Record*, Oct, 27, 1939, pp. 1662–1663). In asking for the passage of that Act, which repealed the embargo on the shipment of arms to countries at war, President Roosevelt pledged to the Congress and to the country that the Act was and would be used as a step towards peace (in his Message of Sept. 21, 1939). As recently as the end of the 1940 campaign, he stated in a speech at New York:

> . . . the Neutrality Act and . . . other steps . . . were measures to keep us at peace. And through all the years of war since 1935 there has been no entanglement and there will be no entanglement. (Quoted in *Saturday Evening Post*, Sept, 27, 1941.)

The Act further sought to eliminate war-provoking "incidents" by requiring that the title to goods sold to countries at war be transferred out of American hands before the goods left American soil (Sec. 2). "Cash-and-carry" was the keynote of the Act; we were not to insure or attempt delivery of goods sold into war zones.

No Convoys

Opponents of the Lend-Lease bill charged that its provisions could be used to emasculate the Neutrality Act, but the Congressional sponsors of the bill denied that there was any intent to affect the Neutrality Act (*Congressional Record*, March 8, 1941, pp. 2116, 2112). In order to allay the fears voiced, and to indicate once more the intention of Congress that the plan of the Neutrality Act was to remain the law of the land, the original form of the Lease-Lend bill was amended to incorporate amendments which expressly forbade the use of convoys under its provisions (Sec. 3D), and stated expressly that lease-lend aid was not to be used to allow the entry of American ships into a combat area in violation of the Neutrality Act (Sec. 3E). In order to make certain that lease-lend aid could not be interpreted as imposing upon the United States any duty to "deliver" the goods across the ocean or into war zones, or any duty to build a "bridge of ships" into the war zones, the original provision of the bill permitting the "transfer" of goods to foreign countries was amended unanimously to provide that the title to all goods and defense articles disposed of to any foreign government was to be transferred before those articles left our shores (Sec. 3A (2)).

Convoys by Any Other Name

Shortly after the passage of the Lease-Lend law, interventionists, and ultimately the President and leading Cabinet members, began to speak of our duty to build a "bridge of ships" across the ocean, and of our duty to insure delivery of the war supplies we produced and made available to Britain—all in the face of the express prohibitions of the Lease-Lend law. Public sentiment opposed the use of convoys, for it recalled the President's statement that "convoys mean shooting, and shooting means war" (*Congressional Record*, March 31, 1941, p. 2765). In the place of convoys, a series of steps were undertaken under various guises, but all designed to achieve the results forbidden by the law of the land. The naval and air patrols of the Atlantic waters which the President established in April, 1941 (*New York Times*, April 29, 1941) were designed less for actual American defense purposes than for the purpose of aiding British convoy shipments. Such patrols, because they give actual assistance and advice to British warships, have been denounced by one constitutional authority as unconstitutional "acts of war" (Henry Frazer, *Syracuse Post Standard*, May 11, 1941). They necessarily place American warships and American sailors and aviators in shooting zones.

Iceland Ho!

The occupation of Iceland was undertaken under the theory that it was necessary for the defense of the Western Hemisphere (although Iceland is in the Eastern Hemisphere) and the additional theory that the occupation was necessary in order to insure the delivery of lease-lend aid (see Did You Know #7). Moreover, in informing the Congress and the nation that Iceland was being occupied, the President stated that our troops were to replace the British there (*New York Times*, July 8, 1941). But Iceland was then and still is simultaneously occupied by British troops, at war with the Nazis, and is located in the war zone proclaimed by the Nazis. Moreover, with the arrival in Iceland of a recent contingent of Regular Army troops, it became known that *all American troops there are under the command of a British officer* (*New York Times*, Oct. 2, 1941). When American ships were directed to carry supplies to Iceland, and when still later, the President instructed the Navy to "shoot first" in order to clear the sea lanes to Iceland (*New York Times*, Sept. 12, 1941), American merchant ships and American warships were thrust into danger zones, where war-provoking incidents would inevitably occur—all under the theory that "lease-lend aid" justified such a policy. But that policy violated unmistakably the spirit of the Lease-Lend law and the spirit of its mandates against convoying and against the entry of American ships into danger zones.

Ships in War Trade

But even that policy could not justify sending supplies directly to countries at war, in American-flag ships. Consequently, the device was adopted of transferring American ships to the flag of Panama. Sixty-three American-owned ships suitable for trans-atlantic trade have been transferred to the flag of Panama between the outbreak of the European war (Sept. 1, 1939) and July 1, 1941. Some ships have been armed by the United States, becoming warships under international law (*New York Times*, Sept. 26, 27, 1941). It is now openly admitted that these transfers were made in order to evade the restrictions of the Neutrality Act (*Washington Times-Herald*, Sept. 13, 1941; *New York Times*, Sept. 23, 1941). Thus, on the one hand, the Administration sought to place American ships in the war trade forbidden by our laws, by placing them under *foreign flags*, and, on the other hand, claimed that *American* ships were being attacked when those foreign-flag ships ran the risks to which that policy necessarily subjected them (see Did You Know, #3, 22).

Convoys Unmasked

Nor can the President's "shoot on sight" order be justified, as he claims, as necessary to protect lease-lend aid. It must be recalled that American armed protection is to be given, not only to American ships, but also to the ships of any flag, and that the waters in which that protection is to be given extend to an undefined width (even to the Pacific Ocean), to any waters the President chooses to declare vital to our "defense". This would enable our fleet to give what amounts to "convoy protection" to British ships or the ships of any other allied nation, as well as American ships, carrying war supplies for Britain or Russia or China. It would enable American patrols even to convoy British ships right into English ports, since the President has stated that he did not feel that the Neutrality Law prevented American warships from entering the war zones he established under that law (*New York Times*, April 29, 1941).

One-Man War

Thus it is that we have been precipitated into a limited naval war by decree of the President, and without the consent of Congress (see Did You Know #22). And we have reached that pass despite the steady, although slow, betterment of our own defensive position, and the rapidly improving situation of Britain. As British Prime Minister Churchill announced recently, Britain's shipping losses have decreased materially, she now has control of the air, and her island defenses have been strengthened (*New York Times*, Oct. 1, 1941).

Russia Calls

It may be that the call for this new lease-lend fund arises in part from Russia's needs for war supplies. The Lease-Lend law would allow the President to direct that war supplies be made directly available to Russia (Sec. 3A (1)), or to authorize Britain to turn over to Russia lease-lend supplies received from the United States (Sec. 4). Even were the new appropriation bill amended to forbid any aid to Russia, it would still be possible for Britain to turn over to Russia her own supplies, while receiving lease-lend supplies from the United States. And, of course, the Administration has already granted some loans to Russia, and has promised more (*United States News*, Sept. 26, 1941). Aid to Russia has a prominent place in the Administration's program, for Secretary of Commerce Jones has announced that he contemplates a vast expansion of American plant capacity in order to supply Russian needs (*New York Herald Tribune*, Sept. 24, 1941).

Apart from these considerations, however, the new appropriation should be denied because it would eliminate Congressional control over vast sums of money, and because the effect of lease-lend aid to date has been detrimental to our own defense program and to our domestic economy.

The Torrent and The Trickle

As Senator Robert LaFollette, Jr., has pointed out, the second lease-lend request "is an attempt to project a program for years into the future with no further Congressional control over expenditures" (*The Progressive*, Sept. 27, 1941). So little actual lease-lend aid has been rendered that the "torrent" of aid which was promised so eloquently is described by even interventionist publications as a mere "trickle" (*New Republic*, Sept. 22, 1941; *The Nation*, Sept. 20, 1941; *Life*, Sept. 20, 1941; *New York Times*, Sept. 21, 1941; *Washington Star*, Sept. 19, 1941; *Washington Post*, Sept. 16, 1941). The President's figures show that Lend-Lease has actually paid out of its seven billion dollar fund only $389,000,000, or about 3% of the fund (Senate Document 112, p. 9). There still remains over six and a half billion to be spent for articles completed or being manufactured before the fund will be exhausted. Lend-Lease hasn't even gotten around to ordering supplies (by letting contracts) in the case of almost three and a half billion of the original fund (ibid., p. 9).

Time-Lag

The President's hope for improved production in the future can not justify this new request. Even making all allowances for a vastly accelerated rate of production in the near future, the evidence demonstrates that it will take many, many months, if not much longer, before the vast unspent balance of lease-lend funds can be translated into war supplies and materials. Since the European War began, our factories have been working at a constantly accelerated rate to produce supplies under British war contracts made before Lease-Lend. Yet, as the President's report shows, our total exports to the British Empire since the beginning of the war, combining British contracts and lease-lend aid, amounts to $4,400,000,000 (ibid., p. v). Thus, our production for Britain has averaged $2,200,000,000 per year. The most optimistic allowance for accelerated production cannot bridge the gap of $10,785,000,000 between that performance and the fund which would be appropriated were this new request to be granted. Even the Treasury anticipates that only three and a half billion dollars can be spent under Lend-Lease by June, 1942 (*Congressional Record*, Sept. 25, 1941, p. A4658). That would still leave three billion unspent.

Congress Eliminated

The real reason for the request is not "continuity of production." The real reason lies in the fact that the Lease-Lend law sets a time limit on the blanket power granted to the President in the handling of authorized lease-lend funds. Contracts must be made before July 1, 1943, and must be completed before July 1, 1946 (Sec. 5C). By making this request now (although there is no real need yet for additional funds), and following it up with other requests within short periods of time, it becomes possible for the President to exercise unlimited powers over vast sums of money, and, to that extent, hamstring Congressional control over the purse-strings. That is entirely in keeping with the nature of the President's foreign policy, whose one-man formulation and execution have led us to the verge of all-out war.

We Told You So

Small as has been the volume of actual lease-lend aid, it has exercised an incalculably severe effect upon our own defense program and upon our domestic economy. In February, 1941, while the Lease-Lend bill was before Congress, the Research Bureau of the America First Committee issued a study entitled *The Economic Consequences of the Lease-Lend Program* in which we demonstrated that even America's vast and ingenious industrial plant and expansion capacity was not unlimited; that we might be able to *share* our arms production with the British, but that to *superimpose* a huge arms program for Britain upon our own large defense program (since then increased manyfold) would jeopardize our own defense program and would cause serious economic dislocations. The accuracy of that analysis is demonstrated by the evidence available today.

Production Bottleneck

There is not space for consideration of all the evidence, but some aspects may be noted. The cry that "continuity of production" requires the new appropriation scarcely accords with the evidence that our productive capacities are overloaded, and that production for lease-lend aid necessarily competes with production for our own defense program. It will take years to carry out our presently-projected program, for one estimate is that about 85% of defense funds are still unspent (*Washington Post*, Sept, 15, 1941). Official figures point still more strongly to the time-lag:

> Approximately $56,000,000,000 has been appropriated in direct appropriations or contract authorizations for national defense since June 1940. During the fiscal year 1941, $6,048,000,000 of this was spent. During the fiscal year 1942 the Treasury estimates that $15,900,000,000 will be spent. Thus, at the end of the fiscal year 1942 there will have been expended $21,948,000,000 of the $56,000,000,000 that has been appropriated or for which contract authorizations have been provided since June 1940. That would leave about $35,000,000,000 of this sum unexpended at the end of the current fiscal year. (*Congressional Record*, Sept. 29, 1941, p. 7774.)

Defense Jam

How are both lease-lend funds and British contracts to be translated into war materials unless our own program is subordinated? *United States News* reports that "war industry capacity for next year or more already is overloaded with orders" (Sept. 26, 1941). It is reported that it will be late 1942 before the contracts of Britain and her allies (chiefly made before Lend-Lease) are completed (*New York Times*, Sept. 21, 1941)—contracts which amount to almost four billion dollars (*Washington News*, Sept. 23, 1941).

Real lease-lend operations must wait until then. A recent survey points out that: "At the rate the payments have been going it will be next spring before last spring's appropriations (for defense) are being spent." (*Washington News*, Sept. 26, 1941.) A few of the many possible examples demonstrate the overloading of our major industries. Bethlehem Steel, in mid-July, 1941, had unfilled defense orders of a billion and a quarter dollars; General Motors had unfilled defense orders in the middle of September, 1941 amounting to $1,200,000,000 (*Washington Post*, Sept. 18, 1941). In the airplane industry, whose estimated total production for 1941 is 700 million dollars, Pacific Coast airplane plants alone had unfilled defense orders on July 1, 1941 of two and a half billion dollars (*Christian Science Monitor*, Sept. 20, 1941); Curtiss-Wright in September had a defense-order backlog of over a billion dollars (*Washington Post*, Sept. 18, 1941); and Consolidated Aircraft had a backlog of 750 millions (*Christian Science Monitor*, Sept. 17, 1941). Senator LaFollette points out that, on the basis of Department of Commerce figures, new orders have been outrunning completed orders to a large degree during the past year throughout our industrial plant (*The Progressive*, Sept. 27, 1941).

Who Gets Bombers?

But one of many possible examples will demonstrate the competition with our own defense needs which must result if British requests for lease-lend aid are to prevail. The British are begging for all the bombers we can produce, for "there is no doubt as to the superiority of the U.S. bomber" (*Fortune*, October, 1941, pp. 81, 166). Yet, can we furnish them to the British in the state of our own bomber program?

> . . . the objective was a peak production rate of 500 four-engine bombers a month, . . . In truth, the rate was far short of even that figure (figure of bomber production cited by Senator Byrd [Harry F. Byrd, D-Va.]). In April, so far as can be learned, the nation produced only twenty-seven four-engine bombers; in June, ten; in July, thirteen; and in August, twenty—all of which, it should be understood, were under preprogram contracts. (Ibid., pp. 169,176.)

Lend-Lease Depression

Small as has been the actual aid rendered under lease-lend, it has had an unmeasurable but nevertheless definite role in creating the unemployment and business depression brought about by our system of "priorities" for vital materials. We pointed out in our February study that the initiation of a huge defense program, upon which an aid-to-Britain program was superimposed, without proper expansion of plant capacity, would compel the rationing of our supplies of industrial materials. That rationing has now been in force for some time. So tight is the priority situation that any new or additional contract for war supplies which is executed acts like a catalyst in a chemical solution, and exerts an industrial influence far out of proportion to its monetary value. Once a contract is let, efforts must be made well in advance to secure priorities for supplies of needed materials. Allocation of such materials to a contract makes it difficult or impossible for other contracts to be carried out because of the heightened shortage of materials. This, in turn, creates similar shortages in connection with other contracts, and ultimately has far-reaching repercussions throughout our industrial set-up. Even the small amount of actually completed lease-lend supplies has contributed greatly to that situation, as have the three and a half billion dollars of contracts which have been made under lease-lend and as have the large British contracts which were made before the Lease-Lend law was adopted. The result of that priority system is widespread: present unemployment and the destruction of thousands of small businesses in the midst of the war "boom" and the threatened more serious unemployment and depression (see Did You Know #25).

Taxed to Death

Lease-Lend, further, constitutes a heavy burden upon the national income. The combined lease-lend total, should the new bill be passed, would impose a burden of about $100 on every man, woman and child in the country. Since the national income per capita for 1941 is estimated to be about $620 (Oliver McKee, in *Washington Star*, July 23, 1941), this would mean a burden amounting to about 16% of the national income. The American people face tax collections of about $165 per capita from a $620 income, even excluding the new lease-lend fund. With the new tax law, and making allowance for state and local taxes as well as federal taxes, the American people, still at peace, are now taxed more heavily than the embattled British (Washington Review, U.S. Chamber of Commerce, Sept. 29, 1941). In the light of this burden upon our national debt and income, what justification is there for adoption of another six billion dollar burden?

DOCUMENT 57

"The Economic Consequences of American Intervention"

Lawrence Dennis
unpublished manuscript, undated [1941]

. . . Whether the Germans can achieve the economic unification of Europe may be considered doubtful. But whether they can or cannot succeed in doing so, it seems that we have no real cause for concern over their success or failure. In a German-led economic United States of Europe, should such an achievement be realized, there would be greater forces making for disunity and civil war than in our United States of America. This is not saying that civil war would inevitably overtake Hitler's United States of Europe. It is merely saying that the danger of civil war would be greater there than here. Here the processes of assimilation and amalgamation have gone far. In Hitler's United States of Europe they have hardly begun. Certainly we have less group conflicts than Europe. To begin with, we have not the European problem of nearly two score nationalities, each of which has a language, a culture, and a government, recent if not actual, of its own. Then we have not the diversity of economic tastes and types of production which complicate the problem of rationalizing production and distribution over there. We have highly standardized tastes and markets. Europe has not, as yet. These problems will greatly complicate the German task of economically unifying Europe.

The chief reason why so many intelligent observers see nothing but disaster or, at best, a steadily falling standard of living ahead for the American people if Hitler wins the war is that they apply the standards of the old to the new economics. They foresee a victorious Hitler using his combined economic and military power to undersell America in world markets and thus to deprive us of all means either of procuring needed imports or of maintaining full employment in our mass production industries. That in many markets Hitler's Europe can undersell us in nearly everything that can be sold there goes without saying. That in all markets Hitler's Europe will be able to undersell us in many things is equally probable. America can't compete with Germany or Japan for the world's five and ten cent store trade. Russia will buy few American products competing with those of Hitler's Europe. But what of it? We should need almost nothing in the way of exports from Russia, as we have a similar endowment of raw materials.

. . . Most current talk about Germany's taking the Latin America market away from us is sheer poppycock. German trade with Latin America stands to increase if Germany wins the war but has no chance of excluding American trade there. Since the last war we have led all other nations in trade with South America. Britain has run second and Germany a poor-third, though German trade naturally came up after the war of 1914–1918 and regained its pre-war rank, the ratios being roughly three for the United States, two for Britain and one for Germany.

The great fear of Latin America, so far as Germany is concerned, is not economic domination of Germany but loss or curtailment of European export market in the Nazi new order. Everything South America has to offer Europe can be obtained within Europe, Africa and the Near East. The key to an understanding of post-war trade in a German led new European economy is the elementary fact that the big objective will be procurement of needed supplies, not monopolization of distant markets just to shut the United States out. There would be no advantage for a European planned economy in the monopolization of the Latin American market even if it could be achieved. A European planned economy must not for its own strength and security be highly dependent on imports from far off Latin America.

In the new order planned economies, economic planning, of course, has to be done with a view to such contingencies as war. What use to Germany in this war are the foreign investments of Germany under American or British control? Of what use to Germany in the war are German controlled raw material sources in Latin America? A sufficiency in war time cannot be insured by the mere possession of foreign credits or gold. To be sure of a sufficiency of rubber imports in war time, the United States should promote the production of rubber in Brazil or Central America while Germany promotes the production of synthetic rubber in German controlled areas of Europe. In either case, the cost is a secondary consideration. The first consideration is a sufficient supply of an essential commodity. Neither Germany nor the United States should ever be concerned with capturing the world's rubber market. And neither would be worried about being denied the plantation rubber of the Malaisia [*sic*] in times of peace. What else could the Japanese or any other people in control of Straits rubber do with it but trade it off to America and western Europe?

The commodities which the United States has now to import from beyond the limits of this hemisphere are few in number and, with almost no exceptions, their total bulk is not great. The bulk of our rubber, silk, tungsten, nickel, and manganese imports is not great as compared with the bulk of Germany's necessary imports of fats and fodder. The commodities we need to import are easily procurable, even in time of war, due to the small amount of shipping space they take up. America needs few really bulky imports.

. . . The notion that Germany is out to conquer the world and that the

Nazis, once victorious in Europe, will pursue this objective through economic penetration of South America is widely current in America today. If the Nazis really are out to conquer the world, their strategy will certainly not be to waste their economic resources in trying to undersell us in Latin America or to establish there military bases which will be useless for the invasion of the United States. Bases five hundred or more miles south of the Panama Canal would be of little or no use for attacking the territory or sea borne commerce of the United States. For the Germans to maintain military bases in South America south of the equator and further from any point in the United States than German controlled bases on the European Continent would weaken the German potential for making war on the United States.

German military strategists cannot want bases in the principal countries of South America as a means of attacking the United States. If they want bases in the Caribbean, Mexico and Central America, the Germans know they will first have to defeat our navy to get them. Such bases, of course, would be useful for an attempt at invading the United States. If the Germans want bases in South America, south of the Equator, the Germans know they will have to fight a naval war with us while they seize and develop such bases. Finally and more fundamentally still, if the Germans want to conquer the world, they know they will have to conquer the United States and that this can only be a military and naval accomplishment. If it be the German purpose to conquer America after winning the war in Europe, it would seem logical under the circumstances to give them battle over here and not over there. As the governing factors and considerations for a military war between the United States and Germany are mainly strategic and not economic, we ought not to confuse the two sets of factors and considerations in this discussion.

The only reason for referring to the military problems of an American-German conflict is to point out the speciousness of the argument that if Germany wins the war, Germany will enhance her economic strength for attack on the United States and that Germany will drive the entering wedge of that attack through the economic penetration of Latin America. Such notions make plausible talk but will not bear analysis.

If Germany aspires to a military conquest of the United States, Germany will be well advised to leave South America alone and, within the area under German control in Europe, Russia, Asia, the Near East and Africa, to concentrate on building a navy and an air force to defeat ours. And, of course, if Germany wants to knock out the United States in military battle, the very best course of events to serve that German purpose would be what our American interventionists want, namely for the United States to send expeditionary forces to scattered points in Europe and Africa and the Near and Far East where German forces or Japanese forces could outnumber them and overwhelm them one by one. This would certainly suit the ends of German conquest of the United States better than German bases in South

America equidistant and over five thousand miles from either German occupied Europe or the United States.

There is every reason to suppose that if Germany wins the war, she will have her hands full consolidating her gains, and that no German of influence on German policy today entertains the notion Germany can conquer the world or should attempt it. Germany, by her recent conquests, has not been rolling up a snowball which is soon to pass over and envelop us in a German world system. Germany by her recent conquests has been rolling up problems for German statesmanship, economic administration and military control. The greater those problems, the safer will be the United States, assuming we suffer no moral disintegration such as we might suffer following the discovery on the sands of the Asian and African deserts or in the Malayan jungles that we were not God. The economic ends of German expansion are visibly not world-wide but limited to a rather large but definitely circumscribed economic zone which cannot exceed Europe in the Ural Mountains, the Near East and Africa, if it can take in so much territory. Just what may now be its working boundaries it now seems idle to guess. Equally fatuous is speculation as to its success or failure. This may mean an economically or militarily powerful Germany, and it may also mean a somewhat shrunken and demoralized British Empire, but it does not mean an economically or militarily weaker United States. It is likely to mean a far stronger United States, militarily and economically enhanced by reason of the complete integration into our system of Canada and all the British possessions in the western hemisphere.

. . . Can the Nazis get the better of us in fixing the terms of trade? It would seem that on any overall balance of trade they could not for fundamentally the same reasons that the American farmers did not get the better of the American industrialists during the depression. The probabilities are that neither the American nor the Nazi government could get the better of the other to any important extent in international trade bargaining. The reason: both bargainers would have the means of staying out of the other's market. This was not true of the bargaining duel between American farm and industrial prices. The farmer was under greater pressure to sell than the large corporation; he was also under greater pressure to produce and not to curtail production. The United States Government versus a Nazi European Planning Commission would be like General Motors versus Chrysler in the competitive field. Neither national planning authority, in the event of a German victory, would be under irresistible pressure to sell or to buy competitively with the other. Certainly, the United States would not be under much pressure.

. . . In our post-war trade relations with a Nazi controlled European economy, it will be natural for them to want in an early post-war year, say, five million bales of our cotton, which, at 10 cents a pound, would be $250,000,000; $100,000,000 worth of our tobacco and 300 million bushels of our wheat or another $300,000,000 worth of our exports. This would amount to $650,000,000 dollars of exports of three principal staple commodities. These particular goods in the quantities just mentioned would certainly not be imported by the Nazi economy on a cash or non-barter basis. These imports from America the Nazi economy could use most advantageously, but it could also do without them, or, with some difficulty, it could obtain the Nazi area's minimum requirements of cotton, tobacco and wheat imports from other sources than the United States. If we wanted to sell these particular goods of which we have a glut (the United States government has some 8 million bales of cotton in storage; the total cotton carry-over is over 10 million bales or a year's normal markings) we should have to accept the Nazi bid to sell these goods against a corresponding value of German goods.

In a big barter deal of this character, between the United States and Nazi Europe, involving American cotton, wheat and tobacco, it is quite evident there would be some hard bargaining. The Germans would strive mainly for two things: to make us take payment in their merchandise; to obtain as much of our goods for as little of their goods as possible. This is, obviously, the opposite of dumping. The Germans would probably have the bargaining advantage over us in negotiating such a deal since we should probably be more pressed to sell than they to buy. Or, to put it differently, the Germans could obtain their cotton, wheat and tobacco minimum requirements in other markets more easily than we could market these quantities of cotton, wheat and tobacco elsewhere more advantageously to ourselves than in Nazi controlled Europe. The simple fact of Nazi advantage as a buyer in a buyer's market lends itself to wild interventionist statements about our being at Hitler's mercy in world trade, should he win. No conclusion could be less warranted. We don't have to sell our cotton, wheat and tobacco surpluses at all. We can destroy them, as Brazil has done with millions of bags of coffee, give them away to our own people or eliminate them altogether by better agricultural management. Besides, any price in Nazi goods which we received on a barter deal for our own unsalable surpluses would be more than we have been getting for these surpluses over the past few years. Any Nazi barter payment for an American pork surplus would be better for our welfare than slaughtering pigs as we did in the early days of the New Deal.

The proof that surpluses of wheat and cotton have been unsalable is the record of our large and accumulating carry-overs of these commodities since the depth of the 1932–1933 depression. The notion that the disposition of these surpluses by barter deals favorable to the Nazi economy would constitute a Nazi exploitation of our economy seems the more absurd when one considers the interventionist alternative. This would be (1) to fight a long war to force Europe to use gold, all of which would cost untold billions of dollars; then, (2) assuming we won such a war and succeeded in forcing the monetary use of gold and economic freedom in the world, to lend Europe the gold and dollar credits, as in the twenties, to buy more from us than we bought from them. The barter method calls for an exchange of goods for goods, an exchange in which the seller is compelled,—this is where the sacrifice of liberty comes in,—to receive as much in goods as he delivers in goods. Certainly we should not feel put upon to be forced in the forties to take Nazi merchandise instead of enjoying as in the twenties the democratic liberty of taking now nearly worthless German bonds.

. . . Barter is the only feasible formula of exchanging and utilizing the world's surpluses today. Barter is inconvenient. Barter does to a very slight extent restrict individual liberty. Barter does hamper trade. But unmovable surpluses and unemployable workers are a challenge which cannot again be met by a retrial of the experiments of the twenties, the experiments which culminated in the crisis of commodity surpluses and mass unemployment during the thirties.

America can adjust herself to New Economics better than any other nation. In this adjustment America has the size and strength to be a leader nation within its economic zone. It need not fear the fate of a technologically incompetent nation like Russia for America is not technically incompetent. It need not fear conquest of the world by Germany because no such thing has ever yet happened. But it should not attempt the conquest of the world by America and Britain.

Germany had to fight for the chance to try to build a new order in Europe. It remains to be seen whether Germany can win by war this chance, or whether if Germany wins by war this chance, Germany can take advantage of the chance in peace successfully to build a new order in Europe. Be that as it may, America has the chance to try to build a new order in this hemisphere without having to fight for such a chance. America does not have to fight outside this hemisphere for that chance. We should be prepared, if necessary, to fight within this hemisphere to defend that chance. If we fought outside this hemisphere, we should not be fighting for an opportunity to build a new order here; we should be fighting to prevent another power from building a new order over there. If we won that fight, the gain, if any, would be purely negative. We should not, thereby, have built another and better order abroad or at home. We should thereby have weakened and impoverished ourselves for the building of a new order at home. Would stopping the present builders of a new order in Europe advance or retard the building of our new order in this hemisphere? Our great fortune is that we don't have to fight for our chance to build here, though we may have to fight to defend it. Let us answer the call of our destiny which is to build over here and not to destroy over here. In the words of the Father of this country, "Why quit our own to fight on foreign soil?"

DOCUMENT 58

"The Economic Consequences of the Lease-Lend Program"

undated memorandum [1941]

Dangers of Over-Expansion of the Defense Program Necessitated by the Bill

It is apparent from the above considerations that the present American defense plan is of sufficient scope to tax the productive facilities of the economy. We are now in a position to assess the economic effects of a super-program, such as envisaged by the lease-lend bill, combining American requirements with additional volumes of supplies for the British.

(A) The Effect upon Prices.   There are at the present time sound reasons for holding that the general inflationary price rise of the first world war need not be repeated now. There may develop, however, partial price rises affecting the defense sector of the economy. While excess capacity exists in nearly all consumer-goods industries, thus affording a general check to prices in this field, the same favorable condition does not prevail in the heavy industries. Already price increases of considerable magnitude have occurred in a variety of products required for the arms industries. The following price increases occurred between August 16 and Dec. 31, 1940:

Steel scrap	17 percent
Lead	16 percent
Zinc	11 percent
Copper	12 percent
Hides	27 percent
Wool	24 percent

By the end of last December the industrial stocks of various strategic nonferrous metals dwindled alarmingly and prices rose accordingly. Copper stocks on hand represented six weeks supply; lead stocks, four weeks supply; and zinc, one week; as consumption of these indispensable raw materials increased continuously and production could not increase equally.

Now, as the American defense program expands, there is widespread conviction among economists and market men that prices of materials required for the arms industries will increase considerably, nothwithstanding the Price Stabilization Division. If the prices of farm commodities rise

10 to 20 percent in the next 18 months, as expected, it is reasonable to expect industrial materials and finished defense supplies to rise even more sharply, even under a system of priorities and despite Mr. Henderson. How large the price increase may be cannot be estimated. But it is certain that the faster the government undertakes to expand defense expenditures, the sharper the rise will prove.

The flow of defense materials cannot be increased simply by larger Congressional appropriations or by increased expenditures by defense agencies, except slowly by spending directly in creating new plants. If the defense program is over-expanded, or expanded too rapidly, the result is easily predictable: higher prices will be paid by the government but the flow of armaments will not increase proportionately.

The experience of the first world war is applicable in this respect to the present situation. It will be recalled that there was virtually no increase in the general volume of industrial production after the United States began to pour federal expenditures into the market for war supplies. For the limits of manufacturing capacity had been about reached in the United States during the first world war in the early years of the conflict as the result of war orders from abroad. Industrial production reached its peak in 1916, rising sharply from depression levels in 1914, and receding during the remaining years of the war. The spending of money could not produce more goods; it could produce only higher prices. The index of wholesale prices of the Bureau of Labor Statistics rose from 70 in 1916 to 135 in 1918, while the total output of commodities fell.

In the present situation, if the attempt is made to force the program before capacity is expanded in the critical sectors of the economy, prices will rise but not production. The cost to the government will be multiplied without any comparable advance in the defense effort.

This is the meaning of the threat of inflation in the present situation. It need not take place. It can occur only if a sharp rise in prices in the defense industries causes speculative behavior in all parts of the economy. This is a definite possibility that would not only increase the cost of the defense program but would lead to the familiar disruptive effects throughout the whole economic system.

The dangers implicit in such a situation are described by the economist Jacob Marschak in the current issue of Social Research for February, 1941:

The price "rise will throw overboard all cost calculations, thus favoring the speculator at the expense of the carefully planning entrepreneur; will expropriate the middle class in so far as it consists of savers or of people with fixed money incomes; will penalize the workers, who are usually unable to adjust their incomes to rising prices. Injustice and political upheaval will threaten to frustrate the defense effort."

One of the imperatives of the present situation, then, is that defense expenditures be kept within economic limits. The effects of an economic breakdown, occasioned by over rapid expansion, are incalculable. The United States cannot be made the arsenal of the British Empire merely by our wishing so. Our potential armament production is definitely limited, and the total can be shared with the British but cannot be increased beyond a certain point at any given time.

(B) The Effect upon Labor. No one questions the fact that the American defense program as now planned will increase employment. The program now actually under way is so huge that it may mean three million new jobs in 1941. Yet, huge as it is, it seems small against our army of eight to ten million unemployed (Wage and Hour Division Annual Report for 1940, p. 2, Jan., 1941). While this is all to the good, it does not follow that a larger defense program would mean greater gains to labor. Quite the contrary is the case. Even the present program will mean serious sacrifices to labor as well as benefits; and a larger one would magnify the costs to labor more than it would increase any offsetting advantages. In fact the superimposing of a large British program on top of the growing American one would result in serious dangers to labor over and above the consequences to the general economy discussed in the preceding sections.

Let us suppose, for example, that a consumer-goods industry such as the automotive industry is required to curtail its consumption of steel to make way for armaments as may soon happen. Many similar instances are possible. The result will be large-scale stoppage of production in the industries affected. Hundreds of thousands of persons will be without work for an indefinite period of time. Theoretically they would be available for employment in the defense industries. The diversion of raw materials to the arms industries will facilitate an increase of military goods, but will not necessarily provide employment for all, or even most, of the men laid off. On the contrary it is quite reasonable to suppose that large pools of unemployment will be created at the same time that the defense industries will need more skilled men than are available. The experience of England in the current war supports this supposition. In November, 1940, after more than a year of frenzied industrial efforts there were still over 600,000 unemployed (London Economist, Dec. 28, 1940).

There is no gainsaying the fact that priorities affecting consumer-goods industries will create unemployment on a broad scale. What is more the process is a cumulative one. Unemployment in the automobile industry, for example, will have effects upon the sellers and producers of a long list of other goods, because of the decrease in purchasing power on the part of the men laid off. The consequences will then be multiplied as production in these fields is curtailed. This is not mere surmise but the actual experience of England in the current war. R. G. D. Allen writing in the *Journal* of the Royal Statistical Society (Part II, 1940) reports: "The figures make it clear how severely the outbreak of the war hit the building and contracting industries, the printing trade and all the services. Recruitment of men and transference to other industries have not prevented a considerable rise in unemployment in these previously expanding trades."

A spokesman for the Advisory Commission of the Council of National Defense, Calvin B. Hoover, writing in the New York Times Magazine for February 16, 1941, indicates quite clearly that we may expect priorities to affect wide areas of American industry. He writes:

"Even now, on account of the speed which is absolutely necessary, we shall probably have more specific disruption of production for civilian uses in the near future than there was during the period of rearmament in Germany. A need for a particular kind of steel for armament might seriously hamper production of automobiles, for example, even though men and most materials are readily available. A shortage of copper might curtail production of electrical equipment for civilian uses in the same way. . . .

"We might even have to refrain from building houses which we badly need in order that steel should be available for armament uses or for housing construction in areas where defense industry must expand."

It is not to be suggested that the defense program should be carried only so far as it contributes to prosperity along "business as usual" lines. But the dislocations and postwar problems created by an over-rapid expansion of the defense program should be borne in mind in making legislative decisions as to the size of the defense program to be attempted. Our armament program will, of course, require the shifting of men from one occupation, or industry, or geographical location to another. Housing shortages will naturally become acute in defense areas.

Sacrifices of this kind by labor are expected, and gladly accepted, for the needs of the American defense effort. But the aggravation of the problem by unnecessary or unwise expansion will cause incalculable suffering after the defense industries close down, when defense towns become deserted and workers possessing highly specialized skills become migratory workers attached to no stable community.

The attempt to enlarge the defense program too much, or too rapidly, will have many other immediate and long-run dangers to labor. The shortages of skilled labor already developing at a time when the defense program is still in its infancy will become a more acute problem as time goes on. The larger the defense expenditures, the more serious the problem. Unless there is to be conscription of labor, one solution of the shortage, apart from training programs (which take time), is for industry to break down the industrial process into more simple operations. This dilution of labor skills is a matter of serious concern to labor.

Organized labor is cooperating to the fullest extent in the defense program, and Congress cannot treat lightly or ignore the danger to labor of the dilution of skills that is bound to result even from the existing American arms program. For a man's skill in his occupation is his greatest asset. Quite naturally it is a concern of labor unions to protect the position of their members. While it can be argued that this dilution of skills is, in any case, an inevitable development in modern industry, it can likewise be argued that much human suffering results if the process of change is rapid rather than slow and gradual. The faster we speed up the process, the greater problems we heap up for ourselves in the postwar period.

It is not only the worker occupying a highly skilled position who is endangered. The young recruits to industry who are being trained for one highly specialized task—filing gun triggers, for example—will have received their basic occupational training and experience in an occupation which prepares them for no job afterwards.

Nor can it be simply argued that simplification of the industrial process in the defense industries is a great boon in itself, aside from immediately increasing the output of arms, and that objection to it is obstruction of industrial progress. The minute subdivision of labor that will be pushed to great lengths in the absence of skilled labor, if the defense industries grow prematurely, will not necessarily be applicable in general to peace-time industry. The net result of this excursion into simplified industrial processes may be, aside from the experience gained by industrial engineers, that our peace-time industries will find themselves without necessary skilled labor. To the extent, however, that the over-expanded defense program introduces changes in industrial methods that become a permanent part of our industrial life, the result will be that skilled workers will find themselves competing with relatively unskilled labor for their jobs. On the other hand, the young workers trained to perform simple tasks in a more simplified mode of production will have no training except as relatively unskilled workers.

Quite frankly, labor leaders in the United States find themselves confronted on the one hand by a desire to do everything in their power to contribute to the success of the defense effort and on the other hand by the realization of the danger to their members and their organizations after the war emergency is over. The problem can be complicated unduly by the size of an arms program that tries to superimpose British requirements on top of American. We have said elsewhere that such an attempt is futile, for there are limits to the volume that can be produced in any case, and that it is the one possibility of inflation in this country. But aside from the resulting dangers to consumers and labor of this eventuality, such a program will contribute to the special problems that are bound to face workers and their organizations in the postwar period. These problems will be all the worse, of course, if a postwar depression is not avoided. The aftermath of the first world war is still fresh in the minds of workers. Faced by a declining labor market as the result of the depression that followed the war, whatever gains labor may have made during the war melted away.

These are not picayune fears or objections on the part of labor. The whole history of postwar Germany is the history of a country faced by problems of readjustment that could not be easily solved. In our present case the resumption of peacetime industry may prove as difficult as the transition to a wartime economy. It may then appear easier to maintain the armament economy than risk the danger of abandoning it, once it has become the backbone of the whole economy. Youth thrown out of work, with no skills, amid widespread unemployment that may follow the cessation of military production, amid political upheaval occasioned by economic distress, may well prove good recruits for fascism. Social tension will arise between those with jobs and those without, and labor unions will then be called upon by statesmen to pursue policies expensive to themselves to preserve the social fabric—an accomplishment that not even the well organized German labor movement succeeded in doing. Thus we may save the world from fascism only to find we have created the conditions for it at home.

(C) The Effect upon Consumers. Under the defense program as now outlined in the budget forecasts, calling for expenditures up to $6½ billion in the fiscal year 1941, and $11 billion in the following fiscal year, there should be little question that an increased volume of consumer goods will be produced simultaneously. The growth in consumption will be much smaller than is commonly supposed, for economic reasons that will be indicated later. Consumer-goods production will rise more slowly than durable goods production, of course, but will definitely increase. What is true of a program of this scope, however, is not true of a larger program.

Calvin B. Hoover, the defense spokesman we have already quoted, wrote in the same article in the New York Times Magazine for Feb. 16 a confirmation of this fact: "It seems almost certain that the production of consumption goods will increase at least through 1941, in addition to the great increase in production of the capital goods and armament industries." Mr. Hoover is well aware of the fact that early in 1942 when defense spending begins to exceed an annual rate of approximately $10 million that there is little chance of any further increase in the production of consumption goods. Further extension of the program at that time will mean actually the choice between guns and consumption.

It has already been indicated earlier that as soon as bottlenecks of capacity or skilled labor are reached, the government will necessarily resort to the exercise of priorities on a broad scale. Consumer goods of a wide variety that compete with armaments for strategic war materials or skilled labor will be curtailed by government fiat. Automobiles, refrigerators, other electrical and household appliances, metallic articles of all kinds, perhaps rubber tires, and a long list of smaller items are likely to be affected. For the standard of living of the American family this means that they will be forced to spend their incomes on second choices, and not in the way that they would most prefer. This represents a reduction of their real consumption in the same way that a general rise in prices would reduce the level of their real income. We may again quote from Calvin B. Hoover for official support of this point of view:

"Long before the stage of full employment is reached there will be innumerable specific instances in which we must choose between a particular kind of consumption goods and the progress of our defense program. Consumer whims and unimportant preferences can, of course, be disregarded." Such preferences may, however, be important for the consumer if not for the Consultant to the Advisory Commission of the Council of National Defense.

Despite the hopes of the President that the cost of the defense program will be borne by progressive income taxes out of the increased level of income, there are considerations leading to the conclusion that the American consumer will be required to make substantial contributions toward financing the defense program without reference to any increase in personal income that he may, or may not, receive.

In the recent revision of the American tax structure higher rates were imposed on a broad list of consumptive items. There is no assurance that this kind of taxation will not be extended. On the other hand, there will exist incentives for the government to impose higher consumption taxes as a means of restricting consumption in general or as a means of supplementing priorities in those instances where defense policy dictates curtailment of consumption of specific kinds. From this point of view taxes upon consumption are more effective than the more progressive income tax that, in general, affects savers and investors more than the mass of consumers.

It should be borne in mind, moreover, that income taxes represent a rather small part of the total federal-local tax system. The whole system is not likely to be transformed from a regressive to progressive system under the exigencies of a large defense effort. At the same time there will be attempts on the part of some to minimize borrowing as a means of financing the program by increasing whatever taxes that appear easiest to increase. This view will be supported by the need to curtail consumption and to divert as much of current income and production to the supplying of defense material.

As defense expenditures mount there will develop pressure to induce the mass of consumers to save more and more by investing in liberty loans or baby bonds of some other kind as a means of financing the war. This is tantamount to a reduction of current consumption. Such a drive will be dictated not by the difficulty of governmental borrowing, which will not prove hard, but as an indirect means of curtailing consumption. If the defense program is inflated, along lines suggested by the lease-lend legislation, novel proposals will be presented in imitation of Mr. Keynes suggestions for England as a means of preventing inflation by sterilizing consumer incomes. These plans may call for the forced savings of all overtime or of increases resulting from advances in hourly rates of pay that may take place, or for an arbitrary percentage of all wages and salaries. While such policies may be appropriate for England, they are policies dictated by extreme emergency for an economy near its breaking point. Such action could be justified only by the imminence of inflation resulting from the small volume of consumer goods available compared with the total volume of wages and salaries.

There is little need to emphasize the role of rising prices in undermining the real income of persons with relatively fixed incomes. The experience of the first world war will be recalled. The rise in prices was so marked that not even a rapid rise in wages was sufficient to offset it. The simple fact is that the volume of consumption goods was not increased. There was no possibility for any improvement in the standard of living. While it is not possible to estimate the rise in the cost of living that may occur in the present emergency period, it has already been indicated that a defense program that exceeds the maximum compatible with our economic facilities will result in a striking rise in prices, even in consumer goods, if not extreme inflation throughout the whole economy. Prices will rise more or less depending upon the increase in wages and salaries, flowing from expansion in the defense areas, relative to the increases in the output of consumer goods.

To the degree that the production of articles of consumption is restricted while total income rises with enhanced employment, prices will naturally go up, aside from the consideration of the bidding up of prices by the government in order to force defense output, unless checked by some method of forced saving that keeps consumer incomes off the market. In any case, whether by price rises or forced savings, consumption is reduced, and the general level of non-defense economic activity is depressed.

Consumer's real income in the United States may be reduced not only by priorities, by increased taxes bearing on consumption, forced savings, and rising prices, but likewise by the expected curtailment of many normal government services. Because of the economic cost of a super-armament program, many useful activities of government will be abandoned in the name of economy. If the British requirements for war material are added to our own, the greater will be the incentive to curtail all non-defense expenditures of the federal government. Our public plant will be allowed to deteriorate. Public services that have been developed only after slow realization of their value to the population will be summarily given up. The social utilities flowing from public services are, in many instances, all too difficult for many persons to assess. But they are genuinely real, and their curtailment will reduce the standard of living of the lower income classes.

The economic effects of a large defense program will not include so large an increase in employment or so large an increase in consumer goods production as many people expect. This is the result of the operation of a very simple economic process that is not widely enough appreciated. The stimulating effect of a given volume of investment expenditures, whether for armaments, public works, or private investment in plant, equipment, or housing, will be large or small depending upon the relative size of savings and consumptive expenditures. If a large proportion of national income is saved—that is, not spent for current consumption—it will require a larger volume of investments of all kinds to maintain or increase national income.

Under a huge defense program that requires all sorts of curbs upon production, and that will probably result in a larger proportion of national income going into profits or amortization of plant and a smaller proportion of the total going for wages and salaries, the tendency to consume will naturally be reduced. The stimulating effect of the public expenditures for defense that are made will have a smaller multiplying effect. The corollary of this is that employment opportunities resulting from the defense program will be largely limited to the defense industries alone. It is accordingly unlikely that the defense program will result in either full utilization of our economic resources in consumer-goods industries or full employment of our man-power.

For the postwar period the significance of the above considerations are perhaps even more serious than for the present. In the first place, the beneficial effect of a wise program of public investment will be discredited by the public. It will be associated with a great economic effort, justified by our defense needs or those of the British, which did not improve the lot of the average citizen and which left in its train a host of dislocations in the economy. Secondly, the probable shift in the distribution of income and wealth toward greater concentration will lead to a relatively greater tendency to save in the postwar period. The effect at that time will be to decrease the relative level of consumption, which will require a higher level of combined private and public investment to maintain the level of national income that would otherwise be required in our economy. Finally, the significance of this situation is that the possibility of a serious postwar depression is made more likely, while the only alternative, a great program of public investment for socially useful purposes such as housing, will have been discredited. The financial cost of an over-expanded defense program will result in the demand for retrenchment at the very time that public investment may be required on a large scale to supplement the deficiency in the volume of private investment expenditures. The need for such a program is likely to be accentuated by the dislocations introduced into our economy by the defense effort that will mitigate against the prospects of a high level of peacetime business activity that might in turn stimulate a large volume of private investment.

DOCUMENT 59

A. Whitney Griswold to R. Douglas Stuart, Jr.
January 16, 1941

I am partly reminded by my conscience and partly by my letter files of a memorandum on foreign policy that Dick Bissell [assistant professor of economics, Yale University; later deputy director of plans, Central Intelligence Agency] and I were going to send you last November. I think I owe you a word or two of explanation as to why this memorandum has not been forthcoming. I am speaking now entirely for myself, though I imagine that I am also representing Bissell's views as well.

Events have marched so rapidly in the last two months that I am *frankly confused* in my own mind as to exactly what course of policy to believe in. This is the first reason why I have been unable to draft a memorandum on the subject. I still believe that we can and should refrain from committing ourselves to military involvement in the war and, more particularly, to Utopian visions of world peace, prosperity and democracy advanced by the President in his message to Congress as the basis for his policy. On the other hand, it seems to me that we have already gone so far in stirring up the Axis powers and their satellites against us, that if together or separately they could defeat England and take possession of the British fleet they could, and would certainly be disposed to, do us harm. I deplore and wish undone many of the steps that have led to this position. But the fact is that they have been taken and we face a condition and not a theory. For this reason, I believe it is of considerable importance to us to keep Britain—I mean the United Kingdom and the British navy—out of German hands. Right now, I should not go any further than this in stating my own personal war aims. I should certainly not, at this juncture anyway, endorse a restoration of British hegemony over all Europe or even the prolonged survival of the British imperial *status quo*. Least of all would I sign my name to the Utopian visions alluded to above. But I come back every time to the stubborn fact of the importance of the British navy to American security.

On this point, let me hastily disavow the interpretation of the William Allen White Committee—which is that ever since 1815 the British navy has been a "benevolent" power in the Atlantic. This interpretation is historically unsound. It overlooks the fact of the influence of Canadian security on British naval policy [Griswold reasons that because Canada was part of the British empire, the British had their own vested interest in protecting an Atlantic lifeline.]; it overlooks the British policy toward Texas prior to the Mexican war [Before the Mexican war, Britain had encouraged Texas to remain an independent republic.]; it overlooks the basis of the Alabama Claims [Alabama claims, settled in 1872, were proferred by the United States against Great Britain for the deprivations caused during the Civil War by British-built warships, in particular the *Alabama* and *Florida*]; the British tolerance of French intervention in Mexico during the Maximilian episode [Maximilian, Austrian archduke and brother of the Emperor Francis Joseph, whom Napoleon III persuaded to become puppet emperor of Mexico; in part because of U.S. pressures, in particular those of Secretary of State William E. Seward, Napoleon withdrew his forces, which resulted in Maximilian's death] , as well as the countless instances of British intervention in Latin America, not the least of which was the famous Venezuela boundary dispute. [The Venezuelan boundary dispute was a controversy between Venezuela and Britain over the boundary line of British Guiana. In 1895 Secretary of State Richard Olney precipitated a crisis by declaring that British pressure on Venezuela would violate the Monroe Doctrine, but in 1899 the dispute was arbitrated.] It further overlooks the Anglo-American naval rivalry that existed right up to and during the Washington Conference. [The Washington Conference of 1921–22, designed to reduce naval armaments and reduce conflict in the Far East, established ratios for ship building, froze fortifications in the Far East, and reiterated the Open Door in China.] But, much as I deplore the historical casuistry of the William Allen White people, I do not want myself to lapse into the position of a fundamentalist and use a historical text to obscure a present reality. I don't want to quote the Scriptures against Darwin. Regardless of the motives that guided British naval policy during the past, there is a danger that the British navy today might fall into German hands; and this danger, in my opinion, justifies not only a most comprehensive and thorough-going program of national defense in our own country but also the continuance of sales of war materials to the British.

Now here is where the problem of definition becomes acute. I adhere to the view that all current and future shipments of war materials to Britain should be made on American rather than on British terms. I am not in favor of issuing a blank check of any kind, shape, or description. I deplore the people who make use of the aid to British policy as a means of promoting further involvement in the war. And I know there are many of these people. As I see it, there are innumerable possibilities of barter (which might very easily be carried out through the Export-Import Bank if the capitalization of that were increased substantially) which need not carry any more political involvement than appears right on the bills of lading and receipts for each transaction. That is the kind of policy which I should like to support at this moment.

To this end, I have decided (as I have already explained to you in the past) not to join any of the committees such as your own, organized to influence national policy one way or the other. I still adhere to this decision. The tendency in practical politics is to overstate things, to express things in terms of extremes and logical conclusions, which are altogether foreign to the studious ways that I sincerely believe in. If there is any excuse for my profession, it ought to be able to give a good account of itself in war time as well as in peace, and I for one mean to keep at it as long as I can. In so far as the America First Committee conforms to the general outlines of policy that I have sketched above, I sympathize with its aims. I would sympathize with any committee, even the William Allen White committee, in so far as it stuck to these lines. But I intend to take part in the study and discussion of foreign policy on my own responsibilitiy in the name of my own trade, and under my own letterhead.

DOCUMENT 60

Raymond J. Sontag to Robert E. Wood
February 6, 1941

I have given a good deal of thought to Mrs. Barbara McDonald's letter of February 4, requesting me to speak on behalf of the America First Committee, and also to Mr. Kendrick Lee's letter of January 21, asking me for a statement on H.R. 1776. My conclusion is that, although I subscribed to the original purposes of your Committee and although I still feel it will be folly for us to intervene in the European war, I cannot follow you in flat opposition to H.R. 1776.

Whether we like it or not, Mr. Roosevelt will be in charge of our foreign policy during the next four years. In all questions of foreign policy prestige is one of the most important assets of a nation. Outright defeat of this bill would amount to a repudiation of his leadership and would fatally weaken not only his presence but the prestige of our government in its dealings with other governments.

We cannot abandon democratic processes in foreign affairs, but at the same time, we cannot administer an outright defeat to Mr. Roosevelt. In this situation it seems to me that the objective we should strive for is amendments to this bill which would retain financial control by Congress, and, above everything else, prevent the sailing of our merchant ships and warships in European waters. In these days the difference between being at war and not being at war is one of national emotions, not of a formal declaration. Undoubtedly, if our vessels are sunk, we will go to war emotionally, with what seems to me almost inevitably fatal consequences to the welfare of our country.

Therefore it was my hope that you would concentrate on this most dangerous part of the bill. By calling for outright defeat of the bill, impossible in any circumstances and in my judgment undesirable, it seems to me that you have lost a real opportunity. On January 17, in response to your letter of January 12, I authorized the use of my name in connection with a message to Congress on the subject of convoys. Since you have widened your program to include flat opposition to H.R. 1776, I am compelled to withdraw this authorization. I do this with real regret because I feel that you have missed a real opportunity.

ADDENDUM: (Copy to General Robert E. Wood)

Raymond J. Sontag to Warren Barbour
February 6, 1941

I take the liberty of enclosing a letter which I am sending to General Wood of the America First Committee. I hope that you will find time to read it. The whole discussion of H.R. 1776 has become so confused that this unfortunate bill threatens to weaken our defense effort. Although I feel that we cannot so far repudiate the President as to work for the outright defeat of the bill, I do feel strongly that there is danger that we may find ourselves committed to war before we have attained that national unity which is essential to success in war. On this campus as elsewhere in the country those who are prepared to rush into war have been the most vocal and those who do not want to go to war have been on the defensive or silent, but let me urge you most strongly to look beyond these groups pressing for war. On this faculty, particularly among the younger men but also including some of the most distinguished of my older colleagues, there is a dangerously sullen resentment at the drift towards war. In my conversations also with store-keepers, workmen, and other people whose loyalty must be engaged if we are to fight successfully, I find predominantly a feeling of fear and horror at the drift of our national policy.

Those of us who know that national unity is all-essential if we do get into war will push aside our feeling that war should have been avoided and will bend all our efforts towards the successful prosecution of war if it comes. But it will be very hard to arouse enthusiasm among those who do not realize the dangers of half-hearted effort, and especially among those young people who will be called on to risk their lives in a cause which they are not yet convinced is our own.

I entreat you as a man interested only in the welfare of our country to see that such limitations are placed on H.R. 1776 that we may not find ourselves in war, although spiritually unprepared for war. In particular, I hope that you will make it absolutely impossible to send American warships or the American merchant marine into the war zone.

DOCUMENT 61

John Chamberlain to Mark Prentiss
December 30, 1940

Dear Mark Prentiss:

While I am worried lest we make a fatal blunder that will plunge us fruitlessly into European or Asiatic war, I don't feel at the moment that I want to be listed on any more letterheads or mastheads. The reason for my coyness is the tendency of committees of one sort or another to be pushed to "all-out" extremes.

My personal stand on the war issue is this: I am for aid to Britain, and am cold-blooded enough to see some value to us in trying to keep the scales evened up in Europe and Asia while we re-arm. I don't particularly mind seeing this country becoming an arsenal for England, for in the process we create productive capacity for ourselves. But I would insist that the neutrality legislation remain on the books; and I look with a bilious eye on proposals that allow U.S. bottoms or U.S. naval vessels within the war zones. As for "lease-lend" notions: I should prefer payment for war materials in the form of outright transfer to this country of bases that are important to us: the present 99-year lease program is bound to result in bad blood later on. Britain isn't going to love us when this war is over; no nation ever does love another whose fortune is greater, or whose suffering has been less.

My hope for the future is this: that we can help England build up to the point at which she can get a real negotiated peace, not a fake one that would leave her government and armament in hands sympathetic to Hitler. I should hate to see England compelled to take a peace of "appeasement." But I have no desire to underwrite an Anglo-American invasion of the European continent. In the first place, I don't believe such an expedition can be successfully accomplished short of killing millions of Americans and prostrating ourselves for generations, with a home-grown tyranny as the inevitable by-product; and in the second place I don't believe England and the United States are or ever will be in a position to order the affairs of Poland or Czechoslovakia. "Limitation" is my watchword, and it is no more "appeasement" than drawing a chalkline on the sidewalk and daring a bully to step over it. Incidentally, "limitation" is a word which the world must come to know again if the orgies of blood are not to continue.

To sum up, my position is more or less the stated position of Franklin D. Roosevelt as of late October in 1940. I am fearful, however, that some of the "all-out" hot-heads may push Roosevelt over the "short-of-war" line.

I'd be glad to write an article or articles embodying these views. But I must do so as an individual, not as a member of an organization.

DOCUMENT NO. 62

Lincoln Colcord to Robert E. Wood
January 6, 1941

I am honored to be asked to sign the Message to Congress which the America First Committee proposes to submit at an early date, but I find myself unable to subscribe to the content of this message. I have just sent you the following wire:

"I cannot sign your Message to Congress because in my opinion it does not go far enough or state the case clearly or consistently. It tries to carry water on both shoulders, by taking sides yet wanting to avoid war. I do not see anything in your message fundamentally opposed to the President's policy, except mild references to peace. Am writing fully."

This brief telegram hardly expresses the disagreement I feel with the position outlined in your Message to Congress. It seems to me that this message tries too hard to meet the trend of American opinion, and in doing so loses its point and consistency. It obviously defines war simply as the sending of troops to Europe, and uses this definition to rationalize the real facts out of the picture. This is the cardinal error that most isolationists have allowed themselves to fall into.

As a matter of fact, we are definitely and actively at war with Germany today. Everything the President says and does in the name of government on this issue is an act of war, and has been for many months. There is no such thing, of course, as a "measure short of war." Only a national delusion amounting to hypocrisy could adopt such a phrase, or could continue today to believe that we were not at war with Germany.

What is the point, then, in petitioning Congress not to go to war? The die is already cast; the consequences of total war have already been entailed; and Congress cannot fail to take the next succeeding steps, as the President calls for them. It would seem to me that this situation needs far more drastic and challenging treatment than your message gives it.

My own conviction is that America's position from the first should have been strictly neutral; and when I speak of neutrality I mean it in the true sense. I mean, we should not have taken sides; I mean, the war in Europe should have been no business of ours, since we did nothing to bring it about and since our self-interest was nowhere involved. As a logical corollary to this position, I believe nothing ever has threatened the United States as a result of the present European war. In my opinion, the President's whole premise of fear on which he is basing his foreign policy is without foundation, and will be so shown in history.

In candor, there is a further corollary to this position which needs to be stated. This is that it would not necessarily be fatal to the United States as a nation if Britain were defeated. I personally should be heartsick to see this happen; I come of British stock, with ten generations in New England behind me. I personally should be heartsick to see totalitarianism triumph in Europe; every fibre of my being is democratic, everything I feel and know is opposed to autocracy in any form.

But my personal feelings are one thing, national policy is another. I do not believe that it is the office of my nation to save the British Empire. I do not believe one nation can save another anyway. I believe such a conception is contrary to the history of international relations and to the organic facts of nationalism. It also is contrary to human nature. Hence I believe that the very enterprise the President is now embarking upon in the name of America, is fore-doomed to failure and world disaster.

In short, I believe we should have adopted strict and true neutrality as the only possible basic principle on which we could stand without confusion of the issues. Within this principle, things would have gone on in about the same way, but with a primary difference as to our position. British sea power would have been able to avail itself of our industrial output, while the blockade would have stopped Germany and Italy from utilizing the same resources. Yet we would not have taken sides, would not have compromised our national integrity, and still would be operating on the basis of an honest principle which could be defended with full consistency.

Well, the situation has gone far beyond that now. Yet this is no reason for changing either conviction or position. There still is nothing historically sound for us to cleave to but the pure basic principle of neutrality. I stand for this as an individual, I believe your committee should stand for it if its work is to be of true educational and political value, and I believe the nation should stand for it unless it is to be condemned by history.

DOCUMENT 63

General Memo

Washington Office
January 29, 1941

The fight to impede the Administration's course towards war at present pivots on the lend-lease bill. This bill, at first hailed as commanding the support of a majority of the people, now seems to be running into less fair weather. Confusion in the minds of the people about its purposes, the inevitable reaction in Congress against any demand on the part of the executive for more power, and the absence of any sensational features in the war situation (such as British reverses) have tended to slow up the progress of the bill.

While most observers in Washington—both pro and con—regard its passage—in some form satisfactory to the Administration—as sure, they are now inclined to place the date of its passage as March 15, rather than March 1st as estimated last week. The President's hasty conference with congressional leaders on the night of January 27 indicates Administration concern. It is recalled that the President, during the fight for revision of the Neutrality act in summer of 1939, similarly called a conference of congressional leaders of both parties. As of the last few days, it is said that the Administration now counts on only 32 Senators sure for the bill—while 28 are sure against it, thus leaving 36 unpledged. This picture is not so bright from the non-interventionist view as it seems. Most of the 36 may vote for the bill and are only procrastinating for various personal reasons. While the mail from constituents to members of Congress runs heavily against the bill (from 70% to 90% against), this mail is not as heavy as that received during the conscription fight.

A very large number of amendments seems likely. We should not, however, derive too much hope from either the number or the character of these amendments. The average member of Congress will want to protect himself for future consultation of the record. Thus he may vote for the bill after introducing amendments. If the bill succeeds with the public, his vote for the bill stands. If however the bill turns out to be unpopular, he can always point to the fact that he tried to amend it. Another point: a number of these amendments may well be congressional blackmail of the executive: non-interventionist amendments are proposed with the object of making the Administration buy off with pork the member who proposes them.

Trades, it seems, have already been made. For instance, Sen. Van Nuys, hitherto regarded as anti-Administration and leaning towards non-intervention, was given the chairmanship of the Judiciary committee in preference to Sen. McCarran [Patrick McCarran (D-Nev.)], a strong isolationist. Van Nuys is a member of the vital Senate Foreign Relations Committee, and it is noted that he is now making statements favorable to the Administration. There is speculation, also, about the permanency of the non-intervention stand of Sen. Reynolds, also a member of the committee. Reynold's vote is much desired by the non-intervention members of the committee. The estimated line-up in this Senate committee is now put at 13 for the bill, 9 against it.

A "fake" fight may indeed be made around some amendment of the bill—for instance the two year limitation clause. The Administration may seem to oppose such an amendment and may finally yield—not indeed caring a whit about such a time-limit. The Administration holds strong cards in the generalship of the Congressional fight.

Another factor which may slow up the bill is Latin-American opposition. It is not generally known that the Latin-American republics dislike the bill, for various reasons. For one thing, it violates, by its unilateral action, the collective nature of Pan-American agreements. Furthermore, Latin-American nations which have stubbornly opposed harboring belligerent war vessels—remember the Graf Spee affair in Uruguay—think that the United States are playing them false by the provision admitting warships to ports in the United States. [The *Graf Spee* was a German battleship sunk by the British in the harbor of Montevideo, Uruguay, on December 13, 1939. In the name of the American republics, the president of Panama protested to Britain, France, and Germany belligerent acts committed in American waters.] This opposition from south of the border is not an insuperable obstacle, but it may well retard final enactment. Any pressure brought to bear through Latin-American channels will help the non-interventionists.

One move—and one move only—has appeared to challenge the fundamental nature of the bill. This move is the only satisfactory solution so far of the contradictory wishes of the American people—to aid Britain and at the same time to keep out of war. It is described in this morning's N.Y. Times by Mr. Arthur Krock: "This is the group which holds that the drastic measure is unnecessary to achieve the purpose stated, that an outright gift or loan of money will effectively accomplish the same purpose." The group he refers to is possibly that headed by Senator Taft who has introduced a proposal along these lines. Such a proposal would give the money which the British claim they need, and at the same time it would eliminate the dangerous "dictatorship" powers which the bill confers on the executive. Mark Sullivan, whose piece in yesterday's paper really heralded a campaign for this kind of substitute, pointed out that it would leave responsibility for conducting the war in British rather than Roosevelt hands.

This kind of proposal is considered at least very "interesting" by Washington observers. So far it has not emerged from that stage. But it is understood that it commands increasing support. There is some speculation as to whether the N.Y. Times will give it editorial blessing. (It should be remembered that Mr. Krock's views do not necessarily represent those of the Times; he is regarded as being of an "appeasement" complexion.) Some non-interventionist quarters are cautiously for the Taft bill. These quarters, while admitting that the Taft proposal violates their doctrinaire concepts of neutrality, agree that for tactical reasons it might be well to support such a move. At least it might rally considerable support and slow up the Administration's bill. At most, it might pass and thereby hamper the Administration's warlike tendencies. At any rate, the question of support for such a measure should deserve—for tactical reasons—serious consideration on the part of non-interventionists.

One more fact in regard to the general situation should be mentioned. The more "sophisticated" of Washington observers regard the speech made last week by President Hutchins of the University of Chicago as the most effective statement of the non-interventionist case so far. They are speculating about the possibility of President Hutchins entering further into the fight. They believe he might sway "liberal," "new deal" and "leftist" sentiment more effectively than any other individual or organization at present in the field.

Some consideration of the situation of the European war is important in assessing the general situation in regard to America's entrance into or abstention from the war. The fortunes of the conflict overseas may sway popular and congressional sentiment and force action. Therefore, this letter undertakes to give a picture of the war situation as obtained from high circles in the U.S. Army.

These circles believe that a big air offensive against Britain in the spring is certain. They are inclined to place the opening date in May rather than in April, believing that Germany will expend unusual care on the preparation of air fields and planes, and waiting for the best possible weather. Such an air offensive, they expect, will be of unparalleled violence. The Germans, they think, will keep about three to four thousand planes in actual combat against England every day—which would average about ten times the number in last fall's battles. One assertion is that Germany will have accompanying the bombers a large number of fighters which will exceed the total number of fighters in the whole British air force. These circles are very much impressed by the extraordinary confidence expressed by German military (rather than political) circles that Germany will bring England to its knees by summer. These American circles believe in the possibility of invasion, but only as a last phase, after severe air preparation. Several weeks of such an attack plus the effects of air and submarine attacks of preceding months may put the British government in a mood for a negotiated peace— before any invasion starts. They figure that the air attacks and the economic deterioration of the country under air and submarine attacks may by that time be producing such serious effects that the British government may decide that it cannot afford to carry on much longer while awaiting for effective American assistance. These circles regard the Battle of Britain as of crucial importance and they minimize the long term effects of the fortunes of war in the Mediterranean. If Britain falls, they say, the Mediterranean must necessarily fall to the Axis no matter how brilliant the victories of the British troops are.

The most important factor in the "softening up" of Britain preceding an invasion is the economic factor, according to these circles. They have noted convincing evidences of British economic deterioration, as a result of sub-marine and air attacks. They claim this has now reached a "marked" stage. They speculate on when it will reach a "precipitate" stage. They note that the American public has no knowledge of certain facts like the following: that the raids on Liverpool before Christmas were of much greater impor-tance than the spectacular raids on London because the Liverpool raids destroyed about 60 million dollars worth of foodstuffs. They further point out another unpublished fact—that more than 1,000,000 tons of British shipping lies in British ports either under or waiting repair. Summing up— they estimated Britain's chances of surviving the summer at 50/50.

DOCUMENT 64

Washington News Letter #1

January 31, 1941

The Situation This Week:

The country's opposition to the war dictatorship bill is already beginning to wear it down. Even before debate begins the President has become willing to accept amendments. The hope of its supporters is, of course, that by promptly amending the bill they will break down opposition to its passage. But opponents are convinced that, with the first skirmish a victory for their side, actual defeat of this measure is possible—*provided the strong opposition sentiment in Congress is brought out by repeated encouragement from home.*

As for the amendments so far proposed, anyone familiar with the Washington situation knows that a time limit on a grant of power is worse than nothing, since it gives a false sense of security. *Possession* of power is nine points in the law of *keeping* it. Action taken under powers granted make it impractical to change back to normal on a given date. More than this, opponents of the war bill insist that Congress cannot constitutionally delegate—for a limited or an unlimited time—power to make decisions for which it is responsible under the Constitution. These decisions concern war or peace, the size of the forces this country maintains for its own defense, and the spending of public money.

The other amendments which are being considered by the House Committee as this letter is written are to prohibit the use of our ships as convoys; to require reports to Congress from the President on the operation of the act; and to require the President to consult with the Chief of Staff and the Chief of Naval Operations before any transfer of our arms. That such amendments should have to be considered simply highlights the dangerous character of the bill. The amendments, it should be noted, are being urged by supporters of the bill as originally introduced. Leaders of the opposition are in no way committed to them.

It is from the vantage point of this ground gained in the first weeks that debate in the House and hearings in the Senate will be carried on next week.

House Hearings

Press reports have not reflected what is probably the most important effect of the House hearings on members of Congress, namely dissatisfaction with the lack of concrete information from administration witnesses supporting the bill. Committee members were unable to hold witnesses, notably the Cabinet officers, to its specific provisions. Their testimony was largely a repetition of their alarm over what our situation would be if we did not insist upon an outright defeat of Hitler in Europe. In all the talk of the danger of an overseas invasion of this country, no actual picture of how this was to be accomplished was offered. Nor was there even an attempt to refute the facts and figures by which the opposition showed that invasion of a prepared America was impossible.

Cabinet officers avoided discussion of specific provisions. They refused to state what they thought would actually be done if it were passed. When questioned on the purpose of the measure, Secretary Hull referred the Committee to Secretary Morgenthau, implying it was merely a financial measure. But Mr. Morgenthau in turn referred the Committee back to Mr. Hull. How things stood in the matter of convoys was indicated by Secretary Stimson's opposition to an amendment prohibiting their use.

The House Committee obviously appreciated the frank, pertinent and detailed testimony of opposition witnesses. Notable among them were two members of the National Committee of the America First Committee: Hanford MacNider, former Assistant Secretary of War, Minister to Canada and an early National Commander of the American Legion; and William R. Castle, former Under-Secretary of State and former Ambassador to Japan. General Robert E. Wood, Acting National Chairman of the America First Committee, will be a witness before the Senate Foreign Relations Committee early next week.

In his testimony, Mr. MacNider boldly emphasized his conviction that the bill would involve the United States in war almost immediately, and that we would have to supply from 5 to 10 million men to insure the defeat of the Nazis in Europe.

Mr. Castle's main contention has since been widely picked up by the press. It was that the President under this bill would have to distribute American and American-made armaments as and where he chose. In other words, he would practically dictate the conduct of the war and be responsible for the fate of the nations engaged in the war, both in Europe and in Asia.

"It Depends on the Country"

Men who are fighting the war bill in Washington are able to meet the pressure here for it only with as much pressure as the people put behind them. They say again and again: "The country can defeat this bill—it depends on the country—"

DOCUMENT 65

Washington News Letter #3
February 12, 1941

The Situation This Week:

As the war bill moves to the Senate, opposition leaders encouraged by the size of the "Nay" vote in the House, but unimpressed by the amendments, continue to push for outright defeat of the bill.

The chief significance of the House amendments is that they indicate that the country's out and out opposition to the bill is felt by the Administration. The America First Committee throughout the Senate hearings continued to give telling and persistent expression to this opposition. Following General Robert E. Wood, Acting Chairman of the Committee, Hanford MacNider, former National Commander of the American Legion, and Kingman Brewster, Jr., recent chairman of the Yale Daily News, voiced the protest of two groups highly qualified to speak—those who fought the last war and those who would have to fight the next one.

Basic Attack Planned in Senate

Senate opposition leaders will place no reliance on either the time limit or repeal by concurrent resolution (which may or may not be constitutional) adopted in the House. Other amendments are regarded as small checks on the vast executive power the bill proposes; the financial limitation on what the President can give away binds him only as to present equipment of the Army and Navy; convoying of ships is merely "not authorized"; merchant ships may still be sent to the edge of war areas or may carry goods to neutral ports for transshipment; the requirement that the President merely consult with Army and Navy chiefs before transferring armaments leaves him free to do what he likes in the end; the requirement that he report to Congress every 90 days leaves to his discretion what information he will offer.

What is really in the minds of the bill's proponents can best be judged by the amendments that did not pass. The House voted against these safeguards: a ceiling on expenditures to which the President could commit the country; a prohibition on sending soldiers or sailors out of this Hemisphere; prohibiting the repair of belligerent battleships in our harbors.

Further and stronger amendments will be pressed in the Senate, but leaders of the opposition will direct their attacks against the major premise of the bill which is that the defense of foreign nations chosen by the President is "vital" to the defense of the United States. No amendment can alter the fact that if Hitler has to be defeated in Europe, American men will have to go to Europe to do it. Assurances that Britain does not want American men merely remind Washington of 1917 when Europe also wanted no men and Congress voted for war in the belief no men would be sent overseas.

The Iron Hand

In spite of glib assurances that the bill is "the one way to keep out of war," Washington realizes that the iron hand of war is threatening to close around the country—and that the war bill is the thumb of that hand. Here are some of its fingers: control of industry through priorities and threats to "take over"; control of labor through proposals to prohibit strikes; pressure for a bill to permit wire-tapping; regulations familiar in the last war—fingerprinting of newspaper correspondents, special passes into government buildings, beginnings of censorship, licensing of exports, preparation to take over foreign patents, registry of American-owned ships under a foreign flag, attacks on Administration opponents as unpatriotic or as "giving aid to the enemy."

The most graphic illustration of how matters stand was the revelation that the War Department had ordered 4,500,000 casualty tags and 1,500,000 coffins.

At the same time, most observers are convinced that the hand will not close if the 85 per cent of Americans who are against war will make their voices heard in Washington. No member of Congress, however courageously he fights the bill, can cast more than one vote against it. It is the country and only the country that can see to it there are enough members who make their one vote "no."

DOCUMENT 66

General Memo (Confidential)

Washington Office
February 13, 1941

The Balkan and Mediterranean theatres, while secondary to the Battle of Britain, have now become important and active. Informed military quarters here have received reports from their agents in the Balkans, as follows:

Germany has 500,000 troops in Rumania. German aviators in civilian clothes are now in Bulgaria in large numbers. Bulgaria, in spite of reports to the contrary, will cooperate quite willingly with Germany. Action of German-Bulgarian forces against Greece may be matter of days. The campaign will follow these lines: (1) Bulgarians will mass on Turkish border to immobilize Turkish forces; (2) Germans (possibly 100,000) will join with Bulgarians in moving against Greek frontier posts; (3) a real campaign will probably not start until mid-March, when the weather clears; (4) until then the Axis forces will merely demonstrate against Greece, while diplomacy goes on; (5) this will be aimed at getting Greece to put herself under German "protection," give Bulgaria an outlet on the Aegean and resume the former boundary with Albania; (6) if this succeeds, Jugoslavia will be "Swedenized," that is surrounded and controlled by German spheres and Germany will control all of the Balkans down to Turkey. The one factor that may stop all this is Russia; not war between Russia and Germany, but delay in establishing a complete Russo-German accord on Balkan matters.

These same military quarters expect that Britain will completely drive the Italians out of Libya, thus bringing British and Free French troops up to the border opposite General Weygand's Vichy forces [Maxime Weygand, French delegate general in North Africa]. These quarters however do not anticipate that this will mean Gen. Weygand's union with the Free French and British forces. It will simply mean that such a situation will make Marshall Petain stronger vis-a-vis Germany. His bargaining power will rise and he will extract more and more concessions from Hitler. In short, after British occupation of all of Libya he can wield the threat of Weygand joining the British more strongly over Hitler's head.

My sources in Washington differ as to the dates of the commencement of an all-out German offense against England. State Department sources guess that it will be early—possibly March 15. They attach importance to the American factor in the situation; they believe that Hitler must strike as soon as possible before American aid becomes effective. Military sources take a different view. They discount the factor of American aid as influencing Hitler—in fact they discount American aid as any factor this year. They put the date of the offensive much later—possibly May 1 to May 15. They believe that only military considerations—preparation of enough air fields and weather conditions—will determine the date of Hitler's action. But both State Department and military sources agree that the all-out offensive will be on a scale far vaster and more intense than is generally expected.

In the War Department, opinions on the nature of the German attack split. One school believes that Germany will not attempt invasion unless she wins supremacy of the air—that is a supremacy as great as she had over France in the Battle of Flanders. The other school believes that Germany will attempt invasion after a period of preparation by air bombing, but not necessarily waiting for supremacy of the air to be established. This observer is not competent to decide as between the two schools, but inclines to place more trust in the first view. In the past he has found the officers who take this view more reliable in their forecasts. These latter officers, incidentally, will not make positive predictions as to the outcome of the battle but think the odds are on Germany's side.

It is significant that high members of the Administration, strongly interventionist of course, are reported to be pessimistic (in private conversation) about Britain's chances. This contrasts strongly with the official view of the Administration that Britain will win.

DOCUMENT 67

General Memo (Confidential)
Washington Office
February 18, 1941

The opposition to the lend-lease bill alertly seized an opportunity to embarrass the Administration in the first day of Senate debate. They succeeded in smoking out of both Senators Austin and Pepper [Warren Austin (R-Vt.) and Claude Pepper (D-Fla.)] admissions that the United States might get into war. These admissions received headlines in all sections of the press. It remains to be seen, however, to what extent the country will react against such inflammatory statements. If the reaction is mild, then the predictions of some pessimists among the observers—i.e. that the country has been sufficiently "softened up" by the war propaganda to submit to even entrance into war—would seem to be justified.

On the second day of debate, the speeches of Bennett Clark and Vandenberg [Sens. Bennett Champ Clark (D-Mo.) and Arthur H. Vandenberg (R-Mich.)] were regarded by the press as excellent. However, the basic lack of coordination among the opposition senators developed on this afternoon. Both Clark and Vandenberg made much shorter speeches than they had promised (it had been assumed that they would occupy the whole afternoon) and Nye [Sen. Gerald P. Nye (R-N.D.)] had to be rushed in to deliver an inadequately prepared speech which he had planned to deliver on Thursday. Unless better coordination is effected, next week the opposition may fumble badly, at a time when the Administration senators will be demanding end of the debate. Senator Wheeler today admitted to this observer that the opposition couldn't hope to keep debate going longer than the end of next week.

An omen of what the country may expect once the lease-lend bill is passed appeared during the executive sessions of the Senate Foreign Relations Committee last week. According to one of the opposition senators present, Senator Connally [Tom Connally (D-Tex.)] objected to any amendment limiting the nations to be "asssisted" to Britain, Greece and China. He said that such an amendment might prevent an American aircraft carrier from transporting planes to say French Morocco if General Weygand should revolt against Vichy and join Britain. When it was quickly pointed out by an opposition senator that this would mean sending an American warship into belligerent zone, the Senator hedged and claimed that neither he nor the Administration meant to do any such thing.

Peace rumors. After thorough check-up in various parts of the Government, this observer can find no confirmation of the flood of rumors in the past week to the effect that Italy may make a separate peace with Britain. From State Department sources, it is learned that neither Ambassador Phillips [William Phillips, ambassador to Italy] in Rome, nor Admiral Leahy [William D. Leahy, ambassador to Vichy France; former chief of naval operations] in Vichy could find any truth in the reports. London likewise gave a negative to the story. In official circles here, Italy is regarded as a real "prisoner" of the Reich both from an economic and military standpoint. Economically, Italy is depending on Germany for coal, oil and foodstuffs. Militarily, the Germans could easily take control of the peninsula.

The Turco-Bulgarian non-aggression pact is regarded here as a serious blow to Britain, and especially to Greece. Something like the process described in this letter last week may be expected to follow inevitably, with the odds all on the early submission of Greece. This pact moreover further fortifies the thesis held in these letters last week that Turkey may fall into the sphere of influence of Russia. If Turkey formally breaks her pact with Britain, the latter will have suffered one of the big diplomatic defeats of the war. It would be premature however to expect the Reich to launch a campaign through Turkey against the Suez Canal at any early date. Such a campaign would involve two big diplomatic preparations: (1) with Turkey for passage of troops through her territory; and (2) with the Vichy government for passage through Vichy's Syria. This would take some time.

DOCUMENT 68

General Memo (Confidential)
Washington Office
February 20, 1941

Best opinion on the Hill is still that debate in the Senate on the lend-lease bill will terminate the end of next week. Most opposition senators agree on this. As for the conference period, earlier calculations had put it at a week. Today, this is not certain. Senator Bennett Clark, in conversation with this observer, remarked that unless a number of amendments were passed, the period of conference might not last more than a day. In that case, the bill may be passed in final form during the week of March 3.

Morale among the opposition Senators is poor. A number who will undoubtedly vote against the bill have announced that they won't make a speech against it on the grounds that they believe the fight is lost. A number of last ditchers are now talking about introducing the note of "the fight will go on" (meaning the fight will go on even after the bill is passed) in their speeches. Expert observers in sympathy with our side now predict that the bill will go through with a "whoop"; that the President will not have to proceed cautiously for a few weeks after passage but will immediately make drastic moves in the foreign situation.

This rather pessimistic forecast might have to be modified if a ground-swell from the country should develop. Apparently the White House is carefully watching for popular reactions to the inflammatory we-might-go-to-war-if-necessary statements of Senators Bailey [Josiah W. Bailey (D-NC)], Pepper and Austin. So far the Administration seems sufficiently hesitant about the state of public opinion to refrain from openly following this inflammatory line.

The opposition is now pondering the next move after the bill is passed. Some Senators are strongly for a war referendum proposal. Others are lukewarm to the idea. A decision will have to be made soon.

* * *

It can be positively stated that the Suez Canal has been closed for the past fortnight. It was closed as a result of a German bombing raid. Rumors of this have been current in Washington for the past week. This observer has received positive confirmation of this fact from a high military source. The implications of this are serious. If the Germans can thus cut off the Suez outlet of the Mediterranean and can knock out Gibraltar from the other end, then British operations in Libya, no matter how successful, will be stopped. There is considerable speculation in diplomatic circles in Washington as to whether the British will throw big forces into Greece. Unless they do, they will have lost their chance for the diversion operation on which their dopesters rest so many hopes. The question is whether the British have enough forces to spare, to affect the Greek situation.

DOCUMENT 69

General Memo (Confidential)

Washington Office
February 23, 1941

The Mediterranean situation today is in a state of flux and uncertainty. One of the most marked signs of this uncertainty is the visit of Eden and Dill [Anthony Eden, British foreign minister; General Sir John Dill, chief of Imperial General Staff] to the Near East. American army observers interpret this to mean that a profound re-exploration of the situation and the factors involved has been necessary for the British. On the British decision—and on the Germans'—may depend the course of the whole war in the next few months. Broken up in its components the situation appears as follows to American army experts:

(1) Something—exactly what cannot yet be predicted—is afoot which alters drastically one way or the other the situation in Libya. American army sources say that there is a big ship movement across the Mediterranean to and from Libya. Whether this is a withdrawal of Italian forces from their colony in a sweeping evacuation—or whether it is a strong reinforcement cannot yet be ascertained. In any case, these sources have ascertained that the British air force no longer has mastery of the air over Libya. This may mean that the Luftwaffe has come to cover an Italian retreat, or it may mean that it is covering the landing of large German forces. Our military believe that the presence of even two Panzer divisions would mean checkmate for the British advance.

(2) These sources are very pessimistic about the chances of the British putting any serious military forces into Greece. At present there are no British troops there—only a mission and about 12 squadrons of planes. It is estimated that there are only about 9 British divisions in the eastern Mediterranean and only part of these could safely be diverted to Salonica. Yet, unless the British do send forces to Greece, they will have

lost the last chance for a foothold on the continent—except by the hazardous method of landing on a hostile shore. It is estimated that the British could send not more than three or four divisions to Greece. In that case, they would face, together with that part of the 15 Greek divisions now largely occupied in Albania, some 10 Bulgarian and 25 German divisions. Bulgarian airfields are more numerous than Greek. The Axis position has so improved as a result of the defection of Turkey that it is now felt that no demonstration (as described in a recent letter) is necessary; that the Germans, when they really cross the Danube, will drive right on towards Salonica. Weather conditions at present have turned out to be unusually favorable for the Axis attack. But at present there are all the signs of a furious diplomatic exchange between Germany and Greece naturally to persuade Greece to quit.

(3) The news in the last letter that the Suez Canal was closed because of German attacks now must be slightly modified. It was closed by German planes dropping mines which sank two ships. The British closed the canal in the week of February 3rd to clear away the sunken ships. Last week it was opened again, then closed in the past two days. Reason: the German planes returned and dropped mines again in the canal. No ships have been sunk because the British closed the canal to sweep the mines. But the seriousness of this situation may play a part in the whole Mediterranean situation and in the decisions of Eden and Dill.

(4) American military sources are very suspicious of the entrance of German troops into Spain—whatever is being given out about their "technical" mission to assist devastated Santander. This may be so. But once the infiltration of German troops into Spain starts, it will be hard to check up on—difficult to determine how many troops, what kind and where they are. In such a situation lies the foundation for an attack on Gibraltar, thus pinching the British naval control of the Mediterranean at the two ends. This of course remains highly speculative as little good information about the Spanish situation is being obtained at the present time.

Summing up: The British are confronted by an extremely difficult situation in the Mediterranean—confirming all the pessimism which Churchill is said to have expressed to Willkie and Hopkins about this theater. If Libya is reinforced by the Axis, there is little chance of the British diverting forces to Greece. Even if Libya is evacuated by Italy, British forces available for Greece are so small that they could offer no serious problem to Axis forces. If all the signs so far indicated—Libya, Suez and Spain—turn out to be as favorable for the Axis as the Axis could desire, then the push of Germany into the Balkans may take on a much bigger scope and importance than hitherto assigned to it. Up to now, it has been assumed that Germany has been seeking only to prevent the British from getting a foothold on the continent via Greece. But if Turkey is moving faster in the direction of the Axis—and her desertion of Greece may be a sign of this—then German moves toward Bulgaria may herald an all out attack on British power in, and perhaps on both ends of, the Mediterranean. Such a wide campaign might delay the long awaited attack on Britain. If Turkey, in short, joins the Axis, then a German attack on the Suez, defying Vichy wishes for the neutrality of Syria, might follow. It is important to watch the reports from Istanbul.

DOCUMENT 70

General Memo (Confidential)

Washington Office
March 4, 1941

At a caucus of 15 opposition Senators in Senator Nye's office this morning, it was decided to wind up the series of speeches and prepare to debate amendments beginning Wednesday. It was felt that the effect of prepared speeches was wearing off and speeches relating to the various amendments would give the public fresher interest. It was expected that the Foreign Relations Committee amendments, first to be considered, would take several days. The sentiment of the senators was strongly for opposing any filibuster at the moment. It was felt that the numerous amendments would provide ample opportunity for speeches and the give and take of debate. If the situation developed so as to suggest the possibility of a filibuster, the question could be threshed out then. The most conservative estimates placed the earliest possible date for winding up debate on amendments at the first of next week. Some senators expressed belief that debate on amendments might last two weeks. Two senators, Holman (Ore.) and "Cotton Ed" Smith (So. Car.) [Rufus C. Holman (R-Oreg.) and Ellison S. "Cotton Ed" Smith (D-S.C)] came out against the bill today.

* * *

Now that the Germans have entered Bulgaria and taken up their positions on the frontier, the next move is up to the British. If the British proceed to bomb Bulgaria, then the Germans may be expected to invade Greece. If the British refrain from bombing Bulgaria, then the Germans will merely demonstrate on the frontier, while working diplomatically to bring Greece to peace terms. This is the view of some military quarters here. These quarters are more and more strongly of the opinion that Britain will not send any serious military force to Greece. They feel that now the spotlight has shifted to Turkey. On what Turkey does and more importantly on what Britain does vis-a-vis Turkey depends the shift of events in the Balkans.

At the beginning of the war the British bribed Turkey to join the London Axis with a 60 million pound sterling loan. Today, Britain cannot bribe Turkey with money. Turkey now demands that Britain demonstrate that sufficient British troops are on hand to assist her. Thus Britain may now be facing the necessity of letting Greece go in favor of Turkey, a more important ally. Moreover, to keep sufficient troops ready in Egypt to support Turkey, Britain may have to curtail operations drastically in Libya. It is apparent now that the Germans are arriving in force in Libya, and that German aviation is now at least checking British aviation, if not exerting some superiority. At any rate, the German-Italian air forces now have such air superiority in the central Mediterranean—between Sicily and Africa—that the British no longer can bring convoys through the Mediterranean. Troops and supplies will now have to be brought around the Cape. Military circles here report the following unpublished and unpublishable information: that a British monitor and two British destroyers have been sunk off the coast of Libya. Some military experts here believe that the British may have to evacuate Cyrenaica and retire to Egypt. Such a move would be based on the danger of keeping too long lines of communication open along the north African littoral in face of growing Axis resistance. It would also, according to these speculations, be based on the desirability of keeping large forces ready in Egypt for immediate shipment to Alexandretta should Turkey demand aid.

It is important to keep in mind that the Germans a week ago launched a new submarine drive on shipping to Britain, described by London as being four times as big as last fall. The first communiques on the effects of this should appear the first of next week. Meanwhile, it is reported that a German raider is at large in the Indian Ocean. The British have had to bring five cruisers and an aircraft carrier—from the Mediterranean—to pursue the raider. So far there is no report of her sinking or capture.

DOCUMENT 71

"Highlights of Interviews with Representatives"

Fred Burdick
undated [1941]

"The America First Committee already has prevented the United States from being in the war 100%," according to the analysis of the situation by Rep. Philip A. Bennett of Missouri [former Republican lieutenant governor of Missouri].

"If the lease-lend bill had been rushed through the House and Senate in two or three weeks," said Rep. Bennett, "the President would have been so 'cockey' he would have had us in total war by now. The extended Senate debate helped get the people somewhat acquainted with the war dangers of the measure and made the war mongers realize that the people do not want to get into the war.

"After all, the President is guided a great deal by public opinion. I agree that an articulate public opinion still is our best chance of keeping out of war with our manpower.

"Should shipments of war munitions be planned, the people and the Congress should insist that the ships be manned by volunteer crews under the British flag, and that title to the goods be transferred before leaving our ports.

"Some are saying that we must get into this war because of our world trade considerations. How many years would it take in gross trade, to say nothing of net profits, to pay for a war? From the viewpoint of economics we have no reason for going to war. It would be silly, from the dollars and cents viewpoint, to plunge into this war because of the 5% of our total trade represented by our foreign markets, to say nothing of the costs in deaths, wounded and broken hearts."

* * *

"If the fight over the lease-lend bill had started in the Senate we probably could have beaten it in the House," declared Rep. Carl Mundt of So. Dak. "The long debate in the Upper Chamber aroused the people and softened proponents of the bill in the House."

* * *

"Had it been possible to force the lease-lend bill into conference," said Rep. John M. Vorys of Ohio, "and there had been some objectionable Senate amendments which could have forced another fight on the whole measure in the House, we may have done a lot better. There is no doubt but that sentiment for the bill was on the wane when the Senate got through with it.

"The best chance the United States has of keeping out of the war is for it to end before we can get into it. The situation looks bad to me."

* * *

"The people in general do not know even yet what this lease-lend bill is all about," declared Rep. Henry C. Dworshak [Republican] of Idaho. "I am afraid there is nothing we can do to keep out of the war."

* * *

A. P. reports in local newspapers that certain Representatives finally voted for H.R. 1776 instead of stating the fact that they voted for acceptance of the Senate amendments have gotten a number of Congressmen "in Dutch" with opponents of the bill back home. Many very outspoken critics of the measure voted for the amendments because they thought they improved the bill considerably.

* * *

Democratic floor leader John W. McCormack of Mass., told several Congressmen confidentially that had H.R. 1776 gone to conference the Administration would have taken out the Byrd amendment, which reads:
"On page 3, line 10, after the period, insert the following new sentence: 'Defense articles procured from funds hereafter appropriated shall not be disposed of in any way under authority of this paragraph except to the extent hereafter specifically authorized by the Congress in the Acts appropriating such funds or otherwise.' "

* * *

"The Byrd amendment makes it a much better bill," said Rep. Melvin J. Maas [Republican] of Minn.

* * *

"The bill (H.R. 1776) is much better than when we voted on it in the House," said Rep. Richard M. Simpson [Republican] of Pa. "It shows that the Democratic process works."

* * *

"The Senate amendments are all right," stated Rep. Usher L. Burdick [Republican] of No. Dak. "They could have been stronger, of course, but the moral and psychological effects may prove far-reaching in the future— more so than we can perceive at present."

* * *

It is generally conceded on the Hill that had it not been for the strenuous and determined opposition, the Senate amendments, as well as those originating in the House, would not have been adopted. *Some go so far as to say that it is possible that the amendments may keep the nation out of total war.*

DOCUMENT 72

Union Now?

"Did you know that 'Union Now' means renunciation of the Declaration of Independence, and immediate 'shooting' participation by the United States in the war?"
No. 16, August 6, 1941

The Claim

There is at least a possibility that we are right in believing that we can neither maintain the essentials of our constitutional system, even here at home, nor win the war without establishing a provisional federal union with the British. (Clarence K. Streit, President, to Convention of Federal Union, Inc., on June 28, 1941, reported in *Federal Union,* July-August, 1941, page 2.)

From the war in which accounts between Britain and America are now getting somewhat mixed, the step forward to a common army, navy, and air force—and taxation to pay for them—is not far distant. . . . We in Great Britain have all to gain from a union, and the invitation must come from America. (Colonel Josiah Wedgewood, Member of the British Parliament, in the course of an American "lecture" tour, Washington Times Herald, July 9, 1941.)

The Answer

We, therefore, the Representatives of the United States of America, in General Congress assembled, . . . do . . . solemnly publish and declare, that these United Colonies are, and of Right ought to be Free and Independent States; that they are Absolved from all Allegiance to the British Crown, and that all political connection between them and the State of Great Britain, is and ought to be totally dissolved; . . . And for the support of this Declaration, with a firm reliance on the protection of Divine Providence, we mutually pledge to each other our Lives, our Fortunes and our sacred Honor. (The Declaration of Independence.)

As Others See Us

The American people have expressed their desire to aid Britain by "steps short of war." Attempts are now under way to undermine that policy and to drag the United States into the present war by the devious method of urging alliance with Britain. Symptomatic of these attempts have been the recent statements of British leaders. As public officials of one country, they could not, of course, openly and expressly urge another country to declare war or to form an immediate alliance which necessarily involved participation in war. But their public statements have gone as far as was possible. Thus, Lord Halifax, British Ambassador to the United States, urged recently an Anglo-American alliance after the war for the purpose of establishing a new world order, to which other nations (including the Latin American countries) would be permitted to adhere (Christian Science Monitor, June 20, 1941). Prime Minister Winston Churchill has called for Anglo-American unity of aims, and has proclaimed that "united we can save and guide the world" (Washington Post, June 17, 1941). Australian Minister Richard G. Casey announced in one address that neither the United States nor the British Commonwealth could alone solve post-war problems, and asked for recognition of the "fact" that "we are essential to each other in peace—as essential to each other as one blade of a pair of scissors is to the other" (New York Times, June 14, 1941). In another address, which the press reported as stopping "just short of advocating immediate union of English-speaking peoples . . ." he proclaimed that preservation of the world was in the combined hands of the United States and the British family of nations (Baltimore Sun, July 5, 1941). Dr. R. C. Wallace, principal of Queen's University, in Canada, looked forward to a permanent partnership of the United States and Canada as an outcome of the war, for the ultimate purpose of cementing a permanent Anglo-American alliance (New York Times, June 24, 1941). The most forthright of British propagandists to visit the U.S., Colonel Josiah Wedgewood, called for immediate union and American participation in the war, in such tactless terms (New York Times, June 3, 1941; Washington Times Herald, July 9, 16, 1941) that his visit here was soon terminated by the embarrassed British government.

Lead Kindly Streit

The most important organizational expression of the elements which desire an Anglo-American alliance is Federal Union, Inc., organized in 1939 to promote the plan conceived by Clarence K. Streit, and commonly known as "Union Now." According to the annual report of Dr. Emery W. Balduf,

Executive Director of Federal Union, Inc., this organization now has 93 chapters in as many American cities, and 126 separate organizing groups. During the past year and a half they have produced and distributed more than 1,500,000 pieces of "literature" (*Federal Union World*, July-August, 1941).

In addition to numerous sporadic broadcasts (including the American Forum of the Air on Sunday, August 3rd, 1941), Federal Union has recorded a series of some fifteen radio talks to be rebroadcast over local stations throughout the country. Extensive publicity in contemporary periodicals presents the message of immediate union with Britain to an audience of several million people. During the month of July this propaganda was featured in *Reader's Digest, Liberty*, and *Look*. The September issue of *Screen Life* is presenting a story on the Federal Union plan as explained by those heroes and heroines of Hollywood, suddenly turned foreign affairs experts, who are Union Now devotees. The Book of the Month Club has announced that as their "book-dividend" for September and October they will give away copies of both Clarence Streit's original "Union Now" and his more recent "Union Now with Britain" to from 150,000 to 200,000 of their members. The Executive Director of Federal Union, Inc., boasts further that from March to May of this year his committee obtained 31,686 inches of free newspaper publicity. (E. W. Balduf, Federal Union Convention Report, Cleveland, June 29th, 1941.)

Entangling Alliance

Just what would happen if the United States were to adopt the plan for "Union Now"? According to the literature issued by Federal Union, Inc., and the answers that literature gives to questions about the nature of the plan, these would be the results:

1) *Immediate, "shooting" participation by the United States in the present war*. According to advocates of the plan, "we are already involved, through our guarantees to Canada and Latin America, our aid to Britain, our defense preparations and the conscripting of an army."

2) *An American A.E.F.* would have to fight to defend every or any part of the British Empire, for Federal Union, Inc., points out that, for example, "American boys (would) have to go to war if Japan attacked Australia."

3) *We would be compelled to stay in that war so long as Britain and her Dominions desired to keep fighting,* and Britain and her Dominions could not make peace if we objected. "Union Now" literature points out that "under the federal union arrangement, one country in the Union could no more make a separate peace than the State of New York could

make one for the U.S.A.," and that the British Government could not make a separate peace or surrender its fleet.

4) *There would be a common military machine,* composed of the combined armed forces of Britain and the United States.

5) There would be a *common citizenship,* giving British subjects a voice in effect in American affairs, and Americans a voice in the affairs of the British Empire. One of the first and most significant obligations of this new citizenship would be *common taxation*—on both Americans and British—to pay not only for the cost of the war (which is estimated to be costing Britain now 53 million dollars a day), and for the cost of this combined military machine, but also for the cost of post-war reconstruction of the British Empire. Citizens under this plan would owe allegiance, not to their respective nations, but to a super-government which Clarence K. Streit calls "World Federation for Peace and Democracy."

6) *A common war cabinet,* in which President Roosevelt and Prime Minister Churchill could get together for consultation and decision, would be an important initial feature of this super-government. Lease-Lend Administrator Harry Hopkins has already sat in on a meeting of the British war cabinet (New York Times, July 18, 1941), and the rumors, as yet not authoritatively denied, of a meeting now in progress between the two Chiefs of State may be carrying on the trend towards such a super-government (New York Times, August 6, 1941).

7) *The fate and welfare of the millions of people in the colonies and possessions of the British Empire would become in part our responsibility,* for "Union Now" would make them part of the territorial possessions of the new super-government, without the right to participate in that government. Added to our own problems would then be responsibility for the fate of the 60,000,000 people in British Africa, the 367,086,000 people in British Asia, the 3,249,000 people in British Europe (outside the United Kingdom), the 13,259,000 people in British possessions in the Western Hemisphere, and the 10,516,000 people in Australasia (The Statesman's Yearbook, 1940).

27 to 23

The advantages to an embattled Britain of such a union are obvious. The advantages to the United States are less evident, and supporters of "Union Now" find it necessary to speak in generalities and platitudes in order to sell their plan on this side of the Atlantic. One new feature of Clarence Streit's plan, as revised in his second book, "Union Now With Great Britain," is designed to appeal to those Americans who cherish visions of imperialistic grandeur a la Henry Luce [publisher of *Time, Life, Fortune;* author of editorial "The American Century," *Life*, February 17, 1941]. For example, in his column of March 22nd, 1941 (New York Herald Tribune, March 23rd) Mark Sullivan wrote:

> While Britain is unable, alone, and the United States is unwilling, the two together could readily dominate the world. Britain could continue to be the greatest mercantile sea-going nation. As to naval power, Britain and the United States in union could have dominance beyond any dream of challenge.

Mr. Streit's latest sugar-coating of Federal Union, to increase its palatability for Americans, would provide for American domination of the union by granting to the United States 27 votes in the World Congress as against a total of 23 for the combined British democracies (United Kingdom 11, Canada 3, Australia 3 and 2 votes each for Union of South Africa, New Zealand and Eire). Mr. Streit does not say whether this suggestion has the approval of Mr. Churchill and his government. H. N. Brailsford, well known British journalist, on July 20, 1941, stated that British governmental circles do not look with favor upon this plan (Baltimore Sun).

Sugarcoating

Glossing over their immediate demand to abrogate the sovereign independence of the United States, Mr. Streit and his fellow unionists hasten to assure us of their desire that such a nuclear union between Britain and the United States "shall grow gradually into the United States of Man by peaceful admission of outside peoples to equal membership" as soon as such peoples shall have established their fidelity to the democratic way of life. (Look, July 29th, 1941, pg 38.) By thus envisioning as a *possible* outgrowth of their plan some beatific system of world-wide cooperation for the betterment of man, the federal unionists have corralled into their camp many sincere persons who realize that world peace can only result from universal recognition of the brotherhood of mankind, and who hopefully grasp at Union Now as a tangible movement with such an end as a *possibility*, however remote. These followers are inclined to overlook the imperialist structure of the British Empire, as, indeed, they also overlook the British background of the leading American proponents of Union Now.

British Network

But a more important fact which is overlooked is that "Union Now" is geared to American participation in the war and to Anglo-American world domination—its inevitable, if not its ostensible, result. This is not surprising, when the leading supporters of "Union Now" are identified. The Federal Union organization must be viewed against the long history of attempts in the

United States to promote American participation in the League of Nations and to bring about an Anglo-American alliance. Space is lacking to review here what one informed commentator called the "British Network" (Quincy Howe, "England Expects Every American to Do His Duty" (1937)), but it is clear the Federal Union reflects the influence of such organizations as the League of Nations Association, the English Speaking Union, the Foreign Policy Association, and the Council on Foreign Relations.

Who's Who

Leading interventionists abound in the ranks of Federal Union. Many of the leading supporters of "Union Now" are members or active supporters of such interventionist groups as the Committee to Defend America (formerly the Committee to Defend America by Aiding the Allies), the Fight for Freedom Committee, the Church Peace Union, and the InterFaith Committee for Aid to the Democracies. Many have signed interventionist statements issued by special groups, or have made public statements of an interventionist character. These include (see: New York Times, March 18; April 9; May 9; May 23; June 16; June 15; July 21; July 17, 1941; and Federal Union list of supporters): Margaret Culkin Banning; Stringfellow Barr; Mrs. Emmons Blaine; Clare Boothe; Esther Caukin Brunauer; Lyman Bryson; "Ding" Darling; Russell Davenport; William Alfred Eddy; Charles G. Fenwick; Dorothy Canfield Fisher; Henry W. Hobson; Edwin P. Hubble; Frank Kingdon; Mrs. Thomas W. Lamont; Max Lerner; Bishop Francis J. Mc-Connell; Thomas Mann; Raymond Massey; Helen Hill Miller; Lewis Mumford; Bishop G. Ashton Oldham; Endicott Peabody; Chester Rowell; Robert E. Sherwood; William J. Schieffelin; Ralph W. Sockman; Eugene Staley; Admiral William H. Standley (retired); Lyman Beecher Stowe; Betty Gram Swing; Edmond Taylor; Dorothy Thompson; Mrs. Frank Vanderlip; J. Skottowe Wannamaker; James P. Warburg; William Allen White; Alexander Woolcott; Mary E. Woolley; Rear Admiral H. E. Yarnell (retired); Henry Goddard Leach.

The most cursory examination of the "Partial List of Council of Advisors," printed on Federal Union literature, reveals that an overwhelming majority of the Council fall into the "interventionist" class.

Oxford Accent

Despite the claim of Federal Union that their program is 100% American, the fact remains that many of the organization's leaders—and followers—have close ties with "the motherland." Clarence Streit, founder of the movement, was a Rhodes scholar, receiving his indoctrination at Oxford University in 1920–1921. Apparently, his inspiration for the Federal Union scheme came to him at Geneva, after he had completed his studies at Oxford and was employed as a *Times* correspondent to the League of Nations. Prominent on the National Committee of Federal Union is Mrs. Thomas W. Lamont, wife of the J. P. Morgan partner who served as American purchasing agent for the British Government during the World War. In a letter to the New York Times, dated October 18, 1935, Mr. Lamont defined their mutual attitude:

> We were pro-Ally by inheritance, by instinct, by opinion, and so were almost all the people we knew in the eastern seaboard of the United States.

Another leader of the Federal Union movement in this country is Russell Davenport, Chairman of the Board of Editors of "Fortune," and personal representative of Wendell Willkie in the 1940 Presidential campaign. At the Cleveland Convention of the Federal Union (June 28–29, 1941), Mr. Davenport, who was Chairman of the Resolutions Committee, exhorted his followers to action with these words:

> Now is the time to advocate immediate union with Great Britain, even though this does not meet with the ideal of our ultimate goal. We do not mean to compromise our ideal, but we must seize upon the emergency which will guarantee the advantages that the pooling of all our resources will give. (Cleveland Plain Dealer, June 30, 1941.)

Also on the Council of Advisors for Federal Union we find Dr. Frank Kingdon, English born clergyman-educator, and Dr. Stringfellow Barr, President of St. Johns College, also a Rhodes scholar and a classmate of Clarence Streit at Oxford. Another important member of the National Committee is Frank Aydelotte, Rhodes scholar, American Secretary to Rhodes trustees, former national director of War Issues Course for the War Department Committee on Education and Special Training (1918), now member of the Athenaeum Society of London, author of "The Oxford Stamp," and co-author (with L. A. Crosby) of "Oxford of Today." Another member of the Council of Advisors for Federal Union, Inc., is John Balderston, former editor (1920–23) of "The Outlook," published in London and former London correspondent (1923–31) for the New York World. According to Who's Who for 1940–1941, John Balderston is still a member of the Pilgrims Club in London, and makes his home at 38 Trevor Square, S.W., London, England.

Also listed among the sponsors of the Union Now Plan are Rear Admiral H. E. Yarnell (retired), Admiral William H. Standley (retired), and Brig. General George V. Strong, present Assistant Chief of Staff of the United States Army (Washington Post, June 18th, 1941). This situation was brought to the attention of Congress by Representative George H. Tinkham of Massachusetts on June 17th when he demanded the removal of these officers who support union of the United States with Britain. (Congressional Record, June 17, 1941, p. 5387.)

Required Reading

There are signs of official sanction of the Union Now scheme by other leaders of American destiny. In Senate Document No. 182, Seventy-sixth Congress (a report on schools and training courses in Government departments), it is suggested that there is a "tie-in" between lectures scheduled by the Department of Agriculture Graduate School and the movement sponsored by Federal Union. This report includes the following statement:

> Judging by press releases of the past few months and public utterances of Government officials in high places, the movement has gained such headway as to receive official sanction and advocacy. (Congressional Record, June 17, 1941, page 5387.)

The June, 1941 issue of *Federal Union World* boasts that Clarence Streit's "Union Now" is recommended reading for new officers by the General Staff of the U.S. Army in a list of recent and standard works (U.S. War Dept Training Circular No. 25).

In the Ladies Home Journal (July 1941) Mrs. Eleanor Roosevelt says on her featured page,

> *If You Ask Me*, "I think the Union of all free democracies, whether English-speaking or not, is much to be desired in the future. Without it I see no prospect for eliminating war."

Perhaps it is significant that Robert E. Sherwood, prominent writer and important influence upon recent Roosevelt speeches, is an ardent advocate of the plan for "Union Now." Perhaps, the plan assumes new significance in the light of current rumors that President Roosevelt and Winston Churchill are presently engaged in conference "somewhere in the Atlantic" (United Press from London, August 5th, 1941), following the participation by Lend-Lease Administrator Harry Hopkins in a meeting of the British War Cabinet (New York Times, July 18, 1941).

On June 16th, a member of Congress called for an investigation by the Dies Committee [the House Committee on Un-American Activities led by Martin Dies (D-Tex.)] to determine whether the Union Now movement is an un-American activity (New York Times, June 17, 1941). The Washington Times Herald of June 17th observed:

> The type of British propaganda which incites such disloyalty to America and American institutions is distinctly not admirable.
>
> It is just as dangerous to American unity and American integrity as the Communist propaganda which demands first loyalty of American citizens to Moscow.
>
> All such propaganda to mislead our citizens and abate their loyalty to their own land and institutions should be branded as subversive.
>
> Propaganda to lead us into war in the interests of alien lands is bad enough,

but the attempt to make us sacrifice not only our welfare but our independence for the benefit of any foreign nation should not be tolerated by a self-respecting people.

At this writing, no official Congressional investigation of Federal Union, Inc., has yet been launched.

DOCUMENT 73

Memo on English Defenses

Speakers Bureau
undated [1941]

The difficulty of supplying a modern army and, in particular, of carrying out an all-out aeroplane blitzkreig on England is shown by these expert opinions:

> To make an air blitzkreig on England there would be needed, say, 8000 bombers plus 4000 combat planes. Considering the bombers *only*, their gasoline needs for one trip would be about 6 million gallons. The size of this quantity can best be comprehended thus: the *total* consumption of gasoline by *all* forms of transportation in the U.S. over a period of *two hours* is estimated to be 6.4 million gallons.—Abstracted from an article by Sherman B. Altick in the St. Louis Globe Democrat, February 28, 1941.

Note what a gigantic task it would be to supply only the bombers with gasoline alone. Add to that: oil, bombs, ammunition, the combat planes, anti-aircraft guns, the care of air fields, etc., and it can be understood why such an attack has not yet been attempted.

> To land a thousand parachute troops fully equipped with ammunition, motor cycles, anti-tank guns, etc., it takes 125 assorted planes.—Frederick Sondern, Jr. in Current History and Forum, March, 1941 (abstracted).

Is this a lot of planes? Yes; in the gigantic all-out raids on London, on which tremendous effort is expended, about 500 assorted German planes participate. The sort of trip mentioned in the second paragraph would, on those figures, land about 100,000 parachutists, but no tanks or heavy guns. And England has about 1,500,000 *men* under arms, and plenty of tanks and heavy guns.

DOCUMENT 74

Ruth Sarles to R. Douglas Stuart, Jr.
May 24, 1941

Herewith a few reflections on the Washington atmosphere:

In my judgment, we are in a stronger position than we were a month ago, and that not entirely because of powerful anti-war sentiment. In addition to that very important factor there are at least two others: (1) Apparently it is at last sinking in in official quarters that the British are in a very bad way. General Arnold [Gen. Henry H. ("Hap") Arnold, deputy chief of staff for the Army Air Corps] has brought back reports that have impressed many officials, and so have others. There is a rumor that shaken civilian morale is weakening production. Britain's pilot training program is getting nowhere—story is that there is no air space pilots can train. The N.Y. Times survey I sent Ken Lee last week shows that the ports have taken an awful beating—one dispatch went so far as to say Liverpool was the only remaining fully effective port. It is becoming apparent that even if we were ready to send what it takes to invade the continent, there is no place closer than somewhere in the Near East from which we could base our operations. (2) It is increasingly clear that from the point of view of production we are nowhere near ready to undertake large-scale operations. The papers have been full of it. If we aren't prepared, then some reason must be found to explain our delay giving all-out aid to Britain. As I dope it, the President may let the non-interventionists delay action in one way or another so he can put the blame on them. If there is real debate on the Neutrality law, it may be because the President wanted time.

The convoy issue, while not dead, seems to have taken second or third place. I think it is now clear to the Administration that they could not win the kind of victory necessary for such action on a clearcut convoy issue. That does not mean that tacit approval of convoys may not be secured in some other way, such as repeal of the Neutrality Law. Rep. Curtis has filed a discharge petition on his anti-convoy resolution, which is exactly like Senator Tobey's. I am recommending to Ken Lee that AF urge its members to ask their Congressmen to sign. It would take some time to secure the necessary 218 signatures, and it will probably be a good thing to have this activity going on, even though it is not publicized.

I have canvassed my usual sources of information for dope on the President's speech [Roosevelt was scheduled to give a major policy address on May 27]. I doubt if anyone outside has straight information. Some of the most intelligent guessers think it may contain quite a bit about domestic affairs—the production effort, etc. My guess would be that it will in some way seek to buck up British morale without making definite commitments of stronger action on our part. (The Administration I gather has been hearing some unpleasant truths from Latin American diplomats who resent the "big brother" attitude even in the name of defense!)

At this stage it's anybody's guess as to whether or not the President will call for Neutrality law revision or repeal. We should know after Tuesday. If he does, then I consider it a real victory for our side. A victory—because it means the President concedes he must have congressional approval; repeal will take some time, indicating that he does not want to move immediately. McNary [Sen. Charles L. McNary (R-Oreg.), Republican vice-presidential candidate, 1940] says the Administration doesn't have the votes; I am not sure he's right, although I think it would take some time to vote repeal. It is entirely possible that the Neutrality Law might be superseded in some way, just as the Lease-Lend superseded a lot of laws (including part of the Neutrality Law), without a clearcut vote on repeal.

In any case, I am betting that in the President's speech he will try to make an appealing case for the old freedom of the seas doctrine.

AF ought to be ready to get out a whole new set of literature *if* the President's speech shifts the grounds to the Neutrality Law.

I think we must pay considerable attention to the peace rumors. Senator Connally's statement [Sen. Connally had claimed that peace talk was in progress (*Newsweek*, June 2, 1941, p. 14)] was considered by many as the tip-off that something was actually under way. Newspaper people say they are sure there is "furious activity" along this line behind the scenes. One group in the State Department is pretty certain Hess's visit [Deputy Führer Rudolph Hess flew to Scotland on May 10, 1941, making a parachute landing near Glasgow; his motive was the subject of much speculation] was official, that he brought peace terms that weren't so bad—along the lines of Connally's statement. Two Congressmen—Vorys of Ohio and Mundt [Karl Mundt (R-S. D.), informal adviser to the AFC]—have sent their peace proposals to the President, and have had courteous replies. I hope you are considering recommending to AF groups examination and discussion of peace proposals, and of proposals for organizing the world after the war.

I suppose you are working on plans for the next phase of AF activity, following the series of meetings which probably can't go on after June. I think Mr. Libby [Frederick J. Libby, executive secretary, National Council for the Prevention of War] is writing you about getting speakers before the hundreds of farmers' picnics that are held every summer. Sometimes as many as 10,000 attend one picnic. I think you could use Congressmen for this job, and I should like to see AF use them more. Some of them are just itching to be called on.

I suggest the county fairs as another medium for reaching large numbers. In years past I have known of peace groups that took booths, distributed thousands of pieces of literature, and had something for inquirers to sign.

The thousands of summer conferences and camps—religious and otherwise—are another good medium where you can reach large numbers.

You asked my opinion of hiring Mr. Burdick. On the asset side, he knows his way around the Hill (which is important), he knows a good many men in the House particularly, he distributes a good deal of literature, he is a tireless worker, he is not easily rebuffed and is not afraid to ask members to do something: I understand he had a good deal to do with getting together that first meeting of the informal Senate-House group of which Senator Wheeler is chairman, and that was a good piece of work. On the liability side, he is a lone-wolf worker and it is difficult to cooperate with him, he sometimes gives the impression of being a little starry-eyed, I am not confident of his grasp of the fundamental issues questions of foreign policy. To sum up, if you have the money to put another worker on the Hill, particularly in the House, there is value in having one more person moving around up there, constantly keeping the men stirred up on peace questions. I am not quite clear as to what this Peace Directory he suggests would be. If it is—as I imagine—a compilation of information as to the peace view of members of the House, and other characteristics useful in peace work, that would be useful provided you plan to work by Congressional Districts. If you do hire him, I think the Hill work would proceed more smoothly if his orders come from Chicago, and reports go more directly there, and if you state specifically what you want him to do; I do not think he would relish the prospect of our working as a team.

DOCUMENT 75

Ruth Sarles to Richard A. Moore
June 4, 1941

I'll address this to you, with the request that you show it to anyone who ought to see it.

All that I hear these last few days points to the conclusion that in a very short time we are likely to be in the war, or there will be a sudden peace.

The pressure on the President must be terrific. Apparently those who surround him are getting to the name-calling stage in their resentment at the President's slowness to act. I understand they are now calling the President an isolationist. Alsop and Kintner have been putting tremendous pressure; if you haven't seen their column for the last two or three days, be sure to look it up. Remember their close tie to the White House, as you read the columns.

One story that came from a very good source was that within two weeks we shall have occupied all of the islands except the Canary—that means Martinique, the Azores, Cape Verde Islands, Madeira (I suppose).

Rumor is that Winant has brought back really shocking information about the bad state of the British. Their standard of living is said to be worse than that in Germany; they lack food and clothing (which would probably mean that the textile mills had been badly damaged).

Story is that Churchill is asking *immediate* aid, including manpower, that if we don't come in, all is lost. It is said that Churchill will not make peace with Germany; that he would rather resign, making a flaming speech blaming FDR for not coming in. Hitler, it is said, will not negotiate. He has already made peace proposals to Britain three times and has been turned down. Now it is a matter of take it or leave it. If he is turned down again, he may come back a little later with another set of proposals; but each time he comes back the terms will be less advantageous to Britain.

Congress is really excited about the property seizure bill. There will undoubtedly be real debate. For your information Senator Clark of Missouri will probably make a speech on the Industrial Mobilization Plan. He knows more about this, I think, than anyone else in the Senate, since he studied it seriously during the munitions investigation.

Here is a quote from Rep. May [Andrew J. May (D-Ky.)], chairman of the House Military Affairs Committee, which only the Baltimore Sun carried: "This bill would give the President more power than Woodrow Wilson ever had in the World War. If I were given a week in which to draft something more drastic, I would be at my wit's end. If there is a reason for such legislation as this, someone has got to come up here and tell us what it is. For that purpose we will have hearings."

And Faddis of Pennsylvania [Charles I. Faddis, (D-Pa.)], an ardent supporter of the Administration's foreign policy, said: "If Adolf Hitler wanted a bill to prevent the United States from rearming, he couldn't write a better one than this."

One possible interpretation of the bill interests me in particular: under its provisions, the government could seize bank accounts. Since I understand the bond-selling program is not going well, it is just possible some adaptation of the John Maynard Keynes forced savings plan may have been worked out. Keynes is now in this country.

Please remember that these are today's rumbles. There will be others tomorrow, and possibly quite different. However, I do feel that we are heading toward a showdown.

DOCUMENT 76

Sterling Morton to Robert E. Wood
April 3, 1941

In your speech of October 4, you closed with, in part, these words: "It is up to the American people to decide whether they want to make these sacrifices to preserve not England but the British Empire, and help regulate Europe and Asia. But they should make the decision with all the cards on the table, not misled by artifice and subterfuge. But if that decision is given affirmatively, I think you will find Americans like myself. . . . will be at their posts of duty in the service of this country".

That expressed then and does now my feelings in the matter. You and I, and many others, saw clearly the end of the path. We could not forecast the events marking that path, nor the speed with which we would travel it, but we were not mistaken as to the destination. I believe that in our discussions we even anticipated speeches like Donovan's [Colonel William J. ("Wild Bill") Donovan, roving presidential emissary; later director, Office of Strategic Services. In a radio broadcast given on March 26, 1941, Donovan called for aid to Britain at all costs.]—we had gone so far that we could not turn back. The formula laid down by Mark Twain (used as a foreword to my pamphlet) is working out exactly. [Morton's privately printed pamphlet "Let's Think This Matter Through," dated December 15, 1940, begins with a quotation from Mark Twain's *Mysterious Stranger* warning against war.]

The question which now arises in my mind is whether we have reached the point where the "decision is given affirmatively." If this proves to be the case, opposition becomes obstructionism, Decatur's [Stephen Decatur, whose strategy in the War of 1812 forced the dey of Algiers to end U.S. tribute to the Barbary pirates; author of the maxim, "Our country, right or wrong"] precept applies and must be followed by every good citizen.

We are not actually involved in a shooting war, but shooting may take place at any moment. I believe the President does not wish a shooting war. He must realize that when the first casualty list comes in the people will give more weight to the deeds which have led to that casualty list than to the words which accompanied those deeds. Actual formal war would be the worst possible politics for the administration. It would also be very bad from the German standpoint. They can't want us to declare war any more than the President does. I doubt that convoying—I even doubt that bombing of Berlin by our planes—would bring a war declaration from Germany. Of course, we entirely lack casus belli, except, of course, on the basis of a preventive war (one of the worst forms of aggression).

The Lend-Lease Bill is a law of the land and is, in effect, an official declaration that the safety of this country is bound up with the safety of any and all countries which may resist the Axis. Furthermore, the President has stated that we cannot stop short of complete victory. This can only be taken as an executive declaration of war. The problem in my mind is whether this act of Congress and this statement of the President have not put us in such a position that we cannot withdraw, unless we are willing to be branded as a poltroon nation, unwilling to fight for its very life. If the President and the Congress mean what they have said, then the only honorable course, as Senator Wheeler and others have so well pointed out, is for us to participate in it to the utmost of our strength, sending our men to fight as well as our money and munitions.

Now, do, or do not, these acts and statements set up that condition? If they do, only one course is open to us—you and I and all the rest who have opposed the war must go along with the program, and even urge that the active intervention come at once. "The sooner started, the sooner finished."

Now, if these premises are accepted, the position of America First must, of necessity, change. There is more than enough work for it to do, even though the final act—a declaration of war—should come. This country is full of misguided people who, either through colonial-mindedness or less understandable reasons, feel that everything suggested by Britain is necessarily correct and in our best interests. You were on the ground and of course knew the terrible struggle Pershing [General John J. Pershing, commander of American Expeditionary Force, World War I; later chief of staff] had to keep an American Army, rather than send the men as replacements to British and French units. Admiral Sims [Admiral William S. Sims, commander of U.S. naval forces in Europe during World War I] had much the same problem, mitigated by the actual conditions under which naval warfare is waged. Nevertheless, our ships in European waters were, to all intents and purposes, under the orders of the British Admiralty. I admire the British for their single-minded devotion to British interests; I could only wish that our citizens had that same devotion. As they haven't, America First could well be on guard, even in such minor things as explaining that our soldiers and sailors would appreciate a few knitted sweaters and mufflers.

If this crusade is not to stop until the "four freedoms" are established, we have a pretty tough job ahead of us. We, of course, would have to set a good example by giving up completely our control of the Philippines and Puerto Rico. If New Mexico should vote to rejoin Old Mexico, we would have to assent to it with the best grace possible. Alaska has declared its independence of Ickes; perhaps it might wish to set itself up as a separate country; if so, we would have to consent. But I am not so much worried about the freedoms in the countries now under our flag as I am about what might happen abroad. We certainly would have to be prepared to fight Britain if she would not free India. The former Boer Republics have always been dissatisfied under British rule, so they would have to be turned loose. The Slovenes and Croatians have had a pretty tough time under the rule of the Serbs (the latter being, I believe, the latest recruits to the hosts of democracy!) and, of course, we must restore the former Baltic republics which have been swallowed up by the Russian bear. Exactly what our decision will be in the case of the Jews versus the Arabs in Palestine is something on which I do not care to speculate.

In all of these undertakings, the size and number of which stagger the imagination, there is a very definite place for America First, ever watchful and with an eye solely for the interests of our country.

I realize that a change from opposition to involvement in the war to a demand for immediate and full involvement in it is a very substantial one; but, as I said above, if we accept the President's speech and the passage of the Lend-Lease and associated bills as an expression of executive and legislative intent, there is no other course which can be followed with honor. For us to attempt to hold the President and his late opponent for the Presidency to their pre-election pledges would be, if the facts are as stated, merely to play the part of obstructionists, or worse; for, if the Axis is our enemy, the sooner we smash it to bits the better for all of us. We cannot hold our heads up in the world if we are to hide behind the skirts of those who are doing the fighting.

Passage of the Lend-Lease Bill was an "identifiable" event upon which such a change could have been predicated. I do not doubt that, should you and other members of the Committee feel the change is advisable, timely opportunities for it will present themselves.

All in all, Bob, this letter is just thinking out loud. I have been much troubled in my mind, and undoubtedly you have been in yours, as to when the stirring words with which you closed your speech should become the guidepost of good citizenship.

I am sending copy of this to Bill Castle and to Jack MacNider. I want their opinion, as both of them think these things through very clearly.

DOCUMENT 77

Robert E. Wood to Sterling Morton
April 7, 1941

I read your thoughtful letter of April 3rd a number of times, and I revolved some of the questions mentioned in your letter in my own mind.

To begin with, I do not believe we have as yet reached the point where the opposition becomes obstructionism. The Lend-Lease bill is a law of the land, but the Lend-Lease bill does not commit the Nation to a policy of underwriting a complete victory for Great Britain. It puts us in the position of giving aid for the defense of Great Britain. The strongest proponents of the bill, including Senator George, said the bill made for peace and that it did not commit our entry into the war as an active belligerent.

The America First Committee was formed with the idea to keep this country out of war. True in a sense we are in the war now, but there is a vast difference in the position of being a friendly non-belligerent and the position of an active belligerent. In terms of sacrifices, money and blood there is an enormous difference.

I think the Committee can perform its function by opposing our entrance into the war as an active belligerent.

DOCUMENT 78

Ruth Sarles to Kendrick Lee
May 4, 1941

I hope you were as encouraged as I was at the vote in the Committee Wednesday (Fear people expected more than 9 votes). As a matter of fact, I am rather glad they did not report out the resolution: their failure to gives our men an awfully good talking point and I think helps arouse them. As long as we still have a convoy resolution to fight for I think we are in a better strategic position.

Some of the men on the Hill seem to think that unless public opinion changes, the President will not use convoys without putting the issue before Congress. Perhaps not—but from the point of view of the Germans I wonder if they will resent the patrols as now functioning more than they would convoys. Apparently the President has ordered the patrols to keep submarines or surface raiders in sight, radioing their position, which the British can pick up. In other words, they are to follow them around.

Perhaps you will want to publish the vote in Committee. Those voting against the convoy resolution: George, Harrison [Sen. Pat Harrison (D-Miss.)], Wagner [Sen. Robert F. Wagner (D-N.Y.)], Connally, Thomas of Utah [Sen. Elbert D. Thomas (D-Utah)], Murray, Pepper, Green [Sen. Theodore Francis Green (D-R.I.)], Barkley [Sen. Alben W. Barkley (D-Ky.); Senate majority leader], Guffey [Sen. Joseph F. Guffey (D-Pa.)], Glass [Sen. Carter Glass (D-Va.)], Byrnes [Sen. James F. Byrnes (D-S.C.)] and White [Sen. Wallace H. White, Jr. (R-Me.)]. For the resolution: Van Nuys [Sen. Frederick Van Nuys (D-Ind.)], Reynolds [Sen. Robert Rice Reynolds (D-N.C.)], Gillette [Sen. Guy Gillette (D-Iowa)], Clark of Missouri, Johnson of California [Sen. Hiram Johnson (R-Calif.)], Capper [Sen. Arthur Capper (R-Kans.)], Vandenberg, Shipstead, Nye, LaFollette [Sen. Robert M. La Follette, Jr. (Prog.-Wis.)]. On this vote our men picked up one extra one—Van Nuys. He voted with the Administration, I am told, on the other five ballots.

Just in case you missed it—Nye proposed that representatives from the State and Navy Departments and from OPM [Office of Production Management] be called before the Committee to say just what losses we were suffering in delivering goods to Britain. A few days earlier some Congressman had said we were losing 40 per cent. Nye is convinced that was a plant. The Committee turned down his proposal, which was rather bad—refusing to get the facts about a matter on which they were voting.

It was encouraging that Guffey spoke for convoys on the floor of the Senate. So far, with the exception of Barkley early in the game, the Administration has not answered Tobey. Taft also jumped in the same day. I *think* these boys are beginning to think they had better get in and fight. Incidentally, this system of calling for two or three day recesses every time the Senate meets is probably an Administration tactic to keep the debate from assuming any proportions.

You know by this time that Tobey plans to propose his resolution as an amendment to the ship seizure bill, which will probably come up next Monday, although there is a slight chance it may come up a few days earlier. It will probably not be tried in the House, because in the House an amendment can be ruled out as not germane on a point of order. That cannot be done in the Senate; it would have to be defeated by vote, and Tobey will call for a record vote.

Tobey's mail is increasing.

Congressman Gehrmann of Wisconsin [Bernard J. Gehrmann (Prog.-Wis)] has been taking a poll in his district. So far, about 3,000 letters are against convoys, and 88 for. I enclose the reprint from the record he sent out to his constituents. (Also the column he sends to papers in his district.) I understand that Schulte of Indiana [William T. Schulte (D-Ind.)] is going to conduct a similar poll. Wouldn't it be a good idea to recommend to AF members that they write and urge their Congressmen to take a poll?

Forgot to say that Senator George is said still to be against convoys and firmly convinced that the President must come to Congress for authority to use convoys (George is supposed to be a good constitutional lawyer). Letters should continue to go to George to strengthen his hands.

In general, I think that the stay-out point of view has grown stronger in the last week or two.

And that brings me to this: I am hearing with growing frequency the report that the President is really reluctant to go in any further, that he is withstanding tremendous pressure from some of his advisers. It is said that Hopkins came back from London convinced that England was done for, and that he has influenced the President. A man who spent a few hours with the President at Hyde Park and is a good friend of the President's came away convinced that the President is trying his darnedest to keep us out. Some people here are inclined to believe that if the President is taking that attitude, the isolationists should more or less lie low. I do not agree. I believe that if the President is holding back now, it is largely because of the popular pressure and I should hate to see it lessen. But I do not think we ought to tell people all this about the President, because they might feel less urge to keep on writing and working.

I notice in one of the memos to local branches Mr. Bliss has said something about the possibility of winning on the Tobey resolution when it comes up again. Will you pass on to him my suggestion that it might be best not to hold that up too much as a possibility, because I believe that it will not come to a vote until the Administration is convinced it has the votes to defeat it. And our people will have one more defeat to discourage them. Seems to me it might be better strategy to emphasize opposition to convoys in general, rather than playing up the hope of winning on one legislative measure.

I enclose a couple of things I put together in a hurry for one of the men.

Now about what I've been doing. I have spent the major part of my time in the last two weeks on the Hill and on the telephone. The main thing seemed to be to try to stir up a little action on the part of our men. I've done all I dare do without becoming a nuisance, and I think this week I can get to work digging out some material. Of course, I have planted speech ideas and some material, stuff I have read that I knew certain men were interested in.

I wish you could make a trip to Washington. Do try to work it out.

Is America First urging its local groups to take part in the KAOWC conference here May 30?

Now for your own private enjoyment: Senator Aiken [George D. Aiken (R-Vt.); former state governor] the other day showed me the 1938 Republican Party platform for the State of Vermont. Two paragraphs were to the effect that the country should not get into war under this administration because of the controls that would be clamped on the country, threatening private enterprise etc. The Senator tells me that Dorothy Thompson [columnist for the *New York Herald-Tribune* (1936–1941); later for the Bell Syndicate] came to the platform committee and asked if she couldn't make that contribution—it is her own wording!

Did you see story in NY Times for April 29 on Union for Democratic Action headed by Reinhold Niebuhr [professor of applied Christianity, Union Theological Seminary, New York]—another pro-war group!

DOCUMENT 79

Ruth Sarles to Kendrick Lee
May 18, 1941

The decision to postpone the attempt to bring the anti-convoy measure to a vote, it should be noted, was a *group* decision of several of the non-interventionist Senators—Taft, Tobey, Wheeler, La Follette, D. Worth Clark [D-Idaho], Brooks [C. Wayland ("Curly") Brooks (R-Ill.)]. Might be worth playing up how well they worked together in this case. (I have noticed the newsletter in several Senate offices, and think this might have a healthy effect.)

Of course, the Administration is now trying to play down the convoy question as receding into the limbo of academic matters. You probably saw the N.Y. Times front-page story of May 15 to this effect, by Frank Kluck-hohn, obviously White House inspired. It said that "with the danger from surface raiders to shipping carrying American war supplies greatly reduced by the extension of American naval patrol activities, there was a growing belief in Administration circles that American naval convoys would not be necessary, at least for the present." I do not believe that our men seriously believe this. Obviously, the Administration would do anything to prevent a real debate on the subject.

Unless there is an incident, we can probably just coast along on this issue until the President's speech. Then—well, we shall just have to wait and see. As long as American merchant vessels are going into a danger zone (the Red Sea area), and as long as American naval vessels are doing "patrol" duty, the convoy question is still a live issue, that may be catapulted into the limelight whenever Germany chooses to make it an issue.

Note the close vote on the Clark-Vandenberg amendment to the ship seizure bill—43 to 38. [On May 7 the House voted 266 to 120 to seize foreign vessels tied up in U.S. ports. The Senate voted similarly by 59 to 20 on May 15. The Clark-Vandenberg amendment, which would have prohibited the United States from turning Axis ships over to the British, was defeated, 48 to 43.]

The confidential memo I sent you some time ago on our rumored plans with regard to the eastern Atlantic islands and Dakar is certainly given point by recent happenings. Watch for some new move in Martinique. Some of the non-interventionists think we should take over Martinique in view of the latest Vichy happenings. Might keep in mind the fact that there is still on the island of Martinique that much-discussed shipment of 100 planes originally intended for France before it fell.

The Administration faces quite a dilemma in making any decision regarding possible action with regard to the eastern Atlantic islands. If it moves, it will seriously displease some of the Latin American nations which means a rift in the solidarity we are trying to build up in this hemisphere. Might be a good idea to point out that the Azores, Madeira and Cape Verde islands are Portuguese and Canary, Spanish.

I get the general impression from talking with men on the Hill and with newspaper people that the conviction is growing that the country is hardening against war. It of course works two ways—keeps the President worried, and helps "our" men work harder.

I suppose I ought to say something about the Hess affair. There is some feeling that this had something to do with cancellation of the President's speech. If it did, I feel that it was only one of several things—protests from Latin American diplomats who had been consulted that the President could not speak for all the American nations in taking a more aggressive policy, Hoover's speech, Lindbergh's speech, plus other evidences of growing opposition to war.

Would it be a good idea to mention the talk about a move for peace now? Of course, there are Wheeler's statements the last two days. And there's John Vorys' speech in the House (See Cong. Record, May 8, p. 3964). Did I write you that Mr. Vorys was himself amazed at the interest expressed by other members, men who have been on the other side? They didn't jump on him, they seemed eager to hear more about it, as if it were an entirely new prospect to them. I wish that America First would urge discussion and study of all proposals for peace; it does not need to express an opinion on them. Seems to me that is an educational job of first importance.

The talk here—most of it—is that the President has practically made up his mind as to his course of action. Some think that interviews with Admiral King [Ernest J. King, commander-in-chief of the Atlantic fleet] (I think he is in charge of the Atlantic Fleet) and James Forrestal, Under-Secretary of the Navy, who has been in Britain since the war began, presage some new action on the sea. It is hard for me to believe that the President's mind is definitely made up; I doubt if it will be until shortly before his speech on the 27th.

It's terribly important that the President continue to receive floods of mail expressing not only opposition to convoys, but to any action likely to lead us closer to war. I suppose you will urge a special drive *before* the President's speech as well as afterward.

DOCUMENT 80

Washington News Letter #15
May 30, 1941

The Situation This Week

Both before and after the event, the eyes and ears of all Washington turned to the President's "chat" delivered on Tuesday night. It was a very long speech. It was not specific. It was confusing. The *Newsletter* was held up this week because we wanted to make some considered comments on the speech. However, after three days wait, there is still no unanimity of opinion as to just what the President really means to *do* in order to implement the ideas he *expressed*.

That it was a highly inflammatory speech is obvious. That it does not mean the immediate entrance of America in the war also seems clear.

No one can contend that Roosevelt does not hold more personal power than any other peace-time president in the history of the United States. Briefly, he has almost complete control over labor and capital including the power to suspend the provisions of laws prohibiting the eight-hour day for labor; to suspend trading on stock exchanges for ninety days; to close or take over for government use any radio station; and the power to take possession of any merchant vessels documented under United States laws. It is important to note that these powers did not go into actual effect with the issuance of the emergency proclamation. Actual assumption of any of these powers by the President must be preceded by an individual proclamation.

Government legal experts said there was no clear distinction between a "limited" and an "unlimited" emergency, and that technically the President could call into force his full powers in either case. This indicates that the President issued the proclamation in a further attempt to scare the public into a fatalistic acceptance of the Administration's drive to war. At the same time it indicated that public opinion had expressed itself by mail and telegraph as being overwhelmingly against war, and therefore the President did not dare go all-out as far as *action* is concerned. It was belligerently *worded*, and potentially *can* mean war. But non-interventionists were greatly heartened to realize that the President was still listening to the voice of the people instead of *blindly* following the lead of powerful war-minded individuals.

Day after the President spoke, General Robert E. Wood, speaking for the National Executive committee of the America First Committee, said in part: "The emphasis of his speech last night was on American defense rather than saving the world. To the extent the President adheres to the actual defense of America he will have a united nation behind him. The President has no power whatever to declare war or to carry on armed hostilities without the consent of Congress. The America First Committee urges all Americans, in the interest of democracy and the welfare of this nation, to do everything in their power to maintain peace and avoid participation as a belligerent by this country in the European War now raging. We shall redouble our efforts to crystallize public opinion in support of the President's pledges to Keep America Out of Other People's Wars."

Same day some 50 non-interventionist senators and representatives met in Washington and pledged themselves to intensify their efforts to keep America out of war in Europe, Asia, or Africa. A good many people think it is about time Congress bestirred itself to the extent of taking cognizance of the fact that the President failed to mention Congress once in his emergency speech. The President did say that additional measures necessary to deliver the goods to Great Britain were being devised by military and naval technicians, "who, with me, will work out and *put into effect*" such safeguards. Just where representative government operates in such a situation did not seem to be clear.

The reaction of the hot-for-war-now people was interesting in the light of the President's statement that "we insist upon the vital importance of keeping *Hitlerism* away from any point in the world which could be used as a base of attack against the Americas." On Wednesday Hitlerism reared its ugly head in the President's home state when an interventionist group urged the AMERICA FIRST COMMITTEE to disband and stop talking. Next day, famed Washington columnist Raymond Clapper fell a victim to Hitlerism, when his column announced that free speech can go too far, and that the actions of the non-interventionist bloc in Congress and of the AMERICA FIRST COMMITTEE "amounts in effect to encouraging sedition." Perhaps Mr. Clapper wants us to follow Canadian custom where any person who expresses a belief that Germany may win the war is now guilty of violating the "Defense of Canada Regulations," *regardless of the spirit in which the remark is made.*

The war boys received a terrific setback at the President's press conference late Wednesday afternoon. This conference was called to clarify the previous night's speech. The President announced that he did not intend seeking change or repeal of the Neutrality Act. Someone promptly recalled Mr. Roosevelt's clear statements in the past that the combat zone quarantine did not apply to the nation's *naval* vessels, which were free to go wherever they were sent. He also said that he contemplated no executive orders *at present* to invoke any of the broad powers conferred on him by the emergency proclamation.

DOCUMENT 81

Washington News Letter #16
June 4, 1941

The Situation This Week

For the past two or three weeks Washington has been filled with rumors of peace proposals which Germany is supposed to have offered Great Britain. Chief interest here this week, therefore, is in the return home of Ambassador to Great Britain John Winant. Supposition is that he is to tell Roosevelt the substance of the peace offer. He will also report on the general condition of Great Britain.

The best speech we have seen for some time on the advantages to Great Britain and the world of trying for peace now was made in the House on May 9 by Representative John Vorys. Copies of the speech, entitled "An American Peace Offensive," may be had by writing him at the House Office Building in Washington.

The Situation for the Long Term

What is the domestic economic outlook for the future now that the national defense program has ended its first year?

Plainly, far-reaching changes in our national economy (barely evident as yet) are bound to increasingly affect every phase of business and industry as well as the lives of each individual citizen.

And this is true in varying degree whether or not America enters the European or Asiatic Wars. For we have embarked on a defense program which *already* contemplates the expenditure of between 40 and 50 billion dollars. As the tremendous economic forces of armament building get into fuller sway, the normal aspect of almost every business and industry will disappear. Those industries which are now known as consumer industries and produce such products as refrigerators, vacuum cleaners, and automobiles will find increasing trouble in buying those necessary metals which are also necessary to an armament program. These companies will then either shift (where they can) part of their productive facilities from consumer to armament materials, or they will have to curtail production. Whether they shift what they produce or whether they simply cut production, there will probably be some unemployment as a result. Indeed, there are those who are already saying that the second half of *this* year will see a drop in employment, *in spite of* a rapid increase in defense production, because a shortage of necessary metals will slow down consumer industries *faster* than armament industries can increase production. Such a situation would inevitably bring some population changes as people began to "follow the jobs."

To those cities producing steel, airplanes and airplane motors, tanks, guns, shells, and ships will come a great influx of people. Obviously, this will accentuate any housing shortage in these cities. Cities dependent upon consumer industries will either lose part of their population or find that their relief rolls will increase.

Some time ago it was announced that the automobile industry would make 20% fewer automobiles next year. There seems to be a good chance that they will be "asked" to cut that figure another 25%, i.e. a total decrease over this year of 40%.

Despite the fact that leaders in both the steel and aluminum industries blithely assured the government last year that there would be no shortage of these strategic materials, the opposite is now plainly the case. This means a bogging down in the defense effort and has irritated a good many defense officials. While there seems little likelihood of the government's anti-trust division moving against the Aluminum Company of America's monopoly while the crisis is still with us, there does seem to be good evidence that the government will finance another company in this field. Similar action may be taken in the steel situation.

It is important to remember the place of the Reconstruction Finance Corporation in the defense program. Under legislation recently approved by the Banking and Currency Committees, *any* defense corporation created by the President and the Federal Loan Administrator may have *any and all powers necessary to expedite the defense program*. There is practically no limitation on this authority. This means that the government may build its own plants in those fields in which it experiences difficulty in getting production, or it can finance the establishment of additional privately-owned firms.

Incidentally, it is rumored that one of the fields which will be hit hard by the necessity of cutting down consumer goods purchases will be installment selling. It is said that down payments will be increased and the time given to complete the purchase will be shortened. This will be another means of cutting down purchases, and therefore production, of such items as automobiles, refrigerators, etc. It is also another method to prevent inflation.

The *degree* to which the above changes will take place will be determined by whether or not America enters the Old World's Wars. If the Peppers and the Knoxs and the Stimsons are allowed to push us into a war we never started, such changes as are mentioned above will be only the beginning of a program of complete and dictatorial control of industry and the citizen by a government in which Congress will be little more than a Reichstag rubber stamp, and by a government embarked on the grandiose and futile plan of enforcing the Four Freedoms "everywhere in the world."

Any doubt that the prediction outlined here is not correct was dissipated on Monday of this week when Undersecretary of War Patterson, at the request of the War Department, transmitted a bill to Congress which, if passed, would authorize the President "to requisition and take over, either temporarily or *permanently*, property *of any kind* or character, whether real or personal, tangible or intangible" in the interest of national defense.

What the Battle of Crete Has *Proved*

Before Crete there was still room for argument over the relative merits of sea power and air power. Military men have argued this question ever since the late General William Mitchell was ousted from the United States Army over a decade ago because he shouted too loudly that more attention should be paid to airplanes. Charles Lindbergh ended a tour of Europe a few years ago by telling the British and our own government to build up their air strength. Of course, none of today's war hawks paid any attention to him. Admittedly the proponents of a large air force have been increasing but the Navy boys have held the upper hand.

On the island of Crete, Great Britain held all those advantages which have spelled victory in past wars. Crete is about 70 miles from the nearest Nazi-occupied land. Furthermore the British were strongly intrenched, with an army, tanks, artillery, AND absolute possession of the surrounding waters. Even had the Germans wanted to engage in a naval battle for the island, they had no warships. Plain fact is that for the first time in history, a major military victory has been gained *entirely* by an air force *despite* the presence of a strong and unopposed fleet of warships. Indeed, while the British Navy prevented all but a few Nazis from landing on Crete from boats, it did so only by paying a heavy toll of cruisers and destroyers to the Nazi air arm.

We know now that sea power without air power is no defense at all. The Battle of Crete means that the British Navy is a far less important defense weapon than we had previously thought. Unless England can achieve AIR superiority, the Navy cannot turn the tide of the war, and this remains true even if the United States were to lease her another 50 destroyers or more. For it is plain that while in the last century the fact that Britannia ruled the waves meant that she possessed the greatest offensive weapon of war, mid-twentieth century tactics have shown that the offensive power of a fleet disappears as it nears the shores of an enemy-held country. For enemy land means enemy air bases from which $400,000 long range bombers can scour the seas; search out and destroy great battleships which cost $100,000,000 each and require a much longer time to build.

What all this means to the United States is that the idea that convoys would materially aid in winning the war for Great Britain is shown to be false, unless as those convoys near the land mass of Europe, they are protected by interceptor PLANES. Otherwise, long range bombers or submarines will continue to sink them. (Another factor contributing to the difficulty of the convoy system is that AIR bombings have reduced to ruin all English ports except Liverpool and Glasgow. It is now reported that the turnaround time is three weeks—i.e. the time necessary for a ship to dock, unload, and depart. Obviously, more ships is no answer to this problem.) People who have been asking for convoys should now ask instead that *planes* be sent UNLESS they only want convoys so that shooting will begin. It is still true that convoys would get us into the war.

In the second place, the fact that even a *powerful* Navy, if not sufficiently protected by air power, cannot successfully approach the enemy shore gives a cold, FACTUAL answer to those who have been yelping for another A.E.F. to Europe. The question is—where would they land? AND no interventionist can dispute production *figures* and *export figures*. They may *wish* the situation was different. So does the America First Committee, though for a different reason. The FACT is that plane production in the United States is distressingly small, *especially* production of long range bombers. Furthermore, in a recent column, Boake Carter [radio broadcaster and Hearst columnist] pointed out that we are sending abroad up to 70% of the weapons we would need in any such invasion. An invasion accompanied by our present air force would only mean that we wanted to undergo a Dunkerque in reverse; i.e. not have to retreat from a land position but find ourselves unable to even gain a landhold.

In the third place it demonstrates the truth of what the America First Committee has said, that the United States and the Western Hemisphere *can* be defended *if* we will build a real air force and if that air force has bases close to the shore lines, that our safety does *not* depend upon the British Empire *or* upon the Empire's Navy, that the defense of America depends upon American factories and upon American workmen, and upon American pilots. Rather than a mass army of 5,000,000 men, we need a small army *of men* and a big army *of mechanized equipment*. (There is an excellent article on this subject in the June, 1941 Reader's Digest written by Representative Ross A. Collins, chairman of the House Subcommittee in charge of military appropriation.)

This will take time to build and it will take time to train men in the use of this equipment. We believe America is equal to this task. But American soldiers can never be trained in the use of this equipment if we continue to give away up to 70% of our production. A sane appraisal of our own defense needs would seem to indicate that we can spare precious little in the way of airplanes and mechanized equipment. (The *N.Y. Times* recently pointed out editorially that "before 1938 our own War Department was spending more on *horses, mules, harness and wagons* than on tanks and armed vehicles.")

The fourth lesson of the Battle of Crete is that our huge naval expansion (which will not be completed until 1946) should not be allowed to take necessary material or men away from what should now become our paramount defense effort—a greatly increased program of expansion in our air forces. There is a certain amount of competition here for money, for skilled labor, for machine tools, and for strategic metals. It would appear that where there is such a conflict between the sea and air arms of our fighting forces, that the conflict should be resolved in favor of the air force.

DOCUMENT 82

Memorandum on Contraband Material in the Cargo of the Robin Moor

"Did you know *that the cargo of the Robin Moor contained 1163 items* (or 70% of its cargo) *declared contraband by the British and German contraband lists promulgated in connection with the current war, and that 1133 items were also declared contraband in the United States World War contraband list?*"
No. 1, June 18, 1941

The Facts

The Robin Moor was sunk on May 21, 1941 in waters of the South Atlantic Ocean. The ship was carrying a variegated cargo to Capetown, British South Africa, a portion of the British Empire and territory belonging to a belligerent in the current war. Apparently the sinking occurred outside any combat zone (Washington *Star*, June 13, 1941).

The list of goods carried by the ship, as copied from her manifest, was published in full in the New York *Times* of June 14, 1941. In an interview with the press, the president of the Robin Line, Arthur R. Lewis, Jr., stated that no item in the ship's cargo could be considered contraband material either under international law or under the Neutrality Law of the United States (Washington *Times-Herald*, June 14, 1941). It has been stated that the State Department does not consider that the cargo of the Robin Moor contained contraband, and that the United States has never acquiesced in the contraband lists issued by the belligerent powers—Great Britain and Germany (New York *Times*, June 14, 1941).

The Problem

Now that the passengers and crew of the ship are saved, a consideration of the nature of the Robin Moor's cargo may prove of value in analyzing the status of American commerce with foreign ports and the possibility of similar occurrences in the future. This memorandum is concerned solely with the question whether any of the cargo of the Robin Moor can be considered contraband under either the German or British contraband lists, or under the American contraband list promulgated in connection with the World War or the so-called "contraband" list promulgated under our own Neutrality Law. We do not discuss the wholly unjustifiable manner in which the passengers and crew were treated, nor do we discuss the question whether there has been a violation of the international treaty relating to the search and seizure or merchant ships. But it is clear that if American ships insist upon carrying material declared contraband by a belligerent, they must take the risk.

The Law

At the outbreak of the current World War a list of materials regarded as absolute contraband and as conditional contraband was promulgated by the British government (Congressional Record, October 5, 1939, pp. 278–279). A substantially identical list of contraband was also promulgated by the German government (Congressional Record, October 5, 1939, pp. 278–279). Our own government also issued a list of materials whose export was forbidden or limited, under our Neutrality Law (Proclamation 2237, May 4, 1937, as listed in 22 U.S.C.A., Supplement, pp. 49–50; 22 U.S.C.A., 245j-11, Subd. (1)).

During the World War the United States had promulgated a contraband list which is substantially similar to the German and British contraband lists promulgated for the current war, with the exception that the World War United States list did not specifically include chemical substances and the means of disseminating them (Congressional Record, October 10, 1939, p. 490).

Perusal of the German, British and United States World War contraband lists will reveal that virtually every conceivable commodity can be brought within one or another classification of contraband. It should be noted that both the British and German lists considered foods, foodstuffs, clothing and similar materials as conditional contraband (United States World War list considered even these items as absolute contraband). It should also be noted that Secretary Hull is quoted as having said to a Senate Committee in 1936:

> The situation when the war ended apparently was that the rule or international law on the subject of contraband, absolute and conditional, has been merged into the one subject of contraband, absolute. (Congressional Record, October 10, 1939, p. 490.)

The Cargo of the Robin Moor

The published list of the cargo of the Robin Moor contains an estimated 1667 separate items (Washington Times-Herald, June 14, 1941). These items have been checked against the four contraband lists just mentioned. The Robin Moor's cargo list, in the main, merely states types of goods carried, without indicating how many pieces of each type of goods were included in the cargo. In a few instances, it is stated how many items were shipped in a mentioned category. This memorandum follows the plan of the ship's manifest and counts an item of cargo as one unless the manifest states that more than one piece was included under a mentioned category of goods.

In calculating the number of contraband items in the Robin Moor's cargo, this memorandum excludes non-military items of the cargo (such as advertising matter, paper, razors, lawn mowers, toys, cosmetics and toilet articles) and in addition, excludes numerous items which, although presumably intended for commercial purposes, could conceivably be used in connection with one aspect or another of the equipping or supplying of a military force, or of the carrying on of belligerent operations (such as paints, leather, utensils, flashlights, lanterns, drugs and medicines, soap, adhesives, refrigerators, and refrigerating machinery and lighting fixtures).

Contraband Material

The manifest of the Robin Moor lists *gas masks and canisters as well as some rifles, shotguns and cartridges*. But, in the main, the cargo is not contraband under the requirements of the American "contraband" list adopted under our Neutrality Law, which covers actual weapons of warfare exclusively. *The manifest shows that the ship's cargo of 1667 articles (Washington Times-Herald, June 14, 1941) contained 1133 articles, or 70% of its cargo, which was contraband under the British, the German and the United States World War contraband lists. In addition, 30 more items were banned by both the British and German lists.*

Analysis of Cargo:

1) Articles Violating British, German and United States World War Contraband Lists   1133.

a) Arms and Ammunition　　4.

Comment: The manifest does not list the number of weapons. According to the press, this included 12 rifles, an unspecified number of shotguns, 141 cases of shotgun shells and 4 cases of rifle cartridges (Washington *Times-Herald*, June 14, 1941). The manifest does not give the calibre of the guns or ammunition, but it is claimed that the weapons were sporting guns which do not come under the Neutrality Law "contraband" list. They do come under the British, German and United States World War lists.

b) Articles of Military Equipment　　1.

Comment: This consists of an unspecified number of gas masks and canisters.

c) Means of Transportation (on land, in the sea or the air; including component parts, machinery and tools)　　368.

Comment: This consists chiefly of automobiles, trucks and tractors, together with tools, machinery and parts. The 368 separate items on the manifest include many more vehicles, since many were included in one listing. The press estimates the number of vehicles alone as ranging from 439 (Washington *Times-Herald*, June 14, 1941) to 459 (Washington *Star*, June 14, 1941).

d) Means of Communication (including parts and machinery)　　24.

e) Fuel and Oil　　28.

Comment: The press reports that this included 1000 drums of oil (Washington *Times-Herald*, June 14, 1941).

f) Machinery (including materials, tools, parts, hardware)　　230.

g) Foods, Foodstuffs, Beverages, Tobacco Products　　173.

h) Clothing, Dry Goods, Fabrics　　305.

2) Articles Violating British and German Contraband Lists Alone.

1) Chemicals　　30.

Note: Copies of the contraband lists referred to in this memorandum are available at the office of the Committee.

DOCUMENT 83

Memorandum on Arming United States Merchant Vessels

"Did you know *that our government, before our entry in the World War, declared that armed merchant vessels must be considered as armed for offense purposes and must be considered as auxiliary war ships?*"
No. 2, June 21, 1941

Consequently, the placing of guns on merchantmen at the present day of submarine warfare can be explained only on the ground of a purpose to render merchantmen superior in force to submarines and to prevent warning and visit and search by them. Any armament, therefore, on a merchant vessel would seem to have the character of offensive armament.

I should add that my Government is impressed with the reasonableness of the argument that a merchant vessel carrying an armament of any sort, in view of the character of submarine warfare and the defensive weakness of undersea craft, should be held to be an auxiliary cruiser and so treated by a neutral as well as by a belligerent government, and is seriously considering instructing its officials accordingly. (Proposal to Allies in the World War by the United States, drafted by Secretary of State [Robert] Lansing and approved by President Wilson. Report of Special Senate Committee on Investigation of the Munitions Industry, 74th Congress, Part 5, Pages 123, 124.)

The Facts

Recent press reports cite alleged administration tendencies toward the arming of United States merchant vessels. One report states that "One legislator high in administration confidence said that 'the President is going to have to arm our merchant ships and tell them to protect themselves.' " (Washington *Star*, June 5, 1941.)

In a press conference on June 17, 1941, President Roosevelt announced that the United States had plans ready, and had had them since 1918, for the arming of American merchant ships; that the plans for arming such vessels had not been put into operation, at least not at his request; that he did not know whether Congressional authorization would be needed for the arming of the merchant marine. (Baltimore *Sun*, June 18, 1941.)

The recent sinking of the Robin Moor has furnished a springboard for demands that American merchant vessels be armed. The Robin Moor, an American ship, was sunk in the south Atlantic, in the course of a voyage from the United States to the Union of South Africa, a portion of the British Empire and territory belonging to a belligerent in the current war. Seventy percent of the ship's cargo was contraband under the contraband lists promulgated by the British and German governments in connection with the current war and under the American contraband list promulgated in connection with the World War. ("Did You Know," No. 1—June 18, 1941.)

The Robin Moor is the first American ship sunk by direct belligerent action in the current war. In a speech to Congress on June 20, 1941, President Roosevelt denounced the sinking of the Robin Moor as "outrageous" and "indefensible" and announced that full reparations would be demanded from the German government.

The Law

It seems clear that Congressional action is necessary if American merchant ships are to be armed, despite the President's disclaimer on that subject. The Neutrality Act (22 U.S.C.A.—245 J—5; Nov. 4, 1939) expressly forbids the arming of American merchant vessels:

> Whenever the President shall have issued a proclamation under the authority of section 245j (a), it shall thereafter be unlawful, until such proclamation is revoked, for any American vessel, engaged in commerce with any foreign state to be armed, except with small arms and ammunition therefore, which the President may deem necessary and shall publicly designate for the preservation of discipline aboard any such vessel.

This law was enacted in an effort to prevent a recurrence of the difficulties which, before our entry into the World War, kept us continuously at loggerheads with the German and British governments, and eventually helped cause our entry into that war.

> Most of the controversies respecting neutral rights between this country and Britain during the years 1914–1917 revolved around England's far-reaching extension of the term "contraband," her application and extension of the doctrine of continuous voyage, the new type of blockade established by Britain, British modification of the accepted rule of visit and search on the high seas, mail censorship, and blacklisting of American firms. . . . Our dispute with Germany was chiefly concerned with the legality of the use of the submarine. (Report of Special Senate Committee on Investigation of the Munitions Industry, 74th Congress, Part 5, page 23.)

World War History

The treatment of the passengers and crew of the Robin Moor was unjustified. But in view of the facts that all have been saved and that the cargo contained contraband, the hysteria about the sinking which interventionists have sought to stimulate has little justification. The vehement indignation expressed by the State Department (New York *Times*, June 14, 1941) and by the President (Washington *Times Herald*, June 20, 1941) over the sinking seems uncalled for when compared with the attitude of our government from 1915 to 1917, when our official policy was one of keeping out of war. We did not enter the World War (April 6, 1917) until more than two years after the first American merchant ship had been sunk by direct belligerent action (January 27, 1915). Between the time of that first sinking and the time of our severance of diplomatic relations with Germany (February 3, 1917), 11 American merchant ships were sunk or damaged, and 3 American lives were lost (in the torpedoing of the Gulflight, on May 1, 1915). Nine more ships were sunk or damaged from the rupture of relations until our actual entrance into the war, or a total of 20 American merchant ships sunk or damaged before we entered the World War (Congressional Record, April 18, 1941, page 3252).

Armed Merchant Ships Provoke Submarine Warfare

Secretary of State Lansing pointed out, in an official proposal by this Government to the Allies (which was approved by President Wilson) in the World War, that a submarine's defensive strength rested solely on its power to submerge, and even a merchant ship armed with a small gun could use it effectively for offense against a submarine. He therefore stated:

> If a submarine is required to stop and search a merchant vessel on the high seas and, in case it is found that she is of enemy character and that conditions necessitate her destruction, to remove to a place of safety all persons on board, it would not seem just or reasonable that the submarine should be compelled, while complying with these requirements, to expose itself to almost certain destruction by the guns on board the merchant vessel. (Report of Special Senate Committee on Investigation of the Munitions Industry, 74th Congress, Part 5, pages 123, 124.)

Are Armed Merchant Ships Effective?

Even Administration supporters have expressed doubts as to the wisdom of arming our merchant ships. Senator Norris [George Norris (Ind. Rep.-Nebr.)] has stated that it wouldn't give much protection, and that "even President Wilson admitted that it did not work during the World War" (Washington *Star*, June 19, 1941). Senator Herring [Clyde L. Herring (D-

Iowa)] has said that "I don't believe it would afford any real protection, and it would give submarines and surface raiders an excuse for firing on our boats. . . ." He also stated that such a step would be getting mighty close to war (Washington *Star*, June 19, 1941).

DOCUMENT 84

Freedom of the Seas

"Did you know *that the President's call for 'freedom of the seas' was really a demand for the right to help one country at war defeat another?*

That the right to ship arms and other contraband to one belligerent without interference from its enemy is not recognized under international law, and has been rejected by both England and the United States?

That England has opposed, and would oppose now, genuine 'freedom of the seas,' since England's power to keep all supplies from reaching her enemy is her strongest weapon?"
No. 3, June 26, 1941

Our own Secretary of State admitted during the World War that "freedom of the seas" in wartime was determined by the belligerents:

> The fact that the commerce of the United States is interrupted by Great Britain is consequent upon the superiority of her Navy on the high seas. History shows that whenever a country has possessed that superiority our trade has been interrupted and that few articles essential to the prosecution of the war have been allowed to reach its enemy from this country. (Secretary of State Bryan to Chairman of Senate Committee on Foreign Relations on January 20, 1915; quoted in Report of Special Senate Committee on Investigation of the Munitions Industry, 74th Congress, Part 5, page 163.)

Winston Churchill has pointed out that, at the close of the World War, the representatives of the Allies refused to accept "freedom of the seas" as proposed by President Wilson:

The second Point was then read. "Absolute freedom of navigation upon the seas, outside territorial waters, alike in peace and in war, except as the seas may be closed in whole or in part by international action for the enforcement of international covenants."

This point about what is called the "Freedom of the Seas" naturally aroused British concern. . . . Mr. Lloyd George said he could not accept this clause under any condition. If it had been in operation at the present time we should have lost the power of imposing a blockade. Germany had broken down almost as much from the effects of the blockade as from that of the military operations. . . . Clemenceau and Sonnino agreed with Lloyd George. ("The Aftermath"— 1929, pages 103–104, report of a meeting of representatives of the Allies in the World War to discuss Woodrow Wilson's "Fourteen Points" as the basis for an armistice with Germany.)

The President Demands Freedom of the Seas

In his "unlimited emergency" speech of May 27, 1941, President Roosevelt stated that "we reassert the ancient American doctrine of freedom of the seas." His characterization of the doctrine for which he contended was inaccurate on at least two counts. First, the doctrine he asserted was neither ancient nor "American" in the sense of representing American foreign policy. Second, the doctrine he asserted cannot be called the "freedom of the seas"; what he asked in reality was the "freedom to aid at will one belligerent nation without danger of interference by the other belligerent"— a freedom which our own government and the British government have denied on past occasions, and which the British would be the first to reject now, if it were to their advantage.

The sinking of the Robin Moor, an American ship, in the South Atlantic, afforded the President another opportunity to raise indirectly the question of the "freedom of the seas," in an oratorical message to Congress on June 20, 1941. Of course, the manner in which the ship was sunk and the crew and passengers treated was unjustified and ruthless, but the President failed to mention the Robin Moor was carrying to a belligerent state (the Union of South Africa) a cargo of goods of which 70 per cent was banned as contraband of war by both Britain and Germany (see Did You Know, #1).

Repeal the Neutrality Act?

The Neutrality Act is a substantial barrier to the President's conception of "freedom of the seas." Despite earlier demands for repeal of the Neutrality Act and return to "freedom of the seas" by Secretary of the Navy Knox (New York Times, May 22, 1941) and Secretary of War Stimson (New York Times, May 23, 1941), the President stated at his press conference following the "unlimited emergency" speech that he was not then considering a request asking for repeal or amendment of the Neutrality Act (New York Times, May 29, 1941).

The President's attitude therefore indicates three possibilities: 1) he may have used the phrase "freedom of the seas" merely as a glittering oratorical attraction; or 2) he may plan to seek repeal or amendment of the Neutrality Act later; or 3) his concept of "freedom of the seas" may involve a course of action designed to prevent German warships from interfering with American aid to Great Britain, which may not conflict with the Neutrality Act. In view of the history in American foreign policy of "freedom of the seas," and of the background of the President's remarks, the latter course seems the most likely.

"The Ancient American Doctrine"

In his "unlimited emergency" speech, the President referred to a few historical examples to prove America's devotion to "freedom of the seas." The irrelevance of those examples to the present situation is matched only by the omission from his speech of other and much more important historical instances. He cited our difficulties with the French in 1799, our war against the Barbary pirates a few years later, the War of 1812, and our assistance in ousting the French from Mexico, none of which was analogous to our present claim to the right to supply one belligerent with arms and contraband without interference from the other belligerent. Much more important is the fact that the President failed to mention the Civil War and the World War—not to mention the Neutrality Act and the current war.

In the Civil War, the Union seized British ships which sought to run the Union blockade and to carry goods to the South. (Borchard and Lage, "Neutrality for the United States" (1937), page 15.) In the World War, despite merely formal protests made for the sake of the record, the Wilson Administration actually acquiesced in the British blockade and the all-embracing contraband list adopted by the British, which exposed American trade with the neutrals of Europe and even South America to the complete control of Britain and the Allies (Borchard and Lage, pages 34, 36, 39, 43, 61–62, 65, 72). The Neutrality Act, of course, limits our freedom of trade in time of war, and was adopted as an indication of strength, not weakness, in our desire to keep out of war.

In the current war, despite another mild protest made for the sake of the record, we have again acquiesced in the British blockade and an even more-embracing contraband list. We have acquiesced in the British system of "navicerts," under which our shippers must submit their cargo lists to British agents—even if the cargo is destined for a neutral country—in order to minimize interference with a voyage by British warships. Now, we face a British system of "mailcerts," which amounts to a tax on American mail and operates on the same principle as the "navicerts" (New York Times, June 24, 1941).

Freedom to Aid a Belligerent

The President's remarks showed clearly that what he means by "freedom of the seas" is freedom to send arms and other contraband to Britain and her Allies. This is not the "freedom of the seas" recognized under international law, which means the freedom of American shippers to trade freely with all belligerents. What he means by "freedom of the seas" is shown by his statement that we must help "cut down the losses on the high seas," although at the time of his speech no American ship was known to have been sunk. He is primarily concerned with ousting German ships from Atlantic waters. Whether or not that is wise cannot be determined unless the issue is presented for what it really is.

There is a war in progress. Naturally, Germany will seek to sink or capture British ships carrying arms or contraband, even if the cargoes come from the United States. If American ships carry contraband to ports belonging to part of the British Empire (belligerent territory) it is to be expected that German ships will seek to block such voyages. American ships on such voyages cannot claim exemption from visit and search, or even capture, by German ships, because they can be held liable to capture under the accepted rules of international law, which American courts helped to formulate. (Borchard and Lage, pages 16–17, 118–119.)

Britain Opposes Freedom of the Seas

Obviously, "freedom of the seas" is not the policy of the British government, which rejected it in the World War, and which rejects it in the current war. The British must always reject it, since their strongest weapon is the naval blockade, by which they seek to prevent any supplies from reaching their enemies. No President can profess to seek "freedom of the seas" if he accepts unreservedly the British policy.

DOCUMENT 85

Chester Bowles to R. Douglas Stuart, Jr.
July 15, 1941

I had a most interesting talk with Senator Wheeler last week in Washington.

The principal subject that I discussed with him was the political problems that will face us when the war is over, and this is a subject which I would like to discuss with you the next time you are in New York.

The Communist Party, in my opinion, represents today a far greater threat to our democracy after the war than do the Nazis. I do not mean that the Communists are less desirable than the Nazis, but after all the Communists are here in this country, growing in strength and prestige every day, already an accepted Ally in good standing of our own Ally, Great Britain. The Nazis, barring a few stray subversive elements that may be kicking around in the back streets, are still pretty well concentrated 3,500 miles away.

I have been told that the Communist Party has already secured a far stronger grip on American industry than most of us have dreamed. My authorities are people who tend well towards the Left and who certainly cannot be classed as "Red Baiters."

When the war is over, the country is going to be faced with enormous idle production capacity, widespread unemployment, and millions of disillusioned soldiers and sailors looking for an early delivery on the rainbow which they were promised back in the honeymoon days of 1941.

The Communist Party will have a ready answer to these problems. They will immediately propose that the workers take over the plants and use them to turn out consumer goods of all kinds "for use instead of for profit."

Of course, many things can happen in the meantime to ruin Communist prestige, but it sounds to me as though the Russians are about to join the Belgians, the Dutch, the Norwegians as respected friends and Allies whose day of redemption we must some day bring about.

One answer to this Communist proposal may come from the large group of business men who are now in Washington working for the O.P.M. These business men today are unskilled in politics. Since most of them formerly ran their own businesses, they find it hard to work as members of a team.

Two years from today, however, this situation may have changed drastically. The least adaptable will have gone back to their own companies. The more politically adept, the more flexible and more capable will remain.

With their immense knowledge of our industrial facilities and with far greater knowledge than they have ever boasted before of our bewildering economic and social problems, it is likely that they may attempt to provide an answer to the difficulties that will face us when war production ceases. But their answer, I am afraid, will tend sharply towards Fascism, and it may "temporarily, of course," go the whole way towards Fascism—particularly if the threat of Communism looks dangerous. A civil war at that point is by no means impossible, although it is probably unlikely.

It seems to me that some new movement or new political party must be developed to provide a democratic alternative to these two extremes. The job will not be an easy one, but unless it is done I cannot help but feel rather pessimistic over the future of democratic government in our country.

If we enter the war, a great deal of bitterness will follow the peace. Even though we stay out it is likely that there will be a vast disillusionment when the public becomes aware of the vicious methods that have been used by the interventionists during the last year or two in their efforts to trick us into this mess in Europe.

Moreover, the people in this country have a right to expect the American industrial machine to work at top speed in their behalf. We know what full production can do in providing employment and increased incomes for millions of people. It does not take much imagination to see what this same overpowering productive energy can do if it were concentrated on the production of more consumer goods, better food, better homes, more hospitals.

As I say, the Communists are bound to approach this proposition from one direction. Fascist-minded people will approach it from another. Isn't it vitally necessary to develop a democratic party of the people who will approach it the traditional democratic, American way?

To my mind, Lindbergh may, when the war is over, loom as the logical spokesman for such a group. Unless I am greatly mistaken, his prestige will be very high when the war is over—whether we go in or stay out.

But just as important as his stand on the war is the fact that he, as a technological expert, can talk objectively and convincingly about millions of Americans who lack the proper food, the number who lack the proper housing, proper hospital care, the boost that we can give to the American standard of living if we will only revise our system in a democratic and rational way to meet the problems that it faces.

I have always believed that it would take a great crisis in this country to disrupt the present grip of the Democratic and Republican Party machines. The Republican Party was made possible only by the issue of slavery which split the country from one end to the other. And no new political party has been successfully organized since that time.

The Democratic Party, a mixture of Southern conservatives who sometimes look liberal largely because they hate Wall Street, Northern big city political machines, and a strong sprinkling of middle-of-the-road liberals, which in the past have managed to furnish the glue to hold the Party together, might readily split wide open.

The Republicans might go the same way with the older and more reactionary groups tending towards a Fascist program, and the vast group of relatively conservative but thoroughly democratic, small-town Republicans looking for leadership in some other direction.

This outline of the future, which I have been struggling to express, is admittedly a hazy one. But I feel sure that its general outlines are quite probable. I went over all this in some detail with Senator Wheeler and found him thoroughly in agreement. He is most enthusiastic about the possible role that Lindbergh can play in providing leadership to that vast group and millions upon millions of Americans who are determined to bring about the right kind of economic and social system through traditional American, democratic methods.

Why doesn't Lindbergh run for the Senate from Minnesota in 1942? He would undoubtedly be elected, war or no war. And he would place himself in a vitally important position so far as the future is concerned.

If you think General Wood would be interested in this letter, you are certainly at liberty to show it to him, but please don't let it go any further.

DOCUMENT 86

Chester Bowles to R. Douglas Stuart, Jr. April 25, 1941

Miss Cox just gave me, over the telephone, the figures on the latest Gallup poll, and I am dictating this letter from Essex.

This poll sounds to me like another expression of the same old fundamental confusion, i.e., the American people overwhelmingly want to stay out of war and at the same time overwhelmingly want to save Britain from defeat. They don't yet understand that these two worthy objectives contradict each other.

Although only 15 per cent are actually in favor of our entering the war, 70 per cent, according to the latest Gallup poll, are willing to take the step which would most distinctly put us in the war—according to the President's own admission.

Thus we are faced with the same old difficulty, and you can be sure that the interventionists will take advantage of it—leading us along step by step with the full approval of a public which doesn't understand the ultimate result of the course on which they are being led.

It seems to me that England has very little chance of going through 1941 with or without our aid. I even believe that England herself would be better off if she took a negotiated peace this year rather than to face the certain destruction which would be involved in a long war that she would most likely lose in the end, in spite of the fact that our aid was complete.

A long war of that kind would, in all probability, end in a stalemate since it is likely that we could not defeat Germany any more than she could defeat us.

My own hunch would be that you should stress and re-stress the President's statement of last winter that convoys mean war. With this should probably go what I believe to be a fact that the chances today are overwhelmingly against Britain.

You will notice in the latest Gallup survey that the public doesn't understand this at all. Three or four weeks ago only 4 per cent of the people in this country thought that Germany would win the war. Actually the odds at that time were probably three to one that Germany would win it.

Today, even after the Balkan fiasco, more than half the people still believe that Britain will win. Presumably they feel she will win without our entering the war, since only 15 per cent of them favor our entering the war at this time. This, of course, is ridiculous.

It is my belief that once the people in this country really understand that Britain can't win even with our all-out aid, they will be far more in favor of a negotiated peace. Hence, my suggestions are as follows:

1. Stress the President's statement that convoys mean war.
2. Stress the fact that Britain, with or without our aid, can't win the war. Certainly not within five, six, or ten years.
3. Emphasize, over and over again, the fact that anti-war sympathy is growing, that the non-interventionists' movement is a success, and that thousands upon thousands of people all over the country are growing stronger every hour in their opposition to war.

Let me know, Bob, whether you are going to be in New York again soon. And I certainly hope the ball keeps rolling in spite of the two speeches last night. I believe we have at least an even chance—perhaps better.

DOCUMENT 87

Chester Bowles to Roy Larsen
April 30, 1941

The recent Gallup polls have been both interesting and confusing, although it seems to me that the confusion which they show only reflects (as they should) the confusion of the American people.

There are several sets of figures which are particularly indicative of this:

83% of the people believe that we should not go to war. 17% say that we should.

But 71% favor convoys if a British defeat seems certain without them, although only 41% approve convoys today.

Roughly 70% (I have forgotten the exact figure) believe that Britain will beat Germany.

Roughly 60% (again I have forgotten the exact figure) believe that we should go into the war "if necessary to bring about the defeat of Germany."

These figures, it seems to me, indicate that American public opinion at the moment is thinking as follows:

We definitely do not want to go to war, and right now we can see no reason for going to war, because Germany is pretty sure to get licked by Britain in the long run without our active assistance.

In the meantime, we are inclined to be against convoys, because there is naturally some risk involved. However, we will be perfectly willing to take this risk if it were necessary to do so in order to save England.

In fact we would go further and actually go to war with Germany if it were necessary to do this in order to bring about Hitler's defeat—something we could probably accomplish in relatively short order.

Any such interpretation of the Gallup poll is naturally open to a good deal of argument. In suggesting this one I have tried to judge the figures as objectively as possible regardless of my own viewpoint.

Naturally, if I am right in my interpretation, there is a great deal of confusion in the public's mind. But even worse, I believe, is the fact that there are some very serious misconceptions.

First of all, the public apparently does not agree with the President's statement that "convoys mean shooting and shooting comes pretty close to war." They are inclined to believe that convoys are simply one more *reasonably* risky step in the course of our all-out aid to Britain.

Secondly, the public seems to be totally unaware of the present seriousness of the British situation. Before the Balkan campaign, only 4% of the people in this country (unless my memory is wrong) thought that Germany would beat England, and this figure was probably made up largely of Hitler sympathizers among people of German and Irish descent.

Even today a great majority still feel that Hitler will in some mysterious way collapse, if the British hold out long enough and if we continue to aid them to the full extent of our resources.

You and I will agree, I am sure, Roy, that these beliefs are a long way from the truth. Before the Balkan campaign I would have guessed that the odds against Britain actually beating Germany without our active participation were ten to one. Today it seems to me that the odds in favor of Britain winning, without our active participation, are practically nil, and the odds against her getting even a draw are pretty decisive.

The third point in my interpretation of these Gallup figures is that the public seems to feel that if we did get into the war on Britain's side, it would mean the relatively early end of Mr. Hitler. That theory again seems to me at variance with the probable facts. Any war between Hitler and ourselves would be long and exhausting.

When we talked I maintained that the only possible way to win such a war was by bloody, unrelenting military action on a battlefield or battlefields. You were inclined to feel that sea power would in the end throttle Germany and induce her to sue for peace with a minimum of actual military action.

I hope you are right and I am wrong. But I honestly feel that this idea of a comparatively easy, although perhaps lengthy war, is one of the most dangerous fallacies that confronts us.

It is also my belief that the newspapers, the newsreels, the columnists, the radio commentators and even your own publications, Roy, carry a heavy burden of responsibility for present and past wishful thinking on the part of the American people.

The German military machine has accomplished some amazing things during the last eighteen months. But amazing as they have been, skillful reporting, commentating and news analyses should have done a far better job of preparing our people for the many tragic failures which have taken place.

Based on the reports of countless reporters and experts of various kinds, the public has been led to assume that the German military machine was mechanically imperfect (the stalled and broken down tanks in Hitler's march on Vienna!); that their supplies of gasoline and Diesel oil would not survive an active campaign; that the people in Germany were more or less starving and full of hatred for their leader; that the blockade would bring Germany to her knees within a year or two; that Hitler's Norway campaign had no chance for success; that the German soldier fought only because he was forced to fight; that German equipment was "ersatz" and of poor quality; that the Maginot Line was impregnable and the French Army the greatest in the world; that the Poland campaign was successful only because it was fought against the Poles; that it was impossible for the Germans to carry troops across the Mediterranean; and that the Yugoslavs ("the toughest army in the Balkans") could hold out for the summer.

Now we are told that the progress of our war preparations is ahead of schedule and that 1942 will see us fully prepared for complete war; that aviation parity with Germany lies just ahead; that convoys will save England; that we can lick the Japs in six months; that bombings in Britain have done little military harm; that no American soldiers are wanted abroad; and that Hitler could be defeated by the U.S.A. within a reasonably short time and with only limited inconvenience.

Every scrap of hopeful news has been blown up and multiplied in importance. The many straws that have hinted at failures or damages have been minimized and minimized, until finally many of those straws have grown into facts that could no longer be denied.

During all of this time, the Administration and the interventionists have been telling the American people that they could have their cake and eat it, too.

Since surveys have clearly indicated that the public wants to aid Britain and at the same time stay out of war, the simple expedient was adopted of telling them that these completely opposing ideas were both possible. In fact, it has been maintained, over and over again, that the way to stay out of the war is to become a semi-active belligerent.

The whole operation, to my mind, Roy, has been completely unrealistic in viewpoint and dishonest in action. I believe that we, as a nation, are some day going to be thoroughly ashamed of our behavior during the past eighteen months.

I believe that we are going to be disliked by the British, and I believe we are going to deserve their dislike, for if this is *really* our war we have done exactly what we have accused the British of doing in the past—we have let others do our fighting and our dying.

I believe, Roy, that it is a very dangerous thing not to tell a democratic, free nation the truth. I believe it is a despicable thing to lead our people, as the Administration and the William Allen White group have led them, towards a war which they do not want by the simple device of misrepresenting and disguising each individual step towards that war. When that sort of thing is possible, democracy suffers deeply.

Some day the American people will awaken from their present dream and then their bitterness and their disillusionment are going to be unpleasant things to witness—particularly if we get into a war and the people discover that their path is a much more thorny path than they expected to trod.

As you know, Roy, I feel very deeply on this whole problem and I know that you do, too. It is good to know that you and I can discuss it freely and easily and still respect the other's viewpoint.

I have always maintained that those who really feel that we should go to war, and have felt it all along, stand on honest and firm ground, although I don't happen to agree with them. And I know that this is the stand you have always taken.

Moreover, I agree most heartily with your disappointment over the lack of interest or discussion about the new world which will follow the war. The Union Now Group has at least made an honest effort. But most people are content to say that if Hitler wins, the world will return to barbarism and if Hitler loses all our problems will be solved.

I am sorry that my observation on the Gallup survey turned into such a lengthy and controversial letter. Do let's get together again soon for luncheon.

P.S. Recently I have been developing a hunch that Roosevelt himself is fully aware of many of the points I have made in this letter, and that he is today much more concerned in getting the British and ourselves out of the predicament that we are in through a decent negotiated peace than he is in actually getting us into the war. The next three or four months will prove whether or not I am right on this.

DOCUMENT 88

James P. Selvage to George Gallup, with covering letter to R. Douglas Stuart, Jr.
April 29, 1941

Attached is my answer to Gallup. Bear in mind here that you are not trying to make a news story, for few papers are going to carry this, I think, but to make a case which will drive Gallup into using caution.

I'd be sure that he hears about this, and because of its importance, I would send it to a couple of hundred Washington correspondents (the outstanding bureaus as taken from the Congressional Directory); any list of columnists that you have, and radio commentators; all daily newspaper editors, if you have the money, and if not to 500 or 600.

I would also send a copy to your chapters and ask the chairmen to get someone in each town to write a letter to the editor, particularly those that use Gallup, denouncing these figures from this report under a local signature.

To be sent to all Washington correspondents
                 all daily newspaper editors
                 columnists
                 radio commentators

Dear Dr. Gallup:

I do not have to inform you that grave decisions are before the American people for decision.

Nor that your widely published polls of public opinion can have a tremendous opinion forming influence.

Nor that there are powerful and well-financed organizations propagandizing and pressuring to drag American soldiers and sailors into this war, the latest being the so-called Fight for Freedom Committee which publicly states that it is determined to make America fight now.

In the face of this situation, I cannot believe that you would permit the Gallup polls to be used for furthering this war propaganda. Yet you must have seen and been amazed at the use which has been made of your figures apparently indicating that the people of this country are willing to send our sailors to die on the seven seas as convoys for armaments sent to belligerents.

I do not challenge your good faith.

I do challenge the results of your recent figures on convoys. I do not believe you can defend them in open debate. *They prove each other wrong on their face.*

And, since you have inadvertently permitted your findings to be used as propaganda for war purposes, then I urge that you publicly retract them and denounce those who have spread them far beyond their normal usage in an attempt to mould public sentiment behind the use of convoys, first, then open war, knowing one means the other.

Because of the damage which these polls have done to America, let me ask you to answer the following questions categorically:

On April 21, your Public Opinion Institute asked the question: "Do you think we should send some of our warships manned with American sailors to Europe to help the British?" On that you report as follows: Favor, 27%; Oppose 67%.

On April 23, just two days later, you reported on the question:

"If it appears certain that Britain will be defeated, would you favor or oppose such convoys?" To that, an almost identical question, you reported the following answers: Favor, 71%; Oppose 21%.

Do you really believe that public opinion shifts so swiftly that on April 21 the public was 61% opposed to convoys and two days later it was only 21% opposed?

Do you believe that 46% of the people altered their convictions overnight?

Obviously these questions are one and the same, with a hair-line difference in phrasing. Sending "warships manned with American sailors to help the British" and "using part of our navy" (manned with American sailors) for convoys are identical statements. The difference is that once you mentioned the lives of American boys and spelled out the whole story for your voters, they wanted none of the foreign war.

My second categorical question deals with the phrasing of the question, "If it appears certain that Britain will be defeated unless we use part of our navy to protect ships going to Britain, would you favor or oppose convoys?"

This is an "iffy" or hypothetical question that no scientist seeking accurate information would possibly tolerate.

Had you been seeking the whole truth, and still felt it necessary to hypothecate, you would have presented the entire picture. You would have asked the question:

"If it appears certain that Britain will be defeated unless we use part of our navy to protect ships going to Britain, *and if convoying means war as President Roosevelt and Secretary Knox says it does,* then would you favor or oppose such convoys?"

There is a fair, impartial statement of the question which you asked by appealing to the sympathy of all of us for Great Britain.

It was to that partially hypothecated question that you got your 71% in favor of convoys which the war propagandists are using so avidly.

I assert to you that had you asked the question as I have stated it here, your answers would have been only slightly different from that of April 21 which showed 67% opposed to convoys when those who replied were thinking in terms of American youth dying on another foreign battlefield or in a foreign sea.

Bear in mind that on April 26, three days after you received your hypothetical 71% vote for convoys, you asked the question: "If you were asked today on the question of the United States entering the war against Germany and Italy, how would you vote—to go into the war, or to stay out of the war?" You reported the answers as follows:

Would vote to go in   19%
Would vote to stay out   81%
(There were no "don't knows" here.)

Is it not patent that the American people, or any people, having a clear understanding of the question upon which they were voting could not on April 21 vote against convoys (67%); on April 23 vote for convoys (71%); and on April 26 vote against entry into war (81%) when the President, the Secretary of the Navy, and Chairman George of the Senate Foreign Relations Committee say that convoys means a shooting-war and therefore questions two and three are one and the same?

I invite you, Dr. Gallup, to correct the delusion which you have created and to call to task those who have misused your surveys which fell inadvertently into the predicament of giving aid and comfort to war propagandists.

You owe it to yourself and to the nation to retract these figures which on their own face are incorrect, or else public opinion turns double-handsprings backwards overnight, any night.

DOCUMENT 89

Statement of the New York Chapter

June 23, 1941

Germany attacks Russia! And swiftly the clouds of confusion about this terrible war are lifted. Americans can now see clearly what the war is really about

The attack on Russia is not a new phase. This is what the war was planned for in the first place.

Hitler wanted the Ukraine. He also wanted Baku and Rumania. The Ukraine is a vast Russian state as large as New England, New York, New Jersey, Pennsylvania, Delaware and Maryland all put together. It is the richest grain field in the world. It has fruits, salt, vegetables, tobacco, cattle in abundance. It has 80% per cent of Russia's coal, 95 per cent of her manganese and 70 per cent of her iron. Baku produces nearly 20 per cent of the world's petroleum. If Hitler could get these things plus Rumanian oil his economic problem would be practically solved. And that is what he set out to do.

When he threatened Poland it was to march through that country as the pathway to the Ukraine. This was the primary reason for the present war— that and Hitler's determination to destroy the Communist regime in Russia.

But Britain and France interfered. Frantic, flaming propaganda aroused the populations of Britain and France. And the governments of these countries, knowing they were not prepared for war, got in between Germany and Russia. Their act was dictated partly by the determination of certain war groups in Europe to overthrow Hitler in Germany, partly by the desire of Britain and France to protect their far-flung empires from any seizures by Germany.

They succeeded in destroying France, Denmark, the Low Countries, Norway. They have brought Britain to the verge of ruin. They did not save Poland. They saved only Russia.

Russia made a pact with Germany to gain time and in the hope that Britain and France *might win Russia's battle*. Germany made the pact to keep Russia off her neck while she eliminated the British-French threat. But now France is defeated. The continent, save for Russia, is subdued. England is driven out of the continent and may be dealt with at sea. The moment has arrived to use the plan that was interrupted. If Hitler were to beat Britain *but fail to get the Ukraine* he would *lose the war*.

And so the war settles down to its logical and natural essential business. It is a giant struggle between the two greatest powers on the continent. It is a struggle between two deadly schools of government and life. A war between Germany and Russia; between Fascism and Communism.

England and France in a kind of madness, produced by poisonous propaganda, allowed themselves to get caught in between these two violent forces.

France is crushed. England is nearly crushed. Now she wants us to stick our necks into this cruel combat, as she did. She wants us to repeat her mistake.

Germany wants to overthrow Stalin and Communism and steal Russia's richest province. Stalin wants to overthrow Hitler and grab as much of the Balkans as he can. Hitler wants to make Russia fascist. Russia wants to make Germany Communist.

On which side of this dark contest will we fight? Is it not time we began to think of ourselves? Is it not time England began to make an end of her glamorous pretensions and think about the people of England and of her free dominions and their democracy and less about her empire?

The America First Committee is against Germany. It is against Russia. It is against meddling in their intrigues, their wars. It is *for America*.

More than ever it is for staying out.

DOCUMENT 90

Lease-Lend Aid to Russia

"Did you know *the real implications of the President's refusal to invoke the Neutrality Act against the Soviet Union?*" *No. 4, June 27, 1941*

We are acting to simplify definitions and facts by calling war "war" when armed invasion and a resulting killing of human beings takes place. (President Roosevelt in Armistice Day Speech, 1935.)

Whenever the President . . . shall find that there exists a state of war between foreign states, . . . the President shall issue a proclamation naming the states involved. . . . (Neutrality Act of 1939, section 1).

The President had authorized him to say, Mr. Welles [Sumner Welles; under secretary of state], explained at his press conference, that he has no intention of issuing a proclamation under the neutrality legislation (New York *Times*, June 26, 1941).

Aren't Russia and Germany at War?

Germany declared war on the Soviet Union on June 22, 1941, and a full-fledged total war is now in progress. The Neutrality Act of 1939 provides that whenever the President finds that foreign countries are at war, and that enforcement of the Neutrality Act is necessary "to promote the security or preserve the peace of the United States or to protect the lives of citizens of the United States," he shall issue a proclamation which will bring the entire Neutrality Act into force. The Congress, by concurrent resolution, can issue such a proclamation, but as a practical matter it has been left to the President in past instances, and President Roosevelt has jealously asserted his right to act first.

Our Impartial Law

The Neutrality Act was intended to keep the United States out of war by imposing limitations upon our own freedom of trade and travel, thus preventing the "incidents" which might drag us into war as they helped do twenty-four years ago. The unmistakable intention of Congress was that the President should apply the Act as soon as any war between foreign countries began, and that he was not to use the Act to favor one side against another. The Administration has agreed to this interpretation of the law; former Counselor of the State Department, R. Walton Moore, while testifying in regard to a similar provision in an earlier neutrality law, stated President Roosevelt's position as follows:

> He has not thought that he had the authority to delay, and I can say with the utmost confidence that is the interpretation placed upon that language by the present Executive. (Hearing before House Foreign Affairs Committee, Jan. 7, 1936.)

"Neutrality" Anywhere

The President's refusal to apply the Neutrality Act to the Nazi-Soviet war would be incomprehensible were it not that in the past he has administered the Act so as to enable him to play power politics anywhere in the world. The Act was intended to keep the United States neutral, yet the President has used it so as to enable virtual intervention by the United States in foreign wars. Now, he seeks by the use of the Lend-Lease law virtually to nullify the Neutrality Act.

Chaco, Ethiopia, Spain

Here is the history of the President's administration of neutrality legislation: In 1934, when the Gran Chaco War between Paraguay and Bolivia was in progress, he sought and obtained from Congress authority to embargo the shipment of arms to both belligerents. His present policy is based upon opposition to aggression; yet he himself requested such an embargo in 1934 after the League of Nations had branded Paraguay the aggressor.

When Italy invaded Ethiopia, the President invoked the new Neutrality Act against both belligerents, with the announced intent and practical effect of helping Ethiopia, since only Italy was in a position to obtain supplies from the United States. A few months after the Spanish Insurgents revolted against the legal Loyalist Government of Spain, the President caused the Neutrality Act to be extended to cover civil wars, and then applied the amendment immediately against both parties. This was in clear violation of the right under international law of a legal government faced with insurrection to purchase arms from other countries. (Borchard and Lage: "Neutrality for the United States," pages 311-312-317-321, 335-336.)

Apparently the President still does not believe that Japan and China are at war. He refused to invoke the Neutrality Law when hostilities broke out, on the pretext that there had been no declaration of war. His own definition of "war," and the tremendous loss of life and property in China, have not been enough to convince him. The real reason for his refusal to apply the Act at the outset was an announced desire to help China. Actually, Japan has received as much aid. The present Administration policy of "appeasing" Japan may account for the President's continuing blindness.

All Aid to Stalin

Now comes the Nazi-Soviet war, and the President finds that it is desirable not to invoke the Neutrality Act. Yet the excuse which enabled him to evade invocation of the Act in the Sino-Japanese War—lack of a declaration of war—is not available. Yet, aid to Soviet Russia is now considered essential under our new lease-lend theory of national defense. The defense of Moscow has become essential to the security of the United States. Consequently, the President announces, through Under-Secretary of State Welles, that the Neutrality Act will not be applied, and that lease-lend aid will be given to Russia if it is requested. (New York *Times,* June 26, 1941.) Since the Neutrality Act has already been invoked against Germany (Proclamation 2374, Nov. 4, 1939), it now becomes possible to aid Soviet Russia alone. This latest action amounts to an attempt by the President to nullify the Neutrality Act by use of the recent lease-lend law (formerly known as H.R. 1776). It should be noted that when the lease-lend bill was being discussed in Congress, Administration spokesmen and supporters were most fervent in their protestations that the bill would not repeal or affect the Neutrality Act. (Congressional Record, March 8, 1941, pages 2116, 2112.)

Peace Preserved?

The President's refusal to apply the Neutrality Act against the Soviet Union is in direct contradiction to the Act's purpose on another count. The official statement that application of the Act was unnecessary "to promote the security or preserve the peace of the United States or to protect the lives of citizens in the United States" is subject to serious reservations. That American lives—and property—can be lost through failure to apply the Act is all too possible. An American ship can be sunk in the Pacific on its way to Vladivostok. Invoking the Neutrality Act against the Soviet Union would not by itself afford any protection in the Pacific.

Danger without Combat Zones

U.S. merchantmen still can carry contraband cargo to Vladivostok. For the Act excludes Pacific areas from the ban against U.S. ships' entering belligerent ports—unless Pacific ports are declared to be combat areas (22 U.S.C.A. 245j-1). Suppose the Act is applied and an American ship loaded with motor trucks—which Secretary of State Hull admitted to be "essential war materials" during the Italo-Ethiopian War (Borchard & Lage, page 321)—heads for Vladivostok. Time and again German, and even Italian, raiders have been reported to be loose in the Pacific. Such a ship might be torpedoed or shelled 3,000 miles off San Francisco. Just how so unnecessary a sinking would "promote the security or preserve the peace of the United States" or "protect the lives of citizens of the United States" is not apparent. The Robin Moor was carrying motor trucks and other contraband to the Union of South Africa against whom the Neutrality Act was applied long ago although South African waters have never been declared by the President to be within a combat zone.

Apply the Neutrality Act

A safer course for the American people would seem to be for the President to apply the Act against the Soviet Union and immediately declare Vladivostok and the whole Siberian coast the combat area it is likely to become.

In the light of the President's attitude, it is well to recall his statement in his address at Chautauqua on August 14, 1936:

> The effective maintenance of American neutrality depends today, as in the past, on the wisdom and determination of whoever at the moment occupy the offices of President and Secretary of State.

DOCUMENT 91

Wings over Nome?

"Did you know that a new and false bogey of invasion through Alaska has been invented in order to bolster the policy of aid to Soviet Russia?"
No. 5, July 1, 1941

The Claim

> Control of eastern Siberia by either Germany or Japan, directly or indirectly, would be a source of anxiety. (Columnist Ernest K. Lindley, Washington Post, July 2, 1941.)

> A deal with Russia giving American fighting planes use of the strong Soviet air bases on the Siberian tundra opposite Alaska . . . is being advocated by a number of influential defense strategists here, it was learned tonight. (New York Herald Tribune, June 30, 1941.)

The Answer

> In the hysteria of the moment every area has suddenly become "vital" and "invulnerable"; even Alaska, wilderness of pine and snow, total population of 73,000 people, without a good air target in the territory, has been represented by sources that should know better as highly vulnerable to air attack. (Hanson W. Baldwin, "United We Stand," Page 114.)

Siberia—New Bogey

A cynical old adage has it that military men, if given the chance, would build bases on Mars to defend against invasion from the Moon. The only thing wrong with this adage is that its scope is limited to military men; it should include our present-day interventionists. This week Hitler's invasion of the Soviet Union has given new impetus to the demand for bases on Mars—in this case, Siberia. The professed reason is that a Hitler victory in the latest aggression may mean that the Luftwaffe and the Reichswehr will face the U.S. from eastern Siberia, or it may mean that Japan, taking advantage of a weakened Soviet Union, will move into Siberia's Maritime provinces and Kamchatka peninsula. This is one of the justifications advanced for lease-lend aid to Soviet Russia.

The Interventionist Solution

In either case, the alarmists seem to expect an immediate invasion of North America via Alaska. Advance bases in Siberia, they say, constitute the only solution. Accordingly, they want a deal with the Soviet Union whereby the U.S. can take over the air bases on Siberia's East Cape, up behind narrow Bering Strait, and a number of air and submarine bases on the Bering Sea which were constructed for the Soviet Union by Nazi engineers. Columnist Ernest K. Lindley, who frequently writes with semi-official sanction, has implied approval of such a move. (Washington Post, July 2, 1941.)

Interventionist Errors

Actually the alarmists are talking something close to nonsense. The danger they profess to see does not exist—no matter who holds eastern Siberia. They are discounting the growing formidability of our Alaskan defenses; they are ignoring the strategic difficulty of an attack on Alaska and the strategic difficulty and expense of holding bases in Siberia.

Alaskan Defense Problems

The defense of Alaska falls into three strategic divisions: defense of the island-fringed Panhandle which extends south along the western border of Canada; defense of the Aleutian Islands which extend south and west like a necklace between the Bering Sea and the Pacific Ocean, and which flank the great circle route from Japan to the U.S.; defense of the mainland whose Seward Peninsula is only 60 miles across Bering Strait from Siberia. In the strait—a mile-and-a-half apart—lie the Soviet Union's Big Diomede Island, with its airfield and weather station, and the U.S.-held Little Diomede Island. ("Strategy of the Americas," by Fleming MacLiesh and Cushman Reynolds, pp. 67–71.)

The Panhandle

In the frequently fog-bound Panhandle, whose southern tip is 625 miles north of Seattle, the Navy is developing an air base at Sitka, in the north (900 miles from Seattle), which will eventually service submarines too. The Navy is developing other bases at Juneau and Ketchikan. The Army is developing an air base at Metlakatla.

The Aleutian Islands

In the Aleutian Islands, the Navy has a large base under development on Kodiak Island near the mainland, and has another nearly completed at

Dutch Harbor west of Kodiak on Unalaska Island, which is 2900 miles from Tokyo, 2700 miles north of Hawaii. On other islands still farther west there are Navy "listening posts."

The Mainland

On the mainland, the Army is enlarging its air base and military post at the port of Anchorage, on the south coast. Some 350 miles up the single Alaskan railroad from Anchorage the Army is building an important air base with 10,000 foot runways for "flying fortresses" at Fairbanks, 1600 miles from the main northwestern air base at Spokane, where summer days are 24 hours long and winters are arctic. The Army is also building emergency landing fields on the frozen tundra of the north to supplement the main bases.

Air Bases

In addition to the above, Pan American Airways has bases in the Panhandle, and the Civil Aeronautics Administration is co-operating in the development of emergency fields. What is needed to supplement these bases are some connecting air bases in western Canada which could be arranged for quite easily under the Canadian-American defense agreement. Some experts have thought that a 1200-mile military road over which supplies could be trucked from Seattle to Fairbanks should be built through Canada. The real need for this is not so clear as the need for connecting air bases. However, the basic point is that from this network of bases (see any good map of Alaska), supplied by protected communication lines through the air or along the coast, U.S. submarines and surface raiders and Army and Navy bombers can immediately smash at any invasion attempt and bomb out any bridge head the enemy tries to establish.

Alaska Can't Be Invaded

Regarding the invasion of Alaska, Hanson W. Baldwin, military expert for the New York Times, has the following to say in his recent book, "United We Stand" (pp. 113, 114):

> There has been much talk of "the vulnerability of Alaska to invasion." It is true that we cannot guard all Alaska's coast line against a landing; not all the king's horses and all the king's men could do that. But we could wish for no more ludicrous and fatal error on the part of the enemy than a landing in Alaska. The inhospitable, rugged, and difficult country and the terrible cold would make the Russian difficulties in Finland and the Italian troubles in the mountains of Greece and Albania seem like child's play. Air bases could not be quickly or easily established there by an enemy; if they were, they could be far more easily

reduced by our own forces. And if any enemy ever attempted an overland campaign, striking toward Seattle, he would leave behind him a trail bleached in bones, and, in the words of one officer, the soldiers who started would not reach Seattle. Their grandchildren might reach it, but they would not be an army.

The Siberian Bases

The Siberian bases are difficult to supply from the Soviet Union or from Japan. They are not reached by railroad, but only by ships and planes. From them no vital spot in North America could be bombed by any plane in use today. At best, they could be used as bases from which to bomb our own outlying Alaskan bases. And we can always base forces in Alaska sufficient to beat them. If Japan is the enemy, the industrial cities of the Island Empire will soon be within the reach of our new super-bombers—the B 19's.

DOCUMENT 92

Ruth Sarles to R. Douglas Stuart, Jr. October 3, 1941

Herewith what I hope will be a brief report:

Lease-Lend. The House Appropriations Committee office still thinks the lease-lend measure will be reported to the House next Wednesday. No one seems to know yet just when actual debate on it will start. It is hard to tell at this point just how violent feelings will be on the freedom-of-religion issue by that time but I think it is safe to say there will be several days' debate in the House. I have no polls as to the final outcome that I consider reliable. I hear that some of the men from New York, New Jersey and Pennsylvania who voted against the first lease-lend may go along with this.

In the Senate, I understand there will be some strong pressure while the bill is in Committee. Senator Nye and Senator Adams of Colorado [Alva B. Adams (D-Colo.)] pledged each other during the summer that they would fight future lease-lend measures in Committee. There are six men on that committee who can probably be counted on to force the Administration people to answer a good many searching questions: Adams, Nye, McCarran, Chavez [Dennis Chavez (D-Colo.)], and probably Holman and

Brooks. The tack they will take is to demand a strict accounting of how the money is spent; they will bring out many of the stories that have been floating around about use of lease-lend funds for entertainment, etc.

(The Baltimore Sun carried a long front-page story on Senator Nye's Bridgeport meeting this week, written by one of their best Washington reporters, C. P. Trussell. We were surprised at the length of the story and rather pleased at what seemed to be an attempt to be fair. We now learn that the Sun has assigned a reporter to follow Nye around the country and in reporting his meetings to pay particular attention to the make-up of crowds.)

Neutrality. No line yet as to what form the President's proposal will take. We heard that up to Wednesday noon the President was holding out for outright repeal and that Secretary Hull was insisting that would make things too hard for men who come up for election in 1942, that if revision were adopted they could point to the fact that the neutrality law is still on the books. Today I hear a story from a *fairly* good source that the President will at this time ask only for the arming of merchant ships and later on will bring in a request for lifting the prohibition from combat zones.

Greer Investigation. [On September 4, 1941, the Navy Department announced that the *USS Greer*, a destroyer, had been attacked by German torpedoes that had missed their mark.] No date has been set yet for a hearing. Senator Walsh's office thinks the date will be set early next week when the Senator returns.

Far East. Apparently the situation is still serious but not hopeless. I hear that Secretary Hull has increased his demands; that he does not now want to agree to recognize Manchukuo; that he wishes no U.S. or British troops withdrawn until a settlement is discussed after the war; that he wants reaffirmation of the Nine-Power Pact. One report has it that the President was so sure the situation was smoothing out that he took a great many ships out of the Pacific, leaving only enough so that we would have a parity with Japan. However, our ships are based on Hawaii, and if they were forced into combat with the Japanese navy closer to Japan, they would not have parity because of the decreasing efficiency when far away from base. It is said that Ambassador Grew [Joseph C. Grew, ambassador to Japan] is doing a grand job, and that Mr. Welles is working hard toward some kind of face-saving formula.

Vatican. There is still much curiosity about what Myron Taylor [the president's personal diplomatic representative to the Vatican; former board chairman, United States Steel Corporation] told the Pope and the Pope told Myron Taylor. There seems to be confidence in Matthew's [Herbert Matthews, *New York Times* Rome correspondent] story from Rome, published last week, to the effect that the Pope had turned down Mr. Taylor's request that he bless the war in some way. One State Department man says the Department has had practically no communication with Mr. Taylor, although two diplomatic pouches have left Rome since he has been there. One story going around in newspaper circles here is that Myron Taylor has been converted to Catholicism, which would certainly be embarrassing to the Administration if true. This story continues that Britain's threat to bomb Rome if the Pope did not play ball has resulted in Mr. Taylor's assurance that the Pope could find refuge in this country or somewhere in the Western Hemisphere.

I hear also in the Department of State that Ambassador Phillips is coming home, that he did not *ask* to come, just announced it; the conclusion drawn is that he is probably indignant about Mr. Taylor's handling of relations with the Vatican. There is another story floating around town that the Pope is interested in helping set up some kind of buffer state which Germany would undoubtedly like to have between Germany and the East, after she has taken over European Russia. The story goes on that it would be a Christian state, probably under the White Russians.

Russia. There is acute discomfort in some Administration circles over Russia's strong diplomatic position. It is said Russia makes no secret that she wants an active front on the continent and is making no bones of her willingness to sign a separate peace with Germany if Britain does not play ball. A remark is attributed to Stalin that so far Germany has not taken as much territory as Lenin gave away in the Treaty of Brest-Litovsk. There is a good deal of speculation here as to whether or not Britain will actually invade. Ludwell Denny, Scripps-Howard writer who usually thinks pretty straight, thinks Britain will have to try invasion, that if Russia makes a separate peace Churchill will probably be thrown out.

Africa. We are said to be using Freetown as a naval air base for patrolling the South Pacific. The story has just come to my attention of the report that Colonel Donovan is trying to get General Weygand to join with De Gaulle and hold French Africa; Weygand's price is said to be an A.E.F. plus complete mechanized equipment for two divisions of his own men.

Oceanic Empire. This phrase is becoming the tag for a new kind of "religion" among those who are working for closer relations after the war between the United States and Britain. As I understand it, they see increasing integration of the two with economic integration to be somewhat limited. The conservatives in Britain are said not to want any great degree of "cooperation" but Churchill does and so does labor. It is said that it was at the insistence of the City crowd that the modification—"with due respect for their existing obligation"—was inserted in the fourth of the eight points (this is the point on equal access to trade and raw materials).

The interpretation is that if the City crowd is to stay in power after the war the war will have to be paid for, and the only way it can be paid for is through exports. Thus, Empire tariffs would have to stand since the United States is Britain's greatest competitor.

This interpretation goes on—there will be no freedom of the seas, only Anglo-American sovereignty of the seas. This is an instrument of peace, since no country could under this arrangement get large stocks of raw materials or food as Germany has done.

I am giving you that story in detail because it is being discussed and is one of those things which may sooner or later become a cult.

We hear that an O. P. M. "Big Shot" remarked that the America First Bureau here was the most effective lobby on the Hill.

I gave several of our "Did You Knows" to a member of the State Department staff who does not agree with us but read them over carefully and commented that they were an excellent and sound piece of work.

P.S. Congressman Shafer [Paul W. Shafer (R-Mich.)] of Michigan tells me that when home he was greatly heartened to find that even people who disagreed with him gave him credit for the courageous stand he has taken on the war question.

DOCUMENT 93

Samuel B. Pettengill to Robert E. Wood
October 16, 1941

Herewith another column which will appear next week, "Where Kings Have Always Stood."

I had a long talk with Wheeler yesterday. I outlined the proposal for a vote on war or peace. He is very strong for it. I told him I would let him see a revised draft of a statement which I roughed out for you the other day. The boys at the research office are digging up the quotations showing how the boundaries of action established under lease-lend are being broken down for aggressive war.

There are considerations against adopting the proposed policy, but honestly, I cannot think of any good alternative. In my judgment, only a bold act will bring the nation and Congress right up against the gun. This may not be the bold act to be adopted, but unless something is done we will get into the war inch by inch, and at the same time, all of the Congressmen will go back home and tell their people that they never voted for it!

The arming of ships is almost certain to pass by substantial majority. Wheeler thinks that the Administration will not try to eliminate the combat areas as an amendment in the Senate.

If so, the sequence seems to be the ships will be armed, one of them will be sunk, and then either undeclared war or a declaration for war. Meantime, the President can eliminate all combat areas by proclamation. Pepper has already urged this action which would prevent Congress from passing upon it. Technically and legally the President could do it because the Neutrality Act provides that when war breaks out abroad and when the President thinks the security of the United States requires such action he is then authorized and directed to establish the combat areas. He could now say that the maintenance of combat areas does not promote the security of the United States but the reverse.

Schroeder of Dubuque saw Walsh of Massachusetts yesterday. Walsh is quite blue. He thinks that a month or six weeks from now Congress would go along on a declaration of war. I think this is too dark a picture, but it seems to argue for effect that we put the question to a vote now, when we would be sure to defeat it. If defeated, the moral position of all of our friends on Capitol Hill would be tremendously improved.

I realize that it is unrealistic to assume that a war resolution would be now supported by the President, or could now be brought to a vote. The mere fact, however, that the Administration would flinch from a vote would, in my judgment, be a clear recognition by them that Congress and the country is opposed—in short, it would put us on the majority side.

As arguments against our backing a vote, we have to consider the following:

(1). That it might carry. This, in my judgment, is inconceivable; but, if so, we shall have done our duty.

(2). The danger that the position of America First might be misunderstood or deliberately falsified to the effect that we have abandoned our opposition to war in the same way that the speech of Senator Capper was distorted. It strikes me, however, that this is a minor risk.

(3). It will be argued that we are attempting to force the President's hand when he, in a position of great delicacy, is trying to keep us out of war. The pro-war writers, as we know, do not want the question presented. Ordinarily, however, it is good tactics to do what the opposition does not want you to do. There can be little doubt that it would be very embarrassing to the Administration, but the answer to that is that the Administration is very embarrassing to the American people in leading us inch by inch into total war without the free consent of our people.

(4). There is the danger that the Japanese situation might blow up in our face at the very moment that we were urging Congress to vote on peace or war, and that we might as a result have war, and some people might blame America First for having precipitated the question.

I have presented the case for the proposal and have also suggested all of the arguments against adopting it. We do know that our friends on Capitol Hill think well of it, and their political judgment is an important consideration. The point has been made to me that by taking the whole step now we might frighten the Administration away from war for a month or two, and by that time the situation of Russia will be clearly hopeless and that England will make peace. In that case we win our main objective of keeping this country out.

The fact that not a single British regiment has been in contact with the enemy anywhere in the world during all of this blood letting in Russia takes my mind back to a theory that developed with reference to the Hess flight. That theory was, as you may remember, that Hitler never wanted to go west, that he went west only because England and France declared war, that he desires a rapprochement with Britain, and that a proposal was made that he now be permitted to do what Germany had always wanted, to get the Ukraine and the Caucasian oil fields, and if permitted to do so would then offer peace to Britain. The theory was that Britain was willing to throw Russia to the dogs to save her empire, that she has maintained a token warfare against Germany since July 12 with a few bombings in order not to make too bald a disclosure of her agreement with the Hess proposal and that this accounts for the almost total lack of activity by Britain since the Russian campaign began. Whether there is anything in this theory of a conspiracy between Hitler and Churchill at the expense of Russia, no one knows. The logic of the situation, in any case, however, seems to indicate that Britain and Germany will make peace as soon as the Russian campaign is over, even though it is a bitter pill for Britain to swallow.

With Russia out of action I can't imagine any Congressman voting for American doughboys to take the place of the Russian Army.

DOCUMENT 94

Our African Outpost

"Did you know that, despite pledges that American boys would not invade the Americas, we may invade Africa?"
No. 8, July 11, 1941

Promise

> I repeat again that I stand on the platform of our party; we will not participate in foreign wars and will not send our Army, Naval or Air Force to fight in foreign lands outside of the Americas except in case of attack. (President Roosevelt, campaign speech at Philadelphia, October 23, 1940.)

Prospect

> And that threat extends not only to French North Africa and the western end of the Mediterranean, but also to the Atlantic fortress of Dakar, and to the island outposts of the New World—the Azores and Cape Verde islands. (President Roosevelt, "Unlimited Emergency" speech, May 27, 1941, as reprinted in the New York Times, May 28, 1941.)

> Assurance that such outposts in our defense frontier remain in friendly hands is the very foundation of our national security and of the national security of every one of the independent nations of the New World. (President Roosevelt, Message to Congress on Iceland, July 7, 1941, as reprinted in the New York Times, July 8, 1941.)

Prelude to A.E.F.

In his message to Congress on July 7 announcing the occupation of Iceland, the President also said that U.S. forces had been sent to Trinidad and British Guiana to forestall any Nazi attempt to employ the pincer strategy to the Western Hemisphere. (New York Times, July 8, 1941.) Manning the Trinidad and Guiana bases is one thing. The many justified doubts concerning the necessity of including Iceland in Hemisphere defense (See Did You Know, #7) do not apply to bases guarding the Caribbean and the northeastern coast of South America. But the President did not limit himself to Hemisphere bases in his message, any more than he did in his subsequent press conference. He said: "It is essential that Germany should not be able successfully to employ such tactics through sudden seizure of strategic points in the South Atlantic and in the North Atlantic." (New York Times, July 8, 1941.) The President's failure to restrict those points in the Atlantic to points in the Western Hemisphere has led to the widely-voiced inference that occupation of Iceland is a prelude to occupation of Dakar in west Africa, and of the Cape Verde, Canary and Azores islands by force, if necessary.

Far-off Dakar

Bases in the fjords of sub-Arctic Iceland are essential to Hemisphere defense only by a stretch of the military imagination (See Did You Know, #7). It takes an even greater stretch to include Dakar and the Atlantic islands. Dakar is a steaming, squalid, hurricane-swept tropical port in French Senegal which is loyal to Vichy. It is situated on the Cape Verde peninsula on the western bulge of Africa. It has docking facilities for a score of ships, a coaling station, an oil depot, an airfield, a seaplane base and a small navy yard. Because it is only 1,700 miles across the south Atlantic to Pernambuco and Natal on the bulge of Brazil, and because planes of an Italian air line make that crossing regularly, interventionists dramatize Dakar as the point from which an immediate invasion of the Western Hemisphere would be launched should Hitler gain outright control of it. Accordingly, the interventionists cry constantly for the U.S. to seize Dakar—3,750 miles from the tip of Florida.

Invasion Base?

The interventionists ignore the military facts about Dakar. It is not a suitable invasion base. Seizing it would be a major military venture. An invasion of Brazil, as all the military experts agree, could not be accomplished without first defeating the U.S. Navy and the U.S. Air Forces to gain control of the sea lanes. If such an attack were to be launched from Dakar, it would mean that Dakar would have to have a naval base capable of supplying and *repairing* the combined fleets of Germany and Italy plus whatever is left of the French fleet and a large part of the British fleet; it would also mean that Dakar would have to have an air base capable of supplying and *repairing* a huge fleet of bombing planes—perhaps thousands—with range enough to cross the 1,700 miles to Brazil with bombloads and *return* to Dakar.

Naval Base?

Dakar has no such naval base as would be required. There is a single naval drydock, capable of repairing—one at a time—ships up to 10,000 tons (Major James Ross, Christian Science Monitor, Weekly Magazine Section, June 21, 1941). That means that Dakar could repair one damaged cruiser at a time—or one Nazi pocketbattleship. Dakar cannot repair more than superficial damage to battleships (the 35,000-ton French battleship "Richelieu," torpedoed in the summer of 1940 in Dakar harbor, has not yet been repaired). Damaged battleships, and most lesser ships, would have to limp all the way back to northern Europe to bases 3,000 miles from Dakar. To make Dakar into an important naval base would take years. Navies are tied to their bases. The further they operate from their bases the less efficient they are. According to some estimates they lose 30 per cent per 1,000 miles. One weakness of the British fleet today is that many of its ships must cross the Atlantic to U.S. ports to find adequate repair facilities. A Nazi base at Dakar would be dependent on the steel mills, the electric equipment factories, and the whole industrial complex of northern Europe, 3,000 miles away.

Air Base?

Dakar has no such air base as would be required, nor does Hitler have bombing planes of the range required to bomb Pernambuco. ("Strategy of the Americas," Fleming MacLiesh and Cushman Reynolds, p. 210.) There is an air port at Dakar where there may be as many as 100 French planes (Major James Ross, ibid.). For the defense of Dakar they could be reinforced by German planes flown down from Europe (Colonel Frederick Palmer, Washington Star, June 18, 1941).

Supply Lines

If an attack were to be launched against the Western Hemisphere from Dakar, there would have to be a ponderous supply line from Europe down the coast of Africa—down the nearly 2,000 miles from Gibraltar to Dakar. The bulk of supplies would have to come by sea. The motor road connections from North Africa to Dakar are poor and inadequate (Major James Ross, ibid.). Only a trickle could come by air. The old French imperial dream of a trans-Sahara railroad is still a dream. If the Western Hemisphere were under attack, that supply line would be vulnerable to long-range U.S. submarines, surface raiders and carrier-borne planes.

Advantage Out

Occupying Dakar is another matter. Since Vichy has shown no discernible inclination to turn Dakar over to the U.S., and since Dakar forces, in September 1940, repulsed an attack by Free French and British forces, occupation obviously could be accomplished only by force. If the threat of Dakar to the Western Hemisphere has been magnified out of all proportion, so has the ease with which it could be taken. For us to send an expedition there would mean that all the problems of supply and communications which would beset an enemy attacking the Western Hemisphere would beset U.S. forces. In addition, it would mean accomplishing the most difficult of all military operations, landing on a defended hostile shore. All the advantages would lie with the defenders.

Dakar and Die

In the Washington Star of June 18, 1941, Colonel Frederick Palmer, noted military analyst and war correspondent, wrote as follows: "To send over an expeditionary force in increments to Dakar . . . would be an invitation to massacre in detail. We shall see that our initial force to Dakar should not be less than 100,000 men. With them must go tanks, guns, ammunition, food and all kinds of engineering transport and maintenance equipment. 400,000 tons of shipping would be too modest an estimate for an expedition that might require 100 ships, and a powerful naval escort, inclusive of all types from destroyers to battleships. . . . What a spread of targets, like a flock of ducks in flight over a hunter's head, when the dive-bombers and torpedo-carrying planes, with the aid of submarines, loosed their blitzkrieg on these 100 ships for the last 200 or 300 miles before they were even in sight of the African coast! . . . Suppose half our ships did reach the harbor at Dakar, after silencing the defense batteries. There is insufficient pier space for even 20 ships, and we should still be under bombing attack. So we would be if we tried to establish a beach-head by dribbling men and material ashore in open boats. If we went south to Freetown, British Sierra Leone, we should have to advance through tough tropical country to Dakar, while from French North Africa to Dakar there are available roads for enemy reinforcements which enable quicker transit than for us over 3,400 miles of ocean. . . .

There is also talk of taking the Cape Verde islands. These very small islands would be bull's-eye targets for bombers, based on the African coast 300 miles away, while we were making our landing, leveling volcanic rock for air fields and setting up hasty defense. In any plan of hemispheric defense, both the Dakar and the Cape Verde adventures had better wait until we have a well-equipped and fortified base on the coast of Brazil to cover our side of the Atlantic."

The Atlantic Islands

Everything that is true strategically of Dakar is true of the island groups in the Atlantic which are even less well prepared as "invasion" bases than Dakar. But occupying and holding them is another matter. Colonel Frederick Palmer has dealt effectively with the problem of the Portuguese-owned Cape Verdes (see above). The Canaries, owned by Spain, are less than 300 miles from the coast of Rio de Oro, Spain's big colony in Africa, and only

700 miles from Lisbon. They could be bombed out from bases in Portugal or Rio de Oro. The Portuguese-owned Azores, a favorite among the interventionists for U.S. seizure, would be as difficult for the U.S. to hold—provided the U.S. could take them—as Bermuda, 650 miles off Norfolk, Virginia, would be for Hitler. The Azores are 2,750 miles from New York, 2,350 miles from Puerto Rico, only 785 miles from the Portuguese coast.

Foreign Opposition

Certainly Spain, supporter of the Axis, would resist any attempt by the U.S. to occupy the Canaries. What Portugal's attitude would be has been made clear by two recent protests to the U.S. government. Portugal protested a call for occupation of the Azores and Cape Verdes made on the floor of the Senate early in May by Senator Claude Pepper of Florida. Portugal also protested President Roosevelt's allusions to the Portuguese islands in his speech of May 27 (New York Times, June 11, 1941).

DOCUMENT 95

Our Iceland Outpost

"Did you know *that the occupation of Iceland is closer to Europe's war than it is to defense of the Western Hemisphere?*" *No. 7, July 9, 1941*

I repeat again that I stand on the platform of our party; we will not participate in foreign wars and will not send our Army, Naval or Air Forces to fight in foreign lands outside of the Americas except in case of attack. (President Roosevelt, in campaign speech at Philadelphia, on October 23, 1940.)

The President made something of a joke of attempts to define the Western Hemisphere. . . . When some one recalled that the President himself had marked the area on a previous occasion, and that his line then left most, if not all, of Iceland in the Eastern Hemisphere, the President repeated, with a chuckle, that it all depended on what geographer one talked to last. (Report of President's press conference of July 8, in New York Times of July 9, 1941.)

But these things cannot be done, Iceland cannot be guarded indefinitely without shooting; of this there is no doubt. (Hanson W. Baldwin, military expert, in New York Times, July 9, 1941.)

Now It Can Be Told

On July 7, 1941, a special message from President Roosevelt informed Congress that U.S. Naval forces had that day landed at Iceland, under an agreement secretly concluded six days before between the President and the Prime Minister of Iceland (New York Times, July 8, 1941). Congress was advised that the step had been taken to forestall possible occupation of Iceland by Germany, which would constitute a three-fold threat to the United States: a threat against Greenland and the northern portions of the North American continent; a threat against all North Atlantic shipping; and a threat against the steady flow of munitions to Great Britain.

Reaching towards Europe

To call the occupation of Iceland a "defensive" measure is equivalent to making "a joke of attempts to define the Western Hemisphere rigidly," and to repudiating earlier solemn pledges that American armed forces would not be sent "to fight in foreign lands outside of the Americas." Iceland's capital and chief port, Reykjavik, is only 670 miles from Scotland, and only 915 miles from Norway, both of which are within the combat zones proclaimed by the President in November, 1939, into which American vessels and citizens may not travel. All of Iceland is within the war zone proclaimed by the Nazis on March 25. American troops stationed there are 950 miles closer to Europe than are the troops stationed in Greenland, which is outside the Nazi war zone, and 1950 miles closer to Europe than the troops stationed at our base at St. John's, Newfoundland. Iceland itself is 3200 miles by air from New York, and 2834 miles by the most direct sea route.

In the Shooting Range

There is no doubt but that Reykjavik will continue to be used by the British as a naval and air base (Hanson W. Baldwin, New York Times, July 9, 1941). In that case, Iceland will be subject to attack. Merchant ships have been sunk in Iceland's waters. The Nazi battleship "Bismarck" sank the British battleship "Hood" just south of the Denmark Strait between Greenland and Iceland. The press already has reported reliable predictions that American ships will carry goods for Britain to Iceland, under convoy by the U.S. Navy, and that the American naval patrol will operate from there almost to the coast of Scotland (New York Times, July 9, 1941). Rear Admiral Yates Stirling (retired) admits that the occupation is "a long step nearer to 'shooting war' "

(Washington Post, July 8, 1941). Hanson W. Baldwin's remark that the Iceland occupation marks "our definite participation in a 'shooting war' " is amply justified (New York Times, July 9, 1941). Columnist Mark Sullivan, who supports the Roosevelt foreign policy, admits that the "American force in Iceland will have the same function the British had. The function of the British force was war." (Washington Post, July 9, 1941.)

U.S. Offensive

The circumstances surrounding the agreement with Iceland scarcely support the theory that the occupation was necessary to protect that island against Nazi invasion. It is 915 miles from Nazi bases in Norway—too remote to be another Crete. Were there any real danger of such an attack, the British troops who have been stationed there would not be removed; especially since they are trained troops, better acquainted with the island's defensive problems than our own troops (Hanson W. Baldwin, New York Times, July 9, 1941). The President's message failed to state any known danger or likelihood of attack, and at his press conference of July 8, he refused to state whether he had acted upon information of any projected attack (New York Times, July 9, 1941). The implication was clear that he had acted upon his own theory of an "offensive defense."

Whose Idea?

The agreement itself indicates that our own request may have brought it about. It is presented as originating in Reykjavik. Yet in the Icelandic Prime Minister's note requesting U.S. occupation, it is clear that the island republic had been given the idea by the British Minister to Iceland, who found that the British troops garrisoned there were required elsewhere (New York Times, July 8, 1941). If Hanson W. Baldwin's estimate that the British troops number no more than a third to a half of the 60,000 to 80,000 supposed to be there is accurate (New York Times, July 9), there is no "elsewhere" in the war where they could be so urgently required that other British troops from England could not replace them. In Washington, many believe that the idea actually originated on this side of the Atlantic (Arthur Krock, New York Times, July 8, 1941).

Far-off Islands

The President coupled the occupation of Iceland with defense of the Western Hemisphere by announcing that American forces had been sent to our bases in Trinidad and British Guiana, in the south, to forestall any Nazi attempt to seize strategic points in the Atlantic. Manning these bases, clearly in the Western Hemisphere, is one thing. But his reference to strategic points "in the Atlantic," rather than "in the Western Hemisphere," justifies the conclusion that he is laying the ground for future occupation of the Azores (2750 miles from New York, but only 786 miles from Portugal), the Cape Verde Islands (about 3400 miles from the tip of Florida, but only 300 miles from the coast of Africa), and Dakar (3750 miles from the tip of Florida, on the west coast of Africa)—by seizure should negotiations with Vichy, Spain and Portugal prove impossible.

Politics

The implications of a move into Africa or the Atlantic islands will be discussed in a subsequent study, but it should be said here that the possibility of such a move explains the recent request (New York Times, July 2, 1941) by Chief of Staff Marshall for legislation removing the 12-month limitation on the training period for draftees and National Guardsmen (which the President has approved) and the prohibition against their being sent outside the Western Hemisphere (upon which the President refused to comment) (New York Times, July 9, 1941). General Marshall's request cannot be considered as involving merely technical military questions. Whatever his personal beliefs may be, the Chief of Staff of the U.S. Army holds an appointive position which is partly political in nature. He cannot oppose policy publicly, but can only announce and execute it. Removal of the ban against using draftees and National Guardsmen outside the Western Hemisphere is entirely a matter of foreign policy, not military policy. Lengthening the period of military service (is largely a matter) of foreign policy, not military policy.

Iceland–Eastern Hemisphere

Men will be needed to man these "island outposts" if the foreshadowed policy is carried out. So far as Iceland is concerned, as the British forces gradually leave, there will be calls for units of the U.S. Army to follow the soldiers and marines already there. Under present law, draftees and National Guardsmen could not be sent to Iceland. While it is theoretically possible to consider the Western Hemisphere as including a small part of Iceland, the Official Geographer of the United States pointed out some time ago that the normal conception places Iceland in the Eastern Hemisphere (Congressional Record, June 10, 1940). Certainly, that is the historical and common understanding. The other "island outposts" are unquestionably in the Eastern Hemisphere.

Presidential "Defense"

The President's theory of "offensive defense" might be better styled a theory of "elastic defense." Its logic must now compel him to seek further bases as a protection for Iceland. We secured a base at Newfoundland to protect us against Nazi bases on Greenland. Then we secured Greenland to protect us against Iceland. Now that we have occupied Iceland, must we now occupy Ireland, or Norway, or Scotland, to protect Iceland? If we occupy the Azores, must we not then occupy Portugal to protect the Azores? If we occupy the Cape Verde Islands and Dakar, must we not then occupy portions of the African coast to protect those outposts?

Another A.E.F.

That theory leads inevitably to a second American A.E.F., which British General [Archibald] Wavell and his successor, General [Sir Claude J. E.] Auchinleck, have both stated recently would soon be needed (New York Times, July 5, July 8, 1941). In addition, we face the possibility of "shooting" in many parts of the Atlantic, since the President also announced in his Iceland message to Congress that he had ordered the Navy to take all necessary measures to keep the seas clear between the United States and Iceland and our other "strategic outposts." As Mark Sullivan has pointed out, the implications of the President's theory transgresses "what the public understood when it was told we would confine ourselves to defense of the American Hemisphere" (Washington Post, July 9, 1941).

Iceland No Crete

But was hemisphere defense the main reason for the occupation of Iceland? The President stated that German occupation of Iceland would be a threat to the flow of munitions to Britain, which were being sent under a policy approved by Congress. Nazi occupation would be a threat if Iceland could be occupied by the Nazis. But Iceland, 915 miles from Nazi bases in Norway, is not Crete (which was assaulted from air bases only 100 miles away). The Nazis would like to take Iceland, but Britain controls the surrounding seas. The British never intended to abandon the island without arranging for American replacements. The real reason for the occupation is the shipping of lease-lend aid to Britain.

Convoys

Obviously, the occupation of Iceland is another evasion of the convoy issue. By keeping open the sea route to Iceland, the U.S. Navy, in effect, will be convoying British shipping (if it is not already doing so), up to Iceland. Press reports already indicate that American ships may be used to carry lease-lend products up to Iceland for transshipment to England (New York Times, July 9, 1941). The President has therefore used the lease-lend law to justify the use of convoys. This is unmistakably contrary to the intent of Congress, which wrote into the law a specific statement that "nothing in this Act shall be construed to authorize or permit the authorization of convoying vessels by naval vessels of the United States" (Section 3d).

DOCUMENT 96

Ruth Sarles to R. Douglas Stuart, Jr.
August 15, 1941

This is to report some comments following the issuance of the Roosevelt-Churchill statement, made by one in a position to know.

The eight-point statement may well be followed by some concrete demonstration of solidarity between Britain and the U.S. It might be the breaking off of relations with Vichy and the sending of troops to Liberia and Sierra Leone. The idea is to show that what's Britain's is ours and vice versa, so there will be no talk of exchanging bases and such. Regular troops would be sent, not conscripts. With the draft act extended, 500 regulars could be taken from any camp without missing them.

Another demonstration of solidarity might come in the Far East. The whole Far Eastern situation was thoroughly canvassed by Churchill and Roosevelt and they are ready to take immediate action whenever Japan moves. It does not mean that we would fight if Japan moved into Siam, but we would fight if there were a move toward the Dutch East Indies or Singapore. If Japan should move into Siam, we would probably base our fleet at Singapore. Here again it would be shown that what is Britain's is ours and again vice versa.

It is emphasized that we are not bluffing as far as Singapore or the Dutch East Indies is concerned. You probably read the dispatch of last Tuesday that Kaname Wakasugi, adviser to the embassy in Washington, is on his way to Tokyo and telephoned an interview to the newspaper Nichi Nichi from Los Angeles that the U.S. wanted to be friendly and would not take the initiative against Japan. He is a close friend of Prince Konoye [Konoye Fumimaro, prime minister of Japan] and Ambassador Nomura [Nomura Kichisaburo, Japanese ambassador to the United States], and is going back to Japan to convince the powers that be that the U.S. is not bluffing. His telephoned interview was to tip them off to hold everything until he got there.

It is said we still believe that Japan can be "sterilized."

The eight-point pronouncement was probably to undercut the impression that the stories that have been coming out of Ankara, written by Ray Brook, describing Hitler's peace terms, were correct. (The last one I think you will find in the NY Times of August 7.) Our government is steadily receiving reports from trusted sources that the proposals are bona fida.

Reports are also coming steadily (again from trusted sources) that Hitler is likely to call a Congress of Peoples, similar to the Congress of Vienna. To undercut this, we (Britain and U.S.) offer our own program in the form of the eight points.

There is a possibility that Hitler, who will have to offer his people something after the tremendous losses in Russia, after the Russian campaign is over might offer the Ankara proposals. In which case an armistice is not out of the picture.

It was emphasized that we will probably take many steps toward war, although not a shooting war. That is based on the belief that the Germans don't want us to get in and won't shoot. If they did, of course we would reply in kind.

In reading the eight points it should be remembered that it is a diplomatic document; every word and phrase is carefully used and carefully turned. It should be read in chronological order, starting with point one and superimposing one point on the other. The points should not be evaluated separately. For instance, the statement does not mean the destruction of Nazism in Germany is required, nor the break-up of the German state. The Germans have the right to choose their own form of government at well as anyone else, which is a great victory because of the tremendous pressure the refugee governments have put upon London. The third point, where the authors *wish* to see sovereign rights and self government restored, is recognition that some states will never have their sovereignty restored.

This is worth pondering.

DOCUMENT 97

Eight Points for War or Peace:
1) What Do They Mean?

*"Did you know the implications behind the Roosevelt-
Churchill 'Eight Points'?"*
No. 19, August 23, 1941

> I will confess that the Allies are irritating almost beyond endurance. It is
> evident they are trying to force us into war with Germany. Our prosperity and
> growing strength maddens them. I believe this is confined largely to the
> governing class, nevertheless, the danger is the greater because this is true.
> (Col. House, President Wilson's personal representative to the Allies, in his
> World War Diary, Nov. 17, 1916.)

"Peace Without Victory?"

Men of good will have long been troubled by the lack of declared war aims
and peace aims on the part of Great Britain and her Allies, in the current
European War. Non-interventionists and sincere interventionists alike, although sympathizing with and favoring the cause of Britain, have hoped that
Britain would evidence concern with more than the mere military destruction of Hitler and the German people, would demonstrate recognition and
understanding of the causes of Fascism and war, and would indicate a
willingness to take the steps necessary to eliminate such causes. To such
persons, the dramatic significance of the recent conference between President Roosevelt and Prime Minister Churchill (luridly exploited by the
participants and the press) was much less important than the terms and
significance of the agreements reached. Had the political leaders of America
and Britain learned from the sorry experiences of the World War and
Versailles, and their tragic aftermath? Or was there to be a repetition of
Versailles, another conquest motivated by hate and another "peace" containing the seeds of the next war?

"Piteous Platitudes"

To these men of good will, the Eight Points agreed upon by President
Roosevelt and Prime Minister Churchill (New York Times, Aug. 15, 1941),
but not officially disclosed to Congress until a week later (New York Times,

Aug. 22, 1941), were a bitter disappointment, for they evidenced little more than a desire on the part of their sponsors to be all things to all men. The Eight Points failed to have even that effect upon the British public, which had hoped for an announcement of American military participation in the war. To those Britons, the Eight Points seemed "piteous platitudes" (New York Times, Aug. 15, 1941), and "the sense of letdown was acute" (Raymond Clapper, in Washington News, Aug. 18, 1941).

Questions

The significance of the Eight Points is threefold, and is analyzed in this and two succeeding memoranda. This study considers the question: "What Do They Mean?" What type of thinking about the problems of war and peace do they indicate? Did You Know, #20, considers the question: "What Legal Effect Do They Have?" To what extent are the Eight Points binding upon the American people? Did You Know, #21, is concerned with the question: "Can They Work?" Do these Points furnish a practicable and feasible solution to the problems of war and peace?

Secret Covenants

It should be noted at the outset that the British have been able to reconcile their disappointment over the Eight Points. Britons and Canadians alike have been quick to point out that the presence at the conference of the heads of the military and naval forces of the United States and Great Britain was not necessary for assistance in the formulation of general statements of foreign policy such as constitute the Eight Points (Baltimore Sun, Aug. 15, 19, 1941) (New York Times, Aug. 15, 1941). Comment is unanimous that there were agreements, or at least understandings, concerning future cooperation in connection with the prosecution of the war. How far those agreements go has not been disclosed (not even to Congress), but President Roosevelt announced that he and Prime Minister Churchill "had discussed the situation on every continent. Every continent you ever heard of," he added facetiously. (New York Times, Aug. 15, 1941.) The conference was followed by a joint note to Russian Dictator Stalin, asking for a conference between the three countries to discuss "the future allocation of our joint resources" (New York Times, Aug. 16, 1941), and the announcement that American planes would be ferried to Africa via Brazil, for the use of the Allied forces (New York Times, Aug. 19, 1941).

War Aid

It is understandable, therefore, that press comments should characterize these undisclosed military agreements as "the real decisions" and as perhaps more important than the disclosed Eight Points (see, for example, U.S. Week, Aug. 22, 1941), and that British opinion should be reported from London as feeling that the real purpose of the conference was the discussion by the two leaders of military plans (New York Times, Aug. 15, 1941). Canadian Prime Minister King interpreted the Eight Points as "evidence of a resolution in war, of a determination to destroy nazism," and yet was able to consider them as also indicating "the desire for a just, merciful and lasting peace" (New York Times, Aug. 15, 1941). Britons and Canadians alike were portrayed by the press as being more interested in winning the war than in peace aims, and in considering the conference as a prelude to something more effective in the war effort (New York Times, Aug. 15; Baltimore Sun, Aug. 15, 1941).

What Do They Mean?

Yet, despite all this, the Eight Points are worthy of analysis, standing alone, for they are the first joint pronouncement made by the United States and Great Britain in connection with the European war, the first indication of the purposes for which American taxpayers are expending vast sums of money and for whose effectuation sacrifices are demanded of American consumers, American workers and American business.

What do the Eight Points mean? What type of thinking concerning the problems of war and peace do they indicate?

History Repeats Itself

Much of the disappointment with the Eight Points arises out of their similarity to the aims of the Allied Governments in the World War, as embodied in a note to the United States on January 11, 1917 (printed in Report of Special Senate Committee on Investigation of Munitions Industry, Senate Document 944, Part [sic], 74th Congress, 2nd Session, pages 218–220):

Eight Points	World War Allied Aims
"*First,* their countries seek no aggrandizement, territorial or other";	"The Allied nations are conscious that they are not fighting for selfish interests, . . . the Allies wish to liberate Europe from the brutal covetousness of Prussian militarism. . . ."

Eight Points	World War Allied Aims
"Second, they desire to see no territorial changes that do not accord with the freely expressed wishes of the peoples concerned"; *"Third,* they respect the right of all peoples to choose the form of government under which they will live; and they wish to see sovereign rights and self government restored to those who have been forcibly deprived of them";	"The Allied nations are . . . fighting . . . above all to safeguard the independence of peoples, of right, and of humanity. . . . it has never been their design, as has been alleged, to encompass the extermination of the German peoples and their political disappearance. . . . They imply . . . the restitution of provinces or territories wrested in the past from the Allies by force or against the will of their populations, the liberation of Italians, of Slavs, of Roumanians and of Czecho-Slovaks from foreign domination; the enfranchisement of populations subject to the bloody tyranny of the Turks, . . ."
"Fourth, they will endeavor, with due respect for their existing obligations, to further the enjoyment by all states, great and small, victor or vanquished, of access, on equal terms, to the trade and to the raw materials of the world which are needed for their economic prosperity"; *"Fifth,* they desire to bring about the fullest collaboration between all nations in the economic field with the object of securing, for all, improved labor standards, economic advancement and social security";	"the reorganization of Europe, guaranteed by a stable regime and founded as much upon . . . economic development, which all nations, great or small, possess, as upon territorial conventions and international agreements. . . ."
"Sixth, after the final destruction of the Nazi tyranny, they hope to see established a peace which will afford to all nations the means of dwelling in safety within their own boundaries, and which will afford assurance that all the men in all the	"But a discussion of future arrangements designed to insure an enduring peace presupposes a satisfactory settlement of the actual conflict: . . ." ". . . the reorganization of Europe, guaranteed by a stable regime and founded as much

Eight Points	World War Allied Aims
lands may live out their lives in freedom from fear and want";	upon respect of nationalities and full security and liberty . . . as upon territorial conventions and international agreements suitable to guarantee territorial and maritime frontiers against unjustified attacks; . . . That which they desire above all is to insure a peace upon the principles of liberty and justice, upon . . . inviolable fidelity to international obligations. . . ."
"*Seventh*, such a peace should enable all men to traverse the high seas and oceans without hindrance";	". . . Is it necessary to recall . . . the destruction by (German) submarines of passenger steamers and of merchantmen even under neutral flags, . . . ? The execution of such a series of crimes . . . explains to President Wilson the protest of the Allies."
"*Eighth*, they believe that all of the nations of the world, for realistic as well as spiritual reasons, must come to the abandonment of the use of force. Since no further peace can be maintained if land, sea or air armaments continue to be employed by nations which threaten, or may threaten, aggression outside of their frontiers, they believe, . . . that the disarmament of such nations is essential."	"They recognize all the advantages for the cause of humanity and civilization, which the institution of international agreements, designed to avoid violent conflicts between nations, would present; agreements which must imply the sanctions necessary to insure their execution and thus to prevent an apparent security from only facilitating new aggressions . . . the Allies wish to liberate Europe from the brutal covetousness of Prussian militarism, . . ."
"pending the establishment of a wider and permanent system of general security. . . ."	". . . they associate themselves with all their hopes with the project for the creation of a league of nations to insure peace and justice throughout the world."

Eight Points	World War Allied Aims
"They will likewise aid and encourage all other practicable measures which will lighten for peace-loving peoples the crushing burden of armaments."	". . . the reorganization of Europe, guaranteed by a stable regime and founded as much upon respect of nationalities and full security and liberty, . . . as upon territorial conventions and international agreements suitable to guarantee territorial and maritime frontiers against unjustified attacks . . ."

The Fourteen Points Again

Another reason why men of good will found the Eight Points a disappointment arises out of their similarity to the ill-fated Fourteen Points of Woodrow Wilson (listed in New York Times, Aug. 15, 1941, page 2). Even supporters of the Eight Points must admit that "this statement of principles is much less specific than President Wilson's enunciation of the historic Fourteen Points in 1918, but its general objectives are strikingly similar to those of the World War document." (Foreign Policy Bulletin, Aug. 22, 1941.)

Selected Tyrannies

Each of the Eight Points must be examined in detail, but certain general observations upon the entire document can be made at this point. The Eight Points present a "Stop-Hitler" program, not a program designed to eliminate fascism and war. While the preamble refers to the dangers to world civilization arising from the policy of military aggression pursued by the Hitler government and its satellites, none of the Points evidences any intention of seeking to eliminate "Fascism" itself. Point 6 looks beyond "the final destruction of the Nazi tyranny," but says nothing about destroying "Fascism" as a governmental system or as a way of life, and says nothing about destroying Italian fascism or Russian totalitarianism, or the Spanish dictatorship, or Japanese tyranny.

Missing Freedoms

While President Roosevelt, in his message to Congress on Jan. 6, 1941, listed the "four essential human freedoms" (freedom of speech and expression—everywhere in the world; freedom of religion—everywhere in the world; freedom from want—everywhere in the world; freedom from fear—everywhere in the world) as the bases of the world for which we are striving (and repeated them in his "Unlimited Emergency" Speech of May 27, 1941), the declaration of the Eight Points reduces the "essential human freedoms" to two: freedom from want (Points 4 and 5) and freedom from fear (Points 6, 7 and 8). Nowhere in the declaration is there any mention (express or implied) of freedom of religion and freedom of speech and expression. Whether or not these two basic freedoms were omitted in deference to Dictator Stalin (New York Times, Aug. 22, 1941), still the fact is that the Eight Points present a vision of a world of very circumscribed nobility and idealism, a crassly materialistic world based upon the theory that "man liveth by bread alone." Such a world ill accords with the high idealism and the noble morality upon which the President has predicated his foreign policy—in the past. Widespread criticism of the omission of these two freedoms undoubtedly led the President to claim in his message of Aug. 21 to Congress that the Eight Points of course included by inference the two missing freedoms (New York Times, Aug. 22, 1941). Of course, under universally accepted principles of law, the President's afterthought cannot by his sole act legally alter a written document signed originally by another person also (Prime Minister Churchill).

The Missing Partners

It is of interest that the conference was solely an Anglo-American affair. None of the governments-in-exile of the European countries occupied by Axis aggressors were represented, although one professed aim of Britain is the restoration to sovereignty of these conquered countries, and although representatives of those governments could undoubtedly have been brought to the conference from London just as easily as was Prime Minister Churchill. Nor was Soviet Russia, the newest ally of Great Britain (New York Times, July 14, 1941), represented. This is understandable, for the entire Eight Points contemplate, at least for a long time to come, an Anglo-American alliance which shall alone control and police the world. Yet the sincerity of the declaration would have been evidenced more clearly had the small nations whose fate was to be determined by it (Points 2, 3, 6) been given a voice in its formulation.

New and Untrodden Ways

Another important factor is that the Eight Points represent the formulation by the President, on his own initiative, of new foreign policies for the United States, which have neither been submitted to nor approved by Congress or the people. These Points may have merit, and perhaps should be adopted. Whether or not the conference itself and the military discussions carried out the Lease-Lend law's policy of "aid short of war" cannot be determined until the content of the discussions is disclosed. But the President's contention that they did (New York Times, Aug. 22, 1941) does not, and could not, claim that the justification applied to the declaration embodying the actual Eight Points, whose subject matter is foreign to the contents of the Lease-Lend law.

Our Actual National Policy

The words of the President himself (in his "Unlimited Emergency" speech of May 27, 1941) reveal what even he knew and accepted as our national policy:

> Our national policy today, therefore, is this: First, we shall actively resist wherever necessary, and with all our resources, every attempt by Hitler to extend his Nazi domination to the Western Hemisphere, to threaten it. We shall actively resist his every attempt to gain control of the seas. We insist upon the vital importance of keeping Hitlerism away from any point in the world which could be used and would be used as a base of attack against the Americas.
>
> Second, from the point of view of strict naval and military necessity, we shall give every possible assistance to Britain and to all who, with Britain, are resisting Hitlerism or its equivalent with force of arms. Our patrols are helping now to insure delivery of the needed supplies to Britain. All additional measures necessary to deliver the goods will be taken, . . . (New York Times, May 28, 1941).

This national policy is two-fold: to protect the Western Hemisphere, and to furnish aid short of war to Britain and her allies. But it is a far cry from that policy to the policy of the Eight Points, which would commit us to the responsibility of making and enforcing the peace of Europe. Nor have many of the specific Points (which the declaration would compel us to insist should be included in the peace treaty) been even submitted to, let alone approved by, Congress or the people.

Points of Difference

This is discussed in greater detail in the separate analysis of each Point (Did You Know, #21) but this much can be stated here, with reference to some of the points. The United States enjoys a large portion of world trade, and possesses a larger portion of the world's raw materials. Point 4, if carried out sincerely, would require us to abandon our protective tariff system and to make available our resources to all nations. When was this ever adopted as part of our national policy? For that matter, it would require the British Empire to abandon its Imperial preferences system, largely adopted to block American trade with the English Dominions. Point 5 is a variation on the same theme as Point 4, in that it calls for the economic collaboration of all nations. That would probably require a functioning economic league, or, possibly, agreements for the division of world markets. When was that ever adopted as part of our national policy? Point 6 commits us to seeing the war through to "the final destruction of the Nazi tyranny," which obviously can be "destroyed" only by military force. Possibly, that might not require actual military participation by the United States. But the phrase is so vague, and other commitments in the Eight Points so compelling, that such military participation might be required of us. When was that ever adopted as part of our national policy? The President's own words, in his "Unlimited Emergency" speech, did not claim that we were committed to any such policy. His own statement of our policy restricted our military measures to defense of the Western Hemisphere, and his statement that "we will not accept a Hitler dominated world" obviously refers to Hitler's conquest of the Western Hemisphere, for, as he further said:

> I have said on many occasions that the United States is mustering its men and its resources only for purpose of defense—only to repel attack. I repeat that statement now. (New York Times, May 28, 1941.)

More Differences

Point 7 calls for the freedom of the seas. If it is designed to refer to time of peace, it is meaningless, for there is no question about the right of any nation, if it has the shipping, to use the seas in peace-time. If it refers to time of war, then it certainly does not represent our national policy, for our national policy is the Neutrality Act, by which we have voluntarily limited the right of Americans to travel the seas when other nations are engaged in wars and when such travel might endanger our peace. And we have further restricted our own freedom on the seas in the current war by our acquiescence in the British system of "navicerts" and "mailcerts," which subject our shipping and foreign mail to British control and supervision (see Did You Know, #3). Nor does Point 8 represent accepted national policy. In ratifying the Kellogg-Briand Treaty in 1928, we adopted the policy of disarmament for all nations, ultimately, and the abandonment of force as a weapon of national policy. That is a far different thing from the policy embodied in Point 8, which visualizes an international police force (probably Anglo-American for a long time to come), with disarmament of only the aggressor nations (and whichever other nations are considered to be potential or likely aggressors), and a hope that the other nations eventually may take some steps towards disarmament. The policy of Point 8 is much more like the policy of the League of Nations, which the United States rejected, than like that of the Kellogg-Briand Pact.

DOCUMENT 98

Eight Points for War or Peace:
2) What Legal Effect Do They Have?

*"Did you know the legal effect of the Roosevelt-Churchill
'Eight Points' on our foreign policy?"
No. 20, August 23, 1941*

> Some of the most gifted Americans whom I have met—"men of light and
> leading"—as the saying goes, have said "European politicans ought to have
> understood the Constitution of the United States. You ought to have known that
> the President without the Senate could do nothing. You have only yourselves
> to blame if you have suffered through counting on his personal decisions or
> undertakings. They had no validity." (Winston Churchill, in *The Aftermath*, p.
> 149, commenting on President Wilson's powers at the World War Peace Confer-
> ence.)

Nearer Peace?

Having discussed the implications of the Roosevelt-Churchill "Eight Points"
(Did You Know, #19), the question arises of the legal effect of the declaration
of those points on our foreign policy. Does the declaration of the Eight
Points (apart from whatever military or naval agreements may have been
reached at the conference) commit us to participation in the war, or does it
merely involve us in responsibility for the peace to come? It should be
recalled that the President told the press, after his return from the conference, that he would say no, in reply to the question "Are we any closer to
entering the war?" but "he declined, however, to permit direct quotation of
this answer when a reporter asked whether it might be enclosed in quotation
marks" (New York Times, Aug. 17, 1941). He stated further, when reminded
that the Eight Points did not state how "Nazi tyranny" was to be destroyed,
that that was a narrow way to look at it, and that the conference was
primarily an interchange of views, a swapping of information (New York
Times, Aug. 17, 1941). Senator Barkley, Administration leader, also expressed the view in Senate debate that the Eight Points constituted merely
an expression of hopes and aspirations (Congressional Record, Aug. 19, 1941
pages 7370–7371).

Nearer War

But the other side of the medallion appears in more striking colors. The President admitted that he and Mr. Churchill had reached a complete understanding with regard to all aspects of the war situation (New York Times, Aug. 17, 1941), and that a new era was to open in anti-Axis collaboration to achieve the "final destruction of the Nazi tyranny." That meaning was further interpreted by the President in his message of August 21 to the convention of the Young Democrats, wherein he said: ". . . it soon became evident that only by defeating the sinister powers of cynical conquest before they reach our shores could we even have the slightest chance of staying out of actual war" (New York Times, Aug. 22, 1941). In a friendly interpretation, U.S. Week comments of the decisions at the Roosevelt-Churchill conference: "Primarily they concern war and its successful prosecution" (Aug. 22, 1941, p. 7).

The President's Eight Points

Of what binding force are the Eight Points? They were formulated by the President upon his own initiative, without prior consultation with, or approval by, the Senate, or Congress as a whole. In his special message to Congress of Aug. 21, he advised Congress of the declaration, but apparently did not consider it as constituting a treaty or alliance, since he did not ask for any action upon it by Congress. In their present form, the Eight Points call for no specific action at any specified time, and are not formulated in any manner which could be acted upon by Congress or the Senate. Because of the lack of clarity of the Constitutional provisions defining the powers of, and limitations upon, the President, the Senate, and the Congress as a whole, in the field of international relations, the constitutional law and the precedents concerning such declarations is unsettled. But this much can be said with certainty: as the Eight Points stand today, they are not binding upon either the Senate or the Congress. They represent an attempted formulation of foreign policy by the President. They do not have the formal legal status of either a treaty or an alliance. As is indicated later, they might possibly be held to have the character and force of an executive agreement.

President versus Congress

But it would be a mistake to assume from their present failure to bind Congress or the Senate that nothing can be done by the President to carry out the Eight Points. There is no occasion for discussing in detail the long history of the conflict between the President and the Senate (and, occasionally, the House of Representatives) over the power to formulate and control our foreign policy. It is sufficient here to point out that early Presidents

(Washington, Adams, Jefferson, Madison and Monroe) exercised a dominant influence over foreign policy; that during the rest of the nineteenth century, the authority of Congress was predominant; that Theodore Roosevelt greatly expanded the President's control; that President Wilson's power over foreign policy during the World War reached the high point of such control; that from 1918 to 1930, the Senate was the dominating power; and that under the administrations of Franklin D. Roosevelt, Presidential predominance has once more sought to assert itself (see: Corwin, "The President—Office and Powers" (1940), Ch. VI; "The President's Control of Foreign Policy," by James Frederick Green, Foreign Policy Reports, April 1, 1939; "Participation by Congress in Control of Foreign Policy," by Bryant Putney, Editorial Research Reports, Nov. 9, 1939, vol. II, #18; Corwin, "The President's Control of Foreign Relations" (1917)).

Divided Powers

The reasons for the unsettled nature of constitutional law in this field, and the reasons why President Roosevelt can take steps to carry out the Eight Points have thus been summarized by a leading constitutional authority, Edward S. Corwin, Professor, Princeton University, in "The President—Office and Powers," (pages 252–254):

1) The powers which under the Constitution are capable of determining the policy of the National Government towards other governments are divided. . . . The prime division is between the President—sometimes acting with the Senate, more often alone—and Congress, that is, the national legislative power; a secondary division is that between President and Senate. Not only is a struggle for power in this field thus invited; in the absence of a cooperative disposition all around it is well-nigh inevitable.

2) . . . by the principle of concurrent powers neither Congress nor the Senate is constitutionally concluded by anything done by the President, while he—because of his obligation to the law—*is* usually concluded by what Congress has done.

3) The President today is not only the organ of communication of the United States with foreign governments—he is the *only* organ of communication therewith; and as such he is entitled to shape the foreign policies of the United States so far as he is actually able to do so within the conditions which are imposed by the acts of Congress; and more often than not Congress chooses to follow the leadership which his conspicuous advantages of position serve to confer upon him.

4) Moreover, it is necessary to remember that the President is not only the organ of foreign relations but also Chief Executive and Commander-in-Chief, since on the basis of these blended powers he has been able to lay claim successfully to

a kind of international capacity as executive of the Law of Nations, especially when American interests abroad are menaced by other countries. He has thus come to exercise at times the war-making power without prior consultation of Congress, especially in the region of the Caribbean. What is of vastly greater importance, however, is the ability of the President simply by his day-to-day conduct of our foreign relations to create situations from which escape except by the route of war is difficult or impossible.

5) At the same time presidential prerogative in the diplomatic field is not even today unlimited, either theoretically or practically. No President has a mandate from the Constitution to conduct our foreign relations according to his own sweet will. If his power in that field is indefinite, so is Congress's legislative power; and if he holds "the sword," so does Congress hold "the purse-strings."

Congressional Veto

Let us determine the status of the Eight Points in the light of these principles. These Points, as they stand today, do not bind Congress, and there seems to be no reason why the Senate, or the House, could not voice its approval or disapproval of any or all of them, or could not appoint a committee to inquire into their adoption and the manner of their formulation (Corwin, "The President," ibid., pages 205–206, 227–228). While Congressional investigating committees have seldom been authorized in the field of foreign relations, they seem just as proper in that field as in connection with domestic affairs (Corwin, ibid., pages 227–228). Of course, the President might refuse to disclose matters he considered military secrets or affecting the national safety. If the Eight Points should be embodied in a treaty or alliance hereafter negotiated by the President with Britain, ratification by the Senate would be essential, and the Senate could amend, or modify, or reject, the treaty; moreover, the House could refuse to make such appropriations as were sought to carry out the treaty, even if it had been signed by the President (Corwin, ibid., pages 200, 233–234, 235, 240). The case would be the same if the President, in order to avoid the requirement that a treaty must be approved by two-thirds of the Senate, should simply ask Congress to approve a joint resolution endorsing the Eight Points, which requires only a majority vote in each house (Green, ibid., page 12; Putney, ibid., 343–344, 349–351).

On His Own

But there are still steps which the President might take in connection with the Eight Points on his own initiative, and without being subject to Congressional control if he wished to disregard the will of Congress and the people. There are two possible general categories: steps taken under the President's undefined powers as our organ of international relations, and steps taken under powers granted by existing laws. In the first category are "executive agreements" and an undefinable variety of actions which are limited only by the ingenuity of a President. "Executive agreements" are of two kinds: those whose formulation [is] authorized by existing laws, and those which the President may make by virtue of his broad powers as our representative in international relations (Corwin, ibid., pp. 236–238). The former would not apply to the Eight Points, since no existing law authorizes such a declaration. The Eight Points themselves bear none of the earmarks of the normal executive agreement, but the precedents are so vague that they might possibly be considered to constitute such an agreement (see Green, ibid., p. 12). Moreover, President Roosevelt might be able to implement the Eight Points themselves by making executive agreements of a limited nature under the powers granted him by some of the existing laws which are discussed below. Further, he might be able to enter into an executive agreement under his international relations powers, in order to effectuate some or all of the Eight Points. The possible agreements are too numerous to be described here in detail, but it should be noted that previous Presidents dared to authorize or enter into such secret executive agreements as the Taft-Katsura note of 1905, giving Japan a free hand in Korea [In 1905 Secretary of War William Howard Taft, then in Tokyo, met with Count Katsura Taro. The informal agreement approved a free hand for Japan in Korea in return for a pledge of non-aggression in the Philippines. The agreement had no constitutional force binding upon the United States.], the Lansing-Ishii note of 1917, defining Japan's influence in Asia [In 1917 Secretary of State Robert Lansing met in Washington with Viscount Ishii, special Japanese envoy to the United States. Their agreement, embodied in a public exchange of notes on November 2, was couched in deliberately ambiguous language. It recognized Japan had special interests in China, particularly in the part contiguous to her possessions.], and the House-Grey memorandum of 1916, pledging probable American assistance to the Allies [In 1916 Wilson's personal representative, Colonel Edward M. House, met with British Foreign Secretary Sir Edward Grey. They initialed a memorandum indicating that the United States would invite the belligerents to a peace conference under American mediation, which would endeavor to secure peace terms favorable to the Allies; if the conference failed because Germany was unreasonable, the United States would probably join the war on the side of the Allies.] (Green, ibid., p. 12).

More Moves on His Own

There are numerous existing laws granting sweeping powers to the President which he can possibly exercise to implement the Eight Points without effective Congressional control (unless Congress repeals those laws) unless ratification or appropriations by Congress should later be necessary to effectuate them. They are numerous, and but a few can be mentioned here (many of them are listed in Senate Document 64, 77th Congress, listing the "emergency" laws—which have been analyzed in Did You Know, #13 and #14). Some of them deal exclusively with international relations; others deal with domestic affairs, but are capable of use in foreign relations. To cite some of many possible examples, the President, in order to demonstrate publicly the sincerity behind the Eight Points, or in order to convince the Petain government of France or some other Axis satellite whose loyalty to the dictators showed signs of weakening, of the sincerity of the United States in connection with the "economic equality and economic collaboration" points of the Eight Points (Points 4, 5), or to coerce such a government into support of the Allies, might use his powers over foreign exchange, transfer of credit, revaluation of silver, devaluation of the dollar, and the equalization and currency stabilization fund, his power to make reciprocal trade agreements without Congressional approval, his power to lower tariff duties up to 50%, or his power to finance trade with foreign countries (see Green, ibid., pages 17–18), to accomplish such a result.

At the Peace Table

And, of course, in the exercise of his powers as our organ in the international relations, the President could attend (in person or through representatives) the peace conference which would draft the peace treaty at the end of the current war, and could select an American delegation without members of the Senate, as did President Wilson (Putney, ibid., pages 347–348), even if we had not actually entered the war—since the Eight points at least commit us to some responsibility for the peace. The Senate might then have an opportunity to pass upon the peace treaty, and upon the commitments entered into by the President in order to effectuate the Eight Points—after the treaty had been formulated at the peace conference.

67 Presidential Steps

One final factor must be considered in attempting to forecast the actions which might be taken to effectuate the Eight Points—the nature of foreign policy under the Roosevelt Administrations. One observer has listed 45 known instances—from the President's "quarantine" speech on Oct. 5, 1937 to Jan. 1, 1940, in which the President has taken the initiative in attempting to formulate new foreign policy for the United States (Corwin, ibid., pages 421–423). An independent study by the writers, bringing that list up to the date of the Eight Points, reveals 22 additional instances, for a total of 67 between Oct., 1937 and Aug., 1941 whose cumulative result has been to bring the U.S. closer to involvement in the war. Of these, 33 instances represented clear examples of action taken by the President without specific Congressional approval (10 public statements for or against a warring nation; 10 instances of actual aid rendered to a warring nation; 7 instances of punitive action taken against a warring nation; 3 instances of protective alliances, in effect (Canada, Greenland, Iceland); and 3 actions under the claim of "national defense" which heightened the danger of actual involvement). The declaration of the Eight Points, seeking to commit this nation to responsibility for the nature and enforcement of the peace which is to end a war in which we are not a formal participant, is the latest instance of Presidential efforts to determine the foreign policies of the nation.

Democratic Safeguard

From what had been described above, it is clear that, while the President may not have the moral "right" to embark upon a course of action which is not approved by Congress or the people, he has the legal "power" to undertake many dangerous actions on his own initiative because of the lack of clarity of the Constitution in this regard. *The most effective check is the strength of the opposition sentiment in Congress and the support which that sentiment receives from the people of the nation. That check has often proved effective in the past and undoubtedly can be effective in the future. Even President Roosevelt has suffered setbacks in his attempts to control foreign policy. For example, treaties for the St. Lawrence Seaway and adherence to the World Court were rejected* (Green, ibid, p. 11).

DOCUMENT 99

Eight Points for War or Peace:
3) Can They Work?

"Did you know *the difficulties in the way of carrying out the Churchill-Roosevelt 'Eight Points'?*"
No. 21A and B, September 2, 1941

These "Fourteen Points," admirably, if vaguely, phrased consisted in the main of broad principles which could be applied in varying degrees according to the fortunes of war. . . . None of them (the Allies) was concerned to examine the whole speech meticulously or felt committed except in general sympathy.

(Winston Churchill, referring to Wilson's Fourteen Points, in his book *The Aftermath*, p. 99.)

First, their countries seek no aggrandizement, territorial or other.

In Our Hands

This is undoubtedly a sincere statement. But there are many practical difficulties to be considered. The Eight Points are (see Point Eight in Did You Know, #21B) based on the disarming of "aggressor" nations, and on the thesis that the two democratic nations shall retain all the instruments of force in their own hands. Thus Point Eight envisages an Anglo-American domination of the post-war world.

Military Demands

History records many cases in which factors have "driven" nations and empires to overflow their boundaries. Military reasons have led the British Empire to retain its hold on Gibraltar since 1704. Similar factors were behind the United States occupation of Greenland and Iceland (*New York Times*, April 11 and July 8, 1941). Projecting an Anglo-American world police force makes it seem likely that many more strategic parts of the earth will have to be occupied to make *secure*—military control everywhere in the world. And this may be true even though the Anglo-American Union protests that it does not "seek" territorial aggrandizement. For example, although the British Empire withdrew in 1936 (after 54 years) its army of occupation in Egypt, the withdrawal treaty still provided that British troops would defend the Suez Canal. (*Whitaker's Almanack*, 1941, pp. 887, 878.)

Economic Demands

Economic reasons may necessitate the seizure of additional territory. Because the World War had destroyed French coalfields, France demanded, and got, the use of the Saar valley coalfields previously held by Germany. (Winston Churchill, *The Aftermath*, p. 212.) "It was the story of Danzig all over again, the same complicated problem, the same stress on economic arrangements to the disregard of the principle of nationality." (Paul Birdsall, *Versailles Twenty Years After*, p. 226.)

"Make Them Pay"

There is also the question of financial aggrandizement. This question will probably be determined by the political picture existing in the British Empire and the United States when the war comes to an end. So it was in

England after the World War. Prime Minister Lloyd George came to the Peace Conference fresh from a General Election in which the two popular slogans were "Hang the Kaiser" and "Make them Pay." In mentioning his own campaign speeches on this subject, Churchill says: "I cannot pretend not to have been influenced by the electoral currents so far as verbiage was concerned." (Winston Churchill, ibid. p. 35.) And of Lloyd George's conduct in that election he writes: "Mr. Lloyd George . . . played the part . . . by using language which was in harmony with the prevailing sentiment. . . ." (Winston Churchill, ibid. p. 37.) It was therefore inevitable that a crushing debt was laid upon the new and struggling German Republic by the victorious Allies. The debt proved to be the major factor in the subsequent economic debacle in Germany, which in turn paved the way for the triumph of the Hitler Party.

Money or Land

At the end of the European War many of the "small democracies" will be economically disrupted. There would seem to be two ways of helping them: 1) the Anglo-American combination could make huge "loans" or, 2) the "small democracies" could take over either territory, or industrial capacity now belonging to one of the aggressors. Inasmuch as the Eight Points are not signed by any of the Allied Governments-in-exile, there is nothing to prevent territorial aggrandizement by these governments. It is conceivable that an industrially ruined Holland would demand *at least* a temporary mandate over a section of the German *industrial* capacity, even though not actually seizing any territory.

Dominion Appetites

Because Winston Churchill represented only "His Majesty's Government in the United Kingdom" (*New York Times*, August 15, 1941), the Eight Points do not deter any of the Dominions (or Russia) from seizing territory now held by other nations. At the World War Peace Conference the Dominions agreed to the mandatory principle in regard to conquered territory *except* in the cases of territory conquered by *them*. (Winston Churchill, ibid., p. 150.) Although Lloyd George accepted the mandatory principle unreservedly for all territory which the British fleets and armies had wrested from the Turks or Germans, Mr. Churchill tells us that "We could not however speak for the Dominions." (Winston Churchill, ibid., p. 151.) That this situation will not be altered in the present war is indicated by Canadian Prime Minister Mackenzie King's rejection of a suggested imperial war cabinet to be composed of representatives of all the Dominions as well as the United Kingdom. (*Washington Times-Herald*, August 22, 1941.)

'Twixt Cup and Lip

We see then that while two men in a boat may make a general statement to the effect that neither "seeks" aggrandizement, that statement by no means settles the policy of their respective free governments as to what will really be done at some future Peace Conference attended by accredited representatives of all the Allies, including Russia. As the present Prime Minister of the United Kingdom has said only too well: "When wars begin, much is added to the original cause of quarrel and many results follow never aimed at or cared for at the beginning." (Winston Churchill, ibid., p. 130.)

> **Second, they desire to see no territorial changes that do not accord with the freely expressed wishes of the people concerned.**

To the Victors?

Again granting the sincerity of the two men, difficulties loom up when the practical working-out of this idealistic sentiment is considered. Many of these difficulties have been considered under Point One. In addition it may be asked whether or not, at the war's end, it will be *militarily expedient* for Britain and the United States to withdraw their troops from Iceland. Will their new ally, Russia, seek to regain the eastern half of Poland which the Communists took over at the same time the Germans seized the western portion? And if so, to what extent, if any, are the United States and the United Kingdom committed to preventing such action? Will Britain give up Iraq, or will she feel that because of unsettled post-war conditions, and the appetite of the Russian bear, Empire troops must remain stationed there? And for how long? Will Greece feel that because of her sacrifices she is entitled to wrest control of the nearby Dodecanese Islands from Italy? What about the territory now controlled by the Free French forces of General Charles DeGaulle? Oliver Lyttleton, representing the British Government [member of Parliament for Aldershot, made British minister of state in 1941], has written General DeGaulle guaranteeing the Free French "a predominant position in Syria and Lebanon over any other European power," including, of course, Britain. (*New York Times*, August 15, 1941.) Answering the letter, General DeGaulle expressed gratification over Britain's acceptance of the basic principle of France's "pre-eminent and privileged" position in Syria and Lebanon *even after* those States achieve independence. (*New York Times*, August 15, 1941.) In such a case, how would the situation be resolved at the war's end, assuming that Vichy France had been restored to independent status?

Suffrage for All?

If it be assumed that the plebiscite system (of voting by the population concerned) will be resorted to, will Britain also see fit to hold a plebiscite in long-restive India? And if the plebiscite system is agreed upon, will the actual voting be held promptly, or postponed for 17 years as in the case of the Saar plebiscite following the World War? None of these questions is asked in a carping attitude. They are raised only so that we may realize that the mere *stating* of general principles with which most people already agree does not mean the successful carrying out of those ideals. Indeed, as so often happens with shining ideals, they may become extremely tarnished in the shuffle of hard-driving power politics.

> **Third, they respect the right of all peoples to choose the form of government under which they will live; and they wish to see sovereign rights and self government restored to those who have been forcibly deprived of them.**

Dictatorships Exempt

Naturally, with Communist Dictator Stalin as their ally, neither Churchill nor Roosevelt could presume to lay down the type of government which they will permit in the world after the war is over. To have insisted that all governments become democracies would not only have alienated their new ally, but might also have disturbed some of the present heads of Latin American governments whose goodwill is now so essential to the plan of Western Hemisphere defense. The result at the end of the war may be that Russia will dominate Eastern Europe and much of Asia. What that means to the rights of those countries adjacent to Russia can be deduced from the fate which befell Poland and the small Baltic nations into which Russia marched after the 1939 Nazi-Soviet pact.

Nazi-"ism" Remains

It is even more important to recognize that this point, plus the phrase "after the destruction of Nazi *tyranny*" in Point Six, does not mean that Nazism is to be stamped out within Germany. In the first place, the two signers of the Eight Points say only that they "wish" to see rights of self government restored to those who have been *forcibly* deprived of them. Note that Germany was *not* forcibly deprived of her right of self government, rather she *voted away* those rights. Thus, it can be said that once the Nazi "tyranny" (i.e. aggression) is destroyed, the form of government *within* Germany will not be tampered with.

The National Spirit

It may be asked "What about the countries now under Hitler's domination?" The practical difficulties in the way of this pious "wish" are immense and should not be overlooked. It is well to recall that a too intense nationalism is often the cause of war. Indeed, this has been the driving force behind the Hitler movement. After the World War, the League of Nations was instituted as an attempt to build a feeling of internationalism. But at the same time that the League was set up to create internationalism—nationalism was fostered by the Peace Treaty which set up 67 completely independent nations where only 54 had existed previously. And a new cultural and ethnological problem seemed to spring up for each one that was solved. Furthermore, economic difficulties were heightened with each added mile of boundary line. Is this procedure to be followed again? And if it is followed, will it be done with sufficient intelligence so that nationalistic tensions within Europe are not heightened as before?

Crazy-Quilt

What considerations will determine the new boundary lines—economic? military? political? historical? geographic? language? balance of power? If historical precedents are to be considered, what is to be done in the case of Poland, for instance, whose boundary lines have shifted at frequent intervals through the centuries? Which boundary line in what century shall be considered the correct one? The problem has been well stated by the present Prime Minister of the United Kingdom in his writings on the World War Peace Conference in which he says: "All (the victors) being agreed upon the fundamental principle (of self-determination for all nations) it remained to apply it. But if the principle was simple and accepted, its application was difficult and disputable. What was to be the test of nationality? How were the wishes of 'national elements' to be expressed and obtained? . . . .How far could the armed and vehement forces which were everywhere afoot be brought to accept the resulting decisions? . . . Some of the new States had no access to the sea through their own populations, and could not become effective economic units without such access. Some liberated nationalities had for centuries looked forward to regaining the ancient frontiers of their long-vanished sovereignty. . . .Some integral economic communities lay athwart the ethnic frontier; and at many points rival and hostile races were intermingled." (Winston Churchill, ibid., pp. 210, 211.) Some Polish newspapers in Chicago and other American cities are already demanding possession for Poland of East Prussia. Other Poles are willing to trade certain tracts of Western Poland for East Prussia. Still other Poles demand a frontier including the whole of pre-war Poland as well. (*Christian Science Monitor*, August 20, 1941.)

Democratic Monarch?

Point Three also "wishes" to see "sovereign rights" restored to those who have been forcibly deprived of them. It is quite apparent that this wish is directed at restoring the present Allied Governments-in-exile to their former ruling positions. Whether or not such a step would be a move forward for democracy is a question worth pondering. Some of the royal rulers now living in London awaiting their return to thrones are: King Zog of Albania, King Haakon VII of Norway, King Peter of Yugoslavia, and King George of Greece (who after the 1923 revolution in Greece lived in London until restored to the throne in 1935). Unlike the other royal refugees, Queen Wilhelmina of the Netherlands still rules over an empire, although the Netherlands itself is German-occupied territory. Of Wilhelmina's 67,290,000 subjects, only 8,800,000 live in the mother country itself. The rest live across the oceans in the colonial possessions—the Dutch East Indies in the Pacific; the Dutch West Indies in the Caribbean; and Dutch Guiana in South America—all of which continue to take orders from their Queen. (*Washington Post*, August 10, 1941.)

> **Fourth, they will endeavor, with due respect for their existing obligations, to further the enjoyment by all States, great or small, victor or vanquished, of access, on equal terms, to the trade and to the raw materials of the world which are needed for their economic prosperity.**

Free Trade?

On the surface, this point would seem to presage the immediate elimination of the whole system of quotas, allotments, special tariffs, barter agreements, and bilateral trade agreements. In such a world any nation whose prices are above those prevailing in world markets will be at a disadvantage. The threat which such a plan holds for America's high wage system is obvious. A realist in economic foreign policy might be inclined to think that the idea of the United Kingdom and the United States allowing free access to everybody is so much nonsense. It is at least pertinent to note that when Secretary Hull was asked whether the limiting phrase "with due respect for their existing obligations" meant that the British Empire Preference Agreements would not be discarded, he refused to comment. (*New York Times*, August 15, 1941.) It has also been suggested that "free access" might apply only to the colonial territories now held by the Allied Governments. This theory takes the position that the so-called "have" nations would retain their hold on the colonies, but only in the sense that they would be "trustees" for the so-called "have-not" nations, who would be allowed equal economic opportunity.

Colonies No Answer

However, the experience of mandated territories under the League of Nations (which theoretically operated under a somewhat similar principle) casts some doubt on the efficacy of this plan. For despite a technical "open door," the supervising countries under the League of Nations plan found scores of ways to tie up the raw material trade to their own advantage. For example, loans were made with the stipulation that purchases must be made in the supervising country. Businessmen and traders of the supervising country were given special advantages. (*Christian Science Monitor,* August 19, 1941.) Moreover, figures assembled by the Royal Institute of International Affairs show that if all the colonial areas of the world were lumped together, they could not control more than one fifth of the production of any major raw materials, excepting only tin, rubber, and phosphate. (*Christian Science Monitor,* August 19, 1941.) Of all the other basic materials, at least four fifths of the world output comes from non-colonial areas. It is clear then, that it is in the latter areas—the non-colonial areas—that the national monopolies will have to be broken down if the phrase "equal access" is to have any valid meaning.

Wilson's Effort

It is well to recall that although the Third of Wilson's Fourteen Points provided for "the removal, so far as possible, of all economic barriers and the establishment of an equality of trade conditions among all the nations consenting to the peace and associating themselves for its maintenance," the members of the League did no such thing.

Hitler vs. Hitler-"ism"

No one can quarrel with the principle expressed in this point. Surely it is now plain that the wide disparity between the wealthy and the poor nations has only served to throw the disgruntled inhabitants of the poverty-stricken nations into the hands of the fascist-minded elements in society which are seeking grievances to exploit. Admittedly, a solution must be found, if the *cause* of fascism is to be rooted out. Admittedly also, the phrases "with due respect for existing obligations," "will endeavor," "to further" (how far?) are disheartening to those who wish to do more than merely "Stop Hitler"— who wish to Stop Hitler-"ism," by eliminating those features in the world economy which inevitably throw fuel upon fascist fires.

Look At the Record

It has also been proposed that the huge international cartels which now operate to limit production and to raise prices be transferred to international control so that they might be operated for the benefit of the world consumer, rather than against him. Others have carried this idea farther and suggested a huge world-wide cooperative which would control and distribute all the most important raw materials. Following is a list of some of the attempts made in the last two decades to solve the raw material problem: 1) The Italian draft for the League of Nations Covenant contained provisions for free access for everyone to vital raw materials. It was ignored. 2) The subject of raw materials was investigated by a committee during the Peace Conference. Its recommendations were ignored. 3) The first Assembly of the League of Nations debated the subject. 4) The League began an inquiry in 1921, but no action was taken on its report. 5) At the International Economic Conference in 1927, a Convention for the Abolition of Import and Export Prohibitions and Restrictions was drafted. It was never ratified. 6) The World Economic Conference of 1933 ran into equally stubborn resistance on this grave problem. (*Christian Science Monitor,* August 19, 1941.)

Access to Us

Finally, it should be noted that the British Empire and the United States would bear the brunt of furnishing "access." A study a few years ago showed that together they controlled over 30% of the world's supply of wheat, iron ore, chrome ore, and manganese ore; over 40% of the world's supply of tin and copper; over 50% of the world's supply of cocoa, copra, rubber, and coal; over 60% of the corn, groundnuts, wool, petroleum, lead, and zinc; over 70% of the cotton; and over 90% of the world's supply of nickel, jute, and sulphur. (Statistics are from the *London Economist,* October 26, 1935, p. 794, and refer to the year 1934.)

> **Fifth, they desire to bring about the fullest collaboration between all nations in the economic field with the object of securing, for all, improved labor standards, economic adjustment, and social security.**

This point, with the exception of the phrase "improved labor conditions," is mainly a continuance of Point Four. A discussion of many of the problems which would arise here will be found under the preceding point.

> **Sixth, after the final destruction of the Nazi tyranny, they hope to see established a peace which will afford to all nations the means of dwelling in safety within their own boundaries, and which will afford assurance that all the men in all the lands may live out their lives in freedom from fear and want.**

Two-Man Congress

It may be argued that by the Phrase "after the final destruction of the Nazi tyranny," the President has committed us to active participation in the present war. This was the first reaction of even some of the British newspapers. Possibly this is the correct view. But few will claim that this agreement signed at sea by two men is binding upon Congress, or upon the American people, over 80% of whom are opposed to America's entry into the European War. Perhaps the best way to refute any such strained interpretation of Point Six is to quote co-signer Churchill's words regarding former President Wilson's powers at the Peace Conference. "Some of the most gifted Americans whom I have met—'men of light and leading'—as the saying goes, have said 'European politicians ought to have understood the Constitution of the United States. You ought to have known that the President without the Senate could do nothing. You have only yourselves to blame if you have suffered through counting on his personal decisions or undertakings. They had no validity.' " (Winston Churchill, ibid., p. 149.) However, there is apparently no doubt that we are committed to give material aid to Britain until she and her allies have accomplished the *military* (though not necessarily the political) destruction of Nazism. Again note the use of a qualifying word. President Roosevelt and Prime Minister Churchill "hope" to see established a peace which will afford all nations the means of dwelling in safety, and in freedom from fear. Such a peace would apparently be enforced by an Anglo-American military combination (see Point Eight). Freedom from want will depend, in the main, on post-war economic arrangements, which are discussed under Points Four and Five. The writer Heptisax has made an incisive comment on this point in the *New York Herald-Tribune* of August 24, 1941—"If the post-war adjustment grants any one nation enough domestic autonomy to set up the kind of government it wants, the people of that nation will have just as many and as much of Mr. Roosevelt's freedoms, and of various others which he never mentions, as they want and deserve, and no more." One commentator has said that this point is so vague that *all* people can read into it *whatever meaning* they desire.

> **Seventh, such a peace should enable all men to traverse the high seas and oceans without hindrance.**

Civil War

History indicates that a declaration like this has no meaning outside of peacetime. In normal times, any nation enjoys freedom of the seas insofar as it owns, or is able to charter, ships. But in time of war force is the only factor which determines the right of nations, belligerent or not, to sail the oceans in freedom. In the Civil War, we seized British ships which sought to run the Union blocade and to carry goods to the South. (Borchard and Lage, *Neutrality for the United States*, p. 15.)

World War

That force is the only factor determining freedom of the seas was admitted by Secretary of State Bryan [William Jennings Bryan, secretary of state,

1913–1915] in his testimony before the Senate Committee on Foreign Relations in 1915. (*Report of Special Senate Committee on Investigation of the Munitions Industry*, 74th Congress, Part 5, p. 163. Quoted in Did You Know, #3.) Moreover, Secretary of State Lansing (Bryan having resigned in June, 1915) wrote in his *War Memoirs* that: "For a year and a half we had made protest after protest to London because of the illegal practices of the British authorities in their treatment of American commerce and their disregard of American rights on the high seas. . . ." (Quoted in *Report of Special Senate Committee on Investigation of the Munitions Industry*, 74th Congress, Part 5, p. 39.) During a period of five and one half months following the British Order in Council of March 11, 1915, some 301 neutral ships on voyages between the United States and northern neutrals of Europe had been detained by the British fleet. (Edgar Turlington, *Neutrality, Its History, Economics and Law*, Vol. III, pp. 29, 30. Quoted in Charles C. Tansill, *America Goes to War*, p. 519.)

The Peace Treaty

Even after the close of the World War, at a meeting of the representatives of the Allies, the doctrine of "freedom of the seas," as proposed in the Second of Woodrow Wilson's Fourteen Points, was turned down: "This point about what is called the 'Freedom of the Seas' naturally aroused British concern. . . . Mr. Lloyd George [David Lloyd George, British prime minister, 1916–1922] said he could not accept this clause under any condition. If it had been in operation at the present time we should have lost the power of imposing a blockade. . . .Clemenceau and Sonnino [Georges Clemenceau, French premier, 1917–1920; and Baron Sidney Sonnino, Italian foreign minister during World War I] agreed with Lloyd George." (Winston Churchill, ibid., pp. 103, 104.)

The Seas Today

The last decade has witnessed the United States, in a further effort to disentangle itself from foreign wars, limiting its own freedom of the seas by adopting the Neutrality Act which prevents our merchant ships from entering those areas defined by the President as combat zones. Furthermore, less than three months ago the President stated at a press conference that he was not considering a request asking for repeal or amendment of this Act. (*New York Times*, May 29, 1941.) During the present European War, we have followed our ultimate World War course by again acquiescing in the British blockade and in accepting the British contraband list. We have also acquiesced in the British system of "navicerts," under which our shippers must submit their cargo lists to British agents. We have also accepted the British system of "mailcerts," which operates on the same principle as the navicerts, and in addition amounts to a British tax on American mail. (Did You Know, #3.)

In the Future

Obviously then, "freedom of the seas" is not the policy of the British government which rejected it in the World War, and rejects it in the present European War. Just as obviously, no President who unreservedly accepts the British policy can profess to seek "freedom of the seas." A more likely supposition is that the post-war Anglo-American combination, itself controlling most of the world's shipping facilities, will permit "freedom of the seas" to such countries as it deems fit. One observer has stated that this point was inserted for the sole purpose of getting the United States into a shooting war. He reasons that if this principle is acted upon, our vessels will go sailing the seas at random. Sooner or later an "international incident" will have been created, and Congress will be asked to declare war in order to "protect the rights of free men."

> Eighth, they believe that all of the nations of the world, for realistic as well as spiritual reasons, must come to the abandonment of the use of force. Since no future peace can be maintained if land, sea or air armaments continue to be employed by nations which threaten, or may threaten, aggression outside of their frontiers, they believe, pending the establishment of a wider and permanent system of general security, that the disarmament of such nations is essential. They will likewise aid and encourage all other practicable measures which will lighten for peace-loving peoples the crushing burden of armaments.

The Armed Peace

The first sentence is, at the present stage of civilization, of no practical value as the tragic history of the League of Nations, the Kellogg-Briand Pact, and other disarmament attempts shows. It merely states a pious hope—which all men hope will be realized at some future time. The second sentence contains the crux of the Eight Points. It projects a future (but not immediately at the close of the war) "wider and permanent system of general security," perhaps some kind of armed League of Nations, or possibly a variation of the "Union Now" (Did You Know, #16) plan. *But*, "pending the establishment of" such a system, the "nations which threaten, or *may* threaten, aggression outside of their frontiers" must be disarmed. In Mr. Churchill's words: "The United States and Great Britain do not now assume that there will never be any more war again. On the contrary, we intend to take ample precautions to prevent its renewal in any period we can foresee by effectively disarming the guilty nations, while remaining suitably protected ourselves." (*New York Times*, August 25, 1941.) Thus, the Anglo-

American combination will be free to impose its ideas by more practical means than "spiritual" methods. True, the Eighth Point concludes by saying they will "aid and encourage" all other "practicable" measures which will "lighten" the armament burden for non-aggressor peoples. This concluding sentence is reminiscent of Point Four of Wilson's Fourteen Points which read: "Adequate guarantees given and taken that national armaments will be reduced to the lowest point consistent with domestic safety." But the most significant plank in the Eight Points remains—the *heart* of Point Eight means an *Anglo-American world police force*.

Merchants of Death

Lastly, it should be said that disarmament of the aggressors and a self-limitation of arms by the "peace-loving" nations is not enough to maintain future peace. For the facts are that Germany was disarmed after the World War, and other nations entered into arms limitation agreements. The *Report of the Special Senate Committee on Investigation of the Munitions Industry* (74th Congress) would seem to indicate that it is just as important to have the output of war material under international control, or at least taken out of the hands of private capital, which the Eight Points does not discuss.

DOCUMENT 100

Robert E. Wood to Robert R. Reynolds
July 17, 1941

I am informed that you desire to have me testify before the Senate Military Affairs Committee on the recent bill introduced calling for an extended term of service for the draftees and for authority to send the draftees outside the Western Hemisphere. Unfortunately, I have to leave for the Pacific Coast tonight, so will be unable to be present at the Hearings on the bill.

I am unalterably opposed to sending draftees outside of the Western Hemisphere. The sole purpose of the provision would be to get us into the war and involve us in Europe. No question of defense can be urged. Moreover, I understand this provision has been withdrawn.

The first provision involves a direct breach of contract with the draftees and the National Guardsmen now in the service and is bound to create a great deal of hardship to these men. On the other hand, no one wants to disrupt the army at this particular juncture or to injure the defense program.

As I understand it, the reasons advanced for this measure are:

1. Many of the draftees have been sent to bases in Hawaii, Panama, Trinidad and other foreign posts and there is not sufficient tonnage to bring them home. This is undoubtedly true, though in view of the provisions of the draft act, it would seem to have been bad judgment to have sent them in the first place.

2. South America will feel that we will be unable to carry out the protection we have assumed toward her. This seems rather far fetched to me, but I, of course, have no means of proving or disproving it.

It seems to me that some compromise ought to be able to be worked out by which the present army will not be disrupted and yet by which no undue hardships would be voted against the draftees or the National Guardsmen. The best solution, of course, would be to get a sufficient number of the draftees to reenlist for another year. As an inducement a special reenlistment bounty might be offered, amounting to—say $150.00 per man. That might induce a great many to re-enlist. If a sufficient number could not be induced to re-enlist in this fashion, authority might be given to return to the service for an additional period of three to six months draftees who are stationed in foreign possessions.

P.S. The Statistics Department of our America First Committee is compiling some questions and some statistics which we think will be of value to the Military Affairs Committee in considering this bill. Miss Ruth Sarles of our Washington office will deliver them to you.

DOCUMENT 101

Another A. E. F. ?

"Did you know that a bill is pending in Congress which would give the President unlimited power to send another A.E.F. anywhere in the world?"
No. 9, July 15, 1941

The Promises

... we will not participate in foreign wars and will not send our Army, Naval or Air Forces to fight in foreign lands outside of the Americas except in case of attack. (President Roosevelt, in Philadelphia campaign speech, October 23, 1940, reprinted in Congressional Record, July 10, 1941, page 6059.)

There is no demand for sending an American expeditionary force outside our own borders. There is no intention by any member of your Government to send such a force. You can therefore nail any talk about sending armies to Europe as deliberate untruth. (President Roosevelt in December 2, 1940 fireside chat, reprinted in Congressional Record, July 10, 1941, page 6059.)

Persons inducted into the land forces of the United States under this Act shall not be employed beyond the limits of the Western Hemisphere except in the Territories and possessions of the United States, including the Philippine Islands (Selective Training and Service Act of 1940, Section 3e).

The Performance

In his report of July 1, 1941, to the Secretary of War, General George Catlett Marshall, Chief of Staff of the U.S. Army, recommended that "the War Department be given authority to extend the period of service of the Selective Service men, the officers of the Reserve Corps and the units of the National Guard," beyond the one-year term fixed by law (page 18). General language in the report led to press comments that the Chief of Staff also asked for removal of the restriction which forbade the use of such soldiers outside the Western Hemisphere (see *New York Times,* July 4, 1941). Actually, as an Army spokesman later pointed out, the report made no such recommendation (Washington Star, July 13, 1941). That fact is that General Marshall wrote that it was up to Congress and the President to say when and where men in the Army should serve (page 18). Nevertheless, on July 10, at the request of the War Department, three joint resolutions were introduced in the Senate embodying the supposed as well as the actual recommendations General Marshall had made (S. J. Res. 91, 92, 93). Resolution 91 gives the President power to use any members of the armed forces either within or outside the Western Hemisphere at his sole discretion during the period of the unlimited national emergency.

And So to War

What Resolution 91 actually does is to authorize a new A.E.F. should the Administration desire it. The Resolution flatly repeals the established and popular policy of hemisphere defense. While this bill is being shelved temporarily because of the opposition it has aroused in Congress (New York Times, July 15, 1941), it is expected that it will be revived if the other measures are adopted. Another device to accomplish the same end which may be introduced is a bill to have Congress declare a national emergency, which would enable the President to send selectees anywhere. In the light of the background out of which the bill arises and the Administration's foreign policy, it is designed to give the President power to put the country into war. It arises on the heels of the occupation of Iceland (see Did You Know, #7), reports of the projected seizure of Dakar, in Africa, the Cape Verde Islands, and the Azores (see Did You Know, #8), and demands by interventionists for seizure of Soviet bases in Siberia (see Did You Know, #5). It follows the disclosure that American workmen are building a naval base in Northern Ireland (Washington Times-Herald, July 11, 1941), apparently under the direction of U.S. Navy Department employees listed as naval attaches to the American Embassy in London, and after the demand by Wendell Willkie, following a conference with the President, for American bases in Northern Ireland and Scotland—in the heart of the current war (New York Times, July 10, 1941).

National Offense

No reason is presented in the bill for this demand for power to send a new A.E.F. anywhere in the world. It embodies a new foreign policy, not a military policy. This policy was flatly repudiated by the Congress of the United States a year ago when it wrote into the law calling National Guardsmen and Reserve officers into service (50 U.S.C.A., Appendix, Section 401) and into the Selective Training and Service Act (50 U.S.C.A., Appendix, Section 303 (e)), a prohibition against use of such soldiers outside the Western Hemisphere or possessions of the United States. No danger of attack justifies it as a defensive measure. Neither Iceland, nor Siberia, nor Dakar, nor the Azores, nor the Cape Verde Islands offers any real danger. (See Did You Know, #5, 7, 8.) There is no danger of invasion or attack from European shores which justifies our entry into European combat zones along the coasts of Northern Ireland, Scotland, or Norway, where American citizens and ships are now forbidden by law to go. "The argument that we have to establish bases in another hemisphere to protect our own land quickly reaches a strategical absurdity" ("The Realities of Hemisphere Defense," by Hanson W. Baldwin, Reader's Digest, July, 1941, page 117).

Presidential "Defense"

Resolution 91 scraps our established policy of defense of this Hemisphere and enables the execution of the President's new theory of "offensive" or "elastic" defense. By this theory, the boundaries of the Western Hemisphere are as elastic as the President's choice of geographers (see Did You Know, #7). It commits the United States to military experimentation wherever the President—or perhaps the War Department—shall choose. Without prior consultation of, or approval by Congress, it has already placed American troops in Iceland within a war zone proclaimed by a belligerent last spring (see Did You Know, #7), and exposed them to possible attack. The theory has been conceived in rash disregard of the fact, as General Marshall has pointed out, that our Army is poorly trained and that "the necessary amount of critical items is still far short of requirements and only a small portion of the field Army is at present equipped for extended active operations under conditions of modern warfare." (Page 16.)

"America Was Promised"

Most significant of all, Resolution 91 proceeds in violation of the solemn pledges made by the President and the Administration spokesmen to keep America out of war, and the pledges made to the Nation in general and to the selectees and National Guardsmen in particular that the sacrifices exacted of them were asked for the purpose solely of "defense." (President Roosevelt, October 30, 1940, reprinted in Congressional Record, July 10, 1941, page 6059.) Broken pledges scarcely help foster an abiding strength in the democratic form of government.

Compare the British Empire

The true nature of the President's policy is evidenced by a comparison of the laws as they would read if Resolution 91 is adopted with the conscription laws of the British Dominions, belligerent nations engaged in a life-and-death struggle. Neither Canada, Northern Ireland, New Zealand, Australia, the Union of South Africa, nor even semi-colonial British India, has a conscription law requiring service outside the boundaries of the respective State. Eire, the remaining Dominion, is not at war. Neither Northern Ireland nor British India has any conscription law at all (New York Times,

May 28, 1941; Whitaker's Almanack, 1941, pages 727, 732). The New Zealand law gives conscripts the right to choose whether they will serve overseas, or only within the boundaries of New Zealand (Whitaker's Almanack, 1941, page 774; Washington Times-Herald, June 19, 1940). In the other Dominions, men are conscripted solely for "defense," at home, and only volunteers serve outside the boundaries of their respective countries (Canada—New York Times, June 15, 1941; Statement of Canadian Legation, April 4, 1941; *Foreign Policy Reports*, Sept., 1940, page 153; Union of South Africa—Foreign Policy Bulletin, February 7, 1941; Australia—Foreign Policy Bulletin, February 7, 1941; Time, June 20, 1941).

"The People, Yes"

Ironically, this bill for another A.E.F. has the support of the President who once said: "I can at least make certain that no act of the United States helps to produce or promote war" (In address at Chautauqua, August 14, 1936, reprinted in Congressional Record, July 10, 1941, page 6059). Despite the overwhelming popular vote against entry into the current war, evidenced in every public poll, this bill for another A.E.F. has the support of the President who in the same address also said: "But all the wisdom of America is not to be found in the White House or in the Department of State; we need the meditation, the prayer and the positive support of the people of America who go along with us in seeking peace."

DOCUMENT 102

Soldiers Until . . . ?

"Did you know that a bill is pending before Congress which would repudiate the pledge made by our Government to the men drafted into military service?"
No. 10, July 17, 1941

The Promise

Each man inducted . . . shall serve for a training and service period of twelve consecutive months, unless sooner discharged, except that whenever the Congress has declared that the national interest is imperiled, such twelve-month period may be extended by the President to such time as may be necessary in the interests of national defense (Selective Training and Service Act of 1940, Section 3b).

The Breach

. . . the President is hereby authorized to induct from time to time into active military service under the provisions of the . . . Selective Training and Service Act of 1940, such number of men, without limitation, to serve for such period beyond twelve months as the President may deem necessary in the interests of national defense· Provided, That the active military service of persons now on duty under said Act may be similarly extended by the President to such period of time as he may deem necessary in the interests of national defense (Senate Joint Resolution 92, now pending before Congress).

Extended Service

The most momentous questions of the day are the proposals pending before Congress to extend the period of service of selectees drafted into the Army under the Selective Training and Service Act of 1940, and of National Guardsmen and Reserve Officers drafted in 1940. These proposals are Senate Joint Resolutions 92 and 93. Resolution 92 gives the President unlimited power, during the national emergency he has proclaimed, to draft any number of new selectees he may see fit, under the Selective Training and Service Act, for any length of service he may decide upon. In addition, he is empowered to extend the length of service of men already drafted into the Army for any additional period he may decide upon. The life of the Act itself is extended until six months after the end of the unlimited national emergency, but is not to end in any event before 1945—the date fixed in the Act as it now stands. Resolution 93 gives the President similar powers with respect to National Guardsmen and Reserve Officers.

Army Fears

The introduction of these proposals followed the recommendation by Chief of Staff, General George C. Marshall, in his report of July 1 to the Secretary of War, that "the War Department be given authority to extend the period of service of the Selective Service men, the officers of the Reserve Corps and the units of the National Guard" beyond the one-year term fixed by law (page 18). In his report and in his later testimony before an executive session of the Senate Military Affairs Committee, the Chief of Staff argued that releasing these men as their one-year terms expired would cripple the organization and effectiveness of the Army, and that the existing national emergency justified repudiation of the solemn promise that these men would be required to serve one year and one year only (Report, page 18; New York Times, July 16, 1941).

Unfounded Fears

If the facts supported General Marshall's recommendations the Senate resolutions would be essential to national defense. But there are glaring weaknesses which demonstrate that these measures are not essential to national defense, and may even be detrimental. Refusal to adopt them will not cripple the Army. The arguments against them may be roughly classified as moral, political and military.

Our National Honor

Extension of service of men now in arms involves a grave breach of faith on the part of the U.S. Government which could be justified only by an overriding need for such a drastic step. The selectees, National Guardsmen and Reserve officers who left their families and jobs to enter into service did so under the protection of a statutory pledge by Congress that the sacrifices exacted of them were asked for only a year—unless Congress expressly should declare that the danger to the national interest required an extension of their period of service (50 U.S.C.A., Appendix, Section 401; 50 U.S.C.A., Appendix, Section 303b).

Soldiers Unemployed

Resolutions 92 and 93 do not seek a Congressional declaration that the national interest is imperiled. They completely ignore the provisions of the earlier laws. In addition, these men were afforded the protection of special provisions designed to enable them to secure their old jobs back when their service was over. Employers were required to return these men to their jobs unless an individual employer's situation had so changed as to make reinstatement impossible (50 U.S.C.A. Appendix, Sections 308; 401). At the time these provisions were adopted, their sponsors admitted that they were not sure the provisions were constitutional, but the sponsors felt it incumbent upon Congress to make every effort to insure the reinstatement of these men in their jobs (Congressional Record, August 20, 1940, pages 16148–9). Resolutions 92 and 93 emasculate these provisions. If men now in service are kept in service for any appreciable additional period, employers cannot be expected to reinstate them. Every additional week of service makes it more likely that any employer's situation will have changed so as to make reinstatement impossible or unlikely. Even more important, the longer men are away from their jobs, the more likely they are to lose their skills, their all essential "know how." It was consideration of these factors which led Speaker Sam Rayburn, Administration stalwart, to say (Washington Post, July 10, 1941):

> We have made a contract with selectees that they stay in the service for only one year. . . . I am definitely not in favor of amending the law to require their retention on active duty after their one-year term has been served.

The President Raises an Army

From the political point of view, Resolutions 92 and 93 present even graver dangers. They evade the provisions of the earlier laws which would have enabled the extension of service only if Congress declared expressly that the national interest was imperiled. Instead, they remove that Congressional control completely, and confer upon the President alone unlimited power, during the national emergency which only he has proclaimed, to determine how many men shall be drafted into military service and for how long a period they shall serve. This amounts to a transfer to the President of the power, vested in Congress alone by the Constitution, to "raise and support armies" (Article I clause 12). Certainly, national defense does not require the abrogation of the Constitution. The control over the purse-strings which the Congress exerts would be reduced to the mere approval of a "fait accompli" were such broad powers transferred to the President. Moreover, these measures enable the President, or the War Department, to raise the army to war strength without Congressional interference. While General Marshall disclaims any intention of raising the number of men under arms by keeping all those now drafted, and inducting a new crop of conscripts (New York Times, July 16, 1941), still it is possible under these measures to increase the size of the Army from its present "protective mobilization" strength of about 1,400,000 (Marshall report, page 15) to a "war strength" of 2,200,000 men. Such an increase would involve a basic question of foreign policy which these measures remove from consideration by Congress, a question all the more vital in view of the Administration's proposal for power to establish another A.E.F. (see Did you Know, #9). All this is asked by General Marshall in the name of the "emergency" in which the Army as well as the Nation suddenly finds itself, an emergency whose nature the General neither describes nor explains (New York Times, July 16, 1941).

Not the Navy

Presumably, the emergency upon which General Marshall relies also affects the Navy, our first line of defense. Yet it is significant that the Senate Naval Affairs Committee, a short while ago, rejected a bill which would have empowered the Secretary of the Navy to extend for the duration of the President's unlimited national emergency the terms of service of enlisted members of the Navy and the Marines (S.353), while approving action which would put men who enlisted in the future on notice when they enlisted that their terms might be extended for the duration. Senator Walsh, Chairman of the Committee, explained that the extension had been refused with regard to the men now in service because it was felt that such extension would constitute a breach of contract (Wash. Post, June 28, 1941).

DOCUMENT 103

Long-Term Conscription

"Did you know *that our Army will not be crippled if the drafted men are discharged at the end of their one year terms of service?"*
No. 11, July 17, 1941

Yesterday

Each man inducted . . . shall serve for a training and service period of twelve consecutive months, unless sooner discharged, except that whenever the Congress has declared that the national interest is imperiled, such twelve-month period may be extended by the President to such time as may be necessary in the interests of national defense. (Selective Training and Service Act of 1940, Section 3b.)

Tomorrow

. . . the President is hereby authorized to induct from time to time into active military service under the provisions of the . . . Selective Training and Service Act of 1940, such number of men, without limitation, to serve for such period beyond twelve months as the President may deem necessary in the interests of national defense: Provided that the active military service of persons now on duty under said Act may be similarly extended by the President to such period of time as he may deem necessary in the interests of national defense. (Senate Joint Resolution 92.)

Skeleton?

If the effect of mustering out draftees—and National Guardsmen and Reserve Officers—who had served their year would be to strip the U.S.

Army of all its strength, that fact alone might justify over-riding the questions of moral good faith and the transfer of constitutional power raised by Senate Resolutions 92 and 93 (see Did You Know, #10). What these resolutions propose is to give the President unlimited power to draft as many men into the Army as he sees fit and hold them there as long beyond the year allowed by the Selective Training and Service Act and the National Guard Act of 1940 as he desires. Aside from those interventionists who back the proposals automatically, those who support the resolutions have been persuaded by the fear fostered by Chief of Staff General George C. Marshall's statement that the Army would be a "skeleton" if selectees were mustered out when their one-year terms expired (New York Times, July 16, 1941), and the gratuitous slur cast on the Army by the President when he remarked that the Army would "disintegrate" if these measures were not adopted (New York Times, July 16, 1941). The impression has been created that within a few months the bulk of the selectees must be demobilized, leaving an Army utterly devoid of trained man power.

No Mass Exodus

Actually, the Army has six more months before it need muster out any sizeable number of conscripts, and several months before many National Guard units end their terms. There would never be any mass exodus, since conscripts and Guard units alike were inducted at different periods of time, and would end their terms of service on different dates. Meanwhile, 750,000 young men who have reached 21 years of age have since last October become subject to conscription. Few of these new registrants have jobs important to defense; still fewer have dependents. Obviously, most of them will be liable to induction into the Army as soon as the Army wants them. General Marshall has announced that the Army plans to continue inducting new increments of selectees, just as it has done, at intervals, from November, 1940 to date (New York Times, July 16, 1941). In addition, the President recently authorized the induction of up to 900,000 men during the next year under the Selective Training and Service Act of 1940 (New York Times, June 30, 1941).

Discharge Schedule

The breakdown of the number of selectees inducted, by the months of their induction, reveals that only a relatively small number of men are scheduled for discharge in any one month—figuring the period of service as one year. Obviously, there should always be enough new selectees who have completed their thirteen-week, basic-training course to replace the men released from combat units. If there are not, perhaps the Army is to blame, not the Law. Here is the schedule of induction of selectees:

Month of induction	Month when service expires	Number of men involved
Nov. 1940	Nov. 1941	13,806
Dec. 1940	Dec. 1941	5,521
Jan. 1941	Jan. 1942	73,633
Feb. 1941	Feb. 1942	90,238
Mar. 1941	Mar. 1942	153,159
Apr. 1941	Apr. 1942	123,207
May 1941	May 1942	56,896
June 1941	June 1942	79,522
		595,982　TOTAL

Thus, only 19,327 men need be mustered out before January, 1942, and those only in November and December, 1941. By then, those men can be replaced by new selectees who by then will have had more training than the selectees who were inducted between April and June, 1941, now have.

Guardsmen

The National Guard offers a somewhat different problem—partly because of the specialized nature of most National Guard units. Yet, even here, the Army is not faced with a mass exodus. Of the 156 National Guard units now in service, none must be demobilized before September, 1941, and only 56 of the 156 units need be discharged before January 1, 1942:

Number of National Guard units	Month when period of service ends
25	Sept. 1941
15	Oct. 1941
14	Nov. 1941
3	Dec. 1941
47	Jan. 1942
37	Feb. 1942
6	Mar. 1942
7	Apr. 1942
0	May 1942
2	June 1942
TOTAL 156	

The Army itself has admitted that it will not be impossible to replace even these specialized units. In testifying in support of the Selective Training and Service Act of 1940, Lt. Colonel (now General) G. L. Twaddle, representing the General Staff of the War Department, pointed out that although the Regular Army might be spread thin to replace the National Guard units when the Guard's year of service expired, it still could be done (Hearings on S.4164, before Senate Committee on Military Affairs, July 12, 1940, page 370). The Army then recognized the problem and felt itself prepared to cope with it.

Reserve Officers Too

As to the Reserve officers, General Marshall's report states that on June 30, 1941, only 55,000 of them, or 55% of those eligible for service, were on active duty (page 24). He announced that the policy of the Army was to release some of those now in service, in order to bring the remaining officers into training (New York Times, July 16, 1941). In view of the fact that some 50,000 Reserve officers may still be available, that the annual product of the Reserve Officers Training Corps is sufficient to meet the future anticipated requirements, and that training schools for prospective officers from the ranks of the Army are functioning well and will produce a minimum of 10,000 officers a year (Marshall Report, pages 13–14; Appendix, pages 24–26), it seems that, even making due allowance for physical disabilities on the part of some Reserve Officers, there is an ample supply of officer material available for replacements.

Wanted: A Professional Army

A mere basic flaw in Resolutions 92 and 93, and in General Marshall's report, is that they constitute an implied statement that the policy of seeking to raise an efficient army by conscription has failed. Between the lines of these measures, and between the lines of the Marshall report, is recognition of the need for a professional army of soldiers who have undergone a fairly long period of specialized training. Since it is felt unwise to seem to weaken the conscription law, these measures seek to alter the law to permit the setting up of a semi-professional mass army. That, apparently, is why power is sought to extend the period of service. Without openly repealing the present Conscription Law, the Administration is seeking a modification which will yield some of the benefits of a professional, long-term army. It is an open secret that the Army was never enthusiastic about a mass-army law, and never looked with much favor upon the present Selective Training and Service Act. General Marshall testified, before the Senate Committee on Military Affairs, that "the training of young men in large training camps on the basis of compulsory training is something that we cannot manage at the present time" (Hearings on S.4164, July 12, 1940, page 328), but felt constrained for practical (and perhaps political) reasons to endorse the Act.

The Real Reason

Even if it be assumed that all of General Marshall's conclusions are justified, it cannot be claimed that the present unprepared state of our Army is due to the international situation, or to any changes in that situation since 1940. The real cause consists of the defects inherent in the attempt to create a mass army overnight. The need for longer training, requested by General Marshall, does not exist because of any "national emergency" which has just arisen, but because to train a modern army adequately in a year, when that army is a mass army, has been proved impossible. This the Army people foresaw a year ago, when General Marshall and others of his staff stated that 12 months would not be enough, and asked that the Selective Training and Service Act authorize 18 months, or at least 15 months, service for each selectee (Hearings before Senate Committee on Military Affairs, on S.4164, July 12, 1940, pages 341, 366).

There Are Alternatives

However, the Army is far from blameless, and one question at issue is whether selectees now in arms should be penalized because of the errors in judgment of the General Staff. In testifying on the Selective Training and Service Law, General Marshall stated that the Army must choose one of two alternatives, in view of its inability to handle the training of the mass army proposed by that law: Either the existing Regular Army divisions and National Guard units must be kept intact so as not to destroy their organizational powers but must be "diluted" by the addition of selectees, or the existing divisions and units must be broken up and completely new ones formed, composed of Regular Army men and selectees, or National Guardsmen and selectees (Hearings before Senate Committee on Military Affairs, on S.4164, July 12, 1940, pages 328–329). The Army chose the first alternative (Marshall report, pages 11–13). General Marshall did not discuss, nor, apparently, did the Army consider, a third alternative: This was to retain all existing Regular Army divisions, and National Guard units, brought up to full strength by enlistments, if necessary, and to give them intensive training, while placing all selectees and new officers in entirely new units. By this device, while the training of conscripts would have progressed more slowly, the Regular and Guard units would by now be fully trained. We would have perhaps nine (9) fully trained Army divisions, ready for any contingency, plus many partly-trained units. Under the alternative selected by the Army, the existing units have been spread so thin that we now have no more than two well-trained and equipped divisions. Nor would the Army now be faced with the dilemma which the "dilution" process has brought about, that of having the major parts of all but two of its divisions composed of short-term selectees (New York Times, July 16, 1941). The impossibility of accomplishing what the Army sought to do has been pointed out by two recognized military experts, Hanson W. Baldwin (in "United We Stand," page 253), and Maj. George Fielding Eliot (in Congressional Record, August 1, 1940, page 14873).

Dilution

Still another military factor must be considered which casts grave doubt on the possibility of remedying the situation by mere extension of the service period. General Marshall, in his testimony before the Senate Committee on Military Affairs last week, stated that the chief reason why extended service was needed arose out of the "dilution" of the Regular Army divisions and National Guard units with selectees. He said that, with the exception of 2 divisions, from 40% to 85% of the Army units consisted of selectees (New York Times, July 16, 1941). Yet General Marshall, in the same testimony, made clear that the Army planned to continue to induct new selectees in increments. And the General's testimony indicated that few of the selectees now in service would be discharged when their terms expired.

Dilution No Solution

When new conscripts are inducted, it seems evident that further "dilution" of the already too thinly spread trained units of the Army is inevitable—unless the third alternative mentioned above is adopted. The "dilution" will become greater and greater as new men are inducted, just as a stone cast into a placid pool creates one ripple which in turn creates other ripples. This seems to be no remedy at all.

How About Volunteers?

A much more sensible course might be an attempt to persuade men to enlist, of their own volition, for three-year terms. General Marshall estimated that the Army would need at the present time a minimum of 640,000 three-year volunteers, of which it already has 476,000 (New York Times, July 16, 1941)—despite the admitted obstacles placed by the Army in the way of would-be three-year volunteers during the past year (by refusing to allow them to enlist until they had completed their 13-week training period), and despite the fact that the Army has made no real effort to secure volunteers (statement of General [Wade Hampton] Haislip, New York Times, July 16, 1941). In the future, General Marshall said 800,000 such volunteers would be needed at the most. There appears to be no real reason why a genuine effort to overcome this deficit by a vigorous recruiting campaign should not succeed.

Unless . . .

Despite all these facts, the extension of service might be supported if it were necessary to meet an actual or threatened attack. But neither Resolution 92 or 93, nor General Marshall himself, in his report or his testimony, points to any such danger, other than to say that there is an emergency. In view of the impossibility of actual attack in the immediate future upon this country (see Did You Know, #5, 7, 8)—an impossibility which has just been underlined by Hanson W. Baldwin, in his article "The Realities of Hemisphere Defense" (Reader's Digest, July, 1941)—there seems no justification for the proposed Resolutions, unless military ventures into foreign lands are planned (see Did You Know, #9). The serious hardships which these Resolutions would impose upon those now in service should not be lightly imposed, nor imposed because of hysterical and groundless fear.

DOCUMENT 104

" 'Danger Greater'—or A. E. F. ?"

Page Hufty
Bulletin #433, July 23, 1941

In His Message to Congress Monday President Roosevelt Said:
"I do believe—I know—the danger today is infinitely greater" (than a year ago).

* * *

But Is That So Mr. President!!!

1. *One Year Ago*—there was much reason to fear that Hitler might attempt an invasion of Britain.

    Now—that danger has definitely been postponed and the English themselves are confident that no attack can come until next year at the earliest.

2. *One Year Ago*—the British losses at sea were rising.

    Now—they are falling.

3. *One Year Ago*—the British air strength was relatively weak.

Now—England boasts of a much stronger airforce.

4. *One Year Ago*—British cities were being pounded in devastating air-raids.

Now—it is the German cities which are being pounded.

5. *One Year Ago*—our armanent program was still in the blueprint stage.

Now—we are beginning to turn out defense weapons in quantity.

6. *One Year Ago*—Germany was not occupied in the east with a hostile nation of 175 million people, with a huge army and much modern military equipment.

Now—Germany is fighting its strongest opponent on the continent.

7. *One Year Ago*—the scare-mongers said without proof that Hitler had intentions of invading America.

Now—the same people are still making the same assertions. There is still no proof of their assertions.

8. *One Year Ago*—if Hitler had even the remotest notion of invading America he lacked any means for doing so.

Now—Hitler still falls far short of being equipped with means to invade the United States. He lacks transports, a navy to escort them, and sufficient planes to escort the navy.

9. *One Year Ago*—before Hitler could attack America he would have to invade and defeat Britain.

Now—Hitler must knock out both *Britain and Russia* and there is no immediate prospect that he will be able to carry this out.

Mr. President—In face of all these facts where is the "danger infinitely greater?" These would tend to give quite a contrary impression!!!!!

What is this mysterious "danger?" The people of America are entitled to know!

And Mr. President—If it is "invasion" you mean when you say "danger," don't you recall that after the war began and "invasion" was discussed, our army command examined the problem of defending our shores and handed down the decision that half a million (500,000) men, well-trained and well armed, could repel *any* attack? Do you recall that Mr. President? Then why the hysteria now when conditions are much less threatening than a year ago!

* * *

But Mr. President—Since military experts have indicated that 500,000 trained, well equipped men can defend America, does your request for "removal of restrictions in regard to numbers" mean the army will be expanded into millions to prepare for another A. E. F.?

What purpose is there for *millions* of soldiers except for an invasion force?

* * *

Then Mr. President—It is your duty to inform the people of the "danger" hanging so imminently over their heads.

And whether or not the country is in greater "danger," Mr. President it is your duty to prepare the *strongest* possible *defense*.

Not millions of men for an offense, Mr. President!!!!!

Not millions of American youth for another A. E. F.!!!!!!

DOCUMENT 105

Samuel B. Pettengill to R. Douglas Stuart, Jr. July 22, 1941

I was in Washington yesterday and heard the President's message on the floor of the House. Not a single Congressman applauded. This I consider extraordinary. It is universally recognized that it is bitter political medicine.

I also saw Ruth Sarles and Senator Wheeler.

The question arises whether America First should take a position with reference to the extension of the draft. I am planning to come up tomorrow (Wednesday) afternoon to discuss this. I consider the matter important.

As I said the other night, my personal opinion is that America First, as a Committee, should not take a position on this matter. Nothing that America First can do (except to dissolve) would please Secretary Ickes [Harold Ickes, secretary of the interior]. Consequently, we do not need to plan policy to suit him and those who agree with him. We do, however, have to think carefully about the rank and file, fair minded, middle of the ground American citizen who wants to think well of America First. In short, we should keep America First from being subjected to assaults which this fair minded American would not understand and discount.

Some of the reasons against America First taking a position are:

First, that resistance to the extension of the draft would certainly subject us to the charge by Ickes et al, and perhaps to the suspicion by the same American citizen, that our protestations of national defense are not in good faith and that we secretly wish a deterioration of our defensive strength. My feeling is that we must be extremely careful to guard against getting into such a position. Good arguments were made against the draft in the first instance on the ground that we don't need a mass army, as Congressman Collins of Mississippi [Ross Collins (D-Miss.)] said, but rather a strong, highly mechanized professional army of rather permanent service, and paid compensation comparable to firemen and policemen. If so it is wholly likely that there would be sufficient volunteers and no draft necessary. Nevertheless, I do not think America First should make this argument. Others will make it on their own responsibility.

Second, I am inclined to think that the Congress will extend the draft after a hard, mean battle, and we do not strengthen ourselves by being associated with lost causes.

On the other hand we have to consider the arguments for taking a position. The chief of these, I think, are that men like Wheeler, Nye, Taft, Clark, Hiram Johnson, etc., will oppose it and they might feel that America First is letting them down in their fight so that we would not have perhaps as enthusiastic support and cooperation in the future when the big battle, perhaps, has to be fought, won or lost, whatever the odds. Some of these men will expect us to support them in their position.

It might also be argued that the extension of the draft is going to be very unpopular and even if we resist it and lose, we will gain popular support. I think we have got to give our best thought to this matter and I will talk to you about it tomorrow afternoon.

DOCUMENT 106

Nobody Knows the Trouble We're In

"Did you know that Congress is being asked to declare a national emergency whose nature is unknown?"
No. 12, July 24, 1941

Today

> The situation which existed at the time of the passage of the Select-Training and Service Act is quite different from the situation that confronts us today. (General George C. Marshall to the Senate Military Affairs Committee, New York Times, July 16, 1941.)

> I do believe—I know—the danger today is infinitely greater. (President Roosevelt, Message to Congress of July 21, 1941, New York Times, July 22, 1941.)

Yesterday

> Even if there were no British Navy it is not probable that any enemy would be stupid enough to attack us by landing troops in the United States from across thousands of miles of ocean, until it had acquired strategic bases from which to operate. (President Roosevelt, Message to Congress, Jan. 6, 1941, New York Times, Jan. 7, 1941.)

Justification

During the last two weeks, Chief of Staff General George C. Marshall has warned two Congressional committees of a national emergency so grave as to justify passage of Senate resolutions 92 & 93 providing for the retention of Selectees and National Guardsmen for more than twelve months. (New York Times, July 16, July 24.) In his July 21 message to Congress, President Roosevelt said, "I do believe—I know—the danger is infinitely greater" (than a year ago) to justify the same resolutions (New York Times, July 22). The War Department has sent to the House and Senate Military Affairs Committees a bill by which Congress would declare the existence of this emergency—without further ado. Should such a bill become law, its total effect is not precisely determinable, but legal experts are certain of this much: it would surrender to the President power to call up selectees in any number he desired and to keep them and National Guardsmen in service for any length of time he desired; it might even give him power to send them anywhere in the world without regard to the provision limiting them to the Western Hemisphere. (Did You Know #13 will examine in detail the legal implications of such a Congressionally declared emergency.)

Mystery

The actual justification for declaration of such an emergency has not been revealed to the American people. It has not been revealed to Congress, which is asked to declare it! Both General Marshall and the President have refused to describe the nature of the danger. As a consequence Americans can only speculate on the mystery.

What Dangers?

Unless the Administration is planning to put the U.S. into war thousands of miles from its own shores, there could be only one danger sufficient to justify such a declaration: the danger of imminent invasion of the United States or some other nation of the Western Hemisphere by the Nazis or the Japanese. On the face of it the danger seems far less than it was a year ago—if there was any danger then. Hitler can make no attempt to invade this Hemisphere as long as Britain holds out. Any attempt by Hitler to invade Britain seems indefinitely postponed. To attack America, Hitler must first defeat not only Britain but the Soviet Union with its 182,000,000 people and its huge Red Army. And a defeated Soviet Union would have to be policed by hundreds of thousands of Nazi troops. A year ago, France had already fallen and British cities were being blasted by the Luftwaffe. This summer the RAF has bombed Germany far more severely than the Luftwaffe has bombed Britain. This summer British shipping losses have been dropping. A year ago we did not possess the new Atlantic bases. A year ago our own armament program was not even a book of blueprints, but now it is beginning to take effective shape—effective for defense at least. The possibility of invasion can be examined even more closely. It can be narrowed to the study of a few strategic areas—since nobody expects an invading army to land on the marshes and beaches that rim Chesapeake Bay or on the steep rockbound shores of the Golden Gate. What then are the strategic areas of the Western Hemisphere? Is the danger in any area great enough to warrant such a surrender of power by Congress?

Is there danger of invasion from the frozen tundra of eastern Siberia, across the barren wastes of Alaska into western Canada and our own Pacific Northwest?

Ever since the day five weeks ago when Hitler's legions marched into the Soviet Union, interventionists have been voicing the fear that, in the event of a German victory, the bombing planes of the Luftwaffe would bomb out

Alaska from former Soviet bases on the coast of Siberia and the islands of the Bering Sea. After the bombing, Alaska and western Canada would be a highway of invasion. And, according to the interventionists, if it's not the Germans, it will be the Japanese who will take over the bases from a weakened Soviet Union. Consequently, the interventionists have been urging that U.S. forces occupy Soviet bases threatening Alaska to preclude any future invasion from that direction. There have been rumors that these are among the bases which would be occupied by selectees should the Hemisphere restriction on their employment be lifted.

Bleached Bones

But is Alaska a highway of invasion—whoever holds eastern Siberia? Independent experts say "No." Actually the alarmists who talk of invasion via Alaska are talking military nonsense. They ignore 1) the strategic difficulty of supplying and reinforcing the Siberian bases which can be reached only by boat and plane whoever holds them, 2) the growing formidability of our own network of naval and air bases in Alaska. Their fears have been best answered by Hanson W. Baldwin, military analyst for the *New York Times*, in his recent book, "United We Stand" (pp. 111–114): "There has been much talk of 'the vulnerability of Alaska to invasion'. . . . But we could wish for no more ludicrous and fatal error on the part of an enemy than a landing in Alaska. . . . And if an enemy ever attempted an overland campaign striking for Seattle he would leave behind him a trail bleached in bones, and in the words of one officer, the soldiers who started would not reach Seattle. Their grandchildren might, but they would not be an army. . . . In the hysteria of the moment every area has suddenly become 'vital' and 'vulnerable'; even Alaska, wilderness of pine and snow, total population 73,000 people without a good air target in the territory, has been represented by sources that should know better as highly vulnerable to air attack."

The emergency that the President and General Marshall are talking about is not a threat of invasion via Alaska. *Occupation of the Siberian bases can only be justified if the U.S. is contemplating offensive action in the Far East.* (For a full discussion of the defense of Alaska see: Did You Know, #5.)

Is there danger of invasion via Iceland, Greenland, Newfoundland and eastern Canada?

One of the three reasons the President advanced on July 7, 1941, to justify the occupation of Iceland was that the occupation would prevent any possible seizure of Iceland by the Nazis, for use as a stepping stone to Greenland and the eventual invasion of North America. Iceland is well outside the Western Hemisphere and far closer to Europe (only 600 miles from Norway) than to the U.S. And many experts have been skeptical of the "stepping stone" theory. However, if ever there was a threat of invasion via Iceland, Greenland and Newfoundland, that threat has now been blocked. In August 1940, the President concluded a joint defense agreement with Canada. In September 1940, the President secured base rights in Newfoundland from Britain. In April 1941, the President made an executive agreement with the Danish Minister to Washington by which the U.S. secured base rights in Greenland. As if that were not enough, the President has now sent U.S. sailors and marines to Iceland. (On none of these agreements was Congress consulted.) Obviously a threat of invasion from the northeast is not the emergency the President and General Marshall are talking about. (For a full discussion of the occupation of Iceland see Did you Know, #7.)

Is there danger of invasion via the Caribbean, which would drive a wedge between North and South America and threaten the Panama Canal?

If ever there was a serious threat via the Caribbean, it ceased to exist when the new Caribbean bases were acquired from Britain in September 1940. (Whether it was necessary to give away fifty destroyers to acquire them is another question.) The Caribbean now is literally ringed with bases— Guantanamo, Jamaica, Puerto Rico, Virgin Islands, Antigua, Saint Lucia, Trinidad. The southern approach is sealed by bases in British Guiana, the northern approach by a base in the Bahamas, and Vichy-owned Martinique is virtually surrounded. Secretary of the Navy Frank Knox has testified that the Caribbean is now "substantially an American lake" (Hearings on the Lease-Lend Bill before the Senate Committee on Foreign Relations, p. 224). The threat of invasion via the Caribbean is not the emergency the President and General Marshall are talking about.

Is there danger of invasion of Brazil from Dakar in West Africa or from the islands of the Atlantic?

If there is a chink anywhere in the defensive armor of the Western Hemisphere it is the lack, as yet, of an operating base on the bulge of Brazil which is only 1,700 miles from Vichy-owned Dakar on the tip of Africa. Interventionists have urged that the U.S. seize Dakar from the French by force lest Hitler launch an invasion from there against Brazil. The interventionists ignore the military facts of Dakar. A squalid, tropical port, Dakar is not suitable now as an invasion base, and it would take several years to make it suitable. Moreover, there are many indications that lead to the belief that Brazil may be about to enter into a cooperative defense agreement with the U.S. which would include base rights on the Brazilian bulge. Should this happen, the last argument for seizing Dakar—as a defense measure—would disappear. And bases in Brazil would minimize whatever real danger there is of a Fifth Column uprising in Brazil. In *Reader's Digest* for July 1941,

Hanson W. Baldwin writes as follows of Dakar and other West African ports: "None of these ports has adequate drydocks, machine shops or repair facilities to service either naval or air fleets. None has adequate storage capacity for coal or oil or gasoline. None has an ammunition dump of any size. Most of them are unhealthy. To solve these problems would take time—a long time—and until then, no invasion of South America could be started." What is true of Dakar is true of the Atlantic islands—the Cape Verdes, the Canaries, the Azores, Madeira. Moreover, to take Dakar or the islands would require 100,000 men, a huge fleet of perhaps 100 transports, and a large naval escort. Obviously the emergency the President and General Marshall are talking about is not centered in Dakar. (For a full discussion of Dakar and the Atlantic islands see: Did You Know, #8.)

Does Japan's move into French Indo-China threaten the United States?

The interventionists have now seized upon Japan's aggression in French Indo-China as a justification for U.S. action. It takes no military expert to look at a map of the Pacific and recognize the absurdity of thinking that Japan or anyone else could attack the Western Hemisphere from Saigon or Cam-Ranh Bay. But in his statement of July 24, denouncing the Japanese aggression, Under Secretary of State Sumner Welles emphasized the contention that the move jeopardized U.S. supplies of strategic rubber and tin, most of which come from British Malaya and the Netherlands East Indies (New York Times, July 25, 1941). He also mentioned that the Japanese move menaced the Philippines.

Rubber, Tin & Dong Dang

The old rubber & tin argument has been dealt with too often to require much space. Rubber is being produced in the U.S. synthetically; expansion of synthetic production to meet all essential needs would be possible before a serious shortage developed. ("Strategy of the Americas," by Fleming MacLiesh & Cushman Reynolds, pp. 16–23; "United We Stand," by Hanson W. Baldwin, pp. 54, 87, 314; *Fortune*, "Synthetic Rubber," August 1940.) The story of tin is somewhat similar. Tin mined in Bolivia can be smelted in the U.S. A smelter is now being built in Texas. Glass, silver and other materials can be substituted for tin in many instances. (MacLiesh & Reynolds, ibid., pp. 23–30; Baldwin, ibid., pp. 54, 314; New York Times, July 10, 1941.) A threat to the rubber and tin supply line is not the emergency that the President and General Marshall are talking about. American boys need not die for old Dong Dang.

And Manila

The Philippines have been a headache to U.S. strategists for forty years. It is an open secret that many strategical plans regarding them deal with the problem of *retaking* them after losing them in the early stages of a war with Japan. They have been called an indefensible salient. Baldwin calls them "a military, possibly an economic, certainly a political liability" (ibid., p. 56). The islands have been promised their independence in 1946. Japan's latest move may be a threat to the Philippines, but it is not a threat to the Western Hemisphere. The question raised by the Philippines is whether the American people want to fight in the Far East at all.

DOCUMENT 107

The Shape of Things to Come?

"Did you know *that a declaration of national emergency by Congress would give the President virtually undefinable personal power?*"
No. 13, July 30, 1941

> . . . for us to declare a national emergency would invoke powers which I am sure and the committee was sure the Congress of the United States did not want to invoke at this time, no matter how serious they thought the situation was. (Senator Thomas, of Utah, floor manager of Draft-Extension bill, to the U.S. Senate–Congressional Record. July 30, 1941, page 6580.)

Step #1—Extended Service

The Senate Military Affairs Committee has reported to the Senate a bill declaring that "the national interest is imperiled," thus enabling the President, at his sole discretion, to extend for an unlimited time the period of service of selectees, National Guardsmen and Reserve Officers now in the Army, and removing all limitations on the number of selectees who may be drafted for service in the future (S. J. Res. 95). The House Military Affairs Committee has reported a substantially similar measure (H. J. Res. 222). Chief of Staff General George C. Marshall and President Roosevelt, among others, have urged that extension of service is necessary to prevent "disintegration" of the Army (New York Times, July 16, 22, 1941). That contention has been shown to lack merit in previous studies of this series. Did You

Know, #10, pointed out that extension of service would constitute a breach of faith and a transfer of Congressional power to the President. Did You Know, #11, demonstrated that there need be no impairment of the effectiveness of the Army if selectees, Guardsmen and Reserve Officers were discharged at the expiration of their one-year's service period. The mysterious and secret peril, relied upon by the President and General Marshall as justification for such a measure, was examined in Did You Know, #12, and found to lack discernible substance.

Step #2—National Emergency

But the bill for extension of service is only a minor phase of the larger danger of involvement in the war. Presumably, it is a preliminary to other bills. In the coming debate on the extension-of-service bills, Congressional apologists for the Administration's foreign policy will move to substitute a bill calling on Congress to declare an unlimited national emergency. All the evidence supports the belief that such a bill is what the Administration really wants. The resolutions on extension of service, originally introduced at the request of the War Department (into the Senate on July 10 and into the House on July 22), did not follow the wording of the Selective Training and Service Act (50 U.S.C.A. 301) as does the bill adopted now by the Senate committee in declaring "the national interest is imperiled" and then empowering the President to extend the term of service of selectees. Instead, those original resolutions (S. J. Res. 92, 93; H. J. Res, 217, 218) simply gave the President blanket power to extend the service as he saw fit, so long as the national emergency he proclaimed on May 27 should continue. They amounted to a surrender to the President of far greater power than ever was contemplated by the Selective Training and Service law. In addition, other resolutions sought to remove the present prohibitions (50 U.S.C.A. 301, 401) against use of selectees, Guardsmen and Reserve Officers outside the Western Hemisphere (S. J. Res. 91). Congressional and popular opposition forced the withdrawal of these latter resolutions, commonly called the "A. E. F." resolutions (New York Times, July 15, 1941), but presumably only temporarily.

Emergency Wanted

Meanwhile, the demand was again pressed for a declaration by Congress of a national emergency. Chief of Staff Marshall urged it before both the Senate and House Military Affairs committees (New York Times, July 16, 18, 1941). In his message to Congress and the nation on July 21, President Roosevelt urged such a declaration (New York Times, July 22, 1941). In the wake of these utterances, the War Department presented new resolutions calling for the declaration of a national emergency (Senate Report 595, 77th

Congress, pages 10–11), and shelving pending measures then under consideration, which restricted the effect of such an emergency solely to extension of service (S. J. Res. 95, 98, 99; H. J. Res. 220). Further proof that the War Department (and presumably the President) were really interested in something more than mere extension of service is evident from the fact that the War Department rejected Senator Taft's compromise proposal, designed to rotate the service periods of selectees and Guardsmen and still ensure against disintegration of the Army (New York Times, July 25, 1941).

A. E. F. Wanted, Too

The Senate committee's refusal to call for the declaration of an emergency, while a partial rebuff to the Administration, does not settle the issue. It is possible that such a measure will be presented during the debate in Congress as an amendment to, or a substitute for, the extension of service bill, and will be pressed by the supporters of the Administration's "elastic defense" theory (see Did You Know, #7). A Congressional declaration of emergency, in the opinion of some experts, might have the effect of removing the prohibition against use of selectees and others outside the Western Hemisphere (New York Times, July 20, 1941). That this is an all-important Administration goal is evidenced by the statement of Senator Lister Hill [D-Ala.], spokesman in the Senate committee for the Administration's point of view, that recent events in the Pacific now require removal of the Western Hemisphere limitation (Washington Post, July 28, 1941). Senator Hill felt that "it was a foolish thing to have thought in terms of geographical lines in putting a limit on employment of the selective service men and National Guardsmen. The question is one of where the vital interests of the United States lie." (Washington Post, July 28, 1941.) Senators Lee [Joshua W. Lee (D-Okla.)] and Pepper, Administration stalwarts, followed Senator Hill with a statement urging Congress to proclaim the existence of a national emergency (Washington Post, July 29, 1941).

Unlimited Power

A declaration by Congress that a national emergency exists, following upon the similar proclamation by the President on May 27, 1941, would do much more than merely enable the extension of service. It would create an amorphous situation in which drastic powers without definitive limits would become available for exercise by the Administration. This is because of the dearth of binding precedents on the nature and effect of a "national emergency," and because of the host of laws now on the books which become available for use when such an emergency is proclaimed.

Emergency and the Constitution

It is not surprising that few Americans understand the nature and effect of a declaration of "national emergency." It is not expressly mentioned in our Constitution, which confers special powers upon the Congress only in connection with the calling out of the militia in order to "execute the Laws of the Union, suppress Insurrections and repel Invasions" (Article I, Sec. 8). It is a hybrid state of affairs, somewhere in between the state of peace and the state of war which are contrasted by the Constitution (Article I, Sec. 8; Article I, Sec. 9; Third Amendment). Nor does the Constitution expressly confer upon the President any power to declare a "national emergency."

Scarce as Diamonds

Except when the United States has been engaged in war, there have been very few Presidential declarations of "national emergency" and none by the Congress. Diligent search by a federal research agency has found only one proclamation of a national emergency before the incumbency of Franklin D. Roosevelt. That was a declaration by President Wilson on February 5, 1917, before our entrance into the World War, restricted in nature and proclaiming that a national emergency existed solely with regard to transportation by water (39 Stat. 1814–1815). President Roosevelt has invoked the device of an emergency proclamation on five occasions since he entered the White House. On March 6, 1933, he proclaimed that the existence of a national emergency required a banking "holiday," and on March 9, 1933, he continued that proclamation, after Congress had passed a law which validated his proclamation and empowered him to take such action (48 Stat. 1689, 1691). On February 28, 1935, he declared that the continued emergency in cotton production required putting into operation the Cotton Control Act. (49 Stat. 3438). On September 8, 1939, after the outbreak of the current European war, he proclaimed that a "limited" national emergency existed, "limited" in the sense that it was restricted in scope to "the proper observance, safeguarding and enforcing of the neutrality of the United States (and) . . . strengthening our national defense within the limits of peacetime authorizations" (22 U.S.C.A. Supp.). Finally, on May 27, 1941, he proclaimed an unlimited national emergency for the expressed purpose of preventing encirclement of or aggression against the Western Hemisphere (Senate Document 64, 77th Congress, page 10).

Power by Implication

There is no Constitutional provision, nor any law on the statute books, which confers blanket powers upon either the President or Congress when a national emergency is proclaimed. The legal effect of an emergency declaration is that it makes available for use the sweeping powers conferred by a host of separate and specific laws, each dealing with a separate subject matter. In addition, it has been contended that there are other powers, not enumerated in those laws, which can be considered as implied in the powers granted to the President and Congress by the Constitution, and which therefore may be invoked when an emergency has been proclaimed. What Attorney-General Murphy [Frank Murphy, governor of Michigan, 1937–1938; attorney general, 1939–1940; associate justice of the Supreme Court, 1940–1949] wrote to the Senate concerning those implied powers of the President applies equally well to the implied powers belonging to Congress:

> You are aware, of course, that the Executive has powers not enumerated in the statutes—powers derived not from statutory grants but from the Constitution. It is universally recognized that the constitutional duties of the Executive carry with them the constitutional powers necessary for their proper performance. These constitutional powers have never been specifically defined, and in fact cannot be, since their extent and limitations are largely dependent upon conditions and circumstances. (Senate Document 133, 76th Congress, October 4, 1939.)

223 Laws

As a practical matter, the declaration of a national emergency would greatly increase the powers of the President, who as Chief Executive would be charged with the duty of executing the laws brought into operation. As of the date of this study, 223 separate laws might become available for use by the President or executive agencies under Presidential direction if Congress were now to declare that a national emergency existed, following the President's own proclamation of May 27, 1941. A study made by the Legislative Reference Service of the Library of Congress listed 215 laws as of June 1941, which were applicable in emergency situations (see Senate Document 64, 77th Congress), and 8 more such laws have been enacted since.

All Power to the President

Examination of these laws reveals that, should Congress now proclaim a national emergency, sweeping powers would be conferred upon the executive branch of the government to place our armed forces upon a virtual wartime footing, to control labor, industry, agriculture, the merchant marine, and all other agencies of transportation, communication and power. In addition, because of the vagueness of the legal situation and the undefinable scope of the broad constitutional powers vested in the Executive, it would in effect rest mainly with the Executive to determine what powers could be used. The power of Congress over the pursestrings avails little in the face of "fait accompli," as recent American history has disclosed.

Emergency by Intuition

Further complication arises because of the uncertainty as to when these laws may be invoked. Some of the laws come into effect only when the President declares the emergency; others become operative only when Congress so proclaims; still others become effective whenever there is an emergency, without specifying whether that emergency is to be found by Congress or by the President; a few can be put into effect by an executive agency upon the finding by that agency that an emergency situation exists although an executive agency is not headed by an elected officer. There is no definition of what constitutes an "emergency," nor any requirement that any specified factual situation must exist or be found to exist by Congress or the President before an "emergency" can be proclaimed. The determination of whether there is an emergency is left to the discretion of Congress or the President, as the case may be. While some Supreme Court decisions, upon which President Roosevelt professed to rely in part for his power to proclaim the national emergency of May 27 (*New York Times*, May 29, 1941), deal with emergency situations, they do so in such general terms that there is justification for the conclusion of the same federal research agency that there is a dearth of controlling legal precedents on the issues of what is a national emergency, and who may proclaim one.

Conspiracy of Silence

The scope of Presidential power in a national emergency is still cloaked in mystery, despite the recent effort of the U.S. Senate in 1939 to ascertain the nature of that power. In answer to Senate Resolution 185, adopted on September 28, 1939, Attorney General Murphy refused to render a legal opinion upon the President's powers upon the announced ground that the doctrine of "separation of powers" prevented the Attorney General from advising the Congress (Senate Document 133, 76th Congress, 3rd session, Oct. 5, 1939). However, according to the periodical "Time," the Attorney General was "under the strictest White House orders not to talk publicly about the extent of these powers" (Sept. 18, 1939). While many of the 223 emergency laws could be considered as rendered available for use by the President's proclamation of May 27, few of them have been used. Certain it is that a Congressional declaration of emergency would constitute an endorsement of the President's foreign policy, and an incentive to the use of these available powers.

History Lesson

Let us learn from history. Early in the spring of 1933, Adolf Hitler stood before the German Reichstag and requested an "Enabling Act" to meet the "emergency" which faced Germany. The "Enabling Act of 1933," which was speedily passed, was a grant of emergency power. Its duration was to be four years. The four years ended in the spring of 1937, but the "Enabling Act" is still on the German statute books, and is still in use.

DOCUMENT 108

Say, Is This the U.S.A.

"Did you know the extent to which your life would be affected by Congressional reinforcement of the national emergency?"
No. 14, July 31, 1941

For President Roosevelt is without doubt the greatest autocrat in the history of this country. (Colonel (Now Secretary of Navy) Frank Knox, on Feb. 12, 1936, as reported in Congressional Record, July 10, 1940, pages 14224–14226.)

No one likes to think, let alone say we have in Mr. Roosevelt a Chief Executive who has to be continually watched lest he slip over legislation depriving the people of more of their rights. The facts are as they are. (Colonel (Now Secretary of Navy) Frank Knox, in his book, "We Planned It That Way" (1938), Introduction.)

To outline the probable general effects of the declaration of a national emergency by Congress (see Did You Know, #13), and the consequent surrender of still more powers to the President, is not enough. What is more important to Americans is an examination of the specific grants of power, and their probable effects on each American life. For there are many laws, and directly or indirectly they cover every aspect of a citizen's life from the hours he works each week to what he hears when he turns on his radio in the evening. Even constitutional lawyers do not know precisely where the President's powers under his own emergency of May 27 end, and where the powers he would acquire from a Congressionally declared emergency begin—or end. But it is certain that he would acquire a number of specific new powers, and that a Congressionally declared emergency could be interpreted as a clear mandate to exercise powers he has been hesitant to employ heretofore.

223 Varieties

Any analysis of the 223 specific laws which must be considered in a study of emergency powers must take into account the differing natures of these laws. Most of them have been enacted during the last twenty-five years. Many were enacted during the World War period, and many have been enacted since 1932. (These are the two periods in which the trend toward centralization of government has been strongest.) Of the 223 laws, six, including the Neutrality Act, apply to wars between foreign countries (these are already in force and therefore are not to be considered here). There are 52 laws which come into force only when war is declared by this country or when this country is attacked, but the hybrid character of a national emergency in an era of undeclared wars may allow an interpretation bringing them into force during what most people think is peacetime. Seventeen laws (Senate Document 64, 77th Congress, pp. 11–29) apply only to a case when war is "threatened" or "imminent." In view of the nature of the President's "unlimited emergency" proclamation, speaking as it does of contemplated efforts by the Axis powers to conquer all democracies, and of preventing aggression against the Western Hemisphere (Senate Document 64, 77th Congress, page 10), and in view of the hybrid status of a "national emergency," it is likely that those 17 laws might be held applicable should Congress also declare an emergency. They are therefore considered here also. 105 laws are expressly applicable in the case of a national emergency (almost all of these are applicable in time of war) (Senate Document 64, 77th Congress, pp. 11–29). In addition, there are 43 laws in effect in *peace-time*, most of which *protect* the rights of members of the armed forces, the balance of which are a deterrent to *excessive* militarism, which probably would be wiped out in such an emergency as the Administration contemplates (Senate Document 64, 77th Congress, pp. 37–42). Space permits in this study only a consideration of the most important of these laws.

Army

The constitutional power of Congress to raise armies would be effectively transferred to the President. He would have the power, without substantial limitation, to determine where soldiers should be employed, how large the Army should be, who should command the forces, and for how long soldiers should be kept in service.

Outward Bound

At the present time, there is no geographical limitation which prevents the President, as Commander-in-Chief, from sending soldiers of the *Regular Army* anywhere in the world. However, he is forbidden to send selectees, National Guardsmen and Reserve Officers outside the Western Hemisphere (50 U.S.C.A. 301, 401). Should Congress declare a national emergency, that restriction could be considered removed, and the groundwork laid for a new A.E.F. The reasoning in support of that contention would be: in time of war, that all members of the armed forces can be sent anywhere it is thought necessary; the nature of the President's national emergency proclamation of May 27, 1941, speaking as he did of threatened attack, when combined with the hybrid nature of a "national emergency" (see Did You Know, #13), justify a holding that the situation would be so akin to a state of war that all restrictions would disappear. This would follow if Senator Thomas of Utah, floor-leader for the Draft-Extension bill, was correct in stating that the declaration by Congress of a national emergency would confer wartime powers (Congressional Record, July 30, page 6580). The argument against the contention would be that the Selective Service and National Guard Mobilization laws were themselves "emergency" laws, and therefore the Western Hemisphere restriction which they contained could not be removed merely by another statement of "emergency."

Growing Pains

The President could fix the size of the Army. The peacetime limits on the size of the Regular Army would no longer apply, and he could call for as many more volunteers as were desired (10 U.S. Code 602; 54 Stat. 601). On the theory that there was a danger of invasion, he could call into the federal service the militia of the several States (32 U.S. Code 81a). He could call into active duty in the Army, for the duration of the emergency, all of the Reserves of the Army (Reserve Officers, Enlisted Reserve, and Regular Army Reserve—10 U.S. Code 369; 10 U.S. Code 426; 10 U.S. Code Supp. 343). His judgment alone would control. The power of Congress over the pursestrings would be of little practical value, since Congress could scarcely refuse to make appropriations for the Army, after it had endorsed the President's foreign policy by proclaiming a national emergency.

The President's Own

The President's power to decide the leaders of the Army would be increased. He would be able to pick commanders of field forces without being bound by the usual seniority rules (10 U.S. Code 1591). He could promote Army officers at his sole discretion, except as to officers above the rank of brigadier general, who must be confirmed by the Senate (10 U.S. Code 1513; 54 Stat. 875, sec. 101). These powers, obviously, would create stronger Presidential control over the leadership of the Army.

Extended Service

Finally, the President would be able to keep the soldiers now in the Army, whether volunteers or draftees, for as long as he alone should deem necessary or desirable. It seems clear that he would have the power to extend the service of selectees, National Guardsmen and Reserve Officers for an indefinite period beyond the one year period now required of them. While the Selective Service Act allows such extension of service only when Congress declares that "the national interest is imperiled" (Sec. 3) and not expressly upon a declaration of a national emergency, the latter declaration would most likely be construed by the courts as tantamount to a declaration of national peril. Further, under other laws, the President could extend the service of National Guard Officers and members "for the duration" (32 U.S. Code 81; 32 U.S. Code Supp. 81c: 32 U.S. Code 124). All enlistments by volunteers in the future would be for the duration of the emergency plus six months (54 Stat. 213, ch. 194). Regular Army officers and enlisted men could be kept on duty in foreign stations for more than the two-year stretch which is the normal maximum (10 U.S. code 17).

Navy Too

The President would be given increased personal power over the Navy. He could increase its size from 250,000 enlisted men to 300,000 (Act of April 22, 1941, Public Law 39). He could determine with increased freedom who should command the fleets, since he would no longer be required to select them from the active list of rear admirals (34 U.S. Code 864). The Secretary of the Navy, appointed by the President, would be empowered to call into active service, "for the duration," the reserve forces of the Navy (Officers and enlisted men on the Reserve list; Naval Reserves; Coast Guard Reserves—34 U.S. Code 433; 14 U.S. Code 164, 165; 34 U.S. Code 423, 34 U.S. Code Supp. 853c; Act of Feb. 19, 1941, Public Law 8).

Labor's Losses

Once Congress had declared a national emergency, the working conditions of a large portion of our population would become subject to drastic control by the President. With most of the nation's productive capacity engaged in making war supplies, almost every worker engaged in private industry will be engaged in work on contracts with the United States government or on sub-contracts. The present hard-won rights of employees working on public contracts and public works would be at the mercy of the Administration's whim—for instance, the 8-hour day could be eliminated (40 U.S. Code 326; 325; 321). Present provisions concerning the wages of laborers on public building contracts could be suspended (40 U.S. Code Supp. 276a-5). Similarly, many workers employed directly by the government would be affected (54 Stat. 676–680, 714, 1205; Act of June 3, 1941, Public Law 100). By changing a single one of the regulations under which the Selective Service Law is administered (Selective Service Regulations, par. 351) the President would revive the "work or fight" principle to tie seventeen million young American workingmen to their jobs, as is the custom in Nazi Germany and Communist Russia. Citizenship requirements could be relaxed. Present laws pertaining to the citizenship of officers and crew members of the American merchant marine could be suspended (49 Stat. 1993, sec. 302 (h)). The requirement that employees of the War and Navy Departments in the Canal Zone be citizens could be relaxed (Act of May 23, 1941, Public Law 71; Act of May 6, 1941, Public Law 48), and has already been relaxed (Executive Order 8812, June 30, 1941). The present requirements concerning accommodations for sailors on ships owned by the United States government or by U.S. citizens (and, in some circumstances on ships of foreign registry) could be suspended or modified (Act of June 6, 1941, Public Law 101, Section 5b).

The President Rules the Waves

The President would be entitled to assume sweeping personal power over the American merchant marine (50 U.S. Code 36, 191; 46 U.S. code 835; Act of June 6, 1941, Public Law 101). Iron clad control over shipping and trade would be exercisable under the recent Act of July 14, 1941 (Public Law 173), which authorizes the establishment of a warrant system for all ships of American registry, or owned by U.S. citizens. By virtue of its power to deny harbor and loading facilities to ships lacking warrants, and its power to give priority rights to such facilities to ships with warrants, the Maritime Commission—an independent agency under the wing of the executive branch—would be enabled to control the trade, cargoes and voyages of the entire U.S. merchant marine. The Maritime Commission could end the charters of all American vessels, and could itself requisition or take over all privately-owned ships (49 Stat. 1993, sec. 302 (h); 53 Stat. 1254, sec. 1 (d). Until June 30, 1942, the Maritime Commission could also take steps to increase the merchant marine by negotiating contracts for new or rebuilt ships, without being required to call for competitive bids or to advertise publicly, and could secure priorities concerning the material needed for such work (Act of May 2, 1941; Public Law 46).

Industry Drafted

Industry would also become subject to executive control. Under the "draft property" bill, recently passed by the Senate and already approved by the House Military Affairs Committee, the President, until June 30, 1943, could requisition or commandeer any military equipment, supplies or parts, or tools, machinery or materials necessary to manufacture, operate or service them, if they were needed immediately for national defense and could not be secured otherwise, upon paying such fair and just compensation as the President may decree (S. 1759). As the history of the Lease-Lend Law shows (Act of March 11, 1941; Public Law 11, section 2), a large part of the processes and materials used in our industrial economy can be brought within the "draft property" law and rendered subject to requisition as being capable of use in the making or use of military or naval equipment. Under a 1916 law, the President could require any factory to produce arms or other materials, and to give such production preference over all other work, at the risk of a criminal penalty (50 U.S. Code 80). There is also available to the President power to compel manufacturers to produce any desired goods or equipment in preference to all other work, or to suffer seizure of plant and/ or criminal penalties, under the Selective Service and Training Act of 1940 (Sec. 9).

First Freedom

Freedom of speech over the radio is considered by our basic laws to be an integral and essential part of a free society, and the Federal Communications Commission is forbidden to abridge that freedom (47 U.S.C.A. 326). Presumably that freedom is included within the first of the "four freedoms" (freedom of expression), which the President wishes to impose "everywhere in the world" (Message to Congress, January 6; New York Times, January 7, 1941). Yet the President would have the power to destroy freedom of speech over the radio, since he could, by suspending the present regulations which require the impartial discussion of all controversial topics, prevent the use of the radio by any person who wished to criticize his policies (for instance, a speaker who wished to urge him to keep the country out of war) (47 U.S. Code 606). He would have the power to turn the radio into a governmental propaganda machine, since he could close down or take over every station in the country (47 U.S. Code 606).

Power Politics

The use of refrigerators, washing machines and radios could be curtailed more completely than is now proposed by Leon Henderson [director, Office of Price Administration and Civilian Supply]. Whenever the Federal Power

Commission should decide that an emergency existed and that there was danger of an electricity shortage, it could require public utilities to create temporary electricity facilities (16 U.S. Code 824a). This would be accomplished by a decision on the part of the Power Commission ordering the rationing of consumer products to mitigate the shortage. The result might be prohibition of the use of washing machines, refrigerators, milking machines and other electrically driven farm machinery, radios, etc. The Lease Lend program increases the likelihood of a power shortage requiring such rationing by making likely the exercising of the President's authority to take over power houses and dams to feed munitions factories (16 U.S. Code 809).

Railroads

The railroads could be forced to stop transporting passengers and consumer goods. The President would have absolute power to order the railroads to give preference in transportation to any goods the President considered essential (10 U.S. Code 1362; 49 U.S. Code 6(8); 49 U.S. Code 1(15)). Whatever existing arrangements the railroads may have made for the transportation of food, consumer goods or industrial supplies could be set aside, and normal economic life disrupted. Passengers could be denied the use of the railroads for travel, and forced to use less convenient modes of transportation.

Banking

The control which the President could exercise over the banking and financial system would affect every part of the American economy. He would be empowered to exercise complete control over the Federal Reserve Banks, a tremendously powerful weapon, since those banks exercise influence over the policies and operations of the great majority of the banks of the country (12 U.S. Code 95a, 95). He could exert incalculable control over the credit of the country, so essential to a productive economy, through his personal control over the credit policy of the Federal Reserve (31 U.S. Code 821; Act of June 30, 1941, Public Law 142). He could control much of our foreign trade by his power to control foreign exchange, and his power to compel the turning in of all gold, silver and currency, without which transactions with foreign merchants become difficult and often virtually impossible; his power to "freeze" the property and assets of foreigners and foreign countries could be used to carry on economic war with countries he disliked (12 U.S. Code 95a, 95; 54 Stat. 179, ch. 185, Public Res. 69). Some of these powers have already been exercised, but the precise extent of the full powers and the ultimate effect of their exercise is undefinable. This much can be said: these powers, when used, can affect vitally the life of every person in this country, for they enable the President to control the very heart of the economy.

Breadbasket

The farmer would not be immune from special attention. The Secretary of Agriculture, an appointee of the President, could take steps to determine whether increased quantities of such basic farm products as corn, wheat, cotton, rice, tobacco and peanuts were desirable (7 U.S. Code Supp. 1371; Act of April 3, 1941, Public Law 27). The effect of increased production, if ordered, upon farm prices becomes obvious when it is remembered that much of the President's farm policy was based upon the theory that the farmer could not make a living because too much was being produced. This potential threat could be realized in action if the Secretary should exert his power to bring about expanded production of non-basic farm products (Act of July 1, 1941, Public Law 147). Not only do these laws give the President authority to regiment the American farmer, but they allow him to play power politics all over the world with the food the American farmer produces.

Eminent Domain

Property rights would become subordinate to the needs of the country, as determined by the President alone. Any land considered necessary for military purposes could be taken over at once (instead of the usual procedure of waiting until a court had decided what was fair compensation) by merely starting condemnation proceedings, and leaving the matter of the amount of compensation to be determined later (50 U.S. Code 171). Of course, a property owner whose property has already been taken is in no position to refuse to accept the compensation awarded him, and consequently would often compromise on a sum less than he thought just in order to avoid long and expensive litigation. No person or business or industrial plant could use any material which the President considered a strategic or critical material without his approval (50 U.S. Code Supp. 98c). In these days of "total war," virtually every commodity produced or used in industrial life can be considered essential to national defense, as was conceded in the debate on the Lease-Lend law (Act of March 11, 1941, sec. 2) by even its own supporters.

DOCUMENT 109

General Letter
Fred Burdick
August 12, 1941

We scored a big moral victory today! The closeness of the vote was a surprise to nearly every one. Mr. Mundt believes that we are in a better position to slow up the war crowd now than if we had won by a single vote, and I am inclined to agree with him.

For one thing, it is almost certain that *the Administration will not dare to offer their resolution removing restrictions against sending selectees outside the Western Hemisphere.* And as for putting before Congress a declaration of war, that is entirely out of the picture in the foreseeable future and under present international circumstances.

Probably one of the most important angles is that the closeness of this vote will make every Congressman who voted for this war measure do some real thinking regarding his personal responsibility, and likely make dozens of them vow they will never again vote for a war measure and have so much responsibility resting upon their minds. Many will wonder whether their vote may endanger the peace of America and possibly be responsible for hundreds of thousands of American boys losing their lives in foreign wars. And some people may say, *their letter might have changed their Congressman's vote!* And another great advantage resulting from the psychological factor that now exists is that *the people of the nation will be encouraged to redouble their efforts to exert influence upon Congress.* And as we know that 80% of the people are against war, by getting the masses of our citizens to get busy as they have never done before writing letters to their Senators, Representative and President, we have a *much better chance of attaining the objectives of the AFC than at any time since the Committee's organization.* But a tremendous effort has to be made. Now is the time to sell the people on the importance of organization for keeping out of foreign war and making public opinion against war more articulate and effective.

Nearly all of our non-interventionist friends in the House I have talked with during the past half hour or so feel very elated and optimistic over the situation. They all agree that we did gain a moral and psychological victory, gave the interventionist crowd a genuine "run for their money" and put the "Fear of God" into them! They are not a bit likely to try putting over any more war measures for some time to come. And if we can get the people aroused as never before and get deluges of mail going into the offices of the Members who are somewhat "on the fence" on this whole war issue, we may have the war crowds licked for good! At any rate, we can see a patch of blue sky now through the dark war clouds that have been hanging over America.

As to the immediate technical situation in Congress, I understand from Mr. Mundt that either the Senate or the House has to vote on this measure after it goes to conference between committees representing the House and the Senate. It is almost certain that the conferees will let the Senate instead of the House get another vote on the joint resolution. But even in the Senate the chances for defeat are not hopeless, if enough people can be roused and encouraged to flood the offices of doubtful Senators with letters and telegrams and phone calls.

DOCUMENT 110

General Letter

Fred Burdick
August 13, 1941

After talking with a number of leading House non-interventionists today, I am more convinced than ever that probably the way the final vote turned out yesterday was the best thing that could have happened.

It has been pointed out that had we killed the measures in the House the Administration doubtless would have introduced a new 12-month compromise joint resolution, and with tremendous pressure might have put it through. At that, though, it does not seem that pressure could be much greater from the *political angle*, as they had Senators lobbying in the House and many of the "big boys" in the Democratic machine from various parts of the country here in Washington exerting pressure. And the Administration called on members of the National Democratic Committee for help in "holding them in line."

The most important danger from an outright defeat of the measure would be the manufacturing of *"an incident"* to kindle the war spirit amongst the people and the Congress, in an effort to force the joint resolution through Congress. And they might have added, under such circumstances, the proposal to remove restrictions against sending selectees outside the Western Hemisphere.

My forecast of a couple of weeks ago or more that the Administration would seek to create crises in the Far East and in South America proved correct. However, the majority of Senators and Representatives did not "fall" for this sort of strategy concocted by the war crowd.

Mrs. Mundt told me this afternoon that she heard a local broadcaster say that the Administration was "panicky" over the extreme closeness of the vote yesterday, and now know they are not in a position to obtain any legislation making another AEF possible or authorize any moving of selectees outside the Western Hemisphere.

All Congressmen I talked with agreed that our moral victory yesterday very decidedly has succeeded in *slowing up the interventionists*. And we without doubt put those Congressmen who voted for the war measure in a *terrible spot with their constituents*. Mr. Mundt suggested the AFC should encourage people to write to their Representatives who voted wrong on this issue and *ask them for an accounting*, and demand that they let the people, and particularly the writers, know *if their vote means they favor intervention and further steps toward a shooting war* and the sacrificing of the sons of their constituents, etc. By taking full advantage of this unique situation in which these Congressmen find themselves, *we should get them so committed to their constituents that most of them will never dare to want to vote for future war* legislation!

DOCUMENT 111

Samuel B. Pettengill to R. Douglas Stuart, Jr.
August 13, 1941

I will repeat what I said over the phone and send copy to General Wood. I think the no-war people got all out of the situation which they had any chance to expect. In my judgment it is far better for the draft to be extended by one vote than to be defeated by one vote. If the latter had happened the pro-war press and the other agencies for molding public opinion would have gone hysterical. Further, it would have tempted the war party to create an incident which would so arouse public opinion as to force Congress to knuckle to their will. As it is, the no-war party suffered none of these risks, but on the other hand, have made an impressive showing of their strength. I think it definitely postpones our getting into the war, and may have a profound influence upon peace. In short, I consider it a tremendous triumph for our point of view which the Committee and other peace organizations have developed. If Mr. Roosevelt rides through the stop-look-listen sign he does so at his peril. Rather than discourage your members it ought to encourage them. It is a victory in disguise, and a very great victory at that.

It is my judgment from what was said publicly and what members told me privately, that what made this a hairline decision is the Administration getting into bed with Stalin. That, of course, happened since the lease-lend bill was passed and requires reappraisal of the whole policy of the bill. Members of the deep South are particularly fierce in their denunciation in the alliance with Russia because of its effect upon the negro and labor situation. As an illustration, there have been fifteen or more serious sex crimes in Washington since the first of the year. As one southern congress-man told me, Washington is the only capitol in the world where a white woman is not safe. They believe the "coddling" of Communism in high circles here in Washington is partly responsible. I deeply trust no race issue will flare up. Nevertheless, these feelings exist and are factors in the political thinking of southern Congressmen which now are dampening their enthusiasm for war. Aid to Britain was one thing, but in the South at least, the Administration has made a mistake on the Russian alliance.

DOCUMENT 112

John T. Flynn to R. Douglas Stuart, Jr.
August 4, 1941

First on the question of speaking. After much travail we have now gotten our headquarters in pretty good shape so that I bother very little with the administrative detail. Bliss is doing a good job and I can now content myself with daily reports from three or four people and thus keep my finger on what is going on. Moreover we are getting things done. We have been working on our memberships and today we have had the largest mail since the Madison Square Garden meeting. Having brought things to this pass, I now feel that I have more time to devote to the propaganda side of the job. I do not mean publicity—I mean propaganda. And that is a full-time job. I do not, for the time being, therefore, want to absent myself from that as I believe it is critical and much the most important thing we have to do. This gives me time to think about plans and I do not see how I can do this and give to speaking the immense time that it requires. It isn't just making the speech—it is the time it takes to go to a place and come back. So I think you better leave me out of the speaking business for the time being at least.

About the research program, I have gotten along I think beyond my expectations with that. The movie side of it is complete and we have already moved. Here is the program: A. Wheeler sounded off in the Senate on Thursday, denouncing the movies. B. Nye delivered a speech over the radio Friday night which we prepared as part of this drive. He had a big hook-up and I hope you heard it. In any case, I am sending you a copy. C. Friday afternoon Bennett Clark and Nye jointly offered a resolution in the Senate for an investigation of war propaganda in the movies and radio. The plan here is to have this referred to Wheeler's Interstate Commerce Committee. This has been done. Wheeler is appointing Worth Clark, Tobey and Nye a committee to hold hearings on the resolution. We'll present the case that way, getting the benefit of the publicity, and we plan to summon the movie moguls to Washington. Whether we can force them to come in the absence of funds and whether or not they will come voluntarily we do not know. But in any case, it will obtain our objective in focusing attention on the movies and on them. D. We are sending out Nye's speech to all daily and weekly newpapers. We plan a feature story illustrated which we want to send with mats to small papers and weeklies. E. Meantime we will have several other senators and congressmen sound off on the subject. I notice the *Chicago Tribune* gave Nye's speech a good play on Saturday morning. I rushed that speech to them by air-mail Friday and was delighted to see it got to them in time.

In addition to all this of course we have a similar job ready on the radio which we will handle much the same way.

The third phase is to attack the British propaganda penetration, British nationals, the British embassy, the British writers of books and magazine articles, lumping it altogether. We are going to use names always.

Following this we will attack some of the organizations which have been acting as gestapos to supply commentators and others with the calumnities [*sic*] they have been using. There is a whole lot more to this which I cannot put down here. But I think if we keep this rolling it will soon begin to have its effect. To get this material in a hurry has been difficult and has taken an immense amount of time and I plan to go on adding to the material and therefore suggest that everything dealing with this that comes your way be sent along to me.

I honestly feel that I am more service with this sort of thing than by making speeches. It is a whole lot more fun to make speeches, but this is important. Besides we have great plans for beginning next month for widening the circle of our appeal here in the neighborhood.

By the way, I heard your radio speech Friday night and I thought it was excellent, in good taste and well-delivered.

DOCUMENT 113

Samuel E. Romer, Writers Anti-War Bureau, to Sidney Hertzberg
Memo on Network Commentators
December 6, 1940

Network Commentators: The characteristic common to all network commentators except, perhaps, Boake Carter, is an underlying acceptance of the Administration's foreign policy of aid to Britain. Most of them, however, reported the news from abroad without any obvious propaganda.

The most obvious interventionist of the lot is Dorothy Thompson (MBS, Sunday, 8:45 P.M.) who attracts not only her own following but the audience of the "American Forum of the Air" which precedes her on the network. Raymond Gram Swing (MBS, Monday through Friday, 10:00 P.M.) is far more factual; his commentary is, it seems, mainly devoted to minimizing the chances for British victory without American aid. Wythe Williams (MBS, Tuesday and Thursday, 8:00; Sunday, 7:45) harps on the same subject, except that he bolsters his opinions with facts from "confidential sources." Elmer Davis' daily news summary (CBS, 8:55–9:00 P.M.) is usually devoted to factual presentation of the day's foreign news; his 15 minute broadcast (CBS, Saturday, 6:30 P.M.) is, however, much more propagandistic—in the broadcast heard, for instance, he characterized General Wood as a "member of a group which does not like to be called appeasers" and spoke of the Johnson Act as "written under entirely different circumstances." H. V. Kaltenborn (NBC, Blue, Saturday at 7:45; Sunday at 3:15) is more factual in his presentation; nevertheless, he too builds his entire speech upon the assumption that our present foreign policy is correct.

Edwin C. Hill (CBS, Monday through Friday, 6:05–15 P.M.) is probably the least interventionist of that type of broadcaster who seeks only to dramatize and highlight the news. Others in the category are Lowell Thomas (NBC Red, Monday through Friday, 6:45 P.M.), Gabriel Heatter

(MBS, daily except Sunday and Tuesday, 9:00 P.M.), John B. Kennedy (NBC Red, Monday through Friday, 9:30–9:35 P.M.).

Arthur Hale (Confidentially yours, MBS, Mondays, Wednesdays, Fridays at 7:15 P.M.; Tuesday, Thursday and Saturday at 7:30 P.M.) devoted his broadcast to the recital of "confidential information" that betrays neither interventionist nor non-interventionist sentiment. Boake Carter (MBS, Mondays, Wednesdays, Saturdays at 8:30 P.M.) is probably the only commentator who disagrees with the Administration's foreign policy; this is discernible in his willingness to tackle such controversial issues as feeding the occupied countries, etc.

MBS is sponsoring a news sustaining feature. Harold M. Fleming (MBS, Saturday, 9:15 P.M.) is a review from the business man's point of view. His first broadcast did not reveal either interventionist or non-interventionist sentiment.

The two Washington columnists Pearson and Allen, both ardently interventionist in their daily newspaper column, participate in a dual commentary over NBC Red, Sundays, 7:00 P.M. The broadcast heard did not betray any particular anti-interventionist views. This program is evidently sponsored by the United States of Brazil which raises the interesting question of whether the two columnists are registered with the State Department as foreign agents.

No report is available on the Washington political analysts, Fulton Lewis, Jr. (MBS), Albert Warner (CBS) and John Vandercook (NBC).

Recommendations: That commentators with non-interventionist leanings be given continuous material to aid them in the presentation of a fair picture, and further that the more strident pro-interventionist commentators (particularly Thompson, Pearson and Allen, Davis, Swing) be watched carefully for serious breaches. If such cases occur, I would recommend that representations be made not only to the networks but to the sponsoring companies.

Local Commentators: At least eleven commentators on local radio stations were heard and the following analyses were offered:

Maurice C. Dreicer (WINS, Monday through Friday, 9:15 A.M.) is a professional "Two sides to a question" commentator. Nevertheless, he showed non-interventionist sentiments in insisting that the usual questions "Shall We Aid England?" be more correctly worded, "How Much Shall We Risk by Aiding England?"

George H. Combs, Jr. (WHN, daily except Sunday, 7:30 P.M.) is usually factual. When he does express an opinion, it is mildly interventionist.

Lisa Sergio (WQXR, Monday through Friday, 10:00–10:30 P.M.) is mildly interventionist, especially anti-Fascist. I would suggest that Miss Sergio be placed on the mailing list of non-interventionist organizations; she evidently tries very hard to give an unbiased opinion of events.

Estelle Sternberger (WQXR, Monday and Thursday, 5:00) is mildly non-interventionist, although for aid to England.

Quincy Howe (WQXR, Mondays, Wednesday, Fridays, 9:00 P.M.) is strongly non-interventionist although accepting the Administration foreign policy of aid to England.

Sidney Mosely (WMCA, Monday through Friday, 1:00–1:05 P.M.) is an open British propagandist. He is introduced as a "distinguished British author and commentator on international affairs." He makes no secret of his desire for intervention; is bitter in his attacks on "American appeasers."

Johannes Steel (WMCA, Daily, 7:45 P.M.) is also openly interventionist.

Burnett Hershey (WMCA, Monday through Friday, 8:45 P.M.) is the mildest of the three WMCA commentators; he too however is strongly interventionist.

Bryce Oliver (WEVD, Tuesdays, Thursdays, Fridays at 9:45 P.M.) is strongly interventionist. He also speaks on a Latin-American commentary over WMCA Thursdays at 7:00 P.M.

James Waterman Wise (WEVD, Sundays, Tuesdays, Thursday, 10:55 P.M.) is strongly interventionist.

Rev. William C. Kernon of Newark, conductor of the weekly half-hour "Free Speech Forum" (WEVD, Tuesdays, 9:00 P.M.), is an impassioned, emotional speaker, ardently interventionist. His subject was "More Aid for Britain." This time is evidently commercial, paid for by the contributions from his audience.

General Recommendations on Local Stations: Stations WEVD and WMCA are not only unfair in their choice of commentators, but as reference to previous sections of this report will show, generally interventionist in their conduct. I would strongly recommend that all attempts be made to secure proper time to reply upon each possible occasion and further that a careful check be kept of programs to both stations for a period of at least a month for presentations to the Federal Communications Commission in an endeavor to secure a revocation of the broadcasting licenses for partial, biased public disservice.

Network Features: There are regular features which usually do not concern themselves with commentary but which offer regular audiences.

Typical are such features as the semi-official "Farm and Home Hour" broadcast Monday through Saturday over NBC Red from 12:30 P.M.–1:15 P.M. If possible Congressmen should be induced to speak over this program. Another similar program is the "Report to the Nation" prepared by CBS and presented over that network Saturdays at 6:00 P.M. The various women's programs presented during the day offer opportunities for proper contact work; for example, the William Allen White Committee has Madge Evans, an actress and one of the sponsors of the "Star Spangled Hall," appear as a guest of Adelaide Hawley, a CBS women's commentator, Tuesday morning at 8:45 A.M.

General Recommendations: I would strongly urge that non-interventionist groups take the offensive in attempting to secure sustaining time (either through their own auspices or making use of regular sustaining features). Another feature which would be relatively inexpensive would be the preparation of a 15-minute recorded program featuring Hollywood and Broadcast stars and a well-known person as commentator to be offered free to local non-network stations.

It is, however, most important that a careful check be kept of the networks to watch for interventionist programs which raise controversial issues and which, therefore, are opportunities to get time in reply. Once this policy is expressed, I am certain that both the networks and the commentators would be much more careful in expressing such sentiments.

DOCUMENT 114

Henry W. Hobson to Robert E. Wood
October 21, 1941

You have promised America that "if this country is involved in an undeclared shooting war with Germany or any other country . . . you will find Americans like myself . . . will be at their posts of duty in the service of this country."

Live up to that promise. That time is here. Our country today is at war. The Nazi rattlesnakes in the Atlantic are uncoiled. The shooting has begun. Already nine of our vessels have been struck. Already American boys are missing in the line of duty. Dissension now, General Wood, is aiding our common enemy; it is assisting our defeat.

America First may have begun as an honest illusion, based on the false hope that these United States could ignore the world-wide struggle for freedom going on in every ocean, on every continent.

That mirage has faded. Today America First has become the first fascist party in this nation's history. Its most active recruiting agent is Deutscher-Weckruf und Beobachter, official publication of the German-American Bund.

Its only spokesmen are ex-Colonel Charles A. Lindbergh and a similar handful of dealers in the Nazi technique of terror. Its only substantial backing in a nation that has dedicated itself to the defeat of Hitlerism is found in the heiling minority organized by the Rev. Charles E. Coughlin, the Ku Klux Klan, the bitter group of disappointed, administration-hating politicians who would sell our nation short for a brief moment of Nazi power, and the paid agents of Hitler imported here to disrupt, disunite and mislead most Americans.

On the fingers of one hand can be counted those in your movement who still believe any liberty can be maintained in a world overwhelmed by the Nazi perversions of decency. They are wrong. The symbols of their error are to be seen throughout Europe today.

Nazism was born in the diseased mind of a street corner orator who, with a rag-tag group of degenerates and hoodlums, appealed to business as "safe," to labor as "revolutionary," to the great middle class as "stable."

It is none of these. Those who mistakenly believed it in 15 nations today are in the same concentration camps as the Jews, Negroes, the honest labor leaders, the democratic business men. Hitler makes no distinctions. All conflagration of civilization begun by him destroys all alike.

As a military man, General Wood, as one who served this country bravely during the last war, it is time for you to disband your organ of Nazi terror and hate and join with our liberty-loving brothers in all parts of the world, in the fight for the reality that freedom must become.

Yes, shooting has begun. The nation looks to you to keep your word.

DOCUMENT 115

Chester Bowles to Sidney Hertzberg
January 16, 1941

I think your idea of a New Deal Committee to help keep the President out of war would be really swell if you could get a few well-known people. Unfortunately, I simply have to pull in my neck—or at least not push it out any further.

One of the real signs of the age through which we are living is the complete intolerance and fanaticism of a lot of supposedly sensible people. And, sorry to say, several of our clients feel very emphatic against the stand that I have taken. One of them went so far as to take me out to luncheon the other day to warn me about the dangers that he thought I was facing.

In that way advertising is one helluva business—you never can call your soul your own. And whether you like it or not you are usually more or less owned by the clients for whom you work.

Our clients happen to be swell people right down the line. But as I say their feelings on this subject, in two or three cases, are rather violent.

Aren't there a good many labor people who really could do a job for you on this? What, after all, is the matter with these labor leaders, many of whom, I am sure, feel the way we do and who, for the most part, are afraid to open their mouths? Also, why don't the heads of the farm groups have something to say?

It is my hunch that the producing groups in the country, very broadly speaking—the manufacturers, the workers, the farmers—are, in general, opposed to war which is favored, again very broadly speaking, largely by intellectuals, financially-minded people, university presidents, ministers, etc. etc.

But if I am right on this, isn't it time the labor leaders and the farm leaders stepped forward and had something to say?

Why, for instance, aren't they being called before the Congressional Committee? Is it because they are afraid of criticizing Roosevelt to whom they owe so much on other scores?

I just heard yesterday that Bob Hutchins is really going to cut loose on the radio on this whole subject of war, strongly attacking the interventionist's point of view. I talked to Bill Benton about it and it sounds as though it might be hot. I understand a copy of the speech is being sent to me.

So far as radio people are concerned, I tried to find some suggestions to send to Bob Stuart, but I couldn't locate anyone who sounded any good.

If you will let me know what you can afford to pay and the kind of people you want, I shall try to think of someone for publicity and research work. It is pretty tough to find good people who aren't now in good jobs.

DOCUMENT 116

Chester Bowles to R. Douglas Stuart, Jr.
September 19, 1941

I really don't think this statement by the America First Committee on the Lindbergh speech is a good one. In my mind it doesn't answer the issue raised in this speech.

This statement implies that only the war mongers could possibly draw any anti-Semitic deductions from what Lindbergh said at Des Moines, and I don't believe that this is quite correct.

I know that his remarks sounded definitely anti-Semitic to me. And I also know at least half a dozen other people who are non-interventionists who feel as I do.

Norman Thomas is not a war monger and yet he was sufficiently alarmed about Lindbergh's statement to make a statement of his own criticizing what Lindbergh had to say.

I don't think the article which you have suggested will help to clear the problem, because you simply deny something that I, and other people including Norman Thomas, feel was implied.

I believe that the Committee should take the stand that it cannot be responsible for every individual statement which its members or its representatives make. None of the speeches are gone over by the Committee before they are made. Everyone is free to say what he thinks and believes.

In the opinion of the Committee, Colonel Lindbergh is by no means anti-Semitic. But if he has said things which many people (a large percentage of them perfectly sincere) believe are anti-Semitic, it is up to the Colonel to answer them—for the Committee cannot be responsible.

Naturally if any member of the America First Committee consistently took a stand which was at variance with the principles of free speech, tolerance, good Americanism, etc., he would be asked to resign. But the America First Committee maintains full confidence in Colonel Lindbergh's sincerity and his tolerance of all races and groups.

If his remarks at Des Moines were misinterpreted, the Committee is certain that he can and will at some future time clarify his ideas beyond question, etc.

I really believe, Bob, that the statement as it now stands will make a good many people rather mad, as it implies that all of them who didn't like what Lindbergh said are war mongers or character-smearers. This certainly is not true of Norman Thomas, myself and lots of people, as you well know.

I have the greatest admiration for Colonel Lindbergh. I believe he is one of the truly great citizens of this age. And I believe that some day, perhaps not so far distant, the American people will recognize him as such. If I believed that he was anti-Semitic in even the slightest degree, he would suffer drastically in my estimation.

My own belief is that his statement last Thursday night was simply poorly worded, tactless and in bad judgment. I believe he could readily clear it up the next time he speaks. But, as I suggested above, I don't think that this statement by the Committee helps matters at all. In fact, I believe that it will be irritating to a great many people and hence harmful.

DOCUMENT 117

Frederick J. Libby to R. Douglas Stuart, Jr. September 22, 1941

Norman Thomas tells us that Colonel Lindbergh's speech on September 11 has dwarfed even the President's war speech in popular interest and discussion. Because of the general feeling that it has liberated dangerous anti-Semitic forces in the country I joined with others in approving the statement which the Governing Committee of the Keep America Out of War Congress issued and which was published in the Sunday papers. [The statement declared that the KAOWC "deeply regrets and disagrees with Mr. Lindbergh's implication that the Americans of Jewish extraction or religion are a separate group, apart from the rest of the American people, or that they react as a separate group, or that they are unanimously for our entrance into the European war."] I have not received a copy of our original text and will enclose a clipping from yesterday's New York Herald-Tribune, which contains, I think, practically all of it.

For your private information—and I am enclosing a copy of this letter for you to forward to Colonel Lindbergh, if you will—the twenty-five people present, including four Jews, agreed without dissent that Lindbergh's speech was not anti-Semitic. There seemed to be general consent in the group to the position strongly stated by Norman Thomas with my support that Lindbergh himself is not anti-Semitic and that his wish to save the Jews from post-war victimization is one of his reasons, exactly as he stated, for wanting to prevent our involvement in the war and the intolerance that would undoubtedly follow the war. But we agreed also that we must do what we can to prevent anti-Semitism from becoming more open and aggressive as the result of the speech. This is what we have attempted to accomplish by our statement.

You will also recognize the significance of the fact that the statement was written by one of the Jewish members of our committee and was adopted in preference to two other less balanced drafts that had been prepared by other committee members.

Turning now to the future, I am profoundly grateful to your Committee for placing Lindbergh immediately in Fort Wayne, Indiana, for another speech. Lindbergh, Nye and Wheeler are the three chief leaders of the whole anti-war movement. We all must stand by them. When I compare their caliber with that of the Senate leader of the interventionists, Claude Pepper, I realize afresh how fortunate we are.

Senator Gillette, so I understand, told Ruth Sarles that "for the first time we are on the defensive." I have just been talking with Ruth and suggested that a new situation has been created by the exploitation of the issue of anti-Semitism by the interventionists to smear all three of our leaders. It is nothing new and yet it permits our friends, I think, to take the offensive again.

Yesterday's New York Times on Page 10, under the heading "Pecora [Ferdinand Pecora, New York State supreme court justice] Rebukes Hoover on Russia," reported a two-day conference of "fourteen civic and labor organizations" which adopted a resolution described as follows in the report:

A third resolution, as originally put forward by Dr. Frank Kingdon [chairman of the N.Y. chapter, Committee to Defend America by Aiding the Allies and Fight for Freedom; former president, University of Newark], chairman of the sponsoring committee, denounced Senator Nye and Charles A. Lindbergh for "introducing Nazi techniques" by an "appeal to anti-Semitic prejudices." On a motion from the floor the resolution was amended to include the name of Senator Wheeler.

"PM," as you probably know, has been making daily capital of the incident and all the interventionist organizations have passed resolutions that have gone far beyond the truth. Don't you think that it would help to settle things if one of your conservative speakers on the radio—or perhaps Senator Wheeler—would make a judicial reference to the facts of the situation? He would point out on the one hand that Lindbergh, Nye and Wheeler are not anti-Semitic and that the last thing they want to do is to promote racial prejudices. He should say, on the other hand, that the current distortion of the facts by the interventionists, in order to smear the three recognized leaders of the anti-war movement, is a plain exploitation of the Jews for the promotion of interventionism and is bound to prove a boomerang.

To put the issue in another way, these interventionists are trying to befog the main issue, which is whether or not America shall join in this war. It is not Semitism or anti-Semitism. Nor is the naming of the owners of the leading moving picture companies to be called "anti-Semitism," as Mr. Willkie would apparently have us think.

Moveover, Americans with German names and of German parentage should not be singled out for separate treatment by the interventionists as has been too frequently done in reports of America First meetings, any more than Americans with Jewish names should be singled out for separate treatment.

Actually we have leaned over backwards to omit the President's Jewish advisers, such as Justice Frankfurter [Felix Frankfurter, associate justice of the Supreme Court] and Judge Rosenman [Samuel I. Rosenman, jurist and presidential adviser], among leaders of the war party in order to avoid even the appearance of anti-Semitism. We have the right to expect that the interventionist organizations will be equally careful not to brand "Americans with German names or German accent" as agents of Hitler.

Please forward the enclosed carbon of this letter to Colonel Lindbergh and express to him my undiminished appreciation of the magnificent work he is doing and will do to keep our country from further involvement in this war. Again I say, we must not lose sight of the fact that that is our main job, from which nothing must turn us aside.

DOCUMENT 118

Teletype messages between John T. Flynn, Robert E. Wood, and R. Douglas Stuart, Jr. September 12, 1941

Flynn to Wood and Stuart—I am profoundly disturbed about the speech of Col. Lindbergh last nite. It seems incredible to me that Col. Lindbergh without consulting anyone literally committed the America First movement to an open attack upon the Jews. The newspapers have not yet gotten in touch with me here, but I cannot for the life of me think of anything to say when they do reach me. But one thing is certain, we cannot have the Colonel playing a lone hand as he has been doing. I thought his speech at Oklahoma City was a most unfortunate one, but the one in Des Moines might almost be fatal to us. Certainly someone must talk to the Colonel and make him understand that his prominence in this movement is such that a statement by him is far more serious than one by a minor speaker, and that he ought not to embark upon any new form of attack without getting the collective judgment of others. In view of this speech, I think it would be a grave mistake to have Col. Lindbergh talk in Washington. Please let me hear of your reactions at once.

Stuart to Flynn—I agree with your general principle that on matters of major policy Lindbergh should consult with key members of National Committee, although his judgment is usually extremely sound. The reactions of others such as yourself and General Wood can avoid costly errors. I also feel that the Des Moines address might have been handled differently. But notwithstanding this, I am convinced what was said had to be said, and that it behooves us all to close ranks and stand fast with Colonel Lindbergh at a time when any evidence of dissention in our ranks would tend to heighten the attack made upon us. It is terribly important to back him up. I think the General would be interested in your reactions. He can be reached at Fisher's Island % N.A.M. In closing, urge you go the limit to support Colonel Lindbergh's stand even tho' you may want to qualify.

Flynn to Stuart—I am writing Colonel Lindbergh today very freely and frankly my criticisms of his speech. As to closing ranks and standing firm, I understand the necessity of having no split. Therefore, I can think of nothing to do but avoid the newspapers. However, there is going to be no ducking this issue. It has been rising in intensity, and here in the East, we are right on the firing line. I am at my wits' end what to say. But you can gamble that I am not going to say to anybody that I am behind Colonel Lindbergh in that statement. I think Colonel Lindbergh has got to be made to understand that he cannot drag us into the No Man's land of this debate on any issue that he chooses to adopt. I think you have no idea how much concern there is here about the whole thing, including his ill-advised statement at Oklahoma City that we may have to fight the British before this thing is done. I do not agree with you that this thing had to be said— but certainly if it had to be said, Colonel Lindbergh was the last man to say it. It is all the more tragic, in view of the immense patience and industry we have been going through to bring this issue to light in an entirely different way—and just as that is blossoming into almost undreamed of success, Colonel Lindbergh has to "blab" the issue out and hand it on America First. This is just another one of those incidents which is going to get this committee into deep water, and I want to make a very formal protest now against any repetition of this sort of thing. I will have nothing more to do with this movement, if I have got to be put in a position of supporting any course of action of policy of so questionable a nature without being even so much as asked about it. And then told I have to stand behind the Colonel when he does it. On the movie issue, I didn't take a step until I had consulted all the Senators in Washington at a formal meeting and talked it over fully with you and Colonel Lindbergh. We feel that we dare not put our street speakers out tonight or any night until we can find our way out of this fog. We are all completely confused and do not know what to do.

DOCUMENT 119

Thomas S. Hammond to Robert E. Wood
September 16, 1941

I'm sorry I can't be at the meeting on Thursday, which, I presume, you are calling because of the shooting taking place as a result of Lindbergh's Des Moines talk. It is necessary that I be in Washington attending a Directors' Meeting of the United States Chamber of Commerce.

Let me say right off: it is inconceivable to me that the America First Committee will do other than support, without reservation, the statements of Lindbergh as they referred to the three groups pushing us on to war.

Some people say there is no Jewish problem. That may, or may not, be so. However, if the people of this country think that the Jews, as a race, are having a prejudiced and disproportionate influence on today's affairs—then that problem does exist, whether certain individuals or groups think so or not.

From where I sit, I see an enormous amount of writing—books, pamphlets, articles—on this Jewish situation. I hear of it in conversation—time and again. From all this, my only conclusion can be that, to many people, the Jews do constitute a definite problem, and a threat to our peace. If this is so, then it is much better to bring about public discussion, rather than a whispering campaign.

To those who would criticize Lindbergh, I say this: an attitude of people which protects un-American activities under a cloak of fear of creating a racial issue is as dangerous to the welfare of our country, and the maintenance of its peace, as the most subversive acts of any fifth columnist.

Lindbergh has again shown that courage for which he is famous. His handling of the subject—the dignity of his discussion—and his evident sympathy for the very people of whom he was speaking—makes his speech rank with me as one of the epics of present day eloquence. And true to history is his warning to the Jew: that should war come, its aftermath would have most serious consequences to his race. That statement should be regarded by them as a real service to their very existence.

DOCUMENT 120

"A Story of America First"
Ruth Sarles

The National Committee met in Chicago on September 18 with the following members present: General Wood, Dr. A. J. Carlson, [physiologist, University of Chicago], Mrs. Bennett Champ Clark, Mrs. Janet Ayer Fairbank [vice chairman, AFC; formerly prominent Democratic leader, novelist, and suffragette], John T. Flynn, Clay Judson [Chicago attorney, firm of Wilson and McIlvaine; former president, Chicago Council of Foreign Relations], Colonel Charles Lindbergh, Mrs. Alice Roosevelt Longworth [daughter of President Theodore Roosevelt and widow of House Speaker Nicholas Longworth],

George N. Peek [former president, Moline Plow Company; former administrator of Agricultural Adjustment Administration], Amos R. E. Pinchot [New
York attorney and reformer], R. Douglas Stuart, Jr.

Colonel Lindbergh had written the speech six months before he delivered it, believing that sooner or later its subject must be brought out in the
open for frank discussion. To him, the question was not, "Are you or are you
not anti-Semitic?" but rather, "Is there a problem?" He had made the
speech on September 11 because he believed the country was close to war,
and he felt he must define the problem before war clamped down on
freedom of speech. At the September 18 meeting, he proposed to the
National Committee that he issue a public statement making clear that at
Des Moines he had spoken for himself alone and not for America First.

These were some of the considerations voiced by members of the
National Committee during the eight hour discussion:

1. America First had never followed the practice of asking that its
speakers submit their manuscripts in advance—it was clear from the outset
that men and women who spoke on America First platforms would differ
among themselves in their analyses of the problem of keeping the country
out of war. The situation would have been intolerable if every speech had to
be approved in advance. This tacit—if unspoken—agreement implied that if
America First had enough confidence in its speakers to sponsor them
without prior approval of their speeches, it would stand by what was said.
No one of the National Committee or staff had been apprised officially or
unofficially in advance of the delivery of the Des Moines speech or its
contents.

2. The text of Colonel Lindbergh's remarks was not anti-Semitic; he had
not criticized the Jews on grounds of race or religion; he had not advocated
discrimination of any kind against the Jews; his statement:

> It is not difficult to understand why Jewish people desire the overthrow of Nazi
> Germany. The persecution they suffered in Germany would be sufficient to
> make bitter enemies of any race. . . . I am not attacking the Jewish or the British
> people. Both races I admire. But I am saying that the leaders of both the British
> and the Jewish races, for reasons which are as understandable from their
> viewpoint as they are inadvisable from ours, for reasons which are not Ameri-
> can, wish to involve us in the war. We cannot blame them for looking out for
> what they believe to be their own interests, but we also must look out for ours.
> We cannot allow the natural passions and prejudices of other peoples to lead our
> country to destruction . . .

showed complete understanding of any Jewish desire for the crushing of the
persecutors of their race. There was no more impropriety in saying that
Jewish people were interventionist than in applying the same term to the
President or the British, or the Dutch. No group in a democracy is entitled
to immunity from criticism. It was hard to believe that any group in America

could be regarded as occupying a position where its attitude on any public question should be unmentionable, and that anyone who did mention them should be accused of trying to incite prejudice. Colonel Lindbergh did not create anti-Semitism in the 1941 struggle between interventionists and non-interventionists. He had described it and personally disavowed it.

3. The barrage of criticism of Colonel Lindbergh's speech in general was not leveled at the Colonel's statements of facts, but *at his saying them*. The Colonel's critics might have made a case on the basis of fact since there was disagreement as to the proportionate number of Jews who were for intervention. On the one hand, Dr. Jerome Frank, eminent Jewish author [judge, U.S. Court of Appeals; author of *Save America First: How to Make Our Democracy Work* (1938)], in his *Saturday Evening Post* article of December 6, 1941 ["Red, White and Blue Herring"], declared that Jews in America were no more nor no less interventionist than the United States population as a whole:

> . . . the views of the overwhelming majority of Jews concerning intervention are not Jewish. Their views on that subject are American . . . under the impact of the amazing Nazi victories the attitudes of many Americans have changed. Just so have those of many American Jews.

On the other hand, Dr. Anton J. Carlson, widely known, much respected professor of physiology at the University of Chicago said:

> I have seen no statistics on the question, but of the Jews of my acquaintance 90 to 95 percent are for United States participation in the present war, particularly since hostilities started between Russia and Germany. Before that time many Jews of Russian extraction were hardened opponents towards entrance into this war.

The one criticism of Colonel Lindbergh's speech on the basis of fact that cropped up more than once was his statement regarding "their large ownership and influence in our motion pictures, our press, our radio, and our government." It was noted that he had not dealt in percentages, that a distinction could be made between quantitative and qualitative influence.

4. It was regretted that more Jewish people had not spoken out in opposition to intervention. America First had steadily believed that a sizeable proportion of the Jews were non-interventionists; it had sought Jewish spokesmen of the non-interventionist point of view. If the quarrel with Colonel Lindbergh's remarks was that their *effect* was anti-Semitic, in all fairness should it not also be said that the failure of Jewish leaders to speak out against intervention had the *effect* of implying that Jews were not against intervention.

Several times stories were recalled of Jewish patriots of 1776 like Robert Morris and Haym Solomon who had identified themselves for all time with the clear course of American independence. They had stripped themselves to finance the war of the Revolution so as to achieve an independence for America.

5. The interventionist press and organization leaders were making capital of the incident in order to discredit the entire non-interventionist movement. They were exploiting the Jews for the purpose of promoting the interventionist point of view.

A prominent interventionist lecturer was reported to have said privately in Washington:

> You know this uproar on our side against Lindbergh on account of his Des Moines speech about the Jews is largely synthetic—a lot of our crowd has been saying the same thing as Lindbergh.

The belief that interventionists were taking advantage of the situation was encouraged by the knowledge of specific anti-Semitic actions by individuals connected with interventionist organizations.

"One hundred clubs and hotel foyers," said the *Christian Century* editorially, "rang with denouncement of Lindbergh on the morning after his Des Moines speech—clubs and hotels barring their doors to Jews."

DOCUMENT 121

Norman Thomas to R. Douglas Stuart, Jr. September 29, 1941

Thanks for your letter and its enclosure, the letter to the Chapter Chairmen.

That is an excellent piece of work, I congratulate you on it, it ought to do a lot of good at a time when good of that sort is necessary.

Unfortunately I can't say so much for the public statement released to the press. It would almost have been better to make no statement at all. Every sort of group thinks that the repudiation of anti Semitism in it was perfunctory. That's true, not only of your opponents, but of your wrong sort of friends. I hope that Col. Lindbergh can say something that will help the situation when he next speaks, but I'm not too sanguine.

You see it isn't a question merely of the honesty and directness of one's motives, as they might be understood in normal times; it is a question of one's skill and willingness to face abnormal situations and to deal with them so as to do the maximum of good and minimum of harm for one's own cause. Good intentions aren't enough. Whatever may be true of the future, at present when we need some figure around to rally our forces in Washington, and the country, Lindbergh isn't the man and there is no one else in his place.

It is still necessary to plan the best campaign that can be planned to awake the public partly in resignation of the belief that you can have a war without much shooting.

If General Wood and Mr. Villard [Oswald Garrison Villard, journalist and editor], who I believe if his health permits will be in Washington this week for the K.A.O.W., can really work out a plan and get Senators and representatives to back them up, something may yet be accomplished. One great speech in the Senate at a time when we had been led to expect it and our forces organized to give it publicity, it might yet be a clarion call. We have good Senators, but not one of them is precisely the man we want. The Borah [William E. Borah (R-Idaho)] of younger days or the elder La Follette might have done it. Perhaps Bob La Follette could be persuaded to do it as well as anyone else. Other Senators ought to be given specific jobs to push.

DOCUMENT 122

One-Man War

"Did you know that the President's 'shoot on sight' speech initiates an undeclared war, without the consent of the American people?"
No. 22, September 13, 1941

The Congress shall have power. . . . To declare War, . . . and make rules concerning captures on land and water; . . . (United States Constitution, Art. I, Sec. 8.)

. . . Shooting means war. (President Roosevelt, as quoted in *Congressional Record*, March 21, 1941, p. 2765.)

That means, very simply and clearly, that our patrolling vessels and planes will protect all merchant ships—not only American ships but ships of any flag—engaged in commerce in our defensive waters. . . . The orders which I have given as Commander-in-Chief to the United States Army and Navy are to carry out that policy—at once. (President Roosevelt, in Sept. 11, 1941 speech, reported in *New York Times*, Sept. 12, 1941.)

Shoot on Sight

In his speech on September 11, 1941, President Roosevelt informed the nation that, without consultation with, or approval by, the Congress of the United States, he had ordered our naval and air patrols to clear all German and Italian warships from any waters considered vital to American defense, and had, in effect, ordered our armed forces to "shoot on sight." (*New York Times*, Sept. 12, 1941.) His asserted justification for this sudden move, admittedly involving danger of involvement in a "shooting war," arose out of the sinking of three merchant ships and attacks on two American warships.

"Simple Arithmetic"

There is not space to consider the many and curious inconsistencies in the President's speech. Note must be taken, however, of the lack of faith in the strength and ingenuity of America evidenced by the President's statement that we can survive only if the British Navy survives. That contention, coming curiously enough from the Commander-in-Chief of the Army and Navy, was based upon the claim that it is "simple arithmetic" that an Axis-dominated world can outbuild us in shipping capacity. The arithmetic is not "simple"; it is inaccurate. For Hanson W. Baldwin, Annapolis graduate and noted military and naval expert of the *New York Times*, has pointed out in the *Reader's Digest* that

> Our navy is strong enough now, and more than strong enough, to face the combined navies of the totalitarian powers. . . . We need not fear being outbuilt in a naval race, even should Hitler be able to turn all Europe and England to the task.

Pointing out that the *total* shipbuilding capacity of Germany, the occupied lands, the Axis satellites, and Britain together equal 5,700,000 tons per year, Mr. Baldwin demonstrates that we can outdo that challenge, for in 1941–1943 we shall build 9,000,000 tons of merchant shipping alone. Moreover,

> And simultaneously we are pushing forward a naval building program just about equal to the combined programs of *all the rest of the world including the British Empire*.
>
> Furthermore, we can expand shipbuilding incomparably more than can Europe. . . . Shipbuilding is limited by steel and armor production. One

American steel company will this year produce more steel than all of Germany; our expanded capacity soon will outmatch all the rest of the world. Our armor production, steadily increasing, is believed already to exceed that of England plus that of Germany. (*Reader's Digest*, "What of the British Fleet," August, 1941, pages 1–2.)

The Real Reasons

But the more important criticisms of the President's speech are these: 1) shooting war is not justified; 2) it circumvents the spirit of the Neutrality Act and the Lease-Lend Law; 3) the doctrine which the President calls "freedom of the seas" is really "freedom to aid one country at war without interference from that country's enemies"; 4) it takes the war-making power away from Congress.

Robin Moor

Examination of the circumstances under which occurred the attacks upon American ships cited by the President demonstrates clearly that they fail utterly to justify participation in a "shooting war." The three merchant ships were the Robin Moor, the Steel Seafarer and the Sessa. The Robin Moor was sunk in the South Atlantic while carrying contraband to British South Africa, a country at war. Although there was no loss of life, the treatment of her passengers and crew was ruthless and unjustified. But 70% of her cargo consisted of items which were declared contraband of war under both the British and the German contraband lists in the current war, and even under the United States contraband list in the World War (see Did You Know, #1). A large part of the cargo consisted of motor vehicles and parts, which Secretary of State Hull conceded in the past were "essential war materials" (Borchard and Lage, *Neutrality for the United States*, page 321).

Steel Seafarer

The Steel Seafarer was sunk without loss of life in the Red Sea, some 12,000 miles from the United States, while carrying war supplies for Britain, a country at war (*New York Times*, Sept. 9, 1941). The ship was legally in the Red Sea only because President Roosevelt had revoked his earlier proclamation under the Neutrality Act declaring the Red Sea a war zone and forbidding American ships to travel there, and had allowed such travel on the stated ground that war conditions no longer existed there (*Federal Register*, April 12, 1941). While he did so in order to enable the shipment of supplies for British forces, he was unmistakably put on notice that shooting would probably continue in that region for some time to come (*New York Times*, May 10, 1941).

Sessa

The Sessa was not even sailing under the American flag when sunk. She was a Danish ship which had been taken over by the Maritime Commission, and had been transferred to the flag of Panama in order that she might be used to carry supplies into war zones in clear violation of the intent of the Neutrality Act (*New York Times*, Sept. 10, 1941). She was being operated under contract by an American firm, which was earning some of the "fool's gold" of war trade which the President once so vigorously denounced (Chautauqua address, August 14, 1936). She was sunk near Iceland, on her way there, while carrying supplies owned by the government of Iceland. Iceland is in the Eastern Hemisphere, and is occupied in part by British troops (*New York Times*, July 9, 1941). The one American member of her crew was lost. It should be recalled that between October 26, 1939, and January 31, 1941, 56 American ships were transferred to Panama registry in order that they might engage in war trade in clear violation of the intent of the Neutrality Act (Maritime Commission *Reports*). Many of those ships have been reported sunk in the course of the current war, without creating Presidential indignation.

The Greer

The attacks upon the destroyer Greer and an unnamed battleship (*New York Times*, Sept. 5 and 12, 1941) were of course unjustified. But those attacks arose because of the one-man policy pursued by the President of occupying Iceland (nearer to the heart of the European war zone than to the United States) and of keeping American troops there along with the British (see Did You Know, #7). That is a policy whose implementation requires the use of American naval vessels for patrol purposes in order to keep the surrounding waters clear. It is inevitable that they will come into conflict with Nazi warships which are seeking British ships in those waters, part of the Nazi-declared war zone (*New York Times*, March 26, 1941). Certainly these five attacks, resulting in no loss of American lives on any ship operating under the American flag, do not justify American participation in a "shooting" war.

Broken Promises

The President's policy is even more culpable in that it clearly violates the intent of the Neutrality Act and the Lease-Lend law. The President sought amendment of the Neutrality Act in 1939 in order to allow the sale of arms on a "cash and carry" basis to belligerent nations. In a special message on Sept. 21, 1939, he urged this change as a step towards peace and explained:

> I say this because with the repeal of the embargo this Government clearly and definitely will insist that American citizens and American ships keep away from

the immediate perils of the actual zones of conflict. . . . I believe that American merchant vessels should, so far as possible, be restricted from entering danger zones.

The Lease-Lend law was adopted to aid Britain, but it was the expressed intent of Congress that such aid was also to be on a "carry" basis. Title to goods given Britain under lease-lend were to be transferred here, so that American ships were kept out of the war zones (Sec. 3a(2)). The law expressly stated that lease-lend aid was not to authorize convoys (Sec. 3d). The country was also assured by the administration sponsors that the Lease-Lend law was not intended to repeal or affect the Neutrality Act (*Congressional Record*, March 8, 1941, 2112, 2116), and the law so provides (Sec. 3e).

Danger Through Subterfuge

The President has sought to use the national policy of aid short of war to Britain in order to circumvent the Neutrality Act. The "bridge of ships" across the Atlantic of which he frequently speaks, the occupation of Iceland chiefly for the purpose of enabling shipment of war supplies there in American ships, thence to be transshipped to British or other Allied ships (see Did You Know, #7) are steps which necessarily place American ships and citizens in danger zones. The naval and air patrols of the Atlantic waters which the President established in April, 1941 (*New York Times*, April 29, 1941) were designed less for actual American defense purposes than for the purpose of aiding British convoy shipments. Such patrols, because they give actual assistance and advice to British warships, have been denounced by one constitutional authority as unconstitutional "acts of war" (Henry Frazer, *Syracuse Post Standard*, May 11, 1941). They necessarily place American warships and American sailors and aviators in shooting zones. The widespread transfer of American ships to the flag of Panama, even State Department officials now admit, was done in order to circumvent the Neutrality Act and to allow those ships to travel in war zones (*Washington Times-Herald*, Sept. 13, 1941).

Convoys

Nor can the President's "shoot on sight" order be justified, as he claims, as necessary to protect "freedom of the seas." It must be recalled that American armed protection is to be given, not only to American ships, but also to the ships of any flag, and that the waters in which that protection is to be given extend to an undefined width (even to the Pacific Ocean), to any waters the President chooses to declare vital to our "defense." This would enable our fleet to give what amounts to "convoy protection" to British ships or the ships of any other allied nation, as well as American ships, carrying war supplies for Britain or Russia or China. It would enable American patrols even to convoy British ships right into English ports, since the President has stated that he did not feel that the Neutrality Law prevented American warships from entering the war zones he established under that law (*New York Times*, April 29, 1941).

Freedom of the Seas

What the President calls "freedom of the seas" is a misnomer. It is neither the "traditional American doctrine," nor any doctrine recognized in international law. What he asked in reality was the "freedom to aid at will one belligerent nation without danger of interference by the other belligerent"— a freedom which our own government and the British government have denied on past occasions, and which the British would be the first to reject now, if it were to their advantage.

Civil and World Wars

The historical examples cited by the President to justify his course were, as usual, inapposite. The use by Presidents Adams and Jefferson of the Navy to clear the seas of pirates was done to protect American shipping, not, as President Roosevelt would use the Navy, to protect ships of foreign nations and convoys. Much more important is the fact that the President failed to mention the Civil War and the World War—not to mention the Neutrality Act—and our abandonment of freedom of the seas in the current war. In the Civil War, the Union seized British ships which sought to run the Union blockade and to carry goods to the South (Borchard and Lage, *Neutrality for the United States* (1937), page 15). In the World War, despite merely formal protests made for the sake of the record, the Wilson Administration actually acquiesced in the British blockade and the all-embracing contraband list adopted by the British, which exposed American trade with the neutrals of Europe and even South America to the complete control of Britain and the Allies (Borchard and Lage, pages 34, 36, 39, 43, 61–62, 65, 72). Winston Churchill has admitted that Britain and her Allies rejected Wilson's Second Point for the "freedom of the seas," at the close of the World War (*The Aftermath* (1929), pages 103–104).

European War

The Neutrality Act, of course, limits our freedom of trade in time of war, and was adopted as an indication of strength, not weakness, in our desire to keep out of war. In the current war, despite another mild protest made for the sake of the record, we have again acquiesced in the British blockade and an even more-embracing contraband list. We have acquiesced in the British system of "navicerts," under which our shippers must submit their cargo lists to British agents—even if the cargo is destined for a neutral country—in order to minimize interference with a voyage by British warships. Now, we face a British system of "mailcerts," which amounts to a tax on American mail and operates on the same principle as the "navicerts" (*New York Times,* June 24, 1941). American ships carrying contraband to belligerent territory cannot claim exemption from visit and search, or even capture, by German ships, because they can be held liable to capture under the accepted rules of international law, which American courts helped to formulate (Borchard and Lage, pages 16–17, 118–119).

Congress "Eliminated"

The most serious ultimate consequence of the President's "shoot on sight" order is its effect on our form of representative government. His order does not eliminate submarines; as one newspaper editorial points out, it eliminates Congress (*Washington Times-Herald,* Sept. 13, 1941). The President unquestionably acted without consultation with Congress because of his knowledge that the overwhelming majority of Congress, like the American people, are opposed to participation in a "shooting war." His action seeks to arrogate unto himself the warmaking power entrusted by our Constitution to Congress alone. His powers as Commander-in-Chief of the Army and Navy clearly cannot be used to destroy another constitutional provision, the war-making power of Congress, since, as the Supreme Court has pointed out, even his powers in the field of international relations must be exercised in compliance with the mandates of the Constitution (U.S. v. Curtiss-Wright Export Corp.; 299 U.S., 304, 319–22).

The Remedy

Woodrow Wilson, who desired to avoid entry into the World War, sought by diplomatic protest to eliminate attacks on American ships. When that failed, he asked Congress for authority to exercise forcible measures. President Roosevelt ignores Congress and the Constitution. But there is a remedy, a means of checking the drive towards an all-out shooting war. Congress still has the constitutional power to assert its control over the war power (see Did You Know, #20). Congress can still assert its control over the purse-strings to refuse appropriations which may be used to finance a shooting war or the use of our patrols for shooting purposes. Congress can still investigate and bring to the public view the orders given our patrols and their implications. Investigation of the Greer incident has already been sought in pending Senate resolutions (S.Res. 164, 165) introduced by Senators Nye (of North Dakota) and Clark (of Missouri). Assertion by the American people of their will to remain out of war, and of their intention to retain our constitutional form of government, can compel the repudiation of Presidential war moves. It is late, but not yet too late.

DOCUMENT 123

Hanford MacNider to Robert E. Wood
September 20, 1941

I think that America First has come to the end of the road—as far as what has become its first objective (keeping out of foreign wars) is concerned. I have always thought that we were putting too much emphasis on a negative program, and I have so expressed myself many times. We started out to demand an impregnable national defense. Certainly going to other people's wars is not building up our defenses but we have, perhaps because of its definite appeal, allowed it to completely dominate the presentation of our cause.

The other night the President announced that he had declared war—illegally, it's true, but definitely enough to bring out the necessary incidents to make it real. He short circuited the Constitution, violated the Neutrality Act, showed his contempt for Congress by not even bothering to consult them. Congress could stop it, but there are no signs whatsoever that it intends to do so. Hitler still has his choice. The President has left us none.

I see no good reason for our committee to continue being dragged along with our heels dug in, stirring up dust, but accomplishing little else in our present hopeless cause. For that is what it has become, whether we like it or not. We must have a positive program. We can demand an immediate decision from the Congress as to whether this is our war, or whether it is not. That is, Congress must declare war, or it must take us clear out of war. If Congress says war, we can go and get it over with. That would be better for our country in the long run than the disunity, the moral degradation of financing mercenaries to fight what are claimed to be our battles, the fear and hysteria fostered by the President and the slowly closing hand of despotic government upon all that we like to call American.

I think we can make a stirring appeal to get this ghastly business over with one way or the other, so the people can get back to the rebuilding of the nation before it's too late.

Keeping out of war is important but to me war might well be far less destructive than the indefinite prolongation of what the Administration is doing to us right now. We could at least come out of war as Americans. I'm not at all sure that's where this kind of business will leave us.

If we as a Committee take the offensive—either that we get in with everything we have, or get out with whatever we have left—we have a chance. As we are going now, we have none. We won't have to retract one word or retreat one inch from our previous position. Unless some such program can be undertaken and at once, we shall in my opinion be doing the people of the nation a disservice, because the choice of staying out of the war is no longer theirs. It has been taken from them. In this way we can put it back into their hands.

I am not for continuing our present procedure a single additional day. My proposal may not be the proper one, but if the Committee feels that it should stay on its present course, I have no choice but to jump off and swim home as best I can.

With nothing, General, but admiration and gratitude for your magnificent and unselfish efforts to help defend our country against those who consciously or unconsciously are contributing toward its destruction,

DOCUMENT 124

Jay C. Hormel to Robert E. Wood
December 4, 1941

I am sorry to tell you that this letter is my resignation from the America First Committee.

I am grateful for the moments which my membership has permitted me to spend with you, and I am proud to have had my name associated with yours.

I am particularly proud because I realize—as your own modesty has probably kept you from doing—how it has been your name, your reputation, and your personal integrity which have made America First the influence for good which it has been, and which, under your leadership, it must continue to be. I have been in many a hot argument with rabid interventionists who have categorically flayed the motives of everyone connected with America First, and never once have I failed to stop them by simply saying, "wait a minute, how about General Wood?"

It is the personal esteem accorded to you which has inspired millions of people to look through and beyond the superficial and emotional confusions which have tended to pervert our national thinking, and has led them to adhere to the basic and right principles for which you stand.

Although I would like to pay something of the same compliment to certain other members and supporters of the committee, I am sorry to say that I cannot approve of the pattern of the procedures and the conduct of the committee as a whole. As you know, I have been loudly protesting the procedures of the committee for more than a year.

To me, it is incongruous to be anti anything. Instead, we must be *for* something. We must be for our own principles, rather than to be against people who hold other ideas, for the simple reason that we don't want to build an emotional resistance to our own principles.

A year ago I thought America First might well take the stand that the first duty of each member of the Congress is to avoid war, and I then recommended that America First organize in each state and in each Congressional district to impose that objective upon each senator and each congressman. However, it is my idea that it is the end result that we are advocating—not the means. Today we are engaged in limited naval warfare. We have substantially dedicated our economy to war. Whereas, a year ago, I think a small voice might have effectively said to Congress: "Watch where you lead us, because if you lead us to war, the judgment of the people against you when they realize what you have done will be inexorable," today I believe the degree of our involvement is such that our problem is to end this thing. I don't believe it is practicable for us to end it by invading Europe, but I don't see how, at this late date, we can call on our congressmen to avoid "participation" in the war.

I could continue as a member of America First on the platform that the United States must build a national defense so impregnable that no foreign power nor group of powers would ever dare to attack us,

—with an America First which had a program so constructive and so busy as to leave no room for America to undertake the judging, monitoring and policing of the post-war world;

—enthusiastically, with an America First which could conceive a means of bringing the holocaust to an end, or, at least, end our participation in it;

—providing America First confined itself to promoting its principles to the exclusion of criticism of those who might not agree.

My reverence for your leadership in this great cause makes me regret my belief that I should not continue as a member of the committee. I believe your leadership will continue to be important to the welfare of this nation. I am sorry that my own ideas are at such variance with the procedures of the committee as to make my services on the committee ineffective. And, of course, if I cannot be effective, I feel that I have no place on it.

DOCUMENT 125

Jekyll-and-Hyde Ships

"Did you know that the freighter Pink Star *under the flag of Panama was engaged in war trade for the profit of a private American firm, with the support of the Administration?"*
No. 24, September 23, 1941

"Incidents"

The sinking of the freighter *Pink Star*, announced yesterday, is being headlined by certain interventionist newspapers as another justification for "shooting" participation by the United States in the European war. This most recent sinking, when viewed together with the sinkings in past months of the freighters *Montana*, *Sessa*, *Steel Seafarer* and *Robin Moor*, discloses that the Administration has followed a consistent policy which violates the clear intent of the Neutrality Act, the Lease-Lend law, and the recent law authorizing the seizure of foreign ships in American ports. This Administration policy must inevitably *result* in the creation of "incidents" such as these sinkings around which a war-drive could be fomented, if, indeed, the policy was not deliberately *intended* to bring about such incidents. Furthermore, that policy itself has hindered the promotion of our own national defense.

Ships in War Trade

The Nazi technique of submarine warfare is unquestionably ruthless. But examination of the facts involved in these sinkings demonstrates that the Administration is scarcely in a position to claim that the ships which were sunk were legally immune from attack and entitled to the protection of the American flag. The *Pink Star* was a Danish ship which had been seized by the United States under the recent law for the seizure of foreign ships in American ports. It was chartered by the Maritime Commission to the United States Lines, a private concern, and registered under the flag of Panama. It was therefore not an American-flag ship and was not entitled to the protection of the United States. No American citizens were on the ship, when she was sunk between Iceland and Greenland, *on her way to Britain* (Washington Times Herald, Sept. 23, 1941). The *Sessa* and the *Montana* were also Danish ships which had been seized similarly, chartered to a private American firm, and also registered under the flag of Panama. Both were sunk near Iceland while carrying cargoes to Iceland (*New York Times*, Sept. 10, 13, 1941). Only one American was on board the *Sessa,* and none on the *Montana*. As has been pointed out (see Did You Know, #22), the *Steel Seafarer*, sailing under the American flag, was sunk in the Red Sea, 12,000 miles from the U.S., while carrying contraband war supplies for Britain. The ship was legally present in that area only because President Roosevelt had revoked his proclamation declaring the Red Sea a war zone and forbidding American ships to travel there—a proclamation made in compliance with the mandate of the Neutrality Act. The *Robin Moor*, also under the American flag, was carrying contraband to another country at war (British South Africa), and was sunk in the South Atlantic (Did You Know, #2). In neither, case were any American lives lost.

Seafaring Panama

The cases of the *Pink Star,* the *Sessa* and the *Montana* are of the most interest because they illustrate strikingly the type of subterfuge used by the Administration to evade the clear intent of the Neutrality Act and the Lease-Lend law. These three ships and sixty other American-owned ships suitable for transatlantic trade have been transferred to the flag of Panama between the outbreak of the European war (Sept. 1, 1939) and July 1, 1941. The 63 transferred ships comprise a tonnage of 358,460 tons—a tonnage large enough to rank little Panama as one of the leading shipping nations in the world (Bulletin of American Bureau of Shipping, Sept., 1941; figures supplied by U.S. Maritime Commission). The absurdity of the situation is evident when it is recalled that Panama's area (33,667 sq. miles) is less than that of the state of Indiana, which itself ranks 37th among the states of the Union in area, and that the population of Panama is less than that of the District of Columbia (World Almanac, 1940). Among the 63 transferred ships are 28 tankers (Bulletin of the American Bureau of Shipping, Sept., 1941). Yet the Administration recently claimed (until that claim was exploded by Congressional inquiry—see Senate Report 676, and Did You Know, #18) that there was an oil shortage on the East Coast because of the lack of tankers.

President's Neutrality Pledge

The Neutrality Act of 1939 expressly forbade American ships and American citizens to travel to countries proclaimed by the President to be at war, and further forbade such travel into combat zones which he should declare (Sec. 2, 3—Congressional Record, Oct. 27, 1939, pages 1662–1663). In asking for the passage of that Act, which repealed the embargo on the shipment of arms to countries at war, President Roosevelt pledged to the Congress and to the country that the Act was and would be used as a step towards peace (in his Message of Sept. 21, 1939):

> . . . by the repeal of the embargo the United States will more probably remain at peace than if the law remains as it stands today. I say this because with the repeal of the embargo this Government clearly and definitely will insist that American citizens and American ships keep away from the immediate perils of the actual zone of conflict. . . . This means less likelihood of incidents and controversies which tend to draw us into conflict, as they did in the last World War. There lies the road to peace!

Lease-Lend for Peace

Similarly, Lease-Lend aid was urged by the President and members of his Cabinet as a measure which was designed, and would be used, to keep us out of war (President Roosevelt's "fireside chat," Dec. 29, 1940; Secretary Stimson—Hearing before Senate Committee on Foreign Relations on S.275, page 125; Hearing before House Committee on Foreign Relations, on H.R. 1776, p. 118; Secretary Knox—Hearing before Senate Committee on Foreign Relations on S.275, p. 209, 242). The law itself expressly forbade the use of convoys under its provisions (Sec. 3D), and stated expressly that lease-lend aid was not to be used to allow the entry of American ships into a combat area in violation of the Neutrality Act (Sec. 3E), and further provided that the title to all goods and defense articles disposed of to any foreign government was to be transferred before those articles left our shores (Sec. 3A (2)). These provisions indicated the unmistakable intention of Congress that the purpose of the Neutrality Act must be carried out and thus dangerous "incidents" avoided.

Lease-Lend for War

The occupation of Iceland was undertaken under the theory that it was necessary for the defense of the Western Hemisphere (although Iceland is in the Eastern Hemisphere) and the additional theory that the occupation was necessary in order to insure the delivery of lease-lend aid (see Did You Know, #7). Moreover, in informing the Congress and the nation that Iceland was being occupied, the President stated that our troops were to replace the British there (New York Times, July 8, 1941). But Iceland was then and still is simultaneously occupied by British troops, at war with the Nazis, and is located in the war zone proclaimed by the Nazis. When American ships were directed to carry supplies to Iceland, and when still later, the President instructed the Navy to "shoot first" in order to clear the sea lanes to Iceland (New York Times, Sept. 12, 1941), American merchant ships and American warships were thrust into danger zones, where war-provoking incidents would inevitably occur—all under the theory that "lease-lend aid" justified such a policy. But that policy violated unmistakably the spirit of the Lease-Lend law and the spirit of its mandates against convoying and against the entry of American ships into danger zones.

Ships of Dual Personality

But even that policy could not justify sending supplies directly to countries at war, in American-flag ships. Consequently, the device was adopted of transferring American ships to the flag of Panama. It is now openly admitted that these transfers were made in order to evade the restrictions of the Neutrality Act (*Washington Times-Herald*, Sept. 13, 1941; *New York Times*, Sept. 23, 1941). Thus, on the one hand, the Administration seeks to place American ships in the war trade forbidden by our laws, by placing them under foreign flags, and, on the other hand, claims that *American* ships are being attacked when those foreign-flag ships run the risks to which that policy necessarily subjects them. The *Pink Star*, carrying a cargo to Britain, illustrates the dilemma perfectly. But even the Administration must be reminded that it can't eat its cake and have it, too. Nor can it be claimed that we must protect these ships under the Panama flag on the theory that such protection is essential to hemisphere defense. These ships, carrying cargoes to countries at war in Europe, are not engaged in any activity essential to the defense of the Western Hemisphere.

War Profits

Another aspect of these Panama transfers deserves consideration. Admiral [Emory Scott] Land, head of the Maritime Commission, has admitted that ships were transferred to foreign flags, to those of belligerent countries as well as that of Panama, in order to enable the continuance of American trade with Britain, our "greatest foreign market":

> The enactment of the Neutrality Act restrictions on American-flag tonnage had made necessary the substitution of foreign-flag tonnage for American-flag

tonnage forced out of the British trade with the United States. In fact the substituted foreign-flag tonnage was formerly tonnage operated under the American flag. (Memoranda on H.R. 4088 submitted by the Maritime Commission, #13, April 15, 1941, page 106.)

Such transfers were not necessary to keep American ships and sailors in employment, for Admiral Land further admitted that "the American-flag ships forced out of the North Atlantic trade and later the Mediterranean trade had found employment elsewhere" (page 107). The transfers of the *Pink Star*, the *Sessa*, and the *Montana*, as well as the other transfers to Panama registry, were therefore made in order to enable American shippers to engage in the lucrative war trade which the Neutrality Act sought to prevent. Most of the transferred ships are operated by private shipping firms which reap the profits of their much-sought trade. Is this not the "fool's gold" which the President once so bitterly denounced (in his Chautauqua address, Aug. 14, 1936):

> . . . . if war should break out again in another continent, let us not blink the fact that we should find in this country thousands of Americans who, seeking immediate riches—fool's gold—would attempt to break down or evade our neutrality. . . . To resist the clamor of that greed, if war should come, would require the unswerving support of all Americans who love peace. If we face the choice of profits or peace, the Nation will answer—must answer—"we choose peace."

National Defense Last

Perhaps even more important is the fact that these ship transfers, not only to Panama registry, but to belligerent countries, have seriously crippled our own defense efforts. In February, 1941, Maritime Commission officials indicated that there was an acute shortage of ships for the carriage of materials vital to our own defense program (*New York Times*, Feb. 27, 1941). A month earlier, Admiral Land had urged passage of the Emergency Cargo Ship Construction Bill on the ground that "there will be a shortage of bottoms for strategic material for national defense" (Hearing before subcommittee of Senate Appropriations Committee on H.J. Res. 77, p. 7). The same plea of a grave shortage of ships to meet the needs of our home defense program for strategic and critical materials, the needs of the Army and Navy, and the needs of our overseas bases ran incessantly through the later memoranda (April 15, 1941) of Admiral Land in support of the bill to enable the seizure of foreign ships in American ports (Memoranda on H.R. 4088, ibid. pp. 103, 111, 112), in the report of the House Committee on that bill (House Report 440, 77th Congress, pp. 4–6), and in the report of the House Committee on Appropriations on July 24, 1941 on the First Supplemental National Defense Appropriation Bill, 1942, p. 9–11. Other evidence has shown how the ship shortage has crippled our efforts at hemisphere defense (see Did You Know, #23A). Admiral Land's statement pointed out that "construction programs, either long-range or emergency, will not solve the need for ships for the year 1941 and probably not for 1942, unless sudden changes occur" (ibid. page 112). Yet in the past two years, we have transferred 267 ships capable of trans-oceanic trips, aggregating 1,443,308 tons, to foreign flags, of which 126 ships went to British registry and 63 ships to Panama registry, for a combined tonnage of over one million tons (Bulletin of American Bureau of Shipping, Sept., 1941).

Another Broken Pledge

The *Pink Star*, the *Sessa* and the *Montana* demonstrate at once the dangers of the Administration's policy and its scant regard for pledges. Seizure of these three ships, along with the 60 other foreign ships in American ports, was necessary, it was asserted, to meet the immediate needs of our own defense program. President Roosevelt himself placed the necessity for the seizure squarely and exclusively on that ground:

> It is therefore essential, both to our defense plans and to our domestic economy, that we shall not permit the continuance of the immobilization in our harbors of shipping facilities. (House Report 440, 77th Congress, page 3.)

Despite assurance of the purpose for which these ships were to be used it now appears that these three, and undoubtedly many others, were transferred to foreign registry for use in the "fool's gold" of war trade. Moreover, it has just been revealed that 7 more of the seized foreign ships have been assigned to private firms under Panama registry. (*Washington Star*, Sept. 23, 1941.)

(Note: As this bulletin went to press, the President revealed that the *Pink Star* was an armed merchant ship and was travelling in a convoy escorted by Canadian warships (*Washington Times-Herald*, September 24, 1941). This does not affect the analysis contained in this memorandum.)

DOCUMENT 126

Ruth Sarles to Page Hufty
September 14, 1941

This is to confirm our telephone conversation of yesterday.

It looks as though there could be a real fight on the Lease-Lend bill, which should be put in early next week. (The President's report of expenditures under the seven billion dollar bill is supposed to be out Monday.) The amount of the new bill has not been officially published but it is expected to be around four or five billion.

There will of course be demands for a thorough accounting of how the seven billion is being spent before authorizing additional funds. But I gather that the main fight will be on aid to Russia. Senator LaFollette understands that the Administration will resist any attempts to amend the bill to prohibit aid to Russia, but will authorize Administration leaders to give verbal assurances on the floor that funds will not be used for Russia. The opposition will show that there are so many unfilled orders for Britain under the seven billion dollar authorization that cannot be filled for some time, that it *must* be aid to Russia that is contemplated under the new Lease-Lend bill.

I am asking James Lipsig [research assistant, AFC Washington bureau] to look into the matter of loans. I vaguely recall that Jesse Jones [secretary of commerce] said some time ago that we could make loans to Russia; if that is so, we ought to air that thoroughly.

The question of arming merchant ships will probably come up soon. (Today's papers confirm this.) My judgment is that if any legislative fight is to be waged on questions of policy in the Atlantic, the Administration would stand a better chance on the question of arming merchant ships than amending the section of the Neutrality Law keeping our ships out of war zones. The President has already in effect altered the war zone provision, and hardly needs to ask Congress for repeal of that section.

The Senate Naval Affairs Committee will hold hearings Wednesday or Thursday on the Nye and Clark resolutions. [The Nye and Clark resolutions called for investigating the *Greer* incident.] I am not able to confirm whether they will be open or closed, but since the Committee hopes to have members of the Greer crew on the stand, they will probably be executive hearings. I understand that Senator Walsh is pretty thoroughly aroused over this, and can be depended upon to air the matter thoroughly on the Senate floor if there is anything in the story that the Greer fired first. One Senator told me there was little question that the Greer was firing literally for hours before the submarine attacked. If that is borne out by testimony of the crew, the Committee would have to make a report.

Hearings of the Movie committee go on tomorrow; it is expected that they will adjourn until Thursday when Schenck [Nicholas M. Schenck, president of Loew's, Inc.] will be on the stand. Senator Nye expects confirmation then of his charge that the Administration put pressure on the movie companies to produce war-mongering pictures.

There is little to report on reactions to the President's speech. [On September 11, Roosevelt gave a nationally broadcast radio address in which he focused on the sinking of the *Greer* and revealed that he was giving U.S. navy ships orders to fire upon Axis submarines in U.S. defense zones.] There seems to be general acceptance on both sides that it involves a limited naval war—how limited to be decided by Hitler. This bears out the reports I have been sending you for some time.

Senator LaFollette thinks we should hammer on the President's statement that we are to protect merchant ships that are not American.

I believe we should grab Hull's reported statement as to what constitutes defensive waters, and play up the elasticity of the definition. [On September 12 Hull admitted that Roosevelt's speech of September 11 was elastic in defining what constituted waters where self-defense applied.]

I shall ask James Lipsig to dig out the story of the fight on arming merchant ships before we got into the last war. I think there is a bulletin for us there, particularly the pressure on Congress. You will remember that that was the occasion for [President Woodrow] Wilson's comment about the little group of willful men. [When, in March 1917, a small group of western and southern senators attempted to block Wilson's efforts to wage an undeclared naval war, the president called them a "little group of willful men."]

I notice in today's papers that the Indianapolis America First chairman has criticized Lindbergh's speech. What reactions are you having from other chapters?

In connection with the new Lease-Lend bill, I neglected to tell you that Senator Bennett Clark has agreed to go on the radio when he returns from the trip he is now on, tying up Lease-Lend expenditures with the terrifically increased tax bill. We are preparing material for him; we hope to break down the tax schedule and show how much taxpayers in various income brackets will be forking over to aid Britain.

I have a sense that the non-interventionists here are beginning to pant for battle. I rather think that when the House members come back, they will confirm that guess; but I'll know more about that after Tuesday.

DOCUMENT 127

Ruth Sarles to R. Douglas Stuart, Jr.
October 16, 1941

I have just come from the House where the non-interventionists are putting up a good fight against the armed merchant ships bill. They are fighting it in the House (and it will be fought the same way in the Senate) as if it were the last real legislative struggle before a vote comes on a declaration of war. Note that I do not say they *feel* it is the last ground—but they must act as if it were.

So far as I know, there have been no polls taken that could be considered comprehensive. Guesses of the men I have talked with today range from 50 to 100 votes against the bill. Mr. Mundt and Mr. Vorys have done a grand job of marshalling the opposition, both in committee and on the floor of the House. Incidentally, letters to them patting them on the back would be a good idea—from the General if possible.

It is sad the way mail has fallen off in the last few weeks. This "defalcation" of the people has contributed much, I believe, to the so-called abdication of Congress. When you add to this any number of minor annoyances here in Washington that the non-interventionists are suffering—such as the non-cooperative attitude of government departments when some of them have sought factual information—it is not surprising that some of them are not making much of a fight. It's a war of nerves.

I have just glanced through the last month's bulletins from Chicago headquarters, and I am surprised that there are practically no suggestions about writing letters to Congress. You have used an excerpt from Spike Movius' Scribner article [Gerald W. Movius, "When You Write to Congress—," *Scribner's Commentator*, August 1941, pp. 63–68], which I think was fine, but that's about all. You did reprint the Scripps-Howard editorial "Is Congress Abdicating?" but did not suggest letters to overcome the apparent abdication. I do feel that as long as America First stays in business we are falling down unless we at least make an effort to keep up the mail. Have you sent out any orders to put the mail brigades into action?

Incidentally, I have wondered why you didn't send out any bulletins on Lend-Lease. I have no feeling that we should have waged any campaign on it, but I did think we ought to keep our members informed. I sent Page [Page Hufty, director of AFC organization] some stuff which I hoped would at least suggest an idea for a bulletin.

Just to fill in the record—yesterday afternoon somewhere between 75 and 100 members of the House met together for a sort of pep meeting prior to today's debate. There were a few Democrats present. Following that meeting, a small steering group met to plan floor strategy. Following that meeting I tried to get some of you by telephone to let you know what men needed bolstering from their own districts, but could not reach you until this morning. (Right here may I suggest that from now on it be possible to reach you or Page or Dick [Richard E. Moore, director of AFC publicity; special counsel to President Nixon, 1971–1974] at any time of the day or night—that is, one of you; I got to the office around seven last night, but couldn't locate any of you three. Things are happening fast here). I am glad that you could go right to work this morning and get out telegrams to A. F. groups in the districts of the wobbling men. This afternoon I learned that telegrams were coming in, so you must have worked fast.

Now for the Senate: day before yesterday Senator Johnson had a pep meeting in his office, where the men decided on an all-out fight. The same group met again this afternoon and was still meeting when I left the Hill. The Foreign Relations Committee is scheduled to meet next Monday when the question of hearings on the armed ship bill should be decided. As I told you over the telephone, Bob, there was a slight fear that there might not be hearings in the Senate, although it is unlikely the Administration would dare try such tactics. It is expected that there will be about a week of hearings. Senator Johnson's Miss Connor told me around four today that the Senator would probably telephone you as soon as today's meeting was over, that you had phoned him about witnesses this morning. I will follow this up and let you know as soon as I find out anything definite. It is expected that there will be about two weeks' debate on the floor of the Senate.

Now a word of explanation about my recent activities: I have since last Friday been working very closely with Mr. Mundt and Mr. Vorys. I met with them Saturday afternoon, and with the opposition bloc of the House Foreign Affairs Committee on Sunday afternoon when they planned the strategy for the Committee hearings. I am aware that the House is not my bailiwick but I felt it advisable to take the amount of time necessary because what happens in the House this week will have very great influence on what happens in the Senate in the next few weeks. You have of course seen newspaper stories to the effect that if the opposition in the House is not too great, an attempt may be made in the Senate to attach an amendment lifting the combat zones restriction; then, send it to a Conference Committee which will make recommendations direct to the House and Senate: the House would finally have to vote on the question of sending ships into combat zones without ever having had hearings.

Jimmie Lipsig has an idea which we got into the hearing last Monday in the House: it is rather generally established under international law that when a merchant ship is armed it takes on the character of an auxiliary warship. It is generally understood that the Neutrality Law does not apply to warships. Thus, the President could, after the ban on arming merchant ships is removed, order armed merchant ships into the war zones without further appeal to Congress.

I understand the State Department takes the view the President has the power to order ships into combat zones; if Congress gives him authorization, all right; if not, alright. But it is not expected that the President would give such orders for some time. Britain now has more ships under her own flag available for carrying Lease-Lend materials than are needed for goods we can produce.

I hear that the State Department is impressed with the "apathy" of the people. Meetings of the Fight for Freedom Committee and America First are being clocked. The State Department has been informed that larger crowds attend America First meetings. Some of the men in the Department wish the President would take measures to whip the public into line, and regret that so far he has not done more of this.

The Policies Committee (I think this is what it is called) of the General Staff is reported to have made a report to the President, through Mr. Stimson, to the effect that a minimum of eight million men would be needed for an AEF. Complete militarization of the country would be required since eighteen men are now required in the mills, mines, and for transportation for every one man in the field. It was also reported that the General Staff had no qualms about meeting Hitler anywhere in the Western Hemisphere.

I hear from a good source that these reports of real aid to Russia are nonsense. Five ships are reported to be loading or waiting in U.S. ports, but have not been dispatched. The reason given is that Britain does not want them sent by any other route than through the Middle East; asks that they be sent to Egypt.

Churchill is reported to be in the worst spot yet. It is noted that in the reports of Parliamentary debate day before yesterday, apparently not one Conservative came to his defense. Beaverbrook's paper [Lord Beaverbrook edited the London *Daily Express*] continues to criticize. The conclusion is that the President is going to have a tough time to keep Churchill in power.

There are still rumors of peace, but it would probably take a shift in the British Cabinet. Lloyd George is reported to be quite active; the assumption is that if he were made Prime Minister there might be a peace with Germany.

There is one report that Hitler wanted to make peace with Russia several weeks ago but the German military would have none of it and Hitler went along. One report says that Russia could stabilize her frontier east of the Volga and probably hold for the winter.

P.S. Joe Martin has been working hard on the floor of the House today against the armed ship bill.

DOCUMENT 128

Are American Bottoms Needed to Deliver Materiel to Britain?

"Did you know *that elimination of the Neutrality Law combat zones means war?*"
No. 28, October 25, 1941 (pp. 2–10)

We cannot, and should not, depend on the strained resources of the exiled nations of Norway and Holland to deliver our goods nor should we be forced to masquerade American-owned ships behind the flags of our sister republics. (From President Roosevelt's Message to Congress on revision of the Neutrality Act. *New York Times*, October 10, 1941.)

(*Note:* British shipping losses ran, in the early and middle months of 1941, to higher rates than had been the case through much of 1940. The increases led to loud outcries by interventionists to the effect that the British merchant fleet was being denuded, and that the losses could not be replaced by the combined British and American ship-building capacities. President Roosevelt said in his speech of May 27, 1941, that shipping was being lost three times as fast as it could be replaced by British shipyards, and twice as fast as it could be replaced by British and American facilities combined, as they existed *at that time*. The figures in subsection B show that the sinkings of British and Allied ships have lessened materially in the recent months, and that the rate of sinking for the war to date is less than that for a comparable period of time in the World War. Section I proves that American and British facilities can replace, and are already in operation for that purpose, many times more ships than the Axis can possibly destroy; that the British merchant marine is larger today than before the war; that the American merchant marine is less than before the war; and that the lack of ships, many of which have been made available for British use, seriously hampers our own defense program. A final subsection shows the sinkings to date of American-owned ships, and the figures of American ships sunk before we entered the World War.)

A. The British Merchant Marine

Status, September 1939

21,000,000 tons (Lloyd's Registry). The largest in the world and nearly one-third of the world total of 68,000,000 tons. (*United States News,* March 21, 1941.)

British acquisitions of gross tonnage since the war started

Allied shipping taken over and available for British war effort	7,540,000
Acquired from United States	640,000
President Roosevelt's ship pool available to British	2,000,000
Axis shipping seized	448,000
Replacements (building in British Empire).	2,000,000
Total (*including* prewar total)	33,628,000

(From *Washington Times-Herald,* October 5, 1941, which used as sources: U.S. Maritime Commission, British shipping mission, Lloyds of London, British Press Service, American Bureau of Shipping, officials of exiled governments.)

Table of War Losses

British, Allied and natural losses published by Admiralty up to July 1, 1941 (includes 1,044,843 tons neutral shipping. This tonnage was excluded in figures in subsection B)	7,000,000
Losses for July, August, and September, estimated from Churchill's speech (Sept. 30) revealing losses had been cut by two-thirds	471,000
Losses from causes other than enemy action, such as collision, etc.	400,000
Total	7,871,000

Subtracting the 21,000,000 ton prewar total of British shipping from the 33,628,000 figure, it is apparent that since September 1939 British merchant tonnage rose by 12,628,000 tons. Even when the loss tonnage of 7,871,000 is subtracted from the 12,628,000 ton figure, it is plain that despite severe losses, the tonnage of the British merchant marine has increased by virtually 5,000,000 tons since September 1939.

A net figure of 25,767,000 tons now under British control is arrived at by subtracting the loss figure from the 33,628,000 ton total. These calculations deal only with vessels afloat and do not take into account ships which are under repair.

In view of the fact that world tonnage has shrunk by more than ten million tons net since the war began, this figure of 25,767,000 tons amounts to 45% world tonnage. (*Washington Times Herald,* October 5, 1941.)

On September 28, 1941 *The New York Times* reported that the British merchant fleet of sea-going ships of 2,000 tons or more had increased from 31.4% on January 1, 1940 to 33.4% on January 1, 1941. For the same period of time and for the same category of ships, United States percentages had decreased from 15.2% to 14.1%.

B. Rate of British Merchant Ship Sinkings

As against the yearly average loss for the war of 3,355,260 tons compare the fact that in a normal peace-time year, the British Empire loses or junks almost 1,000,000 tons of shipping (*Lloyd's Registry,* 1939–1940).

British Shipping Position Improved

The heaviest shipping loss sustained by Great Britain in any single month was in March, 1941, when 326,631 tons were sent to the bottom. . . . Combined British and Allied losses of merchant vessels reached a peak of 533,902 tons in June 1940—the month of the evacuation from Dunkerque. (*New York Times,* Aug. 7, 1941.)

* * *

London, Aug. 7 (AP)—First Lord of the Admiralty A. V. Alexander disclosed tonight that convoys, planes and patrols in the North Atlantic had cut July British shipping losses to the lowest in more than a year.

* * *

Winston Churchill, in speech on Sept. 30, 1941 to House of Commons (reported in *New York Herald Tribune,* October 1, 1941):

Apart from anything which may happen this afternoon, losses by enemy action of British, Allied and neutral ships during the quarter of July, August and September have been only one-third of those losses during the quarter of April, May and June. . . . Very few important ships carrying munitions have been lost on the way. Our reserves of food stand higher than at the outbreak of the war—far higher than a year or eighteen months ago.

* * *

U.S.-Owned Ships Carrying Aid to Britain

January–April, 1941:

> Figures to show that only eight ships out of 205 sailing from this country to Great Britain were sunk in the three months beginning January 1, were laid before the Senate Commerce Committee today by Senator Vandenberg, Republican of Michigan, on the authority of Rear Admiral Emory S. Land, chairman of the Maritime Commission. . . .
>
> Senator Vandenberg said the data furnished him by Admiral Land showed that in the four-month period ending April 30, 158 vessels were reported sunk in all parts of the world, representing approximately 800,000 gross tons.
>
> "But," the Senator added, "only 12, of 66,782 tons, cleared from United States ports, and of the 12 only 8 sailed from the United States directly to the United Kingdom." (*Washington Star*, May 7, 1941.)

April–October, 1941:

Our own figures (see *Did You Know*, #27) show that, since April 1941, only 2 ships flying the American flag (the Robin Moor and the Steel Seafarer) have been sunk. Both apparently cleared from United States ports, but neither was destined for Britain. Since *Did You Know*, #27, was issued, the American flag-ship Lehigh was sunk off West Africa on a voyage from Spain to an African port.

C. Axis Shipping Losses

Comparative Losses

Comparing British losses against British merchant marine (see subsection A), and German and Italian losses against their merchant marines, the percentage of Axis losses to Axis shipping resources is obviously much higher.

Admiral Land, Chairman of Maritime Commission, estimated Axis losses, as of September 1941, as between 4 and 4½ million tons (Hearings Second Lease-Lend Appropriation, House, p. 271).

D. Losses of Shipping Now as against World War Losses

A chart in the *New York Times* for May 18, 1941, compares the shipping losses (British, Allied and neutral) in the first 20 months of this war (Sept.

1939–April 1941) with the similar losses during 20 months of the World War (Feb. 1917–Sept. 1918):

| 1917–1918 | 8,397,962 tons |
| 1939–1941 | 6,117,263 tons |

Highest monthly loss in 1917–1918 was 881,027 tons in April 1917. Compare highest monthly rate in this war—533,902 tons in June 1940 because of evacuation of Dunkirk; next highest was about 490,000 tons in March 1941. Remember also that losses have declined ⅔ in the past three months, according to Churchill.

* * *

London, Oct. 21 (UP)—Albert V. Alexander, First Lord of the Admiralty, contended by inference tonight that British, Allied and neutral shipping losses "from all causes" in the last twelve months had totaled less than 5,639,000 tons.

Mr. Alexander, who was broadcasting in commemoration of the 136th anniversary of the Battle of Trafalgar, did not mention any figure, but merely said that the losses were less than those from "submarine attack alone" at the height of the World War. U-boats sank 5,639,000 tons of shipping that year.

"We cannot, for strategic reasons, publish many details about the destruction of enemy submarines, but Hitler and Mussolini know the extent of their great losses," he said (*New York Times*, October 22, 1941).

E. American and British Capacity to Replace Sunk Ships

Subsection B showed an average yearly loss of British shipping of slightly over 3 million tons. The following authorities demonstrate that British and American capacities can easily replace those and even larger losses.

Great Britain

The exact amount of British shipbuilding since the war began is unknown. British shipbuilding capacity before the war began was estimated at 2 million tons of merchant ships per year. Estimates of what she's actually built during the war range from 1 million to 1½ million of merchant ships (*London Economist*, Nov. 23, 1940; *United States News*, March 11, 1941).

United States

a) Testimony of Admiral Land, Chairman of Maritime Commission on Second Lend-Lease Appropriation bill, before House Committee—Sept. 26, 1941:

Mr. Mahon [Congressman George H. Mahon (D-Tex.)]: You think it is a reasonable hope, that with this expanded shipbuilding and ship supplying program we will be able to keep these supplies in the water and going across?

Admiral Land: I am sure it will unless the submarine sinkings are greater than they have ever been before in the history of the world. This country is in a position to build, during 1942 and 1943, in the neighborhood of 12 to 14 million tons of shipping, and there is no record of continuous losses greater than that, with the possible exception of the submarine sinkings for a month or two during the last war. (p. 288)

Mr. Woodrum [Congressman Clifton A. Woodrum (D-Va.)]: You are building about two ships a week now?

Admiral Land: Yes, sir. Nearly three a week.

Mr. Woodrum: And you want to build one a day?

Admiral Land: Yes, sir. Beginning next year, we expect to build one a day, and by the middle of the year we hope to go to two a day. In 1942 and 1943 we hope to average two a day (p. 270).

b) On July 24, 1941, the House of Representatives Appropriations Committee thus analyzed our building program, in its report on the 1942 First Supplemental Defense Appropriation Bill, p. 10:

> Deducting from the above total of ships, the 93 vessels of a total of 1,018,616 tons, which have been completed, leaves a total of 1,153 vessels with a total of 12,410,300 tons to be completed in accordance with the plans of the Commission by the end of the calendar year 1943. These figures do not include 57 vessels with a total of 792,000 tons being built on private account and 60 vessels with a total of 606,000 tons being built for British account.

c) The Bulletin of the American Bureau of Shipping for October 1941 points out that, as of October 1, 1941, there were under construction or on order in U.S. shipyards, 1071 ships aggregating 6,202,090 tons.

d) Back in July 1941, when interventionist furor over the high losses in March and April was at a peak, Lend-Lease Administrator Harry Hopkins told British newspapermen that "this year America is building 1,000,000 tons of merchant shipping and there will be 6,000,000 next year, with substantially more in 1943." (*New York Times*, July 18, 1941.)

e) (Excerpts from an article in the August 1941 *Reader's Digest* by Hanson W. Baldwin, nationally noted military and naval expert of the *New York Times*, and a graduate of the United States Naval Academy at Annapolis.)

> We need not fear being outbuilt in a naval race, even should Hitler be able to turn all Europe and England to the task. One authority has estimated the shipbuilding capacity of Germany, her conquered lands, and her allies, at 3,200,000 tons, and of Britain at 2,500,000 tons—a total of 5,700,000 tons a year.

Assume that Hitler could get the full benefit of this, an assumption which disregards damage already done to shipyards by bombs and ignores the inefficiency of sullen, conquered labor. Still we could meet the challenge, for we shall turn out 1,100,000 tons of merchant ships alone this year, and next year 3,000,000 and more than 5,000,000 tons in 1943. And simultaneously we are pushing forward a naval building program just about equal to the combined programs of all the rest of the world including the British Empire.

F. Effect on U.S. Defense Program of Shipping Aid to Britain

Testimony of Admiral Land (ibid., pp. 272, 270–271): (After discussing tonnage turned over to Army and Navy and sold to foreign nations):

> By the direction of the President, in a letter published to the world, we were directed to turn over, to aid the democracies, 2,000,000 tons. If you will add the four figures together it gives you about 50% of the tonnage we had in 1939, so our merchant marine is actually smaller than it was in 1939. And we will continue to suffer until our new construction comes into being. I hope, as I said, that within the next six months we will begin to make up the shortage. (p. 272)
>
> We are short of bottoms in everything that enters into transportation. The most acute shortage might be in terms of oil, and the next would be in lend-lease material. We are short of shipping throughout the whole United States, and, in fact, throughout the whole hemisphere. All of our ports are suffering for lack of commercial transportation, because we are first taking care of oil, lend-lease, and the strategic and critical materials carried under priorities established by O.P.M. (pp. 270–271).

Oil Tankers

Washington, Oct. 23—. . . . The British arranged by November 30 to release twenty-five tankers from the "shuttle" service between Caribbean ports and Halifax, in addition to the fifteen tankers obtained from the United States which it was agreed originally they would turn back, the Oil Coordinator (Ickes) disclosed. . . .

Late in the afternoon, the Secretary (Ickes) issued a third statement revealing that, in all, the British were returning forty tankers to this country and that curbs on oil sale and use were to be removed. . . . (New York Times, Oct. 24, 1941).

The above news of the return of 40 of the 80 American tankers diverted to British service is particularly interesting when placed beside the following paragraph which is taken from our *Did You Know*, #18, entitled "Oil-Out For Britain," issued on August 11, 1941.

British "Business-as-Usual"

There are other factors which disturb the American people. In the first place, Americans sincerely desire a British victory and are willing to give Britain material help *if* there is actually a shortage of British tankers. But they resent having their sympathies exploited for the sake of British financial interests. A current report says that the recent contract for oil between Japan and American-British-Dutch companies in the Netherlands East Indies provided for delivery in British tankers. A leading Senate authority on oil is reported to have said that the Japanese wanted to take the oil in their own tankers, but the British-Dutch oil combine insisted on the extra profit that would be made if delivery was in British bottoms. (*PM*, August 7, 1941.) Obviously, if Britain has sufficient tankers to carry on "business-as-usual" in the Far East, even supporters of the lease-lend bill would be unwilling to give away American tankers. Moreover, Senator Charles W. Tobey of New Hampshire is still waiting for Oil Co-ordinator Ickes to answer his letter of July 1 asking whether the "transfer of our oil tankers was accomplished under a condition of actual shortage of British oil tankers for war-time purposes or whether British oil interests have used the lease-lend law to further their commercial interests." The Senator quoted a *Wall Street Journal* editorial which said that for war-time purposes Britain required "at the outside, 250 oil tankers. In 1939, just before the war began, she had 498. She later acquired 400 from Norway, Belgium, Holland, and France, giving her a total of 898. About 100 of these have been sunk, leaving a balance of 798 ships, not counting the new tankers she has launched since the war began. This leaves her with 500 tankers in addition to those which she has for her war-time requirements." (*PM*, August 7, 1941.) To this total the United States has already added 80 tankers, with 70 more promised. Again, the question is—how many of these tankers are in the service of normal British commerce, instead of being engaged in supplying Britain's actual war needs?

G. The Ships Sunk by Belligerent Action

Do These Justify American Participation in a Shooting War?

City of Rayville. Flying the American flag, this ship struck a mine, identity unknown, while sailing in Australian waters in 1940.

Charles Pratt. A tanker sailing under the Panama flag and owned by a foreign company, the Panama Transport Company, a subsidiary of Standard Oil Company (New Jersey); sunk off West Africa on December 21, 1940.

Robin Moor.   American owned sailing under American flag; sunk on May 21, 1941 in South Atlantic while carrying contraband to British South Africa, a country at war.

Steel Seafarer.   American owned under American flag; sunk September 7, 1941 in Red Sea (12,000 miles from the United States) in what was formerly Neutrality Act combat zone before President Roosevelt revoked his combat zone proclamation, while carrying contraband war supplies for Britain.

Sessa and *Montana.*   Danish ships seized by U.S. and chartered to a private American firm; registered under Panama flag; sunk near Iceland while carrying cargoes to Ireland. The Sessa was sunk on August 17, 1941. The Montana was sunk on September 11, 1941.

Pink Star.   Danish ship seized by U.S. and chartered to private American firm. Registered under Panama flag; armed by U.S.; traveling in Canadian convoy, convoyed by Canadian warships, sunk September 19, 1941 between Greenland and Iceland; ultimate destination Great Britain.

I. C. White.   American owned, registered under Panama flag; transferred to British service under lease-lend; sunk on September 27, 1941 in South Atlantic while carrying oil (contraband) from Venezuela to South Africa.

Bold Venture.   American owned but flying the Panama flag; sunk October 17, 1941, 500 miles south of Iceland while traveling in a convoy. She was carrying contraband to England.

Lehigh.   American owned and flying the American flag. Sunk on October 20, 1941 while on a trading voyage from Bilbao, Spain to the African gold coast.

Note: No American life has been lost because of belligerent action to date on any merchant ship flying the American flag.

DOCUMENT 129

General Report
Fred Burdick
October 30, 1941

Non-interventionist Senate leaders now believe there is a chance to defeat in the Senate the proposal to permit sending of merchant ships flying the American flag into war zones and belligerent ports! I got this late this evening from Congressman Mundt who was talking this afternoon with some of our principal friends in the Upper House.

Congressman H. Carl Andersen (R) of Minn. told me he thought if we could get 44 votes in the Senate against repeal of Sections 2 and 5 of the Neutrality Act non-interventionists in the Lower House would be so encouraged that they could win the fight to stop the move dead in its tracks to get us into a total shooting war by permitting our contraband-carrying vessels to go right into the heart of the ocean warfare.

The most encouraging development is the breaking way from the Administration on this issue of such Senators from the deep South as Russell of Georgia [Richard B. Russell (D-Ga.)] and Bilbo and Doxey of Mississippi [Sens. Theodore G. Bilbo and Wall Doxey, both Democrats]. Sen. George is far from hopeless. He should get still more pressure, and from outside Georgia, too. It now appears that the most important contribution to a successful conclusion of the fight to defeat the Administration's effort to get our Navy and merchant ships all the way into the war was made by the President himself! His ultra belligerent Navy Day broadcast finally convinced nearly everybody that he wants war! Too many persons before were prone to give him the benefit of the doubt and figure that he was conducting a big bluff and had no intention of taking the last necessary steps to put our nation into a total shooting war for the duration.

Consequently, the people have at long last been awakened to the genuine dangers of his policies and brought to a realization that repealing Sections 2 and 5 of the Neutrality Act means almost certainly the *last* step. And protesting mail and telegrams are beginning to pour into the offices of the Senators in convincing quantities. There may be no more defections amongst the ranks of the Southern Senators. And, what is very important, this breaking up of solid support from Southern Senators will encourage House Democrats from below the Mason and Dixon line to follow suit!

I got hold of a very important document in the office of Congressman Curtis of Nebraska today. It is a file of clever war propaganda from the Omaha office of *Bosell & Jacobs, Inc., national advertising agency* with other offices in Chicago, Indianapolis, Houston and Shreveport. I may be able to borrow the file Monday. It is a report on a survey conducted by the agency amongst Nebraska daily and weekly newspapers. It constitutes concrete proof of how this campaign, engineered by the *Fight for Freedom Committee*, is managed to coerce newspapers to adopt pro-administration editorial policies regarding the war moves by *indirectly threatening them with loss of national advertising if they do not "go along" with the war party! This insidious campaign to stifle freedom of the press in America should be exposed.* By doing so we would be accomplishing a great deal toward stopping the war promoters. And they are using this coercion of the newspaper to influence Congress. Some Members say the financing of this war-propaganda effort probably could be traced back to England. This would mean that American tax-payers will have to foot the bill to pay for propaganda from England to inveigle our country into a disastrous war and into sacrificing possible millions of lives.

DOCUMENT 130

Samuel B. Pettengill to R. Douglas Stuart, Jr. October 8, 1941

I think now I will leave for South Bend tonight or tomorrow. If so, I will phone with the idea of coming up for a conference with you Friday or Saturday.

This afternoon I am going to attend a conference of the non-interventionist Senators and Congressmen. As General Wood has no doubt told you, our day-long discussion of last Thursday developed considerable support for the idea that we should demand a vote on a declaration of war. Tactically, there are certainly some advantages, as in an open letter to the President and as shown by a full page ad in the papers. We could say that the statements of Knox, Stimson, etc., can only mean war. If that is what the Administration actually intends to consider, two considerations require the issue to be submitted to the Constitutional voice of our people. One is the honor of the nation, internationally, and second, the preservation of Constitutional government at home. We could then review the various steps toward war which have been sold to the people as means to preserve peace and that the steps are now shown to be wholly contradictory of a program of total destruction and disarmament of Germany, Italy, and Japan. We could then say to the President that respect for the Constitution and national honor require that the issue be decided. If in the wisdom of Congress it declares for war, there will be no further opposition from America First. If on the other hand, Congress should decide against war, then let the Administration respect that decision and take no further executive steps into the war.

The advantages of making such an offer and challenge as developed in the conversation last Thursday were two at least, so far as the Committee is concerned. First, that it would tend to free the Committee from the charge that it is secretly advised or is financed by foreign governments; and second, if Congress votes against war it will then *justify* the Committee in patriotism supporting Congress and *opposing* further executive steps into the war.

These points are certainly worth considering. While America First and the non-interventionist Senators and Congressmen must expect smears, nevertheless, patriotism and its friends on the Hill must never be subject to legitimate question. Despite its complete honesty of purpose the fact remains that we are fighting a losing rear guard action and are gradually being forced into a wholly undeserved but anomalous position.

There is little doubt that the Administration would fight asking Congress for a declaration of war, or that a declaration would be defeated if brought to a vote. But as I see it today, this program would clear the atmosphere. It would require a rather clear-cut decision on whether we are at war or not. And *if we are not at war* then America First can *continue* in *good faith* to oppose *going* into war by executive decree. I think, too, that a powerfully worded but respectful statement based primarily upon loyalty to the American Constitution and the power of Congress would win respect for this Committee even from those who either oppose or are neutral.

DOCUMENT 131

John T. Flynn to Robert E. Wood
November 16, 1941

I regret deeply that I cannot be in Washington on Monday. I had already promised to go to a meeting in Lawrence, Mass., which our friends in Boston believe to be important because a congressional election is about to take place in that district.

However, I am anxious to get to you a few notions as to what our course should be as I see it from here.

First, of all, the further away I get from that vote of Thursday, the more I am convinced it was a staggerer for the President. I do not overlook the fact that he got what he wanted and that he is in a position to use it toward a disastrous end. But it must be clear to him, from a wholly selfish point of view, that he got his grant of power under circumstances which will make the use of it extremely dangerous. I do not doubt that his blood-thirsty servants, such as Knox and Stimson and Pepper, and his stooge committees will yell for action. But he has got to take the consequences on his chin and that chin is exceedingly sensitive to public opinion. Whatever he does, he has got to come back to Congress sooner or later—and I imagine quite soon—for some further grants of power, perhaps a declaration of war. Under these circumstances, here is what I am disposed to believe our course should be.

1. I think that for one reason—and one reason alone—our committee should, so far as violent and aggressive public action is concerned, remain quiet for a while. The reason is this. A fight such as we have been through generates deep animosities and intolerance. There are some points on our side which can be put over very much stronger if they do not come with the America First label on them. They are points, indeed, which will put themselves over. I speak of that group of terribly irritating subjects with which the administration must now deal. This week it must face a showdown on price control. This, as you know, is full of burrs—what with the farmer, the wage earner and the producer all having contradictory interests. Then there is the administration of priorities. The whole subject of the bad management of defense production is running into all sorts of trouble and scandal. And as bad as any subject is that of taxation along with the growing apprehensions of business men as they head into the appalling sacrifices and dislocations which now stand directly ahead of them. Murmurs, even loud wailings are coming from many quarters wholly unconnected with us. This will grow. We can through our research departments and a proper publicity department do much on this front, but more will be accomplished if this is allowed to boil up without any open and direct heat from us. I think the Senators and Congressmen with us might well keep silent on these points. Let others, including the administration leaders, invite and receive whatever odium goes with advocating these unpopular measures. Of course any Congressmen or Senators conscientiously opposed to higher taxes and price control on our side should speak up, but Congressmen on our side who are for these unpopular things should keep quiet and let the warmakers take the blame.

2. Next I feel our greatest job can now be done by a vigorous publicity department. Doubts, questionings, eagerness for the truth, grave suspicion

of the President's integrity and honesty are beginning to have a wide effect. Good publicity, wisely placed, now can do a wonderful job. I will be glad to go over this with you in fuller detail. As I have said many times, this is a professional job. It ought to have a paid public relations man of the highest abilities. But I know we cannot afford that, not only because he would have to have a large salary but because that kind of critter likes to surround himself with expensive machinery. For this reason there has seemed to be no other solution than for me to undertake it, since that would involve no cost save a small staff and funds for printing and postage and a little travel. I would have been willing to undertake this a long time ago but for the dangers which inhere in this New York chapter which tends to fall more and more into the wrong hands. However some way must be found to get this publicity job going immediately.

3. As you know, with 194 outright votes and 6 pairs, we had on neutrality repeal 200 house members with us and in the Senate 42 senators (counting pairs). Save for a very few of these I think we can count on this vote sticking. What we have to do is to bring another seven senators and ten congressmen over to our side, and as many more as possible. I have asked Karl Mundt and Ham Fish to make up a list of these congressmen who were in fact for us and flopped at the last minute. Also those who were wobbly and might have come with us had they had more pressure. When this list is made we will find that we have about eight senators and about twenty congressmen who are likely candidates for the saw-dust trail and conversion.

Now I do not think we should waste too much of our energies on the 200 congressmen and 42 senators who are now with us. Let us keep up a moderate pressure on them. But let us take those eight senators and 20 congressmen as our special job for the immediate future. This is a highly localized job. If we have chapters in these districts, let us strengthen those chapters. If we have not, let us organize chapters. Let us also bring to bear on them every other form of pressure we can use—and I can think of a dozen ways to do this. This situation thus localizes and concentrates our immediate work. I plan when I get the full list to go down to Washington and make a study of every one of these men from every angle to see what is the best approach to them.

4. There is one other plan. I hesitate to discuss it fully here. I believe the moment has come for a peace offensive. But I do not think America First should sponsor it. I believe that we should get Dr. Fosdick, Archbishop Beckman and a number of leading clergymen to form a committee at once for peace. They should aim at a sponsoring committee of at least 500, and at least 15,000 clergymen of all denominations. We could help to finance and perhaps lend some personnel to it If this could be done swiftly, such a body could go to the radio and perhaps to the movies and

demand time and space for preaching peace—a great peace Sunday, prayers for peace every Sunday, in which the nation would be asked to join, novenas in all Catholic churches for peace. If we could get this going—and I think we can—it would move on its own force. It would be completely free from any of those resistances and calumnies which have been set up against us.

5. Moreover, the congressional elections of next year will be under way soon. The first primary is in January, in Louisiana. These primaries will come along in April, May and June. After December 31, these primaries will begin to get into full swing. Here is another and a powerful place for the anti-war sentiment to make itself felt. The record of every senator and congressman must be studied. Their constituents must know of it. Their campaign promises of two years ago must be recalled, etc.

There is much we can do and plenty to hope for. We are acutely conscious of our own troubles. We probably overlook the difficulties of our opponents. They see their support dwindling in senate and house. The President himself is in a terrible spot. The war-minded madmen around him grow more and more angry with him. Many of them are cursing him. Yet he stands face to face with an opposition to war which he dare not ignore and which can destroy him. In every way, if we leave the element of accident out of the situation, we are stronger than ever. I know the accident factor cannot be eliminated. But I also keep in mind that an accident may mar as well as make the President's war policy.

I am planning to take a brief rest of four days from Thursday (Thanksgiving) to Monday morning. But I will be back then and eager for the battle.

DOCUMENT 132

General Report
Fred Burdick
December 4, 1941

Probably millions of lives of American boys will be saved as a result of the epochal exposé of the secret plans of the war-makers for a gigantic A.E.F. for a suicidal attempt to reconquer parts of Europe and parts of Africa and Asia. The article by Chesly Manly [Washington correspondent, *Chicago*

Tribune] astounded most interventionists and non-interventionists on the Hill. Nearby newsstands were soon sold out of the *Times-Herald* containing the copy-righted story. (I phoned the paper's circulation department and they sent out extra copies to supply the demand on the Hill.) Some Congressmen hoped that a plan could be worked out whereby the article could be reprinted in some form in all newspapers of the nation.

The consensus was that the remarkable revelations contained in Manly's story would result in keeping America out of Europe's war, or at least prove a great contributory factor in that direction. It generally was agreed that the people would be aroused as never before and they would deluge the White House with protests. It caught the war crowd flat-footed. Congressman Clarence Cannon (D) of Mo. made attempts early in the House session to discredit and belittle Manly's article. Later, however, word must have come from the White House that the authenticity of the story could not be denied and Democratic speakers on and off the floor merely scoffed at the significance of the exposé and contended that it always has been the duty of the War Department and Navy Department to have plans prepared for possible eventualities and the existence of such plans does not indicate that they represent the Administration's set policy or purpose.

However, Congressman John Taber (R) of New York declared that he had been a member of Congressional committees for nineteen years and never before had known of a Presidential request for specific war plans such as disclosed in the Manly article. He, being an interventionist, resorted to the war-promoters' pet argument that "We are already in the war and it is too late to back out now," etc. etc.

Non-interventionist Congressmen came back at him with the truism that the Congress had not gone on record as favoring an A.E.F. and that all measures such as lease-lend, draft extension and even Neutrality Act emasculation went through Congress with the assurances of Administration leaders that they were "peace" measures and designed to help keep us out of war, etc.

Numerous remarks and a few speeches were made on the floor by non-interventionist Representatives, the gist of most of which was that the plans divulged by Manly tied in perfectly with statements and moves of the war party, and the recent purchases of huge quantities of soldiers' equipment bears out the proposals for a new A.E.F. of approximately 10,000,000 men. It was bruited on the Hill that the President was "mad as a wet hen" about the great leak. Most Congressmen I talked with felt certain that *today's disclosures would slow up the war crowd as nothing else could have done, that the repercussions from the people will be terrific and that the revelations will provide the best possible "ammunition" for noninterventionist forces in the approaching Congressional primaries and elections*. It also is believed that today's historical developments will serve to assuage the situation in the Far East and make it more difficult to precipitate our nation into a war with Japan. However, many contend that the whole international set-up is loaded with dynamite and efforts to keep the war-promoters in restraint must be kept up at top speed.

I just phoned the Times-Herald and ascertained that they had received no White House denial. Their story in Friday morning's edition states that the President discussed the matter with Secretary Knox. The follow-up also referred to the conference of Democratic leaders on the Hill called to consider the development.

Reactions of some Congressmen I interviewed follow:

H. Carl Andersen (R) Minn.—It but vindicates what we have been saying right along. A blind man could see through it all. Why all the huge purchases of materials for soldiers if a large A.E.F. is not planned? We can use this development today to great advantage in the next year's elections. I do not believe many Democrats would vote for impeachment of the President. Some of them talk a lot but when it comes to following through with votes it's different.

Harry Sauthoff (R) Wis.—Most of the interventionists I have talked with today just say it's "precautionary plans." The noninterventionists are saying, "I told you so." This news may not change many votes in Congress but it should indirectly influence Congress because of public reaction, which should be terrific.

Harold Knutson (R) Minn.—Some Members could not believe its authenticity. Many could not think that he (the President) could be that crazy.

Dan Reed (R) New York—When this story gets around to the people it will strengthen our cause greatly. I was disappointed that it could not be carried in all the newspapers of the country. I personally was astounded.

J. William Ditter (R) Pa.—The most amazing thing was that there was no attempt at denial. Some Administration followers tried to get around it and minimize its importance, but no one contended that it was a fake. It is well known by Congressmen that General Marshall is not a bit enthusiastic about sending a big A.E.F. to Europe. He knows the costs in lives, suffering and aftermath. The reaction from the people should be very helpful to keeping our nation out of war. Protests by the car-load should pour into the White House from outraged mothers and fathers who have been deceived by the President's public statements. An impetus is all that is needed.

William Lambertson (R) Kans.—It will show the people what their boys are in the army for. This story should prove a good excuse, with everything else, to get millions of letters pouring in on the White House.

Louis Ludlow (D) Ind.—This should wake up the people. The Administration had better develop some sense.

DOCUMENT 133

Ruth Sarles to R. Douglas Stuart, Jr.
December 6, 1941

Ches Manly's story has certainly supplied a shot in the arm here. It enlivened the House debate yesterday in encouraging fashion. One man after another popped up and asked questions. There was a feeling of excitement, and certainly of uneasiness. That uneasiness is something we can build on. Of course when it came to the vote, they went along—only five against the eight billion dollar supplemental appropriation bill. Many of them probably took the view expressed by Case of South Dakota [Congressman Francis H. Case (R-S.D.)], that this is a part of a policy laid down by Congress; you can repeal it, but even if you opposed the policy originally you can't cripple it by refusing money to carry it out, once Congress has adopted it.

Of course the story is not new. The plan has been brought up to date naturally. But it is the sort of plan any War Department would have ready if it were at all on their toes; it's the War Department's business. The story that the actual blueprint (or a photostatic copy) had actually been seen by one of the Hill men was kicking around up there for about a week before the Tribune story broke.

But we can take advantage of this break *if we make it stick*. That I believe we must do. I would like to see AF reprint it (excerpts from the Plan) in attractive form and get it out to the country in tens of thousands. I haven't had time to check with Midwest and far west newspapers to see how widely it has been carried, but I think it is probably safe to assume that plenty of people will not have seen it.

I hope that every speaker who goes on the platform for AF will denounce it in ringing terms, that all will hammer "No AEF." Maybe a memo to all speakers from now on would be helpful. If Senator Wheeler introduces a resolution of inquiry when he returns, as he has said he would do, we ought to give it tremendous support. I hope people are already writing in to the White House to ask if it's true.

The danger, I fear, is that if we don't make it stick, as soon as it dies down the Administration will be able to go ahead more quickly, because it will have given the whole thing away, practically, in one big shock; there will be little worse to which the people need to become accustomed, except an actual AEF. Possibly, with this revelation, the Administration may be able to move more quickly than following its step-by-step procedure of the past.

That is what AF will have to prevent.

One sidelight: One of the Senators said that the President when shown this plan didn't like it, presumably because of what it might produce in the way of popular reaction.

Senator Bridges [Styles Bridges (R-N.H.)] told one of my friends that he thought the interventionists were going to lose at the polls.

I have no clear lead on the Far East situation. I have been trying to drum up interest in introducing a resolution calling on the President to give the Senate Foreign Relations Committee information as to the facts on which our present policy is based. Have had no luck so far on getting radio speakers on the Far East but will keep after them; Mr. Burdick is working on it too.

Mr. Mundt has some good talking points on the FE situation: Hitler is the only one who would benefit from a Far Eastern war; let's not be so gullible as to let Hitler determine our Far Eastern policy. China is in a less bad situation now than she has been in the past; why consider war more seriously now than when she was really having a bad time?

It might be useful if someone were to dig out now, just for a chapter bulletin, some of the faithful old arguments about the military difficulty of fighting a war in the Far East; the decreasing efficiency of ships as they go further from their home bases, etc.; at one time Mr. Hull estimated (that was some years ago) that such a war would cost us forty billions.

Another suggestion: how about a chapter bulletin based on the Did You Know, #17, that meets the argument we have to keep the trade routes open to the Far East to guarantee our supply of essential materials?

One story I get is that some of the secret clauses of the Vichy-Japanese treaty regarding French–Indo China are now being invoked; that Japan in moving troops in that direction is carrying out her right assured by the treaty.

DOCUMENT 134

Memo, R. Douglas Stuart, Jr. to Robert E. Wood
December 2, 1941

Rough outline of organization for non-partisan campaign

I'm writing this outline to clarify my own thinking. It is extremely tentative.

1. Our first major problem is securing a political director. This person must not only be politically sagacious—he must have such background that he is able to work easily with members of all parties. He should have a certain amount of prestige.

The only candidates I have in mind at the moment, who are conceivably available, are Sam Pettengill [former Democratic congressman from Indiana (1931–1939); unofficial adviser to the AFC] and Phil La Follette. As you know, there are certain objections to both these men—probably more to Phil La Follette than Sam Pettengill. Therefore I suggest that we should immediately secure the advice of men like Mr. Hoover, Senator Taft and Senator Wheeler as to any other possible candidates.

2. Under the political director there should be a staff consisting of persons capable of working with the various elements throughout the country from which we would derive our political strength.

At the moment, I would suggest the following—subject to their being both available and sound:

Jeffries [Earl Jeffrey, leading AFC field representative]	— Old age and Townsend groups
Schroeder	— Church groups
Leighton Wilkie [Chicago business-man]	— Small business
Ruth Sarles	— Peace groups
Ray McKaig [master of National Grange, Idaho]	— Farm groups

In addition, we will certainly need a labor advisor. In this regard, I suggest we write to Wm. Hutcheson [president, United Brotherhood of Carpenters and Joiners; first vice president, American Federation of Labor] of our national committee, Senator Wheeler, Norman Thomas and perhaps Kathryn Lewis [daughter and personal secretary of John L. Lewis].

3. Under the political director and staff, we will probably need regional directors. These men would serve to coordinate our field activities in defined geographical areas.

The exact geographical divisions can be determined later. But, for example, Fred Chase, who has been the able executive secretary of our Los Angeles chapter and who has agreed to come into this office after January 1, could handle the Pacific Coast. Harry Schnibbe [assistant director of organization, AFC], the Rocky Mountain area.

The qualification of a regional director would seem to be executive ability rather than personal prestige.

4. In the field it will be necessary to have men who can effectively contact state chairmen and congressional district chairmen in order to enlist their active support. Further, these men will have the responsibility of outlining our non-partisan political technique to our members throughout the country.

As you know, our membership consists generally of people who have never had their hand in local politics. So it is most important that our field men be qualified to give our chapters adequate understanding of their job.

Here again, men like Pettengill would be invaluable. Pettengill makes a fine impression on all types of people, has considerable prestige and knows the political score.

I'm not certain how many of these men we'd need—probably one for each region. For this job, I think we can secure men like Frank Murray of South Bend who, Pettengill advises, will not work in harness with others on an office staff but who might be excellent in the field.

5. Finally, our most important job during the next few weeks is that of securing competent personnel. Our objective should be to get persons of the highest possible type—men who are willing to work for the cause because they sincerely believe in it—not professional politicos. One of our greatest strengths has always been that our chapters realized those who were devoting their time to this job were not in it for selfish political reasons but because of disinterested patriotism.

DOCUMENT 135

William R. Castle to R. Douglas Stuart, Jr.
November 22, 1941

I am afraid that to go to Chicago for a luncheon is a little more than I am yet up to. I am very glad you are going to have this meeting, however, because there must be a definite program if the Committee is going to continue.

So far as the present work is concerned, I feel, as I said to General Wood at the Hot Springs, that we have a perfect right to work against participation in the war until we are definitely and formally in the war, either here, or in the Far East. That does not necessarily mean a declaration of war by Congress, but it does mean a formal admission by Congress that we are in a state of war. Unless we insist on something of this sort we are admitting that the President can involve this country in war on his own initiative and without consulting the representatives of the people. To prevent just this was the purpose of the builders of the Constitution in saying very clearly that only Congress should declare war. There is no doubt that we are at present in a war where we have no business to be; that we have been put there by the President, and Stimson, and Knox, and above all by the young and unheard of New Dealers, who see in the war an opportunity to promote their socialist theories.

I think, if we are going to continue, that John Cudahy is right in saying that we must have some affirmative program, if there is yet time for such a program. Would it be possible, for example, to make it a demand in all our speeches that Congress formally register itself in favor of, or against, a declaration of war. Could some method be worked out by which we could reasonably demand a referendum on the subject. Others would know better than I how feasible this is. Of course it could not be any official thing, but I feel very sure that if there were an advisory referendum, which was overwhelmingly against participation, that neither the President nor Congress would go against it.

Now as to your question as to whether we should support politically "those members of Congress who have placed patriotism above politics," in other words those who have opposed the war policy of the Administration. This always worries me a little, as I have written you before. A man may have voted wrong through conviction and have been persuaded later that he was mistaken. He may have been in every other way a first-class citizen, whereas his opponent may be dead right on the war issue and otherwise a complete rotter. It is a little like the Methodist attitude I told you of before of voting always for a man in favor of prohibition even if he were morally rotten in every way. Furthermore, we must consider that, if this country should be in the war definitely at the time of the next election, it would be anything but a popular issue to urge defeat of those who voted for war. By the unthinking masses it would be something pretty much like treason. I should, of course, never oppose such a motion as you suggest unless it is too specific. If such a motion would be earnest non-partisan support of men who, throughout their careers, have proved themselves loyal American citizens, and courageous enough to oppose public clamor and Administration propaganda, by voting against war measures, I should only say Amen!

I wish I could be at the meeting. It is not lack of desire, but really physical inability.

DOCUMENT 136

Hanford MacNider to Robert E. Wood
December 4, 1941

Without attempting to criticize the new program the Committee is about to undertake, I cannot very well go along, much as I sympathize with the good cause to which it is dedicated. I am a Republican, a rabid Republican, and I don't know how to be non-partisan politically. Those members of Congress who have supported the domestic policies of the New Deal—and they are what have led us into our present desperate situation—are just as undesirable and obnoxious to me as those who have supported the foreign policies of this Administration. I believe that the only hope for the nation's future lies in the Republican party, which despite a few desertions to the New Deal's program of intervention, still must stand on its Philadelphia platform until another national convention. I believe that I can do some good along that line in my own state and perhaps elsewhere. I certainly could not if I were backing the candidacies of adherents of the Roosevelt domestic policy, even though they might be non-interventionists of the first water. For example, we have Democratic congressmen out here who follow the Administration blindly in all things except foreign policy. I am not for them. I want no part in their endorsement. I want some hard headed Republicans in their place. My job and that of other like minded members of my party must be to see that we have candidates who are interested in this country first, last and all the time, and to my mind any man who strings along with the New Deal in any way is not in that category.

I believe that right now our one chance to rescue this Republic lies in the rebuilding and revitalizing of the Republican party, that it may constitute a real opposition and that we may preserve the two party system, without which this Republic is bound to disintegrate. For those Republicans who feel as I do there can be no other honest course. For old line Democrats, former New Dealers, and perhaps for others who agree in part with the Rooseveltian program but who oppose intervention, such a movement as you contemplate is quite another thing.

This then constitutes my resignation from America First. The Committee, I am sure, is in good faith pursuing what its members believe to be the best avenue left for worthwhile action, but it is not my course nor one which I could follow with a clear conscience.

Please understand, General, that I have nothing but gratitude and commendation for your magnificient and unselfish efforts. Under your leadership, America First has become a tremendous national force and has accomplished far more than any of us had any right to expect when we recall what we had to combat. I believe that the majority of our countrymen are with us, despite the constant and tremendous barrage of hysteria and fear which has been put down upon them, but nine years of the New Deal have whipped out of them what it takes to stand up like Americans and fight it out. That's what those Republicans who feel as I do must endeavor to put back into the front line troops of our party.

I am grateful for the opportunity to have served with you even in a limited way, and for the chance it has given me to know you personally and to have seen you in action.

With kindest regards and every good wish for success in all your' endeavors.

DOCUMENT 137

John T. Flynn to Robert E. Wood
December 3, 1941

I have been laying out plans for some effective publicity. Let me outline to you what I have in mind:

1. What I am thinking about, of course, is not just publicity on spot

news in the newspapers, but a propaganda job, or what might be called an educational job.

2. This can be done, I think, only by having a program, that is, by knowing what our objective is, what groups we wish to infect and determining on the plan of doing this. I do not mean, however, a program which will take endless weeks to contrive, but something decided on swiftly to meet a situation which is moving swiftly. In other words, we must not proceed on a hit-or-miss plan.

3. I feel that there are definite groups that must be appealed to. Those are (a) those people who are tax conscious; (b) small business men who are hurt by priorities and the price situation, as well as taxes; (c) conservative groups who see growing danger in the government; (d) investors worried by war inflation; (e) farmers; (f) religious groups, etc.

There are various ways of reaching these people. I name a few:

A. The daily newspapers. An effective job can be done with a weekly clip sheet. This can be made abundantly effective if it supplies the kinds of things that most newspapers like to print—short articles with good names at the top (which we can get) picturing the tax, business, economic perils, etc., short editorials which small papers will use, news features all directed not so much at the war story itself as at the growing dangers of national conflicts, losses, etc., etc. It might indeed be well to send a clip sheet out under a name other than America First—let's say some unincorporated subsidiary which we can operate from a desk.

B. The trade magazines. The most important ones are right here in New York. We will contact them about material. It is not difficult to plant stuff there.

C. The religious press, Catholic and Protestant. It reaches two or three million and will be eager to use material which we can furnish in a very small clip sheet.

D. The right kind of literature must now be prepared dealing with the immediate problems.

E. A very wide propaganda agency is the small radio stations. We have been able to get forty, fifty, as high as 100 stations to use transcriptions. This can be done better if the radio address is made to hammer home some special point and specifically for the transcription rather than using a speech at a meeting. This is not terribly expensive. We can get records made for around $1.50 a piece.

Then there are speakers at luncheons, trade association meetings, and also the Senators who can be used to get out statements. The other side has done a good propaganda job in one respect: They have picked out the propaganda ideas and then had all of their speakers and agencies hammer on those ideas. We must do the same thing. We must decide on what we want to say and then get everybody—Senators, speakers, chapters everywhere—to hammer on that one idea.

I have already begun to sketch out a small force for this job. We have a storage and mimeographing room on the 12th floor of our building at 515 Madison and by taking some additional space and combining with our Bulletin office we will have ample additional room. I have two men here, our New York publicity man and the editor of the Bulletin, who are both capable and experienced newspaper men who will help me with this work and I plan to move quickly so as to get under way with the least possible delay. I will keep you completely informed about our plans and about what we do and will keep in close touch with the Chicago office.

Please tell me, however, how you will handle the expenditures. I mean what arrangements will I make about paying bills and any help that I employ? Incidentally, you may depend upon my proceeding in the most economical way and watching the expenditures, but I want to know the procedure.

You have a research office in Washington with Lipsig and Lee. That, I assume, is still functioning and we will want to make a liberal use of those facilities for material, though I will enlist the services of some volunteer research workers here. Won't you let me hear from you about all this as soon as you get this?

I was greatly pleased with the meeting in Chicago. I think the decision to go in for support of our friends and to attack our foes at the polls will steam up our whole organization. On one point I would warn, though I suppose you are aware of it. Naturally an organization like ours tends to attract a considerable number of the hair-brained [*sic*] fringe. When this political activity gets under way it will attract even more dangerous recruits—gentlemen who are by no means hair-brained and know precisely what they want and who are professional besides. And our organization is necessarily made up chiefly of amateurs it is going to be important to find some means of protection from bad political forces, money spenders, job hunters, etc.

DOCUMENT 138

"If Germany could not defeat us alone, might not she and her ally Japan beat us with a war on two fronts?"
Speakers Bureau
undated [1941]

A. Nations act in general in their own best interests. In modern history only the United States is inclined toward romantic crusades. Once people thought the Soviet Union too would be quixotic, but that was a long time ago. Japan is not a romantic nation, she is not going to pull Germany's chestnuts from the fire. Pact or no pact, when war between America and Europe commences in the Atlantic, best bet is that Japan will spread through British Malaya and the Dutch East Indies. We wouldn't be able to do much about it, even though our hearts might bleed for Australia. The Philippines would have to be forgotten and they may have to be anyway. There has never been much of a case for an actual Japanese attack on America (once a war began sporadic cruiser or carrier raids might be attempted for tactical reasons). The contemplated war with Japan always takes place around the Japanese islands, around the Philippines, or in the South China Sea. It is always a war for Empire. There is not much chance that Japan could come east of Hawaii anyway, not even if all but a skeleton force of our fleet were moved to the Atlantic. Admiral Distance is a doughty foe. Japan's signature on the tri-partite pact of September 27 has present strategic value to both Japan and the Rome-Berlin Axis: by threatening to join on Germany's side if we enter on Britain's, Japan makes a threat on our trade lanes to the East which threat, if we then tried to fight Japan, would mean possible curtailment of our aid to Britain; if we move the fleet to the Atlantic, Japan has a free hand in Southeastern Asia. Obviously, however, Japan, more or less bogged down in China, is not overly anxious to fight us. Finally any war with Japan will be fought in the Far East where Japan is carving Empire, and the war will be of our own forcing.

DOCUMENT 139

General Report
Washington Office
February 21, 1941

While some experienced observers here believe that we are more likely to
get into the war via the Orient than via Europe, it is the opinion of this
observer that our entrance into war with Japan is not imminent. This is not
to say however that the tempo of events—already sharply increasing in the
past week—will not give a very war-like impression in the weeks to come.
Best opinion here both officially and among observers holds that although
the "bluff" war will intensify, both sides—Japan and the United States—will
try to avoid the crowning incident which would lead to war: the United
States for the reason that involvement in war with Japan would weaken
(despite the President's "bluff" statement to the contrary) our aid to Britain;
Japan because her Government does not want to start a war with the United
States in any case and especially does not want to start hostile action against
Britain and the Dutch East Indies before Hitler begins his expected spring
campaign or campaigns (plural because the triple threat against Britain,
Gibraltar and the Eastern Mediterranean is a distinct possibility—note the
report today of entrance of German troops into Spain "to succor storm-
wrecked Santander"). There are persistent reports here that the Navy has
assembled a very large train of supply ships at Hawaii which may extend the
range of operations of the fleet considerably; and there is much speculation
about the whereabouts of the fleet (some rumors are afloat to the effect that
the fleet is on the way to Manila).

DOCUMENT 140

General Report
Fred Burdick
August 28, 1941

There is a growing belief on the Hill that the Japanese situation will be
settled amicably. Although the Japanese Ambassador would not talk after
his conference today with the President and Secretary Hull, he had a

genuine smile which certainly would not be appropriate if his nation were on the verge of war with America.

Some believe that the Administration has often been playing a big game of bluff with Japan and that *the real purpose is to have the Nipponese visualize the dire consequences of an armed clash with the United States and Britain* and more fully appreciate and desire the advantages of "playing ball" with America and England, renouncing the tie-up with Germany and Italy, settling the Chinese "incident" and then being assured of all the oil and other materials Japan is sorely in need of, together with restoration of full trade relationships with this country.

From the view of attaining the objectives of the AFC, by far *the best chances of keeping our boys out of shooting wars all over the world is successful avoidance of an armed clash with Japan.* Once we would find ourselves fighting "shoulder-to-shoulder" or "ship-to-ship" with the British as a military ally in the Far West, it doubtless would be only a matter of time before the war-makers would see to it that the exigencies of the situation and the sequence of events would prove plausible excuses for Uncle Sam protecting the British Empire on all fronts and making most of the sacrifices in gold and blood in the avowed effort to destroy the "Nazi Tyranny."

Another factor to be considered is that *it would be considerably easier to get a war declaration through Congress against Japan than against Germany and Italy.*

The belligerent element of our population has been of the opinion for long that a war against Japan is a "natural." It is generally conceded that sentiment on the Pacific Coast is, on the whole, strongly anti-Japanese. Indeed, it would be quite difficult to keep some of the Pacific Coast Congressmen who are in the noninterventionist camp from "flopping."

A logical analysis of the situation is that *most people agree that the war in Europe is Europe's war, while a conflict with Japan,* built upon the fires of race hatred and incitements of the war hawks, *could much more readily be sold to Americans as "our war."*

Senator Arthur Capper (R) of Kansas, told me today that he believed nothing was to be gained by disparaging the "eight points" but acquiesced in the conclusion that the high-sounding ideals expressed could be used as sugar-coating for a very bitter war pill. The Senator continues, of course, to be strongly non-interventionist.

DOCUMENT 141

General Report
Fred Burdick
December 2, 1941

Accepting the premise that the present Far Eastern situation is fraught with danger, all Congressmen I talked with today believed that it would help to have an avalanche of telegrams and mail to pour in on the White House asking in the name of democracy that the Congress and the people be told the facts regarding negotiations with Japan.

By getting Democracy into action in this respect and giving the people an opportunity of expressing their sentiments as to the wisdom of picking a fight in the Far East, it is the consensus of non-interventionist leaders in the House that the President can be slowed up effectively on this issue and war be avoided with Japan.

Concurring in the wisdom of such procedure, Congressman Mundt suggested that it also might prove helpful to *get a Senator to introduce a resolution of inquiry*.

Congressman Roy O. Woodruff, Republican caucus leader, was emphatic in expressing the need for inducing the Administration to cut off concealment.

"Anything from the people that will help to bring the facts into the light of day would be a very fine thing," said Woodruff.

One purpose of beating the war drums in the Far East is to get the American people war minded, according to Congressman Joshua L. Johns (R) of Wisc. He said the President may, if not stopped, go so far that there will be nothing left for Japan to do but go ahead and fight.

"The people are entitled to know the facts," said Mr. Johns. "If the President tells the people the facts we will not get into war. The President does not like to ignore public opinion. Probably one reason the President does not want to tell the people what is going on behind the scenes is because if they had the facts they might make up their minds contrary to what he wants them to do."

Congressman William T. Pheiffer (R) of New York, who voted against Neutrality Act emasculation, thought it would help a great deal to encourage the people to express their sentiments at the White House.

"There is danger of too much bluff," declared Congressman William Lambertson (R) of Kansas. "It would be foolish for us to go into China to defeat Japan. We would be too far away from our bases. The people should be kept active all the time. The people should keep pouring it in that they have not been converted to war yet. Expressions from the people will help. All we have left is the people."

Congressman Ross Rizley (R) of Okla. said there is considerable talk around the Hill that, unless he is checked, the President wants to get us into war with Japan. And some think that Britain figures this avenue might be the most effective way of getting us totally involved in the European and African war. "I don't know anybody in the country who wants to go to war over aggression in the Far East," said Rizley. "As for fighting over Thailand, most people don't even know where it is. One reason for being hopeful about the situation is that those who talk a great deal about fighting seldom do. In the early days in Oklahoma when every man almost invariably carried a gun, the fellows who would 'tell the world' they were going to shoot so-and-so never did. The shooting was done by those who said nothing but just started shooting."

DOCUMENT 142

General Report
Fred Burdick
December 3, 1941

Congressman Louis Ludlow, leading Democratic House non-intervention-ist, also believes it would be helpful to encourage the people to appeal to the President for more light on the Japanese crisis.

"If this is done in sufficient volume," said Mr. Ludlow, "it would help greatly. There is nothing quite so impressive on public servants as an honest-to-God expression from the home folks. It is important, though, that such an expression of public opinion not be half-hearted. The more people who would respond to such a effort the better.

"The present attitude of our Government toward Japan doesn't make sense to me. We so strenuously insist on adherence to the Monroe Doctrine in our Western Hemisphere, when we reach out 10,000 miles into another hemisphere and tell another nation in that hemisphere that they have no rights. It is just crazy."

Mr. Ludlow also agreed with Congressman Mundt that it would help the situation to have some Senator introduce a resolution of inquiry. It was suggested by Mr. Ludlow that to have such a resolution introduced by a non-interventionist Senator who has not been too publicly associated with the non-interventionist cause would be preferable.

He made the point that the best chances of such a resolution proving resultful would be to have a Senator of weight and influence with the Administration make the move. In this connection, he suggested Senators Byrd, Van Nuys, Walsh and Capper.

I explained to Mr. Ludlow that all I would do was to pass along the idea in my report to Chicago. I was unable to consult Ruth Sarles on this matter today. If it is decided that it would be helpful to the cause of keeping our nation out of war to get such a suggested resolution introduced, the negotiations could be conducted by telephone or telegraph directly with the Senators concerned.

Senator Taft told me he thought it would be a good plan to get telegrams and mail pouring into the White House regarding the Japanese crisis. He said unless trouble develops from the Japanese mess he does not anticipate any special new developments relating to foreign policy until after January 1.

Interviewed by a press association representative with whom I was talking in the Senate Office Building corridor when the Senator came along, Taft said he could be quoted as making the suggestion that he thought it would be well for the President to abide by Woodrow Wilson's principle of "Open covenants openly arrived at."

Congressman Frank Keefe (R) of Wis., a leading non-interventionist, added his voice of approval to the idea of inducing the masses of the people to express their views at the White House regarding flirting with a Japanese war, and asking for the facts as to what it is all about.

P.S.   The Senate will convene Thursday for its first session this week. It is believed by some that the Administration planned the virtual week's recess to forestall Senate discussion of the Japanese situation.

DOCUMENT 143

William R. Castle to R. Douglas Stuart, Jr.
December 8, 1941

You have done a great and unselfish work and I think all of us who have worked with you and known you will always appreciate it. I have been a slacker, I know, in the last months, but that was the hand of God, not any desire on my part.

As I wrote General Wood, our work has, at least, enabled this country to get into some shape to carry on a successful war. The very fact that it was arming and was preparing made the danger of war less all the time, and for this the America First organization is largely, I think, responsible. We could not expect any nation to go mad and make the kind of attack Japan made. I still think it would not have happened if there had been real statesmanship in Washington, and a lot more statesmanship than there was in Tokyo. Perhaps it was inevitable. Perhaps the saying is true that the Gods make mad those whom they would destroy, yet I hate to think of the Far East without, what has been until recent years, the stabilizing influence of Japan. You will live to see a reversion, probably, to the old type of special privilege all through the Far East. Certainly Britain will extend its influence as rapidly as possible and other nations will follow suit. All this unless the Soviet carries communism to all those countries, and if that happens it will simply mean years, and perhaps centuries, of degeneration of standards. I don't like the outlook, but there seems nothing at the moment for us to do except fight. America First has always said that it would rally to the support of the country, and that we have to do; later on, of course, there will be a lot of work, if we are given a chance to do it.

[*P.S.*]   It was bad luck that the Herald-Tribune published my letter yesterday but this cannot be helped. [In the issue of December 7, 1941, the *New York Herald-Tribune* published a letter by Castle calling for conciliation with Japan.]

DOCUMENT 144

Ruth Sarles to Robert E. Wood
December 10, 1941

Some items on the military situation I have picked up will interest you particularly.

It is difficult to describe the profound sense of shock experienced by the men on the Hill at the enormity of the catastrophe that has literally overwhelmed us in the Pacific. Yesterday Secretary Knox and Admiral Stark [Harold R. Stark, chief of naval operations] appeared before a secret session of the Senate Naval Affairs Committee. One of the Senators, as he left the meeting, remarked that we would be lucky if we kept Hawaii.

These men told the Senators that one half our effectives are wiped out, that three capital ships have been destroyed and four or five (I think the latter figure is correct) have been put out of commission indefinitely.

The report is true that five days before the Japanese attack our Navy Department was told just what was going to happen; they considered the story so fantastic they did nothing about it. The British tipped off Sumner Welles and he told the Navy Department. (Senator Gillette told me that he had seen the documents our Navy Department knew about six weeks in advance, which accurately described the plan of attack.)

It is true our ships were at anchor, all lined up in such formation that a bomb could do maximum damage. Oil tanks, out in the open, burst from bomb attack; the oil spilled out on the water and caught fire.

The powers that be will sit on the lid as long as possible but it is doubtful the facts can be concealed for long. Tonight, all 96 Senators must know the story and some House members. It won't take long to travel.

We had 17 battleships altogether; according to the best estimate, 4 in the Atlantic and 13 in the Pacific. Take out the 8 destroyed and damaged, and we have 5 left in the Pacific, as against Japan's 15. We would not have parity even in our own waters.

Up to this point, I feel quite safe in vouching for the above facts. The source was excellent. From here on I shall indicate the source if I know it; otherwise, they are rumors repeated frequently enough and by responsible people.

Yesterday Senator Nye's office said the rumor had been confirmed that Secretary Knox's impeachment was imminent.

Admiral Stark was said to be already under some kind of custody.

I have been reminded today that Admiral Kimmel [Husband E. Kimmel, commander in chief of the Pacific fleet, 1941] is the man who was advanced to his present post after Admiral Richardson [James O. Richardson, commander in chief of the Pacific fleet, 1940–1941] said some months ago that conditions at Hawaii were "woeful," and was thereafter relieved of his post. Somebody—said to be the President—reached down some thirty files to advance Kimmel to Richardson's place.

Vincent Sheean [foreign correspondent] is around the Hill with the story that the money appropriated to build an air base either on Wake or Guam (I do not know which) was used to build two golf links.

The Atlantic fleet is said to be on its way to the Pacific.

Yesterday, the story cropped up in several places that Senator Vandenberg was going to the President and urge him to tell the country the truth about the Pacific tragedy in his speech last night, that if the country had any stuff it would stand by him, that the Republicans would stand behind him.

A member of one of the Military Affairs Committees told me today that around November 1 a man from the War Department named Aires (or Ayres) appeared before his committee and said that we had only 136 modern bombers; the rest had been sent to England. He also said that we had given all but seven per cent of our ammunition to Britain, and had only enough to fight three weeks of a 24-hour war.

Several men have commented that this "union sacré" or national unity is only a very temporary truce at best and is already wearing thin. Senators Byrd and Connally less than an hour after the war vote in the Senate were arguing bitterly over their respective bills for curbing strikes. (Incidentally, Senator Aiken says his committee that has these labor bills before it is not going to report out a "bad" labor bill, whatever that means.) Congressman Celler [Emanuel Celler (D-N.Y.)] yesterday in the House bitterly attacked the non-interventionists and was as bitterly rebuked by Congressman Rankin of Mississippi. When the facts are known about the Pacific rout, as they are bound to be soon, there will be less national unity.

Senator Hiram Johnson does not think heads will roll to pay for the Pacific tragedy.

It is just beginning to dawn on some of the men that this Pacific defeat changes the whole world military picture—the balance is completely shifted. There is growing talk that Britain may be forced to make peace with Germany and combine with us to lick Japan. (I believe the story has been confirmed that the British lost the Repulse and the Prince of Wales.)

On the basis of the realization that the strategic balance has shifted, there are rumbles (and this is really confidential) that there will be some kind of move demanding that Congress reexamine our relation to the war on the basis of facts Congress did not have when the war declaration was voted.

DOCUMENT 145

Ruth Sarles to R. Douglas Stuart, Jr.
December 20, 1941

My personal housing problem was suddenly solved on Tuesday so I am back on the job.

The office has been dismantled. The files were mailed to you on Thursday: I find that one folder and the mailing list were omitted from the package so I am bringing them with me on Monday. Mr. Libby has been kind enough to let me store in his office two file case sections and our Congressional Records, until we decide just what to do with them. I am mailing to Mr. Camphausen [F. H. Camphausen, director of the financial department, AFC] today the petty cash report, and will buy a cashier's check on Monday to clear out our account at the bank. (The Did You Knows were mailed I think on Wednesday.)

In the odd moments, I have been getting some ideas in shape for the AF story, and picking up what I could on the Hill.

The thing that interested me most, of course, was Secretary Knox's report [Knox visited Hawaii from December 9 to 12; on December 15 his report was made public]—in view of the information I had secured last week and sent in a letter to the General. I find a good deal of skepticism regarding his report, ranging from "It's a downright lie" (this from responsible people) to "We'll get the story eventually." This skepticism is evidenced not only by the one-time non-interventionists.

Secretary Knox handled the thing excellently: his trip out there, the colorful picture of the heroism he painted, his forthright manner, his frank admission that the Army and Navy forces were not on the alert all combined to reinstate him with the press (and he had been in bad odor with them). The press men seemed to feel he was acting as "one of the boys."

But I have not found anyone who thinks he told the whole story. Several have commented that his report was so worded that if it develops later that the losses were greater than he said, he will not appear as a liar. Hanson Baldwin [military columnist, *New York Times;* author, *United We Stand! Defense of the Western Hemisphere* (1941)] says the report is "undoubtedly an understatement of the damage done." Mark Watson, the other really good military columnist in my judgment, warns against taking "too much cheer" from the report.

With the appointment of the investigating commission, even "our" men are quite willing to await their report. If there is an attempt to whitewash, then I feel sure there are a number who will speak out. Several look upon this as a heaven-sent opportunity to clean out the dead wood in the army and navy command.

The President has sold some reluctant people the idea of waiting, I am told, on the ground that to reveal all at this time would give the Japanese valuable information. For instance, complete news on sinkings might reveal whether or not the channel at Pearl Harbor was blocked.

I hear the President has expressed his "soreness" at the navy; but he has been reminded that it is *his* navy—he has been running it.

I checked with the sources from whom I got the story originally, and they feel the Knox report does not change the original story at all.

If you have any check on how the public generally is reacting to all this I would like to see it. Several here have commented that now the first shock is over, there is very little interest.

Incidentally, war-time Washington is a bit hard to take: some streets poorly lighted, an air raid shelter going up with lightning speed on the White House lawn, traffic congestion terrible, and—supreme indignity—I am escorted by a guard every time I go to Senator Wheeler's office in the capitol building! Everybody who goes up on the gallery floor submits to a search. My bulging purse has been thoroughly looked over four times in the last week by one of the Capitol attendants I have known for months. Then I am asked to remove my coat; the attendant whacks it a few times, then I can go with a guard to the Senator's office. I call it my daily strip-tease.

As you have noted in the papers, "our" men are keeping fairly quiet, and letting others do the talking. I suppose many of them will follow Senator Wheeler's lead: vote for big taxes, etc. in the hope that it will eventually be on the necks of those "who planned it that way." It is too early for constructive criticism, although that may come later. Senator LaFollette feels there are a few straws in the wind indicating that Congress has not yet completely abdicated. As an example, Senator *Connally's* opposition to the Administration proposal for lowering the draft age.

There was a rumor—not more than a whisper—from the State Department that some information has been received indicating there *might* be the beginning of revolution in Germany; it was very vague; but at least several in the State Department for the first time believed the stories of Russian successes and were aware Hitler was experiencing some unpleasantness at home.

Contrasted to this is the view of several I have talked with on the Hill. They set little store by the tales of Russian successes. They feel that Germany is straightening her lines, removing her spearheads from their forward positions and retiring them to a more compact line for the winter. One of the Senators had just talked with General Arnold, who took this view. All warn against wishful thinking at this time, which would probably be encouraged by the Administration.

I hear rumbles of growing British criticism. One Britisher here quite bluntly said the British would not have lost the Repulse and the Prince of Wales if the U.S. had come across with the planes it had promised.

There was a report you may have heard that in the first few days of the Far East war ten U.S. oil tankers on their way to Vladivostok were captured by the Japanese.

WRC [William R. Castle] says Bishop Tucker [Henry St. George Tucker, presiding bishop, Episcopal church] had an interview with the President a few weeks before the war broke who told him (the Bishop) that he had now maneuvered the Japanese into such a position that they had to attack.

Enough for this time. It will be good to see you all next week.

Note that my home address should be used. The office is completely closed.

DOCUMENT 146

R. Douglas Stuart, Jr., to All Chapter Chairmen
December 8, 1941
in Ruth Sarles, "A Story of America First"

The National Committee will meet in Chicago, Thursday, December 11, to consider what course of action the Committee should take in view of the declaration of war against Japan. In order that the Committee may be fully informed of the attitude of its chapters and members, it is of the utmost importance that you communicate to us by telegram the recommendation of your chapter as to our policy for the future.

You have seen the statement issued by the National Committee the evening of December 7. Quite properly, this statement commits us to full support of the war effort against Japan. It makes no reference to our attitude in connection with the war in Europe.

Several courses of action are to be considered at this time. The principal alternatives are as follows:

1. *Dissolution of Committee and cessation of all activity*.

2. *"Adjournment" of all activity*. By this course we would cease activity but keep the organization intact until such time when it is deemed advisable to renew a loyal opposition in the interests of American democracy. Thus, issues may arise wherein the country will need a patriotic group to act as spokesman for a large proportion of the people. Possible issues are:

   a. *Conduct of the war.* As in England, it may be necessary to carry on constructive criticism of the war, especially on such questions as an AEF, inefficiency, etc.

   b. *Preservation of two-party government.* One of the great dangers to democracy would be destruction of the two-party system. There is a strong possibility that Mr. Roosevelt and Mr. Willkie may seek to remove all issues from the 1942 elections and to unite Republicans and Democrats on a platform of internationalism. In such event, it may be essential to renew our program of non-partisan activity in the 1942 elections. Even in England the opposition party remains active during war time and serves the important democratic function of preserving minority rights.

   c. *Peace terms.* The America First Committee may be able to perform an important service in connection with war aims and peace terms. As the war progresses, there may well develop a serious issue of internationalism against Americanism; there may be a distinct trend toward imperialism. On both issues AFC can be the principal spokesman of the American people.

   d. *Union Now.* There may well be a strong movement toward union with Great Britain. The Union Now organization will doubtless continue and become increasingly active. In the interests of the preservation of American independence it may be vitally necessary to continue activity in opposition to Union Now pressure.

   e. *Bill of Rights.* In war time, especially under the extreme conditions of modern war, the statement that "Eternal vigilance is the price of liberty" is doubly true. War especially threatens civil liberties as guaranteed by our Constitution and Bill of Rights. It is possible that the Committee can well continue as the chief guardian of these constitutional guarantees. December 15 is the 150th anniversary of the adoption of our historic Bill of Rights. This may be a fitting time for an announcement that the Committee will dedicate itself to the preservation of our traditional liberties.

N.B. It should be noted that on all these points the Committee will undertake no active program now. Instead it will "adjourn," holding itself in readiness to renew activity when the need arises as set forth above.

3. *Continued opposition to the entry into the European war*. While supporting the war effort against Japan, it is possible that we can continue our opposition to entering the European war. The facts and arguments against intervention in Europe remain the same as they were before the Japanese issue arose. If we enter the European war, it will still be necessary to defeat the Germans on the Continent, to send a huge AEF, and to spend countless billions. All this involves the same threat to our democracy as it has from the outset. Our argument would be that we must not allow the Japanese situation to serve as a pretext upon which to circumvent the determination of the American people to stay out of Europe's war.

4. *Support of national defense and the war effort against Japan*. Special attention should be given to the needs of the American forces, making certain that they are properly equipped. Various possible courses of action come to mind, among them support of such organizations as the Red Cross, USO [United Service Organization, a body providing recreational activity for soldiers], or perhaps some new approach such as "Bundles for America."

These possible courses of action come to mind, at once; you may think of others. Some of them, or all of them, may be impractical. We are especially anxious to obtain your studied reaction as to the possible reception, which would be given to the above suggestions in your area. Consider, especially, whether you can expect financial support and whether war sentiment will make the Committee ineffective. We do not want to undertake any of the above proposals if the possible reaction to the Committee will be so harsh as to endanger its effectiveness and good name.

The forthcoming decision is, of course, the most serious we have ever faced. The Committee is extremely anxious to give full consideration not only to your own views, but to the views of your chapter as represented by your Executive Committee. It is of the utmost importance, therefore, that you call a meeting of your Executive Committee or Advisory Board immediately and discuss fully the questions with which we are faced. We would like to have the different views of your Committee by telegraph so that they may be placed before the National Committee on Thursday. I hope we may have your cooperation on this important matter.

Meantime, please refrain from making any statements on activity relating to the Japanese situation or the future of the Committee. It is vital that in this critical period we all act together. Whatever decision the Committee reaches, I know we will have your full support and cooperation which has contributed so much to the success of the Committee.

DOCUMENT 147

Ruth Sarles to R. Douglas Stuart, Jr.
December 10, 1941

Here are some notes from my conversations with various men on the
Hill regarding America First's future:

Senators LaFollette, Aiken, Hiram Johnson, D. Worth Clark, and Congressmen Mundt, Vorys and Shafer (Michigan) plus Lewis Caldwell, our
lawyer, think America First should go on in some form or other. (Senator
Danaher [John A. Danaher (R-Conn.)], whom I saw for only a moment,
said the same thing but I do not think his mind was really on the problem.)
All these men stress the importance of waiting for a week or two before
making any decision: so much more information is needed to fill out the
picture that to decide this week is too soon.

Here are some of the ideas for continuing:

There is a role some group can play in offering constructive criticism
during a war, if it is not offered as opposition to the course the government
is pursuing. It must be in the interests of the most efficient and speedy
conduct of the war. It might be in the interest of assuring that in the course
of the war as little permanent damage as possible be done to the country,
economically, socially, etc. Such a program would include examination of
appropriations requested and of taxation, watchfulness that undue sacrifice
is not required of any one group (such as small business), guarding civil
liberties so far as it can be done.

We do not even need to call this constructive *criticism;* an organization
can function for the purpose of promoting the ultimate in defense. It could
advocate ever stronger and more efficient defense. It might even go so far
as to become a "War Assistance" organization.

Congressman Vorys, who is deeply interested and has been for some
time in the Far East, keeps distinguishing between the civilian population
in Japan and the military clique now in power; he thinks that the slogan
"Keep Out of War" could become "Get Out of War." He thinks some sort of
appeal should be made to the Japanese people, so that there will be an
honorable way out for them.

Senator LaFollette (and I think Mr. Mundt) made the point that America First has a responsibility to the thousands of people who have been
actively participating in its program; we can't let them down overnight.
Senator Hiram Johnson seems to think that is the strongest talking point for

continuing. While he feels America First should not give up entirely, he does not have a concrete suggestion as to program. However, he is impressed with Senator Taft's point of view.

Mr. Leedle, Senator Taft's right-hand man who does a good deal of his political leg work, thinks there is a bigger place for America First now than ever before. He thinks there are a number of things that can be done under the flag of "What Is America's Interest?" We can urge, for instance, that no more materials be lease-loaned to Britain since we now need them ourselves.

Lewis Caldwell, our lawyer, has a slogan "American First in War As Well As in Peace."

Several have mentioned the possibility of the organization continuing under another name; Frank Hanighen makes this point.

Senator LaFollette was the most definite about America First going on, which surprised me; I can only think that he and his brother have plans that include the America First organization.

While Congressman Shafer of Michigan was the only one who said in so many words that we should continue to support our friends at the polls, I have the sense that the elections were very definitely in several minds as they commented.

Senator Taft thought we should dissolve. He says our job was to keep the country out of war; that job is over. He thinks it might be possible to keep together a small committee of the leaders, and perhaps later on come out for some kind of peace terms; such a committee might even get out a bulletin every once in a while. He feels that America First is in the public eye as opposed to war and opposed to the President; it would be hard to live that reputation down; America First must not give the impression of being unpatriotic.

Congressman Mundt made the point that if it were decided to dissolve (he seemed more cognizant of the possibility that America First might dissolve than some of the others who advocated its continuing), America First could do it with a good statement that would do it credit—we could point out that if it had not been for America First delaying our entry into war we should have been even worse prepared than we are today.

I think without exception everybody I talked with urged no hasty decision.

You asked my view. I wish America First could dissolve. My understanding was that the organization was founded to keep the country out of war. I feel it has done a magnificent job: it delayed the evil day and the

country is going into this war with more information than it otherwise
would have had. It seems to me the course of greatest dignity is to dissolve.

However, it is not so simple. Here are some of the obstacles I think of
now to such a straightforward course:

1. We have a certain responsibility to AF members. While they are not
opposing this war, they don't overnight belong to Fight for Freedom;
where will they go? There is a sense of fellowship among these people.
Here in Washington several have urged that something be continued. They
want to give their support to the war *among their own kind*.

2. I doubt if it is possible for an organizational structure of such size to
dissolve quickly without leaving frayed edges somewhere. I am disturbed at
the prospect of someone taking over one or more of the local chapters, if
the national dissolves, and using them for purposes never intended.

3. If elections are held in 1942 while war is in progress, there are a
number of men who will need and deserve help. They will feel they have
been let down if we don't help them. I do not yet see how it could be done,
on what issues support could be based that would not arouse cries of
disloyalty; maybe it's all-out, efficient defense but I'm not sure. I do not
think this obstacle as important as the first two.

I am wondering if it would be possible for the AF name to be dropped
without dissolving the organization, and withhold a decision on dissolution
for two weeks or a month. The statement to the press (issued after tomorrow's meeting) might say something along these lines:

> The AFC, which has stood in the minds of the American people as a symbol of
> opposition to involvement in war, *as such* no longer exists. It will take some
> time to demobilize the huge organization structure, particularly since many
> members, giving their loyal support to their President, are writing and wiring to
> ask if they cannot continue some kind of organization on the basis of strong and
> efficient defense and preserving democracy at home with as little damage as
> possible done to the country during the course of the war. Within the next few
> weeks, some of the AF leaders *as individuals* may discuss whether there is a
> place for such an organization; if they decide there is, AF members will be
> offered an opportunity to join a new organization whose purpose is to promote
> America's interest. Then would follow a polite form of "I told you so," and
> end up with reference to General Wood's statement issued immediately after
> the Japanese attack.

I don't know whether such a course is technically possible, from the
organization point of view. If it were, it would allow time to consider
carefully what next. It would offer a straw to those individual members who
need something to cling to. It would permit a graceful exit to those leaders

who are through. It would put on record that the "odious" name AF is on the way out. The Executive Committee could meet again in two weeks or a month and make the final decision. While the name "AF" is exactly right, in my judgment it cannot longer be used now that war has broken out; I believe Senator Taft's view on this is sound.

Before the Executive Committee meets again every reasonable idea for a possible future program could be examined. I would particularly hope that you would add to the somewhat nebulous program suggestions offered by those I have talked with so far, the organization of the world to come after the war; I doubt if this would appeal to many AF members, but someone ought to do an effective educational job on this to reduce the prospect of another Versailles.

If AFC is entirely dissolved, I believe the Executive Committee owes it to AF members to tell them on dissolution what groups there are in existence with which they can work: Keep America Out of War Congress (which meets next week to decide on new name and program) and Mr. Libby's organization are the two I think of offhand.

If the Executive Committee tomorrow does not order dissolution and wants to look further into possible programs, I think next week we can get more specific ideas from men on the Hill.

Incidentally, the old order is certainly passing! It looked today as though dear old Hiram Johnson is the only Senator who will vote against removing the AEF ban from the Selective Service Act. It was quite a sight to see some of the noninterventionist Senators plead with him not to hold up the bill to remove it.

I do not envy you your task tomorrow. Strength and wisdom to all of you.

DOCUMENT 148

William R. Castle to R. Douglas Stuart, Jr.
December 10, 1941

I hope this letter may reach you before the meeting, even though it may not be very important.

In my mind the trouble with continuing the America First Committee is

that there is bound always to be suspicion of its activities in the minds of
many people. The Washington Post this morning had a rather nasty article
in which it pointed out that the Committee had not made up its mind to
suspend activities, and insinuating that it should be watched. The Vice
Chairman of the Fight For Freedom Committee was a nice boy, but a
fanatic—his mother having been an English woman and he having been
brought up in England—remarked also in the paper that you could not
afford to ignore the activities of America First. The above refers to the
Chapters.

I should hate to see in Washington, particularly, a rather prominent
office kept open, because it would be continually a source of suspicion. We
must remember that in war time we are likely to get into pretty serious
trouble if we criticise the President, or the conduct of the war. As you
rightly point out, criticism of the Government continues vigorously in
England; in that way England is more democratic than we are. I ran into
this yesterday when I said that I wished the news could be given out calmly
by the Army and Navy instead of by the President, as I thought the
President of the United States should never speak except after great consideration and with complete accuracy. The person with whom I was talking
said that I could not point out any case in which he had not been accurate
so far, and I answered that, as a matter of fact, he had announced at the
very beginning that Manila had been bombed when it had not been. I am
probably now put down as a dissenter of the worst kind. I quote this
merely to show how careful we must be. It seems to me, therefore, that it
is almost beyond argument that the various chapters of America First ought
to close. On the other hand I should hate not to see some kind of central
body kept going just to hold together the records of the organization and
the list of members in order that, in case of necessity, America First could
quickly be called into action again.

I don't think we can any longer oppose war against Germany and Italy,
much as I hate to say this. Those nations are allies of Japan, and I am
inclined to believe, in any case, that the matter will be taken out of our
hands by a German declaration of war on this country; that would, perhaps,
be the best way out of it. Furthermore, if we are at war with Germany, we
cannot oppose the dispatching of an expeditionary force, if that has been
decided on by the general staff. As one looks at it now nothing could be
more insane, but after all we are civilians and we do not have the say in
matters of that kind. The American people have chosen to put themselves
in the hands of men whom you and I, probably, thoroughly distrust, but
nevertheless they were put there through a democratic process and we
cannot, in consequence, oppose them.

I should hate to see the organization turn into a political party, and that is the danger if we try to take definite political action. On the other hand, if somebody can work out an effective method by which we could be a vivifying and uplifting influence, an Americanizing influence in the public life of the country, I should be all for it. I do not yet see the means by which this could be done.

One other matter must be scrutinized carefully, that is that it is going to be very difficult, and progressively more difficult, to get money to run any kind of an ambitious organization. I don't think we want to ape the British and have any "Bundles" for America; that work is presumably being done efficiently by the Red Cross, an already established organization. Bundles for Britain here is just about folding up and I think we shall have no difficulty in keeping our forces well supplied, except for the red tape in official quarters, which always prevents the maximum use of such things as are given. If we could get money enough to run a very small central organization, which would have no publicity whatever, and which would have, if possible, two or three people doing research work, it might be well worthwhile. But if even that is done it must never be suspected as an anti-war group. I hate it just as much you do, but I feel that, to live up to our promises, we must devote ourselves now to helping the country succeed.

DOCUMENT 149

Minutes, National Committee

December 11, 1941

The Members of the America First Committee convened in a special meeting at 1541 North Astor Street, in the city of Chicago, State of Illinois, at 12 o'clock noon, on the 11th day of December, 1941, pursuant to call and notice.

The meeting was called to order by General Robert E. Wood, Acting Chairman of the corporation. R. Douglas Stuart, Jr. served in his capacity as Secretary of the corporation.

The roll-call found the following Members present in person:

A. J. Carlson
Janet Ayer Fairbank
John T. Flynn
Clay Judson
Sterling Morton [*Chicago
investor*]
J. Sanford Otis [*Chicago investor;
national treasurer, AFC*]
Isaac A. Pennypacker
[*Philadelphia attorney;
chairman, Philadelphia AFC*]

Amos R. E. Pinchot
William H. Regnery
Harry L. Stuart [*president,
Halsey, Stuart and Co.
investment banking firm*]
R. Douglas Stuart, Jr.
Edwin S. Webster, Jr. [*New York
investment banker; secretary,
N.Y. Chapter, AFC*]
Robert Young [*financier, board
chairman, Allegheny
Corporation*]
Robert E. Wood

Also present, by invitation of the Members, were: Hon. Philip LaFollette; Hon. Samuel B. Pettengill; Page Hufty; Richard A. Moore.

The Secretary advised the Chairman that written notice, stating the time, place and object of said meeting had been properly addressed and despatched to each Member of this corporation. The Secretary's affidavit to that effect is appended to these Minutes.

Thereupon the Chairman, pursuant to said notice, announced that the meeting had been called for the purpose of submitting to the Members the question whether the corporation should be dissolved or should be continued.

After discussion, Sterling Morton moved that the corporation be dissolved. The motion was seconded by Clay Judson. A ballot then being taken, each Member voting in person, the said motion was adopted by a majority vote of all the Members present.

John T. Flynn then moved that the records of the America First Committee and the records of its chapters be impounded in the custody of General Robert E. Wood, for the purpose of preventing unauthorized use of the name of the America First Committee, no person or group to be granted access to these records unless written permission is secured from a majority of the Board of Directors. The motion was seconded by Janet Ayer Fairbank. A ballot then being taken, each Member voting in person, the said motion was adopted by a majority vote of all members present.

A motion was then duly made and seconded, and carried by a majority vote of all the Members present, to adopt the following public statement and to issue it to the press:

The America First Committee was organized in the summer of 1940 with two primary objectives:

(1) An impregnable defense for our nation.

(2) Avoidance of involvement in the European and Asiatic war.

Our principles were right. Had they been followed, war could have been avoided. No good purpose can now be served by considering what might have been, had our objectives been attained.

On Sunday, December 7, Japan launched an attack upon us.

On Monday, December 8, Congress declared war on Japan.

Today, December 11, Congress declared war on Germany and Japan.

There is no longer any question about our involvement in the conflict in Europe and Asia. We are at war. Today, though there may be many important considerations, the primary objective is not difficult to state. It can be defined in one word—victory.

While the executive branch of the government will take charge of the prosecution of the war, the fundamental rights of American citizens under our Constitution and Bill of Rights must be respected. The long range aims and the policies of our country must be determined by the people through Congress. We hope that secret treaties committing America to imperialistic aims or vast burden in other parts of the world shall be scrupulously avoided to the end that this nation shall become the champion of a just and lasting peace.

The period of democratic debate on the issue of entering the war is over; the time for military action is here. Therefore, the America First Committee has determined immediately to cease all functions and to dissolve as soon as that can legally be done. And finally, it urges all those who have followed its lead to give their full support to the war effort of the nation, until peace is announced.

The Chairman announced that, since those present and voting for the resolution of dissolution did not constitute a majority of the Members of the corporation, this meeting of the Members of the corporation would adjourn to 29th day of January, 1942, at the office of the Committee at 12:00 P.M. so that Members not present today might have the opportunity to vote upon the question of dissolution, either in person or by proxy.

The Chairman then stated that but for R. Douglas Stuart Jr., there would have been no America First Committee, and that the thanks of all its Members were due him. Thereupon, on motion duly made and seconded, the following resolution was unanimously adopted:

Resolved, that the America First Committee hereby expresses its deep appreciation to R. Douglas Stuart, Jr. for his long self-sacrificing service to the Committee, with confidence that the idealism, courage and ability which he has displayed will continue to be of ever-increasing value to this community and country.

There being no further business for consideration at this time, upon motion duly made and seconded, and unanimously carried, the meeting was adjourned to January 29, 1942.

Name Index

Adams, Alva B., 298
Adams, Charles Francis, 55n.41
Adams, John, 326, 406
Adams, Samuel Hopkins, 54n.41
Aiken, George D., 259, 456, 462
Aikman, Duncan, 178–79, 181
Alexander, A. V., 424, 426
Allen, R. G. D., 208–9
Allen, Robert S., 386
Alsop, Joseph, 128, 252
Altick, Sherman B., 248
Andersen, H. Carl, 431, 438
Angell, Norman, 121
Armstrong, O. K., 12, 101
Arnold, Henry H. ("Hap"), 249, 459
Auchinleck, Claude J. E., 312
Austin, Warren, 231, 233
Aydelotte, Frank, 246

Bailey, Josiah W., 233
Baker, Ray Stannard Baker, 121–22
Balderson, John, 246
Baldridge, Cyrus Leroy, 58n.64
Balduf, Emery W., 241–42
Baldwin, Hanson W., 19, 60n.68, 89, 130,
    309, 310, 457; "The Realities of Hemi-
    sphere Defense," 346, 357, 364–65;
    "What of the British Fleet?" 402–3, 427–
    28. See also *United We Stand!*
Ballantine, Arthur, Jr., 88–89
Bankhead, John A., 15
Banning, Margaret Culkin, 245
Barkley, Alben W., 70n.144, 257, 258, 324
Barnes, Harry Elmer, 5
Barr, Stringfellow, 245, 246
Barton, Bruce, 10
Baruch, Bernard, 15, 73n.155, 159, 164
Beals, Carleton, 176, 179, 180–81, 182
Beard, Charles A., 8, 19, 74n.165, 88, 121
Beaverbrook, Lord, 421
Beckman, Francis J. L., 138–39, 434

Belloc, Hilaire, 60n.68
Bennett, Philip A., 238
Benton, William, 12, 100–101, 102, 108, 136,
    390
Berle, A. A., 155, 180, 182
Bilbo, Theodore G., 75n.179, 431
Bingham, Jonathan B., 58n.64, 73n.155
Birdsall, Paul, 331
Bissell, Richard M., 58n.64, 215
Blaine, Mrs. Emmons, 245
Bliss, Robert L., 56n.52, 78n.203, 102, 259,
    383
Boldt, Joseph R., Jr., 56n.52
Boothe, Clare, 245
Borah, William E., 401
Borchard, Edwin M., 7, 14, 40, 105–6. See
    also *Neutrality for the United States*
Bowles, Chester: general foreign policy
    views of, 14, 109–10; on negotiated
    peace, 20, 126–27, 282, 285; on Lind-
    bergh, 28, 280–81; on polls, 29, 281,
    282–86; on domestic communism, 31,
    279–80; on AFC recruitment, 36, 390–
    91; on Des Moines speech, 38, 391–92;
    on political action, 45, 107–9; on dissolv-
    ing AFC, 48; on Friends of Democracy,
    70n.146; on Bliss, 102; on FBI investiga-
    tion, 108; meets Wheeler, 278–81
Brailsford, H. N., 164, 244
Brewster, Kingman, 8, 58n.64, 88–90, 228
Brewster, Ralph Owen, 75n.179
Bridges, Styles, 440
Bromley, Dorothy Dunbar, 71n.147
Brooks, C. Wayland ("Curly"), 260, 299
Brunauer, Esther Caukin, 245
Brundage, Avery, 15
Bryan, William Jennings, 275, 339–40
Bryson, Lyman, 245
Burdick, Fred: on Newfoundland meeting,
    32; on term of military service, 34, 380–
    82; and neutrality act revision, 42, 44,

Burdick, Fred (*continued*)
431–32; on AEF plans, 45, 184n.76, 436–38; and Far East, 47, 77n.193, 440, 449–53; background of, 56n.52; responsibilities of, 57n.55; AFC activity of, 131; on lend-lease, 238–40; Sarles on, 251
Burdick, Usher L., 239
Burton, Harold H., 75n.179, 134
Byrd, Harry F., 75n.179, 198, 453, 456
Byrnes, James F., 257

Caldwell, Lewis, 462, 463
Camphausen, F. H., 457
Cannon, Clarence, 437
Capper, Arthur, 10, 257, 302, 450, 453
Carlson, Anton J., 39, 397, 468
Carter, Boake, 10, 73n.157, 267, 385, 386
Case, Francis H., 439
Case, Otto, 54n.41
Casey, Richard C., 241
Castle, William R.: on AFC national committee, 11; ties to Hoover, 11, 15; on escorts, 11, 64n.99; on negotiated peace, 19; on lend-lease, 23, 227; on AFC recruitment, 36; on Jews, 37, 72n.152; on New Dealers, 37, 72n.152; on political action, 45, 443; on Pearl Harbor, 47, 453–54; on dissolving AFC, 48, 465–66; on repeal of arms embargo, 50; on General Wood, 57–58n.57; on Lindbergh Des Moines speech, 73n.159; on amending 1939 neutrality act, 75n.180; and Washington, D.C., AFC 95; on No Foreign War Campaign, 103
Celler, Emanuel, 456
Chamberlain, John, 24, 219–20
Chamberlin, William Henry, 73n.155
Chaplin, Charlie, 69n.139
Chase, Fred, 442
Chase, Stuart, 13, 54n.35, 152
Chavez, Dennis, 298
Cherne, Leo M., 189
Childs, Marquis W., 190
Churchill, Winston: and Newfoundland meeting, 3, 32, 135, 247, 313–14, 315–42; pleas for U.S. aid, 11, 22, 53n.27; assured of U.S. naval aid, 26; rumors of resignation, 26, 300, 421; on convoys, 41, 68n.126; quoted that crisis ended, 75n.180; admiration of, 124; and negotiated peace, 135, 136, 252, 303; on shipping losses, 195, 424–25, 426; on Anglo-American unity 241; desperation

of, 252; on economic integration with United States, 300. See also *Aftermath, The;* Great Britain
Clapper, Raymond, 263
Clark, Bennett Champ: movie investigation by, 35, 384; and AFC political advisory committee, 76n.185; and lend-lease, 231, 233, 418; and industrial mobilization plan, 252; and convoy resolution, 257; and ship seizure amendment, 260; on term of military service, 360; and *Greer,* 407, 417
Clark, D. Worth, 62n.76, 76n.185, 260, 384, 462
Clark, Miriam M. (Mrs. Bennett Champ), 54–55n.41, 57n.56, 95, 397
Clemenceau, Georges, 276, 340
Cobb, Irving, 54n.41
Colcord, Lincoln, 24, 220–22
Cole, Wayne S., 16, 25–26, 29, 35–36, 46, 49
Collins, Ross A., 60n.68, 267, 360
Combs, George H., Jr., 386
Conant, James B., 23, 122–26
Connally, Tom, 232, 250, 257, 456, 458
Corwin, Edward S., 74n.165, 326–27, 328, 329
Coughlin, Charles E., 37; followers of, 36, 50, 70n.142, 389
Creel, George, 121; propandanda committee of, 5, 121
Crippen, Harlan, 67n.119
Cudahy, John, 19, 76n.185, 126–27, 137, 443
Curtis, Carl, 128, 249, 431

Danaher, John A., 462
Darling, Jay Norwood ("Ding"), 245
Davenport, Russell, 245, 246
Davenport, Walter, 71n.147
Davila, Carlos, 180, 181
Davis, Elmer, 385, 386
Dawes, Charles G., 13, 161
DeGaulle, Charles, 300, 333. *See also* France: Free French
Dennis, Lawrence: background and general views of, 21–22; and AFC, 21–22, 62n.78; economic memo of, 200–205
Denny, Ludwell, 300
Detzer, Dorothy, 73n.159
Dewey, Thomas E., 13, 23
Dies, Martin, 71n.149, 247
Dill, John, 234, 235
Ditter, J. William, 438

Dodge, Mrs. Hartley A. (Geraldine Rockefeller), 99, 102
Dominick, Peter H., 58n.64
Donovan, William J. ("Wild Bill"), 253, 300
Dos Passos, John, 5
Doxey, Wall, 431
Dreicer, Maurice C., 386
Drummond, Roscoe, 132
Dulles, Janet Avery (Mrs. John Foster), 54n.36
Dulles, John Foster, 13, 54n.36
Durant, Will, 13
Dworshak, Henry C., 239

Eddy, William Alfred, 245
Eden, Anthony, 234, 235
Eggleston, George, 99, 102
Eliot, George Fielding, 357
Embick, Stanley D., 57n.56
Englebrecht, H. C., 121
Evans, Madge, 388

Faddis, Charles I., 252
Fairbank, Janet Ayer: on AFC staff, 16, 56 n.51; on AFC continuation, 25; on war resolution, 44; on aid to Britain, 50–51; and Chicago chapter, 56n.53; on extremists, 72n.150; and Lindbergh Des Moines speech, 73n.157, 397; and AFC dissolution, 468
Farley, James A., 14, 99
Farquarson, Mary, 60n.67
Fay, Sidney Bradshaw, 5
Fenwick, Charles G., 245
Férrer, José, 17, 58n.64
Fish, Hamilton, 27, 66n.111, 130, 138, 435
Fisher, Dorothy Canfield, 245
Fitz Simons, Ellen French Vanderbilt, 76n.186
Fleischer, Charles, 72–73n.154
Fleming, Harold M., 386
Flynn, John T.: and 1940 election, 10; background of, 16; "road ahead," 17; and negotiated peace, 20, 138–40, 435–36; on polls, 29; on Hitler's war aims, 30; and movie investigation, 35, 383, 396; on Lindbergh Des Moines speech, 38, 395–96, 397; on neutrality act revision, 44, 138–41; on war resolution, 45, 435; on AFC political action, 45, 447; on Far East, 47; on New Deal, 50; and New York chapter, 56n.53, 95, 101; on Friends of

Democracy, 70n.146; on anti-Semitism, 73n.156, 111; on extremist elements, 110–12; on radio commentators, 383; on publicity, 445–47; and dissolving AFC, 468. See also America First Committee, New York chapter
Ford, Gerald R., 7, 8, 87
Ford, Henry, 15, 59n.65, 64n.106, 98
Forrestal, James, 261
Fosdick, Harry Emerson, 66n.111, 138–39, 435
Frank, Jerome, 60n.68, 399
Frankfurter, Felix, 394
Frazer, Henry, 193, 405
Fuller, Walter D., 189

Gallup, George, 287–89. See also Gallup poll
Gannett, Frank, 73n.154
Garrison, Lloyd, 60n.67
Garrity, Devin A., 58n.64
Gee, W., 122
Gehrmann, Bernard J., 258
George, King of Greece, 336
George, Walter F., 97, 130–31, 256, 257, 289, 431
Gill, Samuel, 66n.111
Gillette, Guy, 38, 257, 393, 455
Gish, Lillian, 14
Glass, Carter, 257
Goebbels, Josef, 116
Goering, Hermann, 116
Gosgriffe, Walter, 57n.53
Grattan, C. Hartley, 51n.9, 60n.68
Green, James Frederick, 326, 327, 328, 329, 330
Green, Theodore Francis, 257
Green, William, 59n.65
Grew, Joseph C., 299
Grey, Edward, 328
Griswold, A. Whitney, 23, 63n.85, 88, 215–17
Guffey, Joseph F., 257, 258
Gunther, Frances (Mrs. John), 72n.151

Haakon VII, King of Norway, 336
Hagood, Johnson, 19, 61n.68, 120–21
Hailslip, Wade Hampton, 356
Hale, Arthur, 386
Halifax, Lord, 241
Halleck, Charles A., 190
Hallgren, Mauritz A., 51n.9
Hammaker, Wilbur E., 54n.41, 73n.159

Hammond, Thomas S., 8, 39, 48, 396–97
Hanighen, Frank, 57n.55, 121, 463
Hanna, Mrs. Carl, 102
Harrison, Pat, 133, 257
Hawley, Adelaide, 388
Hearst, William Randolph: press of, 23, 73n.155
Heatter, Gabriel, 385–86
Hemingway, Ernest, 5
Henderson, Leon, 176, 184, 187, 207, 377
Heptisax, 339
Herring, Clyde L., 274–75
Herring, Hubert, 121, 170, 171, 179
Hershey, Burnett, 387
Hertzberg, Sidney, 37, 54n.40, 56n.52, 58n.61, 72n.151, 96, 103
Hess, Rudolph: flight of, 61n.70, 250, 261, 303
Hill, Edwin C., 385
Hill, Knute, 66n.111, 131
Hill, Lister, 368
Hirschmann, Ira, 72n.151
Hitler, Adolf: economic threat of, 4, 21, 22, 121, 153, 155, 159, 161, 164–67, 169, 200; isolationist seen as naive on, 4–5, 389; anti-interventionists on goals and potential of, 6, 20, 112–13; and negotiated peace, 19, 20, 32, 109, 252, 303, 314; attack on Russia, 20, 30, 290–91, 295, 358, 362–63, 422; Atlantic war, 43, 45, 49, 408; quotations juxtaposed to Wheeler, Nye, 70n.146; attack Western Hemisphere, 97, 109, 126, 141, 146–47, 150, 323, 358, 362, 421; rise of, 113, 115; defeat of, 116, 227, 283–85, 315; Petain and, 230; and attack on Britain, 230, 449, 358; and attack on Dakar, 305; and attack on Azores, 308; and German shipping capacity, 426, 427–28; and Far East, 440; and attack on Mediterranean, 449; domestic troubles of, 458. See also Germany
Hobson, Henry, 36, 245, 388–89
Holman, Rufus C., 236, 298
Holmes, John Haynes, 61n.70
Hoover, Calvin B., 209, 211, 212
Hoover, Herbert: ties to Castle, 11, 15; and AFC, 15, 55–56n.49, 89, 99; food plan of, 15, 40, 99; on Lindbergh Des Moines speech, 38, 73n.155; book endorsed, 60n.68; on AEF plans, 76n.184; and AFC political advisory committee,

76n.185, 441; on No Foreign War Campaign, 103; speech cited, 261; attack 393
Hoover, J. Edgar, 71n.148
Hopkins, Harry, 30, 135, 235, 243, 247, 258
Hormel, Jay, 41, 409–11
House, Edward M., 315, 328
Howard, Graeme, 121
Howard, Perry, 18
Howard, Roy, 52n.16
Howe, Quincy, 73n.154, 245, 387
Hoyt, Lansing, 57n.53
Hubble, Edwin B., 245
Hufty, Page: on Selective Service, 34, 35, 68n.127, 357–59; background of, 56n.52; on impeachment, 58n.59; on H. Baldwin, 60n.68; on franking issue, 70n.144; on Lindbergh Des Moines speech, 74n.161; issues AFC book list, 120–22; and lend-lease, 419; and AFC strategy, 420; and dissolving AFC, 468
Hughes, Charles Evans, 15
Hull, Cordell: and Far East, 46, 133, 440, 449–50; on reciprocal trade, 181; on lend-lease, 227; on contraband, 270, 294, 403; on neutrality repeal, 299; and British preference, 336; on defensive waters, 418
Hurley, Patrick J., 57n.56
Hutcheson, William L., 54n41, 441
Hutchins, Robert M.: on decline in AFC membership, 13, 54n33; and mediation movement, 20, 61n.74, 136–37; and polls, 29, 54n.33, 66n.111, 137; and FDR meeting, 133–34; antiwar views of, 224, 390
Hyde, Herbert K., 73n.155

Ickes, Harold L., 36, 255, 359, 360, 428, 429
Ingalls, Laura, 36
Ingersoll, Ralph, 102
Ishii, Viscount, 328

Jackson, Gardner, 59n.67
Janeway, Eliot, 59–60n.67
Jefferson, Thomas, 326, 406
Jeffrey, Earl, 56n.52, 441
Jessup, Philip, 73n.154, 74n.165
Jewett, Frank B., 52n.16
Johns, Joshua L., 451
Johnson, Hiram, 9, 48, 131, 257, 360, 420, 456, 462–63, 465

Johnson, Hugh, 9–10, 14, 60n.68, 73n.155, 103, 106–7

Jonasson, Herman, 32, 309, 310

Jones, Jesse, 195, 417

Judson, Clay: as AFC leader, 9, 10; general foreign policy views, 9, 23, 92–94, 122–26; favors nonpartisan AFC, 10; on negotiated peace, 19, 125; on naval engagements, 25, 40; and neutrality act revision, 42, 44; and Chicago Council of Foreign Relations, 50; on loans, 53n.28; on Friends of Democarcy, 70n.146; and Lindbergh Des Moines speech, 397; and dissolving AFC, 468

Judson, William V., 124

Kahn, Florence Prather, 37

Kaltenborn, H. V., 385

Katsura, Taro, 328

Keefe, Frank, 453

Kempton, Murray, 57n.55

Kennedy, John B., 386

Kennedy, John F., 17, 58n.63

Kennedy, Joseph P., 15, 58n.63

Kent, Raymond, 66n.111

Kernon, William C., 387

Keynes, John Maynard, 132, 212, 253

Kimmel, Husband E., 455

King, Ernest J., 261

King, Mackenzie, 142, 317, 332

Kingdon, Frank, 245, 246, 393–94

Kintner, Robert, 128, 252

Knox, Frank: and Pearl Harbor, 47, 454, 455, 457, 458; on waging of Atlantic war, 130, 134, 276, 289; attacked, 131, 265, 434, 443; on U.S. naval strength, 148–49; imply U.S. entering war, 186, 432; on Caribbean, 364; on Roosevelt, 372; and AEF plans, 438

Knutson, Harold, 131, 438

Konoye, Fumimaro, 313

Krock, Arthur, 134, 224

La Follette, Philip, 70n.146, 76n.185, 103, 260, 441, 468

La Follette, Robert M., 401

La Follette, Robert M., Jr.: as AFC radio speaker, 10; on dissolving AFC, 48, 462; on second lend-lease request, 195; on defense orders, 198; on convoys, 257; on AFC strategy, 401; on aid to Russia, 417; on neutrality revision, 418; on post–Pearl Harbor Congress, 458

Lage, William Potter. See *Neutrality for the United States*

Lambertson, William, 438, 453

Lamont, Mrs. Thomas W., 245, 246

Land, Emory Scott, 414–16, 425, 426–27, 428

Landon, Alfred M., 56n.52, 76n.185

Lansing, Robert, 272, 274, 328, 340

Larsen, Roy E., 29

Larson, Cedric, 121

Lawrence, David, 61n.70, 128. See also *United States News*

Leach, Henry Goddard, 245

Leahy, William D., 232

Lee, Joshua W., 368

Lee, Kendrick, 27, 57n.52, 129, 217, 447

Lerner, Max, 245

Lewis, Arthur R., Jr., 268

Lewis, Cleona, 160, 165, 167–68

Lewis, Fulton, Jr., 386

Lewis, John L., 18, 59n.65, 187, 441. See also Congress of Industrial Organizations

Lewis, Kathryn, 18, 59n.65, 72n.155, 441

Libby, Frederick J., 38, 103, 250, 392–94, 457, 465. See also National Council for the Prevention of War

Lindbergh, Anne Morrow (Mrs. Charles), 39, 65n.108

Lindbergh, Charles A.: background and general views of, 5, 19, 28–29, 90, 126–27, 266; role in AFC, 28, 50, 64n.106, 65n.107, 74n.167; call for "new leadership," 29, 65n.108; Oklahoma City speech of, 29, 395, 396; on Soviet Union, 30, 67n.118; Des Moines speech of, 37–40, 41, 50, 72–74n.155–163, 391–401, 418; Fort Wayne speech of, 39, 393; and AFC political action, 46; on Pearl Harbor, 47; on dissolving AFC, 48, 77n.199; "Letter to Americans," 60–61n.68, 65n.106; on negotiated peace, 61n.73, 67n.118, 74n.167; on Tobey resolution, 99n.64; on Iceland, 67–68n.123; and No Foreign War Campaign, 103; speech cited, 261; praised, 280–81; attacked, 389; and movie investigation, 396

Lindley, Ernest K., 295, 296

Lippmann, Walter, 22

Lipsig, James, 37, 56n.52, 57n.55, 417, 418, 447

Lloyd George, David, 276, 332, 340, 421

Locke, Eugene, 87
Lodge, Henry Cabot, 75n.179
Lohbeck, Don, 72n.150
Longworth, Alice Roosevelt, 397
Lowden, Frank O., 54n.41
Luce, Henry: 244; publications of, 35, 38, 60n.68. See also *Fortune; Life; Time*
Ludlow, Louis, 30, 438, 452, 453
Lyttleton, Oliver, 333

Maas, Melvin J., 239
MacCracken, Henry Noble, 66n.111
MacLiesh, Fleming. See *Strategy of the Americas*
MacNider, Hanford: on lend-lease, 23, 227, 228; on war declaration, 41; resigns over AFC political action, 45, 444–45; on No Foreign War Campaign, 53n.30, 101, 103; on negotiated peace, 61n.73; on Roosevelt, 75n.170; AFC activity of, 95; on AFC strategy, 408–9
Madison, James, 328
Mahon, George H., 426–27
Maloney, Francis T., 75n.179
Manion, Clarence, 41n.41
Manly, Chesly, 436–37, 439
Mann, Erika, 124
Mann, Thomas, 245
Manning, William, 67n.115
Marquand, Adelaide Hooker (Mrs. John P.), 41n.41
Marschak, Jacob, 207
Marsh, Daniel L., 89
Marshall, George C., 33, 34, 311, 344–57 passim, 361–67, 438
Marshall, Verne, 12, 15, 72n.152
Martin, Joseph W., Jr., 422
Mason, Gregory, 39, 54n.41
Massey, Raymond, 245
May, Andrew J., 252
Mayer, Frank, 97
McCarran, Patrick, 223, 298
McCarter, Thomas N., 55n.41
McConnell, Francis J., 245
McCormick, John W., 239
McCormick, Robert R., 50, 101
McKaig, Ray, 54n.41, 441
McNary, Charles S., 75n.179, 250
Milbank, Jeremiah, 15, 99, 101, 102
Miller, Douglas, 22, 169
Miller, Helen Hill, 245
Millis, Walter, 5, 121

Minor, Julius, 72n.151
Mitchell, William, 266
Mock, James R., 121
Monroe, James, 328
Moore, R. Walton, 292
Moore, Richard A., 17, 44, 58n.64, 420, 468
Morgan, firm of J. P.: 31, 52n.19
Morgenthau, Henry, Jr., 227
Morley, Felix, 13
Morrison, Charles Clayton, 13, 54n.36, 104
Morton, Sterling J.: general views of, 8, 90–92; as AFC leader, 26; on extremists, 36–37; on attacks, 70n.146; on Lindbergh Des Moines speech, 73n.159; on AFC direction, 253–56; on dissolving AFC, 468
Mosely, Sidney, 387
Movius, Gerald W., 419
Mumford, Lewis, 245
Mundt, Karl: on Lindbergh Des Moines speech, 39; as AFC adviser, 39, 57n.53; on dissolving AFC, 48, 462, 463; optimism of, 64n.99; and Selective Service, 134, 380, 382; and neutrality revision, 138, 419, 420, 431, 435; on lend-lease, 238; peace proposal of, 250; on Far East, 440, 451, 452
Murphy, Frank, 370, 371
Murray, Frank, 442
Murray, James J., 190, 257
Murray, Philip, 65n.65
Mussolini, Benito, 116

Nehemkis, Peter, Jr., 186–87
Nelson, Donald, 190
Neuberger, Richard, 60n.67
Niebuhr, Reinhold, 259
Nomura, Kichiaburo, 313, 449–50
Norris, George, 274
Norris, Kathleen, 39
Nye, Gerald P.: as AFC speaker, 28, 50, 299; and movie investigation, 35, 384, 417; and AFC political action, 46; and Friends of Democracy, 70n.146; and Lindbergh Des Moines speech, 73n.160; and lend-lease, 231, 298; and resolution on conveys, 257; on U.S. shipping losses, 257; on Selective Service, 360; and Jews, 393, 394; and *Greer*, 407, 417; on Knox impeachment, 456. See also Special Senate Committee on Investigation of the Munitions Industry

Ogilby, Remsen Brinkerhoff, 88
Oldham, G. Ashton, 245
Oliver, Bryce, 387
Oliver, Eli, 6on.67
Otis, J. Sanford, 54n.41, 468

Palmer, Albert W., 14, 55n.44, 66n.111
Palmer, Frederick, 306, 307
Palmer, Greta (Mrs. Paul), 71n.151
Parry, Albert, 67n.119
Patterson, Eleanor M. ("Cissy"), 57n.56
Patterson, Joseph M., 52n.16, 101
Patterson, Robert P., 132, 266
Payson, Charles Shipman, 99, 101, 102
Peabody, Endicott, 245
Pearson, Drew, 386
Pecora, Ferdinand, 393
Peek, George, 54n.41, 398
Pennypacker, Isaac, 54n.41, 468
Pepper, Claude: debates Cudahy, 137;
    foresees war, 231, 233, 302; on convoys,
    257; attacked, 265, 393, 434; on occupa-
    tion of Azores, Cape Verdes, 308; on
    national emergency, 368
Pershing, John J., 15, 254
Petain, Henri Philippe, 16, 69n.137, 230
Peter, King of Yugoslavia, 336
Pettengill, Samuel; on negotiated peace, 31;
    on Selective Service, 34, 359–60, 382–
    83; and neutrality act revision, 42; on war
    resolution, 44, 301–3, 432–33; back-
    ground of, 67n.118; on Newfoundland
    meeting, 68n.126; on arming merchant
    ships, 302–3; on AFC political action,
    441, 442; and dissolving AFC, 468
Pheiffer, William T., 451
Phillips, William, 232, 300
Pinchot, Amos, 73n.160, 398, 468
Pius XII, 299–300
Pogue, Forrest, 33, 34
Ponsonby, Arthur, 6on.68
Putney, Bryant, 326, 329

Rankin, John E., 456
Rauschenbush, Joan, 51n.9
Rauschenbush, Stephen, 51n.9
Rayburn, Sam, 350
Reed, Daniel A., 438
Reed, David Aiken, 57n.53
Regnery, William H., 8–9, 10, 17, 48, 97,
    468
Reid, Doris Fielding, 68n.68

Reynolds, Cushman, 62n.76. See also
    Strategy of the Americas
Reynolds, Robert Rice, 33–34, 66n.111, 128,
    132, 223, 257
Richardson, H. Smith, 17, 73n.155
Richardson, James O., 455
Richardson, Lunsford, 102
Rickenbacker, Eddie, 14, 15
Rizley, Ross, 452
Roche, Josephine, 59n.67
Rockefeller, Nelson, 177
Rodell, Fred, 7, 58n.64
Rodman, Selden, 73n.155
Romer, Samuel E., 385–88
Roosevelt, Eleanor (Mrs. Franklin D.), 247
Roosevelt, Franklin D., activities of: histori-
    ans and, 2; general interventionist
    policies of, 2–3, 6; and 1939 neutrality
    revision, 2; seeks aid to Britain and
    France in 1940, 2, 11; and destroyer-
    bases deal, 3, 364; and lend-lease, 3, 22,
    25, 217, 222; and Greenland, 3, 26,
    364; and Iceland, 3, 30, 311–12, 364; on
    lend-lease to Russia, 3, 30; and Far East,
    3, 46, 449–50, 451, 452, 458, 459; and
    Newfoundland meeting, 3, 32, 68n.126,
    n.127, 135, 247, 313–14, 315–42; and
    convoys, 3, 26, 32, 41, 45, 76n.183, 193,
    257, 260, 312; war participation and, 3,
    135, 221, 254, 258; reasons for interven-
    tionism, 3–4; opposes isolationism, 4–5;
    effect of AFC on, 6, 49; opposed, 16–17,
    19, 36, 75n.170, 105–6, 443; on religious
    freedom in Russia, 30; and 1941 Selective
    Service, 33–34; investigates AFC, 36;
    and revision of Neutrality Act, 42,
    44, 139, 299, 417, 434; suggested Wood
    meeting, 103; and Cudahy, 127; and Fish
    poll, 130; suggested Hutchins meeting,
    133–34; and negotiated peace, 135, 136,
    137, 139–40, 286; requests second
    lend-lease appropriation, 191–99; and
    taxes, 214; on *Robin Moor*, 274; does not
    invoke neutrality act in Asia, 293; on
    war resolution, 302; and term of military
    service, 352, 382–83; agreement with
    Canada, 364; and emergency powers,
    369, 372–79; and ship seizures, 416; and
    Pink Star, 416; and AEF, 421, 437; and
    Churchill, 421; and ship tonnage, 428;
    post–Pearl Harbor plans of, 460
Roosevelt, Franklin D., speeches and

Roosevelt, Franklin D., (continued)
statements of: November 11, 1935, 291;
August 14, 1936 (Chautauqua speech),
294, 347, 404; October 5, 1937 (quarantine speech), 329; September 21, 1939
(neutrality), 192, 413; November 4
(defines neutrality zone), 2; September 2,
1940 (Chickamauga speech), 184;
October 23 (Philadelphia speech), 304,
308, 344; December 2 (fireside chat), 344;
December 29 (fireside chat), 3–4, 22,
413; January 6, 1941 (message to
Congress), 22, 320–21, 361; January 21
(press conference covering convoys), 26,
193, 282, 283–84, 289, 401; January 29
(third inaugural), 4; May 27 (proclaims
unlimited emergency), 3, 4, 27, 28, 49,
64n.102, 127–28, 159, 160, 249–50, 261,
262–63, 276–78, 304, 322, 323, 369, 371,
372–73, 422; May 28 (press conference),
263; June 17 (press conference), 272;
June 20 (invokes freedom of seas), 28,
273, 276; July 7 (U.S. landings on
Iceland), 31, 193–94, 304–5, 309, 310–
11, 312, 414; July 8 (press conference),
308; July 21 (on term of military service),
33, 34, 357–59, 361–72; August 16
(press conference), 324; August 21 (message to Congress on Atlantic Charter),
321, 325; August 21 (to Young Democrats), 225; September 11 (shoot-on-sight
orders), 3, 40, 41, 74n.165, 194–95, 401–
8, 408, 414, 418, 422; October 9 (arming
merchant ships), 42–43; October 27 (Navy
Day speech), 42, 75n.170, 431; otherwise
quoted, 94, 192
Roosevelt, Theodore, 328
Rosenman, Samuel I., 394
Rosenwald, Lessing, 37, 102
Ross, James, 305, 306
Rowell, Chester, 245
Russell, Richard B., 431
Ryerson, Edward L., Jr., 12, 14, 25, 50–51,
58n.64, 72n.155

Sabath, Adolph J., 134
Salazar, Antonio de Oliveira, 16
Sanger, Margaret, 26
Sarles, Ruth: history of AFC, 2, 39, 87–88,
459–61; on NFWC, 12; background
of, 16, 56n.52; responsibilities of, 16,
57n.55; on negotiated peace, 19–20, 32,
67n.118, 129, 133, 135–36, 250, 251–52;

261, 264, 314, 422; prognosis on European war, 26, 31, 251–52; on Tobey
resolution, 27, 64n.99, 128; on convoys,
27, 64n.99, 132, 249, 257; on Robin
Moor, 27–28; advisory referendum of,
30, 131, 134; on lend-lease to Russia, 30,
417, 421; on Newfoundland meeting,
32, 135, 313–14; on Selective Service,
34, 134, 135; on radio bias, 35; and
neutrality act revision, 42, 43, 44, 417,
418, 419–20, 422; on Far East, 46, 47,
77n.190, 129, 133, 299, 313, 440; on
Pearl Harbor, 47, 454–59; and dissolving
AFC, 48, 462–65; on U.S. hemispheric
domination, 62n.76; and L. Dennis,
62n.78; on U.S. military plans, 76n.184,
135; on FDR national emergency speech,
127–28; on attacks, 128; on presidential
powers, 129; on AFC strength, 130; on
U.S. defense effort, 130; on polls, 130; on
Washington mood, 127–36, 249–253,
257–61, 298–301, 416–22, 439–40, 454–
59, 462–65; on Russo-German war,
132, 422–23; on postwar peace study,
133; activities of, 359, 453; on AEF
plans, 439–40; and AFC political action,
441
Sauthoff, Harry, 66n.111, 438
Schenck, Nicholas M., 417
Schieffelin, William J., 245
Schnibbe, Harry, 56n.52, 442
Schoonmaker, Nancy, 60n.68
Schulte, William T., 258
Selvage, James P., 29, 287–89
Sergio, Lisa, 387
Shafer, Harry, 66n.111
Shafer, Paul W., 301, 462, 463
Sheean, Vincent, 455
Sherwood, Robert E., 44, 89, 245, 247
Shipstead, Henrik, 5, 97, 257
Shriver, R. Sargent, Jr., 17, 58n.64
Simonds, J. G., 164, 167–68
Simpson, Richard M., 239
Sims, William S., 254
Smith, Ellison D. ("Cotton Ed"), 75n.179,
236
Smith, Truman, 136
Snavely, Carl, 54n.41
Sockman, Ralph, 245
Sondern, Frederick, Jr., 248
Sonnenschein, Hugo, 72n.151
Sonnino, Sidney, 276, 340

Sontag, Raymond, 23–24, 63n.85, 217–19
Spivak, John L., 67n.119
Stagner, Ross, 29
Staley, Eugene, 245
Stalin, Josef, 116, 291, 316, 321, 334, 383.
    See also Russia
Stallings, Lawrence, 5
Stamm, Frederick J., 138–39
Standley, William H., 245, 246
Stark, Harold O., 454, 455
Starobin, Joseph, 67n.119
Steel, Johannes, 387
Steele, Richard W., 36
Stein, Rose M., 51n.9
Sterling, Yates, 309
Sternberger, Estelle, 387
Stettinius, Edward R., Jr., 176–77
Stewart, Douglas M., 99, 101, 102
Stewart, Maxwell, 121
Stewart, Potter, 7, 87
Stimson, Henry L.: on franking issue, 36,
    70n.144; and Japan, 91; on United States
    entering war, 186, 432; attacked, 265,
    434, 443; on freedom of seas, 276;
    and AEF, 421
Stowe, Lyman Beecher, 245
Straight, Michael, 72n.151
Streit, Clarence K., 26, 240–47
Strong, George V., 246
Stuart, Barbara, 8
Stuart, Harold L., 17, 468
Stuart, R. Douglas, Sr., 7, 8
Stuart, R. Douglas, Jr.: background of, 7; and
    Yale anti-interventionist activities, 7, 8;
    organizes AFC, 8, 12, 95–100, 101–3; as
    AFC national director, 9, 10, 15–16; on
    aid "short of war," 10, 11; on Britain's
    predicament, 11, 98; on loans, 12, 98; on
    NFWC, 12; as AFC executive secretary,
    16; and *Scribner's Commentator*, 16; on
    impeachment of FDR, 16–17; "A for
    America" and, 19; on negotiated peace,
    20, 136–38; on lend-lease, 23; on strict
    neutrality, 24; on convoys, 26; advisory
    referendum and, 30; on naval war, 31; on
    Iceland, 32, 68n.123; on Luce publica-
    tions, 35, 69–70n.142; on AFC political
    action, 45–46, 441–42; and New Deal,
    50, 57n.57; and pacifism, 55n.44; and
    Hoover, 55–56n.49; and Fairbank,
    56n.51; on Kennedys, 58n.63; and Gris-
    wold, 63n.85; on Russian campaign,

67n.118, 136; on political advisory
    committee, 76n.185; praised, 385, 400,
    453, 469; activities, 391, 432, 433; and
    Lindbergh Des Moines speech, 395, 398;
    and movie investigation, 396; on dissolv-
    ing AFC, 459–61, 467–69
Sullivan, Mark, 224, 244, 310, 312
Summerall, Charles P., 71n.147
Swing, Betty Graham, 245
Swing, Raymond Graham, 385
Symington, Stuart, 15

Taber, John, 437
Taber, Louis, 54n.41
Taft, Martha (Mrs. Robert A.), 95
Taft, Robert A.: presidential candidacy
    backed, 14, 52n.19; on dissolving AFC,
    48, 463, 465; and AFC political advisory
    committee, 76n.185, 108, 441; and
    Cincinatti chapter, 95; on Tobey resolu-
    tion, 128, 258, 260; on negotiated peace,
    133; and lend-lease, 224; on Selective
    Service, 360, 368; and Far East, 453
Taft, William Howard, 328
Tansill, Charles C., 340
Taylor, Edmond, 245
Taylor, Myron, 299–300
Thatcher, M. W., 55n.41
Thomas, Elbert D., 257, 366, 374
Thomas, Lowell, 385
Thomas, Norman: cooperates with AFC, 18;
    book endorsed, 19, 51–52n.9, 121; and
    Lindbergh Des Moines speech, 38,
    39, 391–93, 400–401; and political
    advisory committee, 76n.185, 108, 441;
    on AFC strategy, 401. *See also* Socialists
Thomas, R. J., 189
Thompson, Dorothy, 38, 245, 259, 385, 386
Thomson, Hans, 36
Thorpe, Merle, 52n.16
Tinkham, George Holden, 131, 246
Tobey, Charles W., 64n.99, 384, 429; convoy
    resolution of, 27, 64n.99, 128, 258, 259,
    260
Tolan, John H., 189, 190
Tucker, Henry St. George, 459
Turlington, Edgar, 340
Twaddle, G. L., 354
Tydings, Millard, 75n.179

Utley, Freda, 61n.70, 136

Valentine, Alan, 66n.111
Vandenberg, Arthur H., 131, 231, 257, 260, 425
Vandercook, John, 386
Vanderlip, Mrs. Frank, 245
Van Nuys, Frederick, 223, 257, 453
Van Wagoner, Murray D., 189
Velde, Harold H., 64n.64
Villard, Oswald Garrison, 14, 73n.159, 401
Vorys, John W., 138, 238–39, 419, 420, 464; peace proposal of, 61n.70, 250, 261, 264

Wagner, Robert F., 257
Wakasugi, Kaname, 313
Waldrop, Frank, 57n.56
Wallace, Henry A., 174
Wallace, R. C., 241
Waln, Nora, 124
Walsh, David I., 10, 130, 299, 302, 351, 417, 453
Wannamaker, J. Skottowe, 245
Warburg, James P., 245
Warner, Albert, 386
Washington, George, 92, 205, 326
Watson, Mark, 459
Watson, Morris, 67n.119
Wavell, Archibald, 312
Webster, Edwin S., Jr., 55n.41, 468
Wedemeyer, Albert G., 15
Wedgewood, Josiah, 240, 241
Welles, Sumner, 46, 291–92, 293, 299, 365, 455
Weygand, Maxime, 230, 232, 300
Wheeler, Burton K.: backed by C. Bowles, 14; as AFC speaker, 28, 50; and neutrality act revision, 42, 75; and AFC political action, 46; on dissolving AFC, 48; on Hess flight, 61n.70; and L. Dennis, 62n.78; attacked by Stimson, 70n.144; and Friends of Democracy, 70n.146; and AFC political advisory committee, 76n.185, 108, 441; on use of frank, 96; and resolution on Atlantic war, 130, 131; and lend-lease, 231–32; chairs Senate-House group, 251; general views of, 254; and Tobey resolution, 260; on negotiated peace, 261; on war resolution, 301; on Selective Service, 360; and movie investigation, 384; and Jews, 393, 394; on AEF, 439; post-Pearl Harbor role, 458
Wheeler, John, 56n.53
Wheeler, Lulu M. (Mrs. Burton K.), 54n.41

Whipple, George, H., 55n.41
White, Wallace H., Jr., 257
White, William Allen, 7, 50, 53n.22, 89, 245. See also William Allen White Committee
Whitney, Joan (Mrs. Charles Shipman Payson), 102
Wilbur, Ray Lyman, 14, 66n.111, 74n.165
Wilhelmina, Queen of the Netherlands, 336
Wilkie, Leighton, 441
Williams, Alvord J., 55n.41, 60n.68, 73n.155
Williams, Wythe, 385
Willis, Paul S., 167
Willkie, Wendell: and election of 1940, 3, 10, 52n.19, 89, 94; Cudahy on, 127; trip to Britain, 235; on U.S. bases in Britain, 345; and movie investigation, 394; post-Pearl Harbor plans of, 460
Wilson, Hugh, 13–14, 99, 103
Wilson, Woodrow: administration of, 5; and Sussex, 28; and Fourteen Points, 32–33, 320, 330–31, 337, 342; antiwar motif of, 94; R. S. Baker on, 121–22; and Versailles, 239; on armed merchantmen, 272, 274, 407, 418; and freedom of the seas, 275–76; Churchill on, 324, 330–31, 339, 340; power of, 326, 369; on national emergency, 369; and open covenants, 453
Winant, John, 19, 129, 252, 264
Wirtz, W. Willard, 58n.64
Wise, James Waterman, 387
Wolfe, Bertram D., 51–52n.9
Wood, Robert E.: background of, 8; and New Deal, 8, 50, 52n.19, 56–57n.57; as AFC chairman, 8, 9, 10, 15, 25, 41, 137, 262–63, 401, 432; on NFWC, 12; and Scribner's Commentator, 16; underwrites AFC, 17; on German victory, 19; on negotiated peace, 20, 73n.61; and L. Dennis, 22, 62n.78; on lend-lease, 22–23, 227, 228; on British caution, 26; and Lindbergh, 28, 29; on lend-lease to Russia, 30–31; on Newfoundland meeting, 32, 68n.126; on Selective Service, 33–34, 342–43; on shoot-on-sight orders, 40, 74n.165; and revision of Neutrality Act, 42, 44; on war resolution, 42–43, 44; on AFC political action, 46, 76n.187, 108; on Pearl Harbor, 47, 464; on dissolving AFC, 48, 74n.167, 256, 467–69; on aid to Britain, 50; on 1940 election, 52n.19; praised, 59n.65, 409–

11, 445; on H. Baldwin, 60n.68; on movie investigation, 69n.141; and extremist groups, 72n.150; morale of, 137; Chicago speech of, 92–93, 96, 97, 253; attacked, 385, 388–89; and Lindbergh Des Moines speech, 397
Woodruff, Roy O., 451
Woodrum, Clifton A., 131, 427

Woolcott, Alexander, 245
Woolley, Mary E., 245
Wright, Frank Lloyd, 14, 54n.40

Yarnell, H. E., 245, 246
Young, Robert, 48, 77n.199, 468

Zog, King of Albania, 336

Topic Index

Advisory referendum, 29–30, 130, 131, 135, 233, 443

Africa, 66n.111, 76n.184, 110, 126, 304, 345; North, 129, 160; West, 146–47, 305–8, 365; French, 300, 304. *See also* Dakar; Freetown; *individual countries*

Aftermath, The (Churchill), 275–76, 324, 330–31, 332, 333, 335, 339, 340, 406

"After Mein Kampf," 69n.139

Alabama claims, 216

Alaska, 30, 172, 255, 295–98, 362–63

Albania, 11, 160, 162, 230, 235, 336

Aleutian Islands, 296–97, 363

Algeria, 160

Alsace-Lorraine, 129

America and a New World Order (Howard), 121

America First Committee (AFC): strength of, 6, 11, 23, 63n.83; and lend-lease bill, 6, 13–14, 22–25, 63n.88, 206–14, 222–29, 231–32, 233, 236; and Iceland occupation, 6, 31–32, 308–13; and Atlantic Charter, 6, 31–32, 68n.126, 315–42; and Far East, 6, 46–47, 448, 449; on neutrality revision, 6, 39, 42–44, 417–30; attacks on, 6, 35, 50, 70n.146–47, 263, 388–89, 466; origins, 7–9, 87–89; research bureau of, 7, 16, 23, 28–34 passim, 43, 56, 60n.68, 97, 197, 447; initial publicizing of, 9–12, 95–100; executive committee (also called directors), 9, 10, 15, 25, 41, 53n.28, 56n.50, 70n.146, 262, 461; political leanings of, 10, 13, 16–17; and credits issue, 12, 53n.28, 98; membership of national committee, 12–15, 16, 41, 45, 54–55n.41, 72n.155, 76n.186, 104, 105, 408–11; isolationism and, 13, 104, 120; pacifists and, 14, 18; role of national committee, 15, 29–30, 45, 48, 56n.50, 70n.146, 227, 397–400, 459–61, 467–69; and H. Hoover, 15; structure

of 15–16; Washington staff, 16, 24, 25, 27, 56n.52, 222–37, 262–68, 449; divisions of, 16; and local chapters, 16; speakers bureau, 16, 18–21, 46; on Roosevelt, 16–17, 58n.59; contributors to, 17, 58n.61; colleges and, 17; veterans and, 17; farmers and, 17; labor and, 17–18; blacks and, 18; socialists and, 18; general views on European war, 18–19, 112–120; books and articles promoted, 19, 120–22; negotiated peace and, 19–20; on German military threat, 20–21, 141–51; on German economic threat, 21, 151–55, 159–68; on Latin America, 21, 155–56, 169–84; on strategic materials, 21, 156–58; and L. Dennis, 21–22, 62n.78; on Roosevelt economic policies, 21, 184–90, 197–99, 264–66; Chicago chapter, 23, 56n.53; on British effort, 25–26, 36, 50–51, 70n.142; opposes convoys, 25, 26–28; considers disbanding or adjourning, 25, 41, 74n.167; on Union Now, 26, 240–48; on unlimited national emergency of May 27, 1941, 27, 262–63; and *Robin Moor*, 27–28, 268–71, 273–74, 276–78, 403, 411, 425, 430; on arming U.S. merchant vessels, 28, 272–75; and Selective Service, 28, 33–34, 49, 68n.134, 70n.144, 344–59; and Lindbergh (general), 28–29; and German-Russian war, 30–31; and aid to Russia, 30, 291–98; fears U.S. seize Dakar, Azores, Cape Verde Islands, 31, 304–8, 311–12, 345; and national emergency, 34, 361–79; and motion picture industry, 35, 384; and radio commentators, 35, 385–88; meetings banned, 36, 70n.146–47; and FBI, 36, 70n.148; and undemocratic elements, 36–37, 71–72n.149, 72n.150; and anti-Semitism (general), 37–40; and Lindbergh Des Moines speech, 37–40,

America First Committee (*continued*)
72–74n.155–63, 395–96, 397–400; and
shoot-on-sight orders, 40–41, 401–8; on
ship sinkings, 41, 411–15; and *Reuben
James*, 42; organization department of,
44; and AEF plans, 45, 76n.184; political
activity and, 45–46, 76n.185, 107–8,
441–42; leaders and Pearl Harbor, 47;
dissolution of, 47–48, 77n.199, 459–61,
467–69; role evaluated, 49–51; bulletins
of speakers bureau, 112–20, 141–58, 248,
448; bulletins of research bureau, 159–
99, 240–48, 268–78, 291–98, 304–13,
315–42, 344–57, 361–79, 401–16, 422–30;
on freedom of the seas, 275–78. *See also*
America First Committee, New York
chapter; *varied personnel*
America First Committee, New York chapter:
leadership and staff, 16, 37, 56n.53,
60n.68, 62n.88, 72n.151, 72–73n.155;
founding of, 95, 101; positions taken, 40–
41, 46, 47, 67n.118, 68n.126, 68–
69n.135, 70n.146, 77n.191. *See also*
Flynn, John T.
America Goes to War (Tansill), 340
American Expeditionary Force (AEF): and
Selective Service, 33, 344–47, 359, 465;
War Department plans for, 45, 76n.184,
421, 436–40; and German defeat, 136–
37; and Union Now, 242; and Africa, 300;
post-Pearl Harbor, 460, 461
American Farm Bureau Federation, 17
American Federation of Labor (AFL), 18,
54n.41, 59n.65, 107, 441
American Guardian, 73n.157
American Legion, 12, 17, 53n.30, 95, 227,
228
And So to War (Herring), 121
Antigua, 145, 364
Anti-Semitism, 15, 37, 72n.152, 73n.156,
108, 111. *See also* Lindbergh: Des
Moines speech; Jews
Archangel, 45
Argentina, 21, 171–82 passim
Arming ships. *See* Neutrality repeal
Asia. *See* Far East
Atlantic Charter, 3, 6, 32–33, 68n.126, 313,
314, 315–42, 450
Atlantic Fleet, U.S., 455
Australia, 142, 143, 172, 346, 448
Austria, 116, 141, 160, 162, 285
Azores, 66n.111, 136, 252, 261, 305, 306,
311, 312, 345, 365

Bahamas, 145, 148, 364
Baku, 290
Balkans, 24, 229, 235, 237, 282, 284, 291.
See also *individual countries*
Baltics, 165, 255, 334
Barbary pirates, 277, 406
Bathurst, 146
Belgium, 6, 15, 129, 137, 160, 162, 290, 429
Bermuda, 91, 145, 148, 308
Bismarck, 309
Bismarck, Otto von, 112
Blacks, 17, 383
Bold Venture, 74n.168, 430
Bolivia: tin within, 154, 157, 158, 171, 172–
73; other resources, 170, 172, 173,
178; war with Paraguay, 293
Bosell and Jacobs, 431–32
Brazil: raw materials in, 21, 154, 158, 170,
171, 172, 173, 177, 179, 183, 201;
military aspects of, 31, 132, 146, 305–6,
364; trade and loans of, 178, 179, 182,
204
Brest-Litovsk, Treaty of, 300
British Empire: praised, 13; preservation
discussed, 109, 116–17, 203, 221, 253;
economic activities of, 176; and Union
Now, 243; and U.S. defense, 267; U.S.
shipments to, 278; conquests of, 331–32;
resources controlled by, 338; shipping
losses of, 424. *See also* Great Britain;
individual countries
British Guinea, 145, 172, 304, 310, 364
British Museum, 12, 100–101
Brookings Institution, 160, 165
Bulgaria, 160, 162, 230, 232, 236
Burma Road, 172
Business, 17, 41, 45, 58n.61. *See also*
Economy, U.S.

Canada: as invasion route, 20, 148, 363; and
U.S. control, 62n.76, 203; and U.S.
defense agreement, 117–18, 142, 145,
147, 242, 297, 330; U.S. trade with, 151,
152, 157, 170, 171, 172, 173; and
British ties, 215; Newfoundland meeting,
316–17; domestic policies of, 346, 263
Canary Islands, 252, 261, 305, 307–8, 365
Cape Verde, 26, 31, 66n.111, 252, 261, 307–
8, 311, 312, 345, 365
Caribbean, 20, 145–46, 147, 150, 151, 178,
202, 304, 364
Catholic Laymen for Peace, 66n.111

Caucasus, 303

Central America, 20, 158, 171, 202. See also *individual countries*

Ceylon, 172

Charles Pratt, 429

Chicago Daily News, 94

Chicago Tribune, 45, 50, 73n.157

Chile, 21, 172, 173, 178, 180, 182

China: Japan's war with, 47, 92, 129, 193, 440, 450, 451; U.S. supplies to, 135, 183, 185, 232, 405–6; U.S. economic interests in, 152, 170; Lansing-Ishii and, 328

Christian Century, 13, 73n.159, 104, 400

Christian Science Monitor, 132

Church Peace Union, 245

Citizens Keep America Out of War Committee, 72n.150

Citizens Peace Petition Committee, 61n.70

City of Rayville, 429

Civilian Conservation Corps, 90

Civil War, U.S., 277, 339, 406

College Men for Defense First (CMDF), 17

Collier's, 19, 28, 60–61n.68, 71n.147

Colombia, 172, 178, 183

Committee to Defend America by Aiding the Allies (CDAAA). *See* William Allen White Committee

Common Sense, 56n.52, 73n.155, 108

Commonweal, 73n.159

Communism: domestic, 9, 31, 70n.142, 279–80, 383; foreign, 19, 30, 94, 116, 122, 126. *See also* Russia

Congress of Industrial Organizations (CIO), 18, 59n.65, 107, 134

Congress, U.S. See *individual legislators, committees, proposals*

Conscription, *see* Selective service

Constitution, U.S., 32, 40, 226, 407, 408, 460, 469

"Convoy," 69n.139

Convoys: Roosevelt policies concerning, 3, 26, 32, 41, 45, 76n.183, 193, 257, 260, 312; fears of, 6, 11, 25, 26–27, 42, 49, 192–95, 258, 282, 285, 288–89; observations and predictions about, 26, 31, 128, 132, 249, 254, 260, 261, 266–67. *See also* Crete; Iceland; Lend-lease; Tobey, Charles W.: convoy resolution of

Council on Foreign Relations, 245

Creel Committee, 5

Crete, 27, 266–68

Croats, 255

Cruise of the Nona (Belloc), 60n.68

Cuba, 145, 157–58, 170, 171, 178, 182

Current History, 56n.56, 96

Cyrenaica, 237

Cyprus, 160

Czechoslovakia, 10, 116, 129, 141, 160, 162, 220

Dakar, 26, 32, 146, 260, 305–7, 311, 312, 345, 364, 365

Danzig, 331

Dawes Plan, 161

Deadly Parallel, The (Grattan), 51n.9, 60n.68

Declaration of Independence, U.S., 240–41

Declaration of war on Axis: proposed, 43–44, 301–3, 432–33

Defense: U.S. military, 19, 90, 93, 118–19, 122, 130. *See also* American Expeditionary Force; Selective service

Defense and Economic Dislocation (Research Institute of America), 186, 187

Democracy: loss of domestic feared, 9, 18, 19, 87, 93–94, 114, 118, 119, 123–26 passim, 143–44; as war aim, 113, 116, 118, 119, 122, 137

Democrats: and AFC, 10; and nonpartisan political plans, 76n.186, 444–45; C. Bowles on, 280; in House, 381, 420, 431; and AEF plans, 438; post-Pearl Harbor plans of, 460. *See also* New Deal

Denmark, 6, 32, 137, 141, 160, 162, 290, 412, 430

Destroyer-bases deal, 3, 7, 89, 118

Deutscher-Weckruf und Beobachter 389

Dies Committee, 71n.149, 247

Dodecanese Islands, 333

Draft: military. *See* Selective service

Dutch East Indies: Japan and, 46, 92, 143, 313, 448, 449; and postwar settlement, 129, 336; U.S. supplies to, 135; resources within, 158, 171, 172, 365

Dutch Guinea, 172, 336

Dutch West Indies, 336

East Prussia, 335

Economy, U.S.: and trade, 4, 19, 21, 110, 117, 151–52; and new depression, 21, 184–90, 197–99; and inflation 132; and lend-lease, 197–99, 206–14, 378; and unemployment, 264–66

Ecuador, 178

Egypt, 40, 129, 160, 168, 237, 331, 421

Eire. *See* Ireland

El Salvador, 182

Emergency Cargo Ship Construction Bill, 415

Emergency Committee to Defend America First, 8. *See also* America First Committee

England Expects Every American to Do His Duty (Howe), 245

English-Speaking Union, 245

"Escape," 69n.139

Escorts. *See* Convoys

Ethiopia, 293, 294

European war: causes, nature, and aims, 18–19, 112–17, 127

Export-Import Bank, 182–83, 216

Falkland Islands, 10

Falsehood in War-Time (Ponsonby), 60n.68

Far East: fears of isolationists, 10, 109, 443; peace rumors and, 129, 437, 451; fears of official AFC personnel, 299, 313, 365–66, 381–82, 440, 448, 449; and Selective Service debate, 368; post-Pearl Harbor, 454. *See also individual countries*

Farmers, 17, 36, 250–51, 390, 379, 441

Fascism, domestic: warnings against, 9, 16, 20, 108, 111, 143, 279–81; and AFC, 9, 36–37, 389; L. Dennis and, 21

Fascism: elimination of foreign, 19, 94, 116, 126, 320, 337

Federal Bureau of Investigation (FBI), 36, 71–72n.148–49, 108

Federal Communications Commission, 387

Federal Power Commission, 377–78

Federal Reserve Board, 378

Federal Union. *See* Union Now

Fifth column, 144

Fight for Freedom, 36, 67n.119, 245, 287, 393, 421, 432, 466

Final Choice, The: America between Europe and Asia (Raushenbush and Raushenbush), 52n.9

Finland, 29

Flanders, 143, 230

Flanders Hall, 71n.149

"Flight Command," 69n.139

Flying Fortresses, 7, 8, 10

"Foreign Correspondent," 69n.139

Foreign Policy Association, 245

Foreign Policy for Americans (Beard), 19, 121

Fortune, 153–54, 155, 166–67, 168, 175, 244, 246, 365

Four Freedoms, 255, 320–21, 377

Fourteen Points. *See* Wilson, Woodrow

France: enters war, 2; fall of, 6, 285, 290; starvation within, 15, 137; colonies, 20, 148; fleet, 29; prewar diplomacy, 30, 65n.106, 90, 116, 150, 151, 291, 303, 331, 429; Vichy, 49, 69n.137, 230, 232, 305, 306, 311, 313, 333; and North Africa, 129, 230; in European economy, 160, 162; and Free French, 230, 300, 306, 333

Freedom of the seas, 28, 105–6, 250, 275–78, 301, 323, 339–42, 406–7. *See also* Roosevelt, speech of June 20, 1941, Mailcerts; Navicerts

Freetown, 300, 307

French Guinea, 172

Friends of Democracy, Inc., 36, 70n.144

Fruits of Victory, The (Angell), 121

Gallup poll, 10, 25, 29, 43, 46, 74n.167, 281–89

Gambia, 146

German-American Bund, 71n.149, 389

German-American National Alliance, 71n.149

Germany; enters war, 2; presented as military threat, 3–4, 20, 27; presented as economic threat, 4, 21, 22; presented as ideological threat, 4; challenged as military threat, 6, 20; ability to invade Western Hemisphere challenged, 8, 91, 109, 123–24, 126, 141, 144–48, 295, 358–59, 362–65; war aims perceived, 19, 114; difficult to defeat, 23, 65n.106, 125, 136, 220, 282; lack of economic threat, 21–22, 153, 154–55, 159–68, 175–76, 200–206; backs U.S. isolationists, 36; declares war on United States, 48, 77n.199; Lindbergh on cooperation with, 65n.107; agencies of endorse AFC, 70n.144; totalitarianism of, 113, 114, 116, 124; U.S. aims toward, 138, 338–39, 432; shipping losses of, 425–26; possible revolution within, 458. *See also* Great Britain; Hitler; Russo-German war; Tripartite Pact

Gibraltar, 129, 233, 235, 331, 449

Giddy Minds and Foreign Quarrels (Beard), 121

Gold standard, 21, 154–55, 204–5

Good Neighbors (Herring), 170, 171, 179

Gran Chaco War, 293

Graf Spee, 23

Great Britain: enters war, 2, 113; shipping losses of, 6, 11, 95, 98; major military aid favored to, 7; seen in peril, 7, 11, 53n.27; major military aid opposed to, 9, 10–11, 87, 93, 117; past relations with United States, 10, 215–16; credits opposed to, 12, 53n.28, 100–101; fleet of, 20–21, 23, 129, 142, 146, 149–51, 215–16, 266–67; isolationists favoring aid to, 23, 50–51, 99, 219–20; German attack feared by, 24, 127, 142–43, 225, 230–31; weakness in Balkans and Mediterranean, 24, 225, 229–30, 233–37, 449; Commonwealth of, 25, 65, 129; imperial preference system of, 25, 32, 300–301,322–23, 336; AFC attitudes toward, 25–26, 36, 50–51, 70n.142; general weaknesses of, 26, 112, 249, 252, 258, 282, 290; strength of, 26, 43, 195, 248, 357–58, 421, 422–29, 456; Lindbergh on, 29, 65n.106, 107; prewar diplomacy of, 18, 30, 91, 291, 303; war aims of, 112–15; nature of regime, 124; domestic life of, 129, 190, 460; trade of, 151; U.S. production sent to, 196–98, 257; and Italy, 232, 300; and "token" war, 303; conquests of, 331; propaganda of, 384, 432; criticism of United States, 459. *See also* Atlantic Charter; British Empire; Churchill, Winston; Union Now

"Great Dictator, The," 69n.139

Greece: military activity in, 11, 24, 230, 232, 234–35, 236–37; and European economy, 160, 162; postwar aims of, 333, 336

Greenland, 3, 26, 31, 309, 312, 330, 331, 363–64. *See also Montana; Sessa*

Greer, 3, 40, 299, 407, 417

Guam, 455

Guantanamo Bay, 145, 364

Guatemala, 182

Guinea. *See* British Guinea

Gulflight, 274

Haiti, 183

Harper's, 60n.68, 89

Hawaii, 47, 143, 299, 343, 449. *See also* Pearl Harbor

Hell-Bent for War (Johnson), 60n.68

Hitlerism. *See* Hitler, Adolf; Nazism

Hitler-Stalin Pact, 113

Holland. *See* Netherlands

Honduras, 10, 182

Hood, 309

House Committee on Un-American Activities, 71n.149, 247

How We Advertised America (Creel), 121

Hungary, 11, 160, 162

Iceland: U.S. troops land, 3, 6, 31–32, 35, 330, 331; U.S. occupation of opposed, 32, 42, 67–68n.123, 304–5, 308–13, 405; U.S. escorts provided to, 41; U.S. shipping to, 43, 193–94, 413–14; no danger from, 345, 363–64. *See also Montana; Sessa*

I. C. White, 74n.168, 430

"I Married a Nazi," 69n.139

Imperialist war, 18–19

India, 77n.192, 110, 142, 255, 334–35, 346

Indochina, 3, 46, 365, 440

Industrial Mobilization Plan. *See* "Property Seizure Bill"

Inter-American Development Commission, 184

Inter-Faith Committee for Aid to the Democracies, 245

International Labor Office, 129

International law, 27

Interstate Commerce Committee, Senate, 384

Iran. *See* Persia

Ireland, 31, 142, 312, 345, 346

Isolationism: defined, 4; attacked, 4, 128; and AFC, 13, 104, 120; C. Bowles on, 108–9

Italy: as Axis ally, 11, 48, 142, 432, 450, 466; political system of, 116, 320; naval strength of, 148, 150, 425; economic role of, 160, 162, 176, 232; invades Ethiopia, 293, 294; Rome threatened, 300; postwar settlement, 333. *See also* Tripartite Pact

Jamaica, 145, 364

Japan: U.S. relations with, 6, 32, 46–47; economic aspects of, 8, 22, 91–92, 155, 156, 158, 200, 201; fear of conflict with, 11, 46–47, 91–92, 451–53; rumors regarding (winter 1940–41), 46, 449 (spring 1941), 46 (summer 1941), 46–47, 77n.192, 129, 133, 135, 313 (fall 1941), 47, 77n.193, 139, 299, 303, 440, 449–50; as military presence, 109, 143, 150, 285, 295, 298, 363, 365–66, 448; naval strength of, 148–49, 150, 299; war with China, 293; political system of, 320; Taft-

Japan (continued)
  Katsura agreement, 328; post-Pearl
  Harbor views on, 454, 461, 462. See also
  Far East; Indochina; Pearl Harbor;
  Tripartite Pact
Jews, 29, 37, 72n.151, 102, 111, 255. See also
  Anti-Semitism; Lindbergh, Charles A.:
  Des Moines speech
Johnson Act, 12, 53n.28
Jugoslavia. See Yugoslavia

Kearny, 3, 42, 43
Keep America Out of War (Thomas and
  Wolfe), 51–52n.9
Keep America Out of War Congress
  (KAOWC), 16, 59n.66, 259, 392–93, 401,
  465
Kellogg-Briand Pact, 323, 341
Korea, 172, 328
Ku Klux Klan, 389

Labor, 17, 36, 45–46, 59n.65, 208–11, 390,
  375–76, 383, 441, 456. See also individual organizations
Lansing-Ishii note, 328
Latin America: trade of, 21, 91, 152, 154,
  155–58, 170, 174–84, 200–202; United
  States rule of, 62n.76; invasion of
  difficult, 91, 151; and German threat,
  136; Britain and, 216; opposes lend-
  lease, 223–24; and Roosevelt administration, 250, 261, 334; defense of northern,
  304; crises in, 381–82. See also individual countries
League of Nations, 13, 91, 115, 245, 293,
  323, 335–41 passim
League of Nations Association, 245
Lebanon, 160, 333
Lehigh, 74n.168, 425, 430
Lend-lease: provisions, 3, 22, 192–93, 337,
  379, 405; opposed by AFC, 6, 13–14, 22–
  25, 28, 49; proposed by FDR, 22;
  General Wood alternative to, 23; R.
  Sontag and, 23–24, 217–19; J. Chamberlain and, 24, 219; AFC evaluations of
  progress of bill, 24, 63n.88, 222–29, 231–
  32, 233, 236; congressional interviews
  on, 25, 238–40; signed, 25; bill evaluated, 25–26; seen as violated, 41, 301,
  411–14; AFC on economic consequences, 185–89, 196–99, 206–14; A. W.
  Griswold and, 216. See also Economy,
  U.S.; Lend-lease: second appropriation

Lend-lease: second appropriation, 3, 21, 25,
  30–31, 132, 191, 195–96, 298–99, 416–
  17, 419, 439
Liberia, 313
Liberty, 242
Libya, 11, 160, 233, 234, 235, 237
Life, 19, 29, 35, 60n.68, 66n.111, 69–
  70n.142, 126, 244
Luxembourg, 160, 162, 290

Madagascar, 171
Madeira, 252, 261, 365
Maginot Line, 285
Mailcerts, 277, 323, 340–41, 407
Malaya, 46, 110, 171, 172, 201, 203, 365, 448
Manchukuo, 299
Manchuria, 92, 299
"Manhunt," 69n.139
Manila, 77n.192, 135, 449, 466
Maritime Commission, U.S., 131, 376, 404,
  412, 415. See also Land, Emory S.
Martinique, 252, 260–61, 364
M-Day, 5
M-Day: The First Day of War (Stein), 51n.9
Mediterranean area, 24, 129, 225, 233–36,
  237, 449. See also individual countries
Merchants of Death (Englebrecht and
  Hanighen), 121
Mers-el-Kebir, 29
Mexico, 10, 145, 170–78 passim, 182, 202,
  216, 255, 277
Middle East. See Near East
Ministers No War Committee, 59n.66
Mobilization Day, 5
Monroe Doctrine, 10, 92
Montana, 41, 411, 412, 415, 416, 430
Moore-McCormack Line, 177
Morocco, 160, 232
"Mortal Storm, The," 69n.139
Mosquito boats, 7
Motion picture industry, 35, 69n.141, 384,
  394, 396, 417
Munich Conference, 10
"Mystery Sea Raider," 69n.139

Napoleon, 112
Natal, 146, 305
National Committee on Food for the Small
  Democracies, 15, 40, 99
National Council for the Prevention of War,
  16, 59n.66, 103, 250, 465. See also
  Libby, Frederick J.

National Defense Advisory Commission, 153–54
National Industrial Conference Board, 186
National Industrial Recovery Administration, 9, 57n.57, 103
National Labor Relations Board, 57n.57
National Small Business Men's Association, 8, 90
Navicerts, 277, 323, 340, 406–7
Navy, U.S.: tonnage of, 20, 148–50
Nazism: domestic, 9, 36–37, 70n.146, 71n.149, 114, 279; and world revolution, 18, 114; elimination of, 19, 113, 116, 119, 122, 320, 334, 337
Near East, 76n.184, 126, 160, 234, 249, 421
Negotiated peace: FDR on, 4; AFC on, 19, 20, 61n.70, 61n.73, 61n.74, 232, 264; individual remarks concerning (January 1941) 109 (February), 24, 125, 126–27, 241 (May) 129, 250, 261, 282, 286 (June), 112, 251–52, 264 (July) 19–20, 61n.70, 61n.73, 133–34 (August), 20, 135–36, 314 (September), 67n.118, 74n.167 (October), 20, 61n.70, 67n.118, 136–38, 421 (November), 20, 61n.73, 138–40, 435–36
Negroes. See Blacks
Netherlands, 6, 14, 129, 137, 160, 162, 290, 336, 429; eastern hemisphere colonies of, 20, 148
Netherlands Indies. See Dutch East Indies
Neutrality: discussion of strict, 24, 40, 220–22
Neutrality: Its History, Economics and Law (Turlington), 340
Neutrality act of 1939 (cash and carry): provisions, 2, 12, 53n.28, 131, 192–93, 291–92, 323, 340, 406, 421; desire to preserve, 7, 11, 12, 41, 87, 95, 99, 291–94, 408, 411, 412–14; and General Wood, 8; rationale behind, 118
Neutrality for the United States (Borchard and Lage), 277, 278, 294, 339, 403, 406, 407
Neutrality repeal (includes arming ships): text and course of bill, 3, 41–43, 299; opposed by AFC, 6, 39, 42–44, 75n.174–75, 180; early fears concerning, 28, 133, 250, 263, 272–75; discussion of bill, 138–41, 302, 417–35. See also Freedom of the seas
Neutrality zone, U.S., 2
New Deal: AFC leaders and, 8, 10, 50, 101–

2; opposed, 13, 37, 49, 67n.118, 90, 443, 444–45; efforts fo recruit backers of, 18, 390. See also specialized agencies
New Directions in the New World (Berle), 180, 182
Newfoundland, 145, 148, 172, 309, 312, 364. See also Roosevelt, Franklin D.: and Newfoundland meeting
New Masses, 67n.119
New Republic, 16, 72n.151
Newsweek, 177, 183
New York Daily News, 52n.16, 66n.111
New York Times, 35, 56n.52, 70n.142, 96. See also Baldwin, Hanson W.
New Zealand, 142, 346–47
"Night Train," 69n.139
Nine Power Pact, 299
1919, 5
No Foreign War Campaign, 12, 103
No Foreign War Committee (NFWC), 12, 36, 53n.30
Non-Partisan Committee for Peace through the Revision of the Neutrality Act, 50
Norway: fall of, 6, 91, 143, 285, 290; and projected peace, 129; in European economy, 160, 162; as U.S. war aim, 312, 346; oil tankers of, 429
Nye Committee. See Special Senate Committee on Investigation of the Munitions Industry

Office of Price Administration and Civilian Supply, 187. See also Henderson, Leon
Office of Production Management (OPM), 189, 257, 279, 301
Oil: shortage in United States, 21, 62n.76, 412–13; German desire for, 30, 166–67, 290; Western Hemisphere and, 169–70; tankers, 428–29
Open Door, 152, 216

Pacific. See Far East
Pacific Fleet, U.S., 10, 129, 132, 143, 299, 449. See also Pearl Harbor
Pacifism, 7, 14, 16, 18, 55n.44, 56n.52, 441
Palestine, 110, 169, 255
Panama: as nation, 223–24, 343
Panama: ship registry of, 40, 41, 43, 74n.168, 194, 404, 405, 411–16, 429, 430. See also individual ships
Panama Canal, 145–46, 147
Pan America (Beals), 176, 180, 181, 182
Paraguay, 172, 178, 293

Pearl Harbor, 47, 454–59
People and Politics of Latin America, The (Williams), 184
Persia, 129
Peru, 171, 172, 178
Petsamo, 29
Philippines: fear of attack on, 46; as U.S. war aim, 110, 143, 255; resources of, 158, 171; and Taft-Katsura agreement, 328; seen as undefensible, 365–66, 448
Pink Star, 41, 411, 412, 414, 415, 416, 430
PM, 37, 52n.19, 102, 394
Poland: as combatant, 2, 285, 290, 334; starvation in, 15; British guarantee to, 30; in European economy, 160, 162; postwar order and, 220, 33, 335
Polls: national, 7, 29, 32, 33, 48–49; AFC and, 29, 49, 66n.111; Hutchins, 54n.33, 66n.111; congressional, 66n.111, 130, 258. *See also* Gallup poll
Portugal, 45, 136, 160, 162, 261, 308, 311, 312
Presidential powers, 80, 129, 262, 325–31, 421; Roosevelt request for emergency, 361–79. *See also* Roosevelt speech of May 27, 1941
President—Office and Powers, The (Corwin), 326–29
Price Stabilization Division, 206
Prince of Wales, 456, 459
"Property Seizure Bill," 132, 252–53, 377
Puerto Rico, 145, 255, 364

Radio commentators, 35, 385–88
Railroad brotherhoods, 18
"Ramparts We Watched, The," 69n.139
Raw materials, 21, 153–54, 156–59, 169–73, 189. *See also* Oil; Rubber; Tin
Reader's Digest, 60n.68, 61n.70, 242
Reconstruction Finance Corporation, 265
Red Cross, 99, 461, 467
Red Sea, 27, 403, 412
Republicans: election of 1940, 10, 52n.19; AFC and, 10; and nonpartisan political plans, 45, 76n.186, 444–45; House organization, 134–35; C. Bowles on, 280–81; post–Pearl Harbor, 456, 460
Repulse, 456, 459
Research Institute of America, Inc., 186, 189
Reuben James, 3, 42
Road to War (Millis), 121
Robin Line, 268

Robin Moor: incident, 27; AFC on, 27–28, 268–71, 273–74, 276–78, 403, 411, 425, 430; contraband issue and, 268–71, 274, 276, 412
Romania, 11, 160, 162, 230, 290
Rubber: U.S. needs, 21, 169, 171–72; and Southeast Asia, 46, 92, 158, 201; synthetic, 153–54, 158, 171, 365; Germany and, 168; hemispheric sources of, 171–72, 201; colonies and, 337
Rumania. *See* Romania
Russia: U.S. aid sought and delivered, 17, 30, 135, 183, 185; freedom of religion in, 30, 66–67n.115, 298; lend-lease to opposed, 30, 35, 185, 291–98, 406; isolationists on, 30–31, 91, 116, 125, 383, 421, 448, 454; peace terms affecting, 129; German appeasement of, 147; naval strength of, 149; as gold producer, 155; raw materials of, 157, 158, 171, 200; as German market, 163, 164–68; Newfoundland meeting and, 320, 321, 332, 333, 334; U.S. South and, 383. *See also* Alaska; Archangel; Lend-lease: second appropriation; Russo-German war; Siberia
Russo-German war: military prognosis of, 21, 164–68, 314, 358, 422, 458–59; and negotiations, 67n.118, 74n.167, 138, 140, 303; analyzed, 130; Congress on, 131. *See also* Lend-lease: second appropriation
Russo-Japanese War, 91

Saar, 331, 334
Santa Lucia, 145, 364
Save America First (Frank), 60n.68, 399
Scotland, 309, 312, 345, 346
Scribner's Commentator, 16, 60n.68, 99, 101, 102, 103
Scripps-Howard press, 9, 16, 52n.16, 103, 300
Selective service act of 1940, 2–3, 7, 8, 33, 89
Selective service act of 1941: provisions of, 3, 33–34; AFC organization and, 28, 33–34, 49, 68–69n.134–35, 70n.144, 344–59; Roosevelt administration and, 33–34; AFC leaders on, 33–35, 342–43, 359–60, 380–83; Sarles on, 34, 130, 134–35, 136; Hiram Johnson and, 465
Senegal, 146, 305
Serbs, 255

"Sergeant York," 69n.139

Sessa, 40, 403, 404, 411, 412, 415, 416, 430

Shall We Send Our Youth to War? (Hoover), 60n.68

Ship Seizure Bill, 27, 258, 260, 411

Siam, 46, 47, 77n.192, 135, 313, 452

Siberia, 30, 294, 295–96, 298, 345, 363, 459

Sierra Leone, 136, 307

Singapore, 46, 143, 313

Slovakia, 11

Slovenes, 255

Small business committees, congressional, 190

Smoke-Screen (Pettengill), 67n.118

Socialists, 16, 18, 56n.52, 57n.55, 73n.157. *See also* Thomas, Norman

South Africa, Union of, 142, 255, 346. See also *Robin Moor*

South America. *See* Latin America

Soviet-Nazi Pact, 113

Soviet Union. *See* Russia

Spain, 90, 116, 160, 162, 235, 293, 320, 449. *See also* Canary Islands; Cape Verde

Special Senate Committee on Investigation of the Munitions Industry, 5, 272, 273, 274, 317, 340, 342

State Department, U.S., 301, 421, 458

Steel Seafarer, 40, 403, 411, 412, 425, 430

Strategy of the Americas (MacLiesh and Reynolds), 57n.55, 60n.68, 169, 170, 172–73, 179, 296, 306, 365

Suez Canal, 24, 70n.144, 232, 233, 235, 236, 331

Sullivan and Cromwell, 54n.36

Supply Priorities and Allocation Board, U.S., 190

Sweden, 160, 162

Switzerland, 160, 162

Syria, 160, 232, 236, 333

Taft-Katsura note, 328

Thailand. *See* Siam

"That Hamilton Woman," 69n.139

"They Dare Not Love," 69n.139

Time, 12, 35, 36, 56n.52, 60n.68, 69n.70n.142, 96, 180, 244, 371

Tin, 21, 46, 153–54, 158, 169, 171, 172–73, 337, 365

Tolan committee, 190

Tragic Fallacy: A Study of America's War Policies, The (Hallgren), 51n.9

Trinidad, 91, 145, 304, 310, 343, 364

Tripartite Pact, 11, 448, 450

Tunisia, 160

Turkey, 160, 171, 230, 232, 236, 237

Ukraine, 290, 303

Uncensored, 57n.55, 121

Union for Democratic Action, 259

Union Now, 26, 115, 240–48, 286, 341, 460

Union Now (Streit), 63n.93, 242, 247

Union Now with Britain (Streit), 63n.93, 242, 243–44

United Service Organization (USO), 461

United States Lines, 412

United States News, 128, 190

United States v. Curtiss-Wright Export Corporation, 407

United We Stand! Defense of the Western Hemisphere (Baldwin), 120, 169, 170, 295, 297–98, 336, 356, 363, 365, 366

Uruguay, 177, 178, 223

US Week, 67n.119, 325

Vatican, 299–300

Venezuela, 10, 178, 216

Versailles conference and treaty, 5, 18, 20, 335, 338, 339

Veterans, 17. *See also* American Legion

Vichy France. *See* France

Virgin Islands, 145, 364

Wake Island, 455

War Department, U.S., 45, 131, 439, 456. *See also* Selective service

Washington Conference of 1921–22, 216

Washington Post, 466

Washington Times-Herald, 45, 57n.56, 247–48, 407, 437, 438

W. C. Teagle, 75n.168

We Can Defend America (Hagood), 19, 120–21

We Have a Future (Thomas), 51–52n.9, 121

We Planned It That Way (Knox), 372

We Testify (Schoonmaker and Reid), 60n.68

We, the Mothers, Mobilize for America, 72n.150

William Allen White Committee: policies of, 7, 26, 53n.22; backers of, 14, 89, 393; opposed by, 19, 115–17, 215–17, 245, 286; emulated, 95–96, 100, 103

William II of Germany, 112, 124

Women's International League for Peace and Freedom, 59n.66, 73n.159

JUSTUS D. DOENECKE is Professor of History at New College of the University of South Florida, Sarasota, Florida. He earned his doctorate at Princeton University and has served on the faculties of Colgate University and Ohio Wesleyan University. Professor Doenecke is the author of several books, including *Not to the Swift: The Old Isolationists on the Cold War Era* (1979); *The Presidencies of James A. Garfield and Chester A. Arthur* (1981); *When the Wicked Rise: American Opinion-Makers and the Manchurian Crisis of 1931–1933* (1984); and *Anti-Intervention: A Bibliographical Introduction to Isolationism and Pacifism from World War I to the Early Cold War* (1987).

HOOVER ARCHIVAL DOCUMENTARIES
General editors: Milorad M. Drachkovitch (1976–83)
Robert Hessen (1983–)

The documents reproduced in this series (unless otherwise indicated) are deposited in the archives of the Hoover Institution on War, Revolution and Peace at Stanford University. The purpose of their publication is to shed new light on some important events concerning the United States or the general history of the twentieth century.

HERBERT HOOVER AND POLAND: A DOCUMENTARY HISTORY OF A FRIENDSHIP, Foreword by Sen. Mark O. Hatfield
George J. Lerski, compiler

NEGOTIATING WHILE FIGHTING: THE DIARY OF ADMIRAL C. TURNER JOY AT THE KOREAN ARMISTICE CONFERENCE, Foreword by Gen. Matthew B. Ridgway
Allan E. Goodman, editor

PATRIOT OR TRAITOR: THE CASE OF GENERAL MIHAILOVICH, Foreword by Hon. Frank J. Lausche
David Martin, compiler

BEHIND CLOSED DOORS: SECRET PAPERS ON THE FAILURE OF ROMANIAN-SOVIET NEGOTIATIONS, 1931–1932
Walter M. Bacon, Jr., translator and compiler

THE DIPLOMACY OF FRUSTRATION: THE MANCHURIAN CRISIS OF 1931–1933 AS REVEALED IN THE PAPERS OF STANLEY K. HORNBECK
Justus D. Doenecke, compiler

WAR THROUGH CHILDREN'S EYES: THE SOVIET OCCUPATION OF POLAND AND THE DEPORTATION, 1939–1941, Foreword by Bruno Bettelheim
Irena Grudzinska-Gross and Jan Tomasz Gross, editors and compilers

BERLIN ALERT: THE MEMOIRS AND REPORTS OF TRUMAN SMITH, Foreword by Gen. A. C. Wedemeyer
Robert Hessen, editor

LENIN AND THE TWENTIETH CENTURY: A BERTRAM D. WOLFE RETROSPECTIVE, Foreword by Alain Besançon
Lennard Gerson, compiler

A QUESTION OF TRUST: THE ORIGINS OF U.S.-SOVIET DIPLOMATIC RELATIONS: THE MEMOIRS OF LOY W. HENDERSON
George W. Baer, editor

WEDEMEYER ON WAR AND PEACE, Foreword by John Keegan
Keith E. Eiler, editor

LAST CHANCE IN MANCHURIA: THE DIARY OF CHANG KIA-NGAU
Donald G. Gillin and Ramon H. Myers, editors; Dolores Zen, translator

IN DANGER UNDAUNTED: THE ANTI-INTERVENTIONIST MOVEMENT OF 1940–1941 AS REVEALED IN THE PAPERS OF THE AMERICA FIRST COMMITTEE
Justus D. Doenecke, editor

BREAKING WITH COMMUNISM: THE INTELLECTUAL ODYSSEY OF BERTRAM WOLFE
Robert Hessen, editor